The
Poetical Works
of
Burns

THE CAMBRIDGE EDITIONS

The Poetical Works of Burns

Cambridge Edition

Edited by Raymond Bentman

Houghton Mifflin Company Boston

1974

FIRST PRINTING   C

Library of Congress Cataloging in Publication Data

Burns, Robert, 1759–1796.
  The poetical works of Burns.

  I. Bentman, Raymond, ed.   II. Title.
PR4300 1974.B6   821'.6   74-18450
ISBN 0-395-18486-X

Printed in the United States of America

EDITOR'S NOTE

The text and notes of this edition are those of *The Centenary Burns*, edited by William Ernest Henley and Thomas F. Henderson (London, 1896–1897). This edition remains the best text of Burns's poems presented in the order in which they were published. *The Poems and Songs of Robert Burns*, edited by James Kinsley (Oxon, 1968) is the best edition of the poems presented in the order in which they were written. Mr. Kinsley's edition includes some poems discovered since publication of the Henley-Henderson edition.

The poems from *The Merry Muses of Caledonia*, a collection of Burns's bawdy songs, are based on the edition edited by James Barke, Sydney Goodsir Smith, and J. DeLancey Ferguson (Edinburgh, 1959, and New York, 1965). *The Merry Muses* was not published during Burns's lifetime and has had a confused history of publication. The edition by Barke, Smith, and Ferguson was the first serious attempt to establish a correct text of the poems and to attempt to determine which poems were written by Burns. After the 1959 edition, however, G. Legman discovered the manuscript of the first edition of *The Merry Muses* and has been able, on the basis of that document, to correct some of the ascriptions of the 1959 edition. I have included all the poems in the 1959 edition which the editors clearly ascribe to Burns, all poems the editors believed were probably by Burns, and all poems in that edition which Legman's subsequent investigations have demonstrated were probably by Burns. The reader is referred to the Introduction and Notes of the edition by Barke, Smith, and Ferguson, to G. Legman's *The Horn Book: Studies in Erotic Folklore and Bibliography* (New Hyde Park, New York, 1964) and to his edition of *The Merry Muses of Caledonia* (New Hyde Park, New York, 1965) for further discussion.

In the present text of the bawdy poems I have followed the style of the original text in using partial purgation of indecent words (e.g., f—k). The reader may find the method irritatingly prudish. But to fill in the blanks would mean tampering with the source. I had to choose between impertinence and (by current standards) prudery, and decided for the latter. In the case of unfamiliar indecent words, I have retained the dashes but have given the complete word at the foot of the page, with its modern equivalent.

I wish to express my thanks to G. P. Putnam's Sons for their kind permission to reprint poems from *The Merry Muses of Caledonia*.

CONTENTS

INTRODUCTION

Robert Burns is the first truly modern poet in British literature. He is his own man, largely free from the past, from the traditions and concepts of organized religion, and from the conventions of class structure. And yet he is concerned with all of them. This freedom combined with concern results, in part, from his mixed background and personality. The voluminous scholarly and critical writings about him disagree on what traditions he belongs to, on the shape of his poetical career, on his religion, on his national affiliations. They even disagree on what language he wrote in. These disagreements among critics and scholars are unique to Burns because they are not caused by a paucity of facts about his life and writing and do not result primarily from different literary evaluations. They come, rather, from the contradictions within Burns himself, as a man and as a poet, and from the diverse literary, political, intellectual, religious, linguistic milieu into which he was born and in which he lived and wrote. This upheaval, the lack of structure which was part of his life, freed him from allegiance to or dependence on the past. He was left to create his own poetic world out of observation and experience, from his emotions, his sensuality, his senses, and the ordinary events of his life and the life around him.

Burns was born in 1759 in Alloway, Ayrshire, a village in southwest Scotland, the first son of a farmer who struggled all his life without getting free from poverty and indebtedness. His father did manage, with some neighbors, to hire a schoolmaster for the village children for about two years. And he gave his sons instruction on his own. Burns was obviously an exceptionally intelligent boy in an exceptionally intelligent family in a country that valued literacy and education. He read voraciously so that he enlarged on his brief formal education until he acquired substantial learning. But since the books available to him were limited and the guidance was parochial, most of his learning was in eighteenth-century English and Scottish writings and in the Bible, Shakespeare, Milton, a few older Scottish poems, such as "Christis Kirk on the Green," and some French literature (he taught himself to read French).

Burns pursued his father's vocation as a farmer, with as little financial success although with enough hard work to damage his health permanently. He opened a shop as a flaxweaver and failed at that. He had started writing poetry, probably in 1784, but did not consider making a living from writing. He made several plans to emigrate to Jamaica, but never got off, mostly because he could not get the money for passage. But then in 1785 a girl from his village, Jean Armour, became pregnant with Burns's child. He offered to marry her. But her family, rather astonishingly, refused because they considered Burns their social inferior. Their social superiority to Burns was slight, but they still considered the disgrace of an illegitimate grandchild less than the disgrace of marriage out of their class. Burns, totally disgusted with the pretentiousness and hypocrisy, decided to publish his poems in order to earn passage to Jamaica once and for all. He published his first collection in 1786, the Kilmarnock edition, named after its place of publication. The collection was an immediate success and Burns became famous, at least sufficiently famous so that he no longer considered emigration.

The reasons for the success of the Kilmarnock volume are mixed. For some people, Burns fit the fashionable eighteenth-century theory of the "heaven-taught ploughman." He was regarded as something of a noble savage, illustrating the belief that true genius descends direct from heaven, unimpeded by civilization. This view of Burns was to continue through much of the nineteenth century. Its adherents conveniently over-looked Burns's self-education or were unwilling to admit that education was possible outside established institutions. Others of Burns's contemporaries believed he was a kind of rough diamond, that his poetry showed ability but would improve with polish. And they advised Burns to rid his poetry of "Scotticisms," to write in the style and diction of the English tradition — perhaps of Pope. Yet there were others, such as the young William and Mary Wordsworth in 1787, and, only a few years later, Coleridge, Southey, and Lamb, who recognized Burns as a poet of major achievement on the basis of this Kilmarnock volume.

Burns went to Edinburgh in the winter of 1786 to try to find some kind of government job that might support him sufficiently to allow him to continue writing. He was to wait two years before he actually got a job as a tax collector, a job that consumed far too much of his time and energy. But in Edinburgh (in 1786 and later), he was lionized by the aristocracy and literati, partly for what he bitterly referred to as his "novelty," partly for his simple dignity, charm, and wit. His comments on the upper classes of Edinburgh seem to vary, at times admiring, at times envious, at times contemptuous. He carried on an elaborate, effusive, chaste relationship with a married woman, Agnes M'Lehose (they wrote to each other as Sylvander and Clarinda), and then in the middle of it returned to his home and married his old sweetheart, Jean Armour (her family now considered him good enough for her). The remainder of his life he spent in Dumfries, a small town near his birthplace, as a tax collector. He stayed married but not very faithful to Jean, and he devoted much of his spare time to collecting, revising, and writing folk songs. He died in 1796, probably from a heart disease contracted from overwork as a young man.

This brief sketch illustrates some of the inconsistencies that are intrinsic to his life. For example, he seemed to belong to no class in society. He could possibly have climbed into the upper classes of Edinburgh, for British society in the eighteenth century was still fairly mobile and other writers had climbed several social rungs on the basis of their talent. To do so, however, would have required that Burns would have had the desire to, which he never quite did. He seemed to realize that his roots were with the village life of Scotland and with the folk tradition, that his talent lay in writing a kind of folk poetry and his background called for a farm girl for a wife. Yet he was not a peasant; his learning, beliefs, and tastes were partly those of fashionable, sophisticated Edinburgh. And his work as a tax collector put him even more incongruously in the middle class. He lived, personally and poetically, outside the class system yet never disengaged from it.

Burns's language presents another ambiguity. The Highlands of Scotland, the moun-tainous northwest, was occupied by the descendants of the Celts, who spoke a form of Gaelic. The Lowlands, southern and eastern Scotland, was occupied by the descendants of the same Teutonic tribes that had occupied what is now England. They spoke a dialect of English called "Scottish," "Scots," or "Lallan," which is closer to the dialects of northern England than the dialects of northern England are to the dialects of southern England. What we now call "standard" English, the language of English literature and nonliterary writing, the spoken language of educated Englishmen, was also used in Scotland. The Scottish church used the Geneva Bible, which was in English, so the language of the church became English. Early in the seventeenth century James VI of Scotland became James I of England, and in 1707 Scotland and England united, to be ruled by the Parliament in London. So in the eighteenth century the language of courts, law, church, the educated classes, and most of the literary and all of the non-literary writing was in English. The spoken language among farmers, village people, and the uneducated classes of the Lowlands was Scottish. Some of the poetry was written in a mixed language, which took its vocabulary from both English and Scottish and most of its grammar and syntax from English. Burns used this literary language for much of his poetry.

We cannot be sure why Burns wrote in this mixed language. His own comments, like everything else about him, are contradictory. He talks of writing in his "native language" but more frequently refers to his work as containing a "sprinkling" of Scottish words. Perhaps he could have tried to write as he spoke, but few if any poets have succeeded in doing that. He had models for this Scots-English, but he had models who wrote purely in English. Most likely, he tried to use this Scottish sprinkling symbolically, to create a sense of ordinary people speaking, to give the sense of what Wordsworth was later to call a "language really used by men." The many types of characters who speak and appear in his poems and songs, as great a collection of characters as one can find in any nondramatic poetry of Britain (except possibly Chaucer), seem to speak directly out of their experience. An impoverished farmer, a superstitious drunk, a lonely peasant girl deserted by her soldier lover, a gang of celebrating vagrants, a frenzied preacher, an awestruck oaf, an ecstatically happy young man in love, a quietly contented spinning woman, an untrained poet, a man delighted to be newly married, a man wishing his wife were dead, an old woman looking back on a happily married life, an old farmer enjoying the companionship of his mare, a hungry man lamenting about his hungry children — all these characters help to make up a superbly rich composite of moods, economic states, marital states, social levels, which make up the stuff of life. They make up one part of life — Burns does not claim otherwise — but it is a part in which social convention is often unimportant, in which people speak with informality, spontaneity, or considerable emotion. Burns emphasizes this directness of expression by having characters speak in a language which sounds as if it came out of everyday life.

The literary tradition in which Burns wrote is also subject to a variety of interpretations. In eighteenth-century Edinburgh there was an interest in reviving the old, brilliant Scottish tradition in literature. Alan Ramsay, a mildly talented and ambitious wigmaker, anthologized a number of old Scottish writings. Alan Ramsay, Robert Fergusson (a highly talented young poet), and others wrote poetry in the old Scottish forms and in a Scots-English literary language. It is debatable to what extent these men were continuing an old tradition and to what extent they were artificially, self-consciously trying to revive a tradition that had been dead for centuries. Burns's relationship to the Scottish tradition is consequently obscure. He pays lip service to the tradition but probably read no more than a smattering of the great Scottish writers of the fifteenth and sixteenth centuries. He was obviously influenced by Ramsay, Fergusson, and Scottish songs but may have been more influenced by English writers, Alexander Pope, James Thomson, William Cowper, and Oliver Goldsmith. It is simplest and probably most accurate to see Burns as the descendant of a broad British tradition which includes elements from eighteenth-century England and Scotland.

The Scottish poetic forms, especially as used by Fergusson, clearly influenced him. Burns's verse epistles were in the Scottish tradition of a convivial, personal, somewhat bumptious communication which often ended with an agreement to get together for a drinking bout. "The Holy Fair" is in the tradition of a description of a large public event, usually countrified. The verse forms he uses best are from the Scottish tradition, the "Standard Habbie" of the "Epistle to J. Lapraik," "To a Mouse," "To a Louse," et cetera, and the "bob-wheel" of "The Holy Fair," especially the "bob" or short line at the end of the stanza which always concludes with the same word.

But Burns had also read and admired much eighteenth-century English poetry. He seems strongly influenced by the imagery of James Thomson and William Cowper and by one of the greatest satiric versifiers, Alexander Pope. For example, one of Pope's most effective devices is ironic rhyme in which he parallels incongruous ideas and things to demonstrate the lack of sensible values in a disordered society. He shows the superficiality in the court of Queen Anne:

> One speaks the Glory of the *British Queen*,
> And one describes a charming *Indian Screen*.
> ("The Rape of the Lock," stanza III, lines 13–14)

Burns employs a similar device in his use of such Scottish verse forms as the Standard Habbie:

> Do ye envý the city gent,
> Behint a kist to lie an' sklent;   *chest; squint or lie*
> Or purse-proud, big wi' cent. per cent.
>   An' muckle wame,   *big stomach*
> In some bit brugh to represent
>   A bailie's name?   ("Second Epistle to
>   J. Lapraik," stanza XI)

"Sklent" (which has the sense of "side glance," "deviousness") and "cent. per cent." rhyme with and contrast "city gent" and "represent." The class system and political representation are equated, through their sound, with money and dishonesty. Burns uses the short line (here and elsewhere) to throw in afterthoughts, asides, impulsive notions, ironic self-contradictions — all intended to convey easy, informal, conversational rhythms, especially when combined with Scottish diction. Pope's iambic pentameter couplet, on the other hand, is a tightly constructed form which demands order and decries its absence. Burns gets the best of both forms. The parallel and contrasting end-rhymes describe the world as having none of the order it pretends to. They express contempt for the pretentious, ridiculous city gentleman who has a big purse and a "muckle wame," and condemn the world of business, class, and politics for not being the orderly, sensible place it claims to be. But Burns makes this condemnation using a chatty form that does not put much value on order. He can, then, condemn disorder when it leads to injustice and hypocrisy but express the wish for something other than the restoration of order — he wants spontaneity, freedom from formality.

His religious beliefs are complicated and elusive. Scotland was overwhelmingly Calvinist, divided between the orthodox Old Lights and the moderate New Lights. Burns's father and Burns, when he was a Calvinist, adhered to the moderates. But the church at the village level was generally ruled by the orthodox. They taught a harsh doctrine: that man was cursed with the sin of Adam, that only people "elected" before birth would go to heaven, that people not elected were damned to hell no matter how they lived. Although this doctrine would seem to imply that man's actions on earth mattered little, the church at the village level used its considerable secular power, which amounted to a theocracy, to enforce what it considered to be correct moral behavior. For example, a man and a woman convicted of fornication would be required to stand on a stool (the "cutty stool" or "creepie chair") in front of the church congregation for three Sundays and listen to a sermon directed at them. Burns was subjected to this humiliation with Jean Armour (and others) and had no choice but to submit.

At various times in his life Burns was a churchgoing Calvinist. At other times he seems to have accepted the religions that had emerged from the current beliefs among the more advanced thinkers — deism, free thinking, even a kind of agnosticism. Deism was a belief in an impersonal God, one who had created the world, given man a set of principles, revealed himself through the orderliness of the natural world, but who did not participate in man's daily affairs. He did not punish evil or reward good behavior, did not require worship, but remained as a kind of model for orderly, decorous, humane behavior. It is not unusual for the time that Burns moved back and forth between Christianity and deism. Many people, even some of the most important writers of the eighteenth century, did so. But it was one thing to have liberal, fluid, varying beliefs while frequenting the fashionable salons of Paris, London, and Edinburgh, where one could find plenty of others of like expansiveness, and where a firm social structure gave some order to a man's life. It was quite another thing to be theologically independent in a small village where the only intellectual and religious belief was that recognized and enforced by the church and which most people unthinkingly accepted. During much of his life Burns remained a churchgoing Calvinist. In his prose writings, which consist mostly of letters and private journals, he expressed deistic or free thinking beliefs. His poetry, however, expresses a more complicated and subtler view than either his actions or his prose writings, one which seems to result from the equivocal situation he was forced into by his village life.

He rejects and satirizes some of the most important deistic beliefs because they are too schematic. For example, deists did not believe in life after death, but they insisted that the world is good. Denied the Christian justification that evil and suffering are placed on earth to test our worthiness for heaven, they argued for the interdependency of all parts of the world, in which temporary evils contribute to a larger good. The world is divinely structured, each living being has its purpose, each being serves the others, and all contribute to a beautiful, orderly scheme. Burns deals with this belief by reducing it, without fanfare, to the most ordinary everyday experience. A farmer accidentally breaks up a mouse's nest and ruins "Nature's social union" ("To a Mouse"). The only sense the farmer can make out of the world comes from his feelings for his "earth-born companion/ An' fellow mortal!" A louse climbs onto the hat of a

self-impressed, social-climbing young lady in church and breaks the whole scheme of
things — the louse ought to "in some beggar's hauffet (hut) squattle." ("To a Louse")
Burns says there is no universal order and hence we cannot control our lives or foresee
events:

> O Jenny, dinna toss your head
> An' set your beauties a' abroad!   *abroad*
> Ye little ken what cursèd speed   *know*
>   The blastie 's makin!   *blasted creature*

The highly visual "toss your head," suggesting petulant pride, ridicules not only the
snobbish Jenny, but also all those who would try to impose an order — any order —
where the simple facts of life make such order a self-delusion.   The mock-fear of the
speaker conveys a universal truth with amused irony — none of us knows what is going
on even on our own hats.   Evil can be lived with, Burns says, but it cannot be explained
away.

Burns attacks the current belief that we can learn about the way things are from
searching the past ("On the Late Captain Grose's Peregrination thro' Scotland") or
from higher education ("Epistle to J. Lapraik").   He attacks the pretentions of gran-
diose exaltation of ordinary feelings, of sentimental, stylized poetry with its classical
figures and elegant phrases, and substitutes things from ordinary life, such as frank
materialism:

> Awa wi' your witchcraft o' Beauty's alarms,
> The slender bit beauty you grasp in your arms!
> O, gie me the lass that has acres o' charms!
> O, gie me the lass wi' the weel-stockit farms!   ("A Lass wi' a Tocher")

Or he will substitute the plain facts of sexual experience for the high-sounding diction
of idealized, purified nature, as in the bawdy "Ode to Spring":

> When maukin bucks, at early f——s,   *male hares*
>   In dewy grass are seen, Sir;
> And birds, on boughs, take off their m——s,   *finish fucking*
>   Amang the leaves sae green, Sir;
>
> . . . .
>
> There Damon lay, with Sylvia gay,
>   To love they thought no crime, Sir;
> The wild-birds sang, the echoes rang,
>   While Damon's a——e beat time, Sir. —

Burns's attitude toward Christianity, as he expresses it in his poetry, perhaps best
defines his philosophic position.   Some of his more old-fashioned religious satires, such
as "Holy Willie's Prayer" and "The Kirk's Alarm" take the position that religious satires
had been taking for centuries, attacking only the abuses of religion but supporting true
Christianity.   But Burns seems most confident and most poetically effective when he
views Christianity with a kind of amused acceptance, as one of several ethical alterna-
tives.   "The Holy Fair," "Address to the Deil," and the Concluding Hymn of "The
Jolly Beggars" do not offer true belief as the alternative to religious abuse, nor do they
offer deism or nonbelief.   The alternative to religious excess and hypocrisy is a kind

of general acceptance of man as he is, neither advocating nor denouncing Christianity. "The Holy Fair" ends with some people full of "love divine" and some full of brandy, and many headed toward "houghmagandie" (fornication). It is important to see that Burns does not describe the Holy Fair as a place filled with hypocrites seeking drink or sexual opportunity under the guise of seeking Christianity. Rather, most of the young men and women seem uncertain as to why they came to the Fair in the first place. Love divine, brandy, and houghmagandie are all parts of human experience, all to be accepted and enjoyed. Any attempt to raise one above the other, to repress one in favor of the other, to impose a value or create a hierarchy is pretentious and self-deluding, a result of man's prideful desire to impose systems where none exist. And Burns applies his broad tolerance to true Christianity as well as to drinking and fornication. Burns condemns only hypocrisy, pretentiousness, self-importance, repression of others. He condemns these attitudes and acts because they deny the importance of each man's individual feelings. Every aspect of human behavior is precious so long as it values emotions, senses, and ordinary experience.

Burns's poetry presents a disturbingly mixed collection because some of it is so bad. To be sure, most great poets wrote some bad poetry. But Burns's bad poetry is puzzling because it goes so strongly against everything he seems to have believed in, and because he wrote it during the same period he was writing his greatest poetry. In "To a Mountain Daisy" and "The Cotter's Saturday Night" he rails against the foul seducer and takes a sermonizing position which is not only biographically hypocritical (he had a number of illegitimate children, at least one of them after he was married), but also goes against his own joyous acceptance of sexuality. In "The Cotter's Saturday Night" he praises poverty as an ennobling experience, expressing a position which was fashionable among the rich, but which Burns knew perfectly well was absurd. A number of his poems ("Despondency," "Man Was Made to Mourn," "Winter," "The Lament") are written in sentimental, pompous diction. They express grandiloquent, meaningless, pessimistic abstractions, and state the opposite of the beliefs expressed in his best poetry. Burns knew life was hard; he also believed that life had consolations — love, friendship, physical pleasures, unexplained moments of joy, quiet contentment. It is, then, difficult to accept him saying:

> But see him on the edge of life,
>   With cares and sorrows worn;
> Then Age and Want — O ill-match'd pair! —
>   Shew Man was made to mourn.

("Man Was Made to Mourn," stanza V)

Especially when he also wrote:

> Hale be your heart! hale be your fiddle!
> Lang may your elbuck jink an' diddle,   *elbow dart fiddle*
> To cheer you through the weary widdle   *strife, commotion*
>   O' this vile warl',
> Until you on a cummock driddle,   *staff totter*
>   A grey-hair'd carl.   *old man*

("To Major Logan," stanza III)

The first poem is full of abstractions. It despairs without giving the reader reason. Age, in itself, is not cause for mourning, and we are given no sensuous detail to make us feel that it is. The stanza is redundant, obviously "age" comes at the "edge of life" and "cares and sorrows" make one "mourn." The second quotation is rich with vigor although it recognizes that life is hard. The rhyme of "diddle" and "weary widdle" emphasizes the similarity in disparity — the "commotion" suggested by "widdle" reflects the happy activity of the fiddling and the darting elbow. The movement of the fiddling is again reflected comically by the "driddling" on a staff, so that motion runs gaily through the stanza. The comic double rhymes of the long lines counter the terseness of the straightforward, most clearly uncomic short lines. And the image of tottering on a cane, however comic, gives sensuous reality to the fear of old age. Burns sees the world as richly complex. His emotions as expressed in the tone of this superb stanza are a part of this complexity — his feelings about Major Logan and the world he lives in are at once comic and pathetic, joyous and regretful, grimly realistic and gay.

Nothing in Burns's critical or theoretical comments explains why he wrote such dreadful, insincere poems as "Man Was Made to Mourn" when he was able to write such vital, energetic poems as "To Major Logan." It is easy to speculate, and many critics have. All we can say with certainty, however, is that the bad poems are part of the paradoxes and contradictions one finds everywhere in Burns.

"Epistle to James Smith" appears to be aimless and unstructured, merely an informal, rambling note to a friend. But Burns organizes the four subjects of the poem: friendship, poetry writing, poverty, and nature around the theme. The theme is that through personal freedom — in enjoying friendship, in writing poetry without concern for rules and traditions, in enjoying nature by wandering through it — one can endure poverty and, more important, make life good. This theme is particularly expressed through the image of unregulated movement: "I'll wander on, wi' tentless (attentionless) heed," "vacant, careless roamin," "nae rules nor roads observin," "we wander there, we wander here." Other images express pleasurable motion: frisking, dancing, sailing. The images of action, especially of free movement, contrast the static images related to the forces that oppose freedom: the "douce (sedate, prudent) folk" who "live by rule," whose life is a "standing pool" (note the rhymes of "rule," "calm an' cool," "fool," and "standing pool") or a "dyke," who "never stray," have a "steady air," and "ken the road." In poetry, Burns claims to write without undue attention to rules, "I rhyme for fun," "I rhyme away," he has a "random shot/ O' countra wit." When someone says Burns is inferior to poets of learning, "Ither poets, much your betters/ Far seen in Greek, deep men o' letters," he does not argue with the fictional pedant, but is satisfied with a poetry that doesn't need learning, that combines nature, peasant life, freedom:

> Henceforth I'll rove where busy ploughs
>   Are whistling thrang;   *busy*
> An' teach the lanely heights an' howes   *hollows*
>   My rustic sang.   (stanza IX)

The ability to write poetry is a metaphor, an example of the capacity that exists within every person to find joy and purpose in life. The creative power comes from within and enables one to endure poverty and to enjoy friendship, lovemaking, wandering in nature, so long as we give ourselves over to a life without douce rules. Douce folk not only stagnate, but fail to respond to their fellow humans, to nature, or to their own creativity.

The poverty and misfortune he must live with return again and again, the life of "eternal swervin'" can lead to a life "curst with age, obscure an' starvin'." But everytime misfortune appears, Burns overcomes it:

> An anxious e'e I never throws
> Behint my lug, or by my nose;   *ear*
> I jouk beneath Misfortune's blows   *duck*
>   As weel's I may;
> Sworn foe to sorrow, care, and prose,
>   I rhyme away.   (stanza XXV)

The rhymes of "nose," "Misfortune's blows," and "care and prose" jokingly contrast the varieties of his experience. His misfortune can be taken no more seriously than his nose, and all is a bunch of prose. The blows of misfortune are no less severe for being the subject of laughter (note the painful, visual effectiveness of "jouk" and the subtle pathos of the short line, "As weel's I may"). But the way to live with misfortune is to recognize the humor, the ridiculousness of life, to live freely, to write informal, spontaneous poetry, to "rhyme away."

It should be noted that Burns is not writing here about political freedom. He did write some poems about equality, especially "Is There for Honest Poverty," and he was sympathetic with the French Revolution. Throughout his writing he objects to an unfair class system, economic inequality, political repression. But his alternative to these evils, in this poem and throughout his writings, is to change oneself, not to change the society. The freedom he advocates is the kind available to every man.

Stylistically and thematically Burns has it both ways. The easy informality, the apparent lack of structure, the chatty diction, the fluid verse forms, all create a style that is appropriate for a poem that advocates life without rules. But beneath the "rustic sang" the consistent themes and images, the ironic rhymes, the controlled diction, the metrical forms all make "Epistle to James Smith" a highly organized ode to freedom.

"The Jolly Beggars" and "Tam o' Shanter" are probably Burns's greatest long poems. In each Burns creates a whole world of rustic life. "The Jolly Beggars" is a truly original work. There had been poems of that name in English and Scottish literature before, but the beggar usually turns out to be a prince in disguise. "The Jolly Beggars," probably for the first time in British literature, praises impoverished life without patronizing it, sentimentalizing it, pretending it is ennobling, or turning it into something else. Low life is wonderful the way it is, as every emotionally honest aspect of life can be wonderful if one will just accept it fully. The beggars are no heroes; they quarrel over mistresses, brag, steal, have contempt for the law, pawn their clothes for drink when a storm rages outside. The hardships are there; the soldier must "clatter on my stumps." But the rich directness and the personal honesty give the beggars a kind of virtue, attractiveness, and decency. The "martial chuck" tires of her "godly old chaplain" lover,

> Full soon I grew sick of my sanctified sot;
> The regiment at large for a husband I got.

The soldier shows his scars:

> This here was for a wench, and that other in a trench.

Burns does not make the beggars necessarily better or happier than respectable people. Such is exactly his point. It would be perverse to argue that if genuine pleasure, honesty, and beauty can be discovered in improbable places, then they cannot be discovered in probable ones. The cantata is a celebration of life, every part of it.

"Tam o' Shanter" is a kind of a fable, a story that is supposed to point a moral. But it is actually a mock-fable, the moral is illusory. Tam may get a scare, but he gets off free, only the innocent mare suffers. Burns assumes several roles in the poem, most frequently that of a sententious ass, forever moralizing, lecturing Tam, nodding his head over the foolishness of everyone but himself. At times, he assumes elevated diction to emphasize his pompous irrelevancies:

> Inspiring bold John Barleycorn,
> What dangers thou canst make us scorn!   (lines 105–106)

He tells the story with absurd prudishness. When the dance of the witches becomes frantically wild, he will still allow no nakedness in his poem:

> And coost her duddies to the wark,   *tattered clothes*
> And linket at it in her sark.   *tripped, danced   underwear*
>   (lines 149–150)

At times he sermonizes from a moral basis, at times from a financial basis. He is disturbed that Tam is interested in witches, not because they are engaged in the devil's business, but because they wear cheap underwear and are old:

> Louping and flinging on a crummock,   *staff*
> I wonder did na turn thy stomach!   (lines 161–162)

The narrator is himself drawn in when one of the witches turns out to be young and beautiful, especially when he notices her expensive undershirt. Once he has described it, its price, its history, and its moral implications, his muse can go no farther, "Sic (such) flights are far beyond her power." And then Tam's wild flight from the witches ends with his mare losing her tail. Burns again has it both ways, for the sententious and boorish narrator still tells a story that is suspenseful and exciting. "Tam o' Shanter" is a dramatic story, a comic description of drunkenness in all its stages, a satire on superstition, a comic version of the magical tale. It is also a satire on those who, like the narrator, try to impose morality, logic, and sense where none exists and who try to demonstrate that mysterious forces are working to make the world just. There is more sense in the description of Tam's drunken joy:

> Kings may be blest but Tam was glorious,
> O'er a' the ills o' life victorious!   (lines 57–58)

than in all the narrator's attempts to find moral order in a frightening ride through the dark woods.

After 1786 Burns devoted himself almost entirely to revising and collecting songs.

He wrote some poems, but with the exception of "Tam o' Shanter" and "On the Late Captain Grose's Peregrination thro' Scotland," they are bad. "Holy Willie's Prayer" and "The Jolly Beggars" were written earlier, although not published until after 1786. This movement toward songs, viewed by some critics as a decline in his career, is actually a logical and creative development of his poetic power and the beginnings of a major shift in the direction of British poetry.

Most of the better works in the Kilmarnock edition are satires, usually advocating the doctrine of acceptance as an alternative to the human and natural evils in the world and expressing the belief that all men have the capacity for joy and creativity. The song is a simple outpouring of feelings with an artistically constructed statement beneath the apparent simplicity. The song thus symbolizes, in form and content, the universality of beauty and the order that can be derived from emotion. Song writing was, then, a probable direction for Burns to take as his epistles and other poems become less satiric.

Further, British poetry was changing. Satire had been the predominant poetic form in Britain, under the leadership of Dryden and Pope, for a century before Burns. Burns is the last important verse satirist in the eighteenth century. After Burns, Byron is the only important verse satirist in the nineteenth century. Lyric poetry becomes the predominant form, under the leadership of Wordsworth, Shelley, and Keats. The causes for this shift are complicated and subject to speculation. But whatever the reasons may be, the direction of poetry in Britain was away from satire and toward the lyric. In devoting almost all his talents to song writing from 1786 to his death in 1796, Burns participates in a major shift in the style of British poetry.

Burns published most of his songs in two collections, from 1786 to 1796 in James Johnson's *Scots Musical Museum*, which Burns also edited, and from 1792 to 1796 in George Thomson's *A Select Collection of Original Scottish Airs*. Burns also made up a collection of bawdy songs, called *The Merry Muses of Caledonia*, some of which he wrote, some of which he revised from earlier sources, some of which he only collected from popular Scottish folk songs. He did not publish them, apparently intending to use them to amuse his friends. But they were published shortly after he died and have been the subject of controversy ever since. Editions of them have been suppressed, exploited, and faked. It was not, however, until 1959 that a serious edition of the collection was published in which the editors, without prejudice or prudery, and with considerable scholarship, attempted to identify the poems by Burns and to establish the texts accurately. The subsequent discovery of an early manuscript of the first published version has improved considerably the means by which Burns's authorship can be determined.

The songs of *The Merry Muses of Caledonia* are perhaps a little disappointing. They tend to be coarse rather than witty. Many of them are narrated by a woman but do not accurately describe a woman's sexual feelings. Burns was unusually sensitive and sympathetic to women's emotions and was capable of seeing things from a woman's point of view. But when he described sexual experience, he expressed a common masculine misconception of female response, seeing it primarily as an extension of the masculine sensation. In this respect Burns is no exception to an old tradition of bawdy poetry. One wishes, however, that he could have seen beyond the conventional belief, as he could in so many other ways. But there are clearly a considerable number of

interesting songs in the collection.   Many of them show Burns's true creative abilities
and are among the best bawdy poems in British literature.

All his songs are best appreciated with the music but can still be read and enjoyed as
lyric poetry.   They express an enormous range of emotions — almost every emotion
from ecstacy to despondency, from enraptured love:

> O, my luve is like a red, red rose,
>   That's newly sprung in June.   ("A Red, Red Rose")

to obsessive love:

> And maun I still on Menie doat
>   And bear the scorn that's in her e'e?
> For it's jet, jet-black, an' it's like a hawk,
>   An' it winna let a body be.   *will not*
>   ("Composed in Spring")

to undisguised hate:

> Bitter in dool, I licket my winnins   *sorrows   tasted   reward*
> O' marrying Bess, to gie her a slave.
> Blest be the hour she cool'd in her linens,
>   And blythe be the bird that sings on her grave!
>   ("O, Merry hae I been")

Relations between sexes can be loving, tender, gently mingled with a benevolent, natural
world in which the same emotions apply to humans and nature:

> Now simmer blinks on flow'ry braes,
> And o'er the crystal streamlets plays,
> Come, let us spend the lightsome days
>   In the birks of Aberfeldie!   ("The Birks of Aberfeldie")

And relations between the sexes can be purely sensual:

> What could I say, what could I do,
>   I bann'd and sair misca'd him,   *cursed   sore   abused*
> But whiltie-whaltie gaed his a——e, *probably a made-up expression went*
>   The mair that I forbade him:
> He stell'd his foot against a stane,   *fixed*
>   And doubl'd ilka stroke in,   *each*
> Till I gaed daft amang his hands,
>   O the deevil tak sic troggin!   *peddling* ("The Trogger" — from
>   *The Merry Muses of Caledonia*)

He has probably written more poems spoken by a woman than any male poet in Britain.
He is probably the greatest spokesman of manly friendship in British literature. His
songs deal with the joys of drinking, eating, and the pain of hunger, with parting, loneli-
ness, and reconciliation, youth and old age, political freedom and psychological im-
prisonment, peddling, farming, and spinning, desire, denial, and fulfillment, sexual
prowess and impotence — the list could go on and on.

His greatness lies not just in the range of subjects but in the enormous variety of tones, points of view, attitudes he can bring to a single subject. For example, the subject of a woman deserted in love, especially one who is left pregnant or with an illegitimate child. In earlier British literature she was treated with scorn, as an object of fun, as a moral lesson, as a cause for sentimental pity. Burns went beyond all these conventional postures.

He usually assumes the point of view of the suffering girl. Indeed Burns almost always describes emotional states from the viewpoint of the person experiencing it. Most obviously, the deserted woman is lonely and longs for her lover to return:

> Simmer's a pleasant time:
> Flowers of every colour,
> The water rins owre the heugh,   *steep*
> And I long for my true lover.   ("Ay Waukin, O")

In older treatments of the subject, and in Burns's possible source for this song in Scottish folk songs, the traditional poet described nature as beautiful, then inserted a "but" and contrasted it with her unhappiness. Burns leaves the contrast only implied. The girl appears too unhappily listless to bother with nice logical oppositions. Further, the three parallel observations of nature are each undeveloped, the second has no syntactic function, so that the girl's mind seems just to wander from one observation to another, none of them meaning much to her. Yet the images serve to provide the reader with contrasts. The natural pleasantness, variety of color, movement of the water, oppose her sorrow, which has none of them — numb, colorless, unvaried, unchanging.

In "Wha'll Mow Me Now?" Burns makes a prostitute the speaker, a young woman "mowin for its bread," who has been made pregnant by a soldier she loved. The song contains a suggestive intertwining of the several subjects — the woman whose business is impaired by her pregnancy, her suffering the "scornfu' sneer" of the righteous, and her longing for her lover, the father of her child. The tone alternates between pathos, social satire, and comedy:

> O wha'll m—w me now, my jo,
> An' wha'll m—w me now: *fuck*
> A sodger wi' his bandileers   *ammunition box*
> Has bang'd my belly fu'.

The refrain, here quoted, puts matters partly on a business, partly on a sensual basis. She evidently enjoyed her work before her condition made her unattractive. Her complete frankness makes the reader both identify with her and damn the righteous sneerers and the faithless lover:

> But deevil damn the lousy loon,   *rogue*
> Denies the bairn he got!   *child*
> Or lea's the merry a—e he lo'ed,
> To wear a ragged coat!

The last, suggestive detail avoids making the lover a swashbuckling hero or a dastardly villain. He, also, is part of a hard world which can be endured by relying upon intensity of feelings.

In "Duncan Gray" frank comedy becomes the predominant tone.

The girdin brak, the beast cam down,	*binding broke*
I tint my curch and baith my shoon,	*lost kerchief shoes*
And, Duncan, ye 're an unco loun —	*big bastard*
Wae on the bad girdin o't!	

The amusing materialism of the girl describing the intercourse mostly in terms of the loss of her kerchief and "baith" her shoes, the energetic directness of "ye 're an unco loun," the use of the triplet rhyme which lands on the word "loun," all work toward making her statement too frank to be pathetic. She doesn't take the situation too seriously herself. In the last stanza, as frequently in poems on this subject, the girl hopes for her lover's return — and Burns leaves the probability of the event as ambiguous as is life.

Burns is, in my opinion, one of the very great poets in British literature, perhaps the greatest British poet of the eighteenth century. He is, I think, one of the poets who speak most directly to those of us in the late twentieth century who also have begun to question the old rules and who are trying to find a philosophy that derives from ordinary experience. He is probably less popular than he deserves because of the superficial difficulties in his language. He has also suffered from the Scotophiles, who make him into a national monument, the sentimentalists, who still preserve and emphasize his worst works, and from the modern academic critics, who do not find his works sufficiently crammed with verbal complexity or visionary obscurity. And Burns does not fit easily into trends or periods — he is neither Neoclassical nor Romantic, neither purely Scottish nor purely English. It is yet another contradiction in his life and reputation that Burns, who more than any other British poet has urged us to take life for what it is, cannot be taken for what he is.

Perhaps Burns's greatness will eventually be appreciated. He may someday be recognized as a truly articulate exponent of common experience, of ordinary feelings, of everyday life, of the value of simple emotions and impulses. He may be seen as the poet who tried to describe a way of living without conventional religion or schematic or mystical counterparts to it, without reliance on political systems or social conventions either as they were, as they are, or as they might become. He may be seen as a great apostle of the beauty that is available to every man and the essential value of every human being.

RAYMOND BENTMAN

The
Poetical Works
of
Burns

POEMS CHIEFLY IN THE SCOTTISH DIALECT

FOR some time before 1786, Burns had cherished a desire for " guid black prent; " and its fulfilment was hastened in the end by the thought of his removal to Jamaica. " Before leaving my native country," he says, " I resolved to publish my poems." [He issued a prospectus, and after securing a sufficient number of subscribers, the book with the above title was issued by John Wilson, Kilmarnock, appearing July 31, 1786. It was a handsome octavo, bound, except for a few copies in paper covers, in blue boards, with a white back and neat label. It was issued by subscription, and six hundred copies were printed. It contained the following preface.]

The following trifles are not the production of the Poet, who, with all the advantages of learned art, and perhaps amid the elegancies and idlenesses of upper life, looks down for a rural theme, with an eye to Theocrites or Virgil. To the Author of this, these and other celebrated names (their countrymen) are, in their original languages, "a fountain shut up, and a book sealed." Unacquainted with the necessary requisites for commencing Poet by rule, he sings the sentiments and manners he felt and saw in himself and his rustic compeers around him, in his and their native language. Though a Rhymer from his earliest years, at least from the earliest impulses of the softer passions, it was not till very lately that the applause, perhaps the partiality, of Friendship, wakened his vanity so far as to make him think anything of his was worth showing; and none of the following works were ever composed with a view to the press. To amuse himself with the little creations of his own fancy, amid the toil and fatigues of a laborious life; to transcribe the various feelings, the loves, the griefs, the hopes, the fears, in his own breast; to find some kind of counterpoise to the struggles of a world, always an alien scene, a task uncouth to the poetical mind; these were his motives for courting the Muses, and in these he found Poetry to be its own reward.

Now that he appears in the public character of an Author, he does it with fear and trembling. So dear is fame to the rhyming tribe, that even he, an obscure, nameless Bard, shrinks aghast at the thought of being branded as " An impertinent blockhead, obtruding his nonsense on the world; and because he can make a shift to jingle a few doggerel Scotch rhymes together, looks upon himself as a Poet of no small consequence forsooth."

It is an observation of that celebrated Poet [1] — whose divine Elegies do honor to our language, our nation, and our species — that " Humility has depressed many a genius to a hermit, but never raised one to fame." If any Critic catches at the word *genius*, the Author tells him, once for all, that he certainly looks upon himself as possest of some poetic abilities, otherwise his publishing in the manner he has done would be a manœuvre below the worst character which, he hopes, his worst enemy will ever give him : but to the genius of a Ramsay, or the glorious dawnings of the poor, unfortunate Ferguson, he, with equal unaffected sincerity, declares that, even in his highest pulse of vanity, he has not the most distant pretensions. These two justly admired Scotch Poets he has often had in his eye in the following pieces ; but rather with a view to kindle at their flame, than for servile imitation.

To his Subscribers the Author returns his most sincere thanks. Not the mercenary bow over a counter, but the heart-throbbing gratitude of the Bard, conscious how much he is indebted to Benevolence and Friendship for gratifying him, if he deserves it, in that dearest wish of every poetic bosom — to be distinguished. He begs his readers, particularly the Learned and the Polite, who may honor him with a perusal, that they will make every allowance for Education and Circumstances of Life : but if, after a fair, candid, and impartial criticism, he shall stand convicted of Dulness and Nonsense, let him be done by, as he would in that case do by others — let him be condemned without mercy, to contempt and oblivion.

[1] Shenstone.

THE TWA DOGS

A TALE

According to Gilbert Burns, this *Tale* was "composed after the resolution of publishing was nearly taken." During the night before the death of William Burness, Robert's favorite dog, Luath, was killed by some person unknown. He thought at first of certain *Stanzas to the Memory of a Quadruped Friend* — a true Eighteenth-Century inspiration — "but this plan was given up for the *Tale* as it now stands." "I have," he says, in a letter to John Richmond, 17th February, 1786, "likewise completed [since he saw Richmond in November] my poem on the Dogs, but have not shown it to the world." It was Luath's successor — inheriting his name or not — whose appearance at the "penny dance" at Mauchline led Burns to remark, in Jean Armour's hearing, that "he wished he could get any of the lasses to like him as well as his dog did."

'T WAS in that place o' Scotland's isle
That bears the name of auld King Coil,
Upon a bonie day in June,
When wearing thro' the afternoon,
Twa dogs, that were na thrang at hame,
Forgathered ance upon a time.

The first I 'll name, they ca'd him Cæsar,
Was keepit for "his Honor's" pleasure:
His hair, his size, his mouth, his lugs,
Shew'd he was nane o' Scotland's dogs;
But whalpit some place far abroad,
Whare sailors gang to fish for cod.

His locked, letter'd, braw brass collar
Shew'd him the gentleman an' scholar;
But tho' he was o' high degree,
The fient a pride, nae pride had he;
But wad hae spent an hour caressin,
Ev'n wi' a tinkler-gipsy's messin;
At kirk or market, mill or smiddie,
Nae tawted tyke, tho' e'er sae duddie,
But he wad stan't, as glad to see him,
An' stroan't on stanes an' hillocks wi' him.

The tither was a ploughman's collie,
A rhyming, ranting, raving billie,
Wha for his friend an' comrade had him,
And in his freaks had Luath ca'd him,
After some dog in Highland sang,
Was made lang syne — Lord knows how
    lang.

He was a gash an' faithfu' tyke,
As ever lap a sheugh or dyke.
His honest, sonsie, baws'nt face
Ay gat him friends in ilka place;
His breast was white, his tousie back
Weel clad wi' coat o' glossy black;
His gawsie tail, wi' upward curl,
Hung owre his hurdies wi' a swirl.

Nae doubt but they were fain o' ither,
And unco pack an' thick thegither;
Wi' social nose whyles snuff'd an' snowkit;
Whyles mice an' moudieworts they howkit;
Whyles scour'd awa' in lang excursion,
An' worry'd ither in diversion;
Till tir'd at last wi' monie a farce,
They sat them down upon their arse,
An' there began a lang digression
About the "lords o' the creation."

CÆSAR

I 've aften wonder'd, honest Luath,
What sort o' life poor dogs like you have;
An' when the gentry's life I saw,
What way poor bodies liv'd ava.

Our laird gets in his rackèd rents,
His coals, his kain, an' a' his stents:
He rises when he likes himsel;
His flunkies answer at the bell;
He ca's his coach; he ca's his horse;
He draws a bonie silken purse,
As lang 's my tail, whare, thro' the steeks,
The yellow letter'd Geordie keeks.

Frae morn to e'en it 's nought but toil-
    ing,
At baking, roasting, frying, boiling;
An' tho' the gentry first are stechin,
Yet ev'n the ha' folk fill their pechan
Wi' sauce, ragouts, an sic like trashtrie,
That 's little short o' downright wastrie:
Our whipper-in, wee, blastit wonner,
Poor, worthless elf, it eats a dinner,
Better than onie tenant-man
His Honor has in a' the lan';
An' what poor cot-folk pit their painch in,
I own it 's past my comprehension.

LUATH

Trowth, Cæsar, whyles they 're fash't
    eneugh:
A cotter howkin in a sheugh,
Wi' dirty stanes biggin a dyke,
Baring a quarry, an' sic like;

Himsel, a wife, he thus sustains,
A smytrie o' wee duddie weans,
An' nought but his han' darg to keep
Them right an' tight in thack an' rape.

An' when they meet wi' sair disasters,
Like loss o' health or want o' masters,
Ye maist wad think, a wee touch langer,
An' they maun starve o' cauld and hunger:
But how it comes, I never kend yet,
They 're maistly wonderfu' contented;
An' buirdly chiels, an' clever hizzies,
Are bred in sic a way as this is.

CÆSAR

But then to see how ye 're negleckit,
How huff'd, an' cuff'd, an' disrespeckit !
Lord, man, our gentry care as little
For delvers, ditchers, an' sic cattle;
They gang as saucy by poor folk,
As I wad by a stinking brock.

I 've notic'd, on our laird's court-day,
(An' monie a time my heart 's been wae),
Poor tenant bodies, scant o' cash,
How they maun thole a factor's snash:
He 'll stamp an' threaten, curse an' swear
He 'll apprehend them, poind their gear;
While they maun staun', wi' aspect humble,
An' hear it a', an' fear an' tremble !

I see how folk live that hae riches;
But surely poor-folk maun be wretches !

LUATH

They 're nae sae wretched 's ane wad
        think:
Tho' constantly on poortith's brink,
They 're sae accustom'd wi' the sight,
The view o't gies them little fright.

Then chance an' fortune are sae guided,
They 're ay in less or mair provided;
An' tho' fatigu'd wi' close employment,
A blink o' rest 's a sweet enjoyment.

The dearest comfort o' their lives,
Their grushie weans an' faithfu' wives;
The prattling things are just their pride,
That sweetens a' their fire-side.

An' whyles twalpennie worth o' nappy
Can mak the bodies unco happy:
They lay aside their private cares,
To mind the Kirk and State affairs;

They 'll talk o' patronage an' priests,
Wi' kindling fury i' their breasts,
Or tell what new taxation 's comin,
An' ferlie at the folk in Lon'on.

As bleak-fac'd Hallowmass returns,
They get the jovial, ranting kirns,
When rural life, of ev'ry station,
Unite in common recreation;
Love blinks, Wit slaps, an' social Mirth
Forgets there 's Care upo' the earth.

That merry day the year begins,
They bar the door on frosty win's;
The nappy reeks wi' mantling ream,
An' sheds a heart-inspiring steam;
The luntin pipe, an' sneeshin mill,
Are handed round wi' right guid will;
The cantie auld folks crackin crouse,
The young anes ranting thro' the house —
My heart has been sae fain to see them,
That I for joy hae barkit wi' them.

Still it 's owre true that ye hae said
Sic game is now owre aften play'd;
There 's monie a creditable stock
O' decent, honest, fawsont folk,
Are riven out baith root an' branch,
Some rascal's pridefu' greed to quench,
Wha thinks to knit himsel the faster
In favor wi' some gentle master,
Wha, aiblins thrang a parliamentin',
For Britain's guid his saul indentin' —

CÆSAR

Haith, lad, ye little ken about it:
For Britain's guid ! guid faith ! I doubt
        it.
Say rather, gaun as Premiers lead him
An' saying aye or no 's they bid him:
At operas an' plays parading,
Mortgaging, gambling, masquerading:
Or maybe, in a frolic daft,
To Hague or Calais taks a waft,
To mak a tour an' tak a whirl,
To learn bon ton, an' see the worl'.

There, at Vienna or Versailles,
He rives his father's auld entails;
Or by Madrid he taks the rout,
To thrum guitars an' fecht wi' nowt;
Or down Italian vista startles,
Whore-hunting amang groves o' myrtles
Then bowses drumlie German-water,
To mak himsel look fair an' fatter,

An' clear the consequential sorrows,
Love-gifts of Carnival signoras.

For Britain's guid! for her destruction!
Wi' dissipation, feud an' faction.

LUATH

Hech, man! dear sirs! is that the gate
They waste sae monie a braw estate!
Are we sae foughten an' harass'd
For gear ta gang that gate at last?

O would they stay aback frae courts,
An' please themsels wi' countra sports,
It wad for ev'ry ane be better,
The laird, the tenant, an' the cotter!
For thae frank, rantin, ramblin billies,
Fient haet o' them is ill-hearted fellows:
Except for breakin o' their timmer,
Or speakin lightly o' their limmer,
Or shootin of a hare or moor-cock,
The ne'er-a-bit they 're ill to poor folk.

But will ye tell me, master Cæsar:
Sure great folk's life 's a life o' pleas-
ure?
Nae cauld nor hunger e'er can steer them,
The vera thought o't need na fear them.

CÆSAR

Lord, man, were ye but whyles whare I
am,
The gentles, ye wad ne'er envy 'em!

It 's true, they need na starve or sweat,
Thro' winter's cauld, or simmer's heat;
They 've nae sair wark to craze their banes,
An' fill auld-age wi' grips an' granes:
But human bodies are sic fools,
For a' their colleges an' schools,
That when nae real ills perplex them,
They mak enow themsels to vex them;
An' ay the less they hae to sturt them,
In like proportion, less will hurt them.

A countra fellow at the pleugh,
His acre 's till'd, he 's right eneugh;
A countra girl at her wheel,
Her dizzen 's done, she 's unco weel;
But gentlemen, an' ladies warst,
Wi' ev'n down want o' wark are curst:
They loiter, lounging, lank an' lazy;
Tho' deil-haet ails them, yet uneasy:
Their days insipid, dull an' tasteless;
Their nights unquiet, lang an' restless.

An' ev'n their sports, their balls an' races,
Their galloping through public places,
There 's sic parade, sic pomp an' art,
The joy can scarcely reach the heart.

The men cast out in party-matches,
Then sowther a' in deep debauches;
Ae night they 're mad wi' drink an' whor-
ing,
Niest day their life is past enduring.

The ladies arm-in-arm in clusters,
As great an' gracious a' as sisters;
But hear their absent thoughts o' ither,
They 're a' run deils an' jads thegither.
Whyles, owre the wee bit cup an' platie,
They sip the scandal-potion pretty;
Or lee-lang nights, wi' crabbit leuks
Pore owre the devil's pictur'd beuks;
Stake on a chance a farmer's stackyard,
An' cheat like onie unhang'd blackguard.

There 's some exceptions, man an' woman;
But this is Gentry's life in common.

By this, the sun was out o' sight,
An' darker gloamin brought the night;
The bum-clock humm'd wi' lazy drone;
The kye stood rowtin i' the loan;
When up they gat, an' shook their lugs,
Rejoic'd they were na *men*, but *dogs*;
An' each took aff his several way,
Resolv'd to meet some ither day.

SCOTCH DRINK

Gie him strong drink until he wink,
    That 's sinking in despair;
An' liquor guid to fire his bluid,
    That 's prest wi' grief an' care:
There let him bowse, and deep carouse,
    Wi' bumpers flowing o'er,
Till he forgets his loves or debts,
    An' minds his griefs no more.
                    SOLOMON'S PROVERBS, xxxi. 6, 7.

Composed some time between the beginning of November, 1785, and 17th February, 1786 (letter of Burns to Richmond). On 20th March Burns sent a copy to his friend Robert Muir, wine-merchant, Kilmarnock: "May the —— follow with a blessing for your edification." The metre, which has come to be regarded as essentially Scottish (see Prefatory Note to the *Address to the Deil*, p. 12), is that of Fergusson's *Cauler Water*, of which *Scotch Drink* is a kind of parody.

I

Let other poets raise a fracas
'Bout vines, an' wines, an' drucken Bacchus,
An' crabbit names an' stories wrack us,
    An' grate our lug:
I sing the juice Scotch bear can mak us,
    In glass or jug.

II

O thou, my Muse! guid auld Scotch drink!
Whether thro' wimplin worms thou jink,
Or, richly brown, ream owre the brink,
    In glorious faem,
Inspire me, till I lisp an' wink,
    To sing thy name!

III

Let husky wheat the haughs adorn,
An' aits set up their awnie horn,
An' pease an' beans, at e'en or morn,
    Perfume the plain:
Leeze me on thee, John Barleycorn,
    Thou king o' grain!

IV

On thee aft Scotland chows her cood,
In souple scones, the wale o' food!
Or tumbling in the boiling flood
    Wi' kail an' beef;
But when thou pours thy strong heart's blood,
    There thou shines chief.

V

Food fills the wame, an' keeps us livin;
Tho' life's a gift no worth receivin,
When heavy-dragg'd wi' pine an' grievin;
    But oil'd by thee,
The wheels o' life gae down-hill, scrievin,
    Wi' rattlin glee.

VI

Thou clears the head o' doited Lear,
Thou cheers the heart o' drooping Care;
Thou strings the nerves o' Labor sair,
    At 's weary toil;
Thou ev'n brightens dark Despair
    Wi' gloomy smile.

VII

Aft, clad in massy siller weed,
Wi' gentles thou erects thy head;
Yet, humbly kind in time o' need,
    The poor man's wine:

His wee drap parritch, or his bread,
    Thou kitchens fine.

VIII

Thou art the life o' public haunts:
But thee, what were our fairs and rants?
Ev'n godly meetings o' the saunts,
    By thee inspir'd,
When, gaping, they besiege the tents,
    Are doubly fir'd.

IX

That merry night we get the corn in,
O sweetly, then, thou reams the horn in!
Or reekin on a New-Year mornin
    In cog or bicker,
An' just a wee drap sp'ritual burn in,
    An' gusty sucker!

X

When Vulcan gies his bellows breath,
An' ploughmen gather wi' their graith,
O rare! to see thee fizz an' freath
    I' th' lugget caup!
Then Burnewin comes on like death
    At ev'ry chaup.

XI

Nae mercy, then, for airn or steel:
The brawnie, bainie, ploughman chiel,
Brings hard owrehip, wi' sturdy wheel,
    The strong forehammer,
Till block an' studdie ring an' reel,
    Wi' dinsome clamour.

XII

When skirlin weanies see the light,
Thou maks the gossips clatter bright,
How fumbling cuifs their dearies slight;
    Wae worth the name!
Nae howdie gets a social night,
    Or plack frae them.

XIII

When neebors anger at a plea,
An' just as wud as wud can be,
How easy can the barley-brie
    Cement the quarrel!
It 's aye the cheapest lawyer's fee,
    To taste the barrel.

XIV

Alake! that e'er my Muse has reason,
To wyte her countrymen wi' treason!

But monie daily weet their weason
        Wi' liquors nice,
An' hardly, in a winter season,
        E'er spier her price.

XV

Wae worth that brandy, burnin trash !
Fell source o' monie a pain an' brash !
Twins monie a poor, doylt, drucken hash,
        O' half his days;
An' sends, beside, auld Scotland's cash
        To her warst faes.

XVI

Ye Scots, wha wish auld Scotland well !
Ye chief, to you my tale I tell,
Poor, plackless devils like mysel !
        It sets you ill,
Wi' bitter, dearthfu' wines to mell,
        Or foreign gill.

XVII

May gravels round his blather wrench,
An' gouts torment him, inch by inch,
Wha twists his gruntle wi' a glunch
        O' sour disdain,
Out owre a glass o' whisky-punch
        Wi' honest men !

XVIII

O Whisky ! soul o' plays an' pranks !
Accept a Bardie's gratefu' thanks !
When wanting thee, what tuneless cranks
        Are my poor verses !
Thou comes — they rattle i' their ranks
        At ither's arses !

XIX

Thee, Ferintosh ! O sadly lost !
Scotland lament frae coast to coast !
Now colic grips, an' barkin hoast
        May kill us a';
For loyal Forbes' chartered boast
        Is taen awa !

XX

Thae curst horse-leeches o' th' Excise,
Wha mak the whisky stells their prize !
Haud up thy han', Deil ! ance, twice,
        thrice !
        There, seize the blinkers !
An' bake them up in brunstane pies
        For poor damn'd drinkers.

XXI

Fortune ! if thou 'll but gie me still
Hale breeks, a scone, an' whisky gill,
An' rowth o' rhyme to rave at will,
        Tak a' the rest,
An' deal 't about as thy blind skill
        Directs thee best.

THE AUTHOR'S EARNEST CRY AND PRAYER

TO THE RIGHT HONORABLE AND HONORABLE THE SCOTTISH REPRESENTATIVES IN THE HOUSE OF COMMONS

Dearest of distillation ! last and best —
— How art thou lost ! —
Parody on Milton.

I

YE Irish lords, ye knights an' squires,
Wha represent our brughs an' shires,
An' doucely manage our affairs
        In Parliament,
To you a simple Bardie's prayers
        Are humbly sent.

II

Alas ! my roupet Muse is haerse !
Your Honors' hearts wi' grief 't wad pierce.
To see her sittin on her arse
        Low i' the dust,
And scriechin out prosaic verse,
        An' like to brust !

III

Tell them wha hae the chief direction,
Scotland an' me 's in great affliction,
E'er sin' they laid that curst restriction
        On aqua-vitæ;
An' rouse them up to strong conviction,
        An' move their pity.

IV

Stand forth, an' tell yon Premier youth
The honest, open, naked truth:
Tell him o' mine an' Scotland's drouth,
        His servants humble:
The muckle deevil blaw you south,
        If ye dissemble !

V

Does onie great man glunch an' gloom ?
Speak out, an' never fash your thumb !

Let posts an' pensions sink or soom
        Wi' them wha grant 'em:
If honestly they canna come,
        Far better want 'em.

VI

In gath'rin votes you were na slack;
Now stand as tightly by your tack:
Ne'er claw your lug, an' fidge your back,
        An' hum an haw;
But raise your arm, an' tell your crack
        Before them a'.

VII

Paint Scotland greetin owre her thrissle;
Her mutchkin stowp as toom 's a whissle;
An' damn'd excisemen in a bustle,
        Seizin a stell,
Triumphant, crushin 't like a mussel,
        Or lampit shell !

VIII

Then, on the tither hand, present her —
A blackguard smuggler right behint her,
An' cheek-for-chow, a chuffie vintner
        Colleaguing join,
Pickin her pouch as bare as winter
        Of a' kind coin.

IX

Is there, that bears the name o' Scot,
But feels his heart's bluid rising hot,
To see his poor auld mither's pot
        Thus dung in staves,
An' plunder'd o' her hindmost groat,
        By gallows knaves ?

X

Alas ! I 'm but a nameless wight,
Trode i' the mire out o' sight !
But could I like Montgomeries fight,
        Or gab like Boswell,
There 's some sark-necks I wad draw tight,
        An' tie some hose well.

XI

God bless your Honors ! can ye see 't,
The kind, auld, cantie carlin greet,
An' no get warmly to your feet,
        An' gar them hear it,
An' tell them wi' a patriot-heat,
        Ye winna bear it ?

XII

Some o' you nicely ken the laws,
To round the period an' pause,

An' with rhetóric clause on clause
        To mak harangues:
Then echo thro' Saint Stephen's wa's
        Auld Scotland's wrangs.

XIII

Dempster, a true blue Scot I 'se warran;
Thee, aith-detesting, chaste Kilkerran;
An' that glib-gabbet Highland baron,
        The Laird o' Graham;
An' ane, a chap that 's damn'd auldfarran,
        Dundas his name :

XIV

Erskine, a spunkie Norland billie;
True Campbells, Frederick and Ilay;
An' Livistone, the bauld Sir Willie;
        An' monie ithers,
Whom auld Demosthenes or Tully
        Might own for brithers.

XV

Thee, sodger Hugh, my watchman stented,
If Bardies e'er are represented;
I ken if that your sword were wanted,
        Ye 'd lend your hand;
But when there 's ought to say anent it,
        Ye 're at a stand.

XVI

Arouse, my boys ! exert your mettle,
To get auld Scotland back her kettle;
Or faith ! I 'll wad my new pleugh-pettle,
        Ye 'll see 't or lang,
She 'll teach you, wi' a reekin whittle,
        Anither sang.

XVII

This while she 's been in crankous mood,
Her lost Militia fir'd her bluid;
(Deil na they never mair do guid,
        Play'd her that pliskie !)
An' now she 's like to rin red-wud
        About her whisky.

XVIII

An' Lord ! if ance they pit her till 't,
Her tartan petticoat she 'll kilt,
An' durk an' pistol at her belt,
        She 'll tak the streets,
An' rin her whittle to the hilt,
        I' the first she meets !

XIX

For God-sake, sirs ! then speak her fair,
An' straik her cannie wi' the hair,

An' to the Muckle House repair,
   Wi' instant speed,
An' strive, wi' a' your wit an' lear,
   To get remead.

XX

Yon ill-tongu'd tinkler, Charlie Fox,
May taunt you wi' his jeers an' mocks;
But gie him 't het, my hearty cocks !
   E'en cowe the cadie !
An' send him to his dicing box
   An' sportin lady.

XXI

Tell yon guid bluid of auld Boconnock's,
I 'll be his debt twa mashlum bonnocks,
An' drink his health in auld Nanse Tin-
   nock's
   Nine times a-week,
If he some scheme, like tea an' winnocks,
   Wad kindly seek.

XXII

Could he some commutation broach,
I 'll pledge my aith in guid braid Scotch,
He needna fear their foul reproach
   Nor erudition,
Yon mixtie-maxtie, queer hotch-potch,
   The Coalition.

XXIII

Auld Scotland has a raucle tongue;
She 's just a devil wi' a rung;
An' if she promise auld or young
   To tak their part,
Tho' by the neck she should be strung,
   She 'll no desert.

XXIV

And now, ye chosen Five-and-Forty,
May still your mither's heart support
  ye;
Then, tho' a minister grow dorty,
   An' kick your place,
Ye 'll snap your fingers, poor an' hearty,
   Before his face.

XXV

God bless your Honors, a' your days,
Wi' sowps o' kail and brats o' claes,
In spite o' a' the thievish kaes,
   That haunt St. Jamie's !
Your humble Bardie sings an' prays,
   While Rab his name is.

POSTSCRIPT

XXVI

Let half-starv'd slaves in warmer skies
See future wines, rich-clust'ring, rise;
Their lot auld Scotland ne'er envíes,
   But, blythe and frisky,
She eyes her freeborn, martial boys
   Tak aff their whisky.

XXVII

What tho' their Phœbus kinder warms,
While fragrance blooms and Beauty charms,
When wretches range, in famish'd swarms,
   The scented groves;
Or, hounded forth, dishonor arms
   In hungry droves !

XXVIII

Their gun 's a burden on their shouther;
They downa bide the stink o' powther;
Their bauldest thought 's a hank'ring
  swither
   To stan' or rin,
Till skelp — a shot — they 're aff, a' throw'-
  ther,
   To save their skin.

XXIX

But bring a Scotsman frae his hill,
Clap in his cheek a Highland gill,
Say, such is royal George's will,
   An' there 's the foe !
He has nae thought but how to kill
   Twa at a blow.

XXX

Nae cauld, faint-hearted doubtings tease
  him;
Death comes, wi' fearless eye he sees
  him;
Wi' bluidy han' a welcome gies him;
   An' when he fa's,
His latest draught o' breathin lea'es him
   In faint huzzas.

XXXI

Sages their solemn een may steek
An' raise a philosophic reek,
An' physically causes seek
   In clime an' season;
But tell me whisky's name in Greek:
   I 'll tell the reason.

XXXII

Scotland, my auld, respected mither !
Tho' whiles ye moistify your leather,
Till whare ye sit on craps o' heather
　　　Ye tine your dam,
Freedom and whisky gang thegither,
　　　　　Tak aff your dram !

THE HOLY FAIR

A robe of seeming truth and trust
　Hid crafty observation;
And secret hung, with poison'd crust,
　The dirk of defamation:
A mask that like the gorget show'd,
　Dye-varying on the pigeon;
And for a mantle large and broad,
　He wrapt him in Religion.
　　　　Hypocrisy à-la-mode.

" ' Holy Fair ' is a common phrase in the
West of Scotland for a sacramental occasion "
(R. B., in Edinburgh Editions). The satire
is chiefly concerned with the " tent - preach-
ing " outside the church while the Communion
services went on within. In Mauchline the
preaching tent was pitched in the churchyard,
whence a back entrance gave access to Nanse
Tinnock's tavern ; and the " Sacrament " was
observed once a year, on the second Sunday in
August. Critics have classed the piece among
the later ones in the Kilmarnock Edition ; but
in the MS. at Kilmarnock it is dated " Autumn,
1785," and it probably records the events of
that year. This ascription supports the tra-
dition that Burns recited it in the tavern where
the scene is laid, to an audience which in-
cluded Jean Armour, with whom there was no
quarrel till the spring of 1786.

I

Upon a simmer Sunday morn,
　When Nature's face is fair,
I walkèd forth to view the corn,
　An' snuff the caller air.
The rising sun, owre Galston Muirs,
　Wi' glorious light was glintin;
The hares were hirplin down the furs,
　The lav'rocks they were chantin
　　　　　Fu' sweet that day.

II

As lightsomely I glowr'd abroad,
　To see a scene sae gay,
Three hizzies, early at the road,
　Cam skelpin up the way.

Twa had manteeles o' dolefu' black,
　But ane wi' lyart lining;
The third, that gaed a wee a-back,
　Was in the fashion shining
　　　　　Fu' gay that day.

III

The twa appear'd like sisters twin,
　In feature, form, an' claes;
Their visage wither'd, lang an' thin,
　An' sour as onie slaes:
The third cam up, hap-step-an'-lowp,
　As light as onie lambie,
An' wi' a curchie low did stoop,
　As soon as e'er she saw me,
　　　　　Fu' kind that day.

IV

Wi' bonnet aff, quoth I, " Sweet lass,
　I think ye seem to ken me;
I 'm sure I 've seen that bonie face,
　But yet I canna name ye."
Quo' she, an' laughin as she spak,
　An' taks me by the han's,
" Ye, for my sake, hae gi'en the feck
　Of a' the Ten Comman's
　　　　　A screed some day.

V

" My name is Fun — your cronie dear,
　The nearest friend ye hae;
An' this is Superstition here,
　An' that 's Hypocrisy.
I 'm gaun to Mauchline Holy Fair,
　To spend an hour in daffin:
Gin ye 'll go there, yon runkl'd pair,
　We will get famous laughin
　　　　　At them this day."

VI

Quoth I, " Wi' a' my heart, I 'll do 't;
　I 'll get my Sunday's sark on,
An' meet you on the holy spot;
　Faith, we 'se hae fine remarkin ! "
Then I gaed hame at crowdie-time,
　An' soon I made me ready;
For roads were clad, frae side to side,
　Wi' monie a wearie body,
　　　　　In droves that day.

VII

Here farmers gash, in ridin graith,
　Gaed hoddin by their cotters;
There swankies young, in braw braid-claith,
　Are springin owre the gutters.

The lasses, skelpin barefit, thrang,
　In silks an' scarlets glitter;
Wi' sweet-milk cheese, in monie a whang,
　An' farls, bak'd wi' butter,
　　　　Fu' crump that day.

VIII

When by the plate we set our nose,
　Weel heapèd up wi' ha'pence,
A greedy glowr black-bonnet throws,
　An' we maun draw our tippence.
Then in we go to see the show:
　On ev'ry side they're gath'rin;
Some carryin dails, some chairs an' stools,
　An' some are busy bleth'rin
　　　　Right loud that day.

IX

Here stands a shed to fend the show'rs,
　An' screen our countra gentry;
There Racer Jess, an' twa-three whores,
　Are blinkin at the entry.
Here sits a raw o' tittlin jads,
　Wi' heavin breasts an' bare neck;
An' there a batch o' wabster lads,
　Blackguardin frae Kilmarnock,
　　　　For fun this day.

X

Here some are thinkin on their sins,
　An' some upo' their claes;
Ane curses feet that fyl'd his shins,
　Anither sighs an' prays:
On this hand sits a chosen swatch,
　Wi' screw'd-up, grace-proud faces;
On that a set o' chaps, at watch,
　Thrang winkin on the lasses
　　　　To chairs that day.

XI

O happy is that man an' blest!
　Nae wonder that it pride him!
Whase ain dear lass, that he likes best,
　Comes clinkin down beside him!
Wi' arm repos'd on the chair back,
　He sweetly does compose him;
Which, by degrees, slips round her neck,
　An's loof upon her bosom,
　　　　Unkend that day.

XII

Now a' the congregation o'er
　Is silent expectation;
For Moodie speels the holy door,
　Wi' tidings o' damnation:

Should Hornie, as in ancient days,
　'Mang sons o' God present him;
The vera sight o' Moodie's face
　To's ain het hame had sent him
　　　　Wi' fright that day.

XIII

Hear how he clears the points o' Faith
　Wi' rattlin and thumpin!
Now meekly calm, now wild in wrath,
　He's stampin, an' he's jumpin!
His lengthen'd chin, his turn'd-up snout,
　His eldritch squeel an' gestures,
O how they fire the heart devout —
　Like cantharidian plaisters
　　　　On sic a day.

XIV

But hark! the tent has chang'd its voice;
　There's peace an' rest nae langer;
For a' the real judges rise,
　They canna sit for anger:
Smith opens out his cauld harangues,
　On practice and on morals;
An' aff the godly pour in thrangs,
　To gie the jars an' barrels
　　　　A lift that day.

XV

What signifies his barren shine,
　Of moral pow'rs an' reason?
His English style, an' gesture fine
　Are a' clean out o' season.
Like Socrates or Antonine,
　Or some auld pagan heathen,
The moral man he does define,
　But ne'er a word o' faith in
　　　　That's right that day.

XVI

In guid time comes an antidote
　Against sic poison'd nostrum;
For Peebles, frae the water-fit,
　Ascends the holy rostrum:
See, up he's got the word o' God,
　An' meek an' mim has view'd it,
While Common-sense has taen the road,
　An' aff, an' up the Cowgate
　　　　Fast, fast that day.

XVII

Wee Miller niest, the guard relieves,
　An' orthodoxy raibles,
Tho' in his heart he weel believes,
　An' thinks it auld wives' fables:

But faith ! the birkie wants a manse:
　So, cannilie he hums them;
Altho' his carnal wit an' sense
　Like hafflins-wise o'ercomes him
　　　　At times that day.

XVIII

Now butt an' ben the change-house fills,
　Wi' yill-caup commentators;
Here 's crying out for bakes an' gills,
　An' there the pint-stowp clatters;
While thick an' thrang, an' loud an' lang,
　Wi' logic an' wi' Scripture,
They raise a din, that in the end
　Is like to breed a rupture
　　　　O' wrath that day.

XIX

Leeze me on drink ! it gies us mair
　Than either school or college;
It kindles wit, it waukens lear,
　It pangs us fou o' knowledge:
Be 't whisky-gill or penny wheep,
　Or onie stronger potion,
It never fails, on drinkin deep,
　To kittle up our notion,
　　　　By night or day.

XX

The lads an' lasses, blythely bent
　To mind baith saul an' body,
Sit round the table, weel content,
　An' steer about the toddy:
On this ane's dress, an' that ane's leuk,
　They 're makin observations;
While some are cozie i' the neuk,
　An' formin assignations
　　　　To meet some day.

XXI

But now the Lord's ain trumpet touts,
　Till a' the hills are rairin,
And echoes back return the shouts;
　Black Russell is na spairin:
His piercin words, like Highlan' swords,
　Divide the joints an' marrow;
His talk o' Hell, whare devils dwell,
　Our verra "sauls does harrow"
　　　　Wi' fright that day !

XXII

A vast, unbottom'd, boundless pit,
　Fill'd fou o' lowin brunstane,
Whase ragin flame, an' scorchin heat,
　Wad melt the hardest whun-stane !

The half-asleep start up wi' fear,
　An' think they hear it roarin;
When presently it does appear,
　'T was but some neebor snorin
　　　　Asleep that day.

XXIII

'T wad be owre lang a tale to tell,
　How monie stories past;
An' how they crouded to the yill,
　When they were a' dismist;
How drink gaed round, in cogs an' caups,
　Amang the furms an' benches;
An' cheese an' bread, frae women's laps,
　Was dealt about in lunches,
　　　　An' dawds that day.

XXIV

In comes a gawsie, gash guidwife,
　An' sits down by the fire,
Syne draws her kebbuck an' her knife;
　The lasses they are shyer:
The auld guidmen, about the grace,
　Frae side to side they bother;
Till some ane by his bonnet lays,
　An' gies them 't, like a tether,
　　　　Fu' lang that day.

XXV

Waesucks ! for him that gets nae lass,
　Or lasses that hae naething !
Sma' need has he to say a grace,
　Or melvie his braw claithing !
O wives, be mindfu', ance yoursel,
　How bonie lads ye wanted,
An' dinna for a kebbuck-heel
　Let lasses be affronted
　　　　On sic a day !

XXVI

Now Clinkumbell, wi' rattlin tow,
　Begins to jow an' croon;
Some swagger hame the best they dow,
　Some wait the afternoon.
At slaps the billies halt a blink,
　Till lasses strip their shoon:
Wi' faith an' hope, an' love an' drink,
　They 're a' in famous tune
　　　　For crack that day.

XXVII

How monie hearts this day converts
　O' sinners and o' lasses !
Their hearts o' stane, gin night, are gane
　As saft as onie flesh is:

There's some are fou o' love divine;
There's some are fou o' brandy;
An' monie jobs that day begin,
May end in houghmagandie
        Some ither day.

ADDRESS TO THE DEIL

> Ɔ Prince! O Chief of many thronèd pow'rs!
> That led th' embattl'd seraphim to war.
>   MILTON.

Gilbert Burns states that his brother first repeated the *Address to the Deil* in the winter "following the summer of 1784," while they "were going together with carts of coal to the family fire;" but it is clear from Burns's letter to Richmond, 12th February, 1786, that he misdates the poem by a year. The *Address* is, in part, a good-natured burlesque of the Miltonic ideal of Satan; and this is effected "by the introduction," to use the words of Gilbert Burns, "of ludicrous accounts and representations," from "various quarters," of that "august personage." Burns in his despairing moods was accustomed to feign the strongest admiration for Milton's Arch-Fiend and his dauntless superiority to his desperate circumstances; and his farewell apostrophe, although it takes the form of an exclamation of pity — and was accepted merely as such by the too-too sentimental yet austere Carlyle — is in reality a satiric thrust at the old Satanic dogma.

The six-line stave in *rime couée*, built on two rhymes, used in the *Address to the Deil*, was borrowed from the troubadours, and freely used in mediæval English during the thirteenth, fourteenth, and fifteenth centuries. There is small doubt that it was known to mediæval Scotland, but the first Scotsman whose name is attached to it is Sir David Lindsay (1540). It fell into disuse with the decline of popular poetry after the Reformation [but was revived in the *Piper of Kilbarchan* and other ballads, rendered more familiar by Allan Ramsay, and] it so took the Scottish ear that by Fergusson's time, as may be seen in Ruddiman's *Weekly Magazine* (1768-1784), it had become the common inheritance of all such Scotsmen as could rhyme. Through Fergusson, who did his sprightliest work in it, and John Mayne (1759-1836) — author of *The Siller Gun* (1777), who wrote it by cantos — it passed into the hands of Burns, who put it to all manner of uses and informed it with all manner of sentiments: in ambitious and serious poetry like *The Vision;* in *Addresses* — to a Louse, a Mountain Daisy, the Toothache, the Devil, a Haggis, Scotch Drink, to name but these; in *Elegies* — upon Tam Samson and Poor Mailie

and Captain Matthew Henderson; in such satires as *Death and Dr. Hornbook* and *Holy Willie's Prayer;* and in a series of *Epistles* of singular variety and range. His thoughts and fancies fell naturally into the pace which it imposes: as Dryden's into the heroic couplet, as Spenser's into the stanza of *The Faërie Queen*. Indeed, he cannot keep it out of his head, and his Alexandrines often march to the tune of it: —

> "And heard great Bab'lon's doom pronounced
>   By Heaven's command" —

> "And 'Let us worship God,' he says
>   With solemn air " —

> "And curse the ruffian's aim, and mourn
>   Thy hapless fate."

'T is small wonder, therefore, that a very large proportion of his non-lyrical achievement is set forth in it, or that Wordsworth should choose it for the stave of his memorial verses.

I

O THOU! whatever title suit thee —
Auld Hornie, Satan, Nick, or Clootie —
Wha in yon cavern grim an' sootie,
        Clos'd under hatches,
Spairges about the brunstane cootie,
        To scaud poor wretches!

II

Hear me, Auld Hangie, for a wee,
An' let poor damnèd bodies be;
I'm sure sma' pleasure it can gie,
        Ev'n to a deil,
To skelp an' scaud poor dogs like me
        An' hear us squeel.

III

Great is thy pow'r an' great thy fame;
Far kend an' noted is thy name;
An' tho' yon lowin heugh's thy hame,
        Thou travels far;
An' faith! thou's neither lag, nor lame,
        Nor blate, nor scaur.

IV

Whyles, ranging like a roarin lion,
For prey, a' holes an' corners trying;
Whyles, on the strong-wing'd tempest flyin,
        Tirlin the kirks;
Whyles, in the human bosom pryin,
        Unseen thou lurks.

V

I've heard my rev'rend graunie say,
In lanely glens ye like to stray;

Or, where auld ruin'd castles grey
   Nod to the moon,
Ye fright the nightly wand'rer's way
   Wi' eldritch croon.

VI

When twilight did my graunie summon,
To say her pray'rs, douce, honest woman !
Aft yont the dyke she 's heard you bum-
  min,
   Wi' eerie drone;
Or, rustlin, thro' the boortrees comin,
   Wi' heavy groan.

VII

Ae dreary, windy, winter night,
The star shot down wi' sklentin light,
Wi' you mysel, I gat a fright:
   Ayont the lough,
Ye, like a rash-buss, stood in sight,
   Wi' waving sugh.

VIII

The cudgel in my nieve did shake,
Each bristl'd hair stood like a stake;
When wi' an eldritch, stoor "quaick,
  quaick,"
   Amang the springs,
Awa ye squatter'd like a drake,
   On whistling wings.

IX

Let warlocks grim, an' wither'd hags,
Tell how wi' you, on ragweed nags,
They skim the muirs an' dizzy crags,
   Wi' wicked speed;
And in kirk-yards renew their leagues,
   Owre howkit dead.

X

Thence, countra wives, wi' toil an' pain,
May plunge an' plunge the kirn in vain;
For O ! the yellow treasure 's taen
   By witching skill;
An' dawtit, twal-pint hawkie 's gaen
   As yell 's the bill.

XI

Thence, mystic knots mak great abuse
On young guidmen, fond, keen an' croose;
When the best wark-lume i' the house,
   By cantraip wit,
Is instant made no worth a louse,
   Just at the bit.

XII

When thowes dissolve the snawy hoord,
An' float the jinglin icy boord,
Then, water-kelpies haunt the foord,
   By your direction,
An' nighted trav'llers are allur'd
   To their destruction.

XIII

And aft your moss-traversing spunkies
Decoy the wight that late an' drunk is:
The bleezin, curst, mischievous monkies
   Delude his eyes,
Till in some miry slough he sunk is,
   Ne'er mair to rise.

XIV

When Masons' mystic word an' grip
In storms an' tempests raise you up,
Some cock or cat your rage maun stop,
   Or, strange to tell !
The youngest brother ye wad whip
   Aff straught to hell.

XV

Lang syne in Eden's bonie yard,
When youthfu' lovers first were pair'd,
An' all the soul of love they shar'd,
   The raptur'd hour,
Sweet on the fragrant flow'ry swaird,
   In shady bow'r:

XVI

Then you, ye auld, snick-drawing dog !
Ye cam to Paradise incog,
An' play'd on man a cursed brogue
   (Black be your fa' !),
An' gied the infant warld a shog,
   'Maist ruin'd a'.

XVII

D' ye mind that day when in a bizz
Wi' reekit duds, an' reestit gizz,
Ye did present your smoutie phiz
   'Mang better folk;
An' sklented on the man of Uzz
   Your spitefu' joke ?

XVIII

An' how ye gat him i' your thrall,
An' brak him out o' house an' hal',
While scabs an' botches did him gall,
   Wi' bitter claw;

An' lows'd his ill-tongu'd wicked scaul —
    Was warst ava ?

XIX

But a' your doings to rehearse,
Your wily snares an' fechtin fierce,
Sin' that day Michael did you pierce
    Down to this time,
Wad ding a Lallan tongue, or Erse,
    In prose or rhyme.

XX

An' now, Auld Cloots, I ken ye 're thinkin,
A certain Bardie's rantin, drinkin,
Some luckless hour will send him linkin,
    To your black Pit;
But, faith ! he 'll turn a corner jinkin,
    An' cheat you yet.

XXI

But fare-you-weel, Auld Nickie-Ben !
O, wad ye tak a thought an' men' !
Ye aiblins might — I dinna ken —
    Still hae a stake:
I 'm wae to think upo' yon den,
    Ev'n for your sake !

THE DEATH AND DYING WORDS OF POOR MAILIE,

THE AUTHOR'S ONLY PET YOWE : AN UNCO MOURNFU' TALE

One of the few pieces written before 1784. Burns " had, partly by way of frolic, bought a ewe and two lambs from a neighbour, and she was tethered in a field adjoining the house at Lochlie. He and I were going out with our teams, and our two younger brothers to drive for us, at mid-day, when Hugh Wilson, a curious-looking, awkward boy, clad in plaiding, came to us with much anxiety in his face, with the information that the ewe had entangled herself in the tether, and was lying in the ditch. Robert was much tickled with Huoc's appearance and postures on the occasion. Poor Mailie was set to rights, and when we returned from the plough in the evening he repeated to me her *Death and Dying Words* pretty much in the way they now stand." — Gilbert Burns.

As Mailie, an' her lambs thegither,
Was ae day nibblin on the tether,
Upon her cloot she coost a hitch,
An' owre she warsl'd in the ditch:

There, groanin, dying, she did lie,
When Hughoc he cam doytin by.

Wi' glowrin een, an' lifted han's
Poor Hughoc like a statue stan's;
He saw her days were near-hand ended,
But, wae 's my heart ! he could na mend
    it !
He gapèd wide, but naething spak.
At length poor Mailie silence brak: —

" O thou, whase lamentable face
Appears to mourn my woefu' case !
My dying words attentive hear,
An' bear them to my Master dear.

" Tell him, if e'er again he keep
As muckle gear as buy a sheep —
O, bid him never tie them mair,
Wi' wicked strings o' hemp or hair !
But ca' them out to park or hill,
An' let them wander at their will:
So may his flock increase, an' grow
To scores o' lambs, an' packs o' woo' !

" Tell him, he was a Master kin',
An' ay was guid to me an' mine;
An' now my dying charge I gie him,
My helpless lambs, I trust them wi' him.

" O, bid him save their harmless lives,
Frae dogs, an' tods, an' butchers' knives !
But gie them guid cow-milk their fill,
Till they be fit to fend themsel;
An' tent them duly, e'en an' morn,
Wi' teats o' hay an' ripps o' corn.

" An' may they never learn the gaets,
Of ither vile, wanrestfu' pets —
To slink thro' slaps, an' reave an' steal,
At stacks o' pease, or stocks o' kail !
So may they, like their great forbears,
For monie a year come thro' the sheers:
So wives will gie them bits o' bread,
An' bairns greet for them when they 'r ·
    dead.

" My poor toop-lamb, my son an' heir,
O, bid him breed him up wi' care !
An' if he live to be a beast,
To pit some havins in his breast !
An' warn him — what I winna name —
To stay content wi' yowes at hame;
An' no to rin an' wear his cloots,
Like other menseless, graceless brutes.

" An' niest, my yowie, silly thing;
Gude keep thee frae a tether string !
O, may thou ne'er forgather up,
Wi' onie blastit, moorland toop;
But ay keep mind to moop an' mell,
Wi' sheep o' credit like thysel !

" And now, my bairns, wi' my last breath,
I lea'e my blessin wi' you baith:
An' when you think upo' your mither,
Mind to be kind to ane anither.

" Now, honest Hughoc, dinna fail,
To tell my master a' my tale;
An' bid him burn this cursed tether,
An' for thy pains thou 'se get my blether."

This said, poor Mailie turn'd her head,
An' clos'd her een amang the dead !

POOR MAILIE'S ELEGY

I

LAMENT in rhyme, lament in prose,
Wi' saut tears tricklin down your nose;
Our Bardie's fate is at a close,
        Past a' remead !
The last, sad cape-stane of his woes;
        Poor Mailie 's dead !

II

It 's no the loss of warl's gear,
That could sae bitter draw the tear,
Or mak our Bardie, dowie, wear
        The mourning weed:
He 's lost a friend an' neebor dear
        In Mailie dead.

III

Thro' a' the toun she trotted by him;
A lang half-mile she could descry him;
Wi' kindly bleat, when she did spy him,
        She ran wi' speed:
A friend mair faithfu' ne'er cam nigh him,
        Than Mailie dead.

IV

I wat she was a sheep o' sense,
An' could behave hersel wi' mense:
I 'll say 't, she never brak a fence,
        Thro' thievish greed.
Our Bardie, lanely, keeps the spence
        Sin' Mailie 's dead.

V

Or, if he wanders up the howe,
Her livin image in her yowe
Comes bleatin till him, owre the knowe,
        For bits o' bread;
An' down the briny pearls rowe
        For Mailie dead.

VI

She was nae get o' moorlan tips,
Wi' tawted ket, an' hairy hips;
For her forbears were brought in ships,
        Frae 'yont the Tweed:
A bonier fleesh ne'er cross'd the clips
        Than Mailie's dead.

VII

Wae worth the man wha first did shape
That vile, wanchancie thing — a rape !
It maks guid fellows girn an' gape,
        Wi' chokin dread;
An' Robin's bonnet wave wi' crape
        For Mailie dead.

VIII

O a' ye bards on bonie Doon !
An' wha on Ayr your chanters tune !
Come, join the melancholious croon
        O' Robin's reed !
His heart will never get aboon !
        His Mailie 's dead !

EPISTLE TO JAMES SMITH

Friendship, mysterious cement of the soul !
Sweet'ner of Life, and solder of Society !
I owe thee much —
                                BLAIR.

The recipient of this epistle was the son of
Robert Smith, merchant, Mauchline. He was
born 1st March, 1765, and was thus six years
younger than the poet. He lost his father
early, and, perhaps by reason of his stepfather's
rigid discipline, grew something regardless of
restraint. He was, however, clever, affection-
ate, and witty; secured the poet's especial es-
teem by his loyalty during the Armour trou-
bles; was a member of the Court of Equity
(or Bachelors' Club, which met at the White-
foord Arms), and the subject of a humorous
epitaph (see *post*, p. 195) which need not be in-
terpreted too literally; for some time kept a
small draper's shop in Mauchline; in 1787 be-
came partner in the Avon Printworks, Linlith-
gowshire; and about 1788 went to Jamaica,
where he died. Several letters to him are in-

cluded in Burns's correspondence. His sister's "wit" is celebrated in *The Belles of Mauchline.* The *Epistle* was probably written early in 1786, before Burns had quite decided to attempt publication.

I

DEAR SMITH, the slee'st, pawkie thief,
That e'er attempted stealth or rief !
Ye surely hae some warlock-breef
      Owre human hearts;
For ne'er a bosom yet was prief
      Against your arts.

II

For me, I swear by sun an' moon,
And ev'ry star that blinks aboon,
Ye 've cost me twenty pair o' shoon,
      Just gaun to see you;
And ev'ry ither pair that 's done,
      Mair taen I 'm wi' you.

III

That auld, capricious carlin, Nature,
To mak amends for scrimpit stature,
She 's turn'd you off, a human-creature
      On her first plan;
And in her freaks, on ev'ry feature
      She 's wrote the Man.

IV

Just now I 've taen the fit o' rhyme,
My barmie noddle 's working prime,
My fancy yerkit up sublime,
      Wi' hasty summon:
Hae ye a leisure-moment's time
      To hear what 's comin ?

V

Some rhyme a neebor's name to lash;
Some rhyme (vain thought !) for needfu' cash;
Some rhyme to court the countra clash,
      An' raise a din;
For me, an aim I never fash;
      I rhyme for fun.

VI

The star that rules my luckless lot,
Has fated me the russet coat,
An' damn'd my fortune to the groat;
      But, in requit,
Has blest me with a random-shot
      O' countra wit.

VII

This while my notion 's taen a sklent,
To try my fate in guid, black prent;
But still the mair I 'm that way bent,
      Something cries, " Hoolie !
I red you, honest man, tak tent !
      Ye 'll shaw your folly:

VIII

" There 's ither poets, much your betters,
Far seen in Greek, deep men o' letters,
Hae thought they had ensur'd their debtors,
      A' future ages ;
Now moths deform, in shapeless tatters,
      Their unknown pages."

IX

Then farewell hopes o' laurel-boughs
To garland my poetic brows !
Henceforth I 'll rove where busy ploughs
      Are whistling thrang;
An' teach the lanely heights an' howes
      My rustic sang.

X

I 'll wander on, wi' tentless heed
How never-halting moments speed,
Till Fate shall snap the brittle thread;
      Then, all unknown,
I 'll lay me with th' inglorious dead,
      Forgot and gone !

XI

But why o' death begin a tale ?
Just now we 're living sound an' hale;
Then top and maintop crowd the sail,
      Heave Care o'er-side !
And large, before Enjoyment's gale,
      Let 's tak the tide.

XII

This life, sae far 's I understand,
Is a' enchanted fairy-land,
Where Pleasure is the magic-wand,
      That, wielded right,
Maks hours like minutes, hand in hand,
      Dance by fu' light.

XIII

The magic-wand then let us wield;
For, ance that five-an'-forty 's speel'd,
See, crazy, weary, joyless Eild,
      Wi' wrinkl'd face,

Comes hostin, hirplin owre the field,
    Wi' creepin pace.

XIV

When ance life's day draws near the
    gloamin,
Then fareweel vacant, careless roamin;
An' fareweel chearfu' tankards foamin,
    An' social noise:
An' fareweel dear, deluding Woman,
    The joy of joys!

XV

O Life! how pleasant, in thy morning,
Young Fancy's rays the hills adorning!
Cold-pausing Caution's lesson scorning,
    We frisk away,
Like school-boys, at th' expected warning,
    To joy an' play.

XVI

We wander there, we wander here,
We eye the rose upon the brier,
Unmindful that the thorn is near,
    Among the leaves;
And tho' the puny wound appear,
    Short while it grieves.

XVII

Some, lucky, find a flow'ry spot,
For which they never toil'd nor swat;
They drink the sweet and eat the fat,
    But care or pain;
And haply eye the barren hut
    With high disdain.

XVIII

With steady aim, some Fortune chase;
Keen Hope does ev'ry sinew brace;
Thro' fair, thro' foul, they urge the race,
    And seize the prey:
Then cannie, in some cozie place,
    They close the day.

XIX

And others, like your humble servan',
Poor wights! nae rules nor roads observin,
To right or left eternal swervin,
    They zig-zag on;
Till, curst with age, obscure an' starvin,
    They aften groan.

XX

Alas! what bitter toil an' straining —
But truce with peevish, poor complaining!

Is Fortune's fickle *Luna* waning?
    E'en let her gang!
Beneath what light she has remaining,
    Let 's sing our sang.

XXI

My pen I here fling to the door,
And kneel, ye Pow'rs! and warm implore,
" Tho' I should wander *Terra* o'er,
    In all her climes,
Grant me but this, I ask no more,
    Ay rowth o' rhymes.

XXII

" Gie dreeping roasts to countra lairds,
Till icicles hing frae their beards;
Gie fine braw claes to fine life-guards
    And maids of honor;
And yill an' whisky gie to cairds,
    Until they sconner.

XXIII

" A title, Dempster merits it;
A garter gie to Willie Pitt;
Gie wealth to some be-ledger'd cit,
    In cent. per cent.;
But give me real, sterling wit,
    And I 'm content.

XXIV

" While ye are pleas'd to keep me hale,
I 'll sit down o'er my scanty meal,
Be 't water-brose or muslin-kail,
    Wi' cheerfu' face,
As lang 's the Muses dinna fail
    To say the grace."

XXV

An anxious e'e I never throws
Behint my lug, or by my nose;
I jouk beneath Misfortune's blows
    As weel 's I may;
Sworn foe to sorrow, care, and prose,
    I rhyme away.

XXVI

O ye douce folk that live by rule,
Grave, tideless-blooded, calm an' cool,
Compar'd wi' you — O fool! fool! fool!
    How much unlike!
Your hearts are just a standing pool,
    Your lives a dyke!

XXVII

Nae hair-brained, sentimental traces
In your unletter'd, nameless faces!

In *arioso* trills and graces
      Ye never stray;
But *gravissimo*, solemn basses
      Ye hum away.

XXVIII

Ye are sae grave, nae doubt ye 're wise;
Nae ferly tho' ye do despise
The hairum-scairum, ram-stam boys,
      The rattling squad:
I see ye upward cast your eyes —
      Ye ken the road !

XXIX

Whilst I — but I shall haud me there,
Wi' you I 'll scarce gang onie where —
Then, Jamie, I shall say nae mair,
      But quat my sang,
Content wi' you to mak a pair,
      Whare'er I gang.

A DREAM

Thoughts, words, and deeds, the Statute blames with reason;
But surely *Dreams* were ne'er indicted Treason.

The outspokenness of this address — partly traceable to the poet's latent Jacobitism — was distasteful to some of his loyal patrons, who advised that, unless it were modified, it should not be retained in the 1787 Edition. But, as he wrote to Mrs. Dunlop (30th April), he was "not very amenable to counsel" in such a matter; and, his sentiments once published, he scorned either to withdraw them or to dilute his expression. The author of the *Ode* here ridiculed was Thomas Warton. [Burns introduced *A Dream* with the following preface]: —
On reading in the public papers, the Laureate's Ode with the other parade of June 4th, 1786, the Author was no sooner dropt asleep, than he imagined himself transported to the Birth-day Levee : and, in his dreaming fancy, made the following Address: —

I

GUID-MORNIN to your Majesty !
    May Heaven augment your blisses,
On ev'ry new birth-day ye see,
    A humble Poet wishes !
My Bardship here, at your Levee,
    On sic a day as this is,
Is sure an uncouth sight to see,
    Amang thae birth-day dresses
        Sae fine this day.

II

I see ye 're complimented thrang,
    By monie a lord an' lady;
God Save the King 's a cuckoo sang
    That 's unco easy said ay:
The poets, too, a venal gang,
    Wi' rhymes weel-turn'd an' ready,
Wad gar you trow ye ne'er do wrang,
    But ay unerring steady,
        On sic a day.

III

For me ! before a Monarch's face,
    Ev'n there I winna flatter;
For neither pension, post, nor place,
    Am I your humble debtor:
So, nae reflection on your Grace,
    Your Kingship to bespatter;
There 's monie waur been o' the race,
    And aiblins ane been better
        Than you this day.

IV

'T is very true my sovereign King,
    My skill may weel be doubted;
But facts are chiels that winna ding,
    And downa be disputed:
Your royal nest, beneath your wing,
    Is e'en right reft and clouted,
And now the third part o' the string,
    An' less, will gang about it
        Than did ae day.

V

Far be 't frae me that I aspire
    To blame your legislation,
Or say, ye wisdom want, or fire
    To rule this mighty nation:
But faith ! I muckle doubt, my sire,
    Ye 've trusted ministration
To chaps wha in a barn or byre
    Wad better fill'd their station,
        Than courts yon day.

VI

And now ye 've gien auld Britain peace,
    Her broken shins to plaister;
Your sair taxation does her fleece,
    Till she has scarce a tester:
For me, thank God, my life 's a lease,
    Nae bargain wearin faster,
Or faith ! I fear, that wi' the geese,
    I shortly boost to pasture
        I' the craft some day.

VII

I'm no mistrusting Willie Pitt,
  When taxes he enlarges,
(An' Will's a true guid fallow's get,
  A name not envy spairges),
That he intends to pay your debt,
  An' lessen a' your charges;
But, God sake! let nae saving fit
  Abridge your bonie barges
                An' boats this day.

VIII

Adieu, my Liege! may Freedom geck
  Beneath your high protection;
An' may ye rax Corruption's neck,
  And gie her for dissection!
But since I'm here I'll no neglect,
  In loyal, true affection,
To pay your Queen, wi' due respect,
  My fealty an' subjection
                This great birth-day.

IX

Hail, Majesty most Excellent!
  While nobles strive to please ye,
Will ye accept a compliment,
  A simple Bardie gies ye?
Thae bonie bairntime Heav'n has lent,
  Still higher may they heeze ye
In bliss, till Fate some day is sent,
  For ever to release ye
                Frae care that day.

X

For you, young Potentate o' Wales,
  I tell your Highness fairly,
Down Pleasure's stream, wi' swelling sails,
  I'm tauld ye're driving rarely;
But some day ye may gnaw your nails,
  An' curse your folly sairly,
That e'er ye brak Diana's pales,
  Or rattl'd dice wi' Charlie
                By night or day.

XI

Yet aft a ragged cowte's been known,
  To mak a noble aiver;
So, ye may doucely fill a throne,
  For a' their clish-ma-claver:
There, him at Agincourt wha shone,
  Few better were or braver;
And yet, wi' funny, queer Sir John,
  He was an unco shaver
                For monie a day.

XII

For you, right rev'rend Osnaburg,
  Nane sets the lawn-sleeve sweeter,
Altho' a ribban at your lug
  Wad been a dress completer:
As ye disown yon paughty dog,
  That bears the keys of Peter,
Then swith! an' get a wife to hug,
  Or trowth, ye'll stain the mitre
                Some luckless day!

XIII

Young, royal Tarry-breeks, I learn,
  Ye've lately come athwart her —
A glorious galley, stem an' stern
  Weel rigg'd for Venus' barter;
But first hang out that she'll discern
  Your hymeneal charter;
Then heave aboard your grapple-airn,
  An', large upon her quarter,
                Come full that day.

XIV

Ye, lastly, bonie blossoms a',
  Ye royal lasses dainty,
Heav'n mak you guid as weel as braw,
  An' gie you lads a-plenty!
But sneer na British boys awa!
  For kings are unco scant ay,
An' German gentles are but sma':
  They're better just than want ay
                On onie day.

XV

God bless you a'! consider now,
  Ye're unco muckle dantet;
But ere the course o' life be through,
  It may be bitter sautet:
An' I hae seen their coggie fou,
  That yet hae tarrow't at it;
But or the day was done, I trow,
  The laggen they hae clautet
                Fu' clean that day.

THE VISION

The division into "Duans" was borrowed from Ossian: "Duan, a term of Ossian's for the different divisions of a digressive poem. See his *Cath-Loda*, vol. ii. of M'Pherson's Translation." (R. B.) To Duan I., as it appears in the 1786 Edition, seven stanzas were added in that of 1787, and one to Duan II.

DUAN FIRST

I

THE sun had clos'd the winter day,
The curlers quat their roaring play,
And hunger'd maukin taen her way
　　　　To kail-yards green,
While faithless snaws ilk step betray
　　　　Whare she has been.

II

The thresher's weary flingin-tree,
The lee-lang day had tired me;
And when the day had clos'd his e'e,
　　　　Far i' the west,
Ben i' the spence, right pensivelie,
　　　　I gaed to rest.

III

There, lanely by the ingle-cheek,
I sat and ey'd the spewing reek,
That fill'd, wi' hoast-provoking smeek,
　　　　The auld clay biggin;
An' heard the restless rattons squeak
　　　　About the riggin.

IV

All in this mottie, misty clime,
I backward mus'd on wasted time:
How I had spent my youthfu' prime,
　　　　An' done naething,
But stringing blethers up in rhyme,
　　　　For fools to sing.

V

Had I to guid advice but harkit,
I might, by this, hae led a market,
Or strutted in a bank and clarkit
　　　　My cash-account:
While here, half-mad, half-fed, half-sarkit,
　　　　Is a' th' amount.

VI

I started, mutt'ring "Blockhead ! coof !"
An' heav'd on high my waukit loof,
To swear by a' yon starry roof,
　　　　Or some rash aith,
That I henceforth would be rhyme-proof
　　　　Till my last breath —

VII

When click ! the string the snick did draw;
And jee ! the door gaed to the wa';

And by my ingle-lowe I saw,
　　　　Now bleezin bright,
A tight, outlandish hizzie, braw,
　　　　Come full in sight.

VIII

Ye need na doubt, I held my whisht;
The infant aith, half-form'd, was crusht;
I glowr'd as eerie 's I 'd been dusht,
　　　　In some wild glen;
When sweet, like modest Worth, she blusht,
　　　　And steppèd ben.

IX

Green, slender, leaf-clad holly-boughs
Were twisted, gracefu', round her brows;
I took her for some Scottish Muse,
　　　　By that same token;
And come to stop those reckless vows,
　　　　Would soon been broken.

X

A " hair-brain'd, sentimental trace "
Was strongly markèd in her face;
A wildly-witty, rustic grace
　　　　Shone full upon her;
Her eye, ev'n turn'd on empty space,
　　　　Beam'd keen with honor.

XI

Down flow'd her robe, a tartan sheen,
Till half a leg was scrimply seen;
And such a leg ! my bonie Jean
　　　　Could only peer it;
Sae straught, sae taper, tight an' clean
　　　　Nane else came near it.

XII

Her mantle large, of greenish hue,
My gazing wonder chiefly drew;
Deep lights and shades, bold-mingling,
　　　　threw
　　　　　　A lustre grand;
And seem'd, to my astonish'd view,
　　　　A well-known land.

XIII

Here, rivers in the sea were lost;
There, mountains to the skies were toss't;
Here, tumbling billows mark'd the coast
　　　　With surging foam;
There, distant shone Art's lofty boast,
　　　　The lordly dome.

XIV

Here, Doon pour'd down his far-fetch'd
      floods;
There, well-fed Irwine stately thuds:
Auld hermit Ayr staw thro' his woods,
            On to the shore;
And many a lesser torrent scuds
            With seeming roar.

XV

Low, in a sandy valley spread,
An ancient borough rear'd her head;
Still, as in Scottish story read,
            She boasts a race
To ev'ry nobler virtue bred,
            And polish'd grace.

XVI

By stately tow'r, or palace fair,
Or ruins pendent in the air,
Bold stems of heroes, here and there,
            I could discern;
Some seem'd to muse, some seem'd to
  dare,
            With feature stern.

XVII

My heart did glowing transport feel,
To see a race heroic wheel,
And brandish round the deep-dyed steel
            In sturdy blows;
While, back-recoiling, seem'd to reel
            Their suthron foes.

XVIII

His Country's Saviour, mark him well !
Bold Richardton's heroic swell;
The chief, on Sark who glorious fell
            In high command;
And he whom ruthless fates expel
            His native land.

XIX

There, where a sceptr'd Pictish shade
Stalk'd round his ashes lowly laid,
I mark'd a martial race, pourtray'd
            In colours strong:
Bold, soldier-featur'd, undismay'd,
            They strode along.

XX

Thro' many a wild, romantic grove,
Near many a hermit-fancied cove

(Fit haunts for friendship or for love
            In musing mood),
An aged Judge, I saw him rove,
            Dispensing good.

XXI

With deep-struck, reverential awe,
The learned Sire and Son I saw:
To Nature's God, and Nature's law,
            They gave their lore;
This, all its source and end to draw,
            That, to adore.

XXII

Brydon's brave ward I well could spy,
Beneath old Scotia's smiling eye;
Who call'd on Fame, low standing by,
            To hand him on,
Where many a patriot-name on high,
            And hero shone.

DUAN SECOND

I

With musing-deep, astonish'd stare,
I view'd the heavenly-seeming Fair;
A whisp'ring throb did witness bear
            Of kindred sweet,
When with an elder sister's air
            She did me greet.

II

" All hail ! my own inspirèd Bard !
In me thy native Muse regard !
Nor longer mourn thy fate is hard,
            Thus poorly low !
I come to give thee such reward,
            As we bestow.

III

" Know, the great Genius of this land
Has many a light aerial band,
Who, all beneath his high command,
            Harmoniously,
As arts or arms they understand,
            Their labors ply.

IV

" They Scotia's race among them share:
Some fire the soldier on to dare;
Some rouse the patriot up to bare
            Corruption's heart;
Some teach the bard — a darling care —
            The tuneful art.

V

" 'Mong swelling floods of reeking gore,
They, ardent, kindling spirits, pour;
Or, 'mid the venal Senate's roar,
    They, sightless, stand,
To mend the honest patriot-lore,
    And grace the hand.

VI

" And when the bard, or hoary sage,
Charm or instruct the future age,
They bind the wild poetic rage
    In energy;
Or point the inconclusive page
    Full on the eye.

VII

"Hence, Fullarton, the brave and young;
Hence, Dempster's zeal-inspirèd tongue;
Hence, sweet, harmonious Beattie sung
    His *Minstrel* lays,
Or tore, with noble ardour stung,
    The sceptic's bays.

VIII

" To lower orders are assign'd
The humbler ranks of human-kind,
The rustic bard, the laboring hind,
    The artisan;
All chuse, as various they 're inclin'd,
    The various man.

IX

" When yellow waves the heavy grain,
The threat'ning storm some strongly
    rein,
Some teach to meliorate the plain,
    With tillage-skill;
And some instruct the shepherd-train,
    Blythe o'er the hill.

X

" Some hint the lover's harmless wile;
Some grace the maiden's artless smile;
Some soothe the laborer's weary toil
    For humble gains,
And make his cottage-scenes beguile
    His cares and pains.

XI

" Some, bounded to a district-space,
Explore at large man's infant race,
To mark the embryotic trace
    Of rustic bard;

And careful note each opening grace,
    A guide and guard.

XII

" Of these am I — Coila my name:
And this district as mine I claim,
Where once the Campbells, chiefs of fame,
    Held ruling pow'r:
I mark'd thy embryo-tuneful flame,
    Thy natal hour.

XIII

" With future hope I oft would gaze,
Fond, on thy little early ways:
Thy rudely caroll'd, chiming phrase,
    In uncouth rhymes;
Fir'd at the simple, artless lays
    Of other times.

XIV

" I saw thee seek the sounding shore,
Delighted with the dashing roar;
Or when the North his fleecy store
    Drove thro' the sky,
I saw grim Nature's visage hoar •
    Struck thy young eye.

XV

" Or when the deep green-mantled earth
Warm cherish'd ev'ry flow'ret's birth,
And joy and music pouring forth
    In ev'ry grove;
I saw thee eye the gen'ral mirth
    With boundless love.

XVI

" When ripen'd fields and azure skies
Call'd forth the reapers' rustling noise,
I saw thee leave their ev'ning joys,
    And lonely stalk,
To vent thy bosom's swelling rise,
    In pensive walk.

XVII

" When youthful Love, warm - blushing,
    strong,
Keen-shivering, shot thy nerves along,
Those accents grateful to thy tongue,
    Th' adorèd *Name*,
I taught thee how to pour in song
    To soothe thy flame.

XVIII

" I saw thy pulse's maddening play,
Wild-send thee Pleasure's devious way,

Misled by Fancy's meteor-ray,
   By passion driven;
But yet the light that led astray
   Was light from Heaven.

XIX

"I taught thy manners-painting strains
The loves, the ways of simple swains,
Till now, o'er all my wide domains
   Thy fame extends;
And some, the pride of Coila's plains,
   Become thy friends.

XX

"Thou canst not learn, nor can I show,
To paint with Thomson's landscape glow;
Or wake the bosom-melting throe
   With Shenstone's art;
Or pour, with Gray, the moving flow
   Warm on the heart.

XXI

"Yet, all beneath th' unrivall'd rose,
The lowly daisy sweetly blows;
Tho' large the forest's monarch throws
   His army-shade,
Yet green the juicy hawthorn grows
   Adown the glade.

XXII

"Then never murmur nor repine;
Strive in thy humble sphere to shine;
And trust me, not Potosi's mine,
   Nor king's regard,
Can give a bliss o'ermatching thine,
   A rustic Bard.

XXIII

"To give my counsels all in one:
Thy tuneful flame still careful fan;
Preserve the dignity of Man,
   With soul erect;
And trust the Universal Plan
   Will all protect.

XXIV

"And wear thou *this*" — She solemn said,
And bound the holly round my head:
The polish'd leaves and berries red
   Did rustling play;
And, like a passing thought, she fled
   In light away.

HALLOWEEN

Yes! let the rich deride, the proud disdain,
The simple pleasures of the lowly train:
To me more dear, congenial to my heart,
One native charm, than all the gloss of art.
        GOLDSMITH.

A *Halloween* by John Mayne, author of the *Siller Gun*, appeared in Ruddiman's *Weekly Magazine* in November, 1780. It is written in the six-line stave in *rime couée* of *The Piper of Kilbarchan* (see prefatory note to *Address to the Deil*) and suggested little to Burns except, perhaps, his theme. Burns prefaces his verses thus: "The following poem will, by many readers, be well enough understood; but for the sake of those who are unacquainted with the manners and traditions of the country where the scene is cast, notes are added, to give some account of the principal charms and spells of that night, so big with prophecy to the peasantry in the west of Scotland. The passion of prying into futurity makes a striking part of the history of human nature in its rude state, in all ages and nations; and it may be some entertainment to a philosophic mind, if any such should honor the author with a perusal, to see the remains of it among the more unenlightened in our own."

I

Upon that night, when fairies light
 On Cassilis Downans dance,
Or owre the lays, in splendid blaze,
 On sprightly coursers prance;
Or for Colean the rout is taen,
 Beneath the moon's pale beams;
There, up the Cove, to stray and rove,
 Amang the rocks and streams
   To sport that night:

II

Amang the bonie winding banks,
 Where Doon rins, wimplin, clear;
Where Bruce ance ruled the martial ranks,
 An' shook his Carrick spear;
Some merry, friendly, country-folks
 Together did convene,
To burn their nits, an' pou their stocks,
 An' haud their Halloween
   Fu' blythe that night.

III

The lassies feat an' cleanly neat,
 Mair braw than when they 're fine;
Their faces blythe fu' sweetly kythe
 Hearts leal, an' warm, an' kin':

The lads sae trig, wi' wooer-babs
  Weel-knotted on their garten;
Some unco blate, an' some wi' gabs
  Gar lasses' hearts gang startin
            Whyles fast at night.

IV

Then, first an' foremost, thro' the kail,
  Their stocks maun a' be sought ance;
They steek their een, an' grape an' wale
  For muckle anes, an' straught anes.
Poor hav'rel Will fell aff the drift,
  An' wandered thro' the bow-kail,
An' pow't, for want o' better shift,
  A runt, was like a sow-tail,
            Sae bow't that night.

V

Then, straught or crooked, yird or nane,
  They roar an' cry a' throu'ther;
The vera wee-things, toddlin, rin
  Wi' stocks out-owre their shouther:
An' gif the custock 's sweet or sour,
  Wi' joctelegs they taste them;
Syne coziely, aboon the door,
  Wi' cannie care, they 've plac'd them
            To lie that night.

VI

The lasses staw frae 'mang them a',
  To pou their stalks o' corn;
But Rab slips out, an' jinks about,
  Behint the muckle thorn:
He grippet Nelly hard an' fast;
  Loud skirl'd a' the lasses;
But her tap-pickle maist was lost,
  Whan kiutlin in the fause-house
            Wi' him that night.

VII

The auld guid-wife's weel-hoordet nits
  Are round an' round divided,
An' monie lads' an' lasses' fates
  Are there that night decided:
Some kindle couthie, side by side,
  An' burn thegither trimly;
Some start awa wi' saucy pride,
  An' jump out-owre the chimlie
            Fu' high that night.

VIII

Jean slips in twa, wi' tentie e'e;
  Wha 't was, she wadna tell;
But this is *Jock*, an' this is *me*,
  She says in to hersel:

He bleez'd owre her, an' she owre him,
  As they wad never mair part;
Till fuff ! he started up the lum,
  And Jean had e'en a sair heart
            To see 't that night.

IX

Poor Willie, wi' his bow-kail runt,
  Was burnt wi' primsie Mallie;
An' Mary, nae doubt, took the drunt,
  To be compar'd to Willie:
Mall's nit lap out, wi' pridefu' fling,
  An' her ain fit, it burnt it;
While Willie lap, an' swoor by jing,
  'T was just the way he wanted
            To be that night.

X

Nell had the fause-house in her min',
  She pits hersel an' Rob in;
In loving bleeze they sweetly join,
  Till white in ase they 're sobbin:
Nell's heart was dancin at the view;
  She whisper'd Rob to leuk for 't:
Rob, stownlins, prie'd her bonie mou,
  Fu' cozie in the neuk for 't,
            Unseen that night.

XI

But Merran sat behint their backs,
  Her thoughts on Andrew Bell;
She lea'es them gashing at their cracks,
  An' slips out by hersel:
She thro' the yard the nearest taks,
  An' to the kiln she goes then,
An' darklins grapit for the bauks,
  And in the blue-clue throws then,
            Right fear't that night.

XII

An' ay she win't, an' ay she swat —
  I wat she made nae jaukin;
Till something held within the pat,
  Guid Lord! but she was quakin!
But whether 't was the Deil himsel,
  Or whether 't was a bauk-en',
Or whether it was Andrew Bell,
  She did na wait on talkin
            To spier that night.

XIII

Wee Jenny to her graunie says,
  "Will ye go wi' me, graunie ?
I 'll eat the apple at the glass,
  I gat frae uncle Johnie : "

She fuff't her pipe wi' sic a lunt,
  In wrath she was sae vap'rin,
She notic't na an aizle brunt
  Her braw, new, worset apron
      Out thro' that night.

XIV

" Ye little skelpie-limmer's-face !
  I daur ye try sic sportin,
As seek the Foul Thief onie place,
  For him to spae your fortune:
Nae doubt but ye may get a sight !
  Great cause ye hae to fear it;
For monie a ane has gotten a fright,
  An' liv'd an' died deleeret,
      On sic a night.

XV

" Ae hairst afore the Sherra-moor,
  I mind 't as weel 's yestreen —
I was a gilpey then, I 'm sure
  I was na past fyfteen:
The simmer had been cauld an' wat,
  An' stuff was unco green;
An' ay a rantin kirn we gat,
  An' just on Halloween
      It fell that night.

XVI

" Our stibble-rig was Rab M'Graen,
  A clever, sturdy fallow;
His sin gat Eppie Sim wi' wean,
  That lived in Achmachallæ:
He gat hemp-seed, I mind it weel,
  An' he made unco light o't;
But monie a day was by himsel,
  He was sae sairly frighted
      That vera night."

XVII

Then up gat fechtin Jamie Fleck,
  An' he swoor by his conscience,
That he could saw hemp-seed a peck;
  For it was a' but nonsense:
The auld guidman raught down the pock,
  An' out a handfu' gied him;
Syne bad him slip frae 'mang the folk,
  Sometime when nae ane see'd him,
      An' try 't that night.

XVIII

He marches thro' amang the stacks,
  Tho' he was something sturtin;
The graip he for a harrow taks,
  And haurls at his curpin;

And ev'ry now and then, he says,
  " Hemp-seed I saw thee,
An' her that is to be my lass
  Come after me, an' draw thee
      As fast this night."

XIX

He whistl'd up *Lord Lenox' March*,
  To keep his courage cheery;
Altho' his hair began to arch,
  He was sae fley'd an' eerie;
Till presently he hears a squeak,
  An' then a grane an' gruntle;
He by his shouther gae a keek,
  An' tumbl'd wi' a wintle
      Out-owre that night.

XX

He roar'd a horrid murder-shout,
  In dreadfu' desperation !
An' young an' auld come rinnin out,
  An' hear the sad narration:
He swoor 't was hilchin Jean M'Craw,
  Or crouchie Merran Humphie —
Till stop ! she trotted thro' them a';
  An' wha was it but grumphie
      Asteer that night ?

XXI

Meg fain wad to the barn gaen,
  To winn three wechts o' naething;
But for to meet the Deil her lane,
  She pat but little faith in:
She gies the herd a pickle nits,
  An' twa red-cheekit apples,
To watch, while for the barn she sets,
  In hopes to see Tam Kipples
      That vera night.

XXII

She turns the key wi' cannie thraw,
  An' owre the threshold ventures;
But first on Sawnie gies a ca',
  Syne bauldly in she enters:
A ratton rattl'd up the wa',
  An' she cry'd, L—d preserve her !
An' ran thro' midden-hole an' a',
  An' pray'd wi' zeal and fervour
      Fu' fast that night.

XXIII

They hoy't out Will, wi' sair advice;
  They hecht him some fine braw ane;
It chanc'd the stack he faddom't thrice
  Was timmer-propt for thrawin:

He taks a swirlie, auld moss-oak
  For some black gruesome carlin;
An' loot a winze, an' drew a stroke,
  Till skin in blypes cam haurlin
          Aff 's nieves that night.

XXIV

A wanton widow Leezie was,
  As cantie as a kittlin;
But och ! that night, amang the shaws,
  She gat a fearfu' settlin !
She thro' the whins, an' by the cairn,
  An' owre the hill gaed scrievin;
Whare three lairds' lands met at a burn,
  To dip her left sark-sleeve in
          Was bent that night.

XXV

Whyles owre a linn the burnie plays,
  As thro' the glen it wimpl't;
Whyles round a rocky scaur it strays,
  Whyles in a wiel it dimpl't;
Whyles glitter'd to the nightly rays,
  Wi' bickerin, dancin dazzle;
Whyles cookit underneath the braes,
  Below the spreading hazel
          Unseen that night.

XXVI

Amang the brachens, on the brae,
  Between her an' the moon,
The Deil, or else an outler quey,
  Gat up an' gae a croon:
Poor Leezie's heart maist lap the hool;
  Near lav'rock-height she jumpit,
But mist a fit, an' in the pool
  Out-owre the lugs she plumpit
          Wi' a plunge that night.

XXVII

In order, on the clean hearth-stane,
  The luggies three are ranged;
And ev'ry time great care is taen
  To see them duly changed:
Auld uncle John, wha wedlock's joys
  Sin Mar's-year did desire,
Because he gat the toom dish thrice,
  He heav'd them on the fire
          In wrath that night.

XXVIII

Wi' merry sangs, an' friendly cracks,
  I wat they did na weary;
And unco tales, an' funnie jokes —
  Their sports were cheap an' cheery:

Till butter'd sow'ns, wi' fragrant lunt,
  Set a' their gabs a-steerin;
Syne, wi' a social glass o' strunt,
  They parted aff careerin
          Fu' blythe that night.

THE AULD FARMER'S NEW-YEAR MORNING SALUTATION TO HIS AULD MARE, MAGGIE

ON GIVING HER THE ACCUSTOMED RIPP OF CORN TO HANSEL IN THE NEW-YEAR

[Probably composed about the beginning of 1786.]

I

A GUID NEW-YEAR I wish thee, Maggie !
Hae, there 's a ripp to thy auld baggie:
Tho' thou 's howe-backit now, an' knaggie,
    I 've seen the day
Thou could hae gaen like onie staggie,
    Out-owre the lay.

II

Tho' now thou 's dowie, stiff, an' crazy,
An' thy auld hide as white 's a daisie,
I 've seen thee dappl't, sleek, an' glaizie,
    A bonie gray:
He should been tight that daur't to raize thee,
    Ance in a day.

III

Thou ance was i' the foremost rank,
A filly buirdly, steeve, an' swank;
An' set weel down a shapely shank
    As e'er tread yird;
An' could hae flown out-owre a stank
    Like onie bird.

IV

It 's now some nine-an'-twenty year
Sin' thou was my guid-father's meere;
He gied me thee, o' tocher clear,
    An' fifty mark;
Tho' it was sma', 't was weel-won gear,
    An' thou was stark.

V

When first I gaed to woo my Jenny,
Ye then was trottin wi' your minnie:

Tho' ye was trickie, slee, an' funnie,
    Ye ne'er was donsie;
But hamely, tawie, quiet, an' cannie,
    An' unco sonsie.

VI

That day, ye pranc'd wi' muckle pride,
When ye bure hame my bonie bride:
An' sweet an' gracefu' she did ride,
    Wi' maiden air !
Kyle-Stewart I could braggèd wide,
    For sic a pair.

VII

Tho' now ye dow but hoyte and hobble,
An' wintle like a saumont-coble,
That day, ye was a jinker noble,
    For heels an' win' !
An' ran them till they a' did wauble,
    Far, far behin' !

VIII

When thou an' I were young and skiegh,
An' stable-meals at fairs were driegh,
How thou wad prance, an' snore, an' skriegh,
    An' tak the road!
Town's-bodies ran, an' stood abiegh,
    An' ca't thee mad.

IX

When thou was corn't, an' I was mellow,
We took the road ay like a swallow:
At brooses thou had ne'er a fellow,
    For pith an' speed;
But ev'ry tail thou pay't them hollow,
    Whare'er thou gaed.

X

The sma', droop-rumpl't, hunter cattle
Might aiblins waur't thee for a brattle;
But sax Scotch miles thou try't their mettle,
    An' gar't them whaizle:
Nae whip nor spur, but just a wattle
    O' saugh or hazle.

XI

Thou was a noble fittie-lan',
As e'er in tug or tow was drawn:
Aft thee an' I, in aught hours' gaun,
    On guid March-weather,
Hae turn'd sax rood beside our han'
    For days thegither.

XII

Thou never braing't, an' fetch't, an' fliskit;
But thy auld tail thou wad hae whiskit,
An' spread abreed thy weel-fill'd brisket,
    Wi' pith an' pow'r;
Till sprittie knowes wad rair't, an' riskit,
    An' slypet owre.

XIII

When frosts lay lang, an' snaws were deep,
An' threaten'd labour back to keep,
I gied thy cog a wee bit heap
    Aboon the timmer:
I ken'd my Maggie wad na sleep
    For that, or simmer.

XIV

In cart or car thou never reestit ;
The steyest brae thou wad hae fac't it;
Thou never lap, an' sten't, an' breastit,
    Then stood to blaw;
But just thy step a wee thing hastit,
    Thou snoov't awa.

XV

My pleugh is now thy bairntime a',
Four gallant brutes as e'er did draw;
Forbye sax mae I 've sell't awa,
    That thou hast nurst:
They drew me thretteen pund an' twa,
    The vera warst.

XVI

Monie a sair darg we twa hae wrought,
An' wi' the weary warl' fought !
An' monie an anxious day I thought
    We wad be beat !
Yet here to crazy age we 're brought,
    Wi' something yet.

XVII

An' think na, my auld trusty servan',
That now perhaps thou 's less deservin,
An' thy auld days may end in starvin;
    For my last fow,
A heapet stimpart, I 'll reserve ane
    Laid by for you.

XVIII

We 've worn to crazy years thegither;
We 'll toyte about wi' ane anither;
Wi' tentie care I 'll flit thy tether
    To some hain'd rig,
Whare ye may nobly rax your leather
    Wi' sma' fatigue.

THE COTTER'S SATURDAY NIGHT

INSCRIBED TO R. AIKEN, ESQ.

Let not Ambition mock their useful toil,
Their homely joys, and destiny obscure ;
Nor Grandeur hear, with a disdainful smile,
The short and simple annals of the poor.
GRAY.

The Cotter's Saturday Night is included in the list of poems mentioned by Burns in his letter to Richmond, 17th February, 1786 ; it was therefore composed between the beginning of November, 1785, and that date. Gilbert Burns relates that Robert first repeated it to him in the course of a walk one Sunday afternoon. He also states that the "hint of the plan, and the title of the poem," were taken from Fergusson's *Farmer's Ingle.*

This is true, but the piece as a whole is formed on English models. It is the most artificial and the most imitative of Burns's works. Not only is the influence of Gray's *Elegy* conspicuous, but also there are echoes of Pope, Thomson, Goldsmith, and even Milton; while the stanza, which was taken, not from Spenser, whom Burns had not then read, but from Beattie and Shenstone, is so purely English as to lie outside the range of Burns's experience and accomplishment. "These English songs," he wrote long afterwards (1794) to Thomson, "gravel me to death. I have not that command of the language that I have of my native tongue. In fact, I think my ideas are more barren in English than in Scottish." This is so far true as to make one wish that here, as elsewhere, he had chosen a Scots exemplar : that he had taken (say) not merely the scheme but also the stave — *a, b, a, b, c, d, c, d, d* — of *The Farmer's Ingle,* and sought after effects which he could accomplish in a medium of which he was absolute master. As it is, *The Cotter's Saturday Night* is supposed to paint an essentially Scottish phase of life ; but the Scottish element in the diction — to say nothing of the Scottish cast of the effect — is comparatively slight throughout, and in many stanzas is altogether wanting. In the '94 Edition the vernacular was a little coloured by a more general substitution of *an'* for *and, wi'* for *with,* and so on. But it may be that Tytler, rather than Burns, was responsible for this ; and the earlier orthography, being in better keeping with the general English cast, has been retained.

I

My lov'd, my honor'd, much respected friend !
No mercenary bard his homage pays;
With honest pride, I scorn each selfish end,
My dearest meed, a friend's esteem and praise :
To you I sing, in simple Scottish lays,
The lowly train in life's sequester'd scene;
The native feelings strong, the guileless ways ;
What Aiken in a cottage would have been;
Ah ! tho' his worth unknown, far happier there I ween !

II

November chill blaws loud wi' angry sugh;
The short'ning winter-day is near a close ;
The miry beasts retreating frae the pleugh;
The black'ning trains o' craws to their repose:
The toil-worn Cotter frae his labor goes —
This night his weekly moil is at an end,
Collects his spades, his mattocks, and his hoes,
Hoping the morn in ease and rest to spend,
And weary, o'er the moor, his course does hameward bend.

III

At length his lonely cot appears in view,
Beneath the shelter of an aged tree;
Th' expectant wee-things, toddlin, stacher through
To meet their dad, wi' flichterin' noise and glee.
His wee bit ingle, blinkin bonilie,
His clean hearth-stane, his thrifty wifie's smile,
The lisping infant, prattling on his knee,
Does a' his weary kiaugh and care beguile,
And makes him quite forget his labor and his toil.

IV

Belyve, the elder bairns come drapping in,
At service out, amang the farmers roun';
Some ca' the pleugh, some herd, some tentie rin
A cannie errand to a neebor town :
Their eldest hope, their Jenny, woman grown,
In youthfu' bloom, love sparkling in her e'e,
Comes hame; perhaps, to shew a braw new gown,

VI

ap o' leaves an' stibble,
onie a weary nibble !
ned out, for a' thy trouble,
But house or hald,
nter's sleety dribble,
An' cranreuch cauld !

VII

ou art no thy lane,
esight may be vain:
chemes o' mice an' men
Gang aft agley,
ught but grief an' pain,
For promis'd joy !

VIII

blest, compared wi' me !
nly toucheth thee:
backward cast my e'e,
On prospects drear !
tho' I canna see,
I guess an' fear !

TO DAVIE, A BROTHER POET

JANUARY

of this *Epistle* was David Sillar,
atrick Sillar, farmer at Spittle-
ebolton, born in 1760. He made
ance of Burns early in 1781 at
May of that year was admitted a
e Bachelors' Club ; was for some
teacher in the parish school, Tar-
fterwards started an "adventure"
monside; opened a grocer's shop
ards the close of 1783; published
olume of *Poems* in imitation of
helped him to get subscribers;
mpt to get literary work in Edin-
ned to Irvine, where he took up
in, and ultimately became town
d magistrate; died 2d May, 1830.
is *Second Epistle to Davie* (see
h which Sillar prefaced his own
chided him for his neglect of the

han's as you sud ne'er be faiket,
  Be hain't wha like."

timate was not justified : Sillar's
erses are mere commonplace. A
g his recollections of Burns was
n Josiah Walker's Edition (1811),

and has often been reprinted. Sillar, whose
skill as a fiddler may partly explain Burns's
admiration, wrote the air to which *A Rosebud
by my Early Walk* was set in Johnson's
Museum.
"It was, I think, in the summer of 1784"
writes Gilbert Burns, "when in the intervals
of harder labour Robert and I were weeding
in the garden, that he repeated to me the
principal part of this *Epistle.*"

I

WHILE winds frae aff Ben-Lomond blaw,
And bar the doors wi' drivin' snaw,
  And hing us owre the ingle,
I set me down to pass the time,
And spin a verse or twa o' rhyme,
  In hamely, westlin jingle:
While frosty winds blaw in the drift,
  Ben to the chimla lug,
I grudge a wee the great-folk's gift,
  That live sae bien an' snug:
    I tent less, and want less
      Their roomy fire-side;
    But hanker, and canker,
      To see their cursèd pride.

II

It's hardly in a body's pow'r,
To keep, at times, frae being sour,
  To see how things are shar'd;
How best o' chiels are whyles in want,
While coofs on countless thousands rant,
  And ken na how to ware 't;
But Davie, lad, ne'er fash your head,
  Tho' we hae little gear;
We're fit to win our daily bread,
  As lang 's we 're hale and fier:
    "Mair spier na, nor fear na,"
      Auld age ne'er mind a feg;
    The last o't, the warst o't,
      Is only but to beg.

III

To lie in kilns and barns at e'en,
When banes are craz'd, and bluid is thin,
  Is, doubtless, great distress !
Yet then content could make us blest;
Ev'n then, sometimes, we 'd snatch a taste
  Of truest happiness.
The honest heart that 's free frae a'
  Intended fraud or guile,
However Fortune kick the ba',
  Has ay some cause to smile;
    And mind still, you 'll find still,
      A comfort this nae sma';

Or deposite her sair-won penny-fee,
To help her parents dear, if they in hard-
  ship be.

V

With joy unfeign'd, brothers and sisters
    meet,
  And each for other's weelfare kindly
    spiers:
The social hours, swift-wing'd, unnotic'd
    fleet;
  Each tells the uncos that he sees or
    hears.
The parents partial eye their hopeful
    years;
Anticipation forward points the view;
  The mother, wi' her needle and her
    sheers,
Gars auld claes look amaist as weel 's the
    new;
The father mixes a' wi' admonition due.

VI

Their master's and their mistress's com-
    mand
  The younkers a' are warnèd to obey;
And mind their labours wi' an eydent hand,
  And ne'er, tho' out o' sight, to jauk or
    play:
  "And O! be sure to fear the Lord alway,
And mind your duty, duly, morn and night;
  Lest in temptation's path ye gang astray,
Implore His counsel and assisting might:
They never sought in vain that sought the
    Lord aright."

VII

But hark! a rap comes gently to the door;
  Jenny, wha kens the meaning o' the
    same,
Tells how a neebor lad came o'er the moor,
  To do some errands, and convoy her
    hame.
The wily mother sees the conscious flame
Sparkle in Jenny's e'e, and flush her cheek;
  With heart-struck anxious care, enquires
    his name,
While Jenny hafflins is afraid to speak;
Weel-pleas'd the mother hears, it 's nae
    wild, worthless rake.

VIII

With kindly welcome, Jenny brings him ben;
  A strappin' youth, he takes the mother's
    eye;

Blythe Jenny sees the visit 's no ill taen;
  The father cracks of horses, pleughs, and
    kye.
  The youngster's artless heart o'erflows
    wi' joy,
But blate and laithfu', scarce can weel be-
    have;
  The mother, wi' a woman's wiles, can spy
What makes the youth sae bashfu' and sae
    grave;
Weel-pleas'd to think her bairn 's respected
    like the lave.

IX

O happy love! where love like this is
    found:
  O heart-felt raptures! bliss beyond com-
    pare !
I 've pacèd much this weary, mortal round,
  And sage experience bids me this de-
    clare: —
  "If Heaven a draught of heavenly pleas-
    ure spare,
One cordial in this melancholy vale,
  'T is when a youthful, loving, modest
    pair,
In other's arms, breathe out the tender tale
Beneath the milk-white thorn that scents
    the ev'ning gale."

X

Is there, in human form, that bears a heart,
  A wretch ! a villain ! lost to love and
    truth !
That can, with studied, sly, ensnaring art,
  Betray sweet Jenny's unsuspecting youth?
Curse on his perjur'd arts ! dissembling,
    smooth !
Are honor, virtue, conscience, all exil'd ?
Is there no pity, no relenting ruth,
Points to the parents fondling o'er their
    child ?
Then paints the ruin'd maid, and their
    distraction wild ?

XI

But now the supper crowns their simple
    board,
  The healsome parritch, chief o' Scotia's
    food;
The soupe their only hawkie does afford,
  That 'yont the hallan snugly chows her
    cood;
The dame brings forth, in complimental
    mood,

To grace the lad, her weel-hain'd kebbuck, fell;
  And aft he 's prest, and aft he ca's it guid;
The frugal wifie, garrulous, will tell,
  How 't was a towmond auld, sin' lint was i' the bell.

XII

The chearfu' supper done, wi' serious face,
  They, round the ingle, form a circle wide;
The sire turns o'er, wi' patriarchal grace,
  The big ha'-Bible, ance his father's pride.
His bonnet rev'rently is laid aside,
  His lyart haffets wearing thin and bare;
Those strains that once did sweet in Zion glide,
He wales a portion with judicious care,
And "Let us worship God!" he says, with solemn air.

XIII

They chant their artless notes in simple guise,
  They tune their hearts, by far the noblest aim;
Perhaps *Dundee's* wild-warbling measures rise,
  Or plaintive *Martyrs*, worthy of the name;
Or noble *Elgin* beets the heaven-ward flame,
The sweetest far of Scotia's holy lays:
Compar'd with these, Italian trills are tame;
The tickl'd ears no heart-felt raptures raise;
Nae unison hae they, with our Creator's praise.

XIV

The priest-like father reads the sacred page,
  How Abram was the friend of God on high;
Or, Moses bade eternal warfare wage
  With Amalek's ungracious progeny;
Or, how the royal Bard did groaning lie
Beneath the stroke of Heaven's avenging ire;
  Or Job's pathetic plaint, and wailing cry;
Or rapt Isaiah's wild, seraphic fire;
Or other holy Seers that tune the sacred lyre.

XV

Perhaps the Christian volume is the theme:
  How guiltless blood for guilty man was shed;
How He, who bore in Heaven the second name,
  Had not on earth whereon to lay His head;
How His first followers and servants sped;
  The precepts sage they wrote to many a land:
How he, who lone in Patmos banishèd,
Saw in the sun a mighty angel stand,
And heard great Bab'lon's doom pronounc'd by Heaven's command.

XVI

Then kneeling down to Heaven's Eternal King,
  The saint, the father, and the husband prays:
Hope "springs exulting on triumphant wing,"
  That thus they all shall meet in future days,
There, ever bask in uncreated rays,
No more to sigh or shed the bitter tear,
  Together hymning their Creator's praise,
In such society, yet still more dear;
While circling Time moves round in an eternal sphere.

XVII

Compar'd with this, how poor Religion's pride,
  In all the pomp of method, and of art;
When men display to congregations wide
  Devotion's ev'ry grace, except the heart,
The Power, incens'd, the pageant will desert,
  The pompous strain, the sacerdotal stole;
But haply, in some cottage far apart,
May hear, well-pleas'd, the language of the soul,
And in His Book of Life the inmates poor enroll.

XVIII

Then homeward all take off their sev'ral way;
  The youngling cottagers retire to rest:
The parent-pair their secret homage pay,

And proffer up to Heaven the warm request,
  That He who stills the raven's clam'rous nest,
And decks the lily fair in flow'ry pride,
  Would, in the way His wisdom sees the best,
For them and for their little ones provide;
But, chiefly, in their hearts with Grace Divine preside.

XIX

From scenes like these, old Scotia's grandeur springs,
  That makes her lov'd at home, rever'd abroad:
Princes and lords are but the breath of kings,
  "An honest man 's the noblest work of God;"
And certes, in fair Virtue's heavenly road,
The cottage leaves the palace far behind;
  What is a lordling's pomp? a cumbrous load,
Disguising oft the wretch of human kind,
Studied in arts of Hell, in wickedness refin'd!

XX

O Scotia! my dear, my native soil!
  For whom my warmest wish to Heaven is sent!
Long may thy hardy sons of rustic toil
  Be blest with health, and peace, and sweet content!
And O! may Heaven their simple lives prevent
From Luxury's contagion, weak and vile!
  Then, howe'er crowns and coronets be rent,
A virtuous populace may rise the while,
And stand a wall of fire around their much-lov'd Isle.

XXI

O Thou! who pour'd the patriotic tide,
  That stream'd thro' Wallace's undaunted heart,
Who dar'd to, nobly, stem tyrannic pride,
  Or nobly die, the second glorious part:
(The patriot's God, peculiarly Thou art,
His friend, inspirer, guardian, and reward!)
O never, never Scotia's realm desert;

Nae mair then, we 'll care then,
    Nae farther can we fa'.

IV

What tho', like commoners of air,
We wander out, we know not where,
    But either house or hal'?
Yet Nature's charms, the hills and woods,
The sweeping vales, and foaming floods,
    Are free alike to all.
In days when daisies deck the ground,
    And blackbirds whistle clear,
With honest joy our hearts will bound,
    To see the coming year:
      On braes when we please then,
        We 'll sit an' sowth a tune;
      Syne rhyme till 't we 'll time till 't,
        An' sing 't when we hae done.

V

It 's no in titles nor in rank:
It 's no in wealth like Lon'on Bank,
    To purchase peace and rest.
It 's no in makin muckle, mair;
It 's no in books, it 's no in lear,
    To make us truly blest:
If happiness hae not her seat
    An' centre in the breast,
We may be wise, or rich, or great,
    But never can be blest!
      Nae treasures nor pleasures
        Could make us happy lang;
      The heart ay 's the part ay
        That makes us right or wrang.

VI

Think ye, that sic as you and I,
Wha drudge and drive thro' wet and dry,
    Wi' never ceasing toil;
Think ye, are we less blest than they,
Wha scarcely tent us in their way,
    As hardly worth their while?
Alas! how oft, in haughty mood,
    God's creatures they oppress!
Or else, neglecting a' that 's guid,
    They riot in excess!
      Baith careless and fearless
        Of either Heaven or Hell;
      Esteeming and deeming
        It a' an idle tale!

VII

Then let us chearfu' acquiesce,
Nor make our scanty pleasures less
    By pining at our state:

And, even should misfortunes come,
I here wha sit hae met wi' some,
    An 's thankfu' for them yet,
They gie the wit of age to youth;
    They let us ken oursel;
They make us see the naked truth,
    The real guid and ill:
      Tho' losses and crosses
        Be lessons right severe,
      There 's wit there, ye 'll get there,
        Ye 'll find nae other where.

VIII

But tent me, Davie, ace o' hearts!
(To say aught less wad wrang the cartes,
    And flatt'ry I detest)
This life has joys for you and I;
And joys that riches ne'er could buy,
    And joys the very best.
There 's a' the pleasures o' the heart,
    The lover an' the frien':
Ye hae your Meg, your dearest part,
    And I my darling Jean!
      It warms me, it charms me
        To mention but her name:
      It heats me, it beets me,
        And sets me a' on flame!

IX

O all ye Pow'rs who rule above!
O Thou whose very self art love!
    Thou know'st my words sincere!
The life-blood streaming thro' my heart,
Or my more dear immortal part,
    Is not more fondly dear!
When heart-corroding care and grief
    Deprive my soul of rest,
Her dear idea brings relief
    And solace to my breast,
      Thou Being All-seeing,
        O, hear my fervent pray'r!
      Still take her, and make her
        Thy most peculiar care!

X

All hail! ye tender feelings dear!
The smile of love, the friendly tear,
    The sympathetic glow!
Long since, this world's thorny ways
Had number'd out my weary days,
    Had it not been for you!
Fate still has blest me with a friend
    In every care and ill;
And oft a more endearing band,
    A tie more tender still.

It lightens, it brightens
　　The tenebrific scene,
To meet with, and greet with
　　My Davie or my Jean !

XI

O, how that Name inspires my style !
The words come skelpin' rank an' file,
　　Amaist before I ken !
The ready measure rins as fine,
As Phœbus and the famous Nine
　　Were glowrin owre my pen.
My spaviet Pegasus will limp,
　　Till ance he 's fairly het;
And then he 'll hilch, an' stilt, an' jimp,
　　And rin an unco fit;
　　　　But least then, the beast then
　　　　　　Should rue this hasty ride,
　　　　I 'll light now, and dight now
　　　　　　His sweaty, wizen'd hide.

THE LAMENT

OCCASIONED BY THE UNFORTUNATE ISSUE OF A FRIEND'S AMOUR

Alas ! how oft does Goodness wound itself,
And sweet Affection prove the spring of Woe !
　　　　　　　　　　　　　　　　HOME.

"The unfortunate issue," not of a "friend's," but of his own "amour," — when Jean Armour, overborne by paternal authority, agreed to discard him, — was, Burns declares, the "unfortunate story alluded to" in the *Lament:* a "shocking affair" he calls it, which had nearly given him "one or two of the principal qualifications among those who have lost the chart and mistaken the reckoning of rationality." According to Gilbert, the poem was composed "after the first distraction of his feelings had a little subsided."

I

O THOU pale Orb that silent shines
　　While care-untroubled mortals sleep !
Thou seest a wretch who inly pines,
　　And wanders here to wail and weep !
With Woe I nightly vigils keep,
Beneath thy wan, unwarming beam;
　　And mourn, in lamentation deep,
How life and love are all a dream !

II

I joyless view thy rays adorn
　　The faintly-markèd, distant hill;

I joyless view thy trembling horn
　　Reflected in the gurgling rill:
My fondly-fluttering heart, be still !
Thou busy pow'r, Remembrance, cease !
　　Ah ! must the agonizing thrill
For ever bar returning Peace ?

III

No idly-feign'd, poetic pains
　　My sad, love-lorn lamentings claim:
No shepherd's pipe — Arcadian strains;
　　No fabled tortures quaint and tame.
The plighted faith, the mutual flame,
The oft-attested Pow'rs above,
　　The promis'd father's tender name,
These were the pledges of my love !

IV

Encircled in her clasping arms,
　　How have the raptur'd moments flown !
How have I wished for Fortune's charms,
　　For her dear sake, and hers alone !
And, must I think it ! is she gone,
My secret heart's exulting boast ?
　　And does she heedless hear my groan ?
And is she ever, ever lost ?

V

O ! can she bear so base a heart,
　　So lost to honor, lost to truth,
As from the fondest lover part,
　　The plighted husband of her youth ?
Alas ! Life's path may be unsmooth !
Her way may lie thro' rough distress !
　　Then, who her pangs and pains will
　　　　soothe,
Her sorrows share, and make them less ?

VI

Ye wingèd Hours that o'er us pass'd,
　　Enraptur'd more the more enjoy'd,
Your dear remembrance in my breast
　　My fondly treasur'd thoughts employ'd:
That breast, how dreary now, and void,
For her too scanty once of room !
　　Ev'n ev'ry ray of Hope destroy'd,
And not a wish to gild the gloom !

VII

The morn, that warns th' approaching
　　　　day,
　　Awakes me up to toil and woe;
I see the hours in long array,
　　That I must suffer, lingering slow:
Full many a pang, and many a throe,

Keen Recollection's direful train,
  Must wring my soul, ere Phœbus, low,
Shall kiss the distant western main.

VIII

And when my nightly couch I try,
  Sore-harass'd out with care and grief,
My toil-beat nerves and tear-worn eye
  Keep watchings with the nightly thief:
  Or, if I slumber, Fancy, chief,
Reigns, haggard-wild, in sore affright:
  Ev'n day, all-bitter, brings relief
From such a horror-breathing night.

IX

O thou bright Queen, who, o'er th' ex-
    panse
  Now highest reign'st, with boundless
    sway !
Oft has thy silent-marking glance
  Observ'd us, fondly-wand'ring, stray !
  The time, unheeded, sped away,
While Love's luxurious pulse beat high,
  Beneath thy silver-gleaming ray,
To mark the mutual-kindling eye.

X

O scenes in strong remembrance set !
  Scenes, never, never to return !
Scenes if in stupor I forget,
  Again I feel, again I burn !
  From ev'ry joy and pleasure torn,
Life's weary vale I wander thro';
  And hopeless, comfortless, I 'll mourn
A faithless woman's broken vow !

DESPONDENCY

AN ODE

Composed, no doubt, a little after *The La-
ment.*

I

Oppress'd with grief, oppress'd with care,
A burden more than I can bear,
  I set me down and sigh;
O Life ! thou art a galling load,
Along a rough, a weary road,
  To wretches such as I !
Dim-backward, as I cast my view,
  What sick'ning scenes appear !

What sorrows yet may pierce me thro',
  Too justly I may fear !
    Still caring, despairing,
      Must be my bitter doom;
    My woes here shall close ne'er
      But with the closing tomb !

II

Happy ye sons of busy life,
Who, equal to the bustling strife,
  No other view regard !
Ev'n when the wishèd end 's denied,
Yet while the busy means are plied,
  They bring their own reward:
Whilst I, a hope-abandoned wight,
  Unfitted with an aim,
Meet ev'ry sad returning night
  And joyless morn the same.
    You, bustling and justling,
      Forget each grief and pain;
    I, listless yet restless,
      Find ev'ry prospect vain.

III

How blest the Solitary's lot,
Who, all-forgetting, all-forgot,
  Within his humble cell —
The cavern, wild with tangling roots —
Sits o'er his newly-gather'd fruits,
  Beside his crystal well !
Or haply to his ev'ning thought,
  By unfrequented stream,
The ways of men are distant brought,
  A faint-collected dream;
    While praising, and raising
      His thoughts to Heav'n on high,
    As wand'ring, meand'ring,
      He views the solemn sky.

IV

Than I, no lonely hermit plac'd
Where never human footstep trac'd,
  Less fit to play the part;
The lucky moment to improve,
And just to stop, and just to move,
  With self-respecting art:
But ah ! those pleasures, loves, and joys,
  Which I too keenly taste,
The Solitary can despise —
  Can want and yet be blest !
    He needs not, he heeds not
      Or human love or hate;
    Whilst I here must cry here
      At perfidy ingrate !

V

O enviable early days,
When dancing thoughtless pleasure's maze,
  To care, to guilt unknown !
How ill exchang'd for riper times,
To feel the follies or the crimes
  Of others, or my own !
Ye tiny elves that guiltless sport,
  Like linnets in the bush,
Ye little know the ills ye court,
  When manhood is your wish !
    The losses, the crosses
      That active man engage;
    The fears all, the tears all
      Of dim declining Age !

MAN WAS MADE TO MOURN

A DIRGE

In a letter to Mrs. Dunlop, 10th August,
1788, Burns tells of an old grand-uncle who
had gone blind : — "His most voluptuous en-
joyment was to sit down and cry, while my
mother would sing the simple old song of *The
Life and Age of Man.* The old song began
thus : —

    "'T was in the sixteenth hunder year
      Of God and fifty-three
    Frae Christ was born, that bought us dear,
      As writings testifie ;
    On January the sixteenth day,
      As I did lie alone,
    With many a sob and sigh did say,
      Ah ! man was made to moan ! "

I

WHEN chill November's surly blast
  Made fields and forests bare,
One ev'ning, as I wand'red forth
  Along the banks of Ayr,
I spied a man, whose aged step
  Seem'd weary, worn with care,
His face was furrow'd o'er with years,
  And hoary was his hair.

II

"Young stranger, whither wand'rest thou ?"
  Began the rev'rend Sage;
"Does thirst of wealth thy step constrain,
  Or youthful pleasure's rage ?
Or haply, prest with cares and woes,
  Too soon thou hast began
To wander forth, with me to mourn
  The miseries of Man.

III

"The sun that overhangs yon moors,
  Out-spreading far and wide,
Where hundreds labour to support
  A haughty lordling's pride:
I 've seen yon weary winter-sun
  Twice forty times return;
And ev'ry time has added proofs,
  That Man was made to mourn.

IV

"O Man ! while in thy early years,
  How prodigal of time !
Mis-spending all thy precious hours,
  Thy glorious, youthful prime !
Alternate follies take the sway,
  Licentious passions burn:
Which tenfold force gives Nature's law,
  That Man was made to mourn.

V

"Look not alone on youthful prime,
  Or manhood's active might;
Man then is useful to his kind,
  Supported is his right:
But see him on the edge of life,
  With cares and sorrows worn;
Then Age and Want — O ill-match'd
    pair ! —
  Shew Man was made to mourn.

VI

"A few seem favourites of Fate,
  In Pleasure's lap carest;
Yet think not all the rich and great
  Are likewise truly blest:
But oh ! what crowds in ev'ry land,
  All wretched and forlorn,
Thro' weary life this lesson learn,
  That Man was made to mourn.

VII

"Many and sharp the num'rous ills
  Inwoven with our frame !
More pointed still we make ourselves
  Regret, remorse, and shame !
And Man, whose heav'n-erected face
  The smiles of love adorn, —
Man's inhumanity to man
  Makes countless thousands mourn !

VIII

"See yonder poor, o'erlabour'd wight,
  So abject, mean, and vile,

Who begs a brother of the earth
  To give him leave to toil;
And see his lordly fellow-worm
  The poor petition spurn,
Unmindful, tho' a weeping wife
  And helpless offspring mourn.

IX

" If I 'm designed yon lordling's slave —
  By Nature's law design'd —
Why was an independent wish
  E'er planted in my mind?
If not, why am I subject to
  His cruelty, or scorn?
Or why has Man the will and pow'r
  To make his fellow mourn?

X

" Yet let not this too much, my son,
  Disturb thy youthful breast:
This partial view of human-kind
  Is surely not the last !
The poor, oppressèd, honest man
  Had never, sure, been born,
Had there not been some recompense
  To comfort those that mourn !

XI

" O Death ! the poor man's dearest friend,
  The kindest and the best !
Welcome the hour my agèd limbs
  Are laid with thee at rest !
The great, the wealthy fear thy blow
  From pomp and pleasure torn;
But, oh ! a blest relief to those
  That weary-laden mourn ! "

WINTER

A DIRGE

Burns writes in the *First Common Place Book*
under date April, 1784: " There is scarcely any
earthly object gives me more — I don't know
if I should call it pleasure, but something
which exalts me, something which enraptures
me — than to walk in the sheltered side of a
wood or high plantation, in a cloudy winter day,
and hear a stormy wind howling among the
trees and raving o'er the plain. It is my best
season for devotion; my mind is rapt up in a
kind of enthusiasm to Him who, in the pompous
language of Scripture, ' Walks on the wings of
the wind.' In one of these seasons, just after
a tract of misfortunes, I composed the follow-
ing song " — *Winter*, to wit. Gilbert affirms
it to be a " juvenile production ; " and the poet
himself, in his Autobiographic Letter to Dr.
Moore, refers to it as " the eldest of my printed
pieces," and includes it among others composed
in the interval between his return from Kirkos-
wald and his residence in Irvine. It is there-
fore impossible to assign it to a period so late as
that conjectured by Chambers and Scott Doug-
las ; and the " tract of misfortunes " cannot
describe, as the latter held, the disasters at
Irvine, but was probably one of family losses.

I

THE wintry west extends his blast,
  And hail and rain does blaw;
Or the stormy north sends driving forth
  The blinding sleet and snaw:
Wild-tumbling brown, the burn comes
    down,
  And roars frae bank to brae:
While bird and beast in covert rest,
  And pass the heartless day.

II

" The sweeping blast, the sky o'ercast,"
  The joyless winter day
Let others fear, to me more dear
  Than all the pride of May:
The tempest's howl, it soothes my soul,
  My griefs it seems to join;
The leafless trees my fancy please,
  Their fate resembles mine !

III

Thou Pow'r Supreme, whose mighty scheme
  These woes of mine fulfil,
Here, firm I rest, they must be best,
  Because they are Thy will !
Then all I want (O, do Thou grant
  This one request of mine !):
Since to enjoy Thou dost deny,
  Assist me to resign.

A PRAYER IN THE PROSPECT OF DEATH

First Common Place Book, under date August,
1784: " A Prayer when fainting fits, and other
alarming symptoms of a pleurisy or some other
dangerous disorder, which indeed still threaten
me, first put nature on the alarm." A manu-
script in the Burns Monument, Edinburgh, has
the heading : " A Prayer when dangerously
threatened with pleuritic attacks." The piece
has been assigned to 1784, but the entry in the

Common Place Book proves it earlier than the August of that year. It was probably written during Burns's residence in Irvine, when, as would appear from a letter to his father, 27th December, 1781, he had the prospect of " perhaps very soon " bidding " adieu to all the pains, and uneasiness, and disquietudes of this weary life."

O THOU unknown, Almighty Cause
　　Of all my hope and fear !
In whose dread presence, ere an hour,
　　Perhaps I must appear !

If I have wander'd in those paths
　　Of life I ought to shun —
As something, loudly, in my breast,
　　Remonstrates I have done —

Thou know'st that Thou hast formèd me
　　With passions wild and strong;
And list'ning to their witching voice
　　Has often led me wrong.

Where human weakness has come short,
　　Or frailty stept aside,
Do Thou, All-good — for such Thou art —
　　In shades of darkness hide.

Where with intention I have err'd,
　　No other plea I have,
But, Thou art good; and Goodness still
　　Delighteth to forgive.

TO A MOUNTAIN DAISY

ON TURNING ONE DOWN WITH THE PLOUGH IN APRIL, 1786

Enclosed, under the title of *The Gowan*, in a letter of 20th April, 1786, to John Kennedy, clerk to the Earl of Dumfries, at Dumfries House, near Mauchline: " I have here likewise enclosed a small piece, the very latest of my productions. I am a good deal pleased with some sentiments myself, as they are just the native querulous feelings of a heart which, as the elegantly melting Gray says, ' melancholy has marked for her own.' " The last four stanzas conveying the moral are in undiluted English.

I

WEE, modest, crimson-tippèd flow'r,
Thou 's met me in an evil hour;
For I maun crush amang the stoure
　　　　Thy slender stem:

To spare thee now is past my pow'r,
　　　　Thou bonie gem.

II

Alas ! it 's no thy neebor sweet,
The bonie lark, companion meet,
Bending thee 'mang the dewy weet,
　　　　Wi' spreckl'd breast !
When upward-springing, blythe, to greet
　　　　The purpling east.

III

Cauld blew the bitter-biting north
Upon thy early, humble birth;
Yet cheerfully thou glinted forth
　　　　Amid the storm,
Scarce rear'd above the parent-earth
　　　　Thy tender form.

IV

The flaunting flow'rs our gardens yield,
High shelt'ring woods and wa's maun shield:
But thou, beneath the random bield
　　　　O' clod or stane,
Adorns the histie stibble-field,
　　　　Unseen, alane.

V

There, in thy scanty mantle clad,
Thy snawie bosom sun-ward spread,
Thou lifts thy unassuming head
　　　　In humble guise;
But now the share uptears thy bed,
　　　　And low thou lies !

VI

Such is the fate of artless maid,
Sweet flow'ret of the rural shade!
By love's simplicity betray'd,
　　　　And guileless trust;
Till she, like thee, all soil'd, is laid
　　　　Low i' the dust.

VII

Such is the fate of simple Bard,
On Life's rough ocean luckless starr'd !
Unskilful he to note the card
　　　　Of prudent lore,
Till billows rage, and gales blow hard,
　　　　And whelm him o'er !

VIII

Such fate to suffering Worth is giv'n,
Who long with wants and woes has striv'n,

By human pride or cunning driv'n
   To mis'ry's brink;
Till, wrench'd of ev'ry stay but Heav'n,
   He, ruin'd, sink !

IX

Ev'n thou who mourn'st the Daisy's fate,
That fate is thine — no distant date;
Stern Ruin's plough-share drives elate,
   Full on thy bloom,
Till crush'd beneath the furrow's weight
   Shall be thy doom !

TO RUIN

From the lines

 " For one has cut my dearest tie,
  And quivers in my heart " —

it would appear that this piece dates from the
close of Burns's residence at Irvine in 1782,
when, to crown his misfortunes, he was, as he
relates in his Autobiographical Letter, jilted
" with peculiar circumstances of mortification "
by one " who had pledged her soul to marry
him." True, he was greatly distracted by Ar-
mour's conduct in repudiating him ; but there
is no evidence that he was revisited by the
hypochondriacal longing for death to which
expression is given in his second stanza.

I

ALL hail, inexorable lord !
At whose destruction-breathing word,
 The mightiest empires fall !
Thy cruel, woe-delighted train,
The ministers of grief and pain,
 A sullen welcome, all!
With stern-resolv'd, despairing eye,
 I see each aimèd dart;
For one has cut my dearest tie,
 And quivers in my heart.
  Then low'ring and pouring,
   The storm no more I dread;
  Tho' thick'ning and black'ning
   Round my devoted head.

II

And thou grim Pow'r, by Life abhorr'd,
While Life a pleasure can afford,
 O ! hear a wretch's pray'r !
No more I shrink appall'd, afraid;
I court, I beg thy friendly aid,
 To close this scene of care !

When shall my soul, in silent peace,
 Resign Life's joyless day ?
My weary heart its throbbings cease,
 Cold-mould'ring in the clay ?
  No fear more, no tear more
   To stain my lifeless face,
  Enclaspèd and graspèd
   Within thy cold embrace !

EPISTLE TO A YOUNG FRIEND

May —— 1786.

The " young friend " of this *Epistle* was An-
drew Hunter Aiken, son of Robert Aiken of
Ayr. After a successful commercial career in
Liverpool, he became English consul at Riga,
where he died in 1831. His son, Peter Free-
land Aiken, — born 1790, died 3d March, 1877,
— published in 1876 *Memoirs of Robert Burns
and some of his Contemporaries.*
William Niven of Kirkoswald — afterwards
of Maybole, and finally of Kilbride — was
accustomed to complain — not, however, to
Burns, in so far as is known, nor till after his
death — that this *Epistle* was originally ad-
dressed to him. His claim was supported by
the Rev. Hamilton Paul (*Poems and Songs of
Burns*, 1819) ; but, as Niven had no copy to
show, it would seem that, if a rhyming *Epistle*
were sent him, he set little store by the honour.

I

I LANG hae thought, my youthfu' friend,
 A something to have sent you,
Tho' it should serve nae ither end
 Than just a kind memento:
But how the subject-theme may gang,
 Let time and chance determine:
Perhaps it may turn out a sang;
 Perhaps, turn out a sermon.

II

Ye 'll try the world soon, my lad;
 And, Andrew dear, believe me,
Ye 'll find mankind an unco squad,
 And muckle they may grieve ye:
For care and trouble set your thought,
 Ev'n when your end 's attainèd:
And a' your views may come to nought,
 Where ev'ry nerve is strainèd.

III

I 'll no say, men are villains a' :
 The real, harden'd wicked,

Wha hae nae check but human law,
  Are to a few restricked;
But, och! mankind are unco weak
  An' little to be trusted;
If Self the wavering balance shake,
  It 's rarely right adjusted!

IV

Yet they wha fa' in Fortune's strife,
  Their fate we should na censure;
For still, th' important end of life
  They equally may answer:
A man may hae an honest heart,
  Tho' poortith hourly stare him;
A man may tak a neebor's part,
  Yet hae nae cash to spare him.

V

Ay free, aff han', your story tell,
  When wi' a bosom cronie;
But still keep something to yoursel
  Ye scarcely tell to onie:
Conceal yoursel as weel 's ye can
  Frae critical dissection:
But keek thro' ev'ry other man
  Wi' sharpen'd, sly inspection.

VI

The sacred lowe o' weel-plac'd love,
  Luxuriantly indulge it;
But never tempt th' illicit rove,
  Tho' naething should divulge it:
I waive the quantum o' the sin,
  The hazard of concealing;
But, och! it hardens a' within,
  And petrifies the feeling!

VII

To catch Dame Fortune's golden smile,
  Assiduous wait upon her;
And gather gear by ev'ry wile
  That 's justify'd by honour:
Not for to hide it in a hedge,
  Nor for a train-attendant;
But for the glorious privilege
  Of being independent.

VIII

The fear o' Hell 's a hangman's whip
  To haud the wretch in order;
But where ye feel your honour grip,
  Let that ay be your border:
Its slightest touches, instant pause —
  Debar a' side-pretences;

And resolutely keep its laws,
  Uncaring consequences.

IX

The great Creator to revere
  Must sure become the creature;
But still the preaching cant forbear,
  And ev'n the rigid feature:
Yet ne'er with wits profane to range
  Be complaisance extended;
An atheist-laugh 's a poor exchange
  For Deity offended!

X

When ranting round in Pleasure's ring,
  Religion may be blinded;
Or if she gie a random sting,
  It may be little minded;
But when on Life we 're tempest-driv'n —
  A conscience but a canker —
A correspondence fix'd wi' Heav'n
  Is sure a noble anchor!

XI

Adieu, dear, amiable youth!
  Your heart can ne'er be wanting!
May prudence, fortitude, and truth,
  Erect your brow undaunting!
In ploughman phrase, "God send you
    speed,"
  Still daily to grow wiser;
And may ye better reck the rede,
  Than ever did th' adviser!

ON A SCOTCH BARD

GONE TO THE WEST INDIES

Probably among the latest written for the Kilmarnock Edition. While it was in progress, Burns was maturing his plans for emigration, and on 17th July, 1786, he wrote to David Brice, Glasgow: "I am now fixed to go for the West Indies in October."

I

A' ye wha live by sowps o' drink,
A' ye wha live by crambo-clink,
A' ye wha live and never think,
        Come, mourn wi' me!
Our billie 's gien us a' a jink,
        An' owre the sea!

II

Lament him a' ye rantin core,
Wha dearly like a random-splore;
Nae mair he 'll join the merry roar
    In social key;
For now he 's taen anither shore,
    An' owre the sea!

III

The bonie lasses weel may wiss him,
And in their dear petitions place him:
The widows, wives, an' a' may bless him
    Wi' tearfu' e'e,
For weel I wat they 'll sairly miss him
    That 's owre the sea!

IV

O Fortune, they hae room to grumble!
Hadst thou taen aff some drowsy bummle,
Wha can do nought but fyke an' fumble,
    'T wad been nae plea;
But he was gleg as onie wumble,
    That 's owre the sea!

V

Auld, cantie Kyle may weepers wear,
An' stain them wi' the saut, saut tear:
'T will mak her poor auld heart, I fear,
    In flinders flee:
He was her Laureat monie a year,
    That 's owre the sea!

VI

He saw Misfortune's cauld nor-west
Lang-mustering up a bitter blast;
A jillet brak his heart at last,
    Ill may she be!
So, took a birth afore the mast,
    An' owre the sea.

VII

To tremble under Fortune's cummock,
On scarce a bellyfu' o' drummock,
Wi' his proud, independent stomach,
    Could ill agree;
So, row't his hurdies in a hammock,
    An' owre the sea.

VIII

He ne'er was gien to great misguiding,
Yet coin his pouches wad na bide in:
Wi' him it ne'er was under hiding.
    He dealt it **free ;**

The Muse was a' that he took pride in,
    That 's owre the sea.

IX

Jamaica bodies, use him weel,
An' hap him in a cozie biel:
Ye 'll find him ay a dainty chiel,
    An' fou o' glee:
He wad na wrang'd the vera Deil,
    That 's owre the sea.

X

Fareweel, my rhyme-composing billie !
Your native soil was right ill-willie;
But may ye flourish like a lily,
    Now bonilie !
I 'll toast you in my hindmost gillie,
    Tho' owre the sea !

A DEDICATION

TO GAVIN HAMILTON, ESQ.

Gavin Hamilton — to whom Burns here dedicates the First Edition of his poems, because " I thought them something like yoursel," was descended from an old Ayrshire family, the Hamiltons of Kype. The fifth son of John Hamilton of Kype — who was settled as a Writer in Mauchline — by his first wife, Jacobina King, he was born in 1751, probably in November, as he was baptized on the 20th of that month ; succeeded his father as solicitor in Mauchline, occupying a castellated mansion, now partly in ruins, hard by the churchyard ; and sublet the farm of Mossgiel to Burns and his brother Gilbert. Like the poet, he sympathised with liberalism in religion, and they became warm friends. He was prosecuted in the autumn of 1784 by the Kirk-Session of Mauchline for neglect of public ordinances and other irregularities ; and wrote a letter to the Session, affirming that its proceedings were dictated by "private pique and ill-nature." The accusation is corroborated by Cromek, who states that the Rev. William Auld of Mauchline had quarrelled with Hamilton's father (in all probability the true cause of both the quarrel with the father and the Sessional prosecution of the son was the hereditary Episcopacy of the Hamiltons). Ultimately, through the intervention of the Presbytery of Ayr, Gavin Hamilton compelled the Session, on 17th July, 1785, to grant him a certificate that he was " free from public scandal or ground of Church censure known " to them : a triumph celebrated in *Holy Willie's Prayer*. He was again prosecuted by the Session for causing his servants to dig new potatoes in his garden on the " last Lord's day " of July, 1787. He died 5th February, 1805.   Hamilton's character is very fully portrayed in the *Dedication*, and incisively in his *Epitaph* (p. 55). Several letters from Burns to him are published, including a *Rhyming Epistle* and *Stanzas on Naething;* and there are references to him in *Holy Willie's Prayer*, the *Epistle to John M'Math*, and *The Farewell*.

EXPECT na, sir, in this narration,
A fleechin, fleth'rin Dedication,
To roose you up, an' ca' you guid,
An' sprung o' great an' noble bluid,
Because ye 're surnam'd like His Grace,
Perhaps related to the race:
Then, when I 'm tired — and sae are ye,
Wi' monie a fulsome, sinfu' lie —
Set up a face how I stop short,
For fear your modesty be hurt.

This may do — maun do, sir, wi' them wha
Maun please the great-folk for a wamefou';
For me ! sae laigh I need na bow,
For, Lord be thankit, I can plough;
And when I downa yoke a naig,
Then, Lord be thankit, I can beg;
Sae I shall say, an' that 's nae flatt'rin,
It 's just sic poet an' sic patron.

The Poet, some guid angel help him,
Or else, I fear, some ill ane skelp him !
He may do weel for a' he 's done yet,
But only he 's no just begun yet.

The Patron (sir, ye maun forgie me;
I winna lie, come what will o' me),
On ev'ry hand it will allow'd be,
He 's just — nae better than he should be.

I readily and freely grant,
He downa see a poor man want;
What 's no his ain he winna tak it;
What ance he says, he winna break it;
Ought he can lend he 'll no refuse 't,
Till aft his guidness is abus'd;
And rascals whyles that do him wrang,
Ev'n that, he does na mind it lang;
As master, landlord, husband, father,
He does na fail his part in either.

But then, nae thanks to him for a' that;
Nae godly symptom ye can ca' that;
It 's naething but a milder feature
Of our poor, sinfu', corrupt nature:
Ye 'll get the best o' moral works,
'Mang black Gentoos, and pagan Turks,
Or hunters wild on Ponotaxi,
Wha never heard of orthodoxy.
That he 's the poor man's friend in need,
The gentleman in word and deed,
It 's no thro' terror of damnation:
It 's just a carnal inclination,
And och ! that 's nae regeneration.

Morality, thou deadly bane,
Thy tens o' thousands thou hast slain !
Vain is his hope, whase stay an' trust is
In moral mercy, truth, and justice !

No — stretch a point to catch a plack;
Abuse a brother to his back;
Steal thro' the winnock frae a whore,
But point the rake that taks the door;
Be to the poor like onie whunstane,
And haud their noses to the grunstane;
Ply ev'ry art o' legal thieving;
No matter — stick to sound believing.

Learn three-mile pray'rs, an' half-mile graces,
Wi' weel - spread looves, an' lang, wry faces;
Grunt up a solemn, lengthen'd groan,
And damn a' parties but your own;
I 'll warrant then, ye 're nae deceiver,
A steady, sturdy, staunch believer.

O ye wha leave the springs o' Calvin,
For gumlie dubs of your ain delvin !
Ye sons of Heresy and Error,
Ye 'll some day squeel in quaking terror,
When Vengeance draws the sword in wrath,
And in the fire throws the sheath;
When Ruin, with his sweeping besom,
Just frets till Heav'n commission gies him;
While o'er the harp pale Misery moans,
And strikes the ever-deep'ning tones,
Still louder shrieks, and heavier groans !

Your pardon, sir, for this digression:
I maist forgat my Dedication;
But when divinity comes 'cross me,
My readers still are sure to lose me.

So, sir, you see 't was nae daft vapour;
But I maturely thought it proper,
When a' my works I did review,
To dedicate them, sir, to you:
Because (ye need na tak' it ill),
I thought them something like yoursel.

Then patronize them wi' your favor,
And your petitioner shall ever ——
I had amaist said, ever pray,
But that 's a word I need na say;
For prayin, I hae little skill o't;
I 'm baith dead-sweer, an' wretched ill o't;
But I 'se repeat each poor man's pray'r,
That kens or hears about you, sir: ——

" May ne'er Misfortune's gowling bark
Howl thro' the dwelling o' the clerk !
May ne'er his gen'rous, honest heart,
For that same gen'rous spirit smart !
May Kennedy's far-honor'd name
Lang beet his hymeneal flame,
Till Hamiltons, at least a dizzen,
Are frae their nuptial labors risen:
Five bonie lasses round their table,
And sev'n braw fellows, stout an' able,
To serve their king an' country weel,
By word, or pen, or pointed steel !
May Health and Peace, with mutual rays,
Shine on the ev'ning o' his days;
Till his wee, curlie John's ier-oe,
When ebbing life nae mair shall flow,
The last, sad, mournful rites bestow ! "

I will not wind a lang conclusion,
With complimentary effusion;
But, whilst your wishes and endeavours
Are blest with Fortune's smiles and fa-
  vours,
I am, dear sir, with zeal most fervent,
Your much indebted, humble servant.

But if (which Pow'rs above prevent)
That iron-hearted carl, Want,
Attended, in his grim advances,
By sad mistakes, and black mischances,
While hopes, and joys, and pleasures fly
  him,
Make you as poor a dog as I am,
Your " humble servant " then no more?
For who would humbly serve the poor ?
But, by a poor man's hopes in Heav'n !
While recollection's pow'r is giv'n,
If, in the vale of humble life,
The victim sad of Fortune's strife,

I, thro' the tender-gushing tear,
Should recognise my master dear;
If friendless, low, we meet together,
Then, sir, your hand — my FRIEND and
  BROTHER !

TO A LOUSE

ON SEEING ONE ON A LADY'S BONNET AT CHURCH

I

HA ! whare ye gaun, ye crowlin ferlie ?
Your impudence protects you sairly,
I canna say but ye strunt rarely
    Owre gauze and lace,
Tho' faith ! I fear ye dine but sparely
    On sic a place.

II

Ye ugly, creepin, blastit wonner,
Detested, shunn'd by saunt an' sinner,
How daur ye set your fit upon her —
    Sae fine a lady !
Gae somewhere else and seek your dinner
    On some poor body.

III

Swith ! in some beggar's hauffet squattle:
There ye may creep, and sprawl, and
    sprattle,
Wi' ither kindred, jumping cattle,
    In shoals and nations;
Whare horn nor bane ne'er daur unsettle
    Your thick plantations.

IV

Now haud you there ! ye 're out o' sight,
Below the fatt'rils, snug an' tight;
Na, faith ye yet ! ye 'll no be right,
    Till ye 've got on it —
The vera tapmost, tow'ring height
    O' Miss's bonnet.

V

My sooth ! right bauld ye set your nose
    out,
As plump an' grey as onie grozet:
O for some rank, mercurial rozet,
    Or fell, red smeddum,
I 'd gie ye sic a hearty dose o 't,
    Wad dress your droddum.

VI

I wad na been surpris'd to spy
You on an auld wife's flainen toy;
Or aiblins some bit duddie boy,
         On 's wyliecoat;
But Miss's fine Lunardi ! fye !
         How daur ye do 't ?

VII

O Jenny, dinna toss your head,
An' set your beauties a' abroad !
Ye little ken what cursèd speed
         The blastie 's makin !
Thae winks an' finger-ends, I dread,
         Are notice takin !

VIII

O wad some Power the giftie gie us
To see oursels as ithers see us !
It wad frae monie a blunder free us,
         An' foolish notion:
What airs in dress an' gait wad lea'e us,
         An' ev'n devotion !

EPISTLE TO J. LAPRAIK

AN OLD SCOTTISH BARD, APRIL I, 1785

John Lapraik, whose song *When I upon Thy Bosom Lean* " so thirl'd the heart-strings " of Burns, was descended from an old Ayrshire family, which for several generations possessed the estate of Laigh Dalquhram, near Muirkirk. He was born in 1727 ; succeeded to the estate on the death of his father, and also rented the farm and mill of Muirsmill ; lost his estate and all his means by the failure of the Ayr Bank in 1772 ; was inspired by Burns's success to publish *Poems on Several Occasions* (1788) ; and died 7th May, 1807.

Lapraik's song, so warmly praised by Burns, and afterwards sent by him for insertion to Johnson's *Museum,* iii. 214 (1790), closely resembles one in Ruddiman's *Weekly Magazine,* 11th October, 1773, *When on Thy Bosom I Recline,* dated Edinburgh, 11th October, and signed " Happy Husband." It has been too rashly inferred that Lapraik plagiarised from this lyric : he may have written it himself. Another, *When West Winds did Blow,* which Burns also sent to Johnson, is not without merit. The original *Epistle* was at one time in the possession of Sir Robert Jardine, and the piece is also entered in the *First Common Place Book* under date June, 1785.

I

WHILE briers an' woodbines budding
         green,
And paitricks scraichin loud at e'en,
An' morning poussie whiddin seen,
         Inspire my Muse,
This freedom, in an unknown frien'
         I pray excuse.

II

On Fasten-e'en we had a rockin,
To ca' the crack and weave our stockin;
And there was muckle fun and jokin,
         Ye need na doubt;
At length we had a hearty yokin,
         At " sang about."

III

There was ae sang, among the rest,
Aboon them a' it pleas'd me best,
That some kind husband had addrest
         To some sweet wife:
It thirl'd the heart-strings thro' the breast,
         A' to the life.

IV

I 've scarce heard ought describ'd sae weel,
What gen'rous, manly bosoms feel;
Thought I, " Can this be Pope or Steele,
         Or Beattie's wark ? "
They tald me 't was an odd kind chiel
         About Muirkirk.

V

It pat me fidgin-fain to hear 't,
An' sae about him there I spier't;
Then a' that kent him round declar'd
         He had ingíne;
That nane excell'd it, few cam near 't,
         It was sae fine:

VI

That, set him to a pint of ale,
An' either douce or merry tale,
Or rhymes an' sangs he 'd made himsel,
         Or witty catches,
'Tween Inverness an' Teviotdale,
         He had few matches.

VII

Then up I gat, an' swoor an aith,
Tho' I should pawn my pleugh an' graith,
Or die a cadger pownie's death,
         At some dyke-back,

A pint an' gill I 'd gie them baith,
    To hear your crack.

VIII

But, first an' foremost, I should tell,
Amaist as soon as I could spell,
I to the crambo-jingle fell;
    Tho' rude an' rough —
Yet crooning to a body's sel,
    Does weel eneugh.

IX

I am nae poet, in a sense;
But just a rhymer like by chance,
An' hae to learning nae pretence;
    Yet, what the matter ?
Whene'er my Muse does on me glance,
    I jingle at her.

X

Your critic-folk may cock their nose,
And say, " How can you e'er propose,
You wha ken hardly verse frae prose,
    To mak a sang ? "
But, by your leaves, my learned foes,
    Ye 're maybe wrang.

XI

What 's a' your jargon o' your Schools,
Your Latin names for horns an' stools ?
If honest Nature made you fools,
    What sairs your grammers ?
Ye'd better taen up spades and shools,
    Or knappin-hammers.

XII

A set o' dull, conceited hashes
Confuse their brains in college-classes,
They gang in stirks, and come out asses,
    Plain truth to speak;
An' syne they think to climb Parnassus
    By dint o' Greek !

XIII

Gie me ae spark o' Nature's fire,
That 's a' the learning I desire;
Then, tho' I drudge thro' dub an' mire
    At pleugh or cart,
My Muse, tho' hamely in attire,
    May touch the heart.

XIV

O for a spunk o' Allan's glee,
Or Fergusson's, the bauld an' slee,

Or bright Lapraik's, my friend to be,
    If I can hit it !
That would be lear eneugh for me,
    If I could get it.

XV

Now, sir, if ye hae friends enow,
Tho' real friends I b'lieve are few;
Yet, if your catalogue be fow,
    I 'se no insist:
But, gif ye want ae friend that 's true,
    I 'm on your list.

XVI

I winna blaw about mysel,
As ill I like my fauts to tell;
But friends, an' folks that wish me well,
    They sometimes roose me;
Tho', I maun own, as monie still
    As far abuse me.

XVII

There 's ae wee faut they whyles lay to
    me,
I like the lasses — Gude forgie me !
For monie a plack they wheedle frae me
    At dance or fair;
Maybe some ither thing they gie me,
    They weel can spare.

XVIII

But Mauchline Race or Mauchline Fair,
I should be proud to meet you there:
We 'se gie ae night's discharge to care,
    If we forgather;
And hae a swap o' rhymin-ware
    Wi' ane anither.

XIX

The four-gill chap, we 'se gar him clatter,
An' kirsen him wi' reekin water;
Syne we 'll sit down an' tak our whitter,
    To cheer our heart;
An' faith, we 'se be acquainted better
    Before we part.

XX

Awa ye selfish, warly race,
Wha think that havins, sense, an' grace,
Ev'n love an' friendship should give place
    To Catch-the-Plack !
I dinna like to see your face,
    Nor hear your crack.

XXI

But ye whom social pleasure charms,
Whose hearts the tide of kindness warms,
Who hold your being on the terms,
   " Each aid the others,"
Come to my bowl, come to my arms,
   My friends, my brothers !

XXII

But, to conclude my lang epistle,
As my auld pen 's worn to the grissle,
Twa lines frae you wad gar me fissle,
   Who am most fervent,
While I can either sing or whistle,
   Your friend and servant.

SECOND EPISTLE TO J. LAPRAIK

APRIL 21, 1785

Entered in the *First Common Place Book*
under the first *Epistle* with this explanation :
" On receiving an answer to the above I wrote
the following."

I

WHILE new-ca'd kye rowte at the stake
An' pownies reek in pleugh or braik,
This hour on e'enin's edge I take,
   To own I 'm debtor
To honest-hearted, auld Lapraik,
   For his kind letter.

II

Forjesket sair, with weary legs,
Rattlin the corn out-owre the rigs,
Or dealing thro' amang the naigs
   Their ten-hours' bite,
My awkart Muse sair pleads and begs,
   I would na write.

III

The tapetless, ramfeezl'd hizzie,
She 's saft at best an' something lazy:
Quo' she: " Ye ken we 've been sae busy
   This month an' mair,
That trowth, my head is grown right dizzie,
   An' something sair."

IV

Her dowff excuses pat me mad:
" Conscience," says I, " ye thowless jad !

I 'll write, an' that a hearty blaud,
   This vera night;
So dinna ye affront your trade,
   But rhyme it right.

V

" Shall bauld Lapraik, the king o' hearts,
Tho' mankind were a pack o' cartes,
Roose you sae weel for your deserts,
   In terms sae friendly;
Yet ye 'll neglect to shaw your parts
   An' thank him kindly ? "

VI

Sae I gat paper in a blink,
An' down gaed stumpie in the ink:
Quoth I: " Before I sleep a wink,
   I vow I 'll close it:
An' if ye winna mak it clink,
   By Jove, I 'll prose it ! "

VII

Sae I 've begun to scrawl, but whether
In rhyme, or prose, or baith thegither,
Or some hotch-potch that 's rightly neither,
   Let time mak proof;
But I shall scribble down some blether
   Just clean aff-loof.

VIII

My worthy friend, ne'er grudge an' carp,
Tho' Fortune use you hard an' sharp;
Come, kittle up your moorland harp
   Wi' gleesome touch !
Ne'er mind how Fortune waft an' warp;
   She 's but a bitch.

IX

She 's gien me monie a jirt an' fleg,
Sin' I could striddle owre a rig;
But, by the Lord, tho' I should beg
   Wi' lyart pow,
I 'll laugh an' sing, an' shake my leg,
   As lang 's I dow !

X

Now comes the sax-an-twentieth simmer
I 've seen the bud upo' the timmer,
Still persecuted by the limmer
   Frae year to year;
But yet, despite the kittle kimmer,
   I, Rob, am here.

XI

Do ye envý the city gent,
Behint a kist to lie an' sklent;
Or purse-proud, big wi' cent. per cent.
    An' muckle wame,
In some bit brugh to represent
    A bailie's name?

XII

Or is 't the paughty feudal thane,
Wi' ruffl'd sark an' glancing cane,
Wha thinks himsel nae sheep-shank bane,
    But lordly stalks;
While caps an' bonnets aff are taen,
    As by he walks?

XIII

" O Thou wha gies us each guid gift!
Gie me o' wit an' sense a lift,
Then turn me, if Thou please, adrift
    Thro' Scotland wide;
Wi' cits nor lairds I wadna shift,
    In a' their pride!"

XIV

Were this the charter of our state,
"On pain o' hell be rich an' great,"
Damnation then would be our fate,
    Beyond remead;
But, thanks to heaven, that 's no the gate
    We learn our creed.

XV

For thus the royal mandate ran,
When first the human race began:
" The social, friendly, honest man,
    Whate'er he be,
'T is he fulfils great Nature's plan,
    And none but he."

XVI

O mandate glorious and divine!
The followers o' the ragged Nine —
Poor, thoughtless devils! — yet may shine
    In glorious light;
While sordid sons o' Mammon's line
    Are dark as night!

XVII

Tho' here they scrape, an' squeeze, an'
    growl,
Their worthless neivefu' of a soul
May in some future carcase howl,
    The forest's fright;

Or in some day-detesting owl
    May shun the light.

XVIII

Then may Lapraik and Burns arise,
To reach their native, kindred skies,
And sing their pleasures, hopes an' joys,
    In some mild sphere;
Still closer knit in friendship's ties,
    Each passing year!

TO WILLIAM SIMPSON OF OCHILTREE

MAY, 1785

The " winsome Willie " of this *Epistle* was William Simpson, son of John Simpson, farmer in Ten-Pound Land, in the parish of Ochiltree. He was born 23d August, 1758; was educated at the University of Glasgow; became parish schoolmaster of Ochiltree in 1780, and in 1788 of Cumnock; and died 4th July, 1815. It has been inferred that the piece which drew the flattering letter from him was *The Twa Herds*. But the inference is not supported by the evidence adduced — the statement of Burns himself, that he gave a copy of that satire to " a particular friend; " for Burns affirmed to this same friend that he did not know who was the author, and had got a copy by accident.

I

I GAT your letter, winsome Willie;
Wi' gratefu' heart I thank you brawlie;
Tho' I maun say 't, I wad be silly
    And unco vain,
Should I believe, my coaxin billie,
    Your flatterin strain.

II

But I 'se believe ye kindly meant it:
I sud be laith to think ye hinted
Ironic satire, sidelins sklented,
    On my poor Musie;
Tho' in sic phraisin terms ye 've penn'd
    it,
    I scarce excuse ye.

III

My senses wad be in a creel,
Should I but dare a hope to speel,
Wi' Allan, or wi' Gilbertfield,
    The braes o' fame;

Or Fergusson, the writer-chiel,
    A deathless name.

IV

(O Fergusson! thy glorious parts
Ill suited law's dry, musty arts!
My curse upon your whunstane hearts,
    Ye E'nbrugh gentry!
The tythe o' what ye waste at cartes
    Wad stow'd his pantry!)

V

Yet when a tale comes i' my head,
Or lasses gie my heart a screed —
As whyles they 're like to be my dead,
    (O sad disease!)
I kittle up my rustic reed;
    It gies me ease.

VI

Auld Coila, now, may fidge fu' fain,
She 's gotten bardies o' her ain;
Chiels wha their chanters winna hain,
    But tune their lays,
Till echoes a' resound again
    Her weel-sung praise.

VII

Nae Poet thought her worth his while,
To set her name in measur'd style;
She lay like some unkend-of isle
    Beside New Holland,
Or whare wild-meeting oceans boil
    Besouth Magellan.

VIII

Ramsay an' famous Fergusson
Gied Forth an' Tay a lift aboon;
Yarrow an' Tweed, to monie a tune,
    Owre Scotland rings;
While Irwin, Lugar, Ayr, an' Doon
    Naebody sings.

IX

Th' Illissus, Tiber, Thames, an' Seine,
Glide sweet in monie a tunefu' line:
But, Willie, set your fit to mine,
    An' cock your crest!
We 'll gar our streams and burnies shine
    Up wi' the best.

X

We 'll sing auld Coila's plains an' fells,
Her moors red-brown wi' heather bells,

Her banks an' braes, her dens an' dells,
    Whare glorious Wallace
Aft bure the gree, as story tells,
    Frae Suthron billies.

XI

At Wallace' name, what Scottish blood
But boils up in a spring-tide flood?
Oft have our fearless fathers strode
    By Wallace' side,
Still pressing onward, red-wat-shod,
    Or glorious dy'd!

XII

O, sweet are Coila's haughs an' woods,
When lintwhites chant amang the buds,
And jinkin hares, in amorous whids,
    Their loves enjoy;
While thro' the braes the cushat croods
    With wailfu' cry!

XIII

Ev'n winter bleak has charms to me,
When winds rave thro' the naked tree;
Or frosts on hills of Ochiltree
    Are hoary gray;
Or blinding drifts wild-furious flee,
    Dark'ning the day!

XIV

O Nature! a' thy shews an' forms
To feeling, pensive hearts hae charms!
Whether the summer kindly warms,
    Wi' life an' light;
Or winter howls, in gusty storms,
    The lang, dark night!

XV

The Muse, nae poet ever fand her,
Till by himsel he learn'd to wander,
Adown some trottin burn's meander,
    An' no think lang:
O, sweet to stray, an' pensive ponder
    A heart-felt sang!

XVI

The warly race may drudge an' drive,
Hog-shouther, jundie, stretch, an' strive;
Let me fair Nature's face descrive,
    And I, wi' pleasure,
Shall let the busy, grumbling hive
    Bum owre their treasure.

XVII

Fareweel, my rhyme-composing brither !
We 've been owre lang unkend to ither:
Now let us lay our heads thegither,
        In love fraternal:
May Envy wallop in a tether,
        Black fiend, infernal !

XVIII

While Highlandmen hate tolls an' taxes;
While moorlan' herds like guid, fat brax-
        ies;
While Terra Firma, on her axis,
        Diurnal turns;
Count on a friend, in faith an' practice,
        In Robert Burns.

POSTSCRIPT

XIX

My memory 's no worth a preen:
I had amaist forgotten clean,
Ye bade me write you what they mean
        By this New-Light,
'Bout which our herds sae aft hae been
        Maist like to fight.

XX

In days when mankind were but callans;
At grammar, logic, an' sic talents,
They took nae pains their speech to balance,
        Or rules to gie;
But spak their thoughts in plain, braid
        Lallans,
        Like you or me.

XXI

In thae auld times, they thought the moon,
Just like a sark, or pair o' shoon,
Wore by degrees, till her last roon
        Gaed past their viewin;
An' shortly after she was done,
        They gat a new ane.

XXII

This past for certain, undisputed;
It ne'er cam i' their heads to doubt it,
Till chiels gat up an' wad confute it,
        An' ca'd it wrang;
An' muckle din there was about it,
        Baith loud an' lang.

XXIII

Some herds, weel learn'd upo' the Beuk,
Wad threap auld folk the thing misteuk;
For 't was the auld moon turn'd a neuk
        An' out o' sight.
An' backlins-comin to the leuk,
        She grew mair bright.

XXIV

This was deny'd, it was affirm'd;
The herds and hissels were alarm'd;
The rev'rend gray-beards rav'd an' storm'd,
        That beardless laddies
Should think they better were inform'd
        Than their auld daddies.

XXV

Frae less to mair, it gaed to sticks;
Frae words an' aiths, to clours an' nicks;
An' monie a fallow gat his licks,
        Wi' hearty crunt;
An' some, to learn them for their tricks,
        Were hang'd an' brunt.

XXVI

This game was play'd in monie lands,
An' Auld-Light caddies bure sic hands,
That faith, the youngsters took the sands
        Wi' nimble shanks
Till lairds forbade, by strict commands,
        Sic bluidy pranks.

XXVII

But New-Light herds gat sic a cowe,
Folk thought them ruin'd stick-an-stowe;
Till now, amaist on ev'ry knowe
        Ye 'll find ane placed;
An' some, their New-Light fair avow,
        Just quite barefac'd.

XXVIII

Nae doubt the Auld - Light flocks are
        bleatin;
Their zealous herds are vex'd and sweatin;
Mysel, I 've even seen them greetin
        Wi' girnin spite,
To hear the moon sae sadly lie'd on
        By word an' write.

XXIX

But shortly they will cowe the louns !
Some Auld-Light herds in neebor touns
Are mind't, in things they ca' balloons,
        To tak a flight,

An' stay ae month amang the moons
    An' see them right.

XXX

Guid observation they will gie them;
An' when the auld moon's gaun to lea'e
    them,
The hindmost shaird, they 'll fetch it wi'
    them,
    Just i' their pouch;
An' when the New-Light billies see them,
    I think they 'll crouch !

XXXI

Sae, ye observe that a' this clatter
Is naething but a "moonshine matter;"
But tho' dull prose-folk Latin splatter
    In logic tulzie,
I hope we, Bardies, ken some better
    Than mind sic brulzie.

EPISTLE TO JOHN RANKINE

ENCLOSING SOME POEMS

Rankine was farmer at Adamhill, in the parish of Craigie, near Lochlie. His wit, his dreams (invented for the purpose of roasting his dislikes), and his practical jokes were the talk of the country side. His sister, Margaret, was the first wife of John Lapraik, and his daughter, Anne, afterwards Mrs. Merry, vaunted herself the heroine of *The Rigs o' Barley*. Burns also addressed to Rankine a *Reply to an Announcement*, and complimented him in an *Epitaph* as the one " honest man " in " a mixtie-maxtie motley squad."

It is to be noted that the last seven stanzas of this piece set forth an account in good venereal slang — *e. g.* " straik " (*i. e.* " stroke ") = *subagitare ;* " hen," " wame," " tail," " gun," " feathers," and so forth — of Burns's amour with Elizabeth Paton, by whom he had an illegitimate child (November, 1784), and with whom he did penance by order of the Session.

I

O ROUGH, rude, ready-witted Rankine,
The wale o' cocks for fun an' drinkin !
There 's monie godly folks are thinkin'
    Your dreams and tricks
Will send you, Korah-like, a-sinkin
    Straught to Auld Nick's.

II

Ye hae sae monie cracks an' cants,
And in your wicked drucken rants,
Ye mak a devil o' the saunts,
    An' fill them fou';
And then their failings, flaws, an' wants
    Are a' seen thro'.

III

Hypocrisy, in mercy spare it !
That holy robe, O, dinna tear it !
Spare 't for their sakes, wha aften wear it —
    The lads in black;
But your curst wit, when it comes near it,
    Rives 't aff their back.

IV

Think, wicked sinner, wha ye 're skaithing:
It 's just the Blue-gown badge an' claithing
O' saunts; tak that, ye lea'e them naething
    To ken them by
Frae onie unregenerate heathen,
    Like you or I.

V

I 've sent you here some rhyming ware
A' that I bargain'd for, an' mair;
Sae, when ye hae an hour to spare,
    I will expect,
Yon sang ye 'll sen't, wi' cannie care,
    And no neglect.

VI

Tho' faith, sma' heart hae I to sing:
My Muse dow scarcely spread her wing !
I 've play'd mysel a bonie spring,
    An' danc'd my fill !
I 'd better gaen an' sair't the King
    At Bunker's Hill.

VII

'T was ae night lately, in my fun,
I gaed a rovin wi' the gun,
An' brought a paitrick to the grun' —
    A bonie hen;
And, as the twilight was begun,
    Thought nane wad ken.

VIII

The poor, wee thing was little hurt;
I straikit it a wee for sport,
Ne'er thinkin they wad fash me for 't;
    But, Deil-ma-care !

Somebody tells the Poacher-Court
The hale affair.

IX

Some auld, us'd hands had taen a note,
That sic a hen had got a shot;
I was suspected for the plot;
    I scorn'd to lie;
So gat the whissle o' my groat,
    An' pay't the fee.

X

But, by my gun, o' guns the wale,
An' by my pouther an' my hail,
An' by my hen, an' by her tail,
    I vow an' swear!
The game shall pay, owre moor an' dale,
    For this, niest year!

XI

As soon 's the clockin-time is by,
An' the wee pouts begun to cry,
Lord, I 'se hae sportin by an' by
    For my gowd guinea;
Tho' I should herd the buckskin kye
    For 't, in Virginia!

XII

Trowth, they had muckle for to blame!
'T was neither broken wing nor limb,
But twa-three chaps about the wame,
    Scarce thro' the feathers;
An' baith a yellow George to claim
    An' thole their blethers!

XIII

It pits me ay as mad 's a hare;
So I can rhyme nor write nae mair;
But pennyworths again is fair,
    When time 's expedient:
Meanwhile I am, respected Sir,
    Your most obedient.

SONG

TUNE: *Corn Rigs*

In an interleaved copy of Johnson's *Museum*, Burns remarks: "All the old words that ever I could meet to this were the following, which seem to have been an old chorus: —

    "'O corn rigs and rye rigs,
      O corn rigs are bonie,
    And whene'er you meet a bonnie lass,
      Preen up her cockernony.'"

The last song in Ramsay's *Gentle Shepherd*, *My Patie is a Lover Gay*, to the tune *Corn Rigs are Bonny*, concludes as follows: —

    "Then I 'll comply and marry Pate,
      And syne my cockernony
    He 's free to touzle air and late
      Where corn rigs are bonny."

Burns wrote to George Thomson: "*My Pattie is a Lover Gay* — is unequal. 'His mind is never muddy' is a muddy expression indeed.

    "'Then I 'll resign (*sic*) and marry Pate,
      And syne my cockernony,' etc.

This is surely far unworthy of Ramsay, or of your work." With characteristic deference he added: "My song, *Rigs o' Barley*, to the same tune, does not altogether please me, but if I can mend it, I will submit it to your consideration." Thomson disregarded this modest offer: "*My Patie is a Lover Gay*, though a little unequal, is a natural and pleasing song, and I humbly think we ought not to displace it or alter it except the last stanza."

In his Autobiographical Letter to Dr. Moore, Burns includes this admirable lyric among the "rhymes" of his "early days," composed before his twenty-third year. But its accomplishment is finer than he had then compassed, and, as in the case of the lyric that follows, *Now Westlin' Winds*, the early version was probably a mere fragmentary suggestion of the later. Burns was himself accustomed to regard the last stanza as a nearer approach to his ideal of expression and sentiment than he had achieved elsewhere. As to the heroine there is not basis enough even for conjecture, though divers Annies have claimed the honour.

I

IT was upon a Lammas night,
    When corn rigs are bonie,
Beneath the moon's unclouded light,
    I held awa to Annie;
The time flew by, wi' tentless heed;
    Till, 'tween the late and early,
Wi' sma' persuasion she agreed
    To see me thro' the barley.
        Corn rigs, an' barley rigs,
          An' corn rigs are bonie:
        I 'll ne'er forget that happy night,
          Amang the rigs wi' Annie.

II

The sky was blue, the wind was still,
    The moon was shining clearly;
I set her down, wi' right good will,
    Amang the rigs o' barley:

I ken't her heart was a' my ain;
   I lov'd her most sincerely;
I kiss'd her owre and owre again,
   Amang the rigs o' barley.

III

I lock'd her in my fond embrace;
   Her heart was beating rarely:
My blessings on that happy place,
   Amang the rigs o' barley!
But by the moon and stars so bright,
   That shone that hour so clearly!
She ay shall bless that happy night
   Amang the rigs o' barley.

IV

I hae been blythe wi' comrades dear;
   I hae been merry drinking;
I hae been joyfu' gath'rin gear;
   I hae been happy thinking:
But a' the pleasures e'er I saw,
   Tho' three times doubl'd fairly —
That happy night was worth them a',
   Amang the rigs o' barley.
     Corn rigs, an' barley rigs,
      An' corn rigs are bonie:
     I 'll ne'er forget that happy night,
      Amang the rigs wi' Annie.

SONG: COMPOSED IN AUGUST

Burns states in his "autobiographical letter" that this song was the "ebullition" of his passion for a "charming *filette*" (*sic*), Peggy Thomson, who "overset his trigonometry" at Kirkoswald when he was in his seventeenth year. His sister, Mrs. Begg, further affirms that the passion was afterwards revived, and it has been supposed that Thomson is the Peggy of his letter to Thomas Orr (11th November, 1784): "I am very glad Peggy is off my hand." But about this time he had also an "affair" with "Montgomerie's Peggy," "which," as he wrote in the *First Common Place Book*, "it cost some heart-aches to get rid of." Peggy Thomson became the wife of Mr. Neilson of Kirkoswald. Burns — when he was making ready for the West Indies in 1786 — presented her with a copy of his book, on which he inscribed the lines beginning: —

" Once fondly loved and still remembered dear."

I

Now westlin winds and slaught'ring guns
   Bring Autumn's pleasant weather;
The gorcock springs on whirring wings
   Amang the blooming heather:
Now waving grain, wide o'er the plain,
   Delights the weary farmer;
The moon shines bright, as I rove by night
   To muse upon my charmer.

II

The paitrick lo'es the fruitfu' fells,
   The plover lo'es the mountains;
The woodcock haunts the lonely dells,
   The soaring hern the fountains;
Thro' lofty groves the cushat roves,
   The path o' man to shun it;
The hazel bush o'erhangs the thrush,
   The spreading thorn the linnet.

III

Thus ev'ry kind their pleasure find,
   The savage and the tender;
Some social join, and leagues combine,
   Some solitary wander:
Avaunt, away, the cruel sway!
   Tyrannic man's dominion!
The sportsman's joy, the murd'ring cry,
   The flutt'ring, gory pinion!

IV

But, Peggy dear, the evening 's clear,
   Thick flies the skimming swallow,
The sky is blue, the fields in view
   All fading-green and yellow:
Come, let us stray our gladsome way
   And view the charms of Nature;
The rustling corn, the fruited thorn,
   And ilka happy creature.

V

We 'll gently walk, and sweetly talk,
   While the silent moon shines clearly;
I 'll clasp thy waist, and, fondly prest,
   Swear how I lo'e thee dearly:
Not vernal show'rs to budding flow'rs,
   Not Autumn to the farmer,
So dear can be as thou to me,
   My fair, my lovely charmer!

SONG: FROM THEE, ELIZA

TUNE: *Gilderoy*

Burns, on his return to Mauchline from his Border tour, wrote to James Smith, 11th June, 1787: "Your mother, sister and brother, my quondam Eliza, etc., all, all well." This shows that Eliza lived in Mauchline. She was Elizabeth Miller — afterward Mrs. Templeton — celebrated in *The Belles of Mauchline* (*post*, p. 171) as the " Miss Betty " who 's " braw." See also *A Mauchline Wedding* (*post*, p. 114).

I

FROM thee, Eliza, I must go
   And from my native shore:
The cruel fates between us throw
   A boundless ocean's roar;
But boundless oceans, roaring wide
   Between my Love and me,
They never, never can divide
   My heart and soul from thee.

II

Farewell, farewell, Eliza dear,
   The maid that I adore !
A boding voice is in mine ear,
   We part to meet no more !
But the latest throb that leaves my heart,
   While Death stands victor by,
That throb, Eliza, is thy part,
   And thine that latest sigh !

THE FAREWELL

TO THE BRETHREN OF ST. JAMES'S LODGE, TARBOLTON

TUNE : *Good-night, and joy be wi' you a'.*

" At this time the author intended going to Jamaica " (MS. R. B. in a copy of the '86 Edition in the British Museum). Burns was admitted an apprentice of the St. David's Lodge, Tarbolton (formed by the union of the St. James's with the St. David's), 4th July, 1781, and, when a separation of the Lodges occurred in June, 1782, he adhered to the St. James's, of which he was, on 22d July, 1784, elected depute master. The verses, it is supposed, were recited at a meeting of the Lodge held on the 23d June.

I

ADIEU ! a heart-warm, fond adieu;
   Dear Brothers of the *Mystic Tie !*
Ye favour'd, ye enlighten'd few,
   Companions of my social joy !
Tho' I to foreign lands must hie,
   Pursuing Fortune's slidd'ry ba';

With melting heart and brimful eye,
   I 'll mind you still, tho' far awa.

II

Oft have I met your social band,
   And spent the cheerful, festive night;
Oft, honour'd with supreme command,
   Presided o'er the *Sons of Light;*
And by that *Hieroglyphic* bright,
   Which none but *Craftsmen* ever saw !
Strong Mem'ry on my heart shall write
   Those happy scenes, when far awa.

III

May Freedom, Harmony, and Love,
   Unite you in the *Grand Design,*
Beneath th' Omniscient Eye above —
   The glorious *Architect* Divine —
That you may keep th' *Unerring Line,*
   Still rising by the *Plummet's Law,*
Till *Order* bright completely shine,
   Shall be my pray'r, when far awa.

IV

And You, farewell ! whose merits claim
   Justly that *Highest Badge* to wear:
Heav'n bless your honour'd, noble Name,
   To Masonry and Scotia dear !
A last request permit me here,
   When yearly ye assemble a';
One round, I ask it with a tear,
   To him, the Bard that 's far awa.

EPITAPH ON A HENPECKED SQUIRE

Burns states that the subject of this epitaph was " Mr. Campbell of Netherplace," a mansion a little to the west of Mauchline, on the road to Mossgiel. It is probable that Campbell — or perhaps his wife — had given Burns some particular offence.

As father Adam first was fool'd,
   A case that 's still too common,
Here lies a man a woman rul'd:
   The Devil ruled the woman.

EPIGRAM ON SAID OCCASION

O DEATH, had'st thou but spar'd his life,
   Whom we this day lament !

We freely wad exchanged the wife,
An' a' been weel content.

Ev'n as he is, cauld in his graff,
The swap we yet will do 't;
Tak thou the carlin's carcase aff,
Thou 'se get the saul o' boot.

ANOTHER

ONE Queen Artemisa, as old stories tell,
When depriv'd of her husband she lovèd so
    well,
In respect for the love and affection he 'd
    show'd her,
She reduc'd him to dust and she drank up
    the powder.
But Queen Netherplace, of a diff'rent com-
    plexion,
When call'd on to order the fun'ral direc-
    tion,
Would have eat her dead lord, on a slender
    pretence,
Not to show her respect, but — to save the
    expense !

EPITAPHS

ON A CELEBRATED RULING ELDER

In the Author's Edition the Elder's name is
indicated merely by asterisks; in a copy of the
'86 in the British Museum, "Hood" is in-
serted; and in the *First Common Place Book*,
under the date April, 1784, the heading is,
"Epitaph on Wm. Hood, senr. in Tarbolton."

HERE Souter Hood in death does sleep:
    In hell, if he 's gane thither,
Satan, gie him thy gear to keep;
    He 'll haud it weel thegither.

ON A NOISY POLEMIC

James Humphry, a mason in Mauchline,
with no doubt of his ability to debate with
Burns. He died in 1844.

BELOW thir stanes lie Jamie's banes:
    O Death, it 's my opinion,

Thou ne'er took such a bleth'rin bitch
    Into thy dark dominion.

ON WEE JOHNIE

It is common to assume that Burns meant
this for his own printer, John Wilson of Kil-
marnock; but there was a bookseller in Mauch-
line, also of diminutive stature, named John
Wilson. It has further been denoted, by Cham-
bers, that the trifle is a literal translation of a
Latin epigram in *Nugæ Venales*, 1663.

Hic jacet wee *Johnie*

WHOE'ER thou art, O reader, know,
    That Death has murder'd Johnie,
An' here his *body* lies fu' low —
    For *saul* he ne'er had onie.

FOR THE AUTHOR'S FATHER

William Burness died at Lochlie, 13th
February, 1784; and this *Epitaph on my Ever
Honoured Father* was inserted in the *First Com-
mon Place Book* under the date April of that
year. It is engraved on the tombstone in Allo-
way Churchyard.

O YE whose cheek the tear of pity stains,
    Draw near with pious rev'rence, and
        attend !
Here lie the loving husband's dear remains,
    The tender father, and the gen'rous
        friend.

The pitying heart that felt for human
        woe,
    The dauntless heart that fear'd no human
        pride,
The friend of man — to vice alone a foe;
    For "ev'n his failings lean'd to virtue's
        side."

FOR ROBERT AIKEN, ESQ.

KNOW thou, O stranger to the fame
    Of this much lov'd, much honour'd
        name !
(For none that knew him need be told),
    A warmer heart Death ne'er made cold.

FOR GAVIN HAMILTON, Esq.

THE poor man weeps — here Gavin sleeps,
  Whom canting wretches blam'd;
But with such as he, where'er he be,
  May I be sav'd or damn'd.

A BARD'S EPITAPH

I

Is there a whim-inspirèd fool,
Owre fast for thought, owre hot for rule,
Owre blate to seek, owre proud to snool ? —
    Let him draw near;
And owre this grassy heap sing dool,
    And drap a tear.

II

Is there a Bard of rustic song,
Who, noteless, steals the crowds among,
That weekly this aréa throng ? —
    O, pass not by !
But with a frater-feeling strong,
    Here, heave a sigh.

III

Is there a man, whose judgment clear
Can others teach the course to steer,
Yet runs, himself, life's mad career
    Wild as the wave ? —
Here pause — and, thro' the starting tear,
    Survey this grave.

IV

The poor inhabitant below
Was quick to learn and wise to know,
And keenly felt the friendly glow
    And softer flame;
But thoughtless follies laid him low,
    And stain'd his name.

V

Reader, attend ! whether thy soul
Soars Fancy's flights beyond the pole,
Or darkling grubs this earthly hole
    In low pursuit;
Know, prudent, cautious, self-control
    Is wisdom's root.

ADDITIONS IN THE EDINBURGH EDITION OF 1787

ON 30th July [1783], the eve of publication [of the Kilmarnock Edition of *Poems chiefly in the Scottish Dialect*], Burns wrote thus to Richmond : "My hour is now come," and "you and I shall never meet in Britain more." By the end of August nearly the whole impression was subscribed, and Burns, "after deducting all expenses," pocketed, according to his own statement, "nearly twenty pounds : " a much smaller sum than is shown in the account between him and Wilson. "The money," he says, "came in seasonably, as I was about to indent myself for want of money to pay my freight. As soon as I was master of nine guineas, the price of wafting me to the torrid zone, I bespoke a passage in the very first ship that was to sail —

  "'For hungry ruin had me in the wind.'"

Divers circumstances combined to delay his departure, and although on the 14th August he booked to sail on the 1st September, September passed and he was still in Scotland. On the 9th October, after settling accounts with Wilson, he offered him a second edition: "on the hazard of being paid out of the first and readiest." Wilson declined, and the disappointment more strongly confirmed his determination to leave the country. He would inevitably have done so, if he had not chanced to see a letter from Dr. Blacklock to the Rev. Dr. Lawrie, of Newmilns, expressing a strong opinion in favour of a second edition, and affirming that the book might "obtain a more universal circulation than anything of the kind" within the writer's memory. At this time he had taken "the last farewell" of his friends ; his "chest was on the road to Greenock ; " he had devised a song, *The Gloomy Night is Gathering Fast*, as the "last effort" of his "Muse in Caledonia." But the letter upset all his schemes, and determined him to get his verse reissued by an Edinburgh publisher ; so he "posted" to the capital, "without a single acquaintance in town," or "a single letter of recommendation" in his pocket. Through the Earl of Glencairn he was introduced to Creech : with the result that a new Edition (the First Edinburgh) was ready for delivery on the 18th April.

Three thousand copies were printed, for over fifteen hundred subscribers: the book being entitled " *Poems chiefly in the Scottish Dialect.* By Robert Burns. Edinburgh. Printed for the Author and Sold by William Creech. 1787." Many important pieces — some written while the volume was going through the press — were added ; but not even in the Dedication to the Caledonian Hunt was there so much as a hint that this was a Second Edition. [The Dedication is as follows : —]

DEDICATION

TO THE NOBLEMEN AND GENTLEMEN OF THE CALEDONIAN HUNT

My Lords and Gentlemen, — A Scottish Bard, proud of the name, and whose highest ambition is to sing in his Country's service — where shall he so properly look for patronage as to the illustrious Names of his native Land ; those who bear the honours and inherit the virtues of their Ancestors ? The Poetic Genius of my Country found me as the prophetic bard Elijah did Elisha — at the *plough*, and threw her inspiring mantle over me. She bade me sing the loves, the joys, the rural scenes and rural pleasures of my natal Soil, in my native tongue : I tuned my wild, artless notes, as she inspired. She whispered me to come to this ancient metropolis of Caledonia, and lay my Songs under your honoured protection : I now obey her dictates.

Though much indebted to your goodness, I do not approach you, my Lords and Gentlemen,

in the usual style of dedication, to thank you for past favours ; that path is so hackneyed by prostituted Learning, that honest Rusticity is ashamed of it. Nor do I present this Address with the venal soul of a servile Author, looking for a continuation of those favours : I was bred to the Plough, and am independent. I come to claim the common Scottish name with you, my illustrious Countrymen; and to tell the world that I glory in the title. I come to congratulate my Country, that the blood of her ancient heroes still runs uncontaminated ; and that from your courage, knowledge, and public spirit, she may expect protection, wealth, and liberty. In the last place, I come to proffer my warmest wishes to the Great Fountain of Honour, the Monarch of the Universe, for your welfare and happiness.

When you go forth to waken the Echoes, in the ancient and favorite amusement of your Forefathers, may Pleasure ever be of your party ; and may Social-joy await your return ! When harassed in court or camps with the jostlings of bad men and bad measures, may the honest consciousness of injured Worth attend your return to your native Seats ; and may Domestic Happiness, with a smiling welcome, meet you at your gates ! May Corruption shrink at your kindling, indignant glance ; and may tyranny in the Ruler and licentiousness in the People equally find you an inexorable foe !

I have the honour to be, with the sincerest gratitude and highest respect,

My Lords and Gentlemen,
Your most devoted, humble Servant,
ROBERT BURNS.

Edinburgh, April 4, 1787.

DEATH AND DOCTOR HORN-BOOK

A TRUE STORY

According to Gilbert Burns, Hornbook was one John Wilson, parish schoolmaster of Tarbolton. To eke out his salary he opened a grocer's shop, where he " added the sale of a few medicines to his little trade," informing the public in a shop bill that " advice would be given in common disorders at the shop gratis." At a " masonic meeting at Tarbolton in the spring of 1785 " Wilson happened to air " his medical skill " in the presence of Burns, who — says Gilbert — as he parted with him in the evening at " the place where he describes the meeting with Death " was visited by " one of those floating ideas of apparitions he mentions in his letter to Dr. Moore." The visitation sug-

gested a train of thoughts which he began running into *Death and Dr. Hornbook* on his way home. If Lockhart may be believed, the satire ruined Wilson in Tarbolton: not only was he compelled to shut his shop, but also he had presently to close his school. But, as he continued to act as Session-Clerk down to at least 8th January, 1793 (letter in *Burns Chronicle*, 1895, p. 138), Lockhart must have been in some sort misinformed. Nevertheless, Wilson did remove to Glasgow, where he became schoolmaster and Session-Clerk of the Gorbals parish. He died 13th January, 1839.

Hately Waddell, on the authority of a " respected resident " in Tarbolton, brought forward a prototype of Death : one " Hugh Reid of the Langlands," a " lang ghaist-like body," with whom Burns — 't is the Tarbolton tradition — forgathered, as here described, near " Willie's mill."

I

Some books are lies frae end to end,
And some great lies were never penn'd:
Ev'n ministers, they hae been kend,
 In holy rapture,
A rousing whid at times to vend,
 And nail 't wi' Scripture.

II

But this that I am gaun to tell,
Which lately on a night befel,
Is just as true 's the Deil 's in hell
 Or Dublin city:
That e'er he nearer comes oursel
 'S a muckle pity!

III

The clachan yill had made me canty,
I was na fou, but just had plenty:
I stacher'd whyles, but yet took tent ay
 To free the ditches;
An' hillocks, stanes, an' bushes, kend ay
 Frae ghaists an' witches.

IV

The rising moon began to glowr
The distant Cumnock Hills out-owre:
To count her horns, wi' a' my pow'r
 I set mysel;
But whether she had three or four,
 I cou'd na tell.

V

I was come round about the hill,
And todlin down on Willie's mill,
Setting my staff wi' a' my skill
 To keep me sicker;
Tho' leeward whyles, against my will,
 I took a bicker.

VI

I there wi' *Something* does forgather,
That pat me in an eerie swither;
An awfu' scythe, out-owre ae shouther,
 Clear-dangling, hang;
A three-tae'd leister on the ither
 Lay, large an' lang.

VII

Its stature seem'd lang Scotch ells twa;
The queerest shape that e'er I saw,
For fient a wame it had ava;
 And then its shanks,

They were as thin, as sharp an' sma'
 As cheeks o' branks.

VIII

"Guid-een," quo' I; "Friend! hae ye
 been mawin,
When ither folk are busy sawin?"
It seem'd to mak a kind o' stan',
 But naething spak.
At length, says I: "Friend! whare ye
 gaun?
  Will ye go back?"

IX

It spak right howe: "My name is Death,
But be na' fley'd." Quoth I: "Guid
 faith,
Ye 're may be come to stap my breath;
 But tent me, billie:
I red ye weel, take care o' skaith,
 See, there 's a gully!"

X

"Gudeman," quo' he, "put up your whittle,
I 'm no design'd to try its mettle;
But if I did, I wad be kittle
 To be mislear'd:
I wad na mind it, no that spittle
 Out-owre my beard."

XI

"Weel, weel!" says I, "a bargain be 't;
Come, gie 's your hand, an' say we 're
 gree't;
We 'll ease our shanks, an' tak a seat:
 Come, gie 's your news:
This while ye hae been monie a gate,
 At monie a house."

XII

"Ay, ay!" quo' he, an' shook his head,
"It 's e'en a lang, lang time indeed
Sin' I began to nick the thread
 An' choke the breath:
Folk maun do something for their bread,
 An' sae maun Death.

XIII

"Sax thousand years are near-hand fled
Sin' I was to the butching bred,
An' monie a scheme in vain 's been laid
 To stap or scar me;
Till ane Hornbook 's ta'en up the trade,
 And faith! he 'll waur me.

XIV

" Ye ken Jock Hornbook i' the clachan ?
Deil mak his king's-hood in a spleuchan ! —
He 's grown sae weel acquaint wi' *Buchan*
  And ither chaps,
The weans haud out their fingers laughin,
  An' pouk my hips.

XV

" See, here 's a scythe, an' there 's a dart,
They hae pierc'd monie a gallant heart;
But Doctor Hornbook wi' his art
  An' cursed skill,
Has made them baith no worth a fart,
  Damn'd haet they 'll kill !

XVI

" 'T was but yestreen, nae farther gane,
I threw a noble throw at ane;
Wi' less, I 'm sure, I 've hundreds slain;
  But Deil-ma-care !
It just played dirl on the bane,
  But did nae mair.

XVII

" Hornbook was by wi' ready art,
An' had sae fortify'd the part,
That when I lookèd to my dart,
  It was sae blunt,
Fient haet o't wad hae pierc'd the heart
  Of a kail-runt.

XVIII

" I drew my scythe in sic a fury,
I near-hand cowpit wi' my hurry,
But yet the bauld Apothecary
  Withstood the shock:
I might as weel hae try'd a quarry
  O' hard whin-rock.

XIX

" Ev'n them he canna get attended,
Altho' their face he ne'er had kend it,
Just shit in a kail-blade an' send it,
  As soon 's he smells 't,
Baith their disease and what will mend it,
  At once he tells 't.

XX

" And then a' doctor's saws and whittles
Of a' dimensions, shapes, an' mettles,
A' kinds o' boxes, mugs, and bottles,
  He 's sure to hae:

Their Latin names as fast he rattles
  As A B C.

XXI

" Calces o' fossils, earth, and trees;
True *sal-marinum* o' the seas;
The *farina* of beans an' pease,
  He has 't in plenty;
Aqua-fontis, what you please,
  He can content ye.

XXII

" Forbye some new, uncommon weapons,
Urinus spiritus of capons;
Or mite-horn shavings, filings, scrapings
  Distill'd *per se;*
Sal-alkali o' midge-tail-clippings,
  And monie mae."

XXIII

" Waes me for Johnie Ged's Hole now,"
Quoth I, " if that thae news be true !
His braw calf-ward whare gowans grew
  Sae white and bonie,
Nae doubt they 'll rive it wi' the plew:
  They 'll ruin Johnie ! "

XXIV

The creature grain'd an eldritch laugh,
And says: " Ye nedna yoke the pleugh,
Kirkyards will soon be till'd eneugh,
  Tak ye nae fear:
They 'll a' be trench'd wi monie a sheugh
  In twa-three year.

XXV

" Whare I kill'd ane, a fair strae death
By loss o' blood or want o' breath,
This night I 'm free to tak my aith,
  That Hornbrook's skill
Has clad a score i' their last claith
  By drap an' pill.

XXVI

" An honest wabster to his trade,
Whase wife's twa nieves were scarce weel-
  bred,
Gat tippence-worth to mend her head,
  When it was sair;
The wife slade cannie to her bed,
  But ne'er spak mair.

XXVII

" A countra laird had taen the batts,
Or some curmurring in his guts,

His only son for Hornbook sets,
    An' pays him well:
The lad, for twa guid gimmer-pets,
    Was laird himsel.

XXVIII

" A bonie lass — ye kend her name —
Some ill-brewn drink had hov'd her wame;
She trusts hersel, to hide the shame,
    In Hornbook's care;
Horn sent her aff to her lang hame
    To hide it there.

XXIX

"That's just a swatch o' Hornbook's way;
Thus goes he on from day to day,
Thus does he poison, kill, an' slay,
    An's weel paid for 't;
Yet stops me o' my lawfu' prey
    Wi' his damn'd dirt:

XXX

" But, hark! I 'll tell you of a plot,
Tho' dinna ye be speakin o't:
I 'll nail the self-conceited sot,
    As dead 's a herrin;
Niest time we meet, I 'll wad a groat,
    He gets his fairin! "

XXXI

But just as he began to tell,
The auld kirk-hammer strak the bell
Some wee short hour ayont the twal,
    Which raised us baith:
I took the way that pleas'd mysel,
    And sae did Death.

THE BRIGS OF AYR

A POEM

INSCRIBED TO JOHN BALLANTINE, ESQ., AYR

John Ballantine — to whom Burns dedicated this poem, and who was one of his warmest friends — was eldest son of Bailie William Ballantine, banker and merchant in Ayr, and Elizabeth Bowman; born 22d July, 1743; succeeded to his father's business; was a most active citizen, and a prime mover in the project for a new bridge; was elected provost of the burgh in 1787; and died 15th July, 1812.

In a letter to Robert Aiken, 7th October, 1786, Burns, after narrating the failure of his attempts to persuade Wilson to publish a second edition, states that one of his chief regrets was that he was thus deprived of an opportunity for showing his gratitude to Ballantine by publishing *The Brigs of Ayr.* The New Bridge, designed by Robert Adam of London, the most famous of the four brothers, was erected 1785–88. The boast of the "Auld Brig" that it would "be a brig" when its neighbour was a "shapeless cairn" was justified in 1877, when the New Bridge was so injured by floods that it had to be practically rebuilt at a cost of £15,000, additional repairs being found necessary in 1881.

The Brigs of Ayr, like *To Robert Graham of Fintry* (p. 85), is set forth in the heroic couplet. The technical inspiration is unmistakably English in both; and, accordingly, the verse in both is handled with a certain awkwardness, while the effect is often rough, and even ragged. This is the more surprising, as the couplet had a past of its own in Scottish poetry. To say nothing of late and early chaps and tracts, it is the rhythmus of Blind Harry's *Wallace* (c. 1460); of *The Three Priests of Peebles* (c. 1500); of Gavin Douglas's *Eneados* (1513); of that masterly and brilliant piece of comic narrative, generally (and, no doubt, rightly) ascribed to Dunbar, *The Freirs of Berwick;* of Ramsay's *Gentle Shepherd;* and of Fergusson's *Drink* and *Kirkyard* Eclogues, of which last, and of the same poet's *Plainstanes and Causey,* the present piece is strongly reminiscent. It was probably composed between July and October, 1786.

THE simple Bard, rough at the rustic
    plough,
Learning his tuneful trade from ev'ry bough
(The chanting linnet, or the mellow thrush,
Hailing the setting sun, sweet, in the green
    thorn bush;
The soaring lark, the perching red-breast
    shrill,
Or deep-ton'd plovers grey, wild-whistling
    o'er the hill):
Shall he — nurst in the peasant's lowly shed,
To hardy independence bravely bred,
By early poverty to hardship steel'd,
And train'd to arms in stern misfortune's
    field —
Shall he be guilty of their hireling crimes,
The servile, mercenary Swiss of rhymes?
Or labour hard the panegyric close,
With all the venal soul of dedicating prose?
No! though his artless strains he rudely
    sings,
And throws his hand uncouthly o'er the
    strings,

He glows with all the spirit of the bard,
Fame, honest fame, his great, his dear re-
ward.
Still, if some patron's gen'rous care he trace,
Skill'd in the secret to bestow with grace;
When Ballantine befriends his humble
name,
And hands the rustic stranger up to fame,
With heartfelt throes his grateful bosom
swells:
The godlike bliss, to give, alone excels.

'T was when the stacks get on their win-
ter hap,
And thack and rape secure the toil-won
crap;
Potatoe-bings are snuggèd up frae skaith
O' coming winter's biting, frosty breath;
The bees, rejoicing o'er their summer
toils —
Unnumber'd buds' an' flowers' delicious
spoils,
Seal'd up with frugal care in massive waxen
piles —
Are doom'd by man, that tyrant o'er the
weak,
The death o' devils smoor'd wi' brimstone
reek:
The thundering guns are heard on ev'ry
side,
The wounded coveys, reeling, scatter wide;
The feather'd field-mates, bound by Na-
ture's tie,
Sires, mothers, children, in one carnage
lie:
(What warm, poetic heart but inly bleeds,
And execrates man's savage, ruthless
deeds !)
Nae mair the flower in field or meadow
springs;
Nae mair the grove with airy concert rings,
Except perhaps the robin's whistling glee,
Proud o' the height o' some bit half-lang
tree;
The hoary morns precede the sunny days;
Mild, calm, serene, widespreads the noon-
tide blaze,
While thick the gossamour waves wanton
in the rays.

'T was in that season, when a simple Bard,
Unknown and poor — simplicity's re-
ward ! —
Ae night, within the ancient brugh of Ayr,
By whim inspir'd, or haply prest wi' care,

He left his bed, and took his wayward
route,
And down by Simpson's wheel'd the left
about
(Whether impell'd by all-directing Fate,
To witness what I after shall narrate;
Or whether, rapt in meditation high,
He wander'd forth, he knew not where nor
why):
The drowsy Dungeon-Clock had number'd
two,
And Wallace Tower had sworn the fact
was true;
The tide-swoln Firth, with sullen-sounding
roar,
Through the still night dash'd hoarse along
the shore;
All else was hush'd as Nature's closèd
e'e;
The silent moon shone high o'er tower and
tree;
The chilly frost, beneath the silver beam,
Crept, gently-crusting, o'er the glittering
stream.

When, lo ! on either hand the list'ning
Bard,
The clanging sugh of whistling wings is
heard;
Two dusky forms dart thro' the midnight
air,
Swift as the gos drives on the wheeling
hare;
Ane on th' Auld Brig his airy shape up-
rears,
The ither flutters o'er the rising piers:
Our warlock rhymer instantly descried
The Sprites that owre the Brigs of Ayr
preside.
(That bards are second-sighted is nae joke,
And ken the lingo of the sp'ritual folk;
Fays, spunkies, kelpies, a', they can explain
them,
And ev'n the vera deils they brawly ken
them).
Auld Brig appear'd of ancient Pictish race,
The vera wrinkles Gothic in his face;
He seem'd as he wi' Time had warstl'd
lang,
Yet, teughly doure, he bade an unco bang.
New Brig was buskit in a braw new coat,
That he, at Lon'on, frae ane Adams got;
In 's hand five taper staves as smooth 's a
bead,
Wi' virls an' whirlygigums at the head.

The Goth was stalking round with anxious
    search,
Spying the time-worn flaws in ev'ry arch.
It chanc'd his new-come neebor took his
    e'e,
And e'en a vex'd and angry heart had he !
Wi' thieveless sneer to see his modish mien,
He, down the water, gies him this guid-
    een: —

AULD BRIG

" I doubt na, frien', ye 'll think ye 're
    nae sheep shank,
Ance ye were streekit owre frae bank to
    bank !
But gin ye be a brig as auld as me —
Tho' faith, that date, I doubt, ye 'll never
    see —
There 'll be, if that day come, I 'll wad a
    boddle,
Some fewer whigmeleeries in your noddle."

NEW BRIG

" Auld Vandal ! ye but show your little
    mense,
Just much about it wi' your scanty sense:
Will your poor, narrow foot-path of a
    street,
Where twa wheel-barrows tremble when
    they meet,
Your ruin'd, formless bulk o' stane an'
    lime,
Compare wi' bonie brigs o' modern time ?
There 's men of taste would tak the Ducat
    stream,
Tho' they should cast the vera sark and
    swim,
E'er they would grate their feelings wi'
    the view
O' sic an ugly, Gothic hulk as you."

AULD BRIG

"Conceited gowk ! puff'd up wi' windy
    pride !
This monie a year I 've stood the flood an'
    tide;
And tho' wi' crazy eild I 'm sair forfairn,
I 'll be a brig when ye 're a shapeless cairn!
As yet ye little ken about the matter,
But twa-three winters will inform ye better.
When heavy, dark, continued, a'-day rains
Wi' deepening deluges o'erflow the plains;
When from the hills where springs the
    brawling Coil,
Or stately Lugar's mossy fountains boil,

Or where the Greenock winds his moorland
    course,
Or haunted Garpal draws his feeble source,
Arous'd by blustering winds an' spotting
    thowes,
In monie a torrent down the snaw-broo
    rowes;
While crashing ice, borne on the roaring
    speat,
Sweeps dams, an' mills, an' brigs, a' to the
    gate;
And from Glenbuck down to the Ratton-
    Key
Auld Ayr is just one lengthen'd, tumbling
    sea —
Then down ye 'll hurl (deil nor ye never
    rise!),
And dash the gumlie jaups up to the
    pouring skies !
A lesson sadly teaching, to your cost,
That Architecture's noble art is lost ! "

NEW BRIG

" Fine architecture, trowth, I needs must
    say 't o't,
The Lord be thankit that we 've tint the
    gate o't !
Gaunt, ghastly, ghaist-alluring edifices,
Hanging with threat'ning jut, like preci-
    pices;
O'er-arching, mouldy, gloom-inspiring
    coves,
Supporting roofs fantastic — stony groves;
Windows and doors in nameless sculptures
    drest,
With order, symmetry, or taste unblest;
Forms like some bedlam statuary's dream,
The craz'd creations of misguided whim;
Forms might be worshipp'd on the bended
    knee,
And still the second dread Command be
    free:
Their likeness is not found on earth, in air,
    or sea !
Mansions that would disgrace the building
    taste
Of any mason reptile, bird or beast,
Fit only for a doited monkish race,
Or frosty maids forsworn the dear embrace,
Or cuifs of later times, wha held the
    notion,
That sullen gloom was sterling true de-
    votion:
Fancies that our guid brugh denies pro-
    tection,

And soon may they expire, unblest with
  resurrection !"

AULD BRIG

"O ye, my dear - remember'd, ancient
    yealings,
Were ye but here to share my wounded
    feelings !
Ye worthy proveses, an' monie a bailie,
Wha in the paths o' righteousness did toil
    ay;
Ye dainty deacons, an' ye douce conveeners,
To whom our moderns are but causey-
    cleaners;
Ye godly councils, wha hae blest this town;
Ye godly brethren o' the sacred gown,
Wha meekly gie your hurdies to the smit-
    ers;
And (what would now be strange), ye godly
    Writers;
A' ye douce folk I 've borne aboon the broo,
Were ye but here, what would ye say or
    do !
How would your spirits groan in deep
    vexation
To see each melancholy alteration;
And, agonising, curse the time and place
When ye begat the base degen'rate race !
Nae langer rev'rend men, their country's
    glory,
In plain braid Scots hold forth a plain,
    braid story;
Nae langer thrifty citizens, an' douce,
Meet owre a pint or in the council-house:
But staumrel, corky - headed, graceless
    gentry,
The herryment and ruin of the country;
Men three-parts made by tailors and by
    barbers,
Wha waste your weel-hain'd gear on
    damn'd New Brigs and harbours !"

NEW BRIG

"Now haud you there ! for faith ye 've
    said enough,
And muckle mair than ye can mak to
    through.
As for your priesthood, I shall say but little,
Corbies and clergy are a shot right kittle:
But, under favour o' your langer beard,
Abuse o' magistrates might weel be spar'd;
To liken them to your auld-warld squad,
I must needs say, comparisons are odd.
In Ayr, wag-wits nae mair can hae a handle
To mouth 'a Citizen,' a term o' scandal;

Nae mair the council waddles down the
    street,
In all the pomp of ignorant conceit;
Men wha grew wise priggin owre hops an'
    raisins,
Or gather'd lib'ral views in bonds and
    seisins;
If haply Knowledge, on a random tramp,
Had shor'd them with a glimmer of his
    lamp,
And would to common-sense for once be-
    tray'd them,
Plain, dull stupidity stept kindly in to aid
    them."

What farther clish-ma-claver might been
    said,
What bloody wars, if Sprites had blood to
    shed,
No man can tell; but, all before their sight,
A fairy train appear'd in order bright:
Adown the glittering stream they featly
    danc'd;
Bright to the moon their various dresses
    glanc'd;
They footed o'er the wat'ry glass so neat,
The infant ice scarce bent beneath their
    feet;
While arts of minstrelsy among them rung,
And soul-ennobling Bards heroic ditties
    sung.

O, had M'Lauchlan, thairm - inspiring
    sage,
Been there to hear this heavenly band en-
    gage,
When thro' his dear strathspeys they bore
    with Highland rage;
Or when they struck old Scotia's melting
    airs,
The lover's raptured joys or bleeding cares;
How would his Highland lug been nobler
    fir'd,
And ev'n his matchless hand with finer
    touch inspir'd !
No guess could tell what instrument ap-
    pear'd,
But all the soul of Music's self was heard;
Harmonious concert rung in every part,
While simple melody pour'd moving on the
    heart.

The Genius of the Stream in front ap-
    pears,
A venerable chief advanc'd in years;

His hoary head with water-lilies crown'd,
His manly leg with garter-tangle bound.
Next came the loveliest pair in all the ring,
Sweet Female Beauty hand in hand with
    Spring;
Then, crown'd with flow'ry hay, came
    Rural Joy,
And Summer, with his fervid-beaming eye;
All-cheering Plenty, with her flowing horn,
Led yellow Autumn wreath'd with nodding
    corn;
Then Winter's time-bleach'd locks did
    hoary show,
By Hospitality, with cloudless brow.
Next follow'd Courage, with his martial
    stride,
From where the Feal wild-woody coverts
    hide;
Benevolence, with mild, benignant air,
A female form, came from the towers of
    Stair;
Learning and Worth in equal measures
    trode
From simple Catrine, their long-lov'd
    abode;
Last, white-rob'd Peace, crown'd with a
    hazel wreath,
To rustic Agriculture did bequeath
The broken, iron instruments of death:
At sight of whom our Sprites forgat their
    kindling wrath.

THE ORDINATION

For sense, they little owe to frugal Heav'n :
To please the mob they hide the little giv'n.

In a letter to Richmond (17th February,
1786) Burns mentions that he had composed
The Ordination, and describes it as "a poem
on Mr. M'Kinlay's being called to Kilmar-
nock." Probably he intended to publish it
in the '86 Edition, which he was then con-
templating, and had called it *The Ordination*
to that end; nevertheless, as appears from the
letter, not only was it written before the ordi-
nation, which took place 6th April, but also it
was not even written in view thereof — it only
celebrated the presentation. Moreover, an
early copy — MS. — in the possession of Lord
Rosebery, has merely this heading, "*A Scotch
Poem*, by Rab Rhymer."
    James Mackinlay, born at Douglas, Lanark-
shire, in 1756, was first presented to the second
charge of the Laigh Kirk, Kilmarnock, in the
August of 1785. He declined the presentation

on account of certain conditions attached to it.
Presentation to another was made out on 15th
November, but the messenger to the Presby-
tery of Irvine was despoiled of the warrant by
certain parishioners. Thereupon a new presen-
tation was made out for Mackinlay, who was
ordained on 6th April following; was translated
to the first charge, on a petition of the parish-
ioners, 31st January, 1809; was made D. D.,
Aberdeen, 1810; died 10th February, 1841. A
volume of his *Sermons* was published posthu-
mously, with a *Life* by his son, Rev. James
Mackinlay. Like Russell, he had a rousing
voice; but his oratory was more persuasive and
less menacing than Russell's. In a note to
Tam Samson's Elegy Burns describes him "as
a great favourite of the million." In *The Kirk's
Alarm* he is addressed as "Simper James."
His more than partiality for the "fair Killie
dames" drew on him a presbyterial rebuke
some years afterwards.
    In all probability the satire was composed
immediately after the second presentation.

I

KILMARNOCK wabsters, fidge an' claw,
    An' pour your creeshie nations;
An' ye wha leather rax an' draw,
    Of a' denominations;
Swith! to the Laigh Kirk, ane an' a',
    An' there tak up your stations;
Then aff to Begbie's in a raw,
    An' pour divine libations
            For joy this day.

II

Curst Common-sense, that imp o' hell,
    Cam in wi' *Maggie Lauder:*
But Oliphant aft made her yell,
    An' Russell sair misca'd her:
This day Mackinlay taks the flail,
    An' he's the boy will blaud her!
He'll clap a shangan on her tail,
    An' set the bairns to daud her
            Wi' dirt this day.

III

Mak haste an' turn King David owre,
    An' lilt wi' holy clangor;
O' double verse come gie us four,
    An' skirl up the *Bangor:*
This day the Kirk kicks up a stoure:
    Nae mair the knaves shall wrang her;
For Heresy is in her pow'r,
    And gloriously she'll whang her
            Wi' pith this day.

IV

Come, let a proper text be read,
    An' touch it aff wi' vigour,
How graceless Ham leugh at his dad,
    Which made Canáan a nigger;
Or Phineas drove the murdering blade
    Wi' whore-abhorring rigour;
Or Zipporah, the scauldin jad,
    Was like a bluidy tiger
            I' th' inn that day.

V

There, try his mettle on the Creed,
    And bind him down wi' caution, —
That stipend is a carnal weed
    He taks but for the fashion —
And gie him o'er the flock to feed,
    And punish each transgression;
Especial, rams that cross the breed,
    Gie them sufficient threshin:
            Spare them nae day.

VI

Now auld Kilmarnock, cock thy tail,
    An' toss thy horns fu' canty;
Nae mair thou 'lt rowte out-owre the dale,
    Because thy pasture 's scanty;
For lapfu's large o' gospel kail
    Shall fill thy crib in plenty,
An' runts o' grace, the pick an' wale,
    No gien by way o' dainty,
            But ilka day.

VII

Nae mair by Babel's streams we 'll weep
    To think upon our Zion;
And hing our fiddles up to sleep,
    Like baby-clouts a-dryin.
Come, screw the pegs wi' tunefu' cheep,
    And o'er the thairms be tryin;
O, rare ! to see our elbucks wheep,
    And a' like lamb-tails flyin
            Fu' fast this day !

VIII

Lang, Patronage, wi' rod o' airn,
    Has shor'd the Kirk's undoin;
As lately Fenwick, sair forfairn,
    Has proven to its ruin:
Our patron, honest man ! Glencairn,
    He saw mischief was brewin;
An' like a godly, elect bairn,
    He 's waled us out a true ane,
            And sound this day.

IX

Now, Robertson, harangue nae mair,
    But steek your gab for ever;
Or try the wicked town of Ayr,
    For there they 'll think you clever;
Or, nae reflection on your lear,
    Ye may commence a shaver;
Or to the Netherton repair,
    An' turn a carpet-weaver
            Aff-hand this day.

X

Mu'trie and you were just a match,
    We never had sic twa drones:
Auld Hornie did the Laigh Kirk watch,
    Just like a winkin baudrons,
And ay he catch'd the tither wretch,
    To fry them in his caudrons;
But now his Honor maun detach,
    Wi' a' his brimstone squadrons,
            Fast, fast this day.

XI

See, see auld Orthodoxy's faes
    She 's swingein thro' the city !
Hark, how the nine-tailed cat she plays !
    I vow it 's unco pretty;
There, Learning, with his Greekish face,
    Grunts out some Latin ditty;
And Common-Sense is gaun, she says,
    To mak to Jamie Beattie
            Her plaint this day.

XII

But there 's Morality himsel,
    Embracing all opinions;
Hear, how he gies the tither yell
    Between his twa companions !
See, how she peels the skin an' fell,
    As ane were peelin onions !
Now there, they 're packèd aff to hell,
    An' banish'd our dominions,
            Henceforth this day.

XIII

O happy day ! rejoice, rejoice !
    Come bouse about the porter !
Morality's demüre decoys
    Shall here nae mair find quarter:
Mackinlay, Russell, are the boys
    That Heresy can torture;
They 'll gie her on a rape a hoyse,
    And cowe her measure shorter
            By th' head some day.

XIV

Come, bring the tither mutchkin in,
  And here's — for a conclusion —
To ev'ry New Light mother's son,
  From this time forth, confusion!
If mair they deave us wi' their din
  Or patronage intrusion,
We'll light a spunk, and ev'ry skin
  We'll run them aff in fusion,
            Like oil some day.

THE CALF

To the Rev. James Steven, on his text, Malachi iv. 2:
"And ye shall go forth, and grow up as calves of the
stall."

"A nearly extemporaneous production, on a
wager with Mr. Hamilton that I would not pro-
duce a poem on the subject in a given time:"
— R. B., *Letter to Robert Muir*, 8th September,
1786. It was written on Sunday, 3d Septem-
ber, after listening to a sermon by the Rev.
James Steven. As originally composed and
read to Gavin Hamilton and Dr. Mackenzie, it
consisted of four stanzas only; but on the Sun-
day evening at eight o'clock Burns sent a copy
to Dr. Mackenzie with two more — the fourth
and the sixth. It was printed in 1787 (presum-
ably before its appearance in the Edinburgh
Edition), with some other verses, in a tract
called *The Calf; The Unco Calf's Answer;
Virtue to a Mountain Bard; and the Deil's
Answer to his vera worthy Frien Robert Burns.*
An explanation was added that *The Calf* had
been sent to *The Glasgow Advertiser*, but de-
clined. The same year appeared *Burns' Calf
turned a Bull; or Some Remarks on his mean
and unprecedented attack on Mr. S—— when
preaching from Malachi iv. 2.*
James Steven, a native of Kilmarnock, was
licensed to preach 28th June, 1786; acted for
some time as assistant to Robert Dow, min-
ister of Ardrossan; was ordained minister of
Crown Court Chapel, London, 1st November,
1787; was one of the founders of the Lon-
don Missionary Society; was admitted min-
ister of Kilwinning, 28th March, 1803; and
died of apoplexy 15th February, 1824. Wil-
liam Burns, Robert's younger brother, in a
letter of 20th March, 1790, thus chronicles a
visit to Steven's church: "We were at Covent
Garden Chapel this forenoon to hear the *Calf*
preach; he is grown very fat, and is as boister-
ous as ever."

I

RIGHT, sir! your text I'll prove it true,
  Tho' heretics may laugh;
For instance, there's yoursel just now,
  God knows, an unco *calf*.

II

And should some patron be so kind
  As bless you wi' a kirk,
I doubt na, sir, but then we'll find
  You're still as great a *stirk*.

III

But, if the lover's raptur'd hour
  Shall ever be your lot,
Forbid it, every heavenly Power,
  You e'er should be a *stot!*

IV

Tho', when some kind connubial dear
  Your but-an'-ben adorns,
The like has been that you may wear
  A noble head of *horns*.

V

And, in your lug, most reverend James,
  To hear you roar and rowte,
Few men o' sense will doubt your claims
  To rank among the *nowte*.

VI

And when ye're number'd wi' the dead
  Below a grassy hillock,
With justice they may mark your head: —
  "Here lies a famous *bullock!*"

ADDRESS TO THE UNCO GUID

OR THE RIGIDLY RIGHTEOUS

My Son, these maxims make a rule,
  An' lump them ay thegither:
The Rigid Righteous is a fool,
  The Rigid Wise anither;
The cleanest corn that e'er was dight
  May hae some pyles o' caff in;
So ne'er a fellow-creature slight
  For random fits o' daffin.
            SOLOMON (Eccles. vii. 16).

I

O YE, wha are sae guid yoursel,
  Sae pious and sae holy,

Ye 've nought to do but mark and tell
  Your neebours' fauts and folly;
Whase life is like a weel-gaun mill,
  Supplied wi' store o' water;
The heapet happer 's ebbing still,
  An' still the clap plays clatter !

II

Hear me, ye venerable core,
  As counsel for poor mortals
That frequent pass douce Wisdom's door
  For glaikit Folly's portals:
I for their thoughtless, careless sakes
  Would here propone defences —
Their donsie tricks, their black mistakes,
  Their failings and mischances.

III

Ye see your state wi' theirs compared,
  And shudder at the niffer;
But cast a moment's fair regard,
  What makes the mighty differ ?
Discount what scant occasion gave;
  That purity ye pride in;
And (what 's aft mair than a' the lave)
  Your better art o' hidin.

IV

Think, when your castigated pulse
  Gies now and then a wallop,
What ragings must his veins convulse,
  That still eternal gallop !
Wi' wind and tide fair i' your tail,
  Right on ye scud your sea-way;
But in the teeth o' baith to sail,
  It makes an unco lee-way.

V

See Social-life and Glee sit down
  All joyous and unthinking,
Till, quite transmugrify'd, they 're grown
  Debauchery and Drinking:
O, would they stay to calculate,
  Th' eternal consequences,
Or — your more dreaded hell to state —
  Damnation of expenses !

VI

Ye high, exalted, virtuous dames,
  Tied up in godly laces,
Before ye gie poor Frailty names,
  Suppose a change o' cases:
A dear-lov'd lad, convenience snug,
  A treach'rous inclination —

But, let me whisper i' your lug,
  Ye 're aiblins nae temptation.

VII

Then gently scan your brother man,
  Still gentler sister woman;
Tho' they may gang a kennin wrang,
  To step aside is human:
One point must still be greatly dark,
  The moving *why* they do it;
And just as lamely can ye mark
  How far perhaps they rue it.

VIII

Who made the heart, 't is He alone
  Decidedly can try us:
He knows each chord, its various tone,
  Each spring, its various bias:
Then at the balance let 's be mute,
  We never can adjust it;
What 's done we partly may compute,
  But know not what 's resisted.

TAM SAMSON'S ELEGY

An honest man 's the noblest work of God.
                      POPE.

"When this worthy old sportsman went out last muir-fowl season, he supposed it was to be, in Ossian's phrase, ' the last of his fields,' and expressed an ardent wish to die and be buried in the muirs. On this hint the author composed his *Elegy* and *Epitaph* " (R. B.). Samson — a nursery-gardener and seedsman in Kilmarnock, and an ardent sportsman — died 12th December, 1795, in his seventy-third year. The *Epitaph* is inscribed on his tombstone in the yard of the Laigh Kirk, adjoining those of the two ministers, Mackinlay and Robertson, mentioned in the first stanza. The piece is modelled — even to the use of certain lines — on Sempill's *Piper of Kilbarchan*. See *ante*, p. 12, Prefatory Note to *Address to the Deil*. On 18th November, 1786, shortly before setting out for Edinburgh, Burns wrote to his friend Robert Muir: "Inclosed you have *Tam Samson*, as I intend to print him."

I

Has auld Kilmarnock seen the Deil ?
Or great Mackinlay thrawn his heel ?
Or Robertson again grown weel
                To preach an' read ?

" Na', waur than a' ! '' cries ilka chiel,
　　" Tam Samson 's dead ! "

II

Kilmarnock lang may grunt an' grane,
An' sigh, an' sab, an' greet her lane,
An' cleed her bairns — man, wife an'
　　wean —
　　　　In mourning weed;
To Death she 's dearly pay'd the kain:
　　　　Tam Samson 's dead !

III

The Brethren o' the mystic level
May hing their head in woefu' bevel,
While by their nose the tears will revel,
　　　　Like onie bead;
Death 's gien the Lodge an unco devel:
　　　　Tam Samson 's dead !

IV

When winter muffles up his cloak,
And binds the mire like a rock;
When to the loughs the curlers flock,
　　　　Wi' gleesome speed,
Wha will they station at the cock ? —
　　　　Tam Samson 's dead !

V

He was the king of a' the core,
To guard, or draw, or wick a bore,
Or up the rink like Jehu roar
　　　　In time o' need;
But now he lags on Death 's hog-score:
　　　　Tam Samson 's dead !

VI

Now safe the stately sawmont sail,
And trouts bedropp'd wi' crimson hail,
And eels weel-kend for souple tail,
　　　　And geds for greed,
Since, dark in Death 's fish-creel, we wail
　　　　Tam Samson dead !

VII

Rejoice, ye birring paitricks a';
Ye cootie moorcocks, crousely craw;
Ye maukins, cock your fud fu' braw
　　　　Withouten dread;
Your mortal fae is now awa:
　　　　Tam Samson 's dead !

VIII

That wofu' morn be ever mourn'd,
Saw him in shootin graith adorn'd,

While pointers round impatient burn'd,
　　　　Frae couples free'd;
But och ! he gaed and ne'er return'd:
　　　　Tam Samson 's dead !

IX

In vain auld-age his body batters,
In vain the gout his ancles fetters,
In vain the burns cam down like waters,
　　　　An acre braid !
Now ev'ry auld wife, greetin, clatters:
　　　　" Tam Samson 's dead! "

X

Owre monie a weary hag he limpit,
An' ay the tither shot he thumpit,
Till coward Death behint him jumpit,
　　　　Wi' deadly feide;
Now he proclaims wi' tout o' trumpet:
　　　　" Tam Samson 's dead! "

XI

When at his heart he felt the dagger,
He reel'd his wonted bottle-swagger,
But yet he drew the mortal trigger
　　　　Wi' weel-aim'd heed;
" Lord, five ! " he cry'd, an' owre did
　　　　stagger —
　　　　　　" Tam Samson 's dead! "

XII

Ilk hoary hunter mourn'd a brither;
Ilk sportsman-youth bemoan'd a father;
Yon auld gray stane, amang the heather,
　　　　Marks out his head;
Whare Burns has wrote, in rhyming blether:
　　　　" Tam Samson 's dead! "

XIII

There low he lies in lasting rest;
Perhaps upon his mould'ring breast
Some spitefu' moorfowl bigs her nest,
　　　　To hatch an' breed:
Alas! nae mair he 'll them molest:
　　　　" Tam Samson 's dead! "

XIV

When August winds the heather wave,
And sportsmen wander by yon grave,
Three volleys let his memory crave
　　　　O' pouther an' lead,
Till Echo answers frae her cave:
　　　　" Tam Samson 's dead! "

XV

"Heav'n rest his saul whare'er he be!"
Is th' wish o' monie mae than me:
He had twa fauts, or maybe three,
    Yet what remead?
Ae social, honest man want we:
    "Tam Samson's dead!"

THE EPITAPH

Tam Samson's weel-worn clay here lies:
  Ye canting zealots, spare him!
If honest worth in Heaven rise,
  Ye 'll mend or ye win near him.

PER CONTRA

Go, Fame, an' canter like a filly
Thro' a' the streets an neuks o' Killie;
Tell ev'ry social honest billie
    To cease his grievin;
For, yet unskaith'd by Death's gleg gullie,
    Tam Samson's leevin!

A WINTER NIGHT

Poor naked wretches, wheresoe'er you are,
That bide the pelting of this pityless storm!
How shall your houseless heads and unfed sides,
Your loop'd and window'd raggedness, defend you
From seasons such as these?
        SHAKESPEARE.

Probably the piece which Burns sent to
John Ballantine on 20th of November, 1786:
"Enclosed you have my first attempt in that
irregular kind of measure in which many of
our finest odes are wrote. How far I have
succeeded I don't know, but I shall be happy
to have your opinion on Friday first (24th
November), when I intend being in Ayr." The
irregular strophes — imitated from Gray, and
strikingly inferior to the introductory stanzas
— are freely paraphrased from Shakespeare's
Blow, Blow, thou Winter Wind, in *As You
Like It.*

I

WHEN biting Boreas, fell and doure,
Sharp shivers thro' the leafless bow'r;
When Phœbus gies a short-liv'd glow'r,
    Far south the lift,
Dim-dark'ning thro' the flaky show'r
    Or whirling drift:

II

Ae night the storm the steeples rocked;
Poor Labour sweet in sleep was locked;
While burns, wi' snawy wreaths up-choked,
    Wild-eddying swirl,
Or, thro' the mining outlet bocked,
    Down headlong hurl:

III

List'ning the doors an' winnocks rattle,
I thought me on the ourie cattle,
Or silly sheep, wha bide this brattle
    O' winter war,
And thro' the drift, deep-lairing, sprattle
    Beneath a scaur.

IV

Ilk happing bird — wee, helpless thing! —
That in the merry months o' spring
Delighted me to hear thee sing,
    What comes o' thee?
Whare wilt thou cow'r thy chittering wing,
    An' close thy e'e?

V

Ev'n you, on murd'ring errands toil'd,
Lone from your savage homes exil'd,
The blood-stain'd roost and sheep-cote
    spoil'd
    My heart forgets,
While pityless the tempest wild
    Sore on you beats!

VI

Now Phœbe, in her midnight reign,
Dark-muffl'd, view'd the dreary plain;
Still crowding thoughts, a pensive train,
    Rose in my soul,
When on my ear this plaintive strain,
    Slow-solemn, stole : —

VII

"Blow, blow, ye winds, with heavier gust!
And freeze, thou bitter-biting frost!
Descend, ye chilly, smothering snows!
Not all your rage, as now united, shows
    More hard unkindness unrelenting,
    Vengeful malice, unrepenting,
Than heaven-illumin'd Man on brother Man
    bestows!
See stern Oppression's iron grip,
    Or mad Ambition's gory hand,
Sending, like blood-hounds from the slip,
    Woe, Want, and Murder o'er a land!

Ev'n in the peaceful rural vale,
Truth, weeping, tells the mournful tale:
How pamper'd Luxury, Flatt'ry by her
    side,
The parasite empoisoning her ear,
With all the servile wretches in the rear,
Looks o'er proud Property, extended wide;
And eyes the simple, rustic hind,
Whose toil upholds the glitt'ring show —
A creature of another kind,
Some coarser substance, unrefin'd —
Plac'd for her lordly use, thus far, thus vile,
    below !
Where, where is Love's fond, tender
    throe,
With lordly Honor's lofty brow,
    The pow'rs you proudly own ?
Is there, beneath Love's noble name,
Can harbour, dark, the selfish aim,
    To bless himself alone ?
Mark Maiden-Innocence a prey
    To love-pretending snares:
This boasted Honor turns away,
Shunning soft Pity's rising sway,
Regardless of the tears and unavailing
    pray'rs !
Perhaps this hour, in Misery's squalid
    nest,
She strains your infant to her joyless
    breast,
And with a mother's fears shrinks at the
    rocking blast !

VIII

" O ye ! who, sunk in beds of down,
    Feel not a want but what yourselves
    create,
    Think, for a moment, on his wretched
    fate,
Whom friends and fortune quite disown !
    Ill-satisfy'd keen nature's clam'rous
    call,
Stretch'd on his straw, he lays himself to
    sleep ;
While through the ragged roof and chinky
    wall,
    Chill, o'er his slumbers piles the drifty
    heap !
    Think on the dungeon's grim confine,
    Where Guilt and poor Misfortune
    pine !
    Guilt, erring man, relenting view !
    But shall thy legal rage pursue
    The wretch, already crushèd low
    By cruel Fortune's undeservèd blow ?

Affliction's sons are brothers in distress;
A brother to relieve, how exquisite the
    bliss ! "

IX

I heard nae mair, for Chanticleer
    Shook off the pouthery snaw,
And hail'd the morning with a cheer,
    A cottage-rousing craw.

But deep this truth impress'd my mind·
    Thro' all His works abroad,
The heart benevolent and kind
    The most resembles God.

STANZAS WRITTEN IN PRO-
SPECT OF DEATH

I

WHY am I loth to leave this earthly scene ?
    Have I so found it full of pleasing
    charms ?
Some drops of joy with draughts of ill
    between;
    Some gleams of sunshine mid renewing
    storms.
Is it departing pangs my soul alarms ?
    Or death's unlovely, dreary, dark abode ?
For guilt, for guilt, my terrors are in arms:
    I tremble to approach an angry God,
And justly smart beneath his sin-avenging
    rod.

II

Fain would I say : " Forgive my foul
    offence,"
Fain promise never more to disobey.
But should my Author health again dis-
    pense,
    Again I might desert fair virtue's way;
Again in folly's path might go astray;
    Again exalt the brute and sink the man;
Then how should I for heavenly mercy
    pray,
    Who act so counter heavenly mercy's
    plan ?
Who sin so oft have mourn'd, yet to tempta-
    tion ran ?

III

O Thou great Governor of all below ! —
    If I may dare a lifted eye to Thee, —

Thy nod can make the tempest cease to
    blow,
Or still the tumult of the raging sea:
With that controlling pow'r assist ev'n
    me
    Those headlong furious passions to con-
        fine,
For all unfit I feel my pow'rs to be
    To rule their torrent in th' allowèd
        line:
O, aid me with Thy help, Omnipotence
    Divine !

PRAYER: O THOU DREAD POWER

Lying at a reverend friend's house one night, the
author left the following verses in the room where
he slept.

"The first time ever Robert heard the spinet
played was at the house of Dr. Lawrie, then
minister of Loudoun. . . . Dr. Lawrie (has)
several daughters; one of them played; the
father and mother led down the dance; the
rest of the sisters, the brother, the poet, and
the other guests mixed in it. It was a de-
lightful family scene for our poet, then lately
introduced to the world. His mind was roused
to a poetic enthusiasm, and the stanzas were
left in the room where he slept." — Gilbert
Burns. Robert wrote to the son on 13th No-
vember, 1786: "A poet's warmest wishes for
their happiness to the young ladies, particu-
larly the fair musician, whom I think much
better qualified than ever David was, or could
be, to charm an evil spirit out of Saul. In-
deed, it needs not the feelings of the poet to
be interested in the welfare of one of the
sweetest scenes of domestic peace and kindred
love that ever I saw; as I think the peaceful
unity of St. Margaret's Hill can only be ex-
celled by the harmonious concord of the Apo-
calyptic Zion." When he paid this visit his
chest "was on the road to Greenock;" and
but for the fact that Lawrie showed him Dr.
Blacklock's letter, strongly recommending a
second edition of his poems, he would have
sailed in a few days for Jamaica.

I

O Thou dread Power, who reign'st above,
    I know thou wilt me hear,
When for this scene of peace and love
    I make my prayer sincere.

II

The hoary Sire — the mortal stroke,
    Long, long be pleas'd to spare:
To bless his little filial flock,
    And show what good men are.

III

She, who her lovely offspring eyes
    With tender hopes and fears —
O, bless her with a mother's joys,
    But spare a mother's tears !

IV

Their hope, their stay, their darling youth,
    In manhood's dawning blush,
Bless him, Thou God of love and truth,
    Up to a parent's wish.

V

The beauteous, seraph sister-band —
    With earnest tears I pray —
Thou know'st the snares on every hand,
    Guide Thou their steps alway.

VI

When, soon or late, they reach that coast,
    O'er Life's rough ocean driven,
May they rejoice, no wand'rer lost,
    A family in Heaven !

PARAPHRASE OF THE FIRST PSALM

This is probably an early composition, and
dates from about the same time as the next
piece.

I

The man, in life wherever plac'd,
    Hath happiness in store,
Who walks not in the wicked's way
    Nor learns their guilty lore;

II

Nor from the seat of scornful pride
    Casts forth his eyes abroad,
But with humility and awe
    Still walks before his God!

III

That man shall flourish like the trees,
    Which by the streamlets grow:
The fruitful top is spread on high,
    And firm the root below.

IV

But he, whose blossom buds in guilt,
  Shall to the ground be cast,
And, like the rootless stubble, tost
  Before the sweeping blast.

V

For why ? that God the good adore
  Hath giv'n them peace and rest,
But hath decreed that wicked men
  Shall ne'er be truly blest.

PRAYER UNDER THE PRESSURE OF VIOLENT ANGUISH

Inscribed in the *First Common Place Book*
and thus prefaced: "There was a certain
period of life that my spirit was broke by re-
peated losses and disasters, which threatened,
and indeed effected, the utter ruin of my fu-
ture. My body, too, was attacked by that
most dreadful distemper, a Hypochondria, or
confirmed melancholy : in this wretched state,
the recollection of which makes me yet shud-
der, I hung my harp on the willow trees, except
in some lucid intervals, in one of which I com-
posed the following." It was probably writ-
ten about the close of Burns's residence in Ir-
vine, in 1782, and, under the title, *Prayer under
the Presure of Bitter Anguish*, is inscribed —
in an early hand — at the end of a copy of
Fergusson's *Poems*, published that year, now
in the possession of the Earl of Rosebery.

I

O THOU Great Being ! what Thou art
  Surpasses me to know;
Yet sure I am, that known to Thee
  Are all Thy works below.

II

Thy creature here before Thee stands,
  All wretched and distrest;
Yet sure those ills that wring my soul
  Obey Thy high behest.

III

Sure Thou, Almighty, canst not act
  From cruelty or wrath!
O, free my weary eyes from tears,
  Or close them fast in death!

IV

But, if I must afflicted be
  To suit some wise design,
Then man my soul with firm resolves
  To bear and not repine !

THE NINETIETH PSALM VERSIFIED

Probably dating from the same period as
the two last.

I

O THOU, the first, the greatest friend
  Of all the human race !
Whose strong right hand has ever been
  Their stay and dwelling place !

II

Before the mountains heav'd their heads
  Beneath Thy forming hand,
Before this ponderous globe itself
  Arose at Thy command:

III

That Power, which rais'd and still upholds
  This universal frame,
From countless, unbeginning time
  Was ever still the same.

IV

Those mighty periods of years,
  Which seem to us so vast,
Appear no more before Thy sight
  Than yesterday that's past.

V

Thou giv'st the word: Thy creature, man,
  Is to existence brought;
Again Thou say'st: "Ye sons of men,
  Return ye into nought ! "

VI

Thou layest them, with all their cares,
  In everlasting sleep;
As with a flood Thou tak'st them off
  With overwhelming sweep.

VII

They flourish like the morning flower
  In beauty's pride array'd,
But long ere night, cut down, it lies
  All wither'd and decay'd.

TO MISS LOGAN

WITH BEATTIE'S POEMS FOR A NEW
YEAR'S GIFT, JANUARY 1, 1787

The Miss Logan of these verses was the
"sentimental sister Susie" of the *Epistle to
Major Logan* (*post*, p. 133). It is probable that
Burns, when he last met her, had promised
her a New Year's gift from Jamaica; but, his
prospects changing, he sent her Beattie's volumes
instead.

I

AGAIN the silent wheels of time
Their annual round have driv'n,
And you, tho' scarce in maiden prime,
Are so much nearer Heav'n.

II

No gifts have I from Indian coasts
The infant year to hail;
I send you more than India boasts
In Edwin's simple tale.

III

Our sex with guile, and faithless love,
Is charg'd — perhaps too true;
But may, dear maid, each lover prove
An Edwin still to you.

ADDRESS TO A HAGGIS

Hogg states that this spirited extravaganza
was "written in the house of Mr. Andrew
Bruce, Castlehill, Edinburgh, where a haggis
one day made part of the dinner;" but it is
unlikely that Burns set to work on it there
and then. Chambers's story, that the germ
was the last stanza (as first printed) extemporised
as grace at a friend's house, is seemingly
a variation of the same legend. *The Address*
— "never before published" — appeared in
The Caledonian Mercury on 19th December,
1786, and in *The Scots Magazine* for January,
1787.

I

FAIR fa' your honest, sonsie face,
Great chieftain o' the puddin-race !
Aboon them a' ye tak your place,
        Painch, tripe, or thairm:
Weel are ye wordy of a grace
        As lang 's my arm.

II

The groaning trencher there ye fill,
Your hurdies like a distant hill,
Your pin wad help to mend a mill
        In time o' need,
While thro' your pores the dews distil
        Like amber bead.

III

His knife see rustic Labour dight,
An' cut ye up wi' ready slight,
Trenching your gushing entrails bright,
        Like onie ditch;
And then, O what a glorious sight,
        Warm-reekin, rich !

IV

Then, horn for horn, they stretch an' strive:
Deil tak the hindmost, on they drive,
Till a' their weel-swall'd kytes belyve
        Are bent like drums;
Then auld Guidman, maist like to rive,
        "Bethankit !" hums.

V

Is there that owre his French *ragout*,
Or *olio* that wad staw a sow,
Or *fricassee* wad mak her spew
        Wi' perfect sconner,
Looks down wi' sneering, scornfu' view
        On sic a dinner ?

VI

Poor devil ! see him owre his trash,
As feckless as a wither'd rash,
His spindle shank a guid whip-lash,
        His nieve a nit;
Thro' bluidy flood or field to dash,
        O how unfit !

VII

But mark the Rustic, haggis-fed,
The trembling earth resounds his tread,
Clap in his walie nieve a blade,
        He 'll make it whissle;
An' legs, an' arms, an' heads will sned
        Like taps o' thrissle.

VIII

Ye Pow'rs, wha mak mankind your care,
And dish them out their bill o' fare,
Auld Scotland wants nae skinking ware,
        That jaups in luggies;
But, if ye wish her gratefu' prayer,
        Gie her a Haggis !

ADDRESS TO EDINBURGH

This poem and another were enclosed in a letter from Edinburgh, 27th December, 1786, to William Chalmers, in which Burns stated that he "had carded and spun them" since he "passed Glenbuck," the last Ayrshire hamlet on his way to Edinburgh.

I

EDINA! Scotia's darling seat!
  All hail thy palaces and tow'rs,
Where once, beneath a Monarch's feet,
  Sat Legislation's sov'reign pow'rs:
  From marking wildly-scatt'red flow'rs,
As on the banks of Ayr I stray'd,
  And singing, lone, the ling'ring hours,
I shelter in thy honor'd shade.

II

Here Wealth still swells the golden tide,
  As busy Trade his labours plies;
There Architecture's noble pride
  Bids elegance and splendour rise:
  Here Justice, from her native skies,
High wields her balance and her rod;
  There Learning, with his eagle eyes,
Seeks Science in her coy abode.

III

Thy sons, Edina, social, kind,
  With open arms the stranger hail;
Their views enlarg'd, their lib'ral mind,
  Above the narrow, rural vale;
  Attentive still to Sorrow's wail,
Or modest Merit's silent claim:
  And never may their sources fail!
And never Envy blot their name!

IV

Thy daughters bright thy walks adorn,
  Gay as the gilded summer sky,
Sweet as the dewy, milk-white thorn,
  Dear as the raptur'd thrill of joy!
  Fair Burnet strikes th' adoring eye,
Heav'n's beauties on my fancy shine:
  I see the Sire of Love on high,
And own His work indeed divine!

V

There, watching high the least alarms,
  Thy rough, rude fortress gleams afar;
Like some bold vet'ran, grey in arms,
  And mark'd with many a seamy scar:
  The pond'rous wall and massy bar,

Grim-rising o'er the rugged rock,
  Have oft withstood assailing war,
And oft repell'd th' invader's shock.

VI

With awe-struck thought and pitying tears,
  I view that noble, stately dome,
Where Scotia's kings of other years,
  Fam'd heroes! had their royal home:
  Alas, how chang'd the times to come!
Their royal name low in the dust!
  Their hapless race wild-wand'ring roam!
Tho' rigid Law cries out: " 'T was just."

VII

Wild beats my heart to trace your steps,
  Whose ancestors, in days of yore,
Thro' hostile ranks and ruin'd gaps
  Old Scotia's bloody lion bore:
  Ev'n I, who sing in rustic lore,
Haply my sires have left their shed,
  And fac'd grim Danger's loudest roar,
Bold-following where your fathers led!

VIII

Edina! Scotia's darling seat!
  All hail thy palaces and tow'rs;
Where once, beneath a Monarch's feet,
  Sat Legislation's sov'reign pow'rs:
  From marking wildly-scatt'red flow'rs,
As on the banks of Ayr I stray'd,
  And singing, lone, the ling'ring hours,
I shelter in thy honour'd shade.

SONGS

JOHN BARLEYCORN

A BALLAD

Entered in the *First Common Place Book* under date June, 1785, with the title, *John Barleycorn — A Song to its own Tune.* Burns prefaces it with the remark that he had once heard the old song that goes by this name; and that he remembered only the three first verses and "some scraps" which he had "interwoven here and there in the piece." In the '87 Edition he inserted a note: "This is partly composed on the plan of an old *song* known by the same name." In view of these statements, special interest attaches to a set printed in Laing's *Early Metrical Tales* (1826) from a stall copy of 1781, with a few corrections on the authority of two others of later date. Here are the three first stanzas : —

" There came three merry men from the east,
    And three merry men were they,
    And they did sware a solemn oath
       That Sir John Barleycorn they would slay.

" They took a plough, and plough'd him down,
    And laid clods upon his head ;
    And then they swore a solemn oath,
       That Sir John Barleycorn was dead.

" But the spring-time it came on amain,
    And rain towards the earth did fall :
    John Barleycorn sprung up again,
       And so subdued them all."

Robert Jamieson prints a set in his *Popular Ballads and Songs* (1806) as he heard it in Moray when a boy. In its first three verses it closely resembles the Burns ; but Burns's poems were in circulation before Jamieson's boyhood was over, and may have influenced his memory. He prints another set from a black-letter copy in the Pepys Library, Cambridge, as well as sets of the analogous *Allan-a-Maut* ballad, including that in *The Bannatyne MS.* There is, further, a curious chap (1757) which is not included in Jamieson. The ungrammatical " *was* " in Burns's first line was probably suggested by " There was three ladies in a ha'," in Herd's *Ancient and Modern Scottish Songs* (1776).

I

THERE was three kings into the east,
   Three kings both great and high,
And they hae sworn a solemn oath
   John Barleycorn should die.

II

They took a plough and plough'd him down,
   Put clods upon his head,
And they hae sworn a solemn oath
   John Barleycorn was dead.

III

But the cheerful Spring came kindly on,
   And show'rs began to fall;
John Barleycorn got up again,
   And sore surpris'd them all.

IV

The sultry suns of Summer came,
   And he grew thick and strong:
His head weel arm'd wi' pointed spears,
   That no one should him wrong.

V

The sober Autumn enter'd mild,
   When he grew wan and pale;
His bending joints and drooping head
   Show'd he began to fail.

VI

His colour sicken'd more and more,
   He faded into age;
And then his enemies began
   To show their deadly rage.

VII

They 've taen a weapon long and sharp,
   And cut him by the knee;
Then ty'd him fast upon a cart,
   Like a rogue for forgerie.

VIII

They laid him down upon his back,
   And cudgell'd him full sore.
They hung him up before the storm,
   And turn'd him o'er and o'er.

IX

They fillèd up a darksome pit
   With water to the brim,
They heavèd in John Barleycorn —
   There, let him sink or swim !

X

They laid him out upon the floor,
   To work him farther woe;
And still, as signs of life appear'd,
   They toss'd him to and fro.

XI

They wasted o'er a scorching flame
   The marrow of his bones;
But a miller us'd him worst of all,
   For he crushed him between two stones.

XII

And they hae taen his very heart's blood,
   And drank it round and round;
And still the more and more they drank,
   Their joy did more abound.

XIII

John Barleycorn was a hero bold,
   Of noble enterprise;
For if you do but taste his blood,
   'T will make your courage rise.

XIV

'T will make a man forget his woe;
  'T will heighten all his joy:
'T will make the widow's heart to sing,
  Tho' the tear were in her eye.

XV

Then let us toast John Barleycorn,
  Each man a glass in hand;
And may his great posterity
  Ne'er fail in old Scotlànd!

A FRAGMENT: WHEN GUIL-
FORD GOOD

TUNE: *Gillicrankie*

This was probably the "political ballad" which Burns enclosed to Henry Erskine — on the advice of Glencairn — for his opinion as to whether he should or should not publish it. The work of some nameless Loyalist, the old song on which it is moulded is printed in David Laing's *Various Pieces of Fugitive Scottish Poetry*, First Series (1826), which dates it 1689, under the title, *Killychrankie* [the battle was fought in that year], "To be Sung to its Own Tune:"—

> "*Claverse* and his Highland men
> Came down upon a Raw, then,
> Who, being stout, gave many a Clout,
> The Lads began to claw then;"

and so on for eight mortal octaves. The same volume sets forth an *Answer* to the same tune in as many more.

I

WHEN Guilford good our pilot stood,
  An' did our hellim thraw, man;
Ae night, at tea, began a plea,
  Within America, man:
Then up they gat the maskin-pat,
  And in the sea did jaw, man;
An' did nae less, in full Congress,
  Than quite refuse our law, man.

II

Then thro' the lakes Montgomery takes,
  I wat he was na slaw, man;
Down Lowrie's Burn he took a turn,
  And Carleton did ca', man:

But yet, what reck, he at Quebec
  Montgomery-like did fa', man,
Wi' sword in hand, before his band,
  Amang his en'mies a', man.

III

Poor Tammy Gage within a cage
  Was kept at Boston-ha', man;
Till Willie Howe took o'er the knowe
  For Philadelphia, man;
Wi' sword an' gun he thought a sin
  Guid Christian bluid to draw, man;
But at New-York wi' knife an' fork
  Sir-Loin he hackèd sma', man.

IV

Burgoyne gaed up, like spur an' whip,
  Till Fraser brave did fa', man;
Then lost his way, ae misty day,
  In Saratoga shaw, man.
Cornwallis fought as lang 's he dought,
  An' did the buckskins claw, man;
But Clinton's glaive frae rust to save,
  He hung it to the wa', man.

V

Then Montague, an' Guilford too,
  Began to fear a fa', man;
And Sackville doure, wha stood the stoure
  The German chief to thraw, man:
For Paddy Burke, like onie Turk,
  Nae mercy had at a', man;
An' Charlie Fox threw by the box,
  An' lows'd his tinkler jaw, man.

VI

Then Rockingham took up the game,
  Till death did on him ca', man;
When Shelburne meek held up his cheek,
  Conform to gospel law, man:
Saint Stephen's boys, wi' jarring noise,
  They did his measures thraw, man;
For North an' Fox united stocks,
  An' bore him to the wa', man.

VII

Then clubs an' hearts were Charlie's cartes
  He swept the stakes awa', man,
Till the diamond's ace, of Indian race,
  Led him a sair *faux pas*, man:
The Saxon lads, wi' loud placads,
  On Chatham's boy did ca', man;
An' Scotland drew her pipe an' blew:
  "Up, Willie, waur them a', man!"

VIII

Behind the throne then Granville's gone,
    A secret word or twa, man;
While slee Dundas arous'd the class
    Be-north the Roman wa', man:
An' Chatham's wraith, in heav'nly graith,
    (Inspirèd bardies saw, man),
Wi' kindling eyes, cry'd: "Willie, rise !
    Would I hae fear'd them a', man ? "

IX

But, word an' blow, North, Fox, and Co.
    Gowff'd Willie like a ba', man,
Till Suthron raise an' coost their claise
    Behind him in a raw, man:
An' Caledon threw by the drone,
    An' did her whittle draw, man;
An' swoor fu' rude, thro' dirt an' bluid,
    To make it guid in law, man.

MY NANIE, O

Perhaps suggested by a poor thing of Ramsay's : —

" While some for pleasure pawn their health
    'Twixt Lais and the bagnio,
I 'll save myself, and without stealth
    Kiss and caress my Nanny, O."

In Hogg and Motherwell's Edition another version — oral: communicated by Peter Buchan — is printed ; it begins, " As I gaed down thro' Embro' town." In the *First Common Place Book*, where it appears under date of April, 1784, it is headed *Song (Tune, " As I came in by London, O ")*. It is thus prefaced: "As I have been all along a miserable dupe to Love, and have been led into a thousand weaknesses and follies by it, for that reason I put the more confidence in my critical skill in distinguishing foppery and conceit from real passion and nature. Whether the following song will stand the test, I will not pretend to say, because it is my own; only I can say it was, at the time, real."
According to Gilbert Burns, the heroine was Agnes Fleming. She was daughter of John Fleming, farmer at Doura, in the parish of Tarbolton. On the other hand, Mrs. Begg asserts that it was written in honour of Peggy Thomson of Kirkoswald (see *ante*, p. 52, Prefatory Note to *Song: Composed in August*), while Hamilton Paul champions the charms of a Kilmarnock girl.

I

BEHIND yon hills where Lugar flows
    'Mang moors an' mosses many, O,
The wintry sun the day has clos'd,
    And I 'll awa to Nanie, O.

II

The westlin wind blaws loud an' shill,
    The night 's baith mirk and rainy, O;
But I 'll get my plaid, an' out I 'll steal,
    An' owre the hill to Nanie, O.

III

My Nanie 's charming, sweet, an' young;
    Nae artfu' wiles to win ye, O:
May ill befa' the flattering tongue
    That wad beguile my Nanie, O !

IV

Her face is fair, her heart is true;
    As spotless as she 's bonie, O,
The op'ning gowan, wat wi' dew,
    Nae purer is than Nanie, O.

V

A country lad is my degree,
    An' few there be that ken me, O;
But what care I how few they be ?
    I 'm welcome ay to Nanie, O.

VI

My riches a 's my penny-fee,
    An' I maun guide it cannie, O;
But warl's gear ne'er troubles me,
    My thoughts are a' — my Nanie, O.

VII

Our auld guidman delights to view
    His sheep an' kye thrive bonie, O;
But I 'm as blythe that hauds his pleugh,
    An' has nae care but Nanie, O.

VIII

Come weel, come woe, I care na by;
    I 'll tak what Heav'n will send me, O:
Nae ither care in life have I,
    But live, an' love my Nanie, O.

GREEN GROW THE RASHES, O

This little masterpiece of wit and gaiety and movement was suggested either by the fragment, *Green Grow the Rashes, O* in Herd's *Ancient and Modern Scottish Songs*, or by the blackguard old song itself. Herd gives only three stanzas, of which the first is : —

> " Green grows the rashes — O
> Green grows the rashes — O
> The feather-bed is no sae saft
> As a bed amang the rashes."

But the song (or what is left of it) is given in the unique and interesting garland called *The Merry Muses of Caledonia* (c. 1800), probably — almost certainly — collected by Burns for his private use, together with a second and still grosser set attributed, rightly or wrongly, to Burns himself.

Entered by Burns in the *First Common Place Book*, under date August, 1786, the piece is preceded by a dissertation on young men, who are divided into " two grand classes — the grave and the merry," and by the remark : " It will enable any body to determine which of the classes I belong to." It was published in Johnson's *Museum*. i. 77. Thomson proposed to set it to *Cauld Kail in Aberdeen ;* but Burns declared that it would " never suit " that air.

CHORUS

Green grow the rashes, O;
Green grow the rashes, O;
The sweetest hours that e'er I spend,
Are spent among the lasses, O.

I

THERE 's nought but care on ev'ry han',
In every hour that passes, O:
What signifies the life o' man,
An' 't were nae for the lasses, O.

II

The war'ly race may riches chase,
An' riches still may fly them, O;
An' tho' at last they catch them fast,
Their hearts can ne'er enjoy them, O.

III

But gie me a cannie hour at e'en,
My arms about my dearie, O,
An' war'ly cares an' war'ly men
May a' gae tapsalteerie, O !

IV

For you sae douce, ye sneer at this;
Ye 're nought but senseless asses, O;
The wisest man the warl' e'er saw,
He dearly lov'd the lasses, O.

V

Auld Nature swears, the lovely dears
Her noblest work she classes, O:
Her prentice han' she try'd on man,
An' then she made the lasses, O.

CHORUS

Green grow the rashes, O;
Green grow the rashes, O;
The sweetest hours that e'er I spend,
Are spent among the lasses, O.

COMPOSED IN SPRING

TUNE: *Johnny's Grey Breeks*

Burns explains that the chorus is " part of a song composed by a gentleman in Edinburgh, a particular friend of the author's ; " and that " Menie " is the " common abbreviation of Marianne." In all likelihood the song was composed after the rupture with Jean Armour, and the chorus added in Edinburgh by Burns himself.

I

AGAIN rejoicing Nature sees
Her robe assume its vernal hues:
Her leafy locks wave in the breeze,
All freshly steep'd in morning dews.

CHORUS

And maun I still on Menie doat,
And bear the scorn that 's in her e'e ?
For it 's jet, jet-black, an' it 's like a hawk,
An' it winna let a body be.

II

In vain to me the cowslips blaw,
In vain to me the vi'lets spring;
In vain to me in glen or shaw,
The mavis and the lintwhite sing.

III

The merry ploughboy cheers his team,
Wi' joy the tentie seedsman stalks;
But life to me 's a weary dream,
A dream of ane that never wauks.

IV

The wanton coot the water skims,
Amang the reeds the ducklings cry,

The stately swan majestic swims,
　　And ev'ry thing is blest but I.

V

The sheep-herd steeks his faulding slap,
　　And o'er the moorlands whistles shill;
Wi' wild, unequal, wand'ring step,
　　I meet him on the dewy hill.

VI

And when the lark, 'tween light and dark,
　　Blythe waukens by the daisy's side,
And mounts and sings on flittering wings,
　　A woe-worn ghaist I hameward glide.

VII

Come winter, with thine angry howl,
　　And raging, bend the naked tree;
Thy gloom will soothe my cheerless soul,
　　When nature all is sad like me !

CHORUS

And maun I still on Menie doat,
　　And bear the scorn that 's in her e'e ?
For it 's jet, jet-black, an' it 's like a hawk,
　　An' it winna let a body be.

THE GLOOMY NIGHT IS GATHERING FAST

TUNE: *Roslin Castle*

In an interleaved copy of Johnson's *Museum*
Burns inscribed the following note : " I com-
posed this song as I conveyed my chest so far
on the road to Greenock, where I was to
embark in a few days for Jamaica. I meant
it as my farewell dirge to my native land."
In his Autobiographic Letter to Dr. Moore,
" I had composed," he says, " a song, *The
Gloomy Night is Gathering Fast*, which was to
be the last effort of my muse in Caledonia,
when a letter from Dr. Blacklock to a friend
of mine overthrew all my schemes." Professor
Walker, on R. B.'s authority, affirms that he
composed it on the *way home from* Dr. Law-
rie's ; but, as it was to Dr. Lawrie that Black-
lock wrote, we must infer that Walker was so
far mistaken, and that the verses were made
on the way thither.
　Burns gives *Roslin Castle* as the tune to
which this passionate lyric should be sung.
His use of a refrain, however, suggests that
the true model was *The Birks of Invermay*.

I

THE gloomy night is gath'ring fast,
Loud roars the wild inconstant blast;
Yon murky cloud is filled with rain,
I see it driving o'er the plain;
The hunter now has left the moor,
The scatt'red coveys meet secure;
While here I wander, prest with care,
Along the lonely banks of Ayr.

II

The Autumn mourns her rip'ning corn
By early Winter's ravage torn;
Across her placid, azure sky,
She sees the scowling tempest fly;
Chill runs my blood to hear it rave:
I think upon the stormy wave,
Where many a danger I must dare,
Far from the bonie banks of Ayr.

III

'Tis not the surging billows' roar,
'Tis not that fatal, deadly shore;
Tho' death in ev'ry shape appear,
The wretched have no more to fear:
But round my heart the ties are bound,
That heart transpierc'd with many a wound;
These bleed afresh, those ties I tear,
To leave the bonie banks of Ayr.

IV

Farewell, old Coila's hills and dales,
Her heathy moors and winding vales;
The scenes where wretched Fancy roves,
Pursuing past unhappy loves !
Farewell my friends ! farewell my foes !
My peace with these, my love with those—
The bursting tears my heart declare,
Farewell, my bonie banks of Ayr.

NO CHURCHMAN AM I

TUNE: *Prepare, my dear Brethren*

This poor performance, written probably in
1781 or 1782 for the Tarbolton Bachelors'
Club, in imitation of a popular type of English
drinking song, appears to have been suggested
and inspired by a far better piece, *The Women
all Tell Me I'm False to My Lass* (c. 1740: still
to be heard as *Wine, Mighty Wine*), the air of
which may well have been in Burns's ear when
he directed his own words to be sung to the

tune of *Prepare, my Dear Brethren.* It is quoted, according to Mr. Baring Gould (*English Minstrelsie,* 1895, I. xxiii.), in *The Bullfinch* (1746), *The Wreath* (1753), and *The Occasional Songster* (1782); and we have found it, as Burns before us, in *A Select Collection of English Songs* (London, 1763) — an odd volume of which, containing this very lyric, with notes in his handwriting, is before us as we write — and in *Calliope* (Edinburgh, 1788). Here is a stanza which must certainly have been present when he was struggling with the halting lines and the second-rate buckishness of *No Churchman Am I* : —

> "She too might have poisoned the joy of my life
> With nurses, and babies, and squalling, and strife;
> But my wine neither nurses nor babies can bring,
> *And a big-bellied bottle's* a mighty good thing."

The anapest with four accents has carried a bacchanalian connotation from the time of Shadwell's *Psyche* (1672) at least, and the present stave has been the vehicle of innumerable drinking songs, including the English *A Tankard of Ale*, and the Irish *One Bottle More*. Burns himself reverts to it in *The Whistle* (see *post*, p. 99).

I

No churchman am I for to rail and to write,
No statesman nor soldier to plot or to fight,
No sly man of business contriving a snare,
For a big-belly'd bottle's the whole of my care.

II

The peer I don't envy, I give him his bow;
I scorn not the peasant, tho' ever so low;
But a club of good fellows, like those that are here,
And a bottle like this, are my glory and care.

III

Here passes the squire on his brother — his horse,
There centum per centum, the cit with his purse,
But see you *The Crown*, how it waves in the air ?
There a big-belly'd bottle still eases my care.

IV

The wife of my bosom, alas ! she did die;
For sweet consolation to church I did fly;
I found that old Solomon provèd it fair,
That a big-belly'd bottle's a cure for all care.

V

I once was persuaded a venture to make;
A letter inform'd me that all was to wreck;
But the pursy old landlord just waddlèd up stairs,
With a glorious bottle that ended my cares.

VI

"Life's cares they are comforts" — a maxim laid down
By the Bard, what d' ye call him ? that wore the black gown;
And faith I agree with th' old prig to a hair:
For a big-belly'd bottle's a heav'n of a care.

A STANZA ADDED IN A MASON LODGE

Then fill up a bumper and make it o'erflow,
And honours Masonic prepare for to throw:
May ev'ry true Brother of the Compass and Square
Have a big-belly'd bottle, when harass'd with care !

ADDITIONS IN THE EDINBURGH EDITION OF 1793

In April, 1792, Creech proposed another is-
sue, and Burns replied with an offer of fifty new
pages, and the retrenchment and correction
of some old pieces. Reminding his publisher
that these fifty pages were as much his own
" as the thumb-skull I have just now drawn on
my finger, which I unfortunately gashed in
mending my pen," he practically agreed to
Creech's former terms: craving as his sole
recompence a few books which he very much
wanted, " with as many copies of this new edi-
tion of my own works as friendship or grati-
tude shall prompt me to present." Creech was
not the man to boggle at a bargain of the kind,

and the new edition appeared in the February
of 1793, under the title : " *Poems chiefly in the
Scottish Dialect*. By Robert Burns. In two
volumes. The Second Edition Considerably
Enlarged. Edinburgh : Printed for T. Cadell,
London, and William Creech, Edinburgh.
1793." The volumes, with nearly the same
page and the same type, but with many changes
in spelling, and some new readings of lines
and stanzas, were reprinted early in 1794, with
— excepting for the substitution of " a New
Edition " for " the Second Edition " — an ex-
actly similar title. No other Scots reprint ap-
peared in Burns's lifetime.

WRITTEN IN FRIARS CARSE HERMITAGE, ON NITHSIDE

This is the second version of a piece origi-
nally inscribed on a window-pane of Friars
Carse Hermitage in June, 1788 (see *post*, p. 120).
Friars Carse adjoined Ellisland, and the owner,
Captain Robert Riddell of Glenriddell, had
given Burns a key to the grounds and the
little hermitage which he had built there. It
would appear from an undated letter to William
Dunbar (asking him to decide between the two
sets), and from the fact that Burns distributed
copies of both, that he was by no means con-
vinced of the superiority of the second set.

Thou whom chance may hither lead,
Be thou clad in russet weed,
Be thou deckt in silken stole,
Grave these counsels on thy soul.

Life is but a day at most,
Sprung from night, — in darkness lost:
Hope not sunshine ev'ry hour,
Fear not clouds will always lour.

As Youth and Love with sprightly dance
Beneath thy morning star advance,
Pleasure with her siren air
May delude the thoughtless pair:
Let Prudence bless Enjoyment's cup,
Then raptur'd sip, and sip it up.

As thy day grows warm and high,
Life's meridian flaming nigh,
Dost thou spurn the humble vale ?
Life's proud summits would'st thou scale ?

Check thy climbing step, elate,
Evils lurk in felon wait:
Dangers, eagle-pinioned, bold,
Soar around each cliffy hold;
While cheerful Peace with linnet song
Chants the lowly dells among.

As the shades of ev'ning close,
Beck'ning thee to long repose;
As life itself becomes disease,
Seek the chimney-nook of ease:
There ruminate with sober thought,
On all thou 'st seen, and heard, and
      wrought;
And teach the sportive younkers round,
Saws of experience, sage and sound:
Say, man's true, genuine estimate,
The grand criterion of his fate,
Is not, Art thou high or low ?
Did thy fortune ebb or flow ?
Did many talents gild thy span ?
Or frugal Nature grudge thee one ?
Tell them, and press it on their mind,
As thou thyself must shortly find,
The smile or frown of awful Heav'n
To Virtue or to Vice is giv'n;
Say, to be just, and kind, and wise —
There solid self-enjoyment lies;
That foolish, selfish, faithless ways
Lead to be wretched, vile, and base.

Thus resign'd and quiet, creep
To the bed of lasting sleep:
Sleep, whence thou shall ne'er awake,
Night, where dawn shall never break;
Till future life, future no more,

To light and joy the good restore,
To light and joy unknown before.

Stranger, go !   Heav'n be thy guide !
Quod the beadsman of Nithside.

ODE, SACRED TO THE MEMORY OF MRS. OSWALD OF AUCHEN-CRUIVE

In a letter to Dr. Moore, 23d March, 1789, enclosing this *Ode* Burns explains its origin : " In January last, on my road to Ayrshire, I had put up at Bailie Whigham's in Sanquhar, the only tolerable inn in the place.   The frost was keen, and the grim evening and howling wind were ushering in a night of snow and drift.   My horse and I were both much fatigued with the labours of the day, and just as my friend the Bailie and I were bidding defiance to the storm, over a smoking bowl, in wheels the funeral pageantry of the late great Mrs. Oswald ; and poor I am forced to brave all the horrors of a tempestuous night, and jade my horse, my young favourite horse, whom I had just christened Pegasus, twelve miles further on, through the wildest moors and hills of Ayrshire, to New Cumnock, the next inn.   The powers of poesy and prose sink under me, when I would describe what I felt.   Suffice it to say, that when a good fire at New Cumnock had so far recovered my frozen sinews, I sat down and wrote the enclosed ode."   In a letter (unpublished) to Mrs. Dunlop, enclosing the copy of the *Ode*, " Before I reached the other stage," he writes, " I had composed the following, and sent it off at the first post office for the *Courant*," by which, if this be true, it was declined. On May 7, 1789, the piece appeared in Stuart's *Star* with the following preface, here for the first time reprinted : —

" *Mr. Printer,*
" I know not who is the author of the following poem, but I think it contains some equally well-told and just compliments to the memory of a matron who, a few months ago, much against her private inclination, left this good world and twice five good thousands per annum behind her.

" We are told by very respectable authority that ' the righteous die and none regardeth ; ' but as this was by no means the case in point with the departed beldam, for whose memory I have the honour to interest myself, it is not easy guessing why prose and verse have both said so little on the death of the owner of ten thousand a year.

" I dislike partial respect of persons, and am hurt to see the public make such a fuss when a poor pennyless gipsey is consigned over to Jack Ketch, and yet scarce take any notice when a purse-proud Priestess of Mammon is by the memorable hand of death prisoned in everlasting fetters of ill-gotten gold, and delivered up to the arch-brother among the finishers of the law, emphatically called by your bard, the hangman of creation.
" TIM NETTLE."

Mrs. Oswald was the widow of Richard Oswald, second son of Rev. George Oswald, of Dunnet, Caithness.   He purchased Auchencruive in 1772.   He died at an " advanced age," 6th November, 1784, and in the obituary notice in *The Scots Magazine* is described as " an eminent merchant in London, and lately employed at Paris as a commissioner for negotiating a peace with the United States."   From Burns's epithet, " Plunderer of Armies," he would appear to have been also an army contractor.   In his letter to Dr. Moore, Burns states that he knew that Mrs. Oswald was detested by her tenants and servants " with the most heartfelt cordiality."   She died 6th December, 1788, at her house in Great George Street, Westminster, and when Burns was driven from his inn by her " funeral pageantry," the body was on its way to Ayrshire.   Burns himself was proceeding in the same direction (as we learn from a letter to Mrs. Dunlop of 18th December) to the Ayr Fair, held about the 12th January·

DWELLER in yon dungeon dark,
Hangman of creation, mark !
Who in widow-weeds appears,
Laden with unhonoured years,
Noosing with care a bursting purse,
Baited with many a deadly curse ?

STROPHE

View the wither'd beldam's face:
Can thy keen inspection trace
Aught of Humanity's sweet, melting
        grace ?
Note that eye, 't is rheum o'erflows —
Pity's flood there never rose.
See those hands, ne'er stretch'd to save,
Hands that took, but never gave.
Keeper of Mammon's iron chest,
Lo, there she goes, unpitied and unblest,
She goes, but not to realms of everlasting
        rest !

ANTISTROPHE

Plunderer of Armies ! lift thine eyes
    (A while forbear, ye torturing fiends),

Seest thou whose step, unwilling, hither
 bends ?
No fallen angel, hurl'd from upper skies !
'T is thy trusty, quondam Mate,
Doom'd to share thy fiery fate:
She, tardy, hell-ward plies.

EPODE

And are they of no more avail,
Ten thousand glittering pounds a-year ?
In other worlds can Mammon fail,
 Omnipotent as he is here ?
O bitter mockery of the pompous bier !
 While down the wretched vital part is
  driven,
The cave-lodg'd beggar, with a conscience
  clear,
 Expires in rags, unknown, and goes to
  Heaven.

ELEGY ON CAPTAIN MATTHEW HENDERSON

A GENTLEMAN WHO HELD THE PATENT
FOR HIS HONOURS IMMEDIATELY FROM
ALMIGHTY GOD !

> But now his radiant course is run,
> For Matthew's course was bright:
> His soul was like the glorious sun
> A matchless, Heavenly light.

Matthew Henderson was the son of David
Henderson, of Tannockside, and Elizabeth
Brown ; born 24th February, 1737 ; succeeded
in early youth to the estates on his father's
death ; became lieutenant in the Earl of
Home's regiment ; left the army to hold a
government appointment in Edinburgh ; was
a member of the Poker and other convivial
clubs, and a friend of Boswell, who has pre-
served one or two samples of his wit ; died 21st
November, 1788 ; and was buried in Greyfriars'
Churchyard.

On 23d July, 1790, Burns sent "a first fair
copy" to Robert Cleghorn, Saughton, to whom
he stated that Henderson was a man he "much
regarded." On 2d August he sent a copy to
John M'Murdo of Drumlanrig : "You knew
Henderson," he said ; "I have not flattered
his memory." And in enclosing a copy to Dr.
Moore (27th February, 1791) he described the
Elegy as "a tribute to the memory of a man I
loved much."

I

O DEATH ! thou tyrant fell and bloody !
The meikle Devil wi' a woodie
Haurl thee hame to his black smiddie
  O'er hurcheon hides,
And like stock-fish come o'er his studdie
  Wi' thy auld sides !

II

He 's gane, he 's gane ! he 's frae us torn,
The ae best fellow e'er was born !
Thee, Matthew, Nature's sel shall mourn,
  By wood and wild,
Where, haply, Pity strays forlorn,
  Frae man exil'd.

III

Ye hills, near neebors o' the starns,
That proudly cock your cresting cairns !
Ye cliffs, the haunts of sailing yearns,
  Where Echo slumbers !
Come join ye, Nature's sturdiest bairns,
  My wailing numbers !

IV

Mourn, ilka grove the cushat kens !
Ye hazly shaws and briery dens !
Ye burnies, wimplin down your glens
  Wi' toddlin din,
Or foaming, strang, wi' hasty stens,
  Frae lin to lin !

V

Mourn, little harebells o'er the lea;
Ye stately foxgloves, fair to see;
Ye woodbines, hanging bonilie
  In scented bowers;
Ye roses on your thorny tree,
  The first o' flowers !

VI

At dawn, when every grassy blade
Droops with a diamond at his head;
At ev'n, when beans their fragrance shed
  I' th' rustling gale;
Ye maukins, whiddin through the glade;
  Come join my wail !

VII

Mourn, ye wee songsters o' the wood;
Ye grouse that crap the heather bud;
Ye curlews, calling thro' a clud;
  Ye whistling plover;

And mourn, ye whirring paitrick brood:
    He's gane for ever!

VIII

Mourn, sooty coots, and speckled teals;
Ye fisher herons, watching eels;
Ye duck and drake, wi' airy wheels
    Circling the lake;
Ye bitterns, till the quagmire reels,
    Rair for his sake!

IX

Mourn, clam'ring craiks, at close o' day,
'Mang fields o' flow'ring clover gay!
And when you wing your annual way
    Frae our cauld shore,
Tell thae far warlds wha lies in clay,
    Wham we deplore.

X

Ye houlets, frae your ivy bower
In some auld tree, or eldritch tower,
What time the moon, wi' silent glowr,
    Sets up her horn,
Wail thro' the dreary midnight hour
    Till waukrife morn!

XI

O rivers, forests, hills, and plains!
Oft have ye heard my canty strains:
But now, what else for me remains
    But tales of woe?
And frae my een the drapping rains
    Maun ever flow.

XII

Mourn, Spring, thou darling of the year!
Ilk cowslip cup shall kep a tear:
Thou, Simmer, while each corny spear
    Shoots up its head,
Thy gay, green, flowery tresses shear
    For him that's dead!

XIII

Thou, Autumn, wi' thy yellow hair,
In grief thy sallow mantle tear!
Thou, Winter, hurling thro' the air
    The roaring blast,
Wide o'er the naked world declare
    The worth we've lost!

XIV

Mourn him, thou Sun, great source of light!
Mourn, Empress of the silent night!

And you, ye twinkling starnies bright,
    My Matthew mourn!
For through your orbs he's taen his flight,
    Ne'er to return.

XV

O Henderson! the man! the brother!
And art thou gone, and gone for ever?
And hast thou crost that unknown river,
    Life's dreary bound?
Like thee, where shall I find another,
    The world around?

XVI

Go to your sculptur'd tombs, ye Great,
In a' the tinsel trash o' state!
But by thy honest turf I'll wait,
    Thou man of worth!
And weep the ae best fellow's fate
    E'er lay in earth!

THE EPITAPH

I

Stop, passenger! my story's brief,
    And truth I shall relate, man:
I tell nae common tale o' grief,
    For Matthew was a great man.

II

If thou uncommon merit hast,
    Yet spurn'd at Fortune's door, man;
A look of pity hither cast,
    For Matthew was a poor man.

III

If thou a noble sodger art,
    That passest by this grave, man;
There moulders here a gallant heart,
    For Matthew was a brave man.

IV

If thou on men, their works and ways,
    Canst throw uncommon light, man;
Here lies wha weel had won thy praise,
    For Matthew was a bright man.

V

If thou, at Friendship's sacred ca',
    Wad life itself resign, man;
Thy sympathetic tear maun fa',
    For Matthew was a kind man.

VI

If thou art staunch, without a stain,
  Like the unchanging blue, man;
This was a kinsman o' thy ain,
  For Matthew was a true man.

VII

If thou hast wit and fun, and fire,
  And ne'er guid wine did fear, man;
This was thy billie, dam, and sire,
  For Matthew was a queer man.

VIII

If onie whiggish, whingin sot,
  To blame poor Matthew dare, man;
May dool and sorrow be his lot!
  For Matthew was a rare man.

LAMENT OF MARY QUEEN OF SCOTS

ON THE APPROACH OF SPRING

In enclosing this to Dr. John Moore, 27th February, 1791, Burns states that it was begun while he was busy with Percy's *Reliques of English Poetry*: hence its antique flavouring. He sent copies to Mrs. Dunlop, to Mrs. Graham of Fintry, to Clarinda, and to Lady Winifred Constable, and was at pains to tell each of the four the reason why she was thus specially favoured. In an unpublished letter to Mrs. Dunlop (6th June, 1790), he wrote: "You know and with me pity the miserable and unfortunate Mary Queen of Scots. To you and your young ladies I particularly dedicate the following Scots stanzas." It was probably about the same time that in an undated letter — (usually assigned to February, 1791, to accord with the date of that to Moore) — he wrote to Mrs. Graham of Fintry: "Whether it is that the story of our Mary Queen of Scots has a peculiar effect on the feelings of a poet, or whether I have in the enclosed ballad succeeded beyond my usual poetic success, I know not; but it has pleased me beyond any effort of my Muse for a good while past; on that account I enclose it particularly to you." To Clarinda (in an undated letter) he thus expressed himself: "Such, my dearest Nancy, were the words of the amiable but unfortunate Mary. Misfortune seems to take a peculiar pleasure in darting her arrows against 'honest men and bonie lasses.' Of this you are too, too just a proof; but may your future fate be a bright exception to the remark!" To Lady Constable the ode was sent at the same time that he acknowledged the present of a snuff-box, the lid of it inlaid with a miniature of Queen Mary.

I

Now Nature hangs her mantle green
  On every blooming tree,
And spreads her sheets o' daisies white
  Out o'er the grassy lea;
Now Phœbus cheers the crystal streams,
  And glads the azure skies:
But nought can glad the weary wight
  That fast in durance lies.

II

Now laverocks wake the merry morn,
  Aloft on dewy wing;
The merle, in his noontide bow'r,
  Makes woodland echoes ring;
The mavis wild wi' monie a note
  Sings drowsy day to rest:
In love and freedom they rejoice,
  Wi' care nor thrall opprest.

III

Now blooms the lily by the bank,
  The primrose down the brae;
The hawthorn's budding in the glen,
  And milk-white is the slae:
The meanest hind in fair Scotland
  May rove their sweets amang;
But I, the Queen of a' Scotland
  Maun lie in prison strang.

IV

I was the Queen o' bonie France,
  Where happy I hae been;
Fu' lightly rase I in the morn,
  As blythe lay down at e'en:
And I'm the sov'reign of Scotland,
  And monie a traitor there;
Yet here I lie in foreign bands
  And never-ending care.

V

But as for thee, thou false woman,
  My sister and my fae,
Grim vengeance yet shall whet a sword
  That thro' thy soul shall gae!
The weeping blood in woman's breast
  Was never known to thee;
Nor th' balm that draps on wounds of woe
  Frae woman's pitying e'e.

VI

My son ! my son ! may kinder stars
  Upon thy fortune shine;
And may those pleasures gild thy reign,
  That ne'er wad blink on mine !
God keep thee frae thy mother's faes,
  Or turn their hearts to thee;
And where thou meet'st thy mother's
      friend,
  Remember him for me !

VII

O ! soon, to me, may summer suns
  Nae mair light up the morn !
Nae mair to me the autumn winds
  Wave o'er the yellow corn !
And, in the narrow house of death,
  Let winter round me rave;
And the next flow'rs that deck the spring
  Bloom on my peaceful grave.

TO ROBERT GRAHAM OF FIN-
TRY, ESQ.

Burns first met Graham of Fintry at the
Duke of Atholl's during his northern tour in
August, 1787; and in an undated letter in
which he refers to this, solicited his influence
in obtaining an appointment to a division in
the Excise. In a letter dated 10th September,
1788, he made a special request in regard to a
division in the Ellisland district, enclosing at
the same time the poetical epistle, *Requesting
a Favour* (see *post*, p. 140). Obtaining the
division, he acknowledged Fintry's exertions
in the epistle on *Receiving a Favour* (see *post*,
p. 144); and in an *Election Ballad*, made at the
close of the contest for the Dumfries Burghs
in 1790 (see *post*, p. 162), he addressed him
thus : —

    "Fintry, my stay in worldly strife,
     Friend of my Muse, friend of my life : " —

a eulogy amply justified by Fintry's consistent
and considerate kindness to him, through good
and bad report, to the close of his life. The
present *Epistle* was sent 6th October, 1791,
with a letter in which he describes it as " a
sheetful of groans, wrung from me in my
elbow-chair, with one unlucky leg on my stool
before me." There is some poetical licence —
let us call it so — in this description; not as
regards his own condition, for he was then con-
fined to his arm-chair by a bruised leg, but
as regards the *Epistle* itself, for, with the ex-

ception of the introductory and closing lines,
it consists of two revised and retrenched frag-
ments, written near three years before, and
originally intended, according to his own state-
ment — which need not be taken quite seri-
ously — to form part of a *Poet's Progress.*

Graham of Fintry was descended from Sir
Robert Graham of Strathcarron and Fintry,
Stirlingshire, son of Sir William Graham of
Kincardine by Mary Stewart, daughter of
Robert III. The Grahams acquired the lands
of Mains and of Lumlethan, Forfarshire, in
the sixteenth century, and the estate was then
named "Fintry." The portion with the man-
sion-house was sold by Graham of Fintry —
at some unknown date, but probably before
1789 — to Sir James Stirling; and another
portion — Earl's Strathdichty — in 1789 to
Mr. D. Erskine, Clerk to the Signet (by the
trustees of the creditors of Graham of Fintry).
The part sold to Sir James Stirling was bought
by Erskine's trustees in 1801. Graham con-
tinued to be designated " of Fintry; " and the
name of the estate was (according to the con-
ditions of sale) changed to Linlathen. He died
10th January, 1815.

LATE crippl'd of an arm, and now a leg;
About to beg a pass for leave to beg;
Dull, listless, teas'd, dejected, and deprest
(Nature is adverse to a cripple's rest);
Will generous Graham list to his Poet's
    wail
(It soothes poor Misery, hearkening to her
    tale),
And hear him curse the light he first sur-
    vey'd,
And doubly curse the luckless rhyming
    trade ?

  Thou, Nature ! partial Nature ! I ar-
    raign;
Of thy caprice maternal I complain :
The lion and the bull thy care have found,
One shakes the forests, and one spurns the
    ground;
Thou giv'st the ass his hide, the snail his
    shell;
Th' envenom'd wasp, victorious, guards his
    cell;
Thy minions kings defend, control, devour,
In all th' omnipotence of rule and power.
Foxes and statesmen subtile wiles ensure;
The cit and polecat stink, and are se-
    cure;
Toads with their poison, doctors with their
    drug,

The priest and hedgehog in their robes, are
    snug;
Ev'n silly woman has her warlike arts,
Her tongue and eyes — her dreaded spear
    and darts.

But O thou bitter step-mother and hard,
To thy poor, fenceless, naked child — the
    Bard!
A thing unteachable in world's skill,
And half an idiot too, more helpless still:
No heels to bear him from the op'ning dun,
No claws to dig, his hated sight to shun;
No horns, but those by luckless Hymen
    worn,
And those, alas! not Amalthea's horn;
No nerves olfact'ry, Mammon's trusty cur,
Clad in rich Dulness' comfortable fur;
In naked feeling, and in aching pride,
He bears th' unbroken blast from ev'ry
    side :
Vampyre booksellers drain him to the
    heart,
And scorpion critics cureless venom dart.

Critics — appall'd, I venture on the
    name;
Those cut-throat bandits in the paths of
    fame;
Bloody dissectors, worse than ten Monroes:
He hacks to teach, they mangle to expose.

His heart by causeless wanton malice
    wrung,
By blockheads' daring into madness stung;
His well-won bays, than life itself more
    dear,
By miscreants torn, who ne'er one sprig
    must wear;
Foil'd, bleeding, tortur'd in th' unequal
    strife,
The hapless Poet flounders on thro' life:
Till, fled each hope that once his bosom
    fir'd,
And fled each Muse that glorious once
    inspir'd,
Low sunk in squalid, unprotected age,
Dead even resentment for his injur'd page,
He heeds or feels no more the ruthless crit-
    ic's rage!
So, by some hedge, the gen'rous steed de-
    ceas'd,
For half-starv'd snarling curs a dainty
    feast,

By toil and famine wore to skin and bone,
Lies, senseless of each tugging bitch's son.

O Dulness! portion of the truly blest!
Calm shelter'd haven of eternal rest!
Thy sons ne'er madden in the fierce ex-
    tremes
Of Fortune's polar frost, or torrid beams.
If mantling high she fills the golden cup,
With sober, selfish ease they sip it up:
Conscious the bounteous meed they well
    deserve,
They only wonder "some folks" do not
    starve.
The grave, sage hern thus easy picks his
    frog,
And thinks the mallard a sad, worthless
    dog.
When Disappointment snaps the clue of
    hope,
And thro' disastrous night they darkling
    grope,
With deaf endurance sluggishly they bear,
And just conclude "that fools are fortune's
    care."
So, heavy, passive to the tempest's shocks,
Strong on the sign-post stands the stupid
    ox.

Not so the idle Muse's mad-cap train;
Not such the workings of their moon-struck
    brain:
In equanimity they never dwell;
By turns in soaring heav'n or vaulted hell.

I dread thee, Fate, relentless and se-
    vere,
With all a poet's, husband's, father's fear!
Already one strong hold of hope is lost:
Glencairn, the truly noble, lies in dust
(Fled, like the sun eclips'd as noon ap-
    pears,
And left us darkling in a world of tears).
O, hear my ardent, grateful, selfish pray'r!
Fintry, my other stay, long bless and spare!
Thro' a long life his hopes and wishes
    crown,
And bright in cloudless skies his sun go
    down!
May bliss domestic smooth his private path;
Give energy to life; and soothe his latest
    breath,
With many a filial tear circling the bed of
    death!

LAMENT FOR JAMES EARL OF GLENCAIRN

James Cunningham, fourteenth Earl of Glencairn, second son of William, thirteenth earl, and the eldest daughter of Hugh M'Guire, a violinist in Ayr, whose family had been adopted by Governor Macrae of the H. E. I. C., was born in 1749; succeeded to the earldom in 1775; made the acquaintance of Burns — through James Dalrymple of Orangefield — in Edinburgh in 1786, and introduced him to Creech the publisher; succeeded in obtaining for the Edinburgh Edition the patronage of the Caledonian Hunt, and also exerted himself to the utmost to secure subscriptions among the nobility; used his influence in getting Burns an appointment in the Excise, and is always referred to by the poet in terms of the warmest regard. Owing to ill-health, he went to Lisbon in 1790 to pass the winter; but, finding himself rapidly failing, resolved to return, and died, after landing at Falmouth, 30th January, 1791. Learning of his death, Burns wrote thus to his factor, Alexander Dalziel: "Dare I trouble you to let me know privately before the day of interment, that I may cross the country, and steal among the crowd, to pay a tear to the last sight of my ever revered benefactor?"

In a letter to Glencairn's sister, Lady Elizabeth Cunningham — conjecturally (but wrongly) dated by Scott Douglas "March, 1791" (it was written not earlier than September, and most probably in October) — concerning a copy of the Lament, "If," he wrote, "among my children I shall have a son that has a heart, he shall hand it down to his child as a family honour and a family debt that my dearest existence I owe to the noble heart of Glencairn." He named his fourth son (born 12th August, 1794) "James Glencairn Burns." On the 23d October he sent a copy of the poem to Lady Don (MS. now in the University of Edinburgh) with this inscription: "To Lady Harriet Don this poem, not the fictitious creation of poetic fancy, but the breathings of real woe from a bleeding heart, is respectfully and gratefully presented by the author." In the note enclosing it he wrote: "As all the world knows my obligations to the late noble Earl of Glencairn, I wish to make my obligations equally conspicuous by publishing the poem. But in what way shall I publish it? It is too small a piece to publish alone. The way which suggests itself to me is to send it to the publisher of one of the most reputed periodical works — The Bee, for instance. Lady Betty has referred me to you." It did not appear in The Bee.

I

THE wind blew hollow frae the hills;
　By fits the sun's departing beam
Look'd on the fading yellow woods,
　That wav'd o'er Lugar's winding stream.
Beneath a craigy steep a Bard,
　Laden with years and meikle pain,
In loud lament bewail'd his lord,
　Whom Death had all untimely taen.

II

He lean'd him to an ancient aik,
　Whose trunk was mould'ring down with years;
His locks were bleachèd white with time,
　His hoary cheek was wet wi' tears;
And as he touch'd his trembling harp,
　And as he tun'd his doleful sang,
The winds, lamenting thro' their caves,
　To echo bore the notes alang: —

III

"Ye scatter'd birds that faintly sing,
　The reliques of the vernal quire!
Ye woods that shed on a' the winds
　The honours of the agèd year!
A few short months, and, glad and gay,
　Again ye 'll charm the ear and e'e;
But nocht in all revolving time
　Can gladness bring again to me.

IV

"I am a bending aged tree,
　That long has stood the wind and rain;
But now has come a cruel blast,
　And my last hold of earth is gane;
Nae leaf o' mine shall greet the spring,
　Nae simmer sun exalt my bloom;
But I maun lie before the storm,
　And ithers plant them in my room.

V

"I 've seen sae monie changefu' years,
　On earth I am a stranger grown:
I wander in the ways of men,
　Alike unknowing and unknown:
Unheard, unpitied, unreliev'd,
　I bear alane my lade o' care;
For silent, low, on beds of dust,
　Lie a' that would my sorrows share.

VI

"And last (the sum of a' my griefs!)
　My noble master lies in clay;

The flow'r amang our barons bold,
  His country's pride, his country's stay :
In weary being now I pine,
  For a' the life of life is dead,
And hope has left my agèd ken,
  On forward wing for ever fled.

VII

"Awake thy last sad voice, my harp !
  The voice of woe and wild despair !
Awake, resound thy latest lay,
  Then sleep in silence evermair !
And thou, my last, best, only friend,
  That fillest an untimely tomb,
Accept this tribute from the Bard
  Thou brought from Fortune's mirkest
    gloom.

VIII

"In Poverty's low barren vale,
  Thick mists obscure involv'd me round;
Though oft I turn'd the wistful eye,
  Nae ray of fame was to be found;
Thou found'st me, like the morning sun
  That melts the fogs in limpid air:
The friendless Bard and rustic song
  Became alike thy fostering care.

IX

"O, why has Worth so short a date,
  While villains ripen grey with time !
Must thou, the noble, gen'rous, great,
  Fall in bold manhood's hardy prime ?
Why did I live to see that day,
  A day to me so full of woe ?
O, had I met the mortal shaft
  Which laid my benefactor low !

X

"The bridegroom may forget the bride
  Was made his wedded wife yestreen;
The monarch may forget the crown
  That on his head an hour has been;
The mother may forget the child
  That smiles sae sweetly on her knee;
But I 'll remember thee, Glencairn,
  And a' that thou hast done for me! "

LINES TO SIR JOHN WHITE-FOORD, BART.

SENT WITH THE FOREGOING POEM

Sir John Whitefoord was, like Glencairn,
the warm friend of Burns, who wrote *The*
Braes o' Ballochmyle (see *post*, p. 225) in 1783,
on the occasion of the family's being compelled
to sell the estate of that name.

THOU, who thy honour as thy God rever'st,
Who, save thy mind's reproach, nought
    earthly fear'st,
To thee this votive off'ring I impart,
The tearful tribute of a broken heart.
The Friend thou valued'st, I the Patron
    lov'd;
His worth, his honour, all the world ap-
    prov'd:
We 'll mourn till we too go as he has gone,
And tread the shadowy path to that dark
    world unknown.

TAM O' SHANTER

A TALE

Of Brownyis and of Bogillis full is this Buke.
                                GAWIN DOUGLAS.

Alloway Kirk was originally the church of
the *quoad civilia* parish of Alloway; but this
parish having been annexed to that of Ayr in
1690, the church fell more or less to ruin, and
when Burns wrote had been roofless for half
a century. It stands some two hundred yards
to the north of the picturesque Auld Brig of
Doon, which dates from about the beginning
of the Fifteenth Century, and in Burns's time
was the sole means of communication over the
steep-banked Doon between Carrick and Kyle.
The old road to Ayr ran west of the Kirk:
the more direct road dating from the erection
of the New Brig — a little west of the old one
— in 1815.

Burns's birthplace is about three fourths of
a mile to the north ; so that the ground and its
legends were familiar to him from the first.
Writing to Francis Grose (first published in
Sir Egerton Brydges' *Censura Literaria*, 1796),
— "Among the many witch-stories I have
heard," he says, "relating to Alloway Kirk, I
distinctly remember only two or three. Upon
a stormy night, amid whistling squalls of wind
and bitter blasts of hail — in short, on such a
night as the devil would choose to take the air
in — a farmer, or farmer's servant, was plod-
ding and plashing homeward with his plough-
irons on his shoulder, having been getting
some repairs on them at a neighbouring
smithy. His way lay by the Kirk of Alloway ;
and being rather on the anxious look-out in
approaching a place so well known to be a
favourite haunt of the devil, and the devil's

friends and emissaries, he was struck aghast by discovering, through the horrors of the storm and stormy night, a light, which on his nearer approach plainly shewed itself to proceed from the haunted edifice. Whether he had been fortified from above on his devout supplication, as is customary with people when they suspect the immediate presence of Satan, or whether, according to another custom, he had got courageously drunk at the smithy, I will not pretend to determine; but so it was, that he ventured to go up to, nay into, the very Kirk. As luck would have it, his temerity came off unpunished. The members of the infernal junto were all out on some midnight business or other, and he saw nothing but a kind of kettle or cauldron, depending from the roof, over the fire, simmering some heads of unchristened children, limbs of executed malefactors, etc., for the business of the night. It was, in for a penny, in for a pound with the honest ploughman: so without ceremony he unhooked the cauldron from the fire, and pouring out the damnable ingredients, inverted it on his head, and carried it fairly home, where it remained long in the family, a living evidence of the truth of the story. Another story, which I can prove to be equally authentic, was as follows: On a market-day in the town of Ayr, a farmer from Carrick, and consequently whose way lay by the very gate of Alloway Kirkyard, in order to cross the river Doon at the old bridge, which is about two or three hundred yards further on than the said gate, had been detained by his business till by the time he reached Alloway it was the wizard hour between night and morning. Though he was terrified with a blaze streaming from the Kirk, yet, as it is a well-known fact, that to turn back on these occasions is running by far the greatest risk of mischief, he prudently advanced on his road. When he had reached the gate of the Kirkyard, he was surprised and entertained, through the ribs and arches of an old Gothic window, which still faces the highway, to see a dance of witches merrily footing it round their old sooty blackguard master, who was keeping them all alive with the power of his bagpipe. The farmer, stopping his horse to observe them a little, could plainly descry the faces of many old women of his acquaintance and neighbourhood. How the gentleman was dressed, tradition does not say, but that the ladies were all in their smocks: and one of them happening unluckily to have a smock which was considerably too short to answer all the purpose of that piece of dress, our farmer was so tickled that he involuntarily burst out with a loud laugh, 'Weel luppen, Maggy wi' the short sark!' and recollecting himself, in-

stantly spurred his horse to the top of his speed. I need not mention the universally known fact, that no diabolical power can pursue you beyond the middle of a running stream. Lucky it was for the poor farmer that the river Doon was so near, for notwithstanding the speed of the horse, which was a good one, when he reached the middle of the arch of the bridge, and consequently the middle of the stream, the pursuing vengeful hags were so close at his heels that one of them actually sprang to seize him: but it was too late; nothing was on her side of the stream but the horse's tail, which immediately gave way at her infernal grip, as if blasted by a stroke of lightning; but the farmer was beyond her reach. However, the unsightly tailless condition of the vigorous steed was, to the last hour of the noble creature's life, an awful warning to the Carrick farmers not to stay too late in Ayr markets.

"The last relation I shall give, though equally true, is not so well identified as the two former with regard to the scene; but as the best authorities give it for Alloway, I shall relate it. On a summer's evening, about the time nature puts on her sables to mourn the expiry of the cheerful day, a shepherd boy, belonging to a farmer in the immediate neighbourhood of Alloway Kirk, had just folded his charge and was returning home. As he passed the Kirk, in the adjoining field, he fell in with a crew of men and women who were busy pulling stems of the plant ragwort. He observed that as each person pulled a ragwort, he or she got astride of it and called out, 'Up horsie!' on which the ragwort flew off, like Pegasus, through the air with its rider. The foolish boy likewise pulled his ragwort, and cried with the rest, 'Up horsie!' and, strange to tell, away he flew with the company. The first stage at which the cavalcade stopt was a merchant's wine-cellar in Bordeaux, where, without saying by your leave, they quaffed away at the best the cellar could afford until the morning, foe to the imps and works of darkness, threatened to throw light on the matter, and frightened them from their carousals. The poor shepherd lad, being equally a stranger to the scene and the liquor, heedlessly got himself drunk; and when the rest took horse he fell asleep, and was found so next day by some of the people belonging to the merchant. Somebody that understood Scotch, asking him what he was, he said such a one's herd in Alloway; and by some means or other getting home again, he lived long to tell the world the wondrous tale."

[As a vehicle for narrative, the octosyllabic couplet, employed by Burns in this piece, as also in *The Twa Dogs*, became classical in

Scotland through Barbour's *Bruce* (c. 1375).]
The motto is the eighteenth verse of Gavin
Douglas's sixth "Proloug" (*Eneados*), and
should read thus: "Of browneis and of bogillis
full this buke."

Probably Burns drew the suggestion of his
hero, Tam o' Shanter, from the character and
adventures of Douglas Graham — born 6th Jan-
uary, 1739, died 23d June, 1811 — son of Robert
Graham, farmer at Douglastown, tenant of the
farm of Shanter on the Carrick Shore, and
owner of a boat which he had named *Tam o'
Shanter*. Graham was noted for his convivial
habits, which his wife's ratings tended rather
to confirm than to eradicate. Tradition relates
that once, when his long-tailed grey mare had
waited even longer than usual for her master
at the tavern door, certain humourists plucked
her tail to such an extent as to leave it little
better than a stump, and that Graham, on his
attention being called to its state next morn-
ing, swore that it had been depilated by the
witches at Alloway Kirk (*MS. Notes* by D.
Auld of Ayr in Edinburgh University Li-
brary). The prototype — if prototype there
were — of Souter Johnie is more doubtful; but
a shoemaker named John Davidson — born
1728, died 30th June, 1806 — did live for some
time at Glenfoot of Ardlochan, near the farm
of Shanter, whence he removed to Kirkoswald.

In Alloway Kirk and its surroundings, apart
from its uncanny associations, Burns cherished
a special interest. "When my father," says
Gilbert, "feued his little property near Allo-
way Kirk the wall of the churchyard had gone
to ruin, and cattle had free liberty of pastur-
ing in it. My father and two or three other
neighbours joined in an application to the
Town Council of Ayr, who were superiors of
the adjoining land, for liberty to rebuild it,
and raised by subscription a sum for enclosing
this ancient cemetery with a wall; hence he
came to consider it as his burial-place, and we
learned the reverence for it people generally
have for the burial-place of their ancestors."
When, therefore, Burns met Captain Grose —
then on his peregrinations through Scotland —
at the house of Captain Riddell, he suggested
a drawing of the ruin; and "the captain," Gil-
bert says, "agreed to the request, provided
the poet would furnish a witch story to be
printed along with it." It is probable that
Burns originally sent the stories told above for
insertion in the work, and that the narrative
in rhyme was an afterthought. Lockhart, on
Cromek's authority, accepts a statement, said
to have been made by Mrs. Burns, that the
piece was the work of a single day, and on
this very slender evidence divers critics have
indulged in a vast amount of admiration.
Burns's general dictum must, however, be

borne in mind: "All my poetry is the effect
of easy composition, but of laborious correc-
tion;" together with his special verdict on
Tam o' Shanter (letter to Mrs. Dunlop, April,
1791) that it "showed a finishing polish,"
which he despaired of "ever excelling." It
appeared in Grose's *Antiquities* — published in
April, 1791 — the captain's indebtedness being
thus acknowledged: "To my *ingenious* friend,
Mr. Robert Burns, I have been seriously obli-
gated: he was not only at the pains of making
out what was most worthy of notice in Ayr-
shire, the county honoured by his birth, but
he also wrote, expressly for this work, the
pretty tale annexed to Alloway Church."
Ere Grose's work was before the public, the
piece made its appearance in *The Edinburgh
Magazine* for March, 1791; and it was also
published in *The Edinburgh Herald* of 18th
March, 1791.

WHEN chapman billies leave the street,
And drouthy neebors neebors meet;
As market-days are wearing late,
An' folk begin to tak the gate;
While we sit bousing at the nappy,
An' getting fou and unco happy,
We think na on the lang Scots miles,
The mosses, waters, slaps, and styles,
That lie between us and our hame,
Whare sits our sulky, sullen dame,
Gathering her brows like gathering storm,
Nursing her wrath to keep it warm.

    This truth fand honest Tam o' Shanter,
As he frae Ayr ae night did canter:
(Auld Ayr, wham ne'er a town surpasses,
For honest men and bonie lasses).

O Tam, had'st thou but been sae wise,
As taen thy ain wife Kate's advice !
She tauld thee weel thou was a skellum,
A blethering, blustering, drunken blellum;
That frae November till October,
Ae market-day thou was nae sober;
That ilka melder wi' the miller,
Thou sat as lang as thou had siller;
That ev'ry naig was ca'd a shoe on,
The smith and thee gat roaring fou on;
That at the Lord's house, even on Sun-
        day,
Thou drank wi' Kirkton Jean till Monday.
She prophesied, that, late or soon,
Thou would be found deep drown'd in
        Doon,
Or catch'd wi' warlocks in the mirk
By Alloway's auld, haunted kirk.

Ah ! gentle dames, it gars me greet,
To think how monie counsels sweet,
How monie lengthen'd, sage advices
The husband frae the wife despises !

But to our tale : Ae market-night,
Tam had got planted unco right,
Fast by an ingle, bleezing finely,
Wi' reaming swats, that drank divinely;
And at his elbow, Souter Johnie,
His ancient, trusty, drouthy cronie:
Tam lo'ed him like a very brither;
They had been fou for weeks thegither.
The night drave on wi' sangs and clatter;
And ay the ale was growing better:
The landlady and Tam grew gracious
Wi' secret favours, sweet and precious:
The Souter tauld his queerest stories;
The landlord's laugh was ready chorus:
The storm without might rair and rustle,
Tam did na mind the storm a whistle.

Care, mad to see a man sae happy,
E'en drown'd himsel amang the nappy.
As bees flee hame wi' lades o' treasure,
The minutes wing'd their way wi' pleasure:
Kings may be blest but Tam was glorious,
O'er a' the ills o' life victorious !

But pleasures are like poppies spread:
You seize the flow'r, its bloom is shed;
Or like the snow falls in the river,
A moment white — then melts for ever;
Or like the borealis race,
That flit ere you can point their place;
Or like the rainbow's lovely form
Evanishing amid the storm.
Nae man can tether time or tide;
The hour approaches Tam maun ride:
That hour, o' night's black arch the key-
     stane,
That dreary hour Tam mounts his beast in;
And sic a night he taks the road in,
As ne'er poor sinner was abroad in.

The wind blew as 't wad blawn its last;
The rattling showers rose on the blast;
The speedy gleams the darkness swallow'd;
Loud, deep, and lang the thunder bellow'd:
That night, a child might understand,
The Deil had business on his hand.

Weel mounted on his gray mare Meg,
A better never lifted leg,

Tam skelpit on thro' dub and mire,
Despising wind, and rain, and fire;
Whiles holding fast his guid blue bonnet,
Whiles crooning o'er some auld Scots
     sonnet,
Whiles glow'ring round wi' prudent cares,
Lest bogles catch him unawares:
Kirk-Alloway was drawing nigh,
Whare ghaists and houlets nightly cry.

By this time he was cross the ford,
Whare in the snaw the chapman smoor'd;
And past the birks and meikle stane,
Whare drunken Charlie brak 's neck-bane;
And thro' the whins, and by the cairn,
Whare hunters fand the murder'd bairn;
And near the thorn, aboon the well,
Whare Mungo's mither hang'd hersel.
Before him Doon pours all his floods;
The doubling storm roars thro' the woods;
The lightnings flash from pole to pole;
Near and more near the thunders roll:
When, glimmering thro' the groaning
     trees,
Kirk-Alloway seem'd in a bleeze,
Thro' ilka bore the beams were glancing,
And loud resounded mirth and dancing.

Inspiring bold John Barleycorn,
What dangers thou canst make us scorn !
Wi' tippenny, we fear nae evil;
Wi' usquabae, we 'll face the Devil !
The swats sae ream'd in Tammie's noddle,
Fair play, he car'd na deils a boddle.
But Maggie stood, right sair astonish'd,
Till, by the heel and hand admonish'd,
She ventur'd forward on the light;
And, vow ! Tam saw an unco sight !

Warlocks and witches in a dance:
Nae cotillion, brent new frae France,
But hornpipes, jigs, strathspeys, and reels,
Put life and mettle in their heels.
A winnock-bunker in the east,
There sat Auld Nick, in shape o' beast;
A tousie tyke, black, grim, and large,
To gie them music was his charge:
He screw'd the pipes and gart them skirl,
Till roof and rafters a' did dirl.
Coffins stood round, like open presses,
That shaw'd the dead in their last dresses;
And, by some devilish cantraip sleight,
Each in its cauld hand held a light:
By which heroic Tam was able

To note upon the haly table,
A murderer's banes, in gibbet-airns;
Twa span-lang, wee, unchristen'd bairns;
A thief new-cutted frae a rape —
Wi' his last gasp his gab did gape;
Five tomahawks wi' bluid red-rusted;
Five scymitars wi' murder crusted;
A garter which a babe had strangled;
A knife a father's throat had mangled —
Whom his ain son o' life bereft —
The grey-hairs yet stack to the heft;
Wi' mair of horrible and awefu',
Which even to name wad be unlawfu'.

As Tammie glowr'd, amaz'd, and curious,
The mirth and fun grew fast and furious;
The piper loud and louder blew,
The dancers quick and quicker flew,
They reel'd, they set, they cross'd, they cleekit,
Till ilka carlin swat and reekit,
And coost her duddies to the wark,
And linket at it in her sark !

Now Tam, O Tam ! had thae been queans,
A' plump and strapping in their teens !
Their sarks, instead o' creeshie flannen,
Been snaw-white seventeen hunder linen ! —
Thir breeks o' mine, my only pair,
That ance were plush, o' guid blue hair,
I wad hae gi'en them off my hurdies
For ae blink o' the bonie burdies !

But wither'd beldams, auld and droll,
Rigwoodie hags wad spean a foal,
Louping and flinging on a crummock,
I wonder did na turn thy stomach !

But Tam kend what was what fu' brawlie:
There was ae winsome wench and wawlie,
That night enlisted in the core,
Lang after kend on Carrick shore
(For monie a beast to dead she shot,
An' perish'd monie a bonie boat,
And shook baith meikle corn and bear,
And kept the country-side in fear).
Her cutty sark, o' Paisley harn,
That while a lassie she had worn,
In longitude tho' sorely scanty,
It was her best, and she was vauntie. . . .
Ah ! little kend thy reverend grannie,

That sark she coft for her wee Nannie,
Wi' twa pund Scots ('t was a' her riches),
Wad ever grac'd a dance of witches !

But here my Muse her wing maun cour,
Sic flights are far beyond her power:
To sing how Nannie lap and flang
(A souple jad she was and strang),
And how Tam stood like ane bewitch'd,
And thought his very een enrich'd;
Even Satan glowr'd, and fidg'd fu' fain,
And hotch'd and blew wi' might and main;
Till first ae caper, syne anither,
Tam tint his reason a' thegither,
And roars out: " Weel done, Cutty-sark ! "
And in an instant all was dark;
And scarcely had he Maggie rallied,
When out the hellish legion sallied.

As bees bizz out wi' angry fyke,
When plundering herds assail their byke;
As open pussie's mortal foes,
When, pop ! she starts before their nose;
As eager runs the market-crowd,
When " Catch the thief ! " resounds aloud:
So Maggie runs, the witches follow,
Wi' monie an eldritch skriech and hollo.

Ah, Tam ! ah, Tam ! thou 'll get thy fairin !
In hell they 'll roast thee like a herrin !
In vain thy Kate awaits thy comin !
Kate soon will be a woefu' woman !
Now, do thy speedy utmost, Meg,
And win the key-stane of the brig;
There, at them thou thy tail may toss,
A running stream they dare na cross !
But ere the key-stane she could make,
The fient a tail she had to shake;
For Nannie, far before the rest,
Hard upon noble Maggie prest,
And flew at Tam wi' furious ettle;
But little wist she Maggie's mettle !
Ae spring brought off her master hale,
But left behind her ain grey tail:
The carlin claught her by the rump,
And left poor Maggie scarce a stump.

Now, wha this tale o' truth shall read,
Ilk man, and mother's son, take heed:
Whene'er to drink you are inclin'd,
Or cutty sarks run in your mind,
Think ! ye may buy the joys o'er dear:
Remember Tam o' Shanter's mare.

ON SEEING A WOUNDED HARE LIMP BY ME WHICH A FELLOW HAD JUST SHOT AT

On 21st April, 1789, Burns enclosed a copy of this production in an unpublished letter to Mrs. Dunlop: "Two mornings ago, as I was at a very early hour sowing in the fields, I heard a shot, and presently a poor little hare limped by me apparently very much hurt. You will easily guess this set my humanity in tears and my indignation in arms. The following was the result, which please read to the young ladies. I believe you may include the Major too, as whatever I have said of shooting hares I have not spoken one irreverent word against coursing them. This is according to your just right the very first copy I wrote." Enclosing a draft to Alexander Cunningham, 4th May, 1789 (in a letter only partly published in any collection of the *Correspondence*), Burns, after a somewhat similar account of the incident, added: "You will guess my indignation at the inhuman fellow who could shoot a hare at this season, when all of them have young ones; and it gave me no little gloomy satisfaction to see the poor injured creature escape him." On 2d June, 1789, Dr. Gregory sent to Burns a somewhat supercilious criticism, which induced him (however) to change one or two expressions for the better. Regarding the measure Dr. Gregory remarked that it was "not a good one;" that it did not "flow well," and that the rhyme of the fourth line was "almost lost by its distance from the first, and the two interposed close rhymes:" hence, "Dr. Gregory is a good man, but he crucifies me" (R. B.). Burns's use of his stanza is groping and tentative; and the effect of his piece is one of mere frigidity.

I

INHUMAN man! curse on thy barb'rous art,
And blasted be thy murder-aiming eye;
May never pity soothe thee with a sigh,
Nor never pleasure glad thy cruel heart!

II

Go live, poor wanderer of the wood and field,
The bitter little that of life remains!
No more the thickening brakes and verdant plains
To thee shall home, or food, or pastime yield.

III

Seek, mangled wretch, some place of wonted rest,
No more of rest, but now thy dying bed!
The sheltering rushes whistling o'er thy head,
The cold earth with thy bloody bosom prest.

IV

Oft as by winding Nith I, musing, wait
The sober eve, or hail the cheerful dawn,
I'll miss thee sporting o'er the dewy lawn,
And curse the ruffian's aim, and mourn thy hapless fate.

ADDRESS TO THE SHADE OF THOMSON

ON CROWNING HIS BUST AT EDNAM, ROXBURGHSHIRE, WITH A WREATH OF BAYS

When, in 1791, the eccentric Earl of Buchan instituted an annual festival in commemoration of James Thomson, by crowning, with a wreath of bays, a bust of the poet surmounting the Ionic temple erected in his honour on the grounds in Dryburgh, he sent an invitation to Burns and suggested that he might compose an ode. Burns was harvesting, and must needs decline; but, in regard to the second half of the invitation, he (29th August, 1791) wrote as follows: "Your lordship hints at an ode for the occasion; but who would write after Collins? I read over his verses to the memory of Thomson and despaired. I attempted three or four stanzas, in the way of address to the shade of the Bard, on crowning his bust. I trouble your lordship with the enclosed copy of them, which, I am afraid, will be but too convincing a proof how unequal I am to the task you would obligingly assign me." The piece is closely modelled upon Collins's ode.

I

WHILE virgin Spring by Eden's flood
Unfolds her tender mantle green,
Or pranks the sod in frolic mood,
Or tunes Eolian strains between:

II

While Summer, with a matron grace,
　Retreats to Dryburgh's cooling shade,
Yet oft, delighted, stops to trace
　The progress of the spikey blade:

III

While Autumn, benefactor kind,
　By Tweed erects his aged head,
And sees, with self-approving mind,
　Each creature on his bounty fed:

IV

While maniac Winter rages o'er
　The hills whence classic Yarrow flows,
Rousing the turbid torrent's roar,
　Or sweeping, wild, a waste of snows:

V

So long, sweet Poet of the year!
　Shall bloom that wreath thou well has
　　won;
While Scotia, with exulting tear,
　Proclaims that Thomson was her son.

ON THE LATE CAPTAIN GROSE'S PEREGRINATIONS THRO' SCOTLAND

COLLECTING THE ANTIQUITIES OF THAT KINGDOM

The son of Francis Grose, a Swiss, who had settled as a jeweller at Richmond, Surrey, Francis Grose was born at Greenford, Middlesex, about 1731; was educated as an artist, and exhibited at the Royal Academy; in 1755 became Richmond Herald; was made Adjutant in the Hampshire, and latterly Captain and Adjutant in the Surrey militias; published *Antiquities of England and Wales*, 1773–1787; made the acquaintance of Burns during his antiquarian tour in Scotland in 1789 (see *ante*, p. 90, headnote to *Tam o' Shanter*); published *Antiquities of Scotland*, 1789–1791; was author of many treatises in different branches of antiquarian lore, as well as various miscellaneous works — among them an excellent *Dictionary of the Vulgar Tongue* (1785); and died (of apoplexy) 12th May, 1791. His remarkable corpulence is suggested in the *Epigram on Captain Francis Grose* (see *post*, p. 186); and his wanderings are further denoted in the

lively verses beginning "Ken ye ought o' Captain Grose?" (p. 122). He had his own share of humour, and was an "inimitable boon companion."

I

HEAR, Land o' Cakes, and brither Scots
Frae Maidenkirk to Johnie Groat's,
If there's a hole in a' your coats,
　　I rede you tent it:
A chield's amang you takin notes,
　　And faith he'll prent it:

II

If in your bounds ye chance to light
Upon a fine, fat, fodgel wight,
O' stature short but genius bright,
　　That's he, mark weel:
And wow! he has an unco sleight
　　O' cauk and keel.

III

By some auld, houlet-haunted biggin,
Or kirk deserted by its riggin,
It's ten to ane ye'll find him snug in
　　Some eldritch part,
Wi' deils, they say, Lord safe's! colleaguin
　　At some black art.

IV

Ilk ghaist that haunts auld ha' or chamer,
Ye gipsy-gang that deal in glamour,
And you, deep-read in hell's black grammar,
　　Warlocks and witches:
Ye'll quake at his conjúring hammer,
　　Ye midnight bitches!

V

It's tauld he was a sodger bred,
And ane wad rather fa'n than fled;
But now he's quat the spurtle-blade
　　And dog-skin wallet,
And taen the— Antiquarian trade,
　　I think they call it.

VI

He has a fouth o' auld nick-nackets:
Rusty airn caps and jinglin jackets
Wad haud the Lothians three in tackets
　　A towmont guid;
And parritch-pats and auld saut-backets
　　Before the Flood.

VII

Of Eve's first fire he has a cinder;
Auld Tubalcain's fire-shool and fender;
That which distinguishèd the gender
    O' Balaam's ass:
A broomstick o' the witch of Endor,
    Weel shod wi' brass.

VIII

Forbye, he 'll shape you aff fu' gleg
The cut of Adam's philibeg;
The knife that nicket Abel's craig
    He 'll prove you fully,
It was a faulding jocteleg,
    Or lang-kail gullie.

IX

But wad ye see him in his glee —
For meikle glee and fun has he —
Then set him down, and twa or three
    Guid fellows wi' him;
And port, O port! shine thou a wee,
    And then ye 'll see him!

X

Now, by the Pow'rs o' verse and prose!
Thou art a dainty chield, O Grose! —
Whae'er o' thee shall ill suppose,
    They sair misca' thee;
I 'd take the rascal by the nose,
    Wad say, "Shame fa' thee."

TO MISS CRUICKSHANK

A VERY YOUNG LADY

WRITTEN ON THE BLANK LEAF OF A BOOK
PRESENTED TO HER BY THE AUTHOR

Miss Jane Cruickshank, to whom these lines were addressed, was the daughter of the poet's friend, Mr. William Cruickshank, of the High School, Edinburgh, and was then about twelve or thirteen years old. In June, 1804, she married James Henderson, writer, of Jedburgh. She also inspired *A Rosebud by my Early Walk*. The present piece appears to have been written under the inspiration of "Namby-Pamby" Phillips (*d*. 1749).

BEAUTEOUS Rosebud, young and gay,
Blooming on thy early May,
Never may'st thou, lovely flower,

Chilly shrink in sleety shower!
Never Boreas' hoary path,
Never Eurus' pois'nous breath,
Never baleful stellar lights,
Taint thee with untimely blights!
Never, never reptile thief
Riot on thy virgin leaf!
Nor even Sol too fiercely view
Thy bosom blushing still with dew!

May'st thou long, sweet crimson gem,
Richly deck thy native stem;
Till some ev'ning, sober, calm,
Dropping dews and breathing balm,
While all around the woodland rings,
And ev'ry bird thy requiem sings,
Thou, amid the dirgeful sound,
Shed thy dying honours round,
And resign to parent Earth
The loveliest form she e'er gave birth.

SONG: ANNA, THY CHARMS

Scott Douglas, on plausible evidence, conjectured that this song referred to a sweetheart of Alexander Cunningham, and that it was a "vicarious effusion." His conjecture can now be fully substantiated. In an unpublished part of a letter to Cunningham, 4th May, 1789, Burns wrote: "The publisher of *The Star* has been polite. He may find his account for it, though I would scorn to put my name to a newspaper poem — one instance, indeed, excepted. I mean your two stanzas. Had the lady kept her character she should have kept my verses; but as she has prostituted the one [by marrying in January, 1789], and no longer made anything of the other; so sent them to Stuart as a bribe in my earnestness to be cleared from the foul aspersions respecting the D—— of G——" [Duchess of Gordon]. The piece appeared in Stuart's *Star*, 18th April, 1789. Burns also enclosed a copy to Mrs. Dunlop: "The following is a *jeu d'esprit* of t' other day on a despairing lover leading me to see his Dulcinea."

I

ANNA, thy charms my bosom fire,
    And waste my soul with care;
But ah! how bootless to admire
    When fated to despair!

II

Yet in thy presence, lovely Fair,
    To hope may be forgiven:

For sure 't were impious to despair
  So much in sight of Heaven.

ON READING IN A NEWSPAPER THE DEATH OF JOHN M'LEOD, ESQ.

BROTHER TO A YOUNG LADY, A PARTICULAR FRIEND OF THE AUTHOR'S

Burns made the acquaintance of Miss Isabella M'Leod during his first visit to Edinburgh. Her brother, John M'Leod of Rasay — the representative of the main Lewis branch of the clan — died 20th July, 1787. In reference to other misfortunes of the family Burns wrote his *Raving Winds around her Blowing*. In a MS. note, " This poetic compliment," he says, " what few poetic compliments are, was from the heart."

I

SAD thy tale, thou idle page,
  And rueful thy alarms:
Death tears the brother of her love
  From Isabella's arms.

II

Sweetly deckt with pearly dew
  The morning rose may blow;
But cold successive noontide blasts
  May lay its beauties low.

III

Fair on Isabella's morn
  The sun propitious smil'd;
But, long ere noon, succeeding clouds
  Succeeding hopes beguil'd.

IV

Fate oft tears the bosom-chords
  That Nature finest strung:
So Isabella's heart was form'd,
  And so that heart was wrung.

V

Dread Omnipotence alone
  Can heal the wound he gave —
Can point the brimful, grief-worn eyes
  To scenes beyond the grave.

VI

Virtue's blossoms there shall blow,
  And fear no withering blast;

There Isabella's spotless worth
  Shall happy be at last.

THE HUMBLE PETITION OF BRUAR WATER

TO THE NOBLE DUKE OF ATHOLE

Burns spent two days with the family of the Duke of Atholl during his northern tour in August, 1787; and in the *Glenriddell Book*, in which the *Humble Petition* is inscribed, he wrote: " God, who knows all things, knows how my heart aches with the throes of gratitude, whenever I recollect my reception at the noble house of Atholl." In a letter to Professor Josiah Walker, enclosing the poem, he stated that " it was, at least the most part of it, the effusion of a half hour " at Bruar. But, he adds, " I do not mean it was extempore, for I have endeavoured to brush it up as well as Mr. Nicoll's chat and the jogging of the chaise would allow."

I.

My lord, I know, your noble ear
  Woe ne'er assails in vain;
Embolden'd thus, I beg you 'll hear
  Your humble slave complain,
How saucy Phœbus' scorching beams,
  In flaming summer-pride,
Dry-withering, waste my foamy streams,
  And drink my crystal tide.

II

The lightly-jumping, glowrin trouts,
  That thro' my waters play,
If, in their random, wanton spouts,
  They near the margin stray;
If, hapless chance! they linger lang,
  I 'm scorching up so shallow,
They 're left the whitening stanes amang
  In gasping death to wallow.

III

Last day I grat wi' spite and teen,
  As Poet Burns came by,
That, to a Bard, I should be seen
  Wi' half my channel dry;
A panegyric rhyme, I ween,
  Ev'n as I was, he shor'd me;
But had I in my glory been,
  He, kneeling, wad ador'd me.

IV

Here, foaming down the skelvy rocks,
  In twisting strength I rin;
There high my boiling torrent smokes,
  Wild-roaring o'er a linn:
Enjoying large each spring and well,
  As Nature gave them me,
I am, altho' I say 't mysel,
  Worth gaun a mile to see.

V

Would, then, my noble master please
  To grant my highest wishes,
He 'll shade my banks wi' tow'ring trees
  And bonie spreading bushes.
Delighted doubly then, my lord,
  You 'll wander on my banks,
And listen monie a grateful bird
  Return you tuneful thanks.

VI

The sober laverock, warbling wild,
  Shall to the skies aspire;
The gowdspink, Music's gayest child,
  Shall sweetly join the choir;
The blackbird strong, the lintwhite clear,
  The mavis mild and mellow,
The robin, pensive Autumn cheer
  In all her locks of yellow.

VII

This, too, a covert shall ensure
  To shield them from the storm;
And coward maukin sleep secure,
  Low in her grassy form:
Here shall the shepherd make his seat
  To weave his crown of flow'rs;
Or find a shelt'ring, safe retreat
  From prone-descending show'rs.

VIII

And here, by sweet, endearing stealth,
  Shall meet the loving pair,
Despising worlds with all their wealth,
  As empty idle care:
The flow'rs shall vie, in all their charms,
  The hour of heav'n to grace;
And birks extend their fragrant arms
  To screen the dear embrace.

IX

Here haply too, at vernal dawn,
  Some musing Bard may stray,
And eye the smoking, dewy lawn

And misty mountain grey;
Or, by the reaper's nightly beam,
  Mild-chequering thro' the trees,
Rave to my darkly dashing stream,
  Hoarse-swelling on the breeze.

X

Let lofty firs and ashes cool
  My lowly banks o'erspread,
And view, deep-bending in the pool,
  Their shadows' wat'ry bed:
Let fragrant birks, in woodbines drest,
  My craggy cliffs adorn,
And, for the little songster's nest,
  The close embow'ring thorn !

XI

So may, old Scotia's darling hope,
  Your little angel band
Spring, like their fathers, up to prop
  Their honour'd native land !
So may, thro' Albion's farthest ken,
  To social-flowing glasses,
The grace be : " Athole's honest men
  And Athole's bonie lasses ! "

ON SCARING SOME WATER-FOWL IN LOCH TURIT

A WILD SCENE AMONG THE HILLS OF OUGHTERTYRE

Thus presented in the *Glenriddell Book MS.*
"This was the production of a solitary fore-
noon's walk from Oughtertyre House. I lived
there, the guest of Sir William Murray, for two
or three weeks [October, 1787], and was much
flattered by my hospitable reception. What a
pity that the mere emotions of gratitude are so
impotent in this world! 'T is lucky that, as
we are told, they will be of some avail in the
world to come."

WHY, ye tenants of the lake,
For me your wat'ry haunt forsake ?
Tell me, fellow creatures, why
At my presence thus you fly ?
Why disturb your social joys,
Parent, filial, kindred ties ? —
Common friend to you and me,
Nature's gifts to all are free:
Peaceful keep your dimpling wave,
Busy feed, or wanton lave;

Or, beneath the sheltering rock,
Bide the surging billow's shock.

Conscious, blushing for our race,
Soon, too soon, your fears I trace.
Man, your proud, usurping foe,
Would be lord of all below:
Plumes himself in freedom's pride,
Tyrant stern to all beside.

The eagle, from the cliffy brow
Marking you his prey below,
In his breast no pity dwells,
Strong necessity compels:
But Man, to whom alone is giv'n
A ray direct from pitying Heav'n,
Glories in his heart humane —
And creatures for his pleasure slain!

In these savage, liquid plains,
Only known to wand'ring swains,
Where the mossy riv'let strays
Far from human haunts and ways,
All on Nature you depend,
And life's poor season peaceful spend.

Or, if Man's superior might
Dare invade your native right,
On the lofty ether borne,
Man with all his powers you scorn;
Swiftly seek, on clanging wings,
Other lakes, and other springs;
And the foe you cannot brave,
Scorn at least to be his slave.

VERSES WRITTEN WITH A PENCIL

OVER THE CHIMNEY-PIECE, IN THE PAR-
LOUR OF THE INN AT KENMORE, TAY-
MOUTH

Burns visited Taymouth on 29th August,
1787. The piece is inscribed in the *Glenriddell
Book* in the hand of an amanuensis, with the
following note by Burns: "I wrote this with
a pencil over the chimney-piece in the parlour
of the inn at Kenmore, at the outlet of Loch
Tay."

ADMIRING Nature in her wildest grace,
These northern scenes with weary feet I
trace;
O'er many a winding dale and painful steep,

Th' abodes of covey'd grouse and timid
sheep,
My savage journey, curious, I pursue,
Till fam'd Breadalbane opens to my view.
The meeting cliffs each deep-sunk glen
divides:
The woods, wild-scatter'd, clothe their
ample sides;
Th' outstretching lake, imbosomed 'mong
the hills,
The eye with wonder and amazement fills:
The Tay meand'ring sweet in infant pride,
The palace rising on his verdant side,
The lawns wood-fring'd in Nature's native
taste,
The hillocks dropt in Nature's careless
haste,
The arches striding o'er the new-born
stream,
The village glittering in the noontide
beam —
. . . .
Poetic ardors in my bosom swell,
Lone wand'ring by the hermit's mossy cell;
The sweeping theatre of hanging woods,
Th' incessant roar of headlong tumbling
floods —
. . . .
Here Poesy might wake her heav'n-taught
lyre,
And look through Nature with creative
fire;
Here, to the wrongs of Fate half reconcil'd,
Misfortune's lighten'd steps might wander
wild;
And Disappointment, in these lonely bounds,
Find balm to soothe her bitter rankling
wounds;
Here heart-struck Grief might heav'nward
stretch her scan,
And injur'd Worth forget and pardon man.
. . . .

LINES ON THE FALL OF FYERS NEAR LOCH NESS

WRITTEN WITH A PENCIL ON THE SPOT

Burns visited the Fall of Foyers on 5th
September, 1787. In a note in the *Glenrid-
dell Book*, where the poem is inscribed by
an amanuensis, "I composed these lines," he
wrote, "standing on the brink of the hideous
cauldron below the waterfall."

AMONG the heathy hills and ragged woods
The roaring Fyers pours his mossy floods;
Till full he dashes on the rocky mounds,
Where, thro' a shapeless breach, his stream
    resounds.
As high in air the bursting torrents flow,
As deep recoiling surges foam below,
Prone down the rock the whitening sheet
    descends,
And viewless Echo's ear, astonish'd, rends.
Dim-seen through rising mists and cease-
    less show'rs,
The hoary cavern, wide-surrounding, lours:
Still thro' the gap the struggling river
    toils,
And still, below, the horrid caldron boils —

. . . .

ON THE BIRTH OF A POSTHU-
MOUS CHILD

BORN IN PECULIAR CIRCUMSTANCES
OF FAMILY DISTRESS

In the *Glenriddell Book* — where the poem
is inscribed — Burns explains that it is "on
the birth of Mons. Henri, posthumous child to
a Mons. Henri, a gentleman of family and
fortune from Switzerland; who died in three
days' illness, leaving his lady, a sister of Sir
Thomas Wallace, in her sixth month of this
her first child. The lady and her family were
particular friends of the author (she was a
daughter of Mrs. Dunlop). The child was
born in November, '90." On receiving the
news of the birth Burns wrote to Mrs. Dunlop:
"How could such a mercurial creature as a
poet lumpishly keep his seat on receipt of the
best news from his best friend? I seized my
gilt-headed Wangee rod — an instrument indis-
pensably necessary — in my left hand, in the
moment of inspiration and rapture; and stride,
stride — quick and quicker — out skipt I
among the broomy banks of Nith to muse over
my joy by retail. To keep within the bounds
of prose was impossible. . . . I, almost extem-
pore, poured out to him in the following
verses."

I

SWEET flow'ret, pledge o' meikle love,
    And ward o' monie a prayer,
What heart o' stane wad thou na move,
    Sae helpless, sweet, and fair!

II

November hirples o'er the lea,
    Chill, on thy lovely form;
And gane, alas! the shelt'ring tree,
    Should shield thee frae the storm.

III

May He who gives the rain to pour,
    And wings the blast to blaw,
Protect thee frae the driving show'r,
    The bitter frost and snaw!

IV

May He, the friend of Woe and Want,
    Who heals life's various stounds,
Protect and guard the mother plant,
    And heal her cruel wounds!

V

But late she flourish'd, rooted fast,
    Fair on the summer morn,
Now feebly bends she in the blast,
    Unshelter'd and forlorn.

VI

Blest be thy bloom, thou lovely gem,
    Unscath'd by ruffian hand!
And from thee many a parent stem
    Arise to deck our land!

THE WHISTLE

A BALLAD

Thus prefaced by Burns: "As the authen-
tic *Prose* history of the Whistle is curious, I
shall here give it. In the train of Anne of
Denmark, when she came to Scotland with our
James the Sixth, there came over also a Danish
gentleman of gigantic stature and great prow-
ess, and a matchless champion of Bacchus. He
had a little ebony Whistle, which, at the com-
mencement of the orgies, he laid on the table;
and whoever was last able to blow it, every-
body else being disabled by the potency of the
bottle, was to carry off the Whistle, as a trophy
of victory. The Dane produced credentials of
his victories, without a single defeat, at the
courts of Copenhagen, Stockholm, Moscow,
Warsaw, and several of the petty courts in
Germany; and challenged the Scots Baccha-
nalians to the alternative of trying his prow-
ess, or else of acknowledging their inferiority.
After many overthrows on the part of the

Scots, the Dane was encountered by Sir Robert Laurie of Maxwelton, ancestor to the present worthy baronet of that name ; who, after three days and three nights' hard contest, left the Scandinavian under the table, ' and blew on the Whistle his requiem shrill.'

"Sir Walter, son to Sir Robert before mentioned, afterwards lost the Whistle to Walter Riddell of Glenriddell, who had married a sister of Sir Walter's. On Friday, the 16th October, 1790, at Friars-Carse, the Whistle was once more contended for, as related in the Ballad, by the present Sir Robert Laurie of Maxwelton ; Robert Riddell, Esq., of Glenriddell, lineal descendant and representative of Walter Riddell, who won the Whistle, and in whose family it had continued ; and Alexander Ferguson, Esq., of Craigdarroch, likewise descended of the great Sir Robert, which last gentleman carried off the hard-won honors of the field."

In this Prefatory Note Burns misdates the contest by a year, as is proved by (1) the date of a letter — 16th October, 1789 — to Captain Riddell, in which he refers to the contest of the evening ; and (2) by the memorandum of the "Bett," now in the possession of Sir Robert Jardine of Castlemilk, first published in *Notes and Queries*, Second Series, vol. x. (1860), p. 423 : —

DOQUET

The original Bett between Sir Robert Laurie and Craigdarroch, for the noted Whistle, which is so much celebrated by Robert Burns' Poems — in which Bett I was named Judge — 1789.

The Bett decided at Carse — 16th October, 1789.

Won by Craigdarroch — he drank upds. of 5 Bottles of Claret.

MEMORANDUM FOR THE WHISTLE

The Whistle gained by Sir Robert Laurie (now) in possession of Mr. Riddell of Glenriddell, is to be ascertained to the heirs of the said Sir Robert now existing, being Sir R. L., Mr. R. of G., and Mr. F. of C. — to be settled under the arbitration of Mr. Jn. M'Murdo : the business to be decided at Carse, the 16th of October, 1789.

(Signed)　　ALEX. FERGUSON.
　　　　　　 R. LAURIE.
　　　　　　 ROBT. RIDDELL.

COWHILL, 10th October, 1789.

John M'Murdo accepts as Judge.
Geo. Johnston witness, to be present.
Patrick Miller witness, to be pre. if possible.

Minute of Bett between Sir Robert Laurie and Craigdarroch, 1789.

The question whether or not Burns was present has been hotly debated. The references in his letter on the day of the fight, as well as the terms of the "Bett," seem to show

that, tradition notwithstanding, he was not. But there are no data for an absolute conclusion. For the stanza, see *ante*, p. 79, Prefatory Note to *No Churchman Am I.*

I

I SING of a Whistle, a Whistle of worth,
I sing of a Whistle, the pride of the North,
Was brought to the court of our good
　　　　Scottish King,
And long with this Whistle all Scotland
　　shall ring.

II

Old Loda, still rueing the arm of Fingal,
The God of the Bottle sends down from
　　his hall :
"This Whistle 's your challenge, to Scotland get o'er,
And drink them to Hell, Sir ! or ne'er see
　　me more ! "

III

Old poets have sung, and old chronicles
　　tell,
What champions ventur'd, what champions
　　fell :
The son of great Loda was conqueror still,
And blew on the Whistle their requiem
　　shrill.

IV

Till Robert, the lord of the Cairn and the
　　Scaur,
Unmatch'd at the bottle, unconquer'd in
　　war,
He drank his poor god-ship as deep as the
　　sea ;
No tide of the Baltic e'er drunker than
　　he.

V

Thus Robert, victorious, the trophy has
　　gain'd ;
Which now in his house has for ages remain'd ;
Till three noble chieftains, and all of his
　　blood,
The jovial contest again have renew'd.

VI

Three joyous good fellows, with hearts
　　clear of flaw ;
Craigdarroch, so famous for wit, worth,
　　and law ;

And trusty Glenriddel, so skilled in old
coins;
And gallant Sir Robert, deep-read in old
wines.

VII

Craigdarroch began, with a tongue smooth
as oil,
Desiring Glenriddel to yield up the spoil;
Or else he would muster the heads of the
clan,
And once more, in claret, try which was
the man.

VIII

" By the gods of the ancients ! " Glenriddel
replies,
" Before I surrender so glorious a prize,
I 'll conjure the ghost of the great Rorie
More,
And bumper his horn with him twenty
times o'er."

IX

Sir Robert, a soldier, no speech would pre-
tend,
But he ne'er turn'd his back on his foe, or
his friend;
Said: — " Toss down the Whistle, the prize
of the field,"
And, knee-deep in claret, he 'd die ere he 'd
yield.

X

To the board of Glenriddel our heroes re-
pair,
So noted for drowning of sorrow and care;
But for wine and for welcome not more
known to fame
Than the sense, wit, and taste, of a sweet
lovely dame.

XI

A Bard was selected to witness the fray,
And tell future ages the feats of the day;
A Bard who detested all sadness and
spleen,
And wish'd that Parnassus a vineyard had
been.

XII

The dinner being over, the claret they ply,
And ev'ry new cork is a new spring of joy;
In the bands of old friendship and kindred
so set,
And the bands grew the tighter the more
they were wet.

XIII

Gay Pleasure ran riot as bumpers ran o'er;
Bright Phœbus ne'er witness'd so joyous a
core,
And vow'd that to leave them he was quite
forlorn,
Till Cynthia hinted he 'd see them next
morn.

XIV

Six bottles a-piece had well wore out the
night,
When gallant Sir Robert, to finish the fight,
Turn'd o'er in one bumper a bottle of red,
And swore 't was the way that their ances-
tor did.

XV

Then worthy Glenriddel, so cautious and
sage,
No longer the warfare ungodly would wage:
A high Ruling Elder to wallow in wine !
He left the foul business to folks less di-
vine.

XVI

The gallant Sir Robert fought hard to the
end;
But who can with Fate and quart bumpers
contend ?
Though Fate said, a hero should perish in
light;
So uprose bright Phœbus — and down fell
the knight.

XVII

Next uprose our Bard, like a prophet in
drink : —
" Craigdarroch, thou 'lt soar when creation
shall sink !
But if thou would flourish immortal in
rhyme,
Come — one bottle more — and have at the
sublime !

XVIII

" Thy line, that have struggled for freedom
with Bruce,
Shall heroes and patriots ever produce:
So thine be the laurel, and mine be the bay;
The field thou hast won, by yon bright God
of Day ! "

POSTHUMOUS PIECES

[THE poems included in this general division were gathered for the Centenary Edition from various periodicals, from the several series of tracts by Stewart and Meikle, Glasgow, originally published at a penny or twopence each, from similar cheap publications, from the more or less complete editions of Burns's works, and from manuscripts not before printed.]

THE JOLLY BEGGARS

A CANTATA

The Burns of this " puissant and splendid production," as Matthew Arnold calls it — this irresistible presentation of humanity caught in the act and summarised for ever in the terms of art — comes into line with divers poets of repute, from our own Dekker and John Fletcher to the singer of *les Gueux* (1813) and *le Vieux Vagabond* (1830), and approves himself their master in the matter of such qualities as humour, vision, lyrical potency, descriptive style, and the faculty of swift, dramatic presentation to a purpose that may not be gainsaid. It was suggested by a chance visit (in company with Richmond and Smith) to the " doss-house " of Poosie Nansie, as Agnes Gibson was nicknamed (see *post*, p. 334, Note to Recitativo I, line 9), in the Cowgate, Mauchline. This " ken " stood directly opposite Johnie Dow's tavern (The Whitefoord Arms). Thence issuing, the three friends heard a sound of revelry at Poosie Nansie's, whose company they joined. And a few days afterwards Burns recited several bits of the cantata to Richmond.

RECITATIVO

I

WHEN lyart leaves bestrow the yird,
Or, wavering like the bauckie-bird,
  Bedim cauld Boreas' blast;
When hailstanes drive wi' bitter skyte,
And infant frosts begin to bite,
  In hoary cranreuch drest;
Ae night at e'en a merry core
  O' randie, gangrel bodies
In Poosie-Nansie's held the splore,
  To drink their orra duddies:
    Wi' quaffing and laughing
      They ranted an' they sang,
    Wi' jumping an' thumping
      The vera girdle rang.

II

First, niest the fire, in auld red rags
Ane sat, weel brac'd wi' mealy bags
  And knapsack a' in order;
His doxy lay within his arm;
Wi' usquebae an' blankets warm,
  She blinket on her sodger.
An' ay he gies the tozie drab
  The tither skelpin kiss,
While she held up her greedy gab
  Just like an aumous dish:
    Ilk smack still did crack still
      Like onie cadger's whup;
    Then, swaggering an' staggering,
      He roar'd this ditty up: —

AIR

TUNE : *Soldiers Joy*

I

I am a son of Mars, who have been in many
    wars,
  And show my cuts and scars wherever I
    come:
This here was for a wench, and that other
    in a trench
  When welcoming the French at the
    sound of the drum.
                    Lal de daudle, etc.

II

My prenticeship I past, where my leader
    breath'd his last,
  When the bloody die was cast on the
    heights of Abrâm;
And I servèd out my trade when the gallant game was play'd,
  And the Moro low was laid at the sound
    of the drum.

III

I lastly was with Curtis among the floating
    batt'ries,
  And there I left for witness an arm and
    a limb;
Yet let my country need me, with Eliott to
    head me
  I'd clatter on my stumps at the sound
    of the drum.

IV

And now, tho' I must beg with a wooden
    arm and leg
  And many a tatter'd rag hanging over
    my bum,
I'm as happy with my wallet, my bottle,
    and my callet
  As when I us'd in scarlet to follow a
    drum.

V

What tho' with hoary locks I must stand
    the winter shocks,
  Beneath the woods and rocks oftentimes
    for a home?
When the tother bag I sell, and the tother
    bottle tell,
  I could meet a troop of Hell at the sound
    of a drum.
                Lal de daudle, etc.

RECITATIVO

He ended; and the kebars sheuk
  Aboon the chorus roar;
While frighted rattons backward leuk,
  An' seek the benmost bore:
A fairy fiddler frae the neuk,
  He skirl'd out *Encore!*
But up arose the martial chuck,
  An' laid the loud uproar: —

AIR

TUNE: *Sodger Laddie*

I

I once was a maid, tho' I cannot tell when,
And still my delight is in proper young
    men.
Some one of a troop of dragoons was my
    daddie:
No wonder I'm fond of a sodger laddie!
          Sing, lal de dal, etc.

II

The first of my loves was a swaggering
    blade:
To rattle the thundering drum was his
    trade;
His leg was so tight, and his cheek was so
    ruddy,
Transported I was with my sodger laddie.

III

But the godly old chaplain left him in the
    lurch;
The sword I forsook for the sake of the
    church;
He risk'd the soul, and I ventur'd the
    body:
'T was then I prov'd false to my sodger
    laddie.

IV

Full soon I grew sick of my sanctified sot;
The regiment at large for a husband I
    got;
From the gilded spontoon to the fife I was
    ready:
I ask'd no more but a sodger laddie.

V

But the Peace it reduc'd me to beg in de-
    spair,
Till I met my old boy in a Cunningham
    Fair;
His rags regimental they flutter'd so gaudy:
My heart it rejoic'd at a sodger laddie.

VI

And now I have liv'd — I know not how
    long!
But still I can join in a cup and a song;
And whilst with both hands I can hold the
    glass steady,
Here's to thee, my hero, my sodger lad-
    die!
          Sing, lal de dal, etc.

RECITATIVO

Poor Merry-Andrew in the neuk
  Sat guzzling wi' a tinkler-hizzie;
They mind 't na wha the chorus teuk,
  Between themselves they were sae busy.
At length, wi' drink an' courting dizzy,

He stoiter'd up an' made a face;
    Then turn'd an' laid a smack on Grizzie,
Syne tun'd his pipes wi' grave grimace: —

AIR

TUNE: *Auld Sir Symon*

I

Sir Wisdom 's a fool when he 's fou;
    Sir Knave is a fool in a session:
He 's there but a prentice I trow,
    But I am a fool by profession.

II

My grannie she bought me a beuk,
    An' I held awa to the school:
I fear I my talent misteuk,
    But what will ye hae of a fool?

III

For drink I wad venture my neck;
    A hizzie 's the half of my craft:
But what could ye other expect
    Of ane that 's avowedly daft?

IV

I ance was tyed up like a stirk
    For civilly swearing and quaffing;
I ance was abus'd i' the kirk
    For towsing a lass i' my daffin.

V

Poor Andrew that tumbles for sport
    Let naebody name wi' a jeer:
There 's even, I 'm tauld, i' the Court
    A tumbler ca'd the Premier.

VI

Observ'd ye yon reverend lad
    Mak faces to tickle the mob?
He rails at our mountebank squad —
    It 's rivalship just i' the job!

VII

And now my conclusion I 'll tell,
    For faith! I 'm confoundedly dry:
The chiel that 's a fool for himsel,
    Guid Lord! he 's far dafter than I.

RECITATIVO

Then niest outspak a raucle carlin,
Wha kent fu' weel to cleek the sterlin,

For monie a pursie she had hookèd,
An' had in monie a well been doukèd.
Her love had been a Highland laddie,
But weary fa' the waefu' woodie!
Wi' sighs an' sobs she thus began
To wail her braw John Highlandman: —

AIR

TUNE: *O An' Ye Were Dead, Guidman*

I

A Highland lad my love was born,
The Lalland laws he held in scorn,
But he still was faithfu' to his clan,
My gallant, braw John Highlandman.

CHORUS

Sing hey my braw John Highlandman!
Sing ho my braw John Highlandman!
There 's not a lad in a' the lan'
Was match for my John Highlandman!

II

With his philibeg, an' tartan plaid,
An' guid claymore down by his side,
The ladies' hearts he did trepan,
My gallant, braw John Highlandman.

III

We rangèd a' from Tweed to Spey,
An' liv'd like lords an' ladies gay,
For a Lalland face he fearèd none,
My gallant, braw John Highlandman.

IV

They banish'd him beyond the sea,
But ere the bud was on the tree,
Adown my cheeks the pearls ran,
Embracing my John Highlandman.

V

But, Och! they catch'd him at the last,
And bound him in a dungeon fast.
My curse upon them every one —
They 've hang'd my braw John Highland
    man!

VI

And now a widow I must mourn
The pleasures that will ne'er return;
No comfort but a hearty can
When I think on John Highlandman.

CHORUS

Sing hey my braw John Highlandman !
Sing ho my braw John Highlandman !
There 's not a lad in a' the lan'
Was match for my John Highlandman !

RECITATIVO

I

A pigmy scraper on a fiddle,
Wha us'd to trystes an' fairs to driddle,
Her strappin limb an' gawsie middle
    (He reach'd nae higher)
Had hol'd his heartie like a riddle,
    An' blawn 't on fire.

II

Wi' hand on hainch and upward e'e,
He croon'd his gamut, one, two, three,
Then in an *arioso* key
    The wee Apollo
Set off wi' *allegretto* glee
    His *giga* solo: —

AIR

TUNE : *Whistle Owre the Lave O't*

I

Let me ryke up to dight that tear;
An' go wi' me an' be my dear,
An' then your every care an' fear
May whistle owre the lave o't.

CHORUS

I am a fiddler to my trade,
An' a' the tunes that e'er I play'd,
The sweetest still to wife or maid
    Was *Whistle Owre the Lave O't.*

II

At kirns an' weddins we 'se be there,
An' O, sae nicely 's we will fare !
We 'll bowse about till Daddie Care
Sing *Whistle Owre the Lave O't.*

III

Sae merrily the banes we 'll pyke,
An' sun oursels about the dyke;
An' at our leisure, when ye like,
    We 'll — whistle owre the lave o't !

IV

But bless me wi' your heav'n o' charms,
An' while I kittle hair on thairms,
Hunger, cauld, an' a' sic harms
    May whistle owre the lave o't.

CHORUS

I am a fiddler to my trade,
An' a' the tunes that e'er I play'd,
The sweetest still to wife or maid
    Was *Whistle Owre the Lave O't.*

RECITATIVO

I

Her charms had struck a sturdy caird
    As weel as poor gut-scraper;
He taks the fiddler by the beard,
    An' draws a roosty rapier;
He swoor by a' was swearing worth
    To speet him like a pliver,
Unless he would from that time forth
    Relinquish her for ever.

II

Wi' ghastly e'e poor Tweedle-Dee
    Upon his hunkers bended,
An' pray'd for grace wi' ruefu' face,
    An' sae the quarrel ended.
But tho' his little heart did grieve
    When round the tinkler prest her,
He feign'd to snirtle in his sleeve
    When thus the caird address'd her : —

AIR

TUNE : *Clout the Cauldron*

I

My bonie lass, I work in brass,
    A tinkler is my station;
I 've travell'd round all Christian ground
    In this my occupation;
I 've taen the gold, an' been enrolled
    In many a noble squadron;
But vain they search'd when off I march'd
    To go an' clout the cauldron.

II

Despise that shrimp, that wither'd imp,
    With a' his noise an' cap'rin,

An' take a share wi' those that bear
  The budget and the apron !
And by that stowp, my faith an' houpe !
  And by that dear Kilbaigie !
If e'er ye want, or meet wi' scant,
  May I ne'er weet my craigie !

RECITATIVO

I

The caird prevail'd: th' unblushing fair
  In his embraces sunk,
Partly wi' love o'ercome sae sair,
  An' partly she was drunk.
Sir Violino, with an air
  That show'd a man o' spunk,
Wish'd unison between the pair,
  An' made the bottle clunk
        To their health that night.

II

But hurchin Cupid shot a shaft,
  That play'd a dame a shavie:
The fiddler rak'd her fore and aft
  Behint the chicken cavie;
Her lord, a wight of Homer's craft,
  Tho' limpin' wi' the spavie,
He hirpl'd up, an' lap like daft,
  An' shor'd them " Dainty Davie "
        O' boot that night.

III

He was a care-defying blade
  As ever Bacchus listed !
Tho' Fortune sair upon him laid,
  His heart, she ever miss'd it.
He had no wish but — to be glad,
  Nor want but — when he thristed,
He hated nought but — to be sad;
  An' thus the Muse suggested
        His sang that night.

AIR

TUNE: *For A' That, An' A' That*

I

I am a Bard, of no regard
  Wi' gentle folks an' a' that,
But Homer-like the glowrin byke,
  Frae town to town I draw that.

CHORUS

For a' that, an' a' that,
  An' twice as muckle 's a' that,
I 've lost but ane, I 've twa behin',
  I 've wife eneugh for a' that.

II

I never drank the Muses' stank,
  Castalia's burn, an' a' that;
But there it streams, an' richly reams —
  My Helicon I ca' that.

III

Great love I bear to a' the fair,
  Their humble slave an' a' that;
But lordly will, I hold it still
  A mortal sin to thraw that.

IV

In raptures sweet this hour we meet
  Wi' mutual love an' a' that;
But for how lang the flie may stang,
  Let inclination law that !

V

Their tricks an' craft hae put me daft,
  They 've taen me in, an' a' that;
But clear your decks, an' here 's the Sex!
  I like the jads for a' that.

CHORUS

For a' that, an' a that,
  An' twice as muckle 's a' that,
My dearest bluid, to do them guid,
  They 're welcome till 't for a' that!

RECITATIVO

So sung the Bard, and Nansie's wa's
Shook with a thunder of applause,
  Re-echo'd from each mouth !
They toom'd their pocks, they pawn'd
      their duds,
They scarcely left to coor their fuds,
  To quench their lowin drouth.
Then owre again the jovial thrang
  The Poet did request
To lowse his pack, an' wale a sang,
  A ballad o' the best:
    He rising, rejoicing
      Between his twa Deborahs,
    Looks round him, an' found them
      Impatient for the chorus : —

AIR

TUNE: *Jolly Mortals, Fill Your Glasses*

I

See the smoking bowl before us !
Mark our jovial, ragged ring !
Round and round take up the chorus,
And in raptures let us sing:

CHORUS

A fig for those by law protected !
Liberty's a glorious feast,
Courts for cowards were erected,
Churches built to please the priest !

II

What is title, what is treasure,
What is reputation's care ?
If we lead a life of pleasure,
'T is no matter how or where !

III

With the ready trick and fable
Round we wander all the day;
And at night in barn or stable
Hug our doxies on the hay.

IV

Does the train-attended carriage
Thro' the country lighter rove ?
Does the sober bed of marriage
Witness brighter scenes of love ?

V

Life is all a variorum,
We regard not how it goes;
Let them prate about decorum,
Who have character to lose.

VI

Here's to budgets, bags, and wallets !
Here's to all the wandering train !
Here's our ragged brats and callets !
One and all, cry out, Amen !

CHORUS

A fig for those by law protected !
Liberty's a glorious feast,
Courts for cowards were erected,
Churches built to please the priest !

SATIRES AND VERSES

THE TWA HERDS: OR, THE HOLY TULYIE

AN UNCO MOURNFU' TALE

> Blockheads with reason wicked wits abhor,
> But fool with fool is barbarous civil war.
>
> POPE.

This piece and the two next, *Holy Willie's Prayer*, and *The Kirk's Alarm* — with three printed before, *The Holy Fair*, p. 9, *The Address to the Deil*, p. 12, and *The Ordination*, p. 63, — constitute what is certainly the most brilliant series of assaults ever delivered against the practical bigotry of the Kirk. Burns suffered by them in reputation during his life and long afterwards. Even his most amicable critics have generally failed to appreciate, or at least to indicate, their true significance, and have deemed it seemly to qualify admiration of their cleverness with apologies for their irreverence. But, irreverent or not, they did for the populace much the same service as was done by the *Essay on Miracles* for the class of light and leading, and have proved an enduring antidote against the peculiar superstitions with which the many Scots afflicted themselves so desperately and so long.

" The following," wrote Burns in a note to a MS. copy, now in the British Museum, " was the first of my poetical productions that saw the light. I gave a copy of it to a particular friend of mine, who was very fond of these things, and told him 'I did not know who was the author, but that I had got a copy of it by accident.' The occasion was a bitter and shameless quarrel between two Rev. gentlemen, Moodie of Riccarton and Russell of Kilmarnock. It was at the time when the hue and cry against patronage was at its worst." After a similar account in the Autobiographical Letter to Dr. Moore he adds: " With a certain set of both clergy and laity it met with a roar of applause." The quarrel was about parochial boundaries, and in the discussion of the question, says Lockhart, " the reverend divines, hitherto sworn friends and associates, lost all command of temper, and abused each other *coram populo*, with a fiery virulence of personal invective such as has long been banished from all popular assemblies, wherein the laws of courtesy are enforced by those of a certain unwritten code."

I

O A' ye pious godly flocks,
Weel fed on pastures orthodox,

Wha now will keep you frae the fox
        Or worrying tykes ?
Or wha will tent the waifs an' crocks
        About the dykes ?

II

The twa best herds in a' the wast,
That e'er gae gospel horn a blast
These five an' twenty simmers past —
        O, dool to tell ! —
Hae had a bitter, black out-cast
        Atween themsel.

III

O Moodie, man, an' wordy Russell,
How could you raise so vile a bustle ?
Ye 'll see how New-Light herds will whistle,
        An' think it fine !
The Lord's cause gat na sic a twistle
        Sin' I hae min'.

IV

O Sirs ! whae'er wad hae expeckit
Your duty ye wad sae negleckit ?
Ye wha were no by lairds respeckit
        To wear the plaid,
But by the brutes themselves eleckit
        To be their guide !

V

What flock wi' Moodie's flock could rank,
Sae hale an' hearty every shank ?
Nae poison'd, soor Arminian stank
        He let them taste;
But Calvin's fountainhead they drank —
        O, sic a feast !

VI

The thummart, wilcat, brock, an' tod
Weel kend his voice thro' a' the wood;
He smell'd their ilka hole an' road,
        Baith out and in;
An' weel he lik'd to shed their bluid
        An' sell their skin.

VII

What herd like Russell tell'd his tale ?
His voice was heard thro' muir and dale;
He kend the Lord's sheep, ilka tail,
        O'er a' the height;
An' tell'd gin they were sick or hale
        At the first sight.

VIII

He fine a mangy sheep could scrub;
Or nobly swing the gospel club;

Or New-Light herds could nicely drub
        And pay their skin;
Or hing them o'er the burning dub
        Or heave them in.

IX

Sic twa — O, do I live to see 't ? —
Sic famous twa sud disagree 't,
An' names like villain, hypocrite,
        Ilk ither gi'en,
While New-Light herds wi' laughin spite
        Say neither 's liein !

X

A' ye wha tent the gospel fauld,
Thee, Duncan deep, an' Peebles shaul',
But chiefly great apostle Auld,
        We trust in thee,
That thou wilt work them hot an' cauld
        Till they agree !

XI

Consider, sirs, how we 're beset:
There 's scarce a new herd that we get
But comes frae 'mang that cursed set
        I winna name:
I hope frae heav'n to see them yet
        In fiery flame !

XII

Dalrymple has been lang our fae,
M'Gill has wrought us meikle wae,
An' that curs'd rascal ca'd M'Quhae,
        An' baith the Shaws,
That aft hae made us black an' blae
        Wi' vengefu' paws.

XIII

Auld Wodrow lang has hatch'd mischief:
We thought ay death wad bring relief,
But he has gotten to our grief
        Ane to succeed him,
A chield wha 'll soundly buff our beef —
        I meikle dread him.

XIV

An' monie mae that I could tell,
Wha fain would openly rebel,
Forby turn-coats amang oursel:
        There 's Smith for ane —
I doubt he 's but a greyneck still,
        An' that ye 'll fin' !

XV

O a' ye flocks o'er a' the hills,
By mosses, meadows, moors, an' fells,

Come, join your counsel and your skills
      To cowe the lairds,
An' get the brutes the power themsels
      To chuse their herds !

XVI

Then Orthodoxy yet may prance,
An' Learning in a woody dance,
An' that fell cur ca'd Common-sense,
      That bites sae sair,
Be banish'd o'er the sea to France —
      Let him bark there !

XVII

Then Shaw's an' D'rymple's eloquence,
M'Gill's close, nervous excellence,
M'Quhae's pathetic, manly sense,
      An' guid M'Math
Wha thro' the heart can brawly glance,
      May a' pack aff !

HOLY WILLIE'S PRAYER

And send the godly in a pet to pray.
          POPE.

The interlocutor in this amazing achievement in satire, this matchless parody of Calvinistic intercession — so nice, so exquisite in detail, so overwhelming in effect — was a certain William Fisher, son of Andrew Fisher, farmer at Montgarswood, Ayrshire, born in February, 1737; succeeded his father at Montgarswood, and afterwards tenanted the farm of Tongue-in-Auchterless; on 26th July, 1772, was ordained elder in the parish church of Mauchline ; became one of the most strenuous of Auld's assistants (see *post*, p. 336, note to *The Twa Herds*, Stanza x. l. 3) in his rigid surveillance of the parishioners, and was probably the informer against Gavin Hamilton for neglect of ordinances and violation of the Sabbath (see headnote to *Dedication to Gavin Hamilton, Esq., ante*, p. 41); was himself in 1790 rebuked by the minister, in presence of the Kirk-Session, for drunkenness ; and was reputed (see Stanza xvii. of *The Kirk's Alarm*, p. 112) to have utilised his opportunities, as " elder at the plate," to help himself to the kirk offerings, but there is no official record of any such charge. On his way home from Mauchline, in a snow-storm, he died in a ditch by the roadside, 13th February, 1809.

The occasion of the piece is thus explained by Burns in a preface in the *Glenriddell Book* at Liverpool : " ARGUMENT. — Holy Willie was a rather oldish bachelor elder, in the parish of Mauchline, and much and justly famed for that polemical chattering which ends in tippling orthodoxy, and for that spiritualized bawdry which refines to liquorish devotion. In a sessional process with a gentleman in Mauchline — a Mr. Gavin Hamilton — *Holy Willie* and his priest, Father Auld, after full hearing in the Presbytery of Ayr, came off but second best, owing partly to the oratorical powers of Mr. Robert Aiken, Mr. Hamilton's counsel; but chiefly to Mr. Hamilton's being one of the most irreproachable and truly respectable characters in the country. On losing his process, the muse overheard him at his devotions, as follows." A Presbyterial decision in favour of Hamilton was given in January, 1785. The Session appealed to the Synod, but was at last constrained to grant Hamilton a certificate, 17th July, 1785 : to the effect that he was " free from public scandal or ground of church censure known to us."

I

O THOU that in the Heavens does dwell,
Wha, as it pleases best Thysel,
Sends ane to Heaven an' ten to Hell
      A' for Thy glory,
And no for onie guid or ill
      They 've done before Thee !

II

I bless and praise Thy matchless might,
When thousands Thou hast left in night,
That I am here before Thy sight,
      For gifts an' grace
A burning and a shining light
      To a' this place.

III

What was I, or my generation,
That I should get sic exaltation ?
I, wha deserv'd most just damnation
      For broken laws
Sax thousand years ere my creation,
      Thro' Adam's cause !

IV

When from my mither's womb I fell,
Thou might hae plung'd me deep in hell
To gnash my gooms, and weep, and wail
      In burning lakes,
Whare damnèd devils roar and yell,
      Chain'd to their stakes.

V

Yet I am here, a chosen sample,
To show Thy grace is great and ample:

I 'm here a pillar o' Thy temple,
    Strong as a rock,
A guide, a buckler, and example
    To a' thy flock !

VI

But yet, O Lord ! confess I must:
At times I 'm fash'd wi' fleshly lust;
An' sometimes, too, in warldly trust,
    Vile self gets in;
But Thou remembers we are dust,
    Defiled wi' sin.

VII

O Lord ! yestreen, Thou kens, wi' Meg —
Thy pardon I sincerely beg —
O, may 't ne'er be a living plague
    To my dishonour !
An' I 'll ne'er lift a lawless leg
    Again upon her.

VIII

Besides, I farther maun avow —
Wi' Leezie's lass, three times, I trow —
But, Lord, that Friday I was fou,
    When I cam near her,
Or else, Thou kens, Thy servant true
    Wad never steer her.

IX

Maybe Thou lets this fleshly thorn
Buffet Thy servant e'en and morn,
Lest he owre proud and high should turn
    That he 's sae gifted:
If sae, Thy han' maun e'en be borne
    Until Thou lift it.

X

Lord, bless Thy chosen in this place,
For here Thou has a chosen race !
But God confound their stubborn face
    An' blast their name,
Wha bring Thy elders to disgrace
    An' open shame !

XI

Lord, mind Gau'n Hamilton's deserts:
He drinks, an' swears, an' plays at cartes,
Yet has sae monie takin arts
    Wi' great and sma',
Frae God's ain Priest the people's hearts
    He steals awa.

XII

And when we chasten'd him therefore,
Thou kens how he bred sic a splore,
And set the warld in a roar
    O' laughin at us:
Curse Thou his basket and his store,
    Kail an' potatoes !

XIII

Lord, hear my earnest cry and pray'r
Against that Presbyt'ry of Ayr !
Thy strong right hand, Lord, mak it bare
    Upo' their heads !
Lord, visit them, an' dinna spare,
    For their misdeeds!

XIV

O Lord, my God ! that glib-tongu'd Aiken,
My vera heart and flesh are quakin,
To think how we stood sweatin, shakin,
    An' pish'd wi' dread,
While he, wi' hingin lip an' snakin,
    Held up his head.

XV

Lord, in Thy day o' vengeance try him !
Lord, visit him wha did employ him !
And pass not in Thy mercy by them,
    Nor hear their pray'r,
But for Thy people's sake destroy them,
    An' dinna spare !

XVI

But, Lord, remember me and mine
Wi' mercies temporal and divine,
That I for grace an' gear may shine
    Excell'd by nane;
And a' the glory shall be Thine —
    Amen, Amen !

THE KIRK'S ALARM

William M'Gill, minister of Ayr — whose
"heretic blast" aroused the "alarm" here
burlesqued — was youngest son of William
M'Gill, farmer of Carsenestock, Wigtonshire ;
born 1732 ; educated at the University of Glas-
gow ; became assistant at Kilwinning in June,
1760 ; and was ordained to the second charge
of Ayr, 22d October, 1761, as colleague to
William Dalrymple. M'Gill, who received the
degree of D. D. in 1781, published (Edinburgh,
1786) a *Practical Essay on the Death of Christ*,
which set forth doctrines held to be Socinian.
It was commended in his colleague Dalrym-
ple's *History of Christ*, 1787 ; and attacked,
guardedly and by implication, by Dr. William
Peebles — see *post*, p. 327, note to *The Holy Fair*,
stanza xvi. line 3 — in a *Centenary Sermon on*

the Revolution, preached 5th November, 1788, and published soon afterwards. M'Gill replied in *The Benefits of the Revolution*, Kilmarnock, 1789: whereupon a complaint against his *Essay*, as being heterodox, was presented on 15th April to the Synod of Glasgow and Ayr. The Synod ordered the Presbytery of Ayr to take up the case, and the General Assembly, though it quashed the order, added a general recommendation to the Presbytery to see to it that doctrinal purity was maintained. With this general warrant the Presbytery appointed (15th July) a committee to consider and report specifically on M'Gill's doctrines; and on 14th April, 1790, he compromised the matter by offering an explanation and an apology, which the Synod accepted. M'Gill died 30th March, 1807. He was more philosopher than ecclesiastic. A simple and unworldly man and a resolute student, he was at the same time a quaint and cheerful humourist, and was held by his parishioners in singular affection and respect. Burns's regard for him, like his reverence for Dalrymple, dated from childhood; and the doctrines which had so perturbed the "Orthodox" were those which William Burness [we have adopted throughout the Poet's own spelling of his father's name] had embodied in his *Manual of Religious Belief*. The satire was evoked by the action of the Presbytery on 15th July, 1789. Two days later Burns sent a draft of it to Mrs. Dunlop in an unpublished letter: "You will be well acquainted with the persecution that my worthy friend Dr. M'Gill is undergoing among your divines. Several of these reverend lads his opponents have come through my hands before; but I have some thoughts of serving them up in a different dish. I have just sketched the following ballad and as usual send the first rough draft to you."

I

ORTHODOX! orthodox!—
Wha believe in John Knox—
Let me sound an alarm to your conscience:
A heretic blast
Has been blawn i' the Wast,
That what is not sense must be nonsense—
          Orthodox!
That what is not sense must be nonsense.

II

Dr. Mac! Dr. Mac!
You should stretch on a rack,
To strike wicked Writers wi' terror:
To join faith and sense,

Upon onie pretence,
Was heretic, damnable error—
          Dr. Mac!
'T was heretic, damnable error.

III

Town of Ayr! Town of Ayr!
It was rash, I declare,
To meddle wi' mischief a-brewing:
Provost John is still deaf
To the church's relief,
And Orator Bob is its ruin—
          Town of Ayr!
And Orator Bob is its ruin.

IV

D'rymple mild! D'rymple mild!
Tho' your heart's like a child,
An' your life like the new-driven snaw,
Yet that winna save ye:
Auld Satan must have ye,
For preaching that three's ane and twa—
          D'rymple mild!
For preaching that three's ane and twa.

V

Calvin's sons! Calvin's sons!
Seize your sp'ritual guns,
Ammunition you never can need:
Your hearts are the stuff
Will be powther enough,
And your skulls are store-houses o' lead—
          Calvin's sons!
Your skulls are store-houses o' lead.

VI

Rumble John! Rumble John!
Mount the steps with a groan,
Cry: "The book is wi' heresy cramm'd;"
Then lug out your ladle,
Deal brimstone like adle,
And roar every note o' the damn'd—
          Rumble John!
And roar every note o' the damn'd.

VII

Simper James! Simper James!
Leave the fair Killie dames—
There's a holier chase in your view:
I'll lay on your head
That the pack ye'll soon lead,
For puppies like you there's but few—
          Simper James!
For puppies like you there's but few.

VIII

Singet Sawnie ! Singet Sawnie !
Are ye herding the penny,
Unconscious what evils await ?
Wi' a jump, yell, and howl
Alarm every soul,
For the Foul Thief is just at your gate —
Singet Sawnie !
The Foul Thief is just at your gate.

IX

Daddie Auld ! Daddie Auld !
There 's a tod in the fauld,
A tod meikle waur than the clerk:
Tho' ye can do little skaith,
Ye 'll be in at the death,
And gif ye canna bite, ye may bark —
Daddie Auld !
For gif ye canna bite ye may bark.

X

Davie Rant ! Davie Rant !
In a face like a saunt
And a heart that would poison a hog,
Raise an impudent roar,
Like a breaker lee-shore,
Or the Kirk will be tint in a bog —
Davie Rant !
Or the Kirk will be tint in a bog.

XI

Jamie Goose ! Jamie Goose !
Ye hae made but toom roose
In hunting the wicked lieutenant;
But the Doctor 's your mark,
For the Lord's haly ark,
He has cooper'd, and ca'd a wrang pin in 't —
Jamie Goose !
He has cooper'd and ca'd a wrang pin in 't.

XII

Poet Willie ! Poet Willie !
Gie the Doctor a volley,
Wi' your " Liberty's chain " and your wit:
O'er Pegasus' side
Ye ne'er laid a stride,
Ye but smelt, man, the place where he shit —
Poet Willie !
Ye smelt but the place where he shit.

XIII

Andro' Gowk ! Andro' Gowk !
Ye may slander the Book,
And the Book not the waur, let me tell ye:

Ye are rich, and look big,
But lay by hat and wig,
And ye 'll hae a calf's head o' sma' value —
Andro' Gowk !
Ye 'll hae a calf's head o' sma' value.

XIV

Barr Steenie ! Barr Steenie !
What mean ye ? what mean ye ?
If ye 'll meddle nae mair wi' the matter,
Ye may hae some pretence
To havins and sense
Wi' people wha ken ye nae better —
Barr Steenie !
Wi' people wha ken ye nae better.

XV

Irvine-side ! Irvine-side !
Wi' your turkey-cock pride,
Of manhood but sma' is your share:
Ye 've the figure, 't is true,
Even your faes will allow,
And your friends daurna say ye hae mair —
Irvine-side !
Your friends daurna say ye hae mair.

XVI

Muirland Jock ! Muirland Jock !
Whom the Lord gave a stock
Wad set up a tinkler in brass,
If ill manners were wit,
There 's no mortal so fit
To prove the poor Doctor an ass —
Muirland Jock !
To prove the poor Doctor an ass.

XVII

Holy Will ! Holy Will !
There was wit i' your skull,
When ye pilfer'd the alms o' the poor:
The timmer is scant,
When ye 're taen for a saunt
Wha should swing in a rape for an hour —
Holy Will !
Ye should swing in a rape for an hour.

XVIII

Poet Burns ! Poet Burns !
Wi' your priest-skelping turns,
Why desert ye your auld native shire ?
Your Muse is a gipsy,
Yet were she ev'n tipsy,
She could ca' us nae waur than we are —
Poet Burns !
Ye could ca' us nae waur than we are.

POSTSCRIPTS

I

Afton's Laird! Afton's Laird!
When your pen can be spared,
A copy of this I bequeath,
    On the same sicker score
    As I mention'd before,
To that trusty auld worthy, Clackleith —
        Afton's Laird!
To that trusty auld worthy, Clackleith.

2

Factor John! Factor John!
Whom the Lord made alone,
And ne'er made another thy peer,
    Thy poor servant, the Bard,
    In respectful regard
He presents thee this token sincere —
        Factor John!
He presents thee this token sincere.

A POET'S WELCOME TO HIS LOVE–BEGOTTEN DAUGHTER

THE FIRST INSTANCE THAT ENTITLED HIM TO THE VENERABLE APPELLATION OF FATHER

The "wean" of this generous and delightful Address was the poet's daughter Elizabeth, by Elizabeth Paton, for some time a servant at Lochlie. The child was born in November, 1784. She was brought by her father to Mossgiel. On his marriage the child remained under the charge of his mother and his brother Gilbert. She married John Bishop, overseer at Polkemmet, and died 8th January, 1817, leaving several children. *Cf.* Notes to *The Inventory, post,* p. 338, and Prefatory Note to *Epistle to John Rankine, ante,* p. 50.

I

Thou 's welcome, wean! Mishanter fa'
        me,
If thoughts o' thee or yet thy mammie
Shall ever daunton me or awe me,
        My sweet, wee lady,
Or if I blush when thou shalt ca' me
        Tyta or daddie!

II

What tho' they ca' me fornicator,
An' tease my name in kintra clatter?
The mair they talk, I 'm kend the better;
        E'en let them clash!
An auld wife's tongue 's a feckless matter
        To gie ane fash.

III

Welcome, my bonie, sweet, wee dochter!
Tho' ye come here a wee unsought for,
And tho' your comin I hae fought for
        Baith kirk and queir;
Yet, by my faith, ye 're no unwrought for —
        That I shall swear!

IV

Sweet fruit o' monie a merry dint,
My funny toil is no a' tint:
Tho' thou cam to the warl' asklent,
        Which fools may scoff at,
In my last plack thy part 's be in 't
        The better half o't.

V

Tho' I should be the waur bestead,
Thou 's be as braw and bienly clad,
And thy young years as nicely bred
        Wi' education,
As onie brat o' wedlock's bed
        In a' thy station.

VI

Wee image o' my bonie Betty,
As fatherly I kiss and daut thee,
As dear and near my heart I set thee,
        Wi' as guid will,
As a' the priests had seen me get thee
        That 's out o' Hell.

VII

Gude grant that thou may ay inherit
Thy mither's looks an' gracefu' merit,
An' thy poor, worthless daddie's spirit
        Without his failins!
'T will please me mair to see thee heir it
        Than stocket mailins.

VIII

And if thou be what I wad hae thee,
An' tak the counsel I shall gie thee,
I 'll never rue my trouble wi' thee —
        The cost nor shame o't —
But be a loving father to thee,
        And brag the name o't.

THE INVENTORY

IN ANSWER TO A MANDATE BY THE
SURVEYOR OF TAXES

A MS. of this catalogue of plenishing, dated
May, 1786, sent to Lady Harriet Don and
now in the Laing Collection in the University
of Edinburgh, has this heading: "To Mr.
Robt. Aiken in Ayr, in answer to his mandate
requiring an account of servants, carriages, car-
riage horses, riding horses, wives, children," etc.
Currie explains that the mandate enjoined on
every man "to send a signed list of his horses,
servants, wheel-carriages, etc., and whether he
was a married man or a bachelor, and what
children he had." The new tax was levied by
Pitt (May, 1785) with a view to reducing the
National Debt.

SIR, as your mandate did request,
I send you here a faithfu' list
O' guids an' gear an' a' my graith,
To which I 'm clear to gie my aith.

Imprimis, then, for carriage cattle: —
I hae four brutes o' gallant mettle
As ever drew before a pettle:
My lan'-afore 's a guid auld "has been,"
An' wight an' wilfu' a' his days been.
My lan'-ahin 's a weel-gaun fillie,
That aft has borne me hame frae Killie,
An' your auld borough monie a time
In days when riding was nae crime.
(But ance, when in my wooing pride
I, like a blockhead, boost to ride,
The wilf'u creature sae I pat to —
Lord, pardon a' my sins, an' that too! —
I play'd my fillie sic a shavie,
She 's a' bedevil'd wi' the spavie.)
My fur-ahin 's a wordy beast
As e'er in tug or tow was traced.
The fourth 's a Highland Donald hastie,
A damn'd red-wud Kilburnie blastie!
Foreby, a cowte, o' cowtes the wale,
As ever ran afore a tail:
If he be spar'd to be a beast,
He 'll draw me fifteen pund at least.

Wheel-carriages I hae but few:
Three carts, an' twa are feckly new;
An auld wheelbarrow — mair for token,
Ae leg an' baith the trams are broken:
I made a poker o' the spin'le,
An' my auld mither brunt the trin'le.

For men, I 've three mischievous boys,
Run-deils for fechtin an' for noise:
A gaudsman ane, a thrasher t' other,
Wee Davoc hauds the nowte in fother.
I rule them, as I ought, discreetly,
An' aften labour them completely;
An' ay on Sundays duly, nightly,
I on the *Questions* tairge them tightly:
Till, faith! wee Davoc 's grown sae gleg,
Tho' scarcely langer than your leg,
He 'll screed you aff "Effectual Calling"
As fast as onie in the dwalling.

I 've nane in female servan' station
(Lord keep me ay frae a' temptation!):
I hae nae wife — and that my bliss is —
An' ye hae laid nae tax on misses;
An' then, if kirk folks dinna clutch me,
I ken the deevils darena touch me.

Wi' weans I 'm mair than weel contented:
Heav'n sent me ane mair than I wanted!
My sonsie, smirking, dear-bought Bess,
She stares the daddie in her face,
Enough of ought ye like but grace:
But her, my bonie, sweet wee lady,
I 've paid enough for her already;
An' gin ye tax her or her mither,
By the Lord, ye 'se get them a' thegither!

But pray, remember, Mr. Aiken,
Nae kind of licence out I 'm takin:
Frae this time forth, I do declare
I 'se ne'er ride horse nor hizzie mair;
Thro' dirt and dub for life I 'll paidle,
Ere I sae dear pay for a saddle;
I 've sturdy stumps, the Lord be thankit,
And a' my gates on foot I 'll shank it.
The Kirk and you may tak' you that,
It puts but little in your pat:
Sae dinna put me in your beuk,
Nor for my ten white shillings leuk.

This list, wi' my ain hand I 've wrote it,
The day and date as under notit;
Then know all ye whom it concerns,
Subscripsi huic   ROBERT BURNS.

A MAUCHLINE WEDDING

This, one of Burns's best-natured squibs,
was enclosed in a letter to Mrs. Dunlop, 21st
August, 1788, and is here published for the

first time [1] (Lochryan MSS). He explains that
a sister of Miller, then "a tenant" of his heart,
had huffed his "Bardship in the pride of her
new connection." She was the Miss Betty of
The Belles of Mauchline (see *post*, p. 171); and
the Eliza of the *Song* (see *ante*, p. 52). Burns
did not go on to describe the ceremony:
"Against my Muse had come thus far," he
writes, "Miss Bess and I were once more in
unison."

I

WHEN Eighty-five was seven months auld
　And wearing thro' the aught,
When rolling rains and Boreas bauld
　Gied farmer-folks a faught;
Ae morning quondam Mason W . . .,
　Now Merchant Master Miller,
Gaed down to meet wi' Nansie B . . .,
　And her Jamaica siller
　　　　To wed, that day.

II

The rising sun o'er Blacksideen
　Was just appearing fairly,
When Nell and Bess got up to dress
　Seven lang half-hours o'er early !
Now presses clink, and drawers jink,
　For linens and for laces:
But modest Muses only *think*
　What ladies' underdress is
　　　　On sic a day !

III

But we 'll suppose the stays are lac'd,
　And bonie bosoms steekit,
Tho' thro' the lawn — but guess the rest !
　An angel scarce durst keek it.
Then stockins fine o' silken twine
　Wi' cannie care are drawn up;
An' garten'd tight whare mortal wight —

. . . .

As I never wrote it down my recollection does not en-
　tirely serve me.

IV

But now the gown wi' rustling sound
　Its silken pomp displays;
Sure there 's nae sin in being vain
　O' siccan bonie claes !
Sae jimp the waist, the tail sae vast —
　Trouth, they were bonie birdies !
O Mither Eve, ye wad been grieve
　To see their ample hurdies
　　　　Sae large that day !

[1] That is, in the Centenary Edition.

V

Then Sandy, wi 's red jacket braw,
　Comes whip-jee-woa ! about,
And in he gets the bonie twa —
　Lord, send them safely out !
And auld John Trot wi' sober phiz,
　As braid and braw 's a Bailie,
His shouthers and his Sunday's jiz
　Wi' powther and wi' ulzie
　　　　Weel smear'd that day.

ADAM ARMOUR'S PRAYER

Published in *The Scots Magazine*, January,
1808. The interlocutor in this intercession was
Burns's brother-in-law. At this time he had
headed a band of younkers in Mauchline in the
work of stanging — which is riding astride an
unbarked sapling — a loose woman, one Agnes
Wilson, who figures in the Kirk-Session records
of March, 1786, as "the occasion of a late dis-
turbance in this place." The Geordie, whose
"jurr" or maid she was, is described in *The
Scots Magazine* as the village constable; but
this is clearly a mistake. He was, in fact,
one George Gibson, the husband of Poosie
Nansie (see *post*, p. 334, Note to *The Jolly Beg-
gars*, Recitativo i. line 9). As Gibson resented
the outrage on his maid, Armour, dreading the
law's reprisals, absconded. According to the
person who sent the thing to *The Scots Maga-
zine*, Armour chose Burns's house as his hid-
ing-place. The person adds that he got the
manuscript from Armour himself, who told
him "that Burns composed it one Sunday even-
ing just before he took the *Book*," *i. e.* the
Bible.

I

GUDE pity me, because I 'm little !
For though I am an elf o' mettle,
And can like onie wabster's shuttle
　　　Jink there or here,
Yet, scarce as lang 's a guid kail-whittle,
　　　I 'm unco queer.

II

An' now Thou kens our woefu' case:
For Geordie's jurr we 're in disgrace,
Because we stang'd her through the place,
　　　An' hurt her spleuchan;
For whilk we daurna show our face
　　　Within the clachan.

III

An' now we 're dern'd in dens and hollows,
And hunted, as was William Wallace,
Wi' constables — thae blackguard fal-
          lows —
          An' sodgers baith;
But Gude preserve us frae the gallows,
          That shamefu' death !

IV

Auld, grim, black-bearded Geordie's sel' —
O, shake him owre the mouth o' Hell !
There let him hing, an' roar, an' yell
          Wi' hideous din,
And if he offers to rebel,
          Then heave him in !

V

When Death comes in wi' glimmerin blink,
An' tips auld drucken Nanse the wink,
May Sautan gie her doup a clink
          Within his yett,
An' fill her up wi' brimstone drink
          Red-reekin het.

VI

Though Jock an' hav'rel Jean are merry,
Some devil seize them in a hurry,
An' waft them in th' infernal wherry
          Straught through the lake,
An' gie their hides a noble curry
          Wi' oil of aik !

VII

As for the jurr — puir worthless body ! —
She 's got mischief enough already;
Wi' stanget hips and buttocks bluidy
          She 's suffer'd sair;
But may she wintle in a woody
          If she whore mair !

NATURE'S LAW

HUMBLY INSCRIBED TO GAVIN HAMILTON,
ESQUIRE

Great Nature spoke, observant man obeyed.
          POPE.

Written shortly after the event, — "Wish
me luck, Dear Richmond. Armour has just
brought me a fine boy and girl at one throw.
God bless the little dears!

' Green grow the Rashes, O,
Green grow the Rashes, O,
A feather bed is no sae saft
As the bosoms o' the lasses O.'
"MOSSGIEL, Sunday, 3d September, 1786."

The more serious aspect of the situation is
touched in a letter of the 8th September, to
Robert Muir: "You will have heard that
poor Armour has repayed my amorous mort-
gages double. A very fine boy and girl have
awakened a thought and feelings that thrill,
some with tender pressure and some with fore-
boding anguish thro' my soul." The girl (Jean)
died "at fourteen months old" (R. B. in
Bible); the boy (Robert) died 14th May, 1857.

I

LET other heroes boast their scars,
          The marks o' sturt and strife,
But other poets sing of wars,
          The plagues o' human life !
Shame fa' the fun: wi' sword and gun
          To slap mankind like lumber !
I sing his name and nobler fame
          Wha multiplies our number.

II

Great Nature spoke, with air benign: —
          "Go on, ye human race;
This lower world I you resign;
          Be fruitful and increase.
The liquid fire of strong desire,
          I 've poured it in each bosom;
Here on this hand does Mankind stand,
          And there, is Beauty's blossom ! "

III

The Hero of these artless strains,
          A lowly Bard was he,
Who sung his rhymes in Coila's plains
          With meikle mirth and glee:
Kind Nature's care had given his share
          Large of the flaming current;
And, all devout, he never sought
          To stem the sacred torrent.

IV

He felt the powerful, high behest
          Thrill vital thro' and thro';
And sought a correspondent breast
          To give obedience due.
Propitious Powers screen'd the young
          flow'rs
          From mildews of abortion;
And lo ! the Bard — a great reward —
          Has got a double portion !

V

Auld cantie Coil may count the day,
  As annual it returns,
The third of Libra's equal sway,
  That gave another Burns,
With future rhymes an' other times
  To emulate his sire,
To sing auld Coil in nobler style
  With more poetic fire !

VI

Ye Powers of peace and peaceful song,
  Look down with gracious eyes,
And bless auld Coila large and long
  With multiplying joys !
Lang may she stand to prop the land,
  The flow'r of ancient nations,
And Burnses spring her fame to sing
  To endless generations !

LINES ON MEETING WITH LORD DAER

The Lord Daer was Basil William Douglas-Hamilton, second son of the fourth Earl of Selkirk. He was born 16th March, 1763, and educated at the University of Edinburgh, where he boarded with Professor Dugald Stewart, whose guest he was at Catrine when Burns met him at dinner. A warm admirer of the French Revolution, he went in 1789 to Paris, where he lived in terms of friendship with some of its chief promoters. On his return he joined the Society of the Friends of the People ; became a zealous advocate of Reform ; and raised the question of the eligibility of Scots Peers' sons to vote in elections and sit in the Commons (the Court of Session decided against him in 1792). He died of consumption at Ivy Bridge, Devon, 5th November, 1794.

Burns, in sending the lines to Mackenzie, eulogised the Professor, dividing his character into "ten parts, thus : four parts Socrates, four parts Nathaniel, and two parts Shakespeare's Brutus." Of the verses he wrote that they "were really extempore but a little corrected since."

I

THIS wot ye all whom it concerns:
I, Rhymer Rab, *alias* Burns,
  October twenty-third,
A ne'er-to-be-forgotten day,
Sae far I sprachl'd up the brae
  I dinner'd wi' a Lord.

II

I 've been at drucken Writers' feasts,
Nay, been bitch-fou 'mang godly Priests —
  Wi' rev'rence be it spoken ! —
I 've even join'd the honor'd jorum,
When mighty Squireships o' the Quorum
  Their hydra drouth did sloken.

III

But wi' a Lord ! — stand out my shin !
A Lord, a Peer, an Earl's son ! —
  Up higher yet, my bonnet !
An' sic a Lord ! — lang Scotch ell twa
Our Peerage he looks o'er them a',
  As I look o'er my sonnet.

IV

But O, for Hogarth's magic pow'r
To show Sir Bardie's willyart glow'r,
  An' how he star'd an' stammer'd,
When, goavin 's he 'd been led wi' branks,
An' stumpin on his ploughman shanks,
  He in the parlour hammer'd !

V

To meet good Stewart little pain is,
Or Scotia's sacred Demosthénes :
  Thinks I: "They are but men " !
But "Burns " ! — "My Lord" ! — Good
    God ! I doited,
My knees on ane anither knoited
  As faultering I gaed ben.

VI

I sidling shelter'd in a neuk,
An' at his Lordship staw a leuk,
  Like some portentous omen:
Except good sense and social glee
An' (what surpris'd me) modesty,
  I markèd nought uncommon.

VII

I watch'd the symptoms o' the Great —
The gentle pride, the lordly state,
  The arrogant assuming:
The fient a pride, nae pride had he,
Nor sauce, nor state, that I could see,
  Mair than an honest ploughman !

VIII

Then from his Lordship I shall learn
Henceforth to meet with unconcern

One rank as well 's another;
Nae honest, worthy man need care
To meet with noble youthfu' Daer,
For he but meets a brother.

ADDRESS TO THE TOOTHACHE

I

My curse upon your venom'd stang,
That shoots my tortur'd gooms alang,
An' thro' my lug gies monie a twang
      Wi' gnawing vengeance,
Tearing my nerves wi' bitter pang,
      Like racking engines !

II

A' down my beard the slavers trickle,
I throw the wee stools o'er the mickle,
While round the fire the giglets keckle
      To see me loup,
An', raving mad, I wish a heckle
      Were i' their doup !

III

When fevers burn, or ague freezes,
Rheumatics gnaw, or colic squeezes,
Our neebors sympathise to ease us
      Wi' pitying moan;
But thee ! — thou hell o' a' diseases,
      They mock our groan !

IV

Of a' the num'rous human dools —
Ill-hairsts, daft bargains, cutty-stools,
Or worthy frien's laid i' the mools,
      Sad sight to see !
The tricks o' knaves, or fash o' fools —
      Thou bear'st the gree !

V

Whare'er that place be priests ca' Hell,
Whare a' the tones o' misery yell,
An' ranked plagues their numbers tell
      In dreadfu' raw,
Thou, Toothache, surely bear'st the bell
      Amang them a' !

VI

O thou grim, mischief-making chiel,
That gars the notes o' discord squeel,
Till humankind aft dance a reel
      In gore a shoe-thick,
Gie a' the faes o' Scotland's weal
      A towmond's toothache.

LAMENT FOR THE ABSENCE OF WILLIAM CREECH, PUBLISHER

Enclosed in a letter to "William Creech, Esq., London," dated 13th May, 1787: "My Honored Friend — the enclosed I have just wrote, nearly extempore, in a solitary Inn in Selkirk, after a miserable, wet day's riding."

The son of the Rev. William Creech, minister of Newbattle, in Midlothian, Creech was born 21st April, 1745. He completed the Arts course at the University of Edinburgh; attended some medical lectures; was apprenticed to the publishers Kincaid and Bell; in 1770 accompanied Lord Kilmaurs, afterwards the Earl of Glencairn (and the patron of Burns) on a Continental tour; became partner with Kincaid in 1771 and the firm itself in 1773: when his shop, standing to the north of St. Giles', was soon, in Cockburn's phrase, "the natural resort of lawyers, authors, and all sorts of literary allies." In his house, too, he held literary gatherings, which came to be called "Creech's levees." To his social qualities and his ascendancy in literary and municipal Edinburgh the *Lament* bears witness. Another trait in his character — a combination of bad business habits with a certain keenness over money — revealed itself in so unpleasant a fashion to Burns, in connexion with the settlement over the *Poems*, that the men's relations were strained and distant ever after: Burns from this time forth addressing Creech as "Sir," and in a fragment (see p. 181), meant for part of a *Poet's Progress*, describing him as

"A little, upright, pert, tart, tripping wight,
  And still his precious self his dear delight."

Before this, and before writing the *Lament*, Burns had mastered all Creech's peculiarities; and in his *Second Common Place Book* (in the possession of Mr. Macmillan) he gives a portrait which must be regarded as corrective of eulogy and satire alike: "My worthy bookseller, Mr. Creech, is a strange, multiform character. His ruling passions of the left-hand kind are — extreme vanity, and something of the more harmless modifications of selfishness. The one, mixed as it often is with great goodness of heart, makes him rush into all public matters, and take every instance of unprotected merit by the hand, provided it is in his power to hand it into public notice; the other quality makes him, amid all the embarass in which his vanity entangles him, now and then to cast half a squint at his own interest. His parts as a man, his deportment as a gentleman, and his abilities as a scholar, are much above mediocrity. Of all the Edinburgh literati and wits he writes the most like a gen-

tleman. He does not awe you with the pro-
foundness of the philosopher, or strike your
eye with the soarings of genius; but he pleases
you with the handsome turn of his expression,
and the polite ease of his paragraph. His
social demeanour and powers, particularly at
his own table, are the most engaging I have
ever met with."

Creech was publisher of *The Mirror*, *The
Lounger*, and the works of the chief Scots
authors of his day. He contributed a number
of Essays to *The Edinburgh Courant*, which he
reprinted in a volume under the title *Fugitive
Pieces*, 1791 (a second edition, published post-
humously, with an account of his life, appeared
in 1875). His *Account of the Manners and
Customs in Scotland between 1763 and 1783*,
originally contributed to the *Courant*, was
brought down to 1793 and published in the
Statistical Account of Scotland. He was also
the author of *An Account of the Trial of Wm.
Brodie and George Smith* (1789), having sat on
the jury by which the famous Deacon was
tried. He was a founder of the Speculative
Society and the Edinburgh Chamber of Com-
merce. In 1811–13 he was Lord Provost. He
died 14th January, 1815.

I

Auld chuckie Reekie's sair distrest,
Down droops her ance weel burnish'd crest,
Nae joy her bonie buskit nest
     Can yield ava:
Her darling bird that she lo'es best,
     Willie, 's awa.

II

O, Willie was a witty wight,
And had o' things an unco sleight!
Auld Reekie ay he keepit tight
     And trig an' braw;
But now they'll busk her like a fright —
     Willie's awa!

III

The stiffest o' them a' he bow'd;
The bauldest o' them a' he cow'd;
They durst nae mair than he allow'd —
     That was a law:
We've lost a birkie weel worth gowd —
     Willie's awa!

IV

Now gawkies, tawpies, gowks, and fools
Frae colleges and boarding schools
May sprout like simmer puddock-stools
     In glen or shaw:

He wha could brush them down to mools,
     Willie, 's awa!

V

The brethren o' the Commerce-Chaumer
May mourn their loss wi' doolfu' clamour:
He was a dictionar and grammar
     Amang them a'.
I fear they'll now mak monie a stam-
mer:
     Willie's awa!

VI

Nae mair we see his levee door
Philosophers and Poets pour,
And toothy Critics by the score
     In bloody raw:
The adjutant of a' the core,
     Willie, 's awa!

VII

Now worthy Greg'ry's Latin face,
Tytler's and Greenfield's modest grace,
M'Kenzie, Stewart, such a brace
     As Rome ne'er saw,
They a' maun meet some ither place —
     Willie's awa!

VIII

Poor Burns ev'n "Scotch Drink" canna
quicken:
He cheeps like some bewilder'd chicken
Scar'd frae its minnie and the cleckin
     By hoodie-craw.
Grief's gien his heart an unco kickin —
     Willie's awa!

IX

Now ev'ry sour-mou'd, girnin blellum,
And Calvin's folk, are fit to fell him;
Ilk self-conceited critic-skellum
     His quill may draw:
He wha could brawlie ward their bellum,
     Willie, 's awa!

X

Up wimpling, stately Tweed I've sped,
And Eden scenes on crystal Jed,
And Ettrick banks, now roaring red
     While tempests blaw;
But every joy and pleasure's fled:
     Willie's awa!

XI

May I be Slander's common speech,
A text for Infamy to preach,

And, lastly, streekit out to bleach
      In winter snaw,
When I forget thee, Willie Creech,
      Tho' far awa !

XII

May never wicked Fortune touzle him,
May never wicked men bamboozle him,
Until a pow as auld 's Methusalem
      He canty claw !
Then to the blessed new Jerusalem
      Fleet-wing awa !

VERSES IN FRIARS CARSE HERMITAGE

    This is the first version of the *Hermitage*
verses (see *ante*, p. 80); that which was ac-
tually inscribed on the Friars Carse window-
pane — now in the Observatory Museum, Dum-
fries.

THOU whom chance may hither lead,
Be thou clad in russet weed,
Be thou deckt in silken stole,
Grave these maxims on thy soul: —

Life is but a day at most,
Sprung from night in darkness lost;
Hope not sunshine every hour,
Fear not clouds will always lour.
Happiness is but a name,
Make content and ease thy aim.
Ambition is a meteor-gleam;
Fame a restless airy dream;
Pleasures, insects on the wing
Round Peace, th' tend'rest flow'r of spring;
Those that sip the dew alone —
Make the butterflies thy own;
Those that would the bloom devour —
Crush the locusts, save the flower.

For the future be prepar'd:
Guard whatever thou canst guard;
But, thy utmost duly done,
Welcome what thou canst not shun.
Follies past give thou to air —
Make their consequence thy care.
Keep the name of Man in mind,
And dishonour not thy kind.
Reverence with lowly heart
Him, whose wondrous work thou art;
Keep His Goodness still in view —
Thy trust, and thy example too.

Stranger, go ! Heaven be thy guide !
Quod the Beadsman on Nidside.

ELEGY ON THE DEPARTED YEAR 1788

FOR lords or kings I dinna mourn;
E'en let them die — for that they 're born;
But O, prodigious to reflect,
A Towmont, sirs, is gane to wreck !
O Eighty-Eight, in thy sma' space
What dire events hae taken place !
Of what enjoyments thou hast reft us !
In what a pickle thou hast left us !

The Spanish empire 's tint a head,
An' my auld teethless Bawtie 's dead;
The tulyie's teugh 'tween Pitt and Fox,
An' our guidwife's wee birdie cocks:
The tane is game, a bluidie devil,
But to the hen-birds unco civil;
The tither 's dour — has nae sic breedin,
But better stuff ne'er claw'd a midden.

Ye ministers, come mount the poupit,
An' cry till ye be haerse an' roupet,
For Eighty-Eight, he wished you weel,
An' gied ye a' baith gear an' meal:
E'en monie a plack and monie a peck,
Ye ken yoursels, for little feck !

Ye bonie lasses, dight your een,
For some o' you hae tint a frien':
In Eighty-Eight, ye ken, was taen
What ye 'll ne'er hae to gie again.

Observe the vera nowte an' sheep,
How dowff an' dowilie they creep !
Nay, even the yirth itsel does cry,
For Embro' wells are grutten dry !

O Eighty-Nine, thou 's but a bairn,
An' no owre auld, I hope, to learn!
Thou beardless boy, I pray tak care,
Thou now has got thy Daddie's chair:
Nae hand-cuff'd, mizzl'd, half-shackl'd
    Regent,
But, like himsel, a full free agent,
Be sure ye follow out the plan
Nae waur than he did, honest man !
As muckle better as ye can.
    January 1, 1789.

CASTLE GORDON

Burns was introduced to the Duchess of
Gordon in Edinburgh (1786–7). And during
his northern tour in 1787 he called at Gordon
Castle on 7th September, as recorded in his
Journal : " Cross the Spey to Fochabers — fine
palace, worthy of the noble, the polite, the
generous proprietor. Dine. Company : Duke
and Duchess, Ladies Charlotte and Madeline ;
Colonel Abercrombie and Lady, Mr. Gordon,
and Mr. ——, a clergyman, a venerable, aged
figure, and Mr. Hoy, a clergyman too, I sup-
pose — pleasant open manner. The Duke
makes me happier than ever great man did —
noble, princely, yet mild, condescending and
affable, gay and kind ; the Duchess, charming,
witty, and sensible. God bless them." The
piece was suggested by this visit. Burns sent
it to Mr. Hoy, the Duke's librarian, who wrote
to him that the Duchess wished he had written
in Scotch. It is worth recalling how the
Duchess told Sir Walter that Burns was the
only man she had ever met whose conversation
fairly " carried her off her feet."

I

STREAMS that glide in Orient plains,
Never bound by Winter's chains;
   Glowing here on golden sands,
There immixed with foulest stains
   From tyranny's empurpled hands;
These, their richly gleaming waves,
I leave to tyrants and their slaves:
Give me the stream that sweetly laves
   The banks by Castle Gordon.

II

Spicy forests ever gay,
Shading from the burning ray
   Hapless wretches sold to toil;
Or, the ruthless native's way,
   Bent on slaughter, blood and spoil;
Woods that ever verdant wave,
I leave the tyrant and the slave:
Give me the groves that lofty brave
   The storms of Castle Gordon.

III

Wildly here without control
Nature reigns, and rules the whole;
   In that sober pensive mood,
Dearest to the feeling soul,
   She plants the forest, pours the flood.
Life's poor day I 'll, musing, rave,

And find at night a sheltering cave,
Where waters flow and wild woods wave
   By bonie Castle Gordon.

ON THE DUCHESS OF GOR-
DON'S REEL DANCING

Published in Stuart's *Star* for the 31st March
(1789), and here first reprinted. Jane, Duchess
of Gordon, second daughter of Sir William
Maxwell, third Baronet of Monreith, was born
in Hyndford's Close, Edinburgh, in 1746. She
was beautiful, clever, witty, abounding in
gaiety of temperament, of a most frolic habit,
and more or less reckless of the proprieties.
During her childhood a country cousin caught
her one day, hard by her father's house, riding
an Edinburgh pig — (Edinburgh was largely
scavengered by pigs in those years) — her sis-
ter (afterwards Lady Wallace) belabouring her
mount with a stick. On her marriage to Alex-
ander, Duke of Gordon (1767), she became the
queen of Edinburgh Society ; which, under her
rule, appears to have been as merry as cards,
wine, suppers, dances, late hours, and her own
enchanting example and incomparable energy
could make it ; while in London her house was
a chief resort for the Pittites. In 1802 she
went to Paris, with the purpose (so 't is said)
of making a match between her youngest
daughter and Eugène Beauharnais, and re-
turned to boast (so 't was reported) that Napo-
leon would " breakfast in Ireland, dine in Lon-
don, and sup in Gordon Castle." In her later
years she lived apart from her husband. She
died 11th April, 1812.

I

SHE kiltit up her kirtle weel
   To show her bonie cutes sae sma',
And wallopèd about the reel,
   The lightest louper o' them a' !

II

While some, like slav'ring, doited stots
   Stoit'ring out thro' the midden dub,
Fankit their heels amang their coats
   And gart the floor their backsides rub;

III

Gordon, the great, the gay, the gallant,
   Skip't like a maukin owre a dyke:
Deil tak me, since I was a callant,
   Gif e'er my een beheld the like !

ON CAPTAIN GROSE

WRITTEN ON AN ENVELOPE ENCLOSING A LETTER TO HIM

This amusing parody of the funny old song against tale-telling travellers (Herd, 1769) : —

> " Keep ye weel frae Sir John Malcolme,
> *Igo and ago*
> If he 's a wise man, I mistak him
> *Iram, coram, dago*

> " Keep ye weel frae Sandie Don,
> *Igo and ago*
> He 's ten times dafter than Sir John.
> *Iram, coram, dago :* " —

was " written in a wrapper inclosing a letter to Captain Grose," to be left with Mr. Cardonnel, the Edinburgh antiquary. Only two letters from Burns to Grose have been published : one recommending him to call on Professor Stewart ; the other on witch stories connected with Alloway Kirk (see *ante*, p. 88). For a notice of Captain Grose, see *ante*, p. 94.

I

KEN ye ought o' Captain Grose ?
Igo and ago
If he 's among his friends or foes ?
Iram, coram, dago

II

Is he south, or is he north ?
Igo and ago
Or drownèd in the River Forth ?
Iram, coram, dago

III

Is he slain by Hielan' bodies ?
Igo and ago
And eaten like a wether haggis ?
Iram, coram, dago

IV

Is he to Abra'm's bosom gane ?
Igo and ago
Or haudin Sarah by the wame ?
Iram, coram, dago

V

Where'er he be, the Lord be near him !
Igo and ago
As for the Deil, he daur na steer him.
Iram, coram, dago

VI

But please transmit th' enclosèd letter
Igo and ago
Which will oblige your humble debtor
Iram, coram, dago

VII

So may ye hae auld stanes in store,
Igo and ago
The very stanes that Adam bore !
Iram, coram, dago

VIII

So may ye get in glad possession,
Igo and ago
The coins o' Satan's coronation !
Iram, coram, dago

NEW YEAR'S DAY, 1791

[TO MRS. DUNLOP]

Editors have taken for granted that this was written for New Year's Day, 1790 ; but the " grandchild " whose cap is referred to was probably the child of Mrs. Henri, born in November, 1790. Since also Mrs. Dunlop, on 1st January, 1791, snatched " a few moments " to acknowledge receipt of a letter, a poem, and a gilded card from Burns (Lochryan MSS.), it seems most likely that the latter is the true date.

Mrs. Dunlop, whose maiden name was Frances Anne Wallace, was the eldest daughter of Sir Thomas Wallace of Craigie (descended from the uncle of the renowned leader) and Eleanor Agnew, daughter of Colonel Agnew, of Lochryan. She was born 16th April, 1730 ; married in 1748 John Dunlop of Dunlop, Ayrshire, who died in 1785 ; succeeded her father before July, 1777 ; and died 24th May, 1815. Being in a state of profound mental depression — from which, she affirmed, her " only refuge would have been the madhouse or the grave " — she fell to reading the Kilmarnock volume — the gift of a friend. It had an almost magical effect upon her spirits ; and, feeling herself under an " inexpressible debt " to Burns for the relief thus experienced, she wrote to him what proved to be the initial letter of a most engaging correspondence, — a correspondence which shows the poet at his easiest and best as a letter-writer at the same time that it reveals the lady for one of the staunchest and kindest friends he ever had. The persons referred to in the piece were members of her family.

THIS day Time winds th' exhausted chain,
To run the twelvemonth's length again:
I see the old, bald-pated fellow,
With ardent eyes, complexion sallow,
Adjust the unimpair'd machine
To wheel the equal, dull routine.

The absent lover, minor heir,
In vain assail him with their prayer:
Deaf as my friend, he sees them press,
Nor makes the hour one moment less.
Will you (the Major 's with the hounds;
The happy tenants share his rounds;
Coila 's fair Rachel's care to-day,
And blooming Keith 's engaged with Gray)
From housewife cares a minute borrow
(That grandchild's cap will do to-morrow),
And join with me a-moralizing ?
This day 's propitious to be wise in !

First, what did yesternight deliver ?
"Another year has gone for ever."
And what is this day's strong suggestion ?
"The passing moment 's all we rest on ! "
Rest on — for what ? what do we here ?
Or why regard the passing year ?
Will Time, amus'd with proverb'd lore,
Add to our date one minute more ?
A few days may — a few years must —
Repose us in the silent dust :
Then, is it wise to damp our bliss ?
Yes: all such reasonings are amiss !
The voice of Nature loudly cries,
And many a message from the skies,
That something in us never dies;
That on this frail, uncertain state
Hang matters of eternal weight;
That future life in worlds unknown
Must take its hue from this alone,
Whether as heavenly glory bright
Or dark as Misery's woeful night.

Since, then, my honour'd first of friends,
On this poor being all depends,
Let us th' important Now employ,
And live as those who never die.
Tho' you, with days and honours crown'd,
Witness that filial circle round
(A sight life's sorrows to repulse,
A sight pale Envy to convulse),
Others now claim your chief regard :
Yourself, you wait your bright reward.

FROM ESOPUS TO MARIA

The " Maria " lampooned in this inept and unmanly parody of Pope's *Epistle from Eloisa to Abelard*, in which the writer gives himself the lie all round with distressing particularity, was Mrs. Walter Riddell of Woodley Park, whose favour he had lost (see *post*, p. 178, Prefatory Note to *Impromptu on Mrs. Riddell's Birthday*). The Esopus was James Williamson, manager of the Dumfries Theatre, who, like Burns, had been an occasional guest at Woodley Park. The occasion of the piece was the committal to prison by the Earl of Lonsdale of Williamson's company of players as vagrants.

FROM those drear solitudes and frowsy cells,
Where Infamy with sad Repentance dwells;
Where turnkeys make the jealous portal fast,
And deal from iron hands the spare repast;
Where truant 'prentices, yet young in sin,
Blush at the curious stranger peeping in;
Where strumpets, relics of the drunken roar,
Resolve to drink, nay half — to whore — no more;
Where tiny thieves, not destin'd yet to swing,
Beat hemp for others riper for the string:
From these dire scenes my wretched lines I date,
To tell Maria her Esopus' fate.

" Alas ! I feel I am no actor here ! "
'T is real hangmen real scourges bear !
Prepare, Maria, for a horrid tale
Will turn thy very rouge to deadly pale;
Will make thy hair, tho' erst from gipsy poll'd,
By barber woven and by barber sold,
Though twisted smooth with Harry's nicest care,
Like hoary bristles to erect and stare !
The hero of the mimic scene, no more
I start in Hamlet, in Othello roar;
Or, haughty Chieftain, 'mid the din of arms,
In Highland bonnet woo Malvina's charms:
While sans-culottes stoop up the mountain high,
And steal me from Maria's prying eye.

Blest Highland bonnet ! once my proudest
    dress,
Now, prouder still, Maria's temples press !
I see her wave thy towering plumes afar,
And call each coxcomb to the wordy war !
I see her face the first of Ireland's sons,
And even out-Irish his Hibernian bronze !
The crafty Colonel leaves the tartan'd lines
For other wars, where he a hero shines;
The hopeful youth, in Scottish senate bred,
Who owns a Bushby's heart without the
    head,
Comes 'mid a string of coxcombs to dis-
    play
That *Veni, vidi, vici*, is his way;
The shrinking Bard adown the alley
    skulks,
And dreads a meeting worse than Wool-
    wich hulks,
Though there his heresies in Church and
    State
Might well award him Muir and Palmer's
    fate :
Still she, undaunted, reels and rattles on,
And dares the public like a noontide sun.
What scandal called Maria's jaunty stagger
The ricket reeling of a crooked swagger ?
Whose spleen (e'en worse than Burns's
    venom, when
He dips in gall unmix'd his eager pen,
And pours his vengeance in the burning
    line),
Who christen'd thus Maria's lyre-divine,
The idiot strum of Vanity bemus'd,
And even th' abuse of Poesy abus'd ?
Who called her verse a Parish Workhouse,
    made
For motley foundling Fancies, stolen or
    strayed ?

A Workhouse ! Ah, that sound awakes my
    woes,
And pillows on the thorn my rack'd re-
    pose !
In durance vile here must I wake and
    weep,
And all my frowsy couch in sorrow steep :
That straw where many a rogue has lain
    of yore,
And vermin'd gipsies litter'd heretofore.

Why, Lonsdale, thus thy wrath on vagrants
    pour ?
Must earth no rascal save thyself endure ?
Must thou alone in guilt immortal swell,

And make a vast monopoly of Hell ?
Thou know'st the Virtues cannot hate thee
    worse:
The Vices also, must they club their curse ?
Or must no tiny sin to others fall,
Because thy guilt 's supreme enough for
    all ?

Maria, send me too thy griefs and cares,
In all of thee sure thy Esopus shares :
As thou at all mankind the flag unfurls,
Who on my fair one Satire's vengeance
    hurls !
Who calls thee, pert, affected, vain co-
    quette,
A wit in folly, and a fool in wit !
Who says that fool alone is not thy due,
And quotes thy treacheries to prove it
    true !

Our force united on thy foes we 'll turn,
And dare the war with all of woman born:
For who can write and speak as thou and I ?
My periods that decyphering defy,
And thy still matchless tongue that con-
    quers all reply !

NOTES AND EPISTLES

TO JOHN RANKINE

IN REPLY TO AN ANNOUNCEMENT

The "announcement" was "that a girl
[Elizabeth Paton] in that neighbourhood was
with child" by Robert Burns. The *Epistle to
John Rankine, ante*, p. 50, sets forth the se-
quel.

I

I AM a keeper of the law
In some sma' points, altho' not a';
Some people tell me, gin I fa'
        Ae way or ither,
The breaking of ae point, tho' sma',
        Breaks a' thegither.

II

I hae been in for 't ance or twice,
And winna say o'er far for thrice,
Yet never met wi' that surprise
        That broke my rest.
But now a rumour 's like to rise —
        A whaup 's i' the nest !

TO JOHN GOLDIE

AUGUST, 1785

John Goldie or Goudie was the son of a miller in Galston parish, Ayrshire, where he was born in 1717. He prospered first as a cabinet-maker and then as a wine merchant in Kilmarnock, but lost money in mining speculations. He died in 1809. Much of his leisure was given to mechanical and scientific studies; but in later life he was almost equally addicted to advanced theology. He published an *Essay on Various Important Subjects Moral and Divine — being an attempt to distinguish True from False Religion*, 1779 — popularly known as *Goudie's Bible* (the issue of a second edition, 1785, was the occasion of this *Epistle*); *The Gospel Recovered from its Captive State and Restored to its Original Purity*, six vols., London, 1784; and *A Treatise upon the Evidences of a Deity*, 1809. Before his death he had prepared a work on astronomy. Burns, as laureate of the New-Light party, was warmly welcomed by Goldie, who became one of his sureties for the Kilmarnock Edition, and entertained him while he was seeing the book through the press.

I

O Goudie, terror o' the Whigs,
Dread o' black coats and rev'rend wigs !
Sour Bigotry on her last legs
    Girns and looks back,
Wishing the ten Egyptian plagues
    May seize you quick.

II

Poor gapin, glowrin Superstition !
Wae 's me, she 's in a sad condition !
Fye ! bring Black Jock, her state physician,
    To see her water !
Alas ! there 's ground for great suspicion
    She 'll ne'er get better.

III

Enthusiasm 's past redemption
Gane in a gallopin consumption:
Not a' her quacks wi' a' their gumption
    Can ever mend her;
Her feeble pulse gies strong presumption
    She 'll soon surrender.

IV

Auld Orthodoxy lang did grapple
For every hole to get a stapple;
But now she fetches at the thrapple,
    An' fights for breath:

Haste, gie her name up in the chapel,
    Near unto death !

V

'T is you an' Taylor are the chief
To blame for a' this black mischief;
But, gin the Lord's ain folk gat leave,
    A toom tar barrel
An' twa red peats wad bring relief,
    And end the quarrel.

VI

For me, my skill 's but very sma',
An' skill in prose I 've nane ava';
But, quietlenswise between us twa,
    Weel may ye speed !
And, tho' they sud you sair misca',
    Ne'er fash your head !

VII

E'en swinge the dogs, and thresh them
    sicker !
The mair they squeel ay chap the thicker,
And still 'mang hands a hearty bicker
    O' something stout !
It gars an owthor's pulse beat quicker,
    An' helps his wit.

VIII

There 's naething like the honest nappy:
Whare 'll ye e'er see men sae happy,
Or women sonsie, saft, and sappy
    'Tween morn and morn,
As them wha like to taste the drappie
    In glass or horn ?

IX

I 've seen me daez't upon a time,
I scarce could wink or see a styme;
Just ae hauf-mutchkin does me prime
    (Ought less is little);
Then back I rattle on the rhyme
    As gleg 's a whittle.

TO J. LAPRAIK

THIRD EPISTLE

I

Guid speed and furder to you, Johnie,
Guid health, hale han's, an' weather bonie !
Now, when ye 're nickin down fu' cannie
    The staff o' bread,

May ye ne'er want a stoup o' bran'y
    To clear your head !

II

May Boreas never thresh your rigs,
Nor kick your rickles aff their legs,
Sendin the stuff o'er muirs an' haggs
    Like drivin wrack !
But may the tapmost grain that wags
    Come to the sack !

III

I 'm bizzie, too, an' skelpin at it;
But bitter, daudin showers hae wat it;
Sae my auld stumpie-pen, I gat it,
    Wi' muckle wark,
An' took my jocteleg, an' whatt it
    Like onie clark.

IV

It 's now twa month that I 'm your debtor
For your braw, nameless, dateless letter,
Abusin me for harsh ill-nature
    On holy men,
While deil a hair yoursel ye 're better,
    But mair profane !

V

But let the kirk-folk ring their bells!
Let 's sing about our noble sel's:
We 'll cry nae jads frae heathen hills
    To help or roose us,
But browster wives an' whisky stills —
    They are the Muses !

VI

Your friendship, sir, I winna quat it;
An' if ye mak' objections at it,
Then hand in nieve some day we 'll knot
    it,
    An' witness take;
An', when wi' usquabae we 've wat it,
    It winna break.

VII

But if the beast and branks be spar'd
Till kye be gaun without the herd,
And a' the vittel in the yard
    An' theckit right,
I mean your ingle-side to guard
    Ae winter night.

VIII

Then Muse-inspirin aqua-vitæ
Shall mak us baith sae blythe an' witty,

Till ye forget ye 're auld an gatty,
    And be as canty
As ye were nine year less than thretty —
    Sweet ane an' twenty !

IX

But stooks are cowpet wi' the blast,
And now the sinn keeks in the wast;
Then I maun rin amang the rest,
    An' quat my chanter;
Sae I subscribe mysel in haste,
    Yours, Rab the Ranter.

September 13, 1785.

TO THE REV. JOHN M'MATH

INCLOSING A COPY OF "HOLY WILLIE'S PRAYER" WHICH HE HAD REQUESTED, SEPTEMBER 17, 1785

I

WHILE at the stook the shearers cow'r
To shun the bitter blaudin show'r,
Or, in gulravage rinnin, scowr:
    To pass the time,
To you I dedicate the hour
    In idle rhyme.

II

My Musie, tir'd wi' monie a sonnet
On gown an' ban' an' douse black-bonnet,
Is grown right eerie now she 's done it,
    Lest they should blame her,
An' rouse their holy thunder on it,
    And anathém her.

III

I own 't was rash, an' rather hardy,
That I, a simple, countra Bardie,
Should meddle wi' a pack sae sturdy,
    Wha, if they ken me,
Can easy wi' a single wordie
    Louse Hell upon me.

IV

But I gae mad at their grimaces,
Their sighin, cantin, grace-proud faces,
Their three-mile prayers an' hauf - mile
    graces,
    Their raxin conscience,
Whase greed, revenge, an' pride disgraces
    Waur nor their nonsense.

V

There 's Gau'n, misca'd waur than a beast,
Wha has mair honor in his breast
Than monie scores as guid 's the priest
    Wha sae abus't him:
And may a Bard no crack his jest
    What way they 've use't him ?

VI

See him, the poor man's friend in need,
The gentleman in word an' deed —
An' shall his fame an' honor bleed
    By worthless skellums,
An' not a Muse erect her head
    To cowe the blellums ?

VII

O Pope, had I thy satire's darts
To gie the rascals their deserts,
I 'd rip their rotten, hollow hearts,
    An' tell aloud
Their jugglin, hocus-pocus arts
    To cheat the crowd !

VIII

God knows, I 'm no the thing I should
    be,
Nor am I even the thing I could be,
But twenty times I rather would be
    An atheist clean
Than under gospel colors hid be
    Just for a screen.

IX

An honest man may like a glass,
An honest man may like a lass;
But mean revenge an' malice fause
    He 'll still disdain
An' then cry zeal for gospel laws
    Like some we ken.

X

They take Religion in their mouth,
They talk o' Mercy, Grace, an' Truth:
For what ?   To gie their malice skouth
    On some puir wight;
An' hunt him down, o'er right an' ruth,
    To ruin streight.

XI

All hail, Religion ! Maid divine,
Pardon a Muse sae mean as mine,
Who in her rough imperfect line
    Thus daurs to name thee

To stigmatise false friends of thine
    Can ne'er defame thee.

XII

Tho' blotch't and foul wi' monie a stain
An' far unworthy of thy train,
With trembling voice I tune my strain
    To join with those
Who boldly dare thy cause maintain
    In spite of foes:

XIII

In spite o' crowds, in spite o' mobs,
In spite of undermining jobs,
In spite o' dark banditti stabs
    At worth an' merit,
By scoundrels, even wi' holy robes
    But hellish spirit !

XIV

O Ayr ! my dear, my native ground,
Within thy presbyterial bound
A candid lib'ral band is found
    Of public teachers,
As men, as Christians too, renown'd,
    An' manly preachers.

XV

Sir, in that circle you are nam'd;
Sir, in that circle you are fam'd;
An' some, by whom your doctrine 's blam'd
    (Which gies ye honor),
Even, Sir, by them your heart 's esteem'd,
    An' winning manner.

XVI

Pardon this freedom I have taen,
An' if impertinent I 've been,
Impute it not, good sir, in ane
    Whase heart ne'er wrang'd ye,
But to his utmost would befriend
    Ought that belang'd ye.

TO DAVIE

SECOND EPISTLE

I

AULD NEEBOR,
I 'm three times doubly o'er your debtor
For your auld-farrant, frien'ly letter;
Tho' I maun say 't, I doubt ye flatter,
    Ye speak sae fair:

For my puir, silly, rhymin clatter
    Some less maun sair.

II

Hale be your heart, hale be your fiddle !
Lang may your elbuck jink an' diddle
To cheer you thro' the weary widdle
    O' war'ly cares,
Till bairns' bairns kindly cuddle
    Your auld grey hairs !

III

But Davie, lad, I 'm red ye 're glaikit:
I 'm tauld the Muse ye hae negleckit;
An' gif it 's sae, ye sud be lickit
    Until ye fyke;
Sic han's as you sud ne'er be faiket,
    Be hain't wha like.

IV

For me, I 'm on Parnassus' brink,
Rivin the words to gar them clink;
Whyles daez't wi' love, whyles daez't wi'
    drink
    Wi' jads or Masons,
An' whyles, but ay owre late I think,
    Braw sober lessons.

V

Of a' the thoughtless sons o' man
Commen' me to the Bardie clan:
Except it be some idle plan
    O' rhymin clink —
The devil-haet that I sud ban ! —
    They never think.

VI

Nae thought, nae view, nae scheme o' livin,
Nae cares to gie us joy or grievin,
But just the pouchie put the nieve in,
    An' while ought 's there,
Then, hiltie-skiltie, we gae scrievin,
    An' fash nae mair.

VII

Leeze me on rhyme ! It 's ay a trea-
    sure,
My chief, amaist my only pleasure;
At hame, a-fiel', at wark or leisure,
    The Muse, poor hizzie !
Tho' rough an' raploch be her measure,
    She 's seldom lazy.

VIII

Haud to the Muse, my dainty Davie:
The warl' may play you monie a shavie,

But for the Muse, she 'll never leave ye,
    Tho' e'er sae puir;
Na, even tho' limpin wi' the spavie
    Frae door to door !

TO JOHN KENNEDY, DUMFRIES HOUSE

Kennedy was factor to the Earl of Dumfries, and resided at Dumfries House, two miles west of Cumnock. He died at Edinburgh, 19th June, 1812. The first part of the letter is in prose, and refers to a copy of *The Cotter's Saturday Night* enclosed to Kennedy. Burns sent other pieces to him ; and either he or M'Murdo is the "Factor John" of *The Kirk's Alarm,* see *ante,* p. 113.

I

Now, Kennedy, if foot or horse
E'er bring you in by Mauchlin Corss
(Lord, man, there 's lasses there wad force
    A hermit's fancy;
And down the gate in faith ! they 're worse
    An' mair unchancy):

II

But as I 'm sayin, please step to Dow's,
An' taste sic gear as Johnie brews,
Till some bit callan bring me news
    That ye are there;
An' if we dinna hae a bowse,
    I 'se ne'er drink mair.

III

It 's no I like to sit an' swallow,
Then like a swine to puke an' wallow;
But gie me just a true guid fallow
    Wi' right ingíne,
And spunkie ance to mak us mellow,
    An' then we 'll shine !

IV

Now if ye 're ane o' warl's folk,
Wha rate the wearer by the cloak,
An' sklent on poverty their joke
    Wi' bitter sneer,
Wi' you nae friendship I will troke,
    Nor cheap nor dear.

V

But if, as I 'm informèd weel,
Ye hate as ill 's the vera Deil

The flinty heart that canna feel —
   Come, sir, here 's tae you !
Hae, there 's my han', I wiss you weel,
   An' Gude be wi' you !
     ROBT. BURNESS.
MOSSGIEL, 3d March, 1786.

TO GAVIN HAMILTON, ESQ., MAUCHLINE

RECOMMENDING A BOY

Cromek states that Master Tootie was a knavish cattle-dealer in Mauchline.

     MOSSGAVILLE, May 3, 1786.

I HOLD it, Sir, my bounden duty
To warn you how that Master Tootie,
  Alias Laird M'Gaun,
Was here to hire yon lad away
'Bout whom ye spak the tither day,
  An' wad hae don't aff han';
But lest he learn the callan tricks —
  As faith ! I muckle doubt him —
Like scrapin out auld Crummie's nicks,
  An' tellin lies about them,
   As lieve then, I 'd have then
    Your clerkship he should sair,
   If sae be ye may be
    Not fitted otherwhere.

Altho' I say 't, he 's gleg enough,
An' bout a house that 's rude an' rough
  The boy might learn to swear;
But then wi' *you* he 'll be sae taught,
An' get sic fair example straught,
  I hae na onie fear:
Ye 'll catechise him every quirk,
  An' shore him weel wi' " Hell; "
An' gar him follow to the kirk —
  Ay when ye gang yoursel !
   If ye, then, maun be then
    Frae hame this comin Friday,
   Then please, Sir, to lea'e, Sir,
    The orders wi' your lady.

My word of honour I hae gien,
In Paisley John's that night at e'en
  To meet the " warld's worm,"
To try to get the twa to gree,
An' name the airles an' the fee
  In legal mode an' form:
I ken he weel a snick can draw,
  When simple bodies let him;

An' if a Devil be at a',
  In faith he 's sure to get him.
To phrase you an' praise you,
  Ye ken, your Laureat scorns:
The pray'r still you share still
  Of grateful MINSTREL BURNS.

TO MR. M'ADAM OF CRAIGEN–GILLAN

IN ANSWER TO AN OBLIGING LETTER HE SENT IN THE COMMENCEMENT OF MY POETIC CAREER

There is no evidence that Burns had any further correspondence with this M'Adam, whose letter no doubt referred to the Kilmarnock Edition. The son (" Dunaskin's laird " of stanza vii.) is alluded to in the Second Heron Ballad, p. 166, stanza vii. line 8, as " o' lads no the warst."

I

Sir, o'er a gill I gat your card,
  I trow it made me proud.
" See wha taks notice o' the Bard ! "
  I lap, and cry'd fu' loud.

II

Now deil-ma-care about their jaw,
  The senseless, gawky million !
I 'll cock my nose aboon them a':
  I 'm roos'd by Craigen-Gillan !

III

'T was noble, sir; 't was like yoursel,
  To grant your high protection:
A great man's smile, ye ken fu' well,
  Is ay a blest infection.

IV

Tho', by his banes wha in a tub
  Match'd Macedonian Sandy !
On my ain legs thro' dirt and dub
  I independent stand ay;

V

And when those legs to guid warm kail
  Wi' welcome canna bear me,
A lee dyke-side, a sybow-tail,
  An' barley-scone shall cheer me.

VI

Heaven spare you lang to kiss the breath
  O' monie flow'ry simmers,

An' bless your bonie lasses baith
  (I 'm tauld they 're loosome kimmers) !

VII

An' God bless young Dunaskin's laird,
  The blossom of our gentry,
An' may he wear an auld man's beard,
  A credit to his country !

REPLY TO AN INVITATION

Written doubtless in a tavern.

SIR,
  Yours this moment I unseal,
    And faith ! I 'm gay and hearty.
  To tell the truth and shame the Deil,
    I am as fou as Bartie.
  But Foorsday, Sir, my promise leal,
    Expect me o' your partie,
  If on a beastie I can speel
    Or hurl in a cartie.
            Yours, — ROBERT BURNS.
MACHLIN, Monday Night, 10 o'clock.

TO DR. MACKENZIE

AN INVITATION TO A MASONIC GATHERING

Dr. John Mackenzie — one of the poet's
warmest friends — practised at Mauchline, on
completing his medical course at the University
of Edinburgh. He has recorded, in a letter to
Professor Walker (often reprinted), his first
impressions of Burns, whom he met during
the last illness of William Burness. After
removing to Mossgiel, Burns had frequent
opportunities of meeting him at Gavin Hamil-
ton's, the Masonic Lodge, and elsewhere ; and
he introduced the poet to Sir John White-
foord, Professor Dugald Stewart, and other
persons of influence. At a later period Mac-
kenzie settled at Irvine, and in 1827 he retired
to Edinburgh, where he died 11th January,
1837. For Burns's connexion with the lodge,
see ante, p. 53, Prefatory Note to The Fare-
well. He was then depute-master, and so signs
himself ; the procession referred to in the note
took place on 24th June. The Masonic date
signifies 1786.

FRIDAY first 's the day appointed
By our Right Worshipful Anointed
  To hold our grand procession,
To get a blaud o' Johnie's morals,

An' taste a swatch o' Manson's barrels
I' th' way of our profession.
Our Master and the Brotherhood
  Wad a' be glad to see you.
For me, I wad be mair than proud
  To share the mercies wi' you.
    If Death, then, wi' skaith then
      Some mortal heart is hechtin,
    Inform him, an' storm him,
      That Saturday ye 'll fecht him.
            ROBERT BURNS, D. M.
MOSSGIEL, 14th June, A.M. 5790.

TO JOHN KENNEDY

A FAREWELL

Forms the end of a letter sent from Kilmar-
nock, undated, but written some time between
the 3d and 16th August. Burns tells Ken-
nedy that he is about to set out for Jamaica,
and is in daily expectation of orders to repair
to Greenock. Hence these last lines. For
Kennedy see ante, p. 128, Prefatory Note to To
John Kennedy.

FAREWELL, dear friend ! may guid luck
      hit you,
And 'mong her favourites admit you !
If e'er Detraction shore to smit you,
      May nane believe him !
And onie deil that thinks to get you,
      Good Lord, deceive him !

TO WILLIE CHALMERS' SWEET-HEART

Sent to Lady Harriet Don with this expla-
nation : " Mr. Chalmers, a gentleman in Ayr-
shire, a particular friend of mine, asked me to
write a poetic epistle to a young lady, his Dul-
cinea. I had seen her, but was scarcely ac-
quainted with her, and wrote as follows." On
20th November, 1786, Burns, as " Bard-in-
Chief " of Kyle, Cunningham, and Carrick,
sent to Chalmers and another practitioner " in
the ancient and mysterious science of con-
founding right and wrong," a warrant for the
destruction of a certain " wicked song or bal-
lad." He also wrote Chalmers a humorous
letter on his arrival in Edinburgh, enclosing a
copy of his Address to that city. Chalmers
was a lawyer in Ayr.

I

Wi' braw new branks in mickle pride,
    And eke a braw new brechan,
My Pegasus I 'm got astride,
    And up Parnassus pechin:
Whyles owre a bush wi' downward crush
    The doited beastie stammers;
Then up he gets, and off he sets
    For sake o' Willie Chalmers.

II

I doubt na, lass, that weel kend name
    May cost a pair o' blushes:
I am nae stranger to your fame,
    Nor his warm-urgèd wishes:
Your bonie face, sae mild and sweet,
    His honest heart enamours;
And faith! ye 'll no be lost a whit,
    Tho' wair'd on Willie Chalmers.

III

Auld Truth hersel might swear ye 're fair,
    And Honor safely back her;
And Modesty assume your air,
    And ne'er a ane mistak her;
And sic twa love-inspiring een
    Might fire even holy palmers:
Nae wonder then they 've fatal been
    To honest Willie Chalmers !

IV

I doubt na Fortune may you shore
    Some mim-mou'd, pouther'd priestie,
Fu' lifted up wi' Hebrew lore
    And band upon his breastie;
But O, what signifies to you
    His lexicons and grammars ?
The feeling heart 's the royal blue,
    And that 's wi' Willie Chalmers.

V

Some gapin, glowrin countra laird
    May warsle for your favour:
May claw his lug, and straik his beard,
    And hoast up some palaver.
My bonie maid, before ye wed
    Sic clumsy-witted hammers,
Seek Heaven for help, and barefit skelp
    Awa wi' Willie Chalmers.

VI

Forgive the Bard ! My fond regard
    For ane that shares my bosom
Inspires my Muse to gie 'm his dues,
    For deil a hair I roose him.

May Powers aboon unite you soon,
    And fructify your ámours,
And every year come in mair dear
    To you and Willie Chalmers !

TO AN OLD SWEETHEART

WRITTEN ON A COPY OF HIS POEMS

The sweetheart was Peggy Thomson of Kirkoswald (see *ante*, p. 52, Prefatory Note to *Song Composed in August*). Thus prefaced in the *Glenriddell Book*: " Written on the blank leaf of a copy of the first edition of my Poems which I presented to an old sweetheart, then married. 'T was the girl I mentioned in my letter to Dr. Moore, where I speak of taking the sun's altitude. Poor Peggy ! Her husband is my old acquaintance, and a most worthy fellow. When I was taking leave of my Carrick relations, intending to go to the West Indies, when I took farewell of her, neither she nor I could speak a syllable. Her husband escorted me three miles on my road, and we both parted with tears."

I

ONCE fondly lov'd and still remember'd
        dear,
    Sweet early object of my youthful vows,
Accept this mark of friendship, warm, sin-
        cere —
    (Friendship ! 't is all cold duty now al-
        lows);

II

And when you read the simple artless
        rhymes,
    One friendly sigh for him — he asks no
        more —
Who, distant, burns in flaming torrid climes,
    Or haply lies beneath th' Atlantic roar.

EXTEMPORE TO GAVIN HAMIL-
TON

STANZAS ON NAETHING

I

To you, Sir, this summons I 've sent
    (Pray, whip till the pownie is fraeth-
        ing !);

But if you demand what I want,
　I honestly answer you — naething.

II

Ne'er scorn a poor Poet like me
　For idly just living and breathing,
While people of every degree
　Are busy employed about — naething.

III

Poor Centum-per-Centum may fast,
　And grumble his hurdies their claithing;
He 'll find, when the balance is cast,
　He 's gane to the Devil for — naething.

IV

The courtier cringes and bows;
　Ambition has likewise its plaything —
A coronet beams on his brows;
　And what is a coronet ? — Naething.

V

Some quarrel the Presbyter gown,
　Some quarrel Episcopal graithing ;
But every good fellow will own
　The quarrel is a' about — naething.

VI

The lover may sparkle and glow,
　Approaching his bonie bit gay thing ;
But marriage will soon let him know
　He 's gotten — a buskit-up naething.

VII

The Poet may jingle and rhyme
　In hopes of a laureate wreathing,
And when he has wasted his time,
　He 's kindly rewarded with — naething.

VIII

The thundering bully may rage,
　And swagger and swear like a heathen;
But collar him fast, I 'll engage,
　You 'll find that his courage is — naething.

IX

Last night with a feminine Whig —
　A poet she couldna put faith in !
But soon we grew lovingly big,
　I taught her, her terrors were — naething.

X

Her Whigship was wonderful pleased,
　But charmingly tickled wi' ae thing;

Her fingers I lovingly squeezed,
　And kissed her, and promised her —
　　naething.

XI

The priest anathémas may threat —
　Predicament, sir, that we 're baith in;
But when Honor's reveillé is beat,
　The holy artillery 's — naething.

XII

And now I must mount on the wave:
　My voyage perhaps there is death in;
But what is a watery grave ?
　The drowning a Poet is — naething.

XIII

And now, as grim Death 's in my thought,
　To you, Sir, I make this bequeathing:
My service as long as ye 've ought,　　·
　And my friendship, by God, when ye 've
　　— naething.

REPLY TO A TRIMMING EPIS-TLE RECEIVED FROM A TAILOR

The tailor was one Thomas Walker, who re-sided at Pool, near Ochiltree. His remon-strance, with Burns's *Reply*, appeared in one of the tracts " printed for and sold by Stewart and Meikle." Scott Douglas, who had seen the tailor's manuscripts, concludes that Simp-son of Ochiltree (see *ante*, p. 47, Prefatory Note to *Epistle to William Simpson*) had as much to do with the composition of his *Epistle* as himself.

I

What ails ye now, ye lousie bitch,
To thresh my back at sic a pitch ?
Losh, man, hae mercy wi' your natch !
　　Your bodkin 's bauld:
I didna suffer half sae much
　　Frae Daddie Auld.

II

What tho' at times, when I grow crouse,
I gie their wames a random pouse,
Is that enough for you to souse
　　Your servant sae ?
Gae mind your seam, ye prick-the-louse
　　An' jag-the-flae !

III

King David o' poetic brief
Wrocht 'mang the lassies sic mischief
As fill'd his after-life with grief
    An' bloody rants;
An' yet he 's rank'd amang the chief
    O' lang-syne saunts.

IV

And maybe, Tam, for a' my cants,
My wicked rhymes an' drucken rants,
I 'll gie auld Cloven-Clootie's haunts
    An unco slip yet,
An' snugly sit amang the saunts
    At Davie's hip yet !

V

But, fegs ! the Session says I maun
Gae fa' upo' anither plan
Than garrin lasses coup the cran,
    Clean heels owre body,
An' sairly thole their mither's ban
    Afore the howdy.

VI

This leads me on to tell for sport
How I did wi' the Session sort:
Auld Clinkum at the inner port
    Cried three times : — "Robin !
Come hither lad, and answer for 't,
    Ye 're blam'd for jobbin !"

VII

Wi' pinch I put a Sunday's face on,
An' snoov'd awa' before the Session:
I made an open, fair confession —
    I scorn'd to lie —
An' syne Mess John, beyond expression,
    Fell foul o' me.

VIII

A fornicator-loun he call'd me,
An' said my faut frae bliss expell'd me.
I own'd the tale was true he tell'd me,
    "But, what the matter?"
(Quo' I) " I fear unless ye geld me,
    I 'll ne'er be better !"

IX

" Geld you !" (quo' he) " an' what for no ?
If that your right hand, leg, or toe
Should ever prove your sp'ritual foe
    You should remember
To cut it aff; an' what for no
    Your dearest member ?"

X

" Na, na " (quo' I), " I 'm no for that,
Gelding 's nae better than 't is ca't;
I 'd rather suffer for my faut
    A hearty flewit,
As sair owre hip as ye can draw 't,
    Tho' I should rue it.

XI

" Or, gin ye like to end the bother,
To please us a' — I 've just ae ither:
When next wi' yon lass I forgather,
    Whate'er betide it,
I 'll frankly gie her 't a' thegither,
    An' let her guide it."

XII

But, Sir, this pleas'd them warst of a',
An' therefore, Tam, when that I saw,
I said " Guid-night," an' cam awa,
    An' left the Session:
I saw they were resolved a'
    On my oppression.

TO MAJOR LOGAN

Major William Logan, a retired soldier, of
some repute as fiddler and wit, who lived at
Park, near Ayr, must not be confounded with
John Logan of Afton and Knockshinnoch (the
" Afton's Laird " of *The Kirk's Alarm*, p. 113),
with whom Burns also corresponded.

I

HAIL, thairm-inspirin, rattlin Willie !
Tho' Fortune's road be rough an' hilly
To every fiddling, rhyming billie,
    We never heed,
But take it like the unbrack'd filly
    Proud o' her speed.

II

When, idly goavin, whyles we saunter,
Yirr !   Fancy barks, awa we canter,
Up hill, down brae, till some mishanter,
    Some black bog-hole,
Arrests us; then the scathe an' banter
    We 're forced to thole.

III

Hale be your heart ! hale be your fiddle !
Lang may your elbuck jink an' diddle,

To cheer you through the weary widdle
O' this vile warl',
Until you on a cummock driddle,
A grey-hair'd carl.

IV

Come wealth, come poortith, late or soon,
Heaven send your heart-strings ay in tune,
And screw your temper-pins aboon
(A fifth or mair)
The melancholious, sairie croon
O' cankrie Care.

V

May still your life from day to day,
Nae *lente largo* in the play
But *allegretto forte* gay,
Harmonious flow,
A sweeping, kindling, bauld strathspey —
Encore! Bravo!

VI

A' blessings on the cheery gang,
Wha dearly like a jig or sang,
An' never think o' right an' wrang
By square an' rule,
But as the clegs o' feeling stang
Are wise or fool.

VII

My hand-wal'd curse keep hard in chase
The harpy, hoodock, purse-proud race,
Wha count on poortith as disgrace !
Their tuneless hearts,
May fireside discords jar a bass
To a' their parts !

VIII

But come, your hand, my careless bri-
ther !
I' th' ither warl', if there 's anither —
An' that there is, I 've little swither
About the matter —
We, cheek for chow, shall jog thegither —
I 'se ne'er bid better !

IX

We 've faults and failins — granted clear-
ly !
We 're frail, backsliding mortals merely ;
Eve's bonie squad, priests wyte them
sheerly
For our grand fa' ;
But still, but still — I like them dearly . . .
God bless them a' !

X

Ochon for poor Castalian drinkers,
When they fa' foul o' earthly jinkers !
The witching, curs'd, delicious blinkers
Hae put me hyte,
An' gart me weet my waukrife winkers
Wi' girnin spite.

XI

But by yon moon — and that 's high
swearin ! —
An' every star within my hearin,
An' by her een wha was a dear ane
I 'll ne'er forget,
I hope to gie the jads a clearin
In fair play yet !

XII

My loss I mourn, but not repent it ;
I 'll seek my pursie whare I tint it ;
Ance to the Indies I were wonted,
Some cantraip hour
By some sweet elf I 'll yet be dinted :
Then *vive l'amour !*

XIII

Faites mes baissemains respectueusè
To sentimental sister Susie
And honest Lucky : no to roose you,
Ye may be proud,
That sic a couple Fate allows ye
To grace your blood.

XIV

Nae mair at present can I measure,
An' trowth ! my rhymin ware 's nae trea-
sure ;
But when in Ayr, some half-hour's leisure,
Be 't light, be 't dark,
Sir Bard will do himself the pleasure
To call at Park.
ROBERT BURNS.
MOSSGIEL, 30th October, 1786.

TO THE GUIDWIFE OF WAU-CHOPE HOUSE

(MRS. SCOTT)

Written in answer to a rhyming epistle from
"The Guidwife of Wauchope-House to Robert
Burns the Ayrshire Bard, February, 1787."
The lady was Mrs. Elizabeth Scott (born 1729,
daughter of David Rutherford, Edinburgh,

and niece to Mrs. Cockburn, the song-writer), wife of Walter Scott of Wauchope. Burns's visit to her on 10th May following is thus recorded in his *Journal* of the Border tour: "Wauchope — Mr. Scott exactly the figure and face commonly given to Sancho Panza — very shrewd in his farming matters, and not unfrequently stumbles on what may be called a strong thing rather than a good thing. Mrs. Scott all the sense, taste, intrepidity of face, and bold critical decision which usually distinguish female authors." She died 19th February, 1789. After her death a selection from her verses was published (1801), under the title *Alonzo and Cora*, in which Burns's *Epistle* was included.

I

GUID WIFE,
  I mind it weel, in early date,
  When I was beardless, young, and blate,
    An' first could thresh the barn,
  Or haud a yokin at the pleugh,
  An', tho' forfoughten sair eneugh,
    Yet unco proud to learn;
  When first amang the yellow corn
    A man I reckon'd was,
  An' wi' the lave ilk merry morn
    Could rank my rig and lass:
      Still shearing, and clearing
        The tither stookèd raw,
      Wi' clavers an' havers
        Wearing the day awa.

II

E'en then, a wish (I mind its pow'r),
A wish that to my latest hour
  Shall strongly heave my breast,
That I for poor auld Scotland's sake
Some usefu' plan or book could make,
  Or sing a sang at least.
The rough burr-thistle spreading wide
  Amang the bearded bear,
I turn'd the weeder-clips aside,
  An' spar'd the symbol dear.
    No nation, no station
      My envy e'er could raise;
    A Scot still, but blot still,
      I knew nae higher praise.

III

But still the elements o' sang
In formless jumble, right an' wrang,
  Wild floated in my brain;
Till on that hairst I said before,
My partner in the merry core,
  She rous'd the forming strain.

I see her yet, the sonsie quean
  That lighted up my jingle,
Her witching smile, her pauky een
  That gart my heart-strings tingle!
    I firèd, inspirèd,
      At ev'ry kindling keek,
    But, bashing and dashing,
      I fearèd ay to speak.

IV

Hale to the sex! (ilk guid chiel says):
Wi' merry dance on winter days,
  An' we to share in common!
The gust o' joy, the balm of woe,
The saul o' life, the heav'n below
  Is rapture-giving Woman.
Ye surly sumphs, who hate the name,
  Be mindfu' o' your mither:
She, honest woman, may think shame
  That ye 're connected with her!
    Ye 're wae men, ye 're nae men
      That slight the lovely dears;
    To shame ye, disclaim ye,
      Ilk honest birkie swears.

V

For you, no bred to barn and byre,
Wha sweetly tune the Scottish lyre,
  Thanks to you for your line!
The marl'd plaid ye kindly spare,
By me should gratefully be ware;
  'Twad please me to the nine.
I 'd be mair vauntie o' my hap,
  Douce hingin owre my curple,
Than onie ermine ever lap,
  Or proud imperial purple.
    Farewell, then! lang hale, then,
      An' plenty be your fa'!
    May losses and crosses
      Ne'er at your hallan ca'!
                        R. BURNS.

March, 1787.

TO WM. TYTLER, ESQ., OF WOODHOUSELEE

WITH AN IMPRESSION OF THE AUTHOR'S PORTRAIT

Son of Alexander Tytler, an Edinburgh solicitor, William Tytler was born 12th October, 1711; was educated at the High School and University; was admitted Writer to the Signet in 1744; and died 12th September, 1792. He bestowed his leisure upon historical and antiquarian studies, and is known (to those who care to know) as author of an *Inquiry, Historical and Critical, into the Evidence against Mary Queen of Scots*, 1759 (hence the terms of the poet's address) ; a *Poetical Remains of James I. of Scotland*, 1783 ; a *Dissertation on Scottish Music*, 1774 ; and certain papers in the *Transactions of the Society of Antiquaries*. He assisted Johnson with vol. i. of the *Musical Museum*, whereon his place was presently taken by Burns.

The Epistle (as awkward a piece of writing as Burns ever did in English) was accompanied by a copy of the Beugo engraving. A few lines of prose were added (those in brackets have not hitherto[1] been printed): "My Muse jilted me here, and turned a corner on me, and I have not got again into her good graces. [I have two requests to make. Burn the above verses when you have read them, as any little sense that is in them is rather heretical, and] do me the justice to believe me sincere in my grateful remembrance of the many civilities you have honoured me with since I came to Edinburgh, and in assuring you that I have the honour to be, revered sir, your obliged and very humble servant,   ROBERT BURNS.

"LAWN MARKET, *Friday noon.*"

Scott Douglas surmises that the expunged lines contained "some ultra-Jacobite sally ; " but it is now manifest that Tytler would not have it known that he had disregarded Burns's request.

I

REVERÈD defender of beauteous Stuart,
Of Stuart ! — a name once respected,
A name which to love was once mark of a
    true heart,
But now 't is despis'd and neglected !

II

Tho' something like moisture conglobes in
    my eye —
Let no one misdeem me disloyal !
A poor friendless wand'rer may well claim
    a sigh —
Still more, if that wand'rer were royal.

III

My Fathers that name have rever'd on a
    throne;
My Fathers have fallen to right it:

[1] That is, before the Centenary Edition.

Those Fathers would spurn their degenerate son,
That name, should he scoffingly slight it.

IV

Still in prayers for King George I most
    heartily join,
The Queen, and the rest of the gentry;
Be they wise, be they foolish, is nothing of
    mine:
Their title 's avow'd by my country.

V

But why of that epocha make such a fuss
That gave us the Hanover stem ?
If bringing them over was lucky for us,
I 'm sure 't was as lucky for them.

VI

But loyalty — truce ! we 're on dangerous
    ground:
Who knows how the fashions may alter ?
The doctrine, to-day that is loyalty sound,
To-morrow may bring us a halter !

VII

I send you a trifle, a head of a Bard,
A trifle scarce worthy your care;
But accept it, good Sir, as a mark of regard,
Sincere as a saint's dying prayer.

VIII

Now Life's chilly evening dim-shades on
    your eye,
And ushers the long dreary night;
But you, like the star that athwart gilds
    the sky,
Your course to the latest is bright.

TO MR. RENTON OF LAMERTON

Sent to Mr. Renton, Mordington House, Berwickshire, probably during the poet's Border tour — though Renton is not mentioned in his *Journal*.

YOUR billet, Sir, I grant receipt;
Wi' you I 'll canter onie gate,
Tho' 't were a trip to yon blue warl'
Where birkies march on burning marl:
Then, Sir, God willing, I 'll attend ye,
And to His goodness I commend ye.
    R. BURNS.

TO MISS ISABELLA MACLEOD

For Isabella Macleod, see *ante*, p. 96, Prefatory Note to *On Reading in a Newspaper the Death of John M'Leod, Esq.*

EDINBURGH, March 16, 1787.

I

THE crimson blossom charms the bee,
    The summer sun the swallow:
So dear this tuneful gift to me
    From lovely Isabella.

II

Her portrait fair upon my mind
    Revolving time shall mellow,
And mem'ry's latest effort find
    The lovely Isabella.

III

No Bard nor lover's rapture this
    In fancies vain and shallow!
She is, so come my soul to bliss,
    The lovely Isabella!

TO SYMON GRAY

Symon Gray lived near Duns, and while Burns was on his Border tour sent him some verses for his opinion.

I

SYMON GRAY, you 're dull to-day!
Dullness with redoubled sway
Has seized the wits of Symon Gray.

II

Dear Symon Gray, the other day
    When you sent me some rhyme,
I could not then just ascertain
    Its worth for want of time;

III

But now to-day, good Mr. Gray,
    I 've read it o'er and o'er:
Tried all my skill, but find I 'm still
    Just where I was before.

IV

We auld wives' minions gie our opinions,
    Solicited or no;

Then of its fauts my honest thoughts
    I 'll give — and here they go:

V

Such damn'd bombást no age that 's past
    Can show, nor time to come;
So, Symon dear, your song I 'll tear,
    And with it wipe my bum.

TO MISS FERRIER

Jane Ferrier, eldest daughter of James Ferrier, Writer to the Signet — who resided in George Street, Edinburgh — and sister to Miss Ferrier the novelist. She was born in 1767; married General Samuel Graham, for some time deputy-governor of Stirling Castle; with Edward Blore, the architect, published drawings of the carved work in the state-rooms of that fortress under the title, *Lacunar Strevelincnse*, 1817; and died in 1846.

I

NAE heathen name shall I prefix
    Frae Pindus or Parnassus;
Auld Reekie dings them a' to sticks
    For rhyme-inspiring lasses.

II

Jove's tunefu' dochters three times three
    Made Homer deep their debtor;
But gien the body half an e'e,
    Nine Ferriers wad done better!

III

Last day my mind was in a bog;
    Down George's Street I stoited;
A creeping, cauld, prosaic fog
    My very senses doited;

IV

Do what I dought to set her free,
    My saul lay in the mire;
Ye turned a neuk, I saw your e'e,
    She took the wing like fire!

V

The mournfu' sang I here enclose,
    In gratitude I send you,
And pray, in rhyme as weel as prose,
    A' guid things may attend you!

SYLVANDER TO CLARINDA

Clarinda was Mrs. Agnes Maclehose, *née* Craig, daughter of Andrew Craig, surgeon, Glasgow. She was born in April, 1759 — the same year as her poet; and when he met her in Edinburgh (7th December, 1787) she had for some time been separated from her husband. The Bard, who was (as ever) by way of being a buck, accepted an invitation to take tea with her on the 9th; but an accident obliging him to keep his room, he wrote to express his regret, and at the same time intimated his resolve to cherish her "friendship with the enthusiasm of religion." Mrs. Maclehose responding in the same key, the "friendship" proceeded apace. On Christmas Eve she sent him certain verses, signed "Clarinda," *On Burns saying He had nothing else to Do*, three of which he quoted in the *Glenriddell Book* : —

"When first you saw Clarinda's charms,
    What rapture in your bosom grew !
Her heart was shut to Love's alarms,
    But then — you 'd nothing else to do.

"Apollo oft had lent his harp,
    But now 't was strung from Cupid's bow ;
You sung — it reached Clarinda's heart —
    She wish'd you 'd nothing else to do.

"Fair Venus smil'd, Minerva frown'd,
    Cupid observed, the arrow flew :
Indifference (ere a week went round)
    Show'd you had nothing else to do."

Thus challenged, Sylvander — he became Sylvander there and then — replied as in the text; and the romantic terms in which the two went on to conduct their correspondence soon served the ardent youth as a pretext for the expression of fiercer sentiments than Clarinda's "principles of reason and religion" should have allowed. She sent her Arcadian poems, which he amended for Johnson's *Museum ;* and he fell so deeply enamoured that, on leaving Edinburgh (24th March) he must write thus to a friend : "During these last eight days I have been positively crazy." Clarinda (like Maman Vauquer) *avait des idées* — as what lady in the circumstances would not ? And when Clarinda learned, in August, that Burns had married Armour, Clarinda resented her Sylvander's defection as an unpardonable wrong. They were partly reconciled in the autumn of 1791 ; and ere she rejoined her husband in Jamaica, they had an interview on 6th December, which the gallant and romantic little song, *O May, Thy Morn was ne'er sae Sweet*, is held to commemorate. On the 27th he sent her *Ae Fond Kiss and then We Sever*, with the finest lines he ever wrote : —

"Had we never lov'd sae kindly,
Had we never lov'd sae blindly,
Never met — or never parted —
We had ne'er been broken-hearted :"

Behold the Hour, the Boat Arrive, and part of *Gloomy December*, with the remark : "The remainder of this song is on the wheels — Adieu ! Adieu !" Mrs. Maclehose, still unreconciled to her husband, returned to Scotland in August, 1792. Burns and she corresponded occasionally, but never met again. She died 22d October, 1841.

I

WHEN dear Clarinda, matchless fair,
    First struck Sylvander's raptur'd view,
He gaz'd, he listened to despair —
    Alas ! 't was all he dared to do.

II

Love from Clarinda's heavenly eyes
    Transfixed his bosom thro' and thro',
But still in Friendship's guarded guise —
    For more the demon fear'd to do.

III

That heart, already more than lost,
    The imp beleaguer'd all *perdu;*
For frowning Honor kept his post —
    To meet that frown he shrunk to do.

IV

His pangs the Bard refus'd to own,
    Tho' half he wish'd Clarinda knew;
But Anguish wrung the unweeting groan —
    Who blames what frantic Pain must do ?

V

That heart, where motley follies blend,
    Was sternly still to Honor true:
To prove Clarinda's fondest friend
    Was what a lover, sure, might do !

VI

The Muse his ready quill employ'd;
    No nearer bliss he could pursue;
That bliss Clarinda cold deny'd —
    "Send word by Charles how you do !"

VII

The chill behest disarm'd his Muse,
    Till Passion all impatient grew:
He wrote, and hinted for excuse,
    "'T was 'cause he 'd nothing else to do."

VIII

But by those hopes I have above !
  And by those faults I dearly rue !
The deed, the boldest mark of love,
  For thee that deed I dare to do !

IX

O, could the Fates but name the price
  Would bless me with your charms and
    you,
With frantic joy I 'd pay it thrice,
  If human art or power could do !

X

Then take, Clarinda, friendship's hand
  (Friendship, at least, I may avow),
And lay no more your chill command —
  I 'll write, whatever I 've to do.
             SYLVANDER.
Wednesday night.

TO CLARINDA

WITH A PAIR OF WINE-GLASSES

The glasses were sent as a parting gift when
Burns left Edinburgh, 24th March, 1788.

I

FAIR Empress of the Poet's soul
  And Queen of Poetesses,
Clarinda, take this little boon,
  This humble pair of glasses;

II

And fill them up with generous juice,
  As generous as your mind;
And pledge them to the generous toast:
  "The whole of human kind ! "

III

" To those who love us ! " second fill;
  But not to those whom *we* love,
Lest we love those who love not us !
  A third: — " To thee and me, love ! "

TO HUGH PARKER

A brother of Major William Parker of Kil-
marnock, referred to in the song *Ye Sons of*
Old Killie (see *post*, p. 306). Writing to Robert
Muir, 26th August, 1787, Burns sends compli-
ments to Messrs. W. and H. Parker, and hopes
that " Hughoc is going on and prospering with
God and Miss M'Causlin." The Epistle was
written soon after his arrival in Ellisland on
12th June, 1788, whence, on writing to Mrs.
Dunlop, he describes himself (14th June) as
' a solitary inmate of an old smoky spence ; far
from every object I love, or by whom I am
beloved ; nor any acquaintance older than yes-
terday except *Jenny Geddes*, the old mare I
ride on."

IN this strange land, this uncouth clime,
A land unknown to prose or rhyme;
Where words ne'er cros't the Muse's
    heckles,
Nor limpit in poetic shackles:
A land that Prose did never view it,
Except when drunk he stacher't thro' it:
Here, ambush'd by the chimla cheek,
Hid in an atmosphere of reek,
I hear a wheel thrum i' the neuk,
I hear it — for in vain I leuk:
The red peat gleams, a fiery kernel
Enhuskèd by a fog infernal.
Here, for my wonted rhyming raptures,
I sit and count my sins by chapters;
For life and spunk like ither Christians,
I 'm dwindled down to mere existence;
Wi' nae converse but Gallowa' bodies,
Wi' nae kend face but Jenny Geddes.
Jenny, my Pegasean pride,
Dowie she saunters down Nithside,
And ay a westlin leuk she throws,
While tears hap o'er her auld brown nose !
Was it for this wi' cannie care
Thou bure the Bard through many a shire ?
At howes or hillocks never stumbled,
And late or early never grumbled ?
O, had I power like inclination,
I 'd heeze thee up a constellation !
To canter with the Sagitarre,
Or loup the Ecliptic like a bar,
Or turn the Pole like any arrow;
Or, when auld Phœbus bids good-morrow,
Down the Zodíac urge the race,
And cast dirt on his godship's face:
For I could lay my bread and kail
He 'd ne'er cast saut upo' thy tail ! . . .
Wi' a' this care and a' this grief,
And sma', sma' prospect of relief,
And nought but peat reek i' my head,
How can I write what ye can read ? —
Tarbolton, twenty-fourth o' June,

Ye 'll find me in a better tune;
But till we meet and weet our whistle,
Tak this excuse for nae epistle.
                                        ROBERT BURNS.

TO ALEX. CUNNINGHAM

ELLISLAND IN NITHSDALE,
July 27th, 1788.

Alexander Cunningham, when Burns met
him in Edinburgh in the winter of 1786–7, was
practising as a lawyer. Probably Burns was
introduced to him at the Crochallan Club; and
they remained on the friendliest terms until
the poet's death. The Anna of this Epistle
and of the song *Anna* (*ante*, p. 95) was a Miss
Anne Stewart, who (to Cunningham's lasting
chagrin) married Mr. Forest Dewar, surgeon
and town-councillor, Edinburgh (13th January,
1789). Her perfidy suggested *She 's Fair and
Fause*; and, according to Burns himself, it was
Cunningham's misfortune to which he essayed
to do further justice in *Had I a Cave*. Cun-
ningham married in 1792, and went into part-
nership with a goldsmith. He died January
27, 1812. In accordance with an announce-
ment made by Burns in an affecting letter a
fortnight before his death, the Poet's post-
humous child was named Alexander Cunning-
ham Burns. Holograph letters of Cunningham
— with copies of which we have been favoured
by his descendants — show that he it was who
originated both the subscription on behalf of
Mrs. Burns and the scheme for a collected
Edition; and that to him the success of both
enterprises was chiefly due.

I

My godlike friend — nay, do not stare:
  You think the praise is odd-like ?
But " God is Love," the saints declare:
  Then surely thou art god-like !

II

And is thy ardour still the same,
  And kindled still in Anna ?
Others may boast a partial flame,
  But thou art a volcano !

III

Even Wedlock asks not love beyond
  Death's tie-dissolving portal;
But thou, omnipotently fond,
  May'st promise love immortal !

IV

Thy wounds such healing powers defy,
  Such symptoms dire attend them,
That last great antihectic try —
  Marriage perhaps may mend them.

V

Sweet Anna has an air — a grace,
  Divine, magnetic, touching !
She takes, she charms — but who can trace
  The process of bewitching ?

TO ROBERT GRAHAM, ESQ., OF FINTRY

REQUESTING A FAVOUR

This was doubtless the piece referred to in a
note to Miss Chalmers, 16th September, 1788:
" I very lately — to wit, since harvest began
— wrote a poem, not in imitation, but in the
manner of Pope's *Moral Epistles*. It is only a
short essay, just to try the strength of my
Muse's pinion in that way." For an account
of Graham of Fintry, see *ante*, p. 85.

WHEN Nature her great master-piece de-
      sign'd,
And fram'd her last, best work, the human
      mind,
Her eye intent on all the wondrous plan,
She form'd of various stuff the various
      Man.

The useful many first, she calls them
      forth —
Plain plodding Industry and sober Worth:
Thence peasants, farmers, native sons of
      earth,
And merchandise' whole genus take their
      birth;
Each prudent cit a warm existence finds,
And all mechanics' many-apron'd kinds.
Some other rarer sorts are wanted yet —
The lead and buoy are needful to the net:
The *caput mortuum* of gross desires
Makes a material for mere knights and
      squires;
The martial phosphorus is taught to flow;
She kneads the lumpish philosophic dough,
Then marks th' unyielding mass with grave
      designs —

Law, physic, politics, and deep divines;
Last, she sublimes th' Aurora of the poles,
The flashing elements of female souls.

The order'd system fair before her
    stood;
Nature, well pleas'd, pronounc'd it very
    good;
Yet ere she gave creating labour o'er,
Half-jest, she tried one curious labour
    more.
Some spumy, fiery, *ignis fatuus* matter,
Such as the slightest breath of air might
    scatter;
With arch-alacrity and conscious glee
(Nature may have her whim as well as we:
Her Hogarth-art, perhaps she meant to
    show it),
She forms the thing, and christens it — a
    Poet:
Creature, tho' oft the prey of care and
    sorrow,
When blest to-day, unmindful of to-mor-
    row;
A being form'd t' amuse his graver friends;
Admir'd and prais'd — and there the wages
    ends;
A mortal quite unfit for Fortune's strife,
Yet oft the sport of all the ills of life;
Prone to enjoy each pleasure riches give,
Yet haply wanting wherewithal to live;
Longing to wipe each tear, to heal each
    groan,
Yet frequent all unheeded in his own.

But honest Nature is not quite a Turk:
She laugh'd at first, then felt for her poor
    work.
Viewing the propless climber of mankind,
She cast about a standard tree to find;
In pity for his helpless woodbine state,
She clasp'd his tendrils round the truly
    great:
A title, and the only one I claim,
To lay strong hold for help on bounteous
    Graham.

Pity the hapless Muses' tuneful train !
Weak, timid landsmen on life's stormy
    main,
Their hearts no selfish, stern, absorbent
    stuff,
That never gives — tho' humbly takes —
    enough:
The little Fate allows, they share as soon,

Unlike sage, proverb'd Wisdom's hard-
    wrung boon.
The world were blest did bliss on them de-
    pend —
Ah, that "the friendly e'er should want a
    friend ! "
Let Prudence number o'er each sturdy
    son
Who life and wisdom at one race begun,
Who feel by reason, and who give by rule
(Instinct 's a brute, and Sentiment a fool !),
Who make poor "will do" wait upon "I
    should " —
We own they 're prudent, but who owns
    they 're good ?
Ye wise ones, hence ! ye hurt the social
    eye,
God's image rudely etch'd on base alloy !
But come ye who the godlike pleasure
    know,
Heaven's attribute distinguish'd — to be-
    stow !
Whose arms of love would grasp all human
    race:
Come thou who giv'st with all a courtier's
    grace —
Friend of my life, true patron of my
    rhymes,
Prop of my dearest hopes for future times !

Why shrinks my soul, half blushing, half
    afraid,
Backward, abash'd to ask thy friendly aid ?
I know my need, I know thy giving hand,
I tax thy friendship at thy kind command.
But there are such who court the tuneful
    Nine
(Heavens ! should the branded character
    be mine !),
Whose verse in manhood's pride sublimely
    flows,
Yet vilest reptiles in their begging prose.
Mark, how their lofty independent spirit
Soars on the spurning wing of injur'd
    merit !
Seek you the proofs in private life to find ?
Pity the best of words should be but wind !
So to Heaven's gates the lark's shrill song
    ascends,
But grovelling on the earth the carol ends.
In all the clam'rous cry of starving want,
They dun Benevolence with shameless
    front;
Oblige them, patronise their tinsel lays —
They persecute you all your future days !

Ere my poor soul such deep damnation
    stain,
My horny fist assume the plough again !
The pie-bald jacket let me patch once
    more !
On eighteenpence a week I 've liv'd before.
Tho', thanks to Heaven, I dare even that
    last shift,
I trust, meantime, my boon is in thy gift:
That, plac'd by thee upon the wish'd-for
    height,
With man and nature fairer in her sight,
My Muse may imp her wing for some sub-
    limer flight.

IMPROMPTU TO CAPTAIN RID-
DELL

ON RETURNING A NEWSPAPER

Burns's near neighbour at Friars Carse, who
showed him great courtesy, and gave him a
key to his private grounds and the Hermitage
on Nithside (see *ante*, pp. 80, 120). Friars
Carse was also the scene of the drinking bout
celebrated in *The Whistle* (*ante*, p. 99). Burns
wrote his song, *The Day Returns* (*post*, p. 219)
for the anniversary (7th November) of Captain
Riddell's marriage. At the Riddells' fireside
he " enjoyed more pleasant evenings than at all
the houses of the fashionable people put to-
gether; " and his great regard was in no wise
lessened by the quarrel with the Captain's
brother and sister-in-law (see *post*, p. 178, Pre-
fatory Note to *Impromptu on Mrs. Riddell's
Birthday*), by which the hospitable doors of
Glenriddell — a centre of music and books, of
talk and fellowship and wine — were closed on
him, as the sequel was soon to show, for ever.
On Captain Riddell's death, 21st April, 1794,
he hastened to dedicate his *No More, Ye
Warblers of the Wood* (see *post*, p. 179) to his
memory. Riddell was an accomplished musi-
cian, and composed several of the airs to Burns's
songs in Johnson's *Museum*. He is the " wor-
thy Glenriddell so skilled in old coins " of *The
Whistle*. A fellow of the London Society of
Antiquaries, he contributed some important
papers to *Archæologia*. At his special request,
Burns made a selection from his unprinted
poems, which he presented, with a preface
breathing warm affection for himself and his
" amiable lady," and concluding thus : " Let
these be regarded as the genuine sentiments of
a man who seldom flattered any, and never
those he loved."

ELLISLAND, Monday Evening.

I

YOUR News and Review, Sir,
    I 've read through and through, Sir,
With little admiring or blaming:
    The Papers are barren
    Of home-news or foreign —
No murders or rapes worth the naming.

II

Our friends, the Reviewers,
Those chippers and hewers,
Are judges of mortar and stone, Sir;
    But of meet or unmeet
    In a fabric complete
I 'll boldly pronounce they are none, Sir.

III

My goose-quill too rude is
To tell all your goodness
Bestow'd on your servant, the Poet;
    Would to God I had one
    Like a beam of the sun,
And then all the world, Sir, should know it!

REPLY TO A NOTE FROM CAP-
TAIN RIDDELL

ELLISLAND.

DEAR Sir, at onie time or tide
I 'd rather sit wi' you than ride,
Tho' 't were wi' royal Geordie:
And trowth ! your kindness soon and late
Aft gars me to mysel look blate —
The Lord in Heaven reward ye !
                                    R. BURNS

TO JAMES TENNANT OF GLEN-
CONNER

Second son of John Tennant, farmer, of
Glenconner, in the parish of Ochiltree — ances-
tor of the present Sir Charles Tennant of The
Glen — by his first wife. He was born 1755;
kept a mill at Ochiltree ; and died April, 1835.

AULD comrade dear and brither sinner,
How 's a' the folks about Glenconner ?
How do you this blae eastlin wind,
That 's like to blaw a body blind ?
For me, my faculties are frozen,
My dearest member nearly dozen'd.

I 've sent you here, by Johnie Simson,
Twa sage philosophers to glimpse on:
Smith wi' his sympathetic feeling,
An' Reid to common sense appealing.
Philosophers have fought and wrangled,
An' meikle Greek an' Latin mangled,
Till, wi' their logic-jargon tir'd
And in the depth of science mir'd,
To common sense they now appeal —
What wives and wabsters see and feel !
But, hark ye, friend ! I charge you strictly,
Peruse them, an' return them quickly:
For now I 'm grown sae cursed douse
I pray and ponder butt the house;
My shins my lane I there sit roastin,
Perusing Bunyan, Brown, an' Boston;
Till by an' by, if I haud on,
I 'll grunt a real gospel groan.
Already I begin to try it,
To cast my een up like a pyet,
When by the gun she tumbles o'er,
Flutt'ring an' gasping in her gore:
Sae shortly you shall see me bright,
A burning an' a shining light.

My heart-warm love to guid auld Glen,
The ace an' wale of honest men:
When bending down wi' auld grey hairs,
Beneath the load of years and cares,
May He who made him still support him,
An' views beyond the grave comfort him !
His worthy fam'ly far and near,
God bless them a' wi' grace and gear !

My auld schoolfellow, preacher Willie,
The manly tar, my Mason-billie,
And Auchenbay, I wish him joy;
If he 's a parent, lass or boy,
May he be dad and Meg the mither
Just five-and-forty years thegither !
And no forgetting wabster Charlie,
I 'm tauld he offers very fairly.
An', Lord, remember singing Sannock
Wi' hale breeks, saxpence, an' a bannock !
And next, my auld acquaintance, Nancy,
Since she is fitted to her fancy,
An' her kind stars hae airted till her
A guid chiel wi' a pickle siller !
My kindest, best respects, I sen' it,
To cousin Kate, an' sister Janet:
Tell them, frae me, wi' chiels be cautious,
For faith ! they 'll aiblins fin' them fash-
ious;
To grant a heart is fairly civil,
But to grant a maidenhead 's the devil !

An' lastly, Jamie, for yoursel,
May guardian angels tak a spell,
An' steer you seven miles south o' Hell !
But first, before you see Heaven's glory,
May ye get monie a merry story,
Monie a laugh and monie a drink,
And ay eneugh o' needfu' clink !

Now fare ye weel, an' joy be wi' you !
For my sake, this I beg it o' you:
Assist poor Simson a' ye can;
Ye 'll fin' him just an honest man.
Sae I conclude, and quat my chanter,
Yours, saint or sinner,
RAB THE RANTER.

TO JOHN M'MURDO

WITH SOME OF THE AUTHOR'S POEMS

Son of Robert M'Murdo of Drumlanrig.
He became chamberlain to the Duke of
Queensberry, and resided at Drumlanrig. He
is, perhaps, the " Factor John " of *The Kirk's
Alarm* (see *post*, p. 338). Burns was latterly
on terms of peculiar intimacy with him and
his family, especially after 1793, when
M'Murdo kept house near Dumfries. He
died at Bath, 4th December, 1803. M'Murdo
and Colonel de Peyster of the Dumfries Volun-
teers were brothers-in-law, their wives being
daughters of Provost Blair, Dumfries.. The
canvassing of M'Murdo and his " lovely
spouse " in the Dumfries election of 1790 is
thus described in the *Election Ballad to Gra-
ham of Fintry* (*post*, p. 163):

> " She won each gaping burgess' heart,
>   While he, *sub rosâ*, played his part
>   Among their wives and lasses."

But Burns's esteem for both is sufficiently
shown in the present note and in the lines
On John M'Murdo (*post*, p. 178). Two of
their daughters are the respective themes of
Bonie Jean and *Phyllis the Fair*.

I

O, COULD I give thee India's wealth,
  As I this trifle send !
Because thy Joy in both would be
  To share them with a friend !

II

But golden sands did never grace
  The Heliconian stream;

Then take what gold could never buy —
An honest Bard's esteem.

SONNET TO ROBERT GRAHAM, ESQ., OF FINTRY

ON RECEIVING A FAVOUR, 19TH AUGUST, 1789

The favour was the appointment to an excise district on which the writer's farm was situate. For Graham, see *ante*, p. 85. For the stave, it is fair to note that, judging by this and the other two or three essays in the form which Burns has left, he knew nothing about the sonnet except that it must consist of fourteen lines, and that (as his variations in the present case appear to show) he was not always sure of that. The reason is not, of course, that the sonnet (which is described in the *Schorte Treatise* [1585], and of which Montgomerie left some seventy finished and spirited examples) had no past in the vernacular, but that very few sonnets were made in the eighteenth century, and none of these few was the work of either Ramsay or Fergusson.

I CALL no Goddess to inspire my strains:
A fabled Muse may suit a Bard that feigns.
Friend of my life ! my ardent spirit burns,
And all the tribute of my heart returns,
For boons accorded, goodness ever new,
The gift still dearer, as the giver you.

Thou orb of day ! thou other paler light !
And all ye many sparkling stars of night !
If aught that giver from my mind efface,
If I that giver's bounty e'er disgrace,
Then roll to me along your wand'ring spheres
Only to number out a villain's years !

I lay my hand upon my swelling breast,
And grateful would, but cannot, speak the rest.

EPISTLE TO DR. BLACKLOCK

Thomas Blacklock was born at Annan, of English (Cumberland) parents in 1721. At six months smallpox made him blind. He published *Poems* (poor stuff) in 1746; made the acquaintance of David Hume, who (with other friends) partly supported him at the University of Edinburgh; by Hume's advice completed a theological course; in 1762 was presented to the living of Kirkcudbright; but, the parishioners objecting to his blindness, retired in 1764 to Edinburgh, where he lived by taking pupils. He died 7th July, 1791. An edition of his verses appeared in 1793, with a life by Henry Mackenzie. It was owing to Blacklock that Burns resolved upon an Edinburgh Edition.

ELLISLAND, 21st October, 1789.

I

Wow, but your letter made me vauntie !
And are ye hale, and weel, and cantie ?
I kend it still, your wee bit jauntie
Wad bring ye to :
Lord send you ay as weel 's I want ye,
And then ye 'll do !

II

The Ill-Thief blaw the Heron south,
And never drink be near his drouth !
He tauld mysel by word o' mouth,
He 'd tak my letter:
I lippen'd to the chiel in trowth,
And bade nae better.

III

But aiblins honest Master Heron
Had at the time some dainty fair one
To ware his theologic care on
And holy study,
And, tired o' sauls to waste his lear on,
E'en tried the body.

IV

But what d' ye think, my trusty fier ?
I 'm turned a gauger — Peace be here !
Parnassian queires, I fear, I fear,
Ye 'll now disdain me,
And then my fifty pounds a year
Will little gain me !

V

Ye glaikit, gleesome, dainty damies,
Wha by Castalia's wimplin streamies
Lowp, sing, and lave your pretty limbies,
Ye ken, ye ken,
That strang necessity supreme is
'Mang sons o' men.

VI

I hae a wife and twa wee laddies;
They maun hae brose and brats o' duddies:

Ye ken yoursels my heart right proud is —
    I need na vaunt —
But I 'll sned besoms, thraw saugh woodies,
    Before they want.

VII

Lord help me thro' this warld o' care !
1 'm weary — sick o't late and air !
Not but I hae a richer share
    Than monie ithers;
But why should ae man better fare,
    And a' men brithers ?

VIII

Come, firm Resolve, take thou the van,
Thou stalk o' carl-hemp in man !
And let us mind, faint heart ne'er wan
    A lady fair:
Wha does the utmost that he can
    Will whyles do mair.

IX

But to conclude my silly rhyme
(I 'm scant o' verse and scant o' time):
To make a happy fireside clime
    To weans and wife,
That 's the true pathos and sublime
    Of human life.

X

My compliments to sister Beckie,
And eke the same to honest Lucky:
I wat she is a daintie chuckie
    As e'er tread clay:
And gratefully, my guid auld cockie,
    I 'm yours for ay.
            ROBERT BURNS.

TO A GENTLEMAN

WHO HAD SENT A NEWSPAPER, AND
OFFERED TO CONTINUE IT FREE OF
EXPENSE

Probably Peter Stuart of *The London Star.*
He left *The Morning Post* to join with certain
others, including John Mayne, author of *The
Siller Gun,* in founding *The Star and Evening
Advertiser* in the beginning of 1788; but in the
February of 1789 he quarrelled, not, as has
been vaguely supposed, with the proprietors of
some other paper, but with the proprietors of
The Star aforesaid, and on the 13th he brought
out a *Star* of his own. The main ground of
the quarrel was his support of the Prince of
Wales, and he defended his secession in a
lengthy address to the public. Thus for some
six months two several *Stars* appeared in Lon-
don : the old one — the *Dog Star,* Stuart called
it — " published by John Mayne ; " and the
new one, " published by Peter Stuart," ex-pub-
lisher of the old. At first Stuart retained the
old title, with the addition below, *Printed by
P. Stuart;* but on February 24th he changed it
to *Stuart's Star and Evening Advertiser,* and
on April 27th to *The Morning Star.* Some two
months after the journal died.

KIND SIR, I 've read your paper through,
And faith, to me 't was really new !
How guessed ye, Sir, what maist I wanted ?
This monie a day I 've grain'd and gaunted,
To ken what French mischief was brewin;
Or what the drumlie Dutch were doin;
That vile doup-skelper, Emperor Joseph,
If Venus yet had got his nose off;
Or how the collieshangie works
Atween the Russians and the Turks;
Or if the Swede, before he halt,
Would play anither Charles the Twalt;
If Denmark, any body spak o't;
Or Poland, wha had now the tack o't;
How cut-throat Prussian blades were hingin;
How libbet Italy was singing;
If Spaniard, Portuguese, or Swiss
Were sayin or takin aught amiss;
Or how our merry lads at hame
In Britain's court kept up the game:
How royal George — the Lord leuk o'er
    him ! —
Was managing St. Stephen's quorum;
If sleekit Chatham Will was livin,
Or glaikit Charlie got his nieve in;
How Daddie Burke the plea was cookin;
If Warren Hastings' neck was yeukin;
How cesses, stents, and fees were rax'd,
Or if bare arses yet were tax'd;
The news o' princes, dukes, and earls,
Pimps, sharpers, bawds, and opera-girls;
If that daft buckie, Geordie Wales,
Was threshin still at hizzies' tails;
Or if he was grown oughtlins douser,
And no a perfect kintra cooser:
A' this and mair I never heard of,
And, but for you, I might despair'd of.
So, gratefu', back your news I send you,
And pray a' guid things may attend you !
ELLISLAND, Monday Morning.

TO PETER STUART

DEAR PETER, dear Peter,
  We poor sons of metre
Are often negleckit, ye ken:
  For instance your sheet, man
  (Tho' glad I 'm to see 't, man),
I get it no ae day in ten.

TO JOHN MAXWELL, ESQ., OF TERRAUGHTIE

ON HIS BIRTH-DAY

John Maxwell, though descended from a branch of the Maxwells, was born of humble parents at Buittle, 7th February, 1720, and apprenticed to a joiner in Dumfries. His industry and ability enabled him to repurchase the family estate of Terraughtie. Burns's prediction as to his length of days was so far verified, one learns, that he died (25th January, 1814) in his ninety-fourth year. In the *Second Heron Election Ballad* (p. 166) he is designated "Teuch Johnie."

I

HEALTH to the Maxwells' vet'ran Chief!
Health ay unsour'd by care or grief!
Inspir'd, I turn'd Fate's sibyl leaf
      This natal morn:
I see thy life is stuff o' prief,
      Scarce quite half-worn.

II

This day thou metes threescore eleven,
And I can tell that bounteous Heaven
(The second-sight, ye ken, is given
      To ilka Poet)
On thee a tack o' seven times seven,
      Will yet bestow it.

III

If envious buckies view wi' sorrow
Thy lengthen'd days on thy blest morrow,
May Desolation's lang-teeth'd harrow,
      Nine miles an' hour,
Rake them, like Sodom and Gomorrah,
      In brunstane stoure!

IV

But for thy friends, and they are monie,
Baith honest men and lasses bonie,
May couthie Fortune, kind and cannie
      In social glee,
Wi' mornings blythe and e'enings funny
      Bless them and thee!

V

Fareweel, auld birkie! Lord be near ye,
And then the Deil, he daurna steer ye!
Your friends ay love, your foes ay fear ye!
      For me, shame fa' me,
If neist my heart I dinna wear ye,
      While Burns they ca' me!

TO WILLIAM STEWART

IN honest Bacon's ingle-neuk
  Here maun I sit and think,
Sick o' the warld and warld's folk,
  An' sick, damn'd sick, o' drink!
I see, I see there is nae help,
  But still doun I maun sink;
Till some day laigh enough I yelp:—
  "Wae worth that cursed drink!"
Yestreen, alas! I was sae fu'
  I could but yisk and wink;
And now, this day, sair, sair I rue
  The weary, weary drink.
Satan, I fear thy sooty claws,
  I hate thy brunstane stink,
And ay I curse the luckless cause —
  The wicked soup o' drink.
In vain I would forget my woes
  In idle rhyming clink,
For, past redemption damn'd in prose,
  I can do nought but drink.
To you my trusty, well-tried friend,
  May heaven still on you blink!
And may your life flow to the end,
  Sweet as a dry man's drink!

INSCRIPTION TO MISS GRAHAM OF FINTRY

I

HERE, where the Scottish Muse immortal
    lives
  In sacred strains and tuneful numbers
    join'd,
Accept the gift! Though humble he who
    gives,
  Rich is the tribute of the grateful mind.

II

So may no ruffian feeling in thy breast,
Discordant, jar thy bosom-chords among !
But Peace attune thy gentle soul to rest,
Or Love ecstatic wake his seraph song !

III

Or Pity's notes in luxury of tears,
As modest Want the tale of woe reveals;
While conscious Virtue all the strain en-
dears,
And heaven-born Piety her sanction
seals !

ROBERT BURNS.

DUMFRIES, 31st January, 1794.

REMORSEFUL APOLOGY

Probably sent to Mrs. Walter Riddell.

I

THE friend whom, wild from Wisdom's
way,
The fumes of wine infuriate send
(Not moony madness more astray),
Who but deplores that hapless friend ?

II

Mine was th' insensate, frenzied part —
Ah ! why should I such scenes outlive ?
Scenes so abhorrent to my heart !
'T is thine to pity and forgive.

TO COLLECTOR MITCHELL

Written towards the close of '95. Burns was
on very friendly terms with Mitchell, and often
sent him first drafts for criticism.

I

FRIEND of the Poet tried and leal,
Wha wanting thee might beg or steal;
Alake, alake, the meikle Deil
Wi' a' his witches
Are at it, skelpin jig an' reel
In my poor pouches !

II

I modestly fu' fain wad hint it,
That One-pound-one, I sairly want it;

If wi' the hizzie down ye sent it,
It would be kind;
And while my heart wi' life-blood dunted,
I 'd bear 't in mind !

III

So may the Auld Year gang out moanin
To see the New come laden, groanin
Wi' double plenty o'er the loanin
To thee and thine:
Domestic peace and comforts crownin
The hale design !

POSTSCRIPT

IV

Ye 've heard this while how I 've been
licket,
And by fell Death was nearly nicket:
Grim loon ! He got me by the fecket,
And sair me sheuk;
But by guid luck I lap a wicket,
And turn'd a neuk.

V

But by that health, I 've got a share o't,
And by that life, I 'm promis'd mair o't,
My hale and weel, I 'll tak a care o't,
A tentier way;
Then farewell Folly, hide and hair o't,
For ance and ay !

TO COLONEL DE PEYSTER

Colonel Arent Schuyler de Peyster was de-
scended from a Huguenot family settled in
America, and served with distinction in the
American War. He took up house at Mavis
Grove, near Dumfries ; and on 24th May, 1795,
was appointed colonel of the Dumfries Volun-
teers, in which Burns was a private. He was
a brother-in-law of John M'Murdo (see *ante*,
p. 143). He died 26th November, 1822, in his
96th year.

I

MY honor'd Colonel, deep I feel
Your interest in the Poet's weal:
Ah ! now sma' heart hae I to speel
The steep Parnassus,
Surrounded thus by bolus pill
And potion glasses.

II

O, what a canty warld were it,
Would pain and care and sickness spare it,
And Fortune favor worth and merit
    As they deserve,
And ay a rowth — roast-beef and claret ! —
    Syne, wha wad starve ?

III

Dame Life, tho' fiction out may trick her,
And in paste gems and frippery deck her,
Oh ! flickering, feeble, and unsicker
    I 've found her still:
Ay wavering, like the willow-wicker,
    'Tween good and ill !

IV

Then that curst carmagnole, Auld Satan,
Watches, like baudrons by a ratton,
Our sinfu' saul to get a claut on
    Wi' felon ire;
Syne, whip ! his tail ye ne'er cast saut on —
    He 's aff like fire.

V

Ah Nick ! Ah Nick ! it is na fair,
First showing us the tempting ware,
Bright wines and bonie lasses rare,
    To put us daft;
Syne weave, unseen, thy spider snare
    O' Hell's damned waft !

VI

Poor Man, the flie, aft bizzes by,
And aft, as chance he comes thee nigh,
Thy damn'd auld elbow yeuks wi' joy
    And hellish pleasure,
Already in thy fancy's eye
    Thy sicker treasure !

VII

Soon, heels o'er gowdie, in he gangs,
And, like a sheep-head on a tangs,
Thy girnin laugh enjoys his pangs
    And murdering wrestle,
As, dangling in the wind, he hangs
    A gibbet's tassle.

VIII

But lest you think I am uncivil
To plague you with this draunting drivel,
Abjuring a' intentions evil,
    I quat my pen:
The Lord preserve us frae the Devil !
    Amen ! Amen !

TO MISS JESSIE LEWARS

THINE be the volumes, Jessie fair,
And with them take the Poet's prayer:
That Fate may in her fairest page,
With ev'ry kindliest, best presage
Of future bliss enrol thy name;
With native worth, and spotless fame,
And wakeful caution, still aware
Of ill — but chief Man's felon snare !
All blameless joys on earth we find,
And all the treasures of the mind —
These be thy guardian and reward !
So prays thy faithful friend, the Bard.
           ROBERT BURNS.

June 26, 1796.

INSCRIPTION

WRITTEN ON THE BLANK LEAF OF A
COPY OF THE LAST EDITION OF MY
POEMS, PRESENTED TO THE LADY
WHOM, IN SO MANY FICTITIOUS REVER-
IES OF PASSION, BUT WITH THE MOST
ARDENT SENTIMENTS OF REAL FRIEND-
SHIP, I HAVE SO OFTEN SUNG UNDER
THE NAME OF CHLORIS

For Chloris, see Prefatory Note to *Lassie
wi' the Lint-white Locks, post*, p. 289.   The copy
sent to George Thomson, now at Brechin Cas-
tle, corresponds with the text.   An early draft
is in the Clarke-Adam Collection.
    The stanza is that of much English eigh-
teenth century verse : among the rest, of Gold-
smith's *Edwin and Angelina*.

I

'T IS Friendship's pledge, my young, fair
       Friend,
  Nor thou the gift refuse;
Nor with unwilling ear attend
  The moralising Muse.

II

Since thou in all thy youth and charms
  Must bid the world adieu
(A world 'gainst peace in constant arms),
  To join the friendly few;

III

Since, thy gay morn of life o'ercast,
  Chill came the tempest's lour

(And ne'er Misfortune's eastern blast
  Did nip a fairer flower);

IV

Since life's gay scenes must charm no
    more:
  Still much is left behind,
Still nobler wealth hast thou in store —
  The comforts of the mind !

V

Thine is the self-approving glow
  Of conscious honor's part;
And (dearest gift of Heaven below)
  Thine Friendship's truest heart;

VI

The joys refin'd of sense and taste,
  With every Muse to rove:
And doubly were the Poet blest,
  These joys could he improve.
        Une Bagatelle de l' Amitié.
Coila.

THEATRICAL PIECES

PROLOGUE

SPOKEN BY MR. WOODS ON HIS BENEFIT
NIGHT, MONDAY, 16TH APRIL, 1787

William Woods, born 1751, was originally a
printer, but joined (*c.* 1768) a strolling com-
pany at Southampton. After appearing in
London, he removed, about 1771, to Edinburgh,
where he played leading parts in tragedy
and sentimental comedy. He died 14th De-
cember, 1802, and was buried in the Old Cal-
ton Cemetery. He was author of two plays:
The Volunteers (1778) and *The Twins* (1780);
the last one published in '83. Burns's interest
in Woods was probably quickened by the play-
er's friendship with Fergusson, who, in his *Last
Will*, bequeaths him his Shakespeare : —

> " To Woods, whose genius can provoke
> My passions to the bowl or sock ;
> For love to thee and to the Nine,
> Be my immortal Shakespeare thine."

The piece, like the others in this category, is
on the traditional lines originally laid down by
Dryden.

WHEN by a generous Public's kind acclaim
That dearest need is granted — honest
    fame;

When here your favour is the actor's lot,
Nor even the man in private life forgot;
What breast so dead to heavenly Virtue's
    glow
But heaves impassion'd with the grateful
    throe ?

Poor is the task to please a barb'rous
    throng:
It needs no Siddons' powers in Southern's
    song.
But here an ancient nation, fam'd afar
For genius, learning high, as great in war.
Hail, Caledonia, name for ever dear !
Before whose sons I 'm honor'd to ap-
    pear !
Where every science, every noble art,
That can inform the mind or mend the
    heart,
Is known (as grateful nations oft have
    found),
Far as the rude barbarian marks the bound !
Philosophy, no idle pedant dream,
Here holds her search by heaven-taught
    Reason's beam;
Here History paints with elegance and force
The tide of Empire's fluctuating course;
Here *Douglas* forms wild Shakespeare into
    plan,
And Harley rouses all the God in man.
When well-form'd taste and sparkling wit
    unite
With manly lore, or female beauty bright
(Beauty, where faultless symmetry and
    grace
Can only charm us in the second place),
Witness my heart, how oft with panting fear,
As on this night, I 've met these judges
    here !
But still the hope Experience taught to
    live:
Equal to judge, you 're candid to forgive.
No hundred-headed Riot here we meet,
With Decency and Law beneath his feet;
Nor Insolence assumes fair Freedom's
    name:
Like Caledonians you applaud or blame !

O Thou, dread Power, Whose empire-
    giving hand
Has oft been stretch'd to shield the honor'd
    land !
Strong may she glow with all her ancient
    fire;
May every son be worthy of his sire;

Firm may she rise, with generous disdain
At Tyranny's, or direr Pleasure's chain;
Still self-dependent in her native shore,
Bold may she brave grim Danger's loudest
    roar,
Till Fate the curtain drop on worlds to be
    no more !

PROLOGUE SPOKEN AT THE THEATRE OF DUMFRIES

ON NEW YEAR'S DAY EVENING, 1790

Of Sutherland Burns wrote (9th February,
1790) to William Nicol: "A worthier or
cleverer fellow I have rarely met with." To
his brother Gilbert, 11th January, 1790, he
described him as "a man of apparent worth,"
adding that he spouted the prologue "to his
audience with applause." "I shall not be in
the least mortified," wrote Burns, "though
they are never heard of, but if they can be of
any service to Mr. Sutherland and his friends,
I shall kiss my hands to my Lady Muse, and
own myself much her debtor."

No song nor dance I bring from yon great
    city
That queens it o'er our taste — the more 's
    the pity !
Tho', by the bye, abroad why will you
    roam ?
Good sense and taste are natives here at
    home.
But not for panegyric I appear:
I come to wish you all a good New Year !
Old Father Time deputes me here before
    ye,
Not for to preach, but tell his simple story.
The sage, grave Ancient cough'd, and bade
    me say:
"You 're one year older this important
    day."
If wiser too — he hinted some suggestion,
But 't would be rude, you know, to ask the
    question;
And with a would-be-roguish leer and wink
He bade me on you press this one word —
    Think !

Ye sprightly youths, quite flush with
    hope and spirit,
Who think to storm the world by dint of
    merit,

To you the dotard has a deal to say,
In his sly, dry, sententious, proverb way !
He bids you mind, amid your thoughtless
    rattle,
That the first blow is ever half the battle;
That, tho' some by the skirt may try to
    snatch him,
Yet by the forelock is the hold to catch
    him;
That, whether doing, suffering, or forbear-
    ing,
You may do miracles by persevering.

Last, tho' not least in love, ye youthful
    fair,
Angelic forms, high Heaven's peculiar care !
To you old Bald-Pate smoothes his wrinkled
    brow,
And humbly begs you 'll mind the impor-
    tant — Now !
To crown your happiness he asks your
    leave,
And offers bliss to give and to receive.

For our sincere, tho' haply weak endeav-
    ours,
With grateful pride we own your many
    favours;
And howsoe'er our tongues may ill reveal
    it,
Believe our glowing bosoms truly feel it.

SCOTS PROLOGUE FOR MRS. SUTHERLAND

ON HER BENEFIT-NIGHT AT THE THEA-TRE, DUMFRIES, MARCH 3, 1790

What needs this din about the town o'
    Lon'on,
How this new play an' that new song is
    comin ?
Why is outlandish stuff sae meikle courted ?
Does Nonsense mend like brandy — when
    imported ?
Is there nae poet, burning keen for fame,
Will bauldly try to gie us plays at hame ?
For Comedy abroad he need na toil:
A knave and fool are plants of every soil.
Nor need he stray as far as Rome or Greece
To gather matter for a serious piece:
There 's themes enow in Caledonian story
Would show the tragic Muse in a' her glory

Is there no daring Bard will rise and tell
How glorious Wallace stood, how hapless
    fell ?
Where are the Muses fled that could pro-
    duce
A drama worthy o' the name o' Bruce ?
How here, even here, he first unsheath'd
    the sword
'Gainst mighty England and her guilty
    lord,
And after monie a bloody, deathless doing,
Wrench'd his dear country from the jaws
    of Ruin !
O, for a Shakespeare, or an Otway scene
To paint the lovely, hapless Scottish Queen !
Vain all th' omnipotence of female charms
'Gainst headlong, ruthless, mad Rebellion's
    arms !
She fell, but fell with spirit truly Roman,
To glut the vengeance of a rival woman:
A woman (tho' the phrase may seem uncivil)
As able — and as cruel — as the Devil !
One Douglas lives in Home's immortal
    page,
But Douglasses were heroes every age;
And tho' your fathers, prodigal of life,
A Douglas followed to the martial strife,
Perhaps, if bowls row right, and Right
    succeeds,
Ye yet may follow where a Douglas leads !

As ye hae generous done, if a' the land
Would take the Muses' servants by the
    hand;
Not only hear, but patronize, befriend them,
And where ye justly can commend, com-
    mend them;
And aiblins, when they winna stand the test,
Wink hard, and say: "The folks hae done
    their best !"
Would a' the land do this, then I'll be
    caition
Ye'll soon hae Poets o' the Scottish nation
Will gar Fame blaw until her trumpet crack,
And warsle Time, an' lay him on his back !

For us and for our stage, should onie
    spier: —
"Whase aught thae chiels maks a' this
    bustle here ?"
My best leg foremost, I'll set up my
    brow: —
"We have the honor to belong to you !"
We're your ain bairns, e'en guide us as ye
    like,

But like good mithers, shore before ye
    strike;
And gratefu' still, I trust ye'll ever find us
For gen'rous patronage and meikle kindness
We've got frae a' professions, setts an'
    ranks:
God help us ! we're but poor — ye'se get
    but thanks !

THE RIGHTS OF WOMAN

AN OCCASIONAL ADDRESS

SPOKEN BY MISS FONTENELLE ON HER BENEFIT
NIGHT, NOVEMBER 26, 1792

Sent to Miss Fontenelle in a complimentary
letter: "Your charms as a woman would se-
cure applause to the most indifferent actress,
and your theatrical talents would secure admi-
ration to the plainest figure." She is also the
subject of a flattering *Epigram* (p. 189). Miss
Fontenelle won some applause on the London
boards. Her name appears in the obituary of
The Gentleman's Magazine for September, 1800:
"In Charles-town, South Carolina, a victim to
the yellow fever, Miss Fontenelle, who made
her *debut* many years ago at Covent Garden,
and afterwards performed at the Haymarket.
In America she played under the name of Mrs.
Wilkinson."

WHILE Europe's eye is fix'd on mighty
    things,
The fate of empires and the fall of kings;
While quacks of State must each produce
    his plan,
And even children lisp the Rights of Man;
Amid this mighty fuss just let me mention,
The Rights of Woman merit some attention.

First, in the sexes' intermix'd connexion
One sacred Right of Woman is Protection:
The tender flower, that lifts its head elate,
Helpless must fall before the blasts of fate,
Sunk on the earth, defac'd its lovely form,
Unless your shelter ward th' impending
    storm.

Our second Right — but needless here is
    caution —
To keep that right inviolate's the fashion:
Each man of sense has it so full before him,
He'd die before he'd wrong it — 't is De-
    corum !

There was, indeed, in far less polish'd days,
A time, when rough rude Man had naughty
    ways:
Would swagger, swear, get drunk, kick up
    a riot,
Nay, even thus invade a lady's quiet!
Now, thank our stars! these Gothic times
    are fled;
Now, well-bred men — and you are all
    well-bred —
Most justly think (and we are much the
    gainers)
Such conduct neither spirit, wit, nor man-
    ners.

For Right the third, our last, our best, our
    dearest:
That right to fluttering female hearts the
    nearest,
Which even the Rights of Kings, in low
    prostration,
Most humbly own — 't is dear, dear Admi-
    ration!
In that blest sphere alone we live and move;
There taste that life of life — Immortal
    Love.
Smiles, glances, sighs, tears, fits, flirtations,
    airs —
'Gainst such an host what flinty savage
    dares?
When awful Beauty joins with all her
    charms,
Who is so rash as rise in rebel arms?

But truce with kings, and truce with con-
    stitutions,
With bloody armaments and revolutions;
Let Majesty your first attention summon:
Ah! ça ira! the Majesty of Woman!

ADDRESS

SPOKEN BY MISS FONTENELLE ON HER
    BENEFIT NIGHT, DECEMBER 4, 1793,
    AT THE THEATRE, DUMFRIES

STILL anxious to secure your partial favor,
And not less anxious, sure, this night than
    ever,
A Prologue, Epilogue, or some such mat-
    ter,
'T would vamp my bill, said I, if nothing
    better:

So sought a Poet roosted near the skies;
Told him I came to feast my curious eyes;
Said, nothing like his works was ever
    printed;
And last, my prologue-business slily hinted.
"Ma'am, let me tell you," quoth my man
    of rhymes,
"I know your bent — these are no laugh-
    ing times:
Can you — but, Miss, I own I have my
    fears —
Dissolve in pause, and sentimental tears?
With laden sighs, and solemn-rounded sen-
    tence,
Rouse from his sluggish slumbers fell Re-
    pentance?
Paint Vengeance, as he takes his horrid
    stand,
Waving on high the desolating brand,
Calling the storms to bear him o'er a guilty
    land?"

I could no more! Askance the creature
    eyeing: —
"D' ye think," said I, "this face was made
    for crying?
I 'll laugh, that 's poz — nay more, the
    world shall know it;
And so, your servant! gloomy Master
    Poet!"

Firm as my creed, Sirs, 't is my fix'd be-
    lief
That Misery 's another word for Grief.
I also think (so may I be a bride!)
That so much laughter, so much life en-
    joy'd.

Thou man of crazy care and ceaseless sigh,
Still under bleak Misfortune's blasting eye;
Doom'd to that sorest task of man alive —
To make three guineas do the work of five;
Laugh in Misfortune's face — the beldam
    witch —
Say, you 'll be merry, tho' you can't be
    rich!

Thou other man of care, the wretch in love!
Who long with jiltish arts and airs hast
    strove;
Who, as the boughs all temptingly project,
Measur'st in desperate thought — a rope
    — thy neck —
Or, where the beetling cliff o'erhangs the
    deep,

Peerest to meditate the healing leap:
Would'st thou be cur'd, thou silly, moping
    elf ?
Laugh at her follies, laugh e'en at thy-
    self;
Learn to despise those frowns now so ter-
    rific,
And love a kinder: that's your grand spe-
    cific.

To sum up all: be merry, I advise;
And as we're merry, may we still be wise !

POLITICAL PIECES

ADDRESS OF BEELZEBUB

To the Right Honorable the Earl of Breadalbane,
President of the Right Honorable the Highland Society,
which met on the 23rd of May last, at the *Shakespeare*,
Covent Garden, to concert ways and means to frustrate
the designs of five hundred Highlanders who, as the
Society were informed by Mr. M'Kenzie of Applecross,
were so audacious as to attempt an escape from their
lawful lords and masters whose property they were, by
emigrating from the lands of Mr. Macdonald of Glen-
gary to the wilds of Canada, in search of that fantastic
thing — Liberty.

Long life, my lord, an' health be yours,
Unskaith'd by hunger'd Highland boors !
Lord grant nae duddie, desperate beggar,
Wi' dirk, claymore, or rusty trigger,
May twin auld Scotland o' a life
She likes — as lambkins like a knife !

Faith ! you and Applecross were right
To keep the Highland hounds in sight !
I doubt na ! they wad bid nae better
Than let them ance out owre the water !
Then up amang thae lakes and seas,
They'll mak what rules and laws they
    please:
Some daring Hancock, or a Franklin,
May set their Highland bluid a-ranklin;
Some Washington again may head them,
Or some Montgomerie, fearless, lead them;
Till (God knows what may be effected
When by such heads and hearts directed)
Poor dunghill sons of dirt an' mire
May to Patrician rights aspire !
Nae sage North now, nor sager Sackville,
To watch and premier owre the pack vile !
An' whare will ye get Howes and Clin-
    tons

To bring them to a right repentance ?
To cowe the rebel generation,
An' save the honor o' the nation ?
They, an' be damn'd ! what right hae they
To meat or sleep or light o' day,
Far less to riches, pow'r, or freedom,
But what your lordship likes to gie them ?

But hear, my lord ! Glengary, hear !
Your hand's owre light on them, I fear:
Your factors, grieves, trustees, and bailies,
I canna say but they do gaylies :
They lay aside a' tender mercies,
An' tirl the hullions to the birses.
Yet while they're only poind and herriet,
They'll keep their stubborn Highland spirit.
But smash them ! crush them a' to spails,
An' rot the dyvors i' the jails !
The young dogs, swinge them to the labour:
Let wark an' hunger mak them sober !
The hizzies, if they're aughtlins fawsom,
Let them in Drury Lane be lesson'd !
An' if the wives an' dirty brats
Come thiggin at your doors an' yetts,
Flaffin wi' duds an' grey wi' beas',
Frightin awa your deuks an' geese,
Get out a horsewhip or a jowler,
The langest thong, the fiercest growler,
An' gar the tatter'd gypsies pack
Wi' a' their bastards on their back !

Go on, my Lord ! I lang to meet you,
An' in my " house at hame " to greet you
Wi' common lords ye shanna mingle:
The benmost neuk beside the ingle,
At my right han' assigned your seat
'Tween Herod's hip an' Polycrate,
Or (if you on your station tarrow)
Between Almagro and Pizarro,
A seat, I'm sure ye're weel deservin't;
An' till ye come — your humble servant,
                                BEELZEBUB
HELL,
1st June, Anno Mundi 5790.

BIRTHDAY ODE FOR 31ST
DECEMBER, 1787

Without giving his authority, Currie ac-
counts for the piece thus: " It appears that
on the 31st December he (Burns) attended a
meeting to celebrate the birthday of the lineal
descendant of the Scottish race of kings, the
late unfortunate Prince Charles Edward."

More he knew not; but he assumed the " perfect loyalty to the reigning sovereign of all who attended the meeting," and he withheld a large portion of the *Ode* because it was " a kind of rant, for which indeed precedent may be cited in various other odes, but with which it is impossible to go along."

AFAR the illustrious Exile roams,
  Whom kingdoms on this day should hail,
An inmate in the casual shed,
On transient pity's bounty fed,
  Haunted by busy Memory's bitter tale !
Beasts of the forest have their savage homes,
  But He, who should imperial purple wear,
Owns not the lap of earth where rests his royal head:
  His wretched refuge dark despair,
While ravening wrongs and woes pursue,
And distant far the faithful few
  Who would his sorrows share !

False flatterer, Hope, away,
  Nor think to lure us as in days of yore !
We solemnize this sorrowing natal day,
  To prove our loyal truth — we can no more —
And, owning Heaven's mysterious sway,
  Submissive, low, adore.
Ye honor'd, mighty Dead,
  Who nobly perish'd in the glorious cause,
  Your King, your Country, and her laws:
From great Dundee, who smiling Victory led
And fell a Martyr in her arms
(What breast of northern ice but warms !),
To bold Balmerino's undying name,
Whose soul of fire, lighted at Heaven's high flame,
Deserves the proudest wreath departed heroes claim !

Not unrevenged your fate shall lie,
  It only lags, the fatal hour:
Your blood shall with incessant cry
  Awake at last th' unsparing Power.
As from the cliff, with thundering course,
  The snowy ruin smokes along
With doubling speed and gathering force,

Till deep it, crushing, whelms the cottage in the vale,
  So Vengeance' arm, ensanguin'd, strong,
Shall with resistless might assail,
Usurping Brunswick's pride shall lay,
And Stewart's wrongs and yours with tenfold weight repay.

Perdition, baleful child of night,
Rise and revenge the injured right
  Of Stewart's royal race !
Lead on the unmuzzled hounds of Hell,
Till all the frighted echoes tell
  The blood-notes of the chase !
Full on the quarry point their view,
Full on the base usurping crew,
The tools of faction and the nation's curse !
Hark how the cry grows on the wind;
They leave the lagging gale behind;
Their savage fury, pityless, they pour;
With murdering eyes already they devour !
See Brunswick spent, a wretched prey,
His life one poor despairing day,
Where each avenging hour still ushers in a worse !
  Such Havoc, howling all abroad,
    Their utter ruin bring,
  The base apostates to their God
    Or rebels to their King !

ODE TO THE DEPARTED REGENCY BILL

George III. began to show signs of mental derangement on 22d October, 1788; and on 5th December his physicians reported that, although he was not incurable, it was impossible to predict how long his illness might last. Fox and the " Portland Band " (*i. e.* the Whigs) who hoped to return to power through the Prince of Wales, maintained that the Heir-Apparent must take up the Regency with plenary sovereign powers; but on 16th December Pitt brought in resolutions for appointing him Regent with restricted authority. The Bill passed the Commons on 11th February, 1789, but its progress was suspended by the announcement of the Chancellor on the 19th that the King was convalescent; and on 10th March he resumed his state.

DAUGHTER of Chaos' doting years,
Nurse of ten thousand hopes and fears !

Whether thy airy, unsubstantial shade
(The rights of sepulture now duly paid)
Spread abroad its hideous form
On the roaring civil storm,
Deafening din and warring rage
Factions wild with factions wage;
　　Or Underground
　　Deep-sunk, profound
Among the demons of the earth,
　　With groans that make
　　The mountains shake
Thou mourn thy ill-starr'd blighted birth;
Or in the uncreated Void,
　　Where seeds of future being fight,
　　With lighten'd step thou wander wide
To greet thy mother — Ancient Night —
And as each jarring monster-mass is past,
Fond recollect what once thou wast:
In manner due, beneath this sacred oak,
Hear, Spirit, hear! thy presence I in-
　　voke!

By a Monarch's heaven-struck fate;
By a disunited State;
By a generous Prince's wrongs;
By a Senate's war of tongues;
By a Premier's sullen pride
Louring on the changing tide;
By dread Thurlow's powers to awe —
Rhetoric, blasphemy, and law;
By the turbulent ocean,
A Nation's commotion;
By the harlot-caresses
Of Borough addresses;
By days few and evil;
(Thy portion, poor devil!),
By Power, Wealth, and Show — the Gods
　　by men adored;
By nameless Poverty their Hell abhorred;
　　By all they hope, by all they fear,
　　Hear! and Appear!

Stare not on me, thou ghostly Power,
Nor, grim with chain'd defiance, lour!
No Babel-structure would I build
　　Where, Order exil'd from his native sway,
Confusion might the Regent-sceptre wield,
　　While all would rule and none obey.
Go, to the world of Man relate
The story of thy sad, eventful fate;
And call presumptuous Hope to hear
And bid him check his blind career;
And tell the sore-prest sons of Care
　　Never, never to despair!

Paint Charles's speed on wings of fire,
The object of his fond desire,
Beyond his boldest hopes, at hand.
Paint all the triumph of the Portland Band
(Hark! how they lift the joy-exulting voice,
And how their num'rous creditors rejoice!);
But just as hopes to warm enjoyment rise,
Cry "Convalescence!" and the vision flies.

Then next pourtray a dark'ning twilight
　　gloom
　　Eclipsing sad a gay, rejoicing morn,
While proud Ambition to th' untimely tomb
　　By gnashing, grim, despairing fiends is
　　borne!
Paint Ruin, in the shape of high Dundas
　　Gaping with giddy terror o'er the brow:
In vain he struggles, the Fates behind him
　　press,
　　And clamorous Hell yawns for her prey
　　below!
How fallen That, whose pride late scaled
　　the skies!
And This, like Lucifer, no more to rise!
　　Again pronounce the powerful word:
See Day, triumphant from the night, re-
　　stored!

Then know this truth, ye Sons of Men
　　(Thus ends thy moral tale):
　　Your darkest terrors may be vain,
　　Your brightest hopes may fail!

A NEW PSALM FOR THE CHAPEL OF KILMARNOCK

ON THE THANKSGIVING-DAY FOR HIS
MAJESTY'S RECOVERY

In a letter to Mrs. Dunlop of 4th April, 1789,
[probably for 4th May], Burns wrote: " The
following are a few stanzas of new Psalmody
for that 'joyful solemnity' [the Thanks-
giving for the King's recovery] which I sent
to a London newspaper with the date and
preface following: 'Kilmarnock, 25th April.
Mr. Printer, — In a certain chapel, not fifty
leagues from the market cross of this good
town, the following stanzas of Psalmody, it is
said, were composed for, and devoutly sung on,
the late joyful solemnity of the 23d.' " The
paper was Stuart's *Morning Star*, where parody
and letter, dated " Kilmarnock, April 30th,"
and signed " Duncan M'Leerie " — the hero

he of an old Kilmarnock song preserved in
The Merry Muses — appeared on May 14th.

I

O, SING a new song to the Lord!
  Make, all and every one,
A joyful noise, ev'n for the King
  His restoration!

II

The sons of Belial in the land
  Did set their heads together.
" Come, let us sweep them off," said they,
  " Like an o'erflowing river!"

III

They set their heads together, I say,
  They set their heads together:
On right, and left, and every hand,
  We saw none to deliver.

IV

Thou madest strong two chosen ones,
  To quell the Wicked's pride:
That Young Man, great in Issachar,
  The burden-bearing tribe;

V

And him, among the Princes, chief
  In our Jerusalem,
The Judge that's mighty in Thy law,
  The man that fears Thy name.

VI

Yet they, even they with all their strength,
  Began to faint and fail;
Even as two howling, rav'ning wolves
  To dogs do turn their tail.

VII

Th' ungodly o'er the just prevail'd;
  For so Thou hadst appointed,
That Thou might'st greater glory give
  Unto Thine own anointed!

VIII

And now Thou hast restored our State,
  Pity our Kirk also;
For she by tribulations
  Is now brought very low!

IX

Consume that high-place, Patronage,
  From off Thy holy hill;

And in Thy fury burn the book
  Even of that man M'Gill!

X

Now hear our prayer, accept our song,
  And fight Thy chosen's battle!
We seek but little, Lord, from Thee:
  Thou kens we get as little!

INSCRIBED TO THE RIGHT HON. C. J. FOX

Enclosed to Mrs. Dunlop in the same letter
as the preceding piece: " I have another poetic
whim in my head, which I at present dedicate,
or rather inscribe, to the Hon. Charles J. Fox;
but how long the fancy may hold I can't say.
A few of the first lines I have just rough
sketched as follows."

How Wisdom and Folly meet, mix, and
  unite,
How Virtue and Vice blend their black
  and their white,
How Genius, th' illustrious father of fiction,
Confounds rule and law, reconciles contra-
  diction,
I sing. If these mortals, the critics, should
  bustle,
I care not, not I : let the critics go whistle!

But now for a Patron, whose name and
  whose glory
At once may illustrate and honour my
  story : —

Thou first of our orators, first of our wits,
Yet whose parts and acquirements seem
  mere lucky hits;
With knowledge so vast and with judg-
  ment so strong,
No man with the half of 'em e'er could go
  wrong;
With passions so potent and fancies so
  bright,
No man with the half of 'em e'er could go
  right;
A sorry, poor, misbegot son of the Muses,
For using thy name, offers fifty excuses.

Good Lord, what is Man! For as simple
  he looks,
Do but try to develop his hooks and his
  crooks!

With his depths and his shallows, his good
    and his evil,
All in all he 's a problem must puzzle the
    Devil.

On his one ruling passion Sir Pope hugely
    labors,
That, like th' old Hebrew walking-switch,
    eats up its neighbours.
Human Nature 's his show-box — your
    friend, would you know him ?
Pull the string, Ruling Passion — the pic-
    ture will show him.
What pity, in rearing so beauteous a sys-
    tem,
One trifling particular — Truth — should
    have miss'd him !
For, spite of his fine theoretic positions,
Mankind is a science defies definitions.

Some sort all our qualities each to its
    tribe,
And think Human Nature they truly de-
    scribe:
Have you found this, or t'other ?   There 's
    more in the wind,
As by one drunken fellow his comrades
    you 'll find.
But such is the flaw, or the depth of the plan
In the make of that wonderful creature
    called Man,
No two virtues, whatever relation they
    claim,
Nor even two different shades of the same,
Though like as was ever twin brother to
    brother,
Possessing the one shall imply you 've the
    other.

But truce with abstraction, and truce
    with a Muse
Whose rhymes you 'll perhaps, Sir, ne'er
    deign to peruse !
Will you leave your justings, your jars,
    and your quarrels,
Contending with Billy for proud-nodding
    laurels ?
My much-honour'd Patron, believe your
    poor Poet,
Your courage much more than your pru-
    dence you show it.
In vain with Squire Billy for laurels you
    struggle:
He 'll have them by fair trade — if not, he
    will smuggle;

Nor cabinets even of kings would conceal
    'em,
He 'd up the back-stairs, and by God he
    would steal 'em !
Then feats like Squire Billy's, you ne'er
    can achieve 'em;
It is not, out-do him — the task is, out-
    thieve him !

ON GLENRIDDELL'S FOX BREAKING HIS CHAIN

A FRAGMENT, 1791

THOU, Liberty, thou art my theme :
Not such as idle poets dream,
Who trick thee up a heathen goddess
That a fantastic cap and rod has !
Such stale conceits are poor and silly:
I paint thee out a Highland filly,
A sturdy, stubborn, handsome dapple,
As sleek 's a mouse, as round 's an apple,
That, when thou pleasest, can do wonders,
But when thy luckless rider blunders,
Or if thy fancy should demur there,
Wilt break thy neck ere thou go further.

These things premis'd, I sing a Fox —
Was caught among his native rocks,
And to a dirty kennel chained —
How he his liberty regained.

Glenriddell ! a Whig without a stain,
A Whig in principle and grain,
Could'st thou enslave a free-born crea-
    ture,
A native denizen of Nature ?
How could'st thou, with a heart so good
(A better ne'er was sluiced with blood),
Nail a poor devil to a tree,
That ne'er did harm to thine or thee ?

The staunchest Whig Glenriddel was,
Quite frantic in his country's cause;
And oft was Reynard's prison passing,
And with his brother-Whigs canvássing
The rights of men, the powers of women,
With all the dignity of Freemen.

Sir Reynard daily heard debates
Of princes', kings', and nations' fates,
With many rueful, bloody stories
Of tyrants, Jacobites, and Tories :

From liberty how angels fell,
That now are galley-slaves in Hell;
How Nimrod first the trade began
Of binding Slavery's chains on man;
How fell Semiramis — God damn her! —
Did first, with sacrilegious hammer
(All ills till then were trivial matters)
For Man dethron'd forge hen-peck fetters;
How Xerxes, that abandoned Tory,
Thought cutting throats was reaping glory,
Until the stubborn Whigs of Sparta
Taught him great Nature's Magna Charta;
How mighty Rome her fiat hurl'd
Resistless o'er a bowing world,
And, kinder than they did desire,
Polish'd mankind with sword and fire:
With much too tedious to relate
Of ancient and of modern date,
But ending still how Billy Pitt
(Unlucky boy!) with wicked wit
Has gagg'd old Britain, drained her coffer,
As butchers bind and bleed a heifer.

　　Thus wily Reynard, by degrees
In kennel listening at his ease,
Suck'd in a mighty stock of knowledge,
As much as some folks at a college;
Knew Britain's rights and constitution,
Her aggrandisement, diminution;
How Fortune wrought us good from evil:
Let no man, then, despise the Devil,
As who should say: "I ne'er can need
　　him,"
Since we to scoundrels owe our Freedom.

ON THE COMMEMORATION OF RODNEY'S VICTORY

KING'S ARMS, DUMFRIES, 12TH APRIL,
1793

Rodney's action off Dominica, 12th April,
1792, was for some time celebrated year by
year.

INSTEAD of a song, boys, I'll give you a
　　toast:
Here's the Mem'ry of those on the Twelfth
　　that we lost! —
We lost, did I say? — No, by Heav'n,
　　that we found!
For their fame it shall live while the world
　　goes round.

The next in succession I'll give you: the
　　King!
And who would betray him, on high may
　　he swing!
And here's the grand fabric, our Free
　　Constitution
As built on the base of the great Revolu-
　　tion!
And, longer with Politics not to be cramm'd,
Be Anarchy curs'd, and be Tyranny
　　damn'd!
And who would to Liberty e'er prove
　　disloyal,
May his son be a hangman — and he his
　　first trial!

ODE FOR GENERAL WASHING-TON'S BIRTHDAY

"I am just going to trouble your critical
patience with the first sketch of a stanza I
have been framing as I paced along the road.
The subject is Liberty: you know, my honoured
friend, how dear the theme is to me. I de-
sign it as an irregular ode for General Wash-
ington's birthday." (R. B. to Mrs. Dunlop,
25th June, 1794.)

No Spartan tube, no Attic shell,
　　No lyre Æolian I awake.
'Tis Liberty's bold note I swell:
　　Thy harp, Columbia, let me take!
See gathering thousands, while I sing,
A broken chain, exulting, bring
　　And dash it in a tyrant's face,
　　And dare him to his very beard,
　　And tell him he no more is fear'd,
　　　No more the despot of Columbia's
　　　race!
A tyrant's proudest insults brav'd,
They shout a People freed! They hail an
　　Empire sav'd!

Where is man's godlike form?
　　Where is that brow erect and bold,
　　That eye that can unmov'd behold
The wildest rage, the loudest storm
That e'er created Fury dared to raise?
Avaunt! thou caitiff, servile, base,
That tremblest at a despot's nod,
Yet, crouching under the iron rod,
Canst laud the arm that struck th' insult-
　　ing blow!

Art thou of man's Imperial line ?
Dost boast that countenance divine ?
  Each skulking feature answers: No !
But come, ye sons of Liberty,
Columbia's offspring, brave as free,
In danger's hour still flaming in the van,
Ye know, and dare maintain the Royalty
    of Man !

Alfred, on thy starry throne
  Surrounded by the tuneful choir,
  The Bards that erst have struck the
      patriot lyre,
  And rous'd the freeborn Briton's soul of
      fire,
No more thy England own !
Dare injured nations form the great design
  To make detested tyrants bleed ?
  Thy England execrates the glorious
      deed !
  Beneath her hostile banners waving,
  Every pang of honour braving,
England in thunder calls: " The tyrant's
    cause is mine ! "
That hour accurst how did the fiends rejoice,
And Hell thro' all her confines raise th'
    exulting voice !
That hour which saw the generous English
    name
Link't with such damnèd deeds of ever-
    lasting shame !

Thee, Caledonia, thy wild heaths among,
Fam'd for the martial deed, the heaven-
    taught song,
  To thee I turn with swimming eyes !
Where is that soul of Freedom fled ?
Immingled with the mighty dead
  Beneath that hallow'd turf where Wallace
      lies !
Hear it not, Wallace, in thy bed of death !
  Ye babbling winds, in silence sweep !
  Disturb not ye the hero's sleep,
Nor give the coward secret breath !
Is this the ancient Caledonian form,
Firm as her rock, resistless as her storm ?
Show me that eye which shot immortal hate,
  Blasting the Despot's proudest bearing !
Show me that arm which, nerv'd with
    thundering fate,
  Crush'd Usurpation's boldest daring !
Dark-quench'd as yonder sinking star,
No more that glance lightens afar,
That palsied arm no more whirls on the
    waste of war.

THE FÊTE CHAMPÊTRE

TUNE : *Killiecrankie*

This is the earliest of a series of election
ballads, all in some sort parodies of popular
pieces. Regarding the genesis of this one, see
ante, p. 75, Prefatory Note to *When Guilford
Good*, and *post*, p. 227, Prefatory Note to *The
Battle of Sherramuir*. It celebrates an enter-
tainment given by William Cunningham of
Annbank in 1788, on attaining his majority,
but intended (so men held) to serve a political
end as well.

I

O, WHA will to Saint Stephen's House,
  To do our errands there, man ?
O, wha will to Saint Stephen's House
  O' th' merry lads of Ayr, man ?
Or will ye send a man o' law ?
  Or will ye send a sodger ?
Or him wha led o'er Scotland a'
  The meikle Ursa-Major ?

II

Come, will ye court a noble lord,
  Or buy a score o' lairds, man ?
For Worth and Honour pawn their word,
  Their vote shall be Glencaird's, man.
Ane gies them coin, ane gies them wine,
  Anither gies them clatter;
Annbank, wha guess'd the ladies' taste,
  He gies a Fête Champêtre.

III

When Love and Beauty heard the news
  The gay green-woods amang, man,
Where, gathering flowers and busking
    bowers,
  They heard the blackbird's sang, man;
A vow, they seal'd it with a kiss,
  Sir Politics to fetter:
As theirs alone the patent bliss
  To hold a Fête Champêtre.

IV

Then mounted Mirth on gleesome wing,
  O'er hill and dale she flew, man;
Ilk wimpling burn, ilk crystal spring,
  Ilk glen and shaw she knew, man.
She summon'd every social sprite,
  That sports by wood or water,
On th' bonie banks of Ayr to meet
  And keep this Fête Champêtre.

V

Cauld Boreas wi' his boisterous crew
    Were bound to stakes like kye, man;
And Cynthia's car, o' silver fu',
    Clamb up the starry sky, man:
Reflected beams dwell in the streams,
    Or down the current shatter;
The western breeze steals through the
        trees
    To view this Fête Champêtre.

VI

How many a robe sae gaily floats,
    What sparkling jewels glance, man,
To Harmony's enchanting notes,
    As moves the mazy dance, man !
The echoing wood, the winding flood
    Like Paradise did glitter,
When angels met at Adam's yett
    To hold their Fête Champêtre.

VII

When Politics came there to mix
    And make his ether-stane, man,
He circled round the magic ground,
    But entrance found he nane, man:
He blush'd for shame, he quat his name,
    Forswore it every letter,
Wi' humble prayer to join and share
    This festive Fête Champêtre.

THE FIVE CARLINS

TUNE: *Chevy Chase*

The Five Carlins were of course the Dumfries Parliamentary Burghs. On 29th October, 1789, soon after the beginning of the contest, Burns sent a copy of this brilliant *pastiche* of the folk-ballad to Mrs. Dunlop, prefacing it with a minute account of the state of parties, and indicating pretty plainly that his sympathies were with Sir James Johnstone of Westerhall, who had represented the Burghs in the previous parliament. The other candidate, Captain Patrick Miller — a young officer of twenty — the son of his landlord, he describes as the "creature" of the Duke of Queensberry. To Graham of Fintry he wrote on 9th December that he was "too little a man to have any political attachments;" that he had "the warmest veneration for individuals of both parties;" but "that a man who has it in his power to be the father of a country, and who is only known to that country by the mischiefs he does in it, is a character that one cannot speak of with patience." Captain Miller won the election, and represented the Burghs till 1796. It was through him that Mr. Perry of *The Morning Chronicle* proposed that Burns should join his staff in 1794.

I

THERE was five carlins in the South:
    They fell upon a scheme
To send a lad to Lon'on town
    To bring them tidings hame:

II

Nor only bring them tidings hame,
    But do their errands there:
And aiblins gowd and honor baith
    Might be that laddie's share.

III

There was Maggie by the banks o' Nith,
    A dame wi' pride eneugh;
And Marjorie o' the Monie Lochs,
    A carlin auld and teugh;

IV

And Blinkin Bess of Annandale,
    That dwelt near Solway-side;
And Brandy Jean, that took her gill
    In Galloway sae wide;

V

And Black Joán, frae Crichton Peel,
    O' gipsy kith an' kin:
Five wighter carlins were na found
    The South countrie within.

VI

To send a lad to London town
    They met upon a day;
And monie a knight and monie a laird
    This errand fain wad gae.

VII

O, monie a knight and monie a laird
    This errand fain wad gae;
But nae ane could their fancy please,
    O, ne'er a ane but tway !

VIII

The first ane was a belted Knight,
    Bred of a Border band;
And he wad gae to London Town,
    Might nae man him withstand;

IX

And he wad do their errands weel,
  And meikle he wad say;
And ilka ane at London court
  Wad bid to him guid-day.

X

The neist cam in, a Soger boy,
  And spak wi' modest grace;
And he wad gae to London Town,
  If sae their pleasure was.

XI

He wad na hecht them courtly gifts,
  Nor meikle speech pretend;
But he wad hecht an honest heart
  Wad ne'er desert his friend.

XII

Now wham to chuse and wham refuse
  At strife thae carlins fell;
For some had gentle folk to please,
  And some wad please themsel.

XIII

Then out spak mim-mou'd Meg o' Nith,
  And she spak up wi' pride,
And she wad send the Soger lad,
  Whatever might betide.

XIV

For the auld Guidman o' London court
  She didna care a pin;
But she wad send the Soger lad
  To greet his eldest son.

XV

Then up sprang Bess o' Annandale,
  And swore a deadly aith,
Says: — "I will send the belted Knight,
  Spite of you carlins baith !

XVI

"For far-aff fowls hae feathers fair,
  And fools o' change are fain;
But I hae tried this Border Knight:
  I 'll try him yet again."

XVII

Then Brandy Jean spak owre her drink. —
  "Ye weel ken, kimmers a',
The auld Guidman o' London court,
  His back 's been at the wa';

XVIII

"And monie a friend that kiss'd his caup
  Is now a fremit wight;
But it 's ne'er be sae wi' Brandy Jean —
  I 'll send the Border Knight."

XIX

Says Black Joán frae Crichton Peel,
  A carlin stoor and grim: —
"The auld Guidman or the young Guidman
  For me may sink or swim !

XX

"For fools will prate o' right or wrang,
  While knaves laugh in their slieve;
But wha blaws best the horn shall win —
  I 'll spier nae courtier's leave ! "

XXI

Then slow raise Marjorie o' the Lochs,
  And wrinkled was her brow,
Her ancient weed was russet gray,
  Her auld Scots heart was true: —

XXII

"There 's some great folk set light by me,
  I set as light by them;
But I will send to London town
  Wham I lo'e best at hame."

XXIII

Sae how this sturt and strife may end,
  There 's naebody can tell.
God grant the King and ilka man
  May look weel to themsel !

ELECTION BALLAD FOR WESTERHA'

Written on behalf of Sir James Johnstone,
and modelled on the Jacobite ballad *Up and
Waur them A', Willie.* In the letter to Mrs.
Dunlop enclosing the preceding ballad Burns
wrote of the Duke of Queensberry: "His
Grace is keenly attached to the Buff and Blue
party; renegades and Apostates are, you know,
always keen."

  Up and waur them a', Jamie,
    Up and waur them a'!
  The Johnstones hae the guidin o't:
    Ye turncoat Whigs, awa !

I

THE Laddies by the banks o' Nith
  Wad trust his Grace wi' a', Jamie;
But he 'll sair them as he sair'd the King —
  Turn tail and rin awa, Jamie.

II

The day he stude his country's friend,
  Or gied her faes a claw, Jamie,
Or frae puir man a blessin wan —
  That day the Duke ne'er saw, Jamie.

III

But wha is he, his country's boast?
  Like him there is na twa, Jamie!
There 's no a callant tents the kye
  But kens o' Westerha', Jamie.

IV

To end the wark, here 's Whistlebirk —
  Lang may his whistle blaw, Jamie! —
And Maxwell true, o' sterling blue,
  And we 'll be Johnstones a', Jamie.

  Up and waur them a', Jamie,
  Up and waur them a'!
  The Johnstones hae the guidin o't:
  Ye turncoat Whigs, awa!

AS I CAM DOON THE BANKS O' NITH

William Douglas, fourth Duke of Queens-
berry (1724–1810), the notorious "Old Q.," is
"his Grace" of the last ballad and is satirised
again in the following not hitherto[1] printed.
Queensberry supported the proposal that the
Prince of Wales should assume the govern-
ment, with full royal prerogatives, during the
King's illness.

As I cam doon the banks o' Nith
  And by Glenriddell's ha', man,
There I heard a piper play
  Turn-coat Whigs awa, man.

Drumlanrig's towers hae tint the powers
  That kept the lands in awe, man:
The eagle 's dead, and in his stead
  We 've gotten a hoodie-craw, man.

The turn-coat Duke his King forsook,
  When his back was at the wa', man:

[1] That is, before the Centenary Edition.

The rattan ran wi' a' his clan
  For fear the house should fa', man.

The lads about the banks o' Nith,
  They trust his Grace for a', man:
But he 'll sair them as he sair't his King,
  Turn tail and rin awa, man.

ELECTION BALLAD

AT CLOSE OF THE CONTEST FOR REPRE
SENTING THE DUMFRIES BURGHS, 1790

ADDRESSED TO ROBERT GRAHAM OF FINTRY

For Graham of Fintry, see *ante*, p. 85.

I

FINTRY, my stay in worldly strife,
Friend o' my Muse, friend o' my life,
  Are ye as idle 's I am?
Come, then! Wi' uncouth kintra fleg
O'er Pegasus I 'll fling my leg,
  And ye shall see me try him!

II

But where shall I gae rin or ride,
That I may splatter nane beside?
  I wad na be uncivil:
In mankind's various paths and ways
There 's ay some doytin body strays,
  And I ride like a devil.

III

Thus I break aff wi' a' my birr,
An' down yon dark, deep alley spur,
  Where Theologics dander:
Alas! curst wi' eternal fogs,
And damn'd in everlasting bogs,
  As sure 's the Creed I 'll blunder?

IV

I 'll stain a band, or jaup a gown,
Or rin my reckless, guilty crown
  Against the haly door!
Sair do I rue my luckless fate,
When, as the Muse an' Deil wad hae 't,
  I rade that road before!

V

Suppose I take a spurt, and mix
Amang the wilds o' Politics —
  Electors and elected —

Where dogs at Court (sad sons o' bitches !)
Septennially a madness touches,
 Till all the land 's infected ?

VI

All hail, Drumlanrig's haughty Grace,
Discarded remnant of a race
 Once godlike — great in story !
Thy fathers' virtues all contrasted,
The very name of Douglas blasted,
 Thine that inverted glory !

VII

Hate, envy, oft the Douglas bore;
But thou hast superadded more,
 And sunk them in contempt !
Follies and crimes have stain'd the name;
But, Queensberry, thine the virgin claim,
 From aught that 's good exempt!

VIII

I 'll sing the zeal Drumlanrig bears,
Who left the all-important cares
 Of fiddlers, whores, and hunters,
And, bent on buying Borough Towns,
Came shaking hands wi' wabster-loons,
 And kissing barefit bunters.

IX

Combustion thro' our boroughs rode,
Whistling his roaring pack abroad
 Of mad unmuzzled lions,
As Queensberry buff-and-blue unfurl'd,
And Westerha' and Hopeton hurl'd
 To every Whig defiance.

X

But cautious Queensberry left the war
(Th' unmanner'd dust might soil his star;
 Besides, he hated bleeding),
But left behind him heroes bright,
Heroes in Cæsarean fight
 Or Ciceronian pleading.

XI

O, for a throat like huge Mons-Meg,
To muster o'er each ardent Whig
 Beneath Drumlanrig's banner !
Heroes and heroines commix,
All in the field of politics,
 To win immortal honor !

XII

M'Murdo and his lovely spouse
(Th' enamour'd laurels kiss her brows !)

Led on the Loves and Graces:
She won each gaping burgess' heart,
While he, *sub rosâ*, played his part
 Among their wives and lasses.

XIII

Craigdarroch led a light-arm'd core:
Tropes, metaphors, and figures pour,
 Like Hecla streaming thunder.
Glenriddell, skill'd in rusty coins,
Blew up each Tory's dark designs
 And bared the treason under.

XIV

In either wing two champions fought:
Redoubted Staig, who set at nought
 The wildest savage Tory ;
And Welsh, who ne'er yet flinch'd his
  ground,
High-wav'd his magnum-bonum round
 With Cyclopeian fury.

XV

Miller brought up th' artillery ranks,
The many-pounders of the Banks,
 Resistless desolation !
While Maxwelton, that baron bold,
'Mid Lawson's port entrench'd his hold
 And threaten'd worse damnation.

XVI

To these what Tory hosts oppos'd,
With these what Tory warriors clos'd,
 Surpasses my descriving :
Squadrons, extended long and large,
With furious speed rush to the charge,
 Like furious devils driving.

XVII

What verse can sing, what prose narrate
The butcher deeds of bloody Fate
 Amid this mighty tulyie ?
Grim Horror girn'd, pale Terror roar'd,
As Murther at his thrapple shor'd,
 And Hell mix'd in the brulyie.

XVIII

As Highland craigs by thunder cleft,
When lightnings fire the stormy lift,
 Hurl down with crashing rattle,
As flames among a hundred woods,
As headlong foam a hundred floods —
 Such is the rage of Battle !

XIX

The stubborn Tories dare to die :
As soon the rooted oaks would fly
  Before th' approaching fellers !
The Whigs come on like Ocean's roar,
When all his wintry billows pour
  Against the Buchan Bullers.

XX

Lo, from the shades of Death's deep night
Departed Whigs enjoy the fight,
  And think on former daring !
The muffled murtherer of Charles
The Magna Charter flag unfurls,
  All deadly gules its bearing.

XXI

Nor wanting ghosts of Tory fame :
Bold Scrimgeour follows gallant Graham,
  Auld Covenanters shiver . . .
Forgive ! forgive ! much-wrong'd Mon-
  trose !
Now Death and Hell engulph thy foes,
  Thou liv'st on high for ever !

XXII

Still o'er the field the combat burns;
The Tories, Whigs, give way by turns;
  But Fate the word has spoken ;
For woman's wit and strength o' man,
Alas ! can do but what they can :
  The Tory ranks are broken.

XXIII

O, that my een were flowing burns !
My voice a lioness that mourns
  Her darling cubs' undoing
That I might greet, that I might cry,
While Tories fall, while Tories fly
  From furious Whigs pursuing !

XXIV

What Whig but melts for good Sir James,
Dear to his country by the names,
  Friend, Patron, Benefactor ?
Not Pulteney's wealth can Pulteney save;
And Hopeton falls — the generous,
  brave ! —
  And Stewart bold as Hector.

XXV

Thou, Pitt, shalt rue this overthrow,
And Thurlow growl this curse of woe,
  And Melville melt in wailing !

Now Fox and Sheridan rejoice,
And Burke shall sing : — " O Prince, arise !
  Thy power is all prevailing ! "

XXVI

For your poor friend, the Bard, afar
He sees and hears the distant war,
  A cool spectator purely :
So, when the storm the forest rends,
The robin in the hedge descends,
  And, patient, chirps securely.

XXVII

Now, for my friends' and brethren's sakes,
And for my dear-lov'd Land o' Cakes,
  I pray with holy fire : —
Lord, send a rough-shod troop o' Hell
O'er a' wad Scotland buy or sell,
  To grind them in the mire !

BALLADS ON MR. HERON'S
ELECTION, 1795

BALLAD FIRST

In this Election for the Stewartry of Kirk-
cudbright, Heron of Kerroughtrie, the Whig
candidate, was opposed by Thomas Gordon of
Balmaghie. Burns, who had visited Heron in
June, 1794, warmly supported him, not merely
for friendship's sake but out of a special dis-
like to the more conspicuous among Balmagh-
ie's supporters. This ballad and the next he
enclosed in a letter to Mr. Heron, stating that
he had distributed them "among friends all
over the country."

I

WHAM will we send to London town,
  To Parliament and a' that ?
Or wha in a' the country round
  The best deserves to fa' that ?
    For a' that, and a' that,
    Thro' Galloway and a' that,
  Where is the Laird or belted Knight
    That best deserves to fa' that ?

II

Wha sees Kerroughtree's open yett —
  And wha is 't never saw that ? —
Wha ever wi' Kerroughtree met,
  And has a doubt of a' that ?
    For a' that, and a' that,
    Here 's Heron yet for a' that !

The independent patriot,
  The honest man, and a' that !

III

Tho' wit and worth, in either sex,
  Saint Mary's Isle can shaw that,
Wi' Lords and Dukes let Selkirk mix,
  And weel does Selkirk fa' that.
    For a' that, and a' that,
    Here 's Heron yet for a' that !
  An independent commoner
    Shall be the man for a' that.

IV

But why should we to Nobles jeuk,
  And it against the law, that,
And even a Lord may be a gowk,
  Wi' ribban, star, and a' that ?
    For a' that, and a' that,
    Here 's Heron yet for a' that !
  A Lord may be a lousy loon,
    Wi' ribban, star, and a' that.

V

A beardless boy comes o'er the hills
  Wi 's uncle's purse and a' that;
But we 'll hae ane frae 'mang oursels,
  A man we ken, and a' that.
    For a' that, and a' that,
    Here 's Heron yet for a' that !
  We are na to be bought and sold,
    Like nowte, and naigs, and a' that.

VI

Then let us drink: — " The Stewartry,
  Kerroughtree's laird, and a' that,
Our representative to be: "
  For weel he 's worthy a' that !
    For a' that, and a' that,
    Here 's Heron yet for a' that !
  A House of Commons such as he,
    They wad be blest that saw that.

BALLAD SECOND: THE ELECTION

TUNE: *Fy, Let Us A' to The Bridal*

A parody of *The Blythsome Wedding*, the
classic, in Watson's First Part (1706), attrib-
uted to Francis Semple : —

  " Fy, let us All to the Briddel,
    For there will be Lilting there,

For *Jockie* 's to be marry'd to *Maggie*,
  The Lass with the Gauden Hair :
And there will be Lang-kail and Pottage,
  And Bannocks of Barley-Meal ;
And there will be good Salt-herring
  To relish a kog of good Ale."

I

Fy, let us a' to Kirkcudbright,
  For there will be bickerin there;
For Murray's light horse are to muster,
  An' O, how the heroes will swear !
And there will be Murray commander,
  An' Gordon the battle to win:
Like brothers, they 'll stan' by each other,
  Sae knit in alliance and kin.

II

An' there 'll be black-nebbit Johnie,
  The tongue o' the trump to them a':
Gin he get na Hell for his haddin,
  The Deil gets nae justice ava !
And there 'll be Kempleton's birkie,
  A boy no sae black at the bane;
But as to his fine nabob fortune —
  We 'll e'en let the subject alane !

III

An' there 'll be Wigton's new sheriff —
  Dame Justice fu' brawly has sped:
She 's gotten the heart of a Bushby,
  But Lord ! what 's become o' the head ?
An' there 'll be Cardoness, Esquire,
  Sae mighty in Cardoness' eyes:
A wight that will weather damnation,
  For the Devil the prey would despise.

IV

An' there 'll be Douglasses doughty,
  New christening towns far and near:
Abjuring their democrat doings
  An' kissing the arse of a peer !
An' there 'll be Kenmure sae generous,
  Wha's honor is proof to the storm:
To save them from stark reprobation
  He lent them his name to the firm !

V

But we winna mention Redcastle,
  The body — e'en let him escape !
He 'd venture the gallows for siller,
  An' 't were na the cost o' the rape !
An' whare is our King's Lord Lieutenant,
  Sae famed for his gratefu' return ?
The billie is getting his Questions
  To say at St. Stephen's the morn !

VI

An' there 'll be lads o' the gospel:
  Muirhead, wha 's as guid as he 's true;
An' there 'll be Buittle's Apostle,
  Wha 's mair o' the black than the blue;
An' there 'll be folk frae St. Mary's,
  A house o' great merit and note:
The Deil ane but honors them highly,
  The Deil ane will gie them his vote!

VII

An' there 'll be wealthy young Richard,
  Dame Fortune should hang by the neck:
But for prodigal thriftless bestowing,
  His merit had won him respect.
An' there 'll be rich brither nabobs;
  Tho' nabobs, yet men o' the first!
An' there 'll be Collieston's whiskers,
  An' Quinton — o' lads no the warst!

VIII

An' there 'll be Stamp-Office Johnie:
  Tak tent how ye purchase a dram!
An' there 'll be gay Cassencarry,
  An' there 'll be Colonel Tam;
An' there 'll be trusty Kerroughtree,
  Wha's honour was ever his law:
If the virtues were pack't in a parcel,
  His worth might be sample for a'!

IX

An' can we forget the auld Major,
  Wha 'll ne'er be forgot in the Greys?
Our flatt'ry we 'll keep for some other:
  Him only it 's justice to praise!
An' there 'll be maiden Kilkerran,
  An' also Barskimming's guid Knight.
An' there 'll be roaring Birtwhistle —
  Yet luckily roars in the right!

X

An' there frae the Niddlesdale border
  Will mingle the Maxwells in droves:
Teuch Johnie, Staunch Geordie, and Wattie
  That girns for the fishes an' loaves!
An' there 'll be Logan's M'Doual —
  Sculdudd'ry an' he will be there!
An' also the wild Scot o' Galloway,
  Sogering, gunpowther Blair!

XI

Then hey the chaste interest of Broughton,
  An' hey for the blessings 't will bring!
It may send Balmaghie to the Commons —
  In Sodom 't would mak him a King!

An' hey for the sanctified Murray
  Our land wha wi' chapels has stor'd;
He founder'd his horse among harlots,
  But gie'd the auld naig to the Lord!

BALLAD THIRD:
JOHN BUSHBY'S LAMENTATION

TUNE: *Babes In the Wood*

For John Bushby, see *post*, p. 198, Prefatory
Note to *Epitaph on John Bushby;* and for the
personages referred to in the ballad, see Notes,
p. 343, and also Notes to *Ballad Second*, pp.
342, 343.

I

'Twas in the Seventeen Hunder year
  O' grace, and Ninety-Five,
That year I was the wae'est man
  Of onie man alive.

II

In March the three-an'-twentieth morn,
  The sun raise clear an' bright;
But O, I was a waefu' man,
  Ere to-fa' o' the night!

III

Yerl Galloway lang did rule this land
  Wi' equal right and fame,
Fast knit in chaste and holy bands
  With Broughton's noble name.

IV

Yerl Galloway's man o' men was I,
  And chief o' Broughton's host;
So twa blind beggars, on a string,
  The faithfu' tyke will trust!

V

But now Yerl Galloway's sceptre 's broke,
  And Broughton 's wi' the slain,
And I my ancient craft may try,
  Sin' honesty is gane.

VI

'Twas by the banks o' bonie Dee,
  Beside Kirkcudbright's towers,
The Stewart and the Murray there
  Did muster a' their powers.

VII

Then Murray on the auld grey yaud
  Wi' wingèd spurs did ride:

That auld grey yaud a' Nidsdale rade,
  He staw upon Nidside.

VIII

An' there had na been the Yerl himsel,
  O, there had been nae play !
But Garlies was to London gane,
  And sae the kye might stray.

IX

And there was Balmaghie, I ween —
  In front rank he wad shine;
But Balmaghie had better been
  Drinkin' Madeira wine.

X

And frae Glenkens cam to our aid
  A chief o' doughty deed:
In case that worth should wanted be,
  O' Kenmure we had need.

XI

And by our banners march'd Muirhead,
  And Buittle was na slack,
Whase haly priesthood nane could stain,
  For wha could dye the black ?

XII

And there was grave Squire Cardoness,
  Look'd on till a' was done:
Sae in the tower o' Cardoness
  A howlet sits at noon.

XIII

And there led I the Bushby clan:
  My gamesome billie, Will,
And my son Maitland, wise as brave,
  My footsteps follow'd still.

XIV

The Douglas and the Heron's name,
  We set nought to their score;
The Douglas and the Heron's name
  Had felt our weight before.

XV

But Douglasses o' weight had we:
  The pair o' lusty lairds,
For building cot-houses sae fam'd,
  And christenin kail-yards.

XVI

And then Redcastle drew his sword
  That ne'er was stain'd wi' gore

Save on a wand'rer lame and blind,
  To drive him frae his door.

XVII

And last cam creepin Collieston,
  Was mair in fear than wrath;
Ae knave was constant in his mind —
  To keep that knave frae scaith.

THE TROGGER

TUNE: *Buy Broom Besoms*

Written for Heron's election for Kirkcud-
bright in '96. [See *ante*, p. 164, Prefatory
Note to *First Heron Election Ballad*.] Burns
died before the result was known. On this
occasion Heron was opposed by the Hon. Mont-
gomery Stewart, son of the Earl of Galloway.
A trogger is a travelling hawker or packman.
For the persons, see *post*, pp. 342, 343, Notes to
Second Heron Election Ballad.

CHORUS

Buy braw troggin
  Frae the banks o' Dee !
Wha wants troggin
  Let him come to me !

I

WHA will buy my troggin,
  Fine election ware,
Broken trade o' Broughton,
  A' in high repair ?

II

There 's a noble Earl's
  Fame and high renown,
For an auld sang — it 's thought
  The guids were stown.

III

Here 's the worth o' Broughton
  In a needle's e'e.
Here 's a reputation
  Tint by Balmaghie.

IV

Here 's its stuff and lining,
  Cardoness's head —
Fine for a soger,
  A' the wale o' lead.

V

Here 's a little wadset —
Buittle's scrap o' truth,
Pawn'd in a gin-shop,
Quenching holy drouth.

VI

Here 's an honest conscience
Might a prince adorn,
Frae the downs o' Tinwald —
So was never worn !

VII

Here 's armorial bearings
Frae the manse o' Urr:
The crest, a sour crab-apple
Rotten at the core.

VIII

Here is Satan's picture,
Like a bizzard gled
Pouncing poor Redcastle,
Sprawlin like a taed.

IX

Here 's the font where Douglas
Stane and mortar names,
Lately used at Caily
Christening Murray's crimes.

X

Here 's the worth and wisdom
Collieston can boast:
By a thievish midge
They had been nearly lost.

XI

Here is Murray's fragments
O' the Ten Commands,
Gifted by Black Jock
To get them aff his hands.

XII

Saw ye e'er sic troggin ? —
If to buy ye 're slack,
Hornie 's turnin chapman:
He 'll buy a' the pack !

CHORUS

Buy braw troggin
Frae the banks o' Dee
Wha wants troggin
Let him come to me !

THE DEAN OF THE FACULTY

A NEW BALLAD

TUNE: *The Dragon of Wantley*

Burns charged the squib on learning that
Robert Dundas of Arniston — against whom
he had a grudge — (see *post*, p. 174, Prefatory
Note to *On the Death of Lord President Dun-
das*) — had, on 12th January, 1796, been elected
Dean of the Faculty of Advocates by a large
majority over Henry Erskine. Dundas, the
son of the Lord President, was born 6th June,
1758; appointed Lord Advocate in 1789; from
1790 to 1796 sat for Edinburgh; in 1801 was
made Baron of the Exchequer; and died 17th
June, 1819. For Erskine, see *post*, p. 326, Note
to *The Author's Earnest Cry and Prayer*, stanza
xiv. line 1; and also *post*, p. 183, Prefatory
Note to *In the Court of Session*.

I

DIRE was the hate at Old Harlaw
That Scot to Scot did carry;
And dire the discord Langside saw
For beauteous, hapless Mary.
But Scot to Scot ne'er met so hot,
Or were more in fury seen, Sir,
Than 'twixt Hal and Bob for the famous
job,
Who should be the Faculty's Dean, Sir.

II

This Hal for genius, wit, and lore
Among the first was number'd;
But pious Bob, 'mid learning's store
Commandment the Tenth remember'd.
Yet simple Bob the victory got,
And won his heart's desire:
Which shows that Heaven can boil the pot,
Tho' the Deil piss in the fire.

III

Squire Hal, besides, had in this case
Pretensions rather brassy;
For talents, to deserve a place,
Are qualifications saucy.
So their worships of the Faculty,
Quite sick of Merit's rudeness,
Chose one who should owe it all, d' ye see,
To their gratis grace and goodness.

IV

As once on Pisgah purg'd was the sight
Of a son of Circumcision,

So, may be, on this Pisgah height
Bob's purblind mental vision.
Nay, Bobby's mouth may be open'd yet,
Till for eloquence you hail him,
And swear that he has the Angel met
That met the Ass of Balaam.

V

In your heretic sins may ye live and die,
Ye heretic Eight-and-Thirty !
But accept, ye sublime majority,
My congratulations hearty !
With your honors, as with a certain King,
In your servants this is striking,
The more incapacity they bring
The more they 're to your liking.

MISCELLANIES

THE TARBOLTON LASSES

I

If ye gae up to yon hill-tap,
Ye 'll there see bonie Peggy:
She kens her father is a laird,
And she forsooth 's a leddy.

II

There 's Sophy tight, a lassie bright,
Besides a handsome fortune:
Wha canna win her in a night
Has little art in courtin.

III

Gae down by Faile, and taste the ale,
And tak a look o' Mysie:
She 's dour and din, a deil within,
But aiblins she may please ye.

IV

If she be shy, her sister try,
Ye 'll may be fancy Jenny:
If ye 'll dispense wi' want o' sense,
She kens hersel she 's bonie.

V

As ye gae up by yon hillside,
Spier in for bonie Bessy:
She 'll gie ye a beck, and bid ye light,
And handsomely address ye.

VI

There 's few sae bonie, nane sae guid
In a' King George' dominion:

If ye should doubt the truth of this,
It 's Bessy's ain opinion.

THE RONALDS OF THE BEN-
NALS

The Bennals was a farm in Tarbolton parish.
Miss Jean refused Gilbert Burns. The father,
supposed to have " Braid money to tocher them
a', man," went bankrupt in 1789, when Robert
wrote to his brother William: "You will
easily guess that from his insolent vanity in his
sunshine of life, he will now feel a little retalia-
tion from those who thought themselves eclipsed
by him."

I

In Tarbolton, ye ken, there are proper
young men,
And proper young lasses and a', man:
But ken ye the Ronalds that live in the
Bennals ?
They carry the gree frae them a', man.

II

Their father 's a laird, and weel he can
spare 't:
Braid money to tocher them a', man;
To proper young men, he 'll clink in the
hand
Gowd guineas a hunder or twa, man.

III

There 's ane they ca' Jean, I 'll warrant
ye 've seen
As bonie a lass or as braw, man;
But for sense and guid taste she 'll vie wi'
the best,
And a conduct that beautifies a', man.

IV

The charms o' the min', the langer they
shine
The mair admiration they draw, man;
While peaches and cherries, and roses and
lilies,
They fade and they wither awa, man.

V

If ye be for Miss Jean, tak this frae a
frien',
A hint o' a rival or twa, man:
The Laird o' Blackbyre wad gang through
the fire,
If that wad entice her awa, man.

VI

The Laird o' Braehead has been on his
  speed
For mair than a towmond or twa, man:
The Laird o' the Ford will straught on a
  board,
  If he canna get her at a', man.

VII

Then Anna comes in, the pride o' her kin,
  The boast of our bachelors a', man:
Sae sonsy and sweet, sae fully complete,
  She steals our affections awa, man.

VIII

If I should detail the pick and the wale
  O' lasses that live here awa, man,
The faut wad be mine, if they didna shine
  The sweetest and best o' them a', man.

IX

I lo'e her mysel, but darena weel tell,
  My poverty keeps me in awe, man;
For making o' rhymes, and working at
  times,
  Does little or naething at a', man.

X

Yet I wadna choose to let her refuse
  Nor hae 't in her power to say na, man:
For though I be poor, unnoticed, obscure,
  My stomach 's as proud as them a', man.

XI

Though I canna ride in well-booted pride,
  And flee o'er the hills like a craw, man,
I can haud up my head wi' the best o' the
  breed,
  Though fluttering ever so braw, man.

XII

My coat and my vest, they are Scotch o'
  the best;
O' pairs o' guid breeks I hae twa, man,
And stockings and pumps to put on my
  stumps,
  And ne'er a wrang steek in them a',
  man.

XIII

My sarks they are few, but five o' them
  new —
  Twal' hundred, as white as the snaw,
  man !

A ten-shillings hat, a Holland cravat —
  There are no monie Poets sae braw,
  man !

XIV

I never had frien's weel stockit in means,
  To leave me a hundred or twa, man;
Nae weel-tocher'd aunts, to wait on their
  drants
  And wish them in hell for it a', man.

XV

I never was cannie for hoarding o' money,
  Or claughtin 't together at a', man;
I 've little to spend and naething to lend,
  But devil a shilling I awe, man.

I'LL GO AND BE A SODGER

Inspired, it may be, by the destruction of
the shop at Irvine, when the writer was " left,
like a true poet, not worth sixpence."

I

O, WHY the deuce should I repine,
  And be an ill foreboder ?
I 'm twenty-three and five feet nine,
  I 'll go and be a sodger.

II

I gat some gear wi' meikle care,
  I held it weel thegither;
But now it 's gane — and something mair:
  I 'll go and be a sodger.

APOSTROPHE TO FERGUSSON

INSCRIBED ABOVE AND BELOW HIS
PORTRAIT

The copy of Fergusson bearing this passion-
ate but Anglified and imitative protest was
given by Burns, while in Edinburgh in 1787,
to a young woman, herself a writer of verse:
" This copy of Fergusson's Poems is presented
as a mark of esteem, friendship and regard to
Miss R. Carmichael, poetess, by
                ROBERT BURNS.
" EDINBURGH, 19th March, 1787."

A volume of verse by Rebekah Carmichael,
printed and sold by Peter Hill, appeared in
1790 ; and in 1806, under the name of Rebekah

Hay, the same person enclosed a printed poem, *On Seeing the Funeral of Sir William Forbes*, in a letter (now in the British Museum) presumably to some of Forbes's relations, in which she stated that she "was weak and ill," and begged for assistance.

CURSE on ungrateful man, that can be pleas'd
And yet can starve the author of the pleasure!

O thou, my elder brother in misfortune,
By far my elder brother in the Muse,
With tears I pity thy unhappy fate!
Why is the Bard unfitted for the world,
Yet has so keen a relish of its pleasures?

THE BELLES OF MAUCHLINE

Miss Miller is the "Nell" of *A Mauchline Wedding* (see *ante*, p. 114); Miss Markland married Mr. James Findlay, [an exciseman, formerly but wrongly supposed to be the hero of] *Wha is That at My Bower Door* (*post*, p. 236); Miss Smith, the witty sister of the witty James Smith (see *ante*, p. 15), became the wife of another of Burns's especial friends, James Candlish, and the mother of a famous Free Church leader, the Rev. Dr. Candlish of Edinburgh; Miss Betty was the "Eliza" of Burns's song (see *ante*, p. 52) and the "Bess" of *A Mauchline Wedding* aforesaid; Mr. Paterson, a Mauchline merchant, got Miss Morton; and of the other Burns noted in the *Glenriddell Book:* "Miss Armour is now known by the designation of Mrs. Burns."

I

IN Mauchline there dwells six proper young belles,
The pride of the place and its neighbourhood a',
Their carriage and dress, a stranger would guess,
In Lon'on or Paris they'd gotten it a'.

II

Miss Miller is fine, Miss Markland's divine,
Miss Smith she has wit, and Miss Betty is braw,
There's beauty and fortune to get wi' Miss Morton;
But Armour's the jewel for me o' them a'.

AH, WOE IS ME, MY MOTHER DEAR

JEREMIAH, chap. xv. verse 10

I

AH, woe is me, my Mother dear
A man of strife ye've born me.
For sair contention I maun bear;
They hate, revile, and scorn me.

II

I ne'er could lend on bill or band,
That five per cent. might blest me;
And borrowing, on the tither hand,
The deil a ane wad trust me.

III

Yet I, a coin-denyèd wight,
By Fortune quite discarded,
Ye see how I am day and night
By lad and lass blackguarded!

INSCRIBED ON A WORK OF HANNAH MORE'S

PRESENTED TO THE AUTHOR BY A LADY

"I received your kind letter with double pleasure on account of the second flattering instance of Mrs. C.'s notice and approbation. I assure you I

'Turn out the brunt side o' my shin,'

as the famous Ramsay, of jingling memory, says, of such a patroness. Present her my most grateful acknowledgments in your very best manner of telling the truth. I have inscribed the following stanza on the blank leaf of Miss More's works." (R. B. to Robert Aiken, 3d April, 1786.) Mrs. C. is not identified. Scott Douglas suggested Mrs. Cunninghame of Enterkine, but discovered that she was not married until 1794. He then bethought him of the wife of Sir William Cunningham of Robertland, forgetting that she had a handle to her name. Mrs. Cunninghame of Lainshaw subscribed for two copies of the First Edinburgh.

THOU flatt'ring mark of friendship kind,
Still may thy pages call to mind
The dear, the beauteous donor!

Tho' sweetly female ev'ry part,
Yet such a head and — more — the heart
  Does both the sexes honor:
She show'd her taste refin'd and just,
  When she selected thee,
Yet deviating, own I must,
  For so approving me:
      But, kind still, I mind still
        The giver in the gift;
      I 'll bless her, and wiss her
        A Friend aboon the lift.

LINES WRITTEN ON A BANK NOTE

WAE worth thy power, thou cursed leaf !
Fell source of a' my woe and grief,
For lack o' thee I 've lost my lass,
For lack o' thee I scrimp my glass !
I see the children of affliction
Unaided, through thy curs'd restriction.
I 've seen the oppressor's cruel smile
Amid his hapless victims' spoil;
And for thy potence vainly wish'd
To crush the villain in the dust.
For lack o' thee I leave this much-lov'd
    shore,
Never, perhaps, to greet old Scotland more.
                                    R. B.

KYLE.

THE FAREWELL

The valiant, in himself, what can he suffer ?
Or what does he regard his single woes ?
But when, alas ! he multiplies himself,
To dearer selves, to the lov'd tender fair,
To those whose bliss, whose beings hang upon him,
To helpless children, — then, oh then he feels
The point of misery festering in his heart,
And weakly weeps his fortunes like a coward:
Such, such am I ! — undone !
        THOMSON'S *Edward and Eleanora.*

Published in Hamilton Paul (1819). The
piece may contain the germ of *The Gloomy
Night is Gathering Fast;* but it is so conven-
tional and commonplace withal that one is
tempted to doubt its genuineness, despite the
fact that Paul's authority is of some account.

I

FAREWELL, old Scotia's bleak domains,
Far dearer than the torrid plains,
    Where rich ananas blow !
Farewell, a mother's blessing dear,

A brother's sigh, a sister's tear,
    My Jean's heart-rending throe !
Farewell, my Bess ! Tho' thou 'rt bereft
    Of my paternal care,
A faithful brother I have left,
    My part in him thou 'lt share !
        Adieu too, to you too,
            My Smith, my bosom frien';
        When kindly you mind me,
            O, then befriend my Jean !

II

What bursting anguish tears my heart ?
From thee, my Jeany, must I part ?
    Thou, weeping, answ'rest: "No ! "
Alas ! misfortune stares my face,
And points to ruin and disgrace —
    I for thy sake must go !
Thee, Hamilton, and Aiken dear,
    A grateful, warm adieu:
I with a much-indebted tear
    Shall still remember you !
        All-hail, then, the gale then
            Wafts me from thee, dear shore !
        It rustles, and whistles —
            I 'll never see thee more !

ELEGY ON THE DEATH OF ROBERT RUISSEAUX

"Ruisseaux" — French for "brooks" (*i. e.*
"burns") — is an innocent play on the writer's
name.

I

Now Robin lies in his last lair,
He 'll gabble rhyme, nor sing nae mair;
Cauld Poverty wi' hungry stare
            Nae mair shall fear him;
Nor anxious Fear, nor cankert Care,
            E'er mair come near him.

II

To tell the truth, they seldom fash'd him,
Except the moment that they crush'd him;
For sune as Chance or Fate had hush'd 'em,
            Tho' e'er sae short,
Then wi' a rhyme or sang he lash'd 'em,
            And thought it sport.

III

Tho' he was bred to kintra-wark,
And counted was baith wight and stark,

Yet that was never Robin's mark
    To mak a man;
But tell him, he was learned and clark,
    Ye roos'd him then !

VERSES INTENDED TO BE WRIT-TEN BELOW A NOBLE EARL'S PICTURE

A special compliment (and a gross) to the writer's patron, the Earl of Glencairn (see *ante*, p. 87, Prefatory Note to *Lament for James Earl of Glencairn*), who declined, being a person of taste, to have it included in Edition '87.

I

WHOSE is that noble, dauntless brow ?
    And whose that eye of fire ?
And whose that generous princely mien,
    Ev'n rooted foes admire ?

II

Stranger ! to justly show that brow
    And mark that eye of fire,
Would take His hand, whose vernal tints
    His other works admire !

III

Bright as a cloudless summer sun,
    With stately port he moves;
His guardian Seraph eyes with awe
    The noble Ward he loves.

IV

Among the illustrious Scottish sons
    That Chief thou may'st discern:
Mark Scotia's fond-returning eye —
    It dwells upon Glencairn.

ELEGY ON THE DEATH OF SIR JAMES HUNTER BLAIR

Sir James Hunter Blair, son of John Hunter, bailie in Ayr, was born 2d February, 1741; was apprenticed in the banking house of the brothers Coutts, Edinburgh; became, with Sir William Forbes, joint partner in the bank ; assumed the name of Blair when his wife — a daughter of John Blair of Dunskey, Wigtonshire — succeeded to her estates in 1777; greatly improved the estates in agriculture and trade ; partly rebuilt Portpatrick, and started a packet service to Ireland ; was also an active citizen of Edinburgh, for which he was chosen M. P. in 1781 and 1784, and in 1784 Lord Provost ; was created a baronet, 1786 ; and died of putrid fever 1st July, 1787.

To Robert Aiken, Burns wrote : "The melancholy occasion of the foregoing poem affects not only individuals but a country. That I have lost a friend is but repeating after Caledonia." Further, in the *Glenriddell Book* he thus prefaces his *Elegy:* "This performance is but mediocre, but my grief was sincere. The last time I saw the worthy, public-spirited man — a man he was! how few of the two-legged breed that pass for such deserve the designation! — he pressed my hand, and asked me with the most friendly warmth if it was in his power to serve me ; and if so, that I would oblige him by telling him how. I had nothing to ask of him ; but if ever a child of his should be so unfortunate as to be under the necessity of asking anything of so poor a man as I am it may not be in my power to grant it, but by God I shall try."

I

THE lamp of day with ill-presaging glare,
    Dim, cloudy, sank beneath the western
      wave;
Th' inconstant blast howl'd thro' the dark-ening air,
    And hollow whistled in the rocky cave.

II

Lone as I wander'd by each cliff and dell,
    Once the lov'd haunts of Scotia's royal
      train;
Or mus'd where limpid streams, once hallow'd, well,
    Or mould'ring ruins mark the sacred
      Fane.

III

Th' increasing blast roared round the bee-tling rocks,
    The clouds, swift-wing'd, flew o'er the
      starry sky,
The groaning trees untimely shed their locks,
    And shooting meteors caught the startled
      eye.

IV

The paly moon rose in the livid east,
    And 'mong the cliffs disclos'd a stately
      form

In weeds of woe, that frantic beat her
    breast,
And mix'd her wailings with the raving
    storm.

V

Wild to my heart the filial pulses glow:
'T was Caledonia's trophied shield I
    view'd,
Her form majestic droop'd in pensive woe,
    The lightning of her eye in tears im-
    bued;

VI

Revers'd that spear redoubtable in war,
Reclined that banner, erst in fields un-
    furl'd,
That like a deathful meteor gleam'd afar,
    And brav'd the mighty monarchs of the
    world.

VII

" My patriot son fills an untimely grave ! "
    With accents wild and lifted arms, she
    cried;
"Low lies the hand that oft was stretch'd
    to save,
    Low lies the heart that swell'd with hon-
    or's pride.

VIII

" A weeping country joins a widow's tear;
    The helpless poor mix with the orphan's
    cry;
The drooping Arts surround their patron's
    bier;
    And grateful Science heaves the heart-
    felt sigh.

IX

" I saw my sons resume their ancient fire;
    I saw fair Freedom's blossoms richly
    blow.
But ah ! how hope is born but to expire !
    Relentless fate has laid their guardian
    low.

X

" My patriot falls, but shall he lie unsung,
    While empty greatness saves a worthless
    name ?
No: every Muse shall join her tuneful
    tongue,
    And future ages hear his growing fame.

XI

" And I will join a mother's tender cares
    Thro' future times to make his virtues
    last,
That distant years may boast of other
    Blairs ! " —
    She said, and vanish'd with the sweeping
    blast.

ON THE DEATH OF LORD PRE-
SIDENT DUNDAS

Robert Dundas of Arniston, descended from
an old Scottish family, and eldest son of Rob-
ert Dundas, who also was Lord President of
the Court of Session, was born 18th July, 1713.
He was appointed Lord Advocate in 1754, and
in 1760 became Lord President, in which capa-
city he acquired a high repute for courtesy,
fairness, and ability. He died 13th December,
1787. In a letter to Alexander Cunningham,
11th March, 1791, Burns states that he wrote
the verses at the suggestion of Alexander
Wood, Surgeon, and that Wood left them, to-
gether with a letter from the author, in the
house of the Lord President's son (see *ante*, p.
168, Prefatory Note to *The Dean of the Faculty*);
that Mr. Dundas " never took the smallest no-
tice of the letter, the poem, or the poet ; " and
that since then he (Burns) never saw the name
of Dundas in a newspaper but his " heart felt
straitened " in his " bosom." He makes a sim-
ilar statement in an interleaved copy of his
Poems presented to Bishop Geddes, but adds :
" Did the fellow — the gentleman — think I
looked for any dirty gratuity ? " No doubt
Dundas *did* think so : none, either, that Burns,
by this time a person of importance, was hope-
ful of — not a present in money but a place.
In a letter to Charles Hay, Advocate, published
in *The Scots Magazine* (June, 1818), where the
piece appeared, Burns gives a different ac-
count of its origin : " The enclosed poem was
written in consequence of your suggestion,
last time I had the pleasure of seeing you. It
cost me an hour or two of next morning's sleep,
but did not please me ; so it lay by, an ill-
digested effort, till the other day that I gave
it a critic brush. These kind of subjects are
much hackneyed ; and besides, the wailings of
the rhyming tribe over the ashes of the great
are . . . out of all character for sincerity : "
which well enough describes both the quality
and the effect of a performance meriting no
better reception than it got.

LONE on the bleaky hills, the straying
flocks
Shun the fierce storms among the shelter-
ing rocks;
Down foam the rivulets, red with dashing
rains;
The gathering floods burst o'er the distant
plains;
Beneath the blast the leafless forests
groan;
The hollow caves return a hollow moan.
Ye hills, ye plains, ye forests, and ye caves,
Ye howling winds, and wintry swelling
waves,
Unheard, unseen, by human ear or eye,
Sad to your sympathetic glooms I fly,
Where to the whistling blast and water's
roar
Pale Scotia's recent wound I may de-
plore !
O heavy loss, thy country ill could bear !
A loss these evil days can ne'er repair !
Justice, the high vicegerent of her God,
Her doubtful balance eyed, and sway'd her
rod;
Hearing the tidings of the fatal blow,
She sank, abandon'd to the wildest woe.
Wrongs, injuries, from many a darksome
den,
Now gay in hope explore the paths of
men.
See from his cavern grim Oppression rise,
And throw on Poverty his cruel eyes !
Keen on the helpless victim let him fly,
And stifle, dark, the feebly-bursting cry !
Mark Ruffian Violence, distained with
crimes,
Rousing elate in these degenerate times !
View unsuspecting Innocence a prey,
As guileful Fraud points out the erring
way;
While subtile Litigation's pliant tongue
The life-blood equal sucks of Right and
Wrong !
Hark, injur'd Want recounts th' unlisten'd
tale,
And much-wrong'd Mis'ry pours th' unpit-
ied wail !

Ye dark, waste hills, ye brown, unsightly
plains,
Congenial scenes, ye soothe my mournful
strains.
Ye tempests, rage ! ye turbid torrents,
roll !

Ye suit the joyless tenor of my soul.
Life's social haunts and pleasures I re-
sign;
Be nameless wilds and lonely wanderings
mine,
To mourn the woes my country must en-
dure:
That wound degenerate ages cannot cure.

ELEGY ON WILLIE NICOL'S MARE

Probably William Nicol (see *post,* p. 195,
Epitaph for William Nicol) bought the nag
for use in his holidays at Moffat. She got into
poor condition, and Burns offered to take her
to Ellisland to recruit. When, however, he
had got her into good enough condition for
Dumfries Fair, she suddenly died of an unsus-
pected affection of the spine. In the letter,
9th February, 1790, enclosing the *Elegy* he
wrote : " I have likewise strung four or five
barbarous stanzas to the tune of *Chevy Chase,*
by way of Elegy on your poor unfortunate
mare, beginning (the name she got here was
Peg Nicholson): 'Peg Nicholson,'" etc. No
doubt, the mare was named after Margaret
Nicholson, who, being insane, tried to stab
George III. on 2d August, 1786.

I

PEG NICHOLSON was a good bay mare
As ever trod on airn;
But now she 's floating down the Nith,
And past the mouth o' Cairn.

II

Peg Nicholson was a good bay mare,
An' rode thro' thick an' thin;
But now she 's floating down the Nith,
And wanting even the skin.

III

Peg Nicholson was a good bay mare,
And ance she bore a priest;
But now she 's floating down the Nith,
For Solway fish a feast.

IV

Peg Nicholson was a good bay mare,
An' the priest he rode her sair;
And much oppress'd, and bruis'd she was,
As priest-rid cattle are.

LINES ON FERGUSSON

I

ILL-FATED genius ! Heaven-taught Fergus-
son !
What heart that feels, and will not yield
a tear
To think Life's sun did set, e'er well be-
gun
To shed its influence on thy bright
career !

II

O, why should truest Worth and Genius
pine
Beneath the iron grasp of Want and
Woe,
While titled knaves and idiot-greatness
shine
In all the splendour Fortune can be-
stow ?

ELEGY ON THE LATE MISS BURNET OF MONBODDO

Elizabeth Burnet, the "fair Burnet" of the
Address to Edinburgh (*ante*, p. 73), was the
younger daughter of James Burnet, Lord Mon-
boddo. Burns was a frequent visitor to Mon-
boddo's house in 1786–7; and almost wor-
shipped the fair hostess. "His favourite for
looks and manners," wrote Mrs. Alison
Cockburn, "is Bess Burnet — no bad judge
indeed." In a letter to William Chalmers
(27th December, 1786), he describes her as
"the heavenly Miss Burnet," and declares that
"there has not been anything nearly like her
in all the combinations of beauty, grace, and
goodness the great Creator has formed, since
Milton's Eve on the first day of her existence."
Being asked, after his first visit to the house,
by Father Geddes, if he admired the young
lady, "I admired God Almighty more than
ever," he replied; "Miss Burnet is the most
heavenly of all His works." This fair and
gracious creature died (of consumption) 17th
June, 1790, in her twenty-fifth year. In the
Elegy Burns once more "falls to his English;"
and with the wonted result. Yet it was long
on the anvil. In enclosing a copy to Alexander
Cunningham, 23d January, 1791, he states that
he had been hammering at it for months; and
so dissatisfied is he with the result that he still
calls it a fragment. He was wise enough not
to include it in Edition '93.

I

LIFE ne'er exulted in so rich a prize
As Burnet, lovely from her native skies;
Nor envious Death so triumph'd in a blow
As that which laid th' accomplish'd Burnet
low.

II

Thy form and mind, sweet maid, can I
forget ?
In richest ore the brightest jewel set !
In thee high Heaven above was truest
shown,
For by His noblest work the Godhead best
is known.

III

In vain ye flaunt in summer's pride, ye
groves !
Thou crystal streamlet with thy flowery
shore,
Ye woodland choir that chaunt your idle
loves,
Ye cease to charm: Eliza is no more.

IV

Ye heathy wastes immix'd with reedy fens,
Ye mossy streams with sedge and rushes
stor'd,
Ye rugged cliffs o'erhanging dreary glens,
To you I fly: ye with my soul accord.

V

Princes whose cumb'rous pride was all
their worth,
Shall venal lays their pompous exit hail,
And thou, sweet Excellence ! forsake our
earth,
And not a Muse with honest grief bewail ?

VI

We saw thee shine in youth and beauty's
pride
And Virtue's light, that beams beyond
the spheres;
But, like the sun eclips'd at morning tide,
Thou left us darkling in a world of tears.

VII

The parent's heart that nestled fond in
thee,
That heart how sunk, a prey to grief
and care !
So deckt the woodbine sweet yon aged tree,
So, rudely ravish'd, left it bleak and bare.

PEGASUS AT WANLOCKHEAD

Written in Ramage's Inn while the maker's horse's shoes were frosting. On arriving at the village with a companion, John Sloan, he found the smith too busy to attend immediately to his wants. Sloan thereupon applied to Mr. John Taylor, a person of influence, to speak to the smith: "Sloan's best compliments to Mr. Taylor, and it would be doing him and the Ayrshire Bard a particular favour if he would oblige them *instanter* with his agreeable company. The road has been so slippery that the riders and the brutes were equally in danger of getting some of their bones broken. For the Poet his life and limbs are of some consequence to the world; but for poor Sloan it matters very little what may become of him. The whole of this business is to ask the favour of getting the horses' shoes sharpened." Burns presented the verses — which, to be sure, are poor enough — to Taylor before he left the inn.

I

WITH Pegasus upon a day
Apollo, weary flying
(Through frosty hills the journey lay),
On foot the way was plying.

II

Poor slip-shod, giddy Pegasus
Was but a sorry walker;
To Vulcan then Apollo goes
To get a frosty caulker.

III

Obliging Vulcan fell to work,
Threw by his coat and bonnet,
And did Sol's business in a crack —
Sol paid him in a sonnet.

IV

Ye Vulcan's sons of Wanlockhead,
Pity my sad disaster!
My Pegasus is poorly shod —
I 'll pay you like my master!
RAMAGE'S, 3 *o'clock*.

ON SOME COMMEMORATIONS OF THOMSON

A trifle — produced extempore — which Burns, as he acknowledged to Graham of Fintry, 5th January, 1793, had sent to Captain Johnstone's "extremist sheet," *The Edinburgh Gazetteer*. To publish it was almost to stultify himself; for had he not made the verses recited at the Earl of Buchan's ceremony (see *ante*, p. 93)? Still, on reading an account of the proceedings, he may have recognised that the ridiculous Earl had simply utilised him for his own glorification.

I

DOST thou not rise, indignant Shade,
And smile wi' spurning scorn,
When they wha wad hae starved thy life
Thy senseless turf adorn?

II

They wha about thee mak sic fuss
Now thou art but a name,
Wad seen thee damn'd ere they had spar'd
Ae plack to fill thy wame.

III

Helpless, alane, thou clamb the brae
Wi' meikle honest toil,
And claucht th' unfading garland there,
Thy sair-won, rightful spoil.

IV

And wear it there! and call aloud
This axiom undoubted: —
Would thou hae Nobles' patronage?
First learn to live without it!

V

"To whom hae much, more shall be given"
Is every great man's faith;
But he, the helpless, needful wretch,
Shall lose the mite he hath.

ON GENERAL DUMOURIER'S DESERTION

FROM THE FRENCH REPUBLICAN ARMY

Charles François Dumouriez, being recalled by the Convention after Neerwinden (January, 1793), and menaced with a charge of treason, took refuge in the Austrian camp. After many wanderings he settled in England (1804) at Turville Park, near Henley-on-Thames, and died there 14th March, 1823. [Dampierre, one of his generals, and Beurnonville, an emissary of the Convention but a friend of Dumouriez, had disappointed him by retaining their allegiance to the Republic. Dampierre became commander-in-chief on the defection of his superior and was killed in battle soon after. Beurnonville lived to become a peer and Minister of State under Louis XVIII.]

The piece is a rough but spirited and characteristic parody of the old bacchanalian set of *Robin Adair*.

I

You 're welcome to Despots,
        Dumourier !
You 're welcome to Despots,
        Dumourier !
How does Dampierre do ?
Ay, and Beurnonville too ?
Why did they not come along with you,
        Dumourier ?

II

I will fight France with you,
        Dumourier,
I will fight France with you,
        Dumourier,
I will fight France with you,
I will take my chance with you,
By my soul, I 'll dance with you,
        Dumourier !

III

Then let us fight about,
        Dumourier !
Then let us fight about,
        Dumourier!
Then let us fight about
Till Freedom's spark be out,
Then we 'll be damn'd, no doubt,
        Dumourier.

ON JOHN M'MURDO

Cunningham states that the verses (such as they are) " accompanied a present of books or verse ; " and that afterwards Burns, being on a visit to the house, took out a diamond, and wrote them, as he was fond of doing, on a pane of glass. For M'Murdo see *ante*, p. 143, Prefatory Note to *To John M'Murdo*.

Blest be M'Murdo to his latest day !
No envious cloud o'ercast his evening ray !
No wrinkle furrow'd by the hand of care,
Nor ever sorrow, add one silver hair !
O may no son the father's honor stain,
Nor ever daughter give the mother pain !

ON HEARING A THRUSH SING IN A MORNING WALK IN JANUARY

Enclosed in a letter to Alexander Cunningham, 20th February, 1793 : " I made the following sonnet the other day, which has been so fortunate as to obtain the approbation of no ordinary judge, our friend Sime." It was also sent to Maria Riddell as " a small but sincere mark of esteem."

Sing on, sweet thrush, upon the leafless
        bough,
Sing on, sweet bird, I listen to thy strain:
See aged Winter, 'mid his surly reign,
At thy blythe carol clears his furrowed
        brow.
So in lone Poverty's dominion drear
Sits meek Content with light, unanxious
        heart,
Welcomes the rapid moments, bids them
        part,
Nor asks if they bring ought to hope or
        fear.
I thank Thee, Author of this opening day,
Thou whose bright sun now gilds yon orient
        skies !
Riches denied, Thy boon was purer joys:
What wealth could never give nor take
        away !
Yet come, thou child of Poverty and Care,
The mite high Heav'n bestow'd, that mite
        with thee I 'll share.

IMPROMPTU ON MRS. RIDDELL'S BIRTHDAY

4TH NOVEMBER, 1793

Mrs. Walter Riddell, whose maiden name was Maria Woodley, was the daughter of William Woodley, Commander and Governor of St. Kitts and the Leeward Islands. She married in the West Indies Walter Riddell, younger brother of Captain Robert Riddell, who had an estate in Antigua. In 1791 the couple settled at Goldielea, near Dumfries, which Riddell bought, and which he named Woodley Park in honour of his wife. Burns became a favoured visitor and a warm friend and admirer of the lady, who was handsome, clever, and highly accomplished. In April, 1793, he made a song in her honour. [See *post*,

p. 280, Prefatory Note to *Farewell, thou Stream.*]
It reads like a reckless avowal of passion; but
he disarmed the lady's criticism and resent-
ment — a fact not hitherto [1] set forth — by de-
scribing it as "cold and inanimate," and pro-
testing that "to write a line worth reading on
the subject," it "would be absolutely neces-
sary" for him "to get in love." Then, at a
party at Woodley Park, in January, 1794, he
and the men got drunk in the dining-room.
The talk ran on the Rape of the Sabines, and
they seem to have gone to the drawing-room
with the design of giving a friendly imitation
of the Romans. This, so far as can be divined,
they did: Burns — who was in liquor, and
may well have lost his head in other ways —
laying rude hands on his hostess. On the mor-
row he sent her a desperate apology "from
the regions of hell, amid the horrors of the
damned." "To the men of the company," he
added, "I will make no apology: — Your hus-
band, who insisted on my drinking more than
I chose, has no right to blame me; and the
other gentlemen were partakers of my guilt."
But the indignant lady disregarded this and
other overtures, and Woodley Park was for
some time shut to him. Also, when Mrs. Rid-
dell disliked or disdained, she was apt (as
Burns had noted in a letter to Smellie, 22d
January, 1792) "to make no more secret of
it" than when she respected and esteemed;
and he was rewarded for his too-too practical
proof of admiration, not only with the loss of
Captain Riddell's friendship, but with estrange-
ment also from Maria's intimates. This roused
the cad in him, and he perpetrated the ignoble
Esopus to Maria (ante, p. 123), and a number of
"epigrams" on her husband and herself (see
post) which have neither wit nor decent feel-
ing. These notwithstanding, by the February
of 1795 Mrs. Riddell's anger had begun to cool.
She sent her Bard a book, together with a song
of her own inditing: —

> "For there he rov'd that broke my heart,
> Yet to that heart, ah! still how dear!"

and the old, broken friendship, howbeit in a
more chastened strain, was gradually renewed.
While he was at Brow, Mrs. Riddell, who was
staying in the neighbourhood, invited the dy-
ing man to dinner. His greeting was: "Well,
madam, have you any commands for the other
world?" He expressed to her "great concern
about the care of his literary fame;" regretted
the existence of "letters and verses written
with unguarded and improper freedom;" and
lamented "that he had written many epigrams
on persons against whom he entertained no
enmity, and whose characters he should be
sorry to wound." After his death she wrote
a sketch of his character so admirable in tone,

[1] That is, before the Centenary Edition.

and withal so discerning and impartial in under-
standing, that it remains the best thing written
of him by contemporary critic. Being left a
widow (Walter Riddell, who was something
of a wastrel, had got rid of Woodley Park)
Maria married (1807) Philipps Lloyd Fletcher,
a Welsh gentleman; but died on the 15th De-
cember, 1808. She published (1) *Voyages to
the Madeira and Leeward and Caribbean Isles,
with Sketches of the Natural History of these
Islands* (Edinburgh, 1792), printed by William
Smellie, to whom she dedicated the book; and
(2) *The Metrical Miscellany* (1802), with eigh-
teen songs of her own.

I

OLD Winter, with his frosty beard,
Thus once to Jove his prayer preferred: —
"What have I done of all the year,
To bear this hated doom severe?
My cheerless suns no pleasure know;
Night's horrid car drags dreary slow;
My dismal months no joys are crowning,
But spleeny, English hanging, drowning.

II

Now Jove, for once be mighty civil:
To counterbalance all this evil
Give me, and I 've no more to say,
Give me Maria's natal day!
That brilliant gift shall so enrich me,
Spring, Summer, Autumn, cannot match
     me."
" 'T is done!" says Jove; so ends my story,
And Winter once rejoiced in glory.

SONNET ON THE DEATH OF ROBERT RIDDELL OF GLEN-RIDDELL

For Captain Riddell, who died 20th April,
1794, see *ante*, p. 142, Prefatory Note to *Im-
promptu to Captain Riddell.*

No more, ye warblers of the wood, no more,
Nor pour your descant grating on my soul!
Thou young-eyed Spring, gay in thy ver-
     dant stole,
More welcome were to me grim Winter's
     wildest roar!
How can ye charm, ye flowers, with all
     your dyes?
Ye blow upon the sod that wraps my
     friend.

How can I to the tuneful strain attend ?
That strain flows round the untimely tomb
   where Riddell lies.
Yes, pour, ye warblers, pour the notes of
   woe,
And sooth the Virtues weeping o'er his bier !
The man of worth — and "hath not left
   his peer" ! —
Is in his "narrow house" for ever darkly
   low.
Thee, Spring, again with joy shall others
   greet;
Me, memory of my loss will only meet.

A SONNET UPON SONNETS

We have done our utmost to determine
whether this copy of verses — one of the
crowd of pieces produced in imitation of Lope
de Vega on the Sonnet : —

   " Un soneto me manda hacer Violante," etc. ;

or of Voiture on the Rondeau : —

   " Ma foy ! C'est fait de moi. Car Isabeau," etc. —

be very Burns or merely a copy of Burns's
handwriting ; and we have also taken counsel
with such experts as Dr. Garnett and Mr.
Austin Dobson. It seems to be unknown ; and
we have assumed that it is one of his few
metrical experiments (see *ante*, p. 144, Prefatory Note to *Sonnet*, etc.).

FOURTEEN, a sonneteer thy praises sings;
What magic myst'ries in that number lie !
Your hen hath fourteen eggs beneath her
   wings
That fourteen chickens to the roost may fly.
Fourteen full pounds the jockey's stone
   must be;
His age fourteen — a horse's prime is past.
Fourteen long hours too oft the Bard must
   fast;
Fourteen bright bumpers — bliss he ne'er
   must see !
Before fourteen, a dozen yields the strife;
Before fourteen — e'en thirteen's strength
   is vain.
Fourteen good years — a woman gives us
   life;
Fourteen good men — we lose that life
   again.
What lucubrations can be more upon it ?
Fourteen good measur'd verses make a
   sonnet.

FRAGMENTS

TRAGIC FRAGMENT

"In my early years nothing less would serve
me than courting the Tragic Muse. I was,
I think, about eighteen or nineteen when I
sketched the outlines of a tragedy, forsooth ;
but the bursting of a cloud of family misfortunes, which had for some time threatened us,
prevented my further progress. In those days
I never wrote down anything ; so, except a
speech or two, the whole has escaped my
memory. The following, which I most distinctly remember, was an exclamation from a
great character — great in occasional instances
of generosity and daring at times in villanies.
He is supposed to meet with a child of misery,
and exclaims to himself : ' All villain,' " etc.
(R. B.) Scott Douglas refers this 'prentice exercise — *he* calls it a " pathetic address " — to
family misfortunes and the study of Shakespeare. Burns's own description is preferable
as regards the intention of the thing.

ALL villain as I am — a damnèd wretch,
A hardened, stubborn, unrepenting sin-
   ner —
Still my heart melts at human wretched-
   ness,
And with sincere, tho' unavailing, sighs
I view the helpless children of distress.
With tears indignant I behold the oppres-
   sor
Rejoicing in the honest man's destruction,
Whose unsubmitting heart was all his
   crime.
Ev'n you, ye hapless crew ! I pity you;
Ye, whom the seeming good think sin to
   pity:
Ye poor, despised, abandoned vagabonds,
Whom Vice, as usual, has turn'd o'er to
   ruin.
Oh ! but for friends and interposing Hea-
   ven,
I had been driven forth, like you forlorn,
The most detested, worthless wretch among
   you!
O injured God ! Thy goodness has en-
   dow'd me
With talents passing most of my com-
   peers,
Which I in just proportion have abused,
As far surpassing other common villains
As Thou in natural parts has given me
   more.

REMORSE

"I entirely agree with that judicious Philosopher, Mr. Smith, in his excellent *Theory of Moral Sentiments*, that Remorse is the most painful sentiment that can embitter the human bosom. Any ordinary pitch of fortitude may bear up tolerably well under those calamities, in the procurement of which we ourselves have had no hand; but when our own follies or crimes have made us miserable and wretched, to bear it up with manly firmness, and at the same time have a proper penitential sense of our misconduct, is a glorious effort of self-command." (R. B.)

Of all the numerous ills that hurt our peace,
That press the soul, or wring the mind with anguish,
Beyond comparison the worst are those
By our own folly, or our guilt brought on:
In ev'ry other circumstance, the mind
Has this to say: — "It was no deed of mine."
But, when to all the evil of misfortune
This sting is added: — "Blame thy foolish self!"
Or, worser far, the pangs of keen remorse,
The torturing, gnawing consciousness of guilt,
Of guilt, perhaps, where we 've involvèd others,
The young, the innocent, who fondly lov'd us;
Nay, more, that very love their cause of ruin!
O burning Hell! in all thy store of torments
There 's not a keener lash!
Lives there a man so firm, who, while his heart
Feels all the bitter horrors of his crime,
Can reason down its agonizing throbs,
And, after proper purpose of amendment,
Can firmly force his jarring thoughts to peace?
O happy, happy, enviable man!
O glorious magnanimity of soul!

RUSTICITY'S UNGAINLY FORM

Enclosed in a volume of songs sent to Mrs. Lawrie of Newmilns. Chambers states that it was intended as a justification of the writer's defence of Miss Peggy Kennedy (see *Young Peggy, post*, p. 201), when he touched on the topic of her "fall" in such a fashion as to make Mrs. Lawrie forbid discussion. But Miss Kennedy's "fall" was still to come.

I

Rusticity's ungainly form
 May cloud the highest mind;
But when the heart is nobly warm,
 The good excuse will find.

II

Propriety's cold, cautious rules
 Warm Fervour may o'erlook;
But spare poor Sensibility
 Th' ungentle, harsh rebuke.

ON WILLIAM CREECH

Sent to Mrs. Dunlop, 23d October, 1788, with the fragment on William Smellie: "These," he wrote, "are embryotic fragments of what may one day be a poem." Another instalment, sent on the 29th, he afterwards incorporated in *To Robert Graham of Fintry* (*ante*, p. 85). His subject was his publisher (see *ante*, p. 118, Prefatory Note to *Lament*, etc.).

A little upright, pert, tart, tripping wight,
And still his precious self his dear delight;
Who loves his own smart shadow in the streets
Better than e'er the fairest She he meets.
Much specious lore, but little understood
(Veneering oft outshines the solid wood),
His solid sense by inches you must tell,
But mete his subtle cunning by the ell!
A man of fashion, too, he made his tour,
Learn'd "Vive la bagatelle et vive l'amour:"
So travell'd monkies their grimace improve,
Polish their grin — nay, sigh for ladies' love!
His meddling vanity, a busy fiend,
Still making work his selfish craft must mend.

ON WILLIAM SMELLIE

William Smellie was, says Burns (undated letter to Peter Hill), "a man positively of the first abilities and greatest strength of mind, as well as one of the best hearts and keenest wits."

that he had "ever met with." The son of Alexander Smellie, an Edinburgh architect, he was born in the Pleasance (Edinburgh) in 1740. Being apprenticed to a firm of printers, he yet contrived to attend the Greek, Latin, and Hebrew classes at the University, and to achieve distinction in them all. His love of knowledge once awakened, he was not content till he had completed the round of literary and scientific study, including the full Medical Course. In 1765 he became partner in a firm which some years later, as Balfour and Smellie, was appointed Printers to the University; and on its dissolution in 1782 he took in Creech, engaging himself the while in literature and — especially — science. He was credited with at least the preparation for the press of Buchan's *Domestic Medicine*, 1770; he supervised and in great part compiled the first *Encyclopædia Britannica*, 1777; he edited *The Edinburgh Magazine and Review*, 1773–1776; he translated Buffon's *Natural History*, 9 vols. 1780–1781; he wrote the *Philosophy of Natural History*, 2 vols. 1790–1799 — to name but these. He died 24th June, 1795. He was the life and soul of the club known as "The Crochallan Fencibles," for whose "use" the collection called *The Merry Muses of Caledonia* is stated (on the title-page) to have been "selected," and which met in an historic tavern kept by the Highlander David Douglas. This same Douglas occasionally entertained his guests by singing the Gaelic song *Chro Challin* = "Cattle of Colin;" and in a whimsical spirit Smellie appropriated the song's name to the brotherhood.

CROCHALLAN came:
The old cock'd hat, the brown surtout the
    same;
His grisly beard just bristling in its might
('T was four long nights and days to shav-
    ing-night);
His uncomb'd, hoary locks, wild-staring,
    thatch'd
A head for thought profound and clear
    unmatch'd;
Yet, tho' his caustic wit was biting rude,
His heart was warm, benevolent, and good.

SKETCH FOR AN ELEGY

Probably the original form of the elegy on Captain Matthew Henderson, although his name is not mentioned.

I

CRAIGDARROCH, fam'd for speaking art
And every virtue of the heart,

Stops short, nor can a word impart
    To end his sentence,
When mem'ry strikes him like a dart
    With auld acquaintance.

II

Black James — whase wit was never laith,
But, like a sword had tint the sheath,
Ay ready for the work o' death —
    He turns aside,
And strains wi' suffocating breath
    His grief to hide.

III

Even Philosophic Smellie tries
To choak the stream that floods his eyes:
So Moses wi' a hazel-rice
    Came o'er the stane;
But, tho' it cost him speaking twice,
    It gush'd amain.

IV

Go to your marble graffs, ye great,
In a' the tinkler-trash of state !
But by thy honest turf I 'll wait,
    Thou man of worth,
And weep the ae best fallow's fate
    E'er lay in earth !

PASSION'S CRY

The earlier written part, beginning line 19, "I burn, I burn," etc., was produced in 1787, after hearing the end of a divorce case in which, on March 7th, the Court of Session decided that the husband might proceed against the lover without divorcing his wife. (The oratorical methods of the leading counsel are quizzed in *In the Court of Session*, p. 183.) The lady, who was heiress of Skerrington, Ayrshire, bore a child to Captain Montgomerie in November, 1784; and the husband chose not to interfere with the marriage settlements, but punished the lover, and maintained the matrimony as of old. Burns's sympathies were strongly with the lover and the lady. "O all ye powers of love unfortunate, and friendless woe," he writes to Gavin Hamilton, "pour the balm of sympathising pity on the grief-worn, tender heart of the hapless fair one !"

MILD zephyrs waft thee to life's farthest
    shore,
Nor think of me and my distresses more !

Falsehood accurst! No! Still I beg a
    place,
Still near thy heart some little, little trace!
For that dear trace the world I would re-
    sign:
O, let me live, and die, and think it mine!

By all I lov'd, neglected, and forgot,
No friendly face e'er lights my squalid
    cot.
Shunn'd, hated, wrong'd, unpitied, unre-
    drest
The mock'd quotation of the scorner's jest;
Ev'n the poor support of my wretched life,
Snatched by the violence of legal strife;
Oft grateful for my very daily bread,
To those my family's once large bounty
    fed;
A welcome inmate at their homely fare,
My griefs, my woes, my sighs, my tears
    they share:
Their vulgar souls unlike the souls re-
    fined,
The fashion'd marble of the polish'd mind.

"I burn, I burn, as when thro' ripen'd
    corn
By driving winds the crackling flames are
    borne."
Now, maddening-wild, I curse that fatal
    night,
Now bless the hour that charm'd my guilty
    sight.
In vain the Laws their feeble force op-
    pose:
Chain'd at his feet, they groan Love's van-
    quish'd foes.
In vain Religion meets my shrinking eye:
I dare not combat, but I turn and fly.
Conscience in vain upbraids th' unhallow'd
    fire.
Love grasps his scorpions — stifled they
    expire.
Reason drops headlong from his sacred
    throne.
Your dear idea reigns, and reigns alone;
Each thought intoxicated homage yields,
And riots wanton in forbidden fields.

By all on high adoring mortals know,
By all the conscious villain fears below;
By what, alas! much more my soul
    alarms —
My doubtful hopes once more to fill thy
    arms —

Ev'n shouldst thou, false, forswear the
    guilty tie,
Thine and thine only I must live and die!

IN VAIN WOULD PRUDENCE

IN vain would Prudence with decorous
    sneer
Point out a censuring world, and bid me
    fear:
Above that world on wings of love I rise,
I know its worst, and can that worst de-
    spise.
"Wrong'd, injur'd, shunn'd, unpitied, un-
    redrest,
The mock'd quotation of the scorner's
    jest,"
Let Prudence' direst bodements on me
    fall,
Clarinda, rich reward! o'erpays them all.

THE CARES O' LOVE

HE

THE cares o' Love are sweeter far
    Than onie other pleasure;
And if sae dear its sorrows are,
    Enjoyment, what a treasure!

SHE

I fear to try, I dare na try
    A passion sae ensnaring;
For light's her heart and blythe's her
    song
That for nae man is caring.

EPIGRAMS

EXTEMPORE IN THE COURT OF SESSION

TUNE: *Killiecrankie*

The oratorical duel thus cleverly thumb-
nailed was between Islay Campbell, Lord Ad-
vocate (for Islay Campbell, see *post*, p. 326, Note
to *The Earnest Cry and Prayer*, Stanza xiv.
Line 2), and Henry Erskine, Dean of Faculty
(for Erskine, see *ib.* Line 1), in a certain divorce
case (1787), as to which see *ante*, p. 182, Prefa-
tory Note to *Passion's Cry*.

LORD ADVOCATE

HE clench'd his pamphlets in his fist,
   He quoted and he hinted,
Till in a declamation-mist
   His argument, he tint it:
He gapèd for 't, he grapèd for 't,
   He fand it was awa, man;
But what his common sense came short,
   He ekèd out wi' law, man.

MR. ERSKINE

Collected, Harry stood awee,
   Then open'd out his arm, man;
His lordship sat wi' ruefu' e'e,
   And ey'd the gathering storm, man;
Like wind-driv'n hail it did assail,
   Or torrents owre a linn, man;
The Bench sae wise lift up their eyes,
   Hauf-wauken'd wi' the din, man.

AT ROSLIN INN

Chambers states that Burns breakfasted at
the inn after a ramble in the Pentlands with
Alexander Nasmyth, the painter. He further
relates that the ramble was taken after trans-
gressing "the rules of sobriety" in Edinburgh,
and sitting "till an early hour in the morn-
ing." Part of this on the authority of a gos-
sip who "lived at Roslin at the time."

MY blessings on ye, honest wife !
   I ne'er was here before;
Ye 've wealth o' gear for spoon and knife:
   Heart could not wish for more.
Heav'n keep you clear o' sturt and strife,
   Till far ayont fourscore,
And by the Lord o' death and life,
   I 'll ne'er gae by your door !

TO AN ARTIST

Chambers states that Burns, entering a
studio in Edinburgh, found the occupant en-
gaged on a *Jacob's Dream*, and wrote the lines
on the back of a little sketch.

DEAR ——, I 'll gie ye some advice,
   You 'll tak it no uncivil:
You shouldna paint at angels, man,
   But try and paint the Devil.

To paint an angel 's kittle wark,
   Wi' Nick there 's little danger:
You 'll easy draw a lang-kent face,
   But no sae weel a stranger.
                                    R. B.

THE BOOK-WORMS

Said to have been written on a splendidly
bound but worm-eaten volume of Shakespeare
in a nobleman's library.

THROUGH and through th' inspirèd leaves,
   Ye maggots, make your windings;
But O, respect his lordship's taste,
   And spare the golden bindings !

ON ELPHINSTONE'S TRANSLA-
TION OF MARTIAL

James Elphinstone — born 1721, died 1809,
— published his egregious translation of Mar-
tial's *Epigrams* in 1782. "A Mr. Elphin-
stone," wrote Burns to Clarinda, "has given
a translation of Martial, a famous Latin poet.
The poetry of Elphinstone can only equal his
prose notes. I was sitting in a merchant's shop
of my acquaintance waiting somebody; he
put Elphinstone into my hand, and asked my
opinion of it. I begged leave to write it on a
blank leaf, which I did." A facsimile of the
inscription — below Elphinstone's "Rhymed
Address to the Subscribers"— was published
in *The Burns Chronicle* for 1894. The epigram
was doubtless suggested by the old one which
served as a model for *On Thanksgiving for a
National Victory* (see *post*, p. 190).

O THOU whom Poesy abhors,
Whom Prose has turnèd out of doors,
Heard'st thou yon groan ? — Proceed no
      further !
'T was laurel'd Martial calling "Murther !"

ON JOHNSON'S OPINION OF
HAMPDEN

Inscribed on a copy of Johnson's *Lives*, pre-
sented by Burns to Alexander Cunningham.
A comment on Johnson's remark: "His mother
was the daughter of John Hampden of Hamp-

den, in the same county, and sister to Hampden, the *zealot of rebellion.*"

For shame !
Let Folly and Knavery
Freedom oppose:
'T is suicide, Genius,
To mix with her foes.

UNDER THE PORTRAIT OF MISS BURNS

Cease, ye prudes, your envious railing !
Lovely Burns has charms: confess !
True it is she had ae failing:
Had ae woman ever less ?

ON MISS AINSLIE IN CHURCH

Miss Ainslie was sister to Burns's friend, Robert Ainslie. Burns, on his Border Tour, arrived at Berrywell, Berwickshire, the farm of Ainslie's father, on 5th May, 1787. On the Sunday, as related in his *Journal*, he accompanied the family to church at Duns, and, being seated next Miss Ainslie, wrote the lines in her Bible, apropos of her search for a text against the impenitent denoted by the preacher. In his *Journal* he sketches the young lady thus: " Her person a little *embonpoint*, but handsome ; her face, particularly her eyes, full of sweetness and good humour ; she unites three qualities rarely to be found together : keen, solid penetration ; sly, witty observation and remark ; and the gentlest, most unaffected female modesty."

Fair maid, you need not take the hint,
Nor idle texts pursue ;
'T was guilty sinners that he meant,
Not angels such as you.

AT INVERARAY

Published in Stewart's *Poems Ascribed to Robert Burns* (1801), with the explanation that Burns found " himself and his companion entirely neglected by the innkeeper, whose whole attention seemed to be occupied " by " some company " on a visit to the Duke of Argyll.

I

Whoe'er he be that sojourns here,
I pity much his case,
Unless he come to wait upon
The Lord their God, " His Grace."

II

There 's naething here but Highland pride
And Highland scab and hunger:
If Providence has sent me here,
'T was surely in an anger.

AT CARRON IRONWORKS

Written on the window of the inn at Carron.

We cam na here to view your warks
In hopes to be mair wise,
But only, lest we gang to Hell,
It may be nae surprise.

But when we tirl'd at your door
Your porter dought na bear us:
Sae may, should we to Hell's yetts come,
Your billie Satan sair us.

ON SEEING THE ROYAL PALACE AT STIRLING IN RUINS

Burns reached Stirling on the afternoon of the Sunday (26th August) which saw him " tirling " at the door of Carron Ironworks. Visiting Harvieston on the Monday, he returned to Stirling that evening. Not improbably these lines were written after the jolly supper mentioned in his *Journal*. The inscription was published, with the intention of showing Burns up, in James Maxwell's rhymed *Animadversions on Some Poets and Poetasters* (1788), and it appears in Cunningham (1834). As we learn from a letter to Clarinda, January, 1788, Burns, on applying for a place in the Excise, was severely questioned about it.

Here Stewarts once in glory reign'd,
And laws for Scotland's weal ordain'd;
But now unroof'd their palace stands,
Their sceptre fallen to other hands:
Fallen indeed, and to the earth,
Whence grovelling reptiles take their birth !

The injured Stewart line is gone,
A race outlandish fills their throne:
An idiot race, to honour lost —
Who know them best despise them most.

ADDITIONAL LINES AT STIR-LING

Published by Cunningham (1834), who states, but, as usual, without giving his authority, that Burns wrote the preceding inscription on the Monday morning, and, being remonstrated with by Nicol on his return from Harvieston, added this mock " reproof to the author."

RASH mortal, and slanderous poet, thy name
Shall no longer appear in the records of Fame !
Dost not know that old Mansfield, who writes like the Bible,
Says, the more 't is a truth, Sir, the more 't is a libel ?

REPLY TO THE THREAT OF A CENSORIOUS CRITIC

WITH Æsop's lion, Burns says: — " Sore I feel
Each other blow: but damn that ass's heel ! "

A HIGHLAND WELCOME

WHEN Death's dark stream I ferry o'er
(A time that surely shall come),
In Heaven itself I 'll ask no more
Than just a Highland welcome.

AT WHIGHAM'S INN, SAN-QUHAR

ENVY, if thy jaundiced eye
Through this window chance to spy,
To thy sorrow thou shalt find
All that 's generous, all that 's kind.
Friendship, virtue, every grace,
Dwelling in this happy place.

VERSICLES ON SIGN-POSTS

" The everlasting surliness of a lion and Saracen's head," etc. — thus does Burns preface them — " or the unchanging blandness of the landlord welcoming a traveller, on some sign-posts, would be no bad similes of the constant affected fierceness of a Bully, or the eternal simper of a Frenchman or a Fiddler."

I

HE looked
Just as your sign-post Lions do,
With aspect fierce and quite as harmless too.

2

(PATIENT STUPIDITY)

So heavy, passive to the tempest's shocks,
Dull on the sign-post stands the stupid ox.

3

HIS face with smile eternal drest
Just like the landlord to his guest,
High as they hang with creaking din
To index out the Country Inn.

4

A HEAD, pure, sinless quite of brain and soul,
The very image of a barber's poll:
Just shews a human face, and wears a wig,
And looks, when well friseur'd, amazing big.

ON MISS JEAN SCOTT

O, HAD each Scot of ancient times
Been, Jeanie Scott, as thou art,
The bravest heart on English ground
Had yielded like a coward.

ON CAPTAIN FRANCIS GROSE

THE Devil got notice that Grose was a-dying,
So whip ! at the summons, old Satan came flying;
But when he approach'd where poor Francis lay moaning,
And saw each bed-post with its burthen a-groaning,

Astonish'd, confounded, cries Satan: — "By
   God,
I 'd want him ere take such a damnable
   load !"

ON BEING APPOINTED TO AN EXCISE DIVISION

The appointment was made in August, 1789.

SEARCHING auld wives' barrels,
   Ochon, the day
That clarty barm should stain my laurels !
   But what 'll ye say ?
These movin' things ca'd wives an' weans
Wad move the very hearts o' stanes.

ON MISS DAVIES

For Miss Davies, see Prefatory Note to
Bonie Wee Thing, post, p. 236.

ASK why God made the gem so small,
   And why so huge the granite ?
Because God meant mankind should set
   That higher value on it.

ON A BEAUTIFUL COUNTRY SEAT

For Maxwell of Cardoness, see *post*, p. 197,
Prefatory Note to *On a Galloway Laird.*

WE grant they 're thine, those beauties all,
   So lovely in our eye:
Keep them, thou eunuch, Cardoness,
   For others to enjoy.

THE TYRANT WIFE

CURS'D be the man, the poorest wretch in
   life,
The crouching vassal to the tyrant wife !
Who has no will but by her high permis-
   sion;
Who has not sixpence but in her posses-
   sion;
Who must to her his dear friend's secret
   tell;
Who dreads a curtain lecture worse than
   hell !
Were such the wife had fallen to my
   part,
I 'd break her spirit, or I 'd break her heart:
I 'd charm her with the magic of a switch,
I 'd kiss her maids, and kick the perverse
   bitch.

AT BROWNHILL INN

[A play upon the name of the landlord,
"honest Bacon" of *To William Stewart, ante,*
p. 146.]

AT Brownhill we always get dainty good
   cheer
And plenty of bacon each day in the year;
We 've a' thing that 's nice, and mostly in
   season:
But why always bacon ? — come, tell me
   the reason ?

THE TOADEATER

OF Lordly acquaintance you boast,
   And the Dukes that you dined with
      yestreen;
Yet an insect 's an insect at most,
   Tho' it crawl on the curl of a Queen !

IN LAMINGTON KIRK

The minister was Thomas Mitchell. He was
presented (1772) to Kinglassie by the Earl of
Rothes ; but, as the parishioners were unani-
mously against him, it was arranged that he
should exchange with the original presentee to
Lamington. He is described as "an accom-
plished scholar." He died 12th March, 1811.

As cauld a wind as ever blew,
A cauld kirk, and in 't but few,
As cauld a minister 's ever spak —
Ye 'se a' be het or I come back !

THE KEEKIN GLASS

Written extempore at Dalswinton, and handed by Burns to Miss Miller, his landlord's daughter, on her informing him that one of the Lords of Justiciary had got so drunk the night before that, coming into the drawing-room, he pointed at her, and asked her father : "Wha 's yon hoolet-faced thing i' the corner ? "

How daur ye ca' me " Howlet-face,"
  Ye blear-e'ed, wither'd spectre ?
Ye only spied the keekin-glass,
  An' there ye saw your picture.

AT THE GLOBE TAVERN, DUM-
FRIES

I

THE greybeard, old Wisdom, may boast of
    his treasures,
Give me with gay Folly to live !
I grant him his calm-blooded, time-settled
    pleasures,
But Folly has raptures to give.

2
(I)

I MURDER hate by field or flood,
  Tho' Glory's name may screen us.
In wars at hame I 'll spend my blood —
  Life-giving wars of Venus.
The deities that I adore
  Are Social Peace and Plenty:
I 'm better pleas'd to make one more
  Than be the death of twenty.

(II)

I would not die like Socrates,
  For all the fuss of Plato;
Nor would I with Leonidas,
  Nor yet would I with Cato;
The zealots of the Church and State
  Shall ne'er my mortal foes be;
But let me have bold Zimri's fate
  Within the arms of Cozbi.

3

MY bottle is a holy pool,
That heals the wounds o' care an' dool,
And pleasure is a wanton trout —
An ye drink it, ye 'll find him out.

4

IN politics if thou would'st mix
  And mean thy fortunes be;
Bear this in mind: Be deaf and blind,
  Let great folks hear and see.

YE TRUE LOYAL NATIVES

The " Loyal Natives Club " of Dumfries was formed in January, 1793. It celebrated the King's birthday on 4th June with a dinner and a ball. Burns's lines were in reply to these : —

THE LOYAL NATIVES' VERSES

" Ye Sons of Sedition, give ear to my song,
Let Syme, Burns, and Maxwell pervade every throng,
With Cracken, the attorney, and Mundell, the quack,
Send Willie, the monger, to hell with a smack.''

YE true " Loyal Natives," attend to my
    song:
In uproar and riot rejoice the night long !
From Envy and Hatred your core is ex-
    empt,
But where is your shield from the darts of
    Contempt ?

ON COMMISSARY GOLDIE'S
BRAINS

Goldie was President of the Loyal Natives.

LORD, to account who does Thee call,
  Or e'er dispute Thy pleasure ?
Else why within so thick a wall
  Enclose so poor a treasure ?

IN A LADY'S POCKET BOOK

GRANT me, indulgent Heaven, that I may
    live
To see the miscreants feel the pains they
    give !
Deal Freedom's sacred treasures free as
    air,
Till Slave and Despot be but things that
    were !

AGAINST THE EARL OF GAL-LOWAY

Burns went a jaunt through Galloway, with John Syme, in the last week of July, 1793. Between Kenmure and Gatehouse the pair got "utterly wet," and, coming to Gatehouse, Burns insisted on getting "utterly drunk." Next morning, in attempting to get his boots on, he tore them to shreds. "Mercy on us," wrote Syme, "how he did fume and rage! Nothing could reinstate him in temper. I tried various expedients, and at last hit on one that succeeded. I showed him the house of Garlieston, across the bay of Wigton. Against the Earl of Galloway, with whom he was offended, he expectorated his spleen, and regained a most agreeable temper."

John Stewart, seventh Earl of Galloway, born 13th March, 1736, succeeded to the peerage 24th September, 1773; was a representative Scottish Peer from 1774 to 1790; supported Pitt, and in 1784 was chosen a Lord of the Bedchamber; was created a Peer of Great Britain 6th June, 1796; and died 13th November, 1806. Being of puritan repute and habit, he was a *persona ingrata* to Burns, who satirised him in *The Heron Election Ballads*. See *ante*, p. 166.

WHAT dost thou in that mansion fair?
　Flit, Galloway, and find
Some narrow, dirty, dungeon cave,
　The picture of thy mind.

ON THE SAME

No Stewart art thou, Galloway:
　The Stewarts all were brave.
Besides, the Stewarts were but fools,
　Not one of them a knave.

ON THE SAME

BRIGHT ran thy line, O Galloway,
　Thro' many a far-famed sire!
So ran the far-famed Roman way,
　And ended in a mire.

ON THE SAME, ON THE AUTHOR BEING THREATENED WITH VENGEANCE

SPARE me thy vengeance, Galloway!
　In quiet let me live:
I ask no kindness at thy hand,
　For thou hast none to give.

ON THE LAIRD OF LAGGAN

Written during the same tour as the Epigrams preceding. Having settled Lord Galloway, he afterwards, wrote Syme, "fell on humbler game. There is one Morine whom he does not love. He had a passing blow at him." Morine had bought the farm of Ellisland.

WHEN Morine, deceas'd, to the Devil went down,
'T was nothing would serve him but Satan's own crown.
"Thy fool's head," quoth Satan, "that crown shall wear never:
I grant thou 'rt as wicked, but not quite so clever."

ON MARIA RIDDELL

Inscribed on the back of a draft copy of *Scots Wha Hae*, now in the possession of Mrs. Locker-Lampson. The heading is, "On my Lord Buchan's vociferating in an argument that 'Women must always be flattered grossly or not spoken to at all.'" For Maria Riddell see *ante*, p. 178, Prefatory Note to *Impromptu on Mrs. Riddell's Birthday*.

"PRAISE Woman still," his lordship roars,
　"Deserv'd or not, no matter!"
But thee whom all my soul adores,
　There Flattery cannot flatter!
Maria, all my thought and dream,
　Inspires my vocal shell:
The more I praise my lovely theme,
　The more the truth I tell.

ON MISS FONTENELLE

"If Miss Fontenelle," wrote Burns, "will accept this honest compliment to her personal charms, amiable manners, and gentle heart from a man too proud to flatter, though too poor to have his compliment of any consequence, it will sincerely oblige her anxious friend and most devoted humble servant."

SWEET naïveté of feature,
　Simple, wild, enchanting elf,

Not to thee, but thanks to Nature
    Thou art acting but thyself.

Wert thou awkward, stiff, affected,
    Spurning Nature, torturing art,
Loves and Graces all rejected,
    Then indeed thou 'dst act a part.

KIRK AND STATE EXCISEMEN

Written on a window in the King's Arms, Dumfries.

YE men of wit and wealth, why all this
    sneering
'Gainst poor Excisemen? Give the cause
    a hearing.
What are your Landlord's rent-rolls? Tax-
    ing ledgers!
What Premiers? What ev'n Monarchs?
    Mighty Gaugers!
Nay, what are Priests (those seeming godly
    wise-men)?
What are they, pray, but Spiritual Excise-
    men!

ON   THANKSGIVING   FOR   A NATIONAL VICTORY

The victory was probably Howe's, off Ushant, 1st June, 1794.

YE hypocrites! are these your pranks?
To murder men, and give God thanks?
Desist for shame! Proceed no further:
God won't accept your thanks for Mur-
    ther.

PINNED TO MRS. WALTER RID-DELL'S CARRIAGE

IF you rattle along like your mistress's
    tongue,
    Your speed will out-rival the dart;
But, a fly for your load, you 'll break down
    on the road,
    If your stuff be as rotten 's her heart.

TO DR. MAXWELL

ON MISS JESSY STAIG'S RECOVERY

For Miss Staig, see Prefatory Note to *Young Jessie* (*post*, p. 276).

Dr. William Maxwell, son of a noted Jacobite, James Maxwell of Kirkconnell, was born in 1760. He was educated at the Jesuits' College at Dinant, and afterwards studied medicine at Paris. In 1792 he started a London sub-scription for the French Jacobins, and he is the Englishman said in Burke's speech (28th December, 1792) to have ordered three thou-sand daggers at Birmingham. As a National Guard he was present at the execution of Louis XVI., and is reported to have dipped his hand-kerchief in the King's blood. When Burns wrote, he had just returned to Scotland and started a practice in Dumfries. Burns and he became fast friends. He attended Burns during the last illness, when the dying man presented him with his pistols. He died 13th October, 1834.

MAXWELL, if merit here you crave,
    That merit I deny:
You save fair Jessie from the grave!—
    An Angel could not die!

TO THE BEAUTIFUL MISS ELIZA J——N

ON HER PRINCIPLES OF LIBERTY AND EQUALITY

How, "Liberty!" Girl, can it be by thee
    nam'd?
"Equality," too! Hussy, art not asham'd?
Free and Equal indeed, while mankind
    thou enchainest,
And over their hearts a proud Despot so
    reignest.

ON CHLORIS

REQUESTING ME TO GIVE HER A SPRIG OF BLOSSOMED THORN

FROM the white-blossom'd sloe my dear
    Chloris requested
A sprig, her fair breast to adorn:

"No, by Heaven !" I exclaim'd, "let me
    perish for ever,
Ere I plant in that bosom a thorn ! "

TO THE HON. WM. R. MAULE OF PANMURE

Here [1] published for the first time. Sent to
Mrs. Dunlop in a letter of 24th October, 1794.
After telling her that the Caledonians had
been at Dumfries for the last fortnight, Burns
adds: "One of the corps provoked my ire the
other day, which burst out as follows."
    The Hon. William Ramsay Maule, the second
son of George Ramsay, Earl of Dalhousie, was
born 27th October, 1771. He succeeded to
Panmure on the death of his uncle, William
Earl of Panmure, in 1787, when he assumed
the surname of Maule; served for some time
in the 11th Dragoons; was chosen M. P. for
Forfar in 1796 as a supporter of Fox; on 9th
September, 1831, was raised to the British
Peerage as Baron Panmure; and died 13th
April, 1852. He appears (with his horse) in
Kay's *Edinburgh Portraits* as "a generous
sportsman." In effect, he was ardent in
racing and cocking, much given to obstreper-
ous practical jokes, and not too exemplary in
his general habits: at the same time that he
was generous to his dependants, and liberal in
regard to schemes for the public welfare. He
bestowed an annuity of £50 on Burns's widow.

THOU Fool, in thy phaeton towering,
    Art proud when that phaeton 's prais'd ?
'T is the pride of a Thief's exhibition
    When higher his pillory 's rais'd.

ON SEEING MRS. KEMBLE IN YARICO

The lady was Mrs. Stephen Kemble, who
appeared at the Dumfries Theatre in October,
1794.

KEMBLE, thou cur'st my unbelief
    Of Moses and his rod:
At Yarico's sweet notes of grief
    The rock with tears had flow'd.

ON DR. BABINGTON'S LOOKS

Burns, in a letter to Mrs. Dunlop, refers to
the subject of his satire "as a well-known

[1] That is, in the Centenary Edition.

character here " — that is, presumably, Dum-
fries. He explains that it was in answer to
one who said "there was falsehood in his
looks."

THAT there is a falsehood in his looks
    I must and will deny:
They say their Master is a knave,
    And sure they do not lie.

ON ANDREW TURNER

IN Se'enteen Hunder 'n Forty-Nine
The Deil gat stuff to mak a swine,
    An' coost it in a corner;
But wilily he chang'd his plan,
An' shap'd it something like a man,
    An' ca'd it Andrew Turner.

THE SOLEMN LEAGUE AND COVENANT

Inscribed by Burns in the Dumfriesshire vol-
ume of Sir John Sinclair's *Statistical Account
of Scotland*, in a footnote to a narrative of the
Persecution in Balmaghie parish.

THE Solemn League and Covenant
    Now brings a smile, now brings a tear.
But sacred Freedom, too, was theirs:
    If thou 'rt a slave, indulge thy sneer.

TO JOHN SYME OF RYEDALE

WITH A PRESENT OF A DOZEN OF PORTER

John Syme, son of a Writer to the Signet in
Edinburgh, was born in 1755. He entered the
army in his nineteenth year, but after his
father's death resided on the little estate of
Barncailzie, Kirkcudbrightshire. Constrained
to sell by the failure of the Ayr Bank, he ob-
tained the office of Distributor of Stamps in
Dumfries in 1791. Burns inhabited the floor
immediately above his office, and presently got
to regard him as his "supreme court of criti-
cal judicature" in literary matters. Syme's
rather glowing description of a passage be-
tween him and Burns (when, being rebuked
for his excesses, the Bard half drew on him)
was made the matter of a piece of criticism by
Walter Scott in a review of Cromek's *Reliques*.
In July, 1793, Burns and Syme went touring in

Galloway, (see *ante*, pp. 188, 189, Prefatory Note to *Against the Earl of Galloway*, and Prefatory Note to *On the Laird of Laggan*), and after Burns's death Syme was Alexander Cunningham's chief coöperator in the work of starting a subscription for his friend's family and projecting the publication of his posthumous poems and letters. It is much to be regretted that he did not undertake the editorship, as at one time it was thought he might, instead of Currie. He died 24th November, 1831.

O, HAD the malt thy strength of mind,
  Or hops the flavour of thy wit,
'T were drink for first of human kind —
  A gift that ev'n for Syme were fit.

JERUSALEM TAVERN,
  DUMFRIES.

ON A GOBLET

The goblet belonged to Syme.

THERE 's Death in the cup, so beware !
  Nay, more — there is danger in touching !
But who can avoid the fell snare ?
  The man and his wine 's so bewitching !

APOLOGY TO JOHN SYME

Published in Currie with the explanation : "On refusing to dine with him, after having been promised the first of company and the first of cookery, 17th December, 1795."

No more of your guests, be they titled or not,
  And cookery the first in the nation :
Who is proof to thy personal converse and wit
  Is proof to all other temptation.

ON MR. JAMES GRACIE

GRACIE, thou art a man of worth,
  O, be thou Dean for ever !
May he be damn'd to Hell henceforth,
  Who fauts thy weight or measure !

AT FRIARS CARSE HERMITAGE

To RIDDELL, much-lamented man,
  This ivied cot was dear :
Wand'rer, dost value matchless worth ?
  This ivied cot revere.

FOR AN ALTAR OF INDEPENDENCE

AT KERROUGHTRIE, THE SEAT OF MR. HERON

For Heron, see *ante*, p. 164, Prefatory Note to *First Heron Election Ballad*.

THOU of an independent mind,
With soul resolv'd, with soul resign'd,
Prepar'd Power's proudest frown to brave,
Who wilt not be, nor have a slave,
Virtue alone who dost revere,
Thy own reproach alone dost fear :
Approach this shrine, and worship here.

VERSICLES TO JESSIE LEWARS

THE TOAST

Inscribed on a crystal goblet presented to Miss Lewars.

FILL me with the rosy wine ;
Call a toast, a toast divine ;
Give the Poet's darling flame ;
Lovely Jessie be her name :
Then thou mayest freely boast
Thou hast given a peerless toast.

THE MENAGERIE

Written on the advertisement of a travelling show, which in May, 1796, was handed to Burns by Mr. Brown, Surgeon, in Jessie's presence.

I

TALK not to me of savages
  From Afric's burning sun !
No savage e'er can rend my heart
  As, Jessie, thou hast done.

II

But Jessie's lovely hand in mine
  A mutual faith to plight —
Not even to view the heavenly choir
  Would be so blest a sight.

JESSIE'S ILLNESS

SAY, sages, what's the charm on earth
  Can turn Death's dart aside?
It is not purity and worth,
  Else Jessie had not died!

HER RECOVERY

BUT rarely seen since Nature's birth
  The natives of the sky!
Yet still one seraph's left on earth,
  For Jessie did not die.

ON MARRIAGE

THAT hackney'd judge of human life,
  The Preacher and the King,
Observes: — "The man that gets a wife
  He gets a noble thing."
But how capricious are mankind,
  Now loathing, now desirous!
We married men, how oft we find
  The best of things will tire us!

GRACES

A POET'S GRACE

BEFORE MEAT

O THOU, who kindly dost provide
  For ev'ry creature's want!
We bless the God of Nature wide
  For all Thy goodness lent.
And if it please Thee, heavenly Guide,
  May never worse be sent;
But, whether granted or denied,
  Lord, bless us with content.

AFTER MEAT

O THOU, in whom we live and move,
  Who made the sea and shore,
Thy goodness constantly we prove,
  And, grateful, would adore;
And, if it please Thee, Power above!
  Still grant us with such store
The friend we trust, the fair we love,
  And we desire no more.

AT THE GLOBE TAVERN

BEFORE MEAT

O LORD, when hunger pinches sore,
  Do Thou stand us in stead,
And send us from Thy bounteous store
  A tup- or wether-head.

AFTER MEAT

I

LORD, [Thee] we thank, and Thee alone,
  For temporal gifts we little merit!
At present we will ask no more:
  Let William Hislop bring the spirit.

2

O LORD, since we have feasted thus,
  Which we so little merit,
Let Meg now take the flesh away,
  And Jock bring in the spirit.

3

O LORD, we do Thee humbly thank
  For that we little merit:
Now Jean may tak the flesh away,
  And Will bring in the spirit.

EPITAPHS

ON JAMES GRIEVE, LAIRD OF BOGHEAD, TARBOLTON

The epitaph is a sort of reversal of that on Gavin Hamilton, *ante*, p. 55.

HERE lies Boghead amang the dead
  In hopes to get salvation;
But if such as he in Heav'n may be,
  Then welcome — hail! damnation.

ON WM. MUIR IN TARBOLTON MILL

William Muir, described in the *First Common Place Book* as "my own friend and my father's friend," was born in 1745. His mill at Tarbolton is mentioned in *Death and Dr. Hornbook* (*ante*, p. 57, stanza v. line 2). Jean Armour, being expelled her father's home, found shelter for a time with the miller's wife (1787–8). Muir died in 1793; and Burns, recalling this piece of kindness, wrote to Gavin Hamilton that, hearing that Mrs. Muir was likely to be "involved in great difficulties" in regard to the settlements, he was ready to "move heaven and earth on her behalf," and would undertake, through his friends in Edinburgh, to get her the best legal assistance free of charge.

AN honest man here lies at rest,
As e'er God with His image blest:
The friend of man, the friend of truth,
The friend of age, and guide of youth:
Few hearts like his — with virtue warm'd,
Few heads with knowledge so inform'd:
If there's another world, he lives in bliss;
If there is none, he made the best of this.

ON JOHN RANKINE

For Rankine, see Prefatory Note to *Epistle to John Rankine*, *ante*, p. 50.

AE day, as Death, that gruesome carl,
Was driving to the tither warl'
A mixtie-maxtie, motley squad
And monie a guilt-bespotted lad:
Black gowns of each denomination,
And thieves of every rank and station,
From him that wears the star and garter
To him that wintles in a halter:
Asham'd himself to see the wretches,
He mutters, glow'ring at the bitches: —
"By God I'll not be seen behint them,
Nor 'mang the sp'ritual core present them,
Without at least ae honest man
To grace this damn'd infernal clan!"
By Adamhill a glance he threw,
"Lord God!" quoth he, "I have it now,
There's just the man I want, i' faith!"
And quickly stoppit Rankine's breath.

ON TAM THE CHAPMAN

As Tam the chapman on a day
Wi' Death forgather'd by the way,
Weel pleas'd he greets a wight so fa-
    mous,
And Death was nae less pleas'd wi' Thomas,
Wha cheerfully lays down his pack,
And there blaws up a hearty crack:
His social, friendly, honest heart
Sae tickled Death, they could na part;
Sae, after viewing knives and garters,
Death takes him hame to gie him quar-
    ters.

ON HOLY WILLIE

For William Fisher, see *ante*, p. 109, Prefatory Note to *Holy Willie's Prayer*.

I

HERE Holy Willie's sair worn clay
    Taks up its last abode;
His saul has taen some other way —
    I fear, the left-hand road.

II

Stop! there he is as sure's a gun!
    Poor, silly body, see him!
Nae wonder he's as black's the grun —
    Observe wha's standing wi' him!

III

Your brunstane Devilship, I see,
    Has got him there before ye!
But haud your nine-tail-cat a wee,
    Till ance you've heard my story.

IV

Your pity I will not implore,
    For pity ye have nane.
Justice, alas! has gi'en him o'er,
    And mercy's day is gane.

V

But hear me, Sir, Deil as ye are,
    Look something to your credit:
A cuif like him wad stain your name,
    If it were kent ye did it!

ON JOHN DOVE, INNKEEPER

Dove was landlord of the Whitefoord Arms, Mauchline.

I

HERE lies Johnie Pigeon:
What was his religion
    Whae'er desires to ken
To some other warl'
Maun follow the carl,
    For here Johnie Pigeon had nane !

II

Strong ale was ablution;
Small beer, persecution;
    A dram was *memento mori ;*
But a full flowing bowl
Was the saving his soul,
    And port was celestial glory !

ON A WAG IN MAUCHLINE

The wag was James Smith. See *ante*, p. 15, Prefatory Note to *Epistle to James Smith.*

I

LAMENT him, Mauchline husbands a',
    He aften did assist ye;
For had ye staid hale weeks awa',
    Your wives they ne'er had missed ye !

II

Ye Mauchline bairns, as on ye pass
    To school in bands thegither,
O, tread ye lightly on his grass —
    Perhaps he was your father !

ON ROBERT FERGUSSON

ON THE TOMBSTONE IN THE CANONGATE CHURCHYARD

On the 6th February, 1787, Burns applied to the Kirk Managers of the Canongate parish, Edinburgh, for permission to "lay a small stone" over the "revered ashes" of Fergusson, to "remain an inalienable property to his deathless fame ; " and his request was unanimously granted on the 22d of the same month. But the mason whom Robert Burn, the architect, employed was so dilatory that the com-mission was not executed until August, 1789. To be quits with his architect, Burns did not pay the account (£5 10s.) until February, 1792. On the 11th August, 1789, the following notice appeared in *The Edinburgh Advertiser*, and on the 13th in *The Evening Courant:* " The Ayrshire Bard, Mr. Burns, has at his own expense erected a monument or headstone in the Canongate Church, over the grave of the late Mr. Fergusson, with the following inscription," etc. On the reverse of the stone is the declaration : " By special grant of the Managers to Robert Burns, who erected this stone, this Burial Place is to remain for ever sacred to the memory of Robert Fergusson."

HERE LIES ROBERT FERGUSSON
BORN SEPT 5TH, 1751
DIED OCT 16TH, 1774

No sculptur'd Marble here, nor pompous lay,
No storied Urn nor animated Bust;
This simple stone directs pale Scotia's way
    To pour her sorrow o'er the Poet's dust.

ADDITIONAL STANZAS

NOT INSCRIBED

I

SHE mourns, sweet tuneful youth, thy hapless fate:
Tho' all the powers of song thy fancy fir'd,
Yet Luxury and Wealth lay by in State,
    And, thankless, starv'd what they so much admir'd.

II

This humble tribute with a tear he gives,
    A brother Bard — he can no more bestow:
But dear to fame thy Song immortal lives,
    A nobler monument than Art can show.

FOR WILLIAM NICOL

William Nicol was born in 1744 at Dumbretton, in the parish of Annan. In early childhood he lost his father; while still a mere youth opened a school in his mother's house; studied, at the University of Edinburgh, first theology and then medicine ; took up teaching again; and in 1774 was appointed a classical master in the High School of Edinburgh. Burns met him in that city as a Crochallan Club man, and in the autumn took him on his Highland tour. His visit to Nicol at Moffat in 1789 is celebrated in O, *Willie Brewed a Peck o' Maut* (*post*, p. 229). After Nicol bought the little property of Laggan, in Glencairn parish (1790), he and Burns met often in the holidays, Burns counting him his " dearest friend " after his own brother. In 1795 Nicol, having assaulted the Rector of the High School, resigned his mastership, and started on his own account; but late hours and liquor had already undermined his health, and he died 21st April, 1797.

> YE maggots, feed on Nicol's brain,
>   For few sic feasts you 've gotten;
> And fix your claws in Nicol's heart,
>   For deil a bit o't 's rotten.

FOR MR. WlLLIAM MICHIE

SCHOOLMASTER OF CLEISH PARISH, FIFE-SHIRE

> HERE lie Willie Michie's banes:
>   O Satan, when ye tak him,
> Gie him the schulin o' your weans,
>   For clever deils he 'll mak them !

FOR WILLIAM CRUICKSHANK, A. M.

William Cruickshank was appointed master of the Canongate High School, Edinburgh, in 1770; was promoted to a classical mastership in the Edinburgh High School in 1772; and died 8th March, 1795. His only daughter, Jenny Cruickshank, was a prime favourite with the Poet. See Prefatory Note to *To Miss Cruickshank*, *ante*, p. 95.

> Now honest William 's gaen to Heaven,
>   I wat na gin 't can mend him:
> The fauts he had in Latin lay,
>   For nane in English kent them.

ON ROBERT MUIR

Robert Muir, son of William Muir, who had the little estate of Loanfoot, near Kilmarnock, was born 8th August, 1758, and became a wine merchant at Kilmarnock. He subscribed with great liberality to both the Kilmarnock and the Edinburgh Editions, and letters to him are included in Burns's *Correspondence*. He died of consumption 22d April, 1788.

"Muir, thy weaknesses were the aberrations of human nature, but thy heart glowed with everything generous, manly, and noble ; and, if ever emanations from the all-good Being animated a human form, it was thine." (R. B.)

> WHAT man could esteem, or what woman
>   could love,
>   Was he who lies under this sod:
> If such Thou refusest admission above,
>   Then whom wilt Thou favour, Good God ?

ON A LAP-DOG

The lap-dog belonged to Mrs. Gordon of Kenmore. The little beast had died just before Burns visited her during his Galloway tour, and she was importunate that he should write its epitaph.

I

> IN wood and wild, ye warbling throng,
>   Your heavy loss deplore:
> Now half extinct your powers of song —
>   Sweet Echo is no more.

II

> Ye jarring, screeching things around,
>   Scream your discordant joys:
> Now half your din of tuneless sound
>   With Echo silent lies.

. MONODY

ON A LADY FAMED FOR HER CAPRICE

The lady was Maria Riddell (see *ante*, p. 178, Prefatory Note to *Impromptu on Mrs. Riddell's Birthday*). "The subject of the foregoing," Burns wrote to Clarinda, "is a woman of fashion in this country, with whom at one period I was well acquainted. By some scandalous conduct to me, and two or three other gentlemen here as well as me, she steered so far to the north of my good opinion, that I have made her the theme of several ill-natured things." For a fairer statement of the case, see as above, the Prefatory Note to *Impromptu*.

I

How cold is that bosom which Folly once
  fired !
  How pale is that cheek where the rouge
  lately glisten'd !
How silent that tongue which the echoes oft
  tired !
  How dull is that ear which to flatt'ry so
  listen'd !

II

If sorrow and anguish their exit await,
  From friendship and dearest affection
  remov'd,
How doubly severer, Maria, thy fate !
  Thou diedst unwept, as thou livedst un-
  lov'd.

III

Loves, Graces, and Virtues, I call not on
  you:
  So shy, grave, and distant, ye shed not a
  tear.
But come, all ye offspring of Folly so true,
  And flowers let us cull for Maria's cold
  bier !

IV

We 'll search through the garden for each
  silly flower,
  We 'll roam thro' the forest for each
  idle weed,
But chiefly the nettle, so typical, shower,
  For none e'er approach'd her but rued
  the rash deed.

V

We 'll sculpture the marble, we 'll measure
  the lay:
  Here Vanity strums on her idiot lyre !
There keen Indignation shall dart on his
  prey,
  Which spurning Contempt shall redeem
  from his ire !

THE EPITAPH

Here lies, now a prey to insulting neglect,
  What once was a butterfly, gay in life's
  beam:
Want only of wisdom denied her respect,
  Want only of goodness denied her es-
  teem.

FOR MR. WALTER RIDDELL

See *ante*, p. 178, Prefatory Note to *Impromptu
on Mrs. Riddell's Birthday.*

So vile was poor Wat, such a miscreant
  slave,
That the worms ev'n damn'd him when laid
  in his grave.
" In his scull there 's a famine," a starved
  reptile cries;
" And his heart, it is poison," another re-
  plies.

ON A NOTED COXCOMB

CAPT. WM. RODDICK, OF CORBISTON

LIGHT lay the earth on Billie's breast,
  His chicken heart 's so tender;
But build a castle on his head —
  His scull will prop it under.

ON CAPT. LASCELLES

WHEN Lascelles thought fit from this
  world to depart,
Some friends warmly spoke of embalming
  his heart.
A bystander whispers: — " Pray don't make
  so much o't —
The subject is poison, no reptile will touch
  it."

ON A GALLOWAY LAIRD

NOT QUITE SO WISE AS SOLOMON

David Maxwell of Cardoness — described to
Mrs. Dunlop as a " stupid, money-loving dun-
derpate," and alluded to with great contempt
in an *Epigram* (see p. 187), and in the *Heron
Election Ballads* (*q. v.*), was created a baronet
in 1804, and died in 1825.

BLESS Jesus Christ, O Cardoness,
  With grateful lifted eyes,
Who taught that not the soul alone
  But body too shall rise !

For had He said: — "The soul alone
From death I will deliver,"
Alas ! alas ! O Cardoness,
Then hadst thou lain for ever !

ON WM. GRAHAM OF MOSS-KNOWE

"Stop thief ! " Dame Nature call'd to
    Death,
As Willie drew his latest breath:
"How shall I make a fool again ?
My choicest model thou hast taen."

ON JOHN BUSHBY OF TINWALD DOWNS

Bushby, the son of a spirit-dealer in Dumfries, became a lawyer and afterwards a private banker in the same town. Business capacity and a good marriage enabled him to purchase Tinwald Downs. He is severely satirised in two of the *Heron Election Ballads*, more particularly *John Bushby's Lamentation* (*ante*, p. 166).

Here lies John Bushby — honest man !
Cheat him, Devil — if you can !

ON A SUICIDE

Cunningham says that Burns was seen to write the trash on a piece of paper, and " thrust it with his fingers into the red mould of the grave."

Here lies in earth a root of Hell
    Set by the Deil's ain dibble:
This worthless body damn'd himsel
    To save the Lord the trouble.

ON A SWEARING COXCOMB

Here cursing, swearing Burton lies,
A buck, a beau, or " Dem my eyes ! "
Who in his life did little good,
And his last words were: — " Dem my
    blood ! "

ON AN INNKEEPER NICKNAMED "THE MARQUIS"

The inn was in a Dumfries close.

Here lies a mock Marquis, whose titles
    were shamm'd.
If ever he rise, it will be to be damn'd.

ON GRIZZEL GRIMME

Mrs. Grizzel Young was the widow of Thomas Young of Lincluden. The ancient nunnery of Lincluden was converted into a college by Archibald the Grim, Earl of Douglas.

Here lyes with Dethe auld Grizzel Grimme
    Lincluden's ugly witche.
O Dethe, an' what a taste hast thou
    Cann lye with siche a bitche !

FOR GABRIEL RICHARDSON

Inscribed on a crystal goblet. Gabriel Richardson was the chief brewer of Dumfries, and Provost of the burgh in 1802–3. He was the father of Sir John Richardson, naturalist and traveller.

Here brewer Gabriel's fire 's extinct,
    And empty all his barrels:
He 's blest — if as he brew'd, he drink —
    In upright, virtuous morals.

ON THE AUTHOR

" Wrote by Burns, while on his deathbed, to John Rankine, Ayrshire, and forwarded to him immediately after the Poet's death." Stewart.

He who of Rankine sang, lies stiff and
    deid,
And a green, grassy hillock hides his
    heid:
Alas ! alas ! a devilish change indeed !

SONGS FROM JOHNSON'S "MUSICAL MUSEUM" AND THOMSON'S "SCOTTISH AIRS"

THE present section consists of songs sent by Burns to Johnson's *Musical Museum* and Thomson's *Scottish Airs*, and duly set forth in these collections. Some he sent which were not used, and some were used which he did not send. These appear in the last section.

Burns's earliest reference to the *Museum* is contained in a letter, written as he was leaving Edinburgh, of the 4th May, 1787. He tells Johnson that he sends a song ("never before known ") for his publication, and that had the acquaintance been a little older, he would have asked the favour of a "correspondence." Only two of his songs appeared in Johnson's First Volume, the Preface to which is dated 22d May, 1787; and it is possible to observe in detail neither the growth of his acquaintance with Johnson himself nor that of his interest in Johnson's venture. He seems, however, to have made special arrangements with Johnson during his visit to Edinburgh in the autumn: at any rate, there are indications that he has resolved — entirely as a labour of love — to do his best for both the man and the book. On the 20th October he informs Mr. Hoy, chamberlain to the Duke of Gordon, that, to "the utmost of his small power," he assists "in collecting the old poetry, or sometimes for a fine air " makes "a stanza when it has no words ;" on the 25th he confides to Skinner, the parson poet, that he has "been absolutely crazed about " the project, and is "collecting old stanzas, and every information respecting their origin, authors," etc. ; and in November he is found asking his friend James Candlish to send him "*Pompey's Ghost*, words and music," and confessing that he has already "collected, begged, borrowed, and stolen all the songs" he could. All this is in the beginning; and of itself it were enough to show that, even had he done no more, still Johnson's debt to him had been considerable.

But there is evidence in plenty that he was very soon a great deal more than a mere contributor, however unwearied and unselfish. Johnson — an engraver, who could neither write grammatically nor even spell — was quite incompetent himself to edit the *Museum;* and at first he was helped by the elder Tytler. But that Burns was virtually editor of the work from the autumn of 1787 until his health began to fail, is proved (1) by what is left of his correspondence with Johnson; (2) by his annotations on the Hastie MSS. (British Mu-

seum) ; and (3) by certain draft-plans of volumes, lists of songs, and other MS. scraps now in the library of Mr. George Gray, Glasgow, which we have been privileged to consult for this Edition.[1] Thus, in November, 1788, he tells Johnson that he has prepared a "flaming preface" for vol. iii. The tone of it is not exactly that of the Preface to vol. ii. ; but Burns was a creature of moods, and he may very well have written both. If he did, he ends the earlier thus : "Ignorance and Prejudice may perhaps affect to sneer at the simplicity of the poetry or music of some of those pieces, but their having been for ages the favourites of Nature's judges, the Common People, was to the Editor a sufficient test of their merit." The next is less humble and more cynical as regards the *Vox Populi*. "As this is not," it runs, "one of those many Publications which are hourly ushered into the World merely to catch the eye of Fashion in her frenzy of a day, the Editor has little to hope or fear from the herd of readers. Consciousness of the well-known merit of our Scottish Music, and the natural fondness of a Scotchman for the productions of his own country, are at once the Editor's motive and apology for the Undertaking ; and where any of the Pieces in the Collection may perhaps be found wanting at the Critical Bar of the First, he appeals to the honest prejudices of the Last." Burns's hand is also plain in the Preface to vol. iv., which ends with this pronouncement : "To those who object that this Publication contains pieces of inferior or little value the Editor answers by referring to his plan. All our songs cannot have equal merit. Besides, as the world have (*sic*) not yet agreed on any unerring balance, any undisputed standard, in matters of Taste, what to one person yields no manner of pleasure, may to another be a high enjoyment." He died before the appearance of vol. v. (there were six in all), but the Preface thereto contains an extract from a letter of his: "You may probably think that for some time past I have neglected you and your work ; but alas, the hand of pain and sorrow and care has these many months lain heavy on me ! Personal and domestic affliction have almost entirely banished that alacrity and life with which I used to woo the rural Muse of Scotia. In the meantime let us finish what we have so well begun."

In the September of 1792 he was invited by

[1] That is, the Centenary Edition.

George Thomson to contribute to his *Scottish Airs*, a more ambitious and — musically speaking — a more elaborate adventure than the *Museum*. He replied that, inasmuch as it would positively add to his enjoyment to comply with the request, he would " enter into the undertaking with all the small portion of the abilities" he had, "strained to the utmost exertion by the impulse of enthusiasm." " As to remuneration," he added, " you may think my songs either above or below price ; for they shall absolutely be the one or the other. In the honest enthusiasm with which I embark in your undertaking, to talk of money, wages, fee, hire, etc.. would be downright sodomy of soul. A proof of each of the songs that I compose or amend I shall receive as a favour. In the rustic phrase of the season : ' God speed the work.' " Thomson returns his " warmest acknowledgment for the enthusiasm with which " Burns has " entered into our undertaking ; " but as he says nothing of Burns's admirable generosity, it is reasonable to infer that the idea of payment would have been unwelcome to his mind.

Even so, it is fair to add that the best of time had passed for Burns ere his connexion with Thomson began. Misfortunes, hardships, follies, excesses in fact and sentiment, success itself, so barren of lasting profit to him — all these had done some part of their work ; and already his way of life was falling into the sere and yellow leaf. Though few, the years had been full exceedingly ; and his inspiration was its old rapturous, irresistible self no longer. Moreover, he had to content Thomson as well as to satisfy himself ; and Thomson, a kind of poetaster, whose taste in verse was merely academic, persuaded him to write more English than was good for him ; being in this matter wholly of his time, he could find nothing to "fire his vocal rage " but the amatory " effusions " of one of the least lyrical schools in letters ; and the consequences were disastrous to his art. The Thomson songs, indeed, some distinguished and delightful exceptions to the contrary, are not in his happier vein. They have not the fresh sweetness and the unflagging spirit of his *Museum* numbers. They are less distinctively Scots than these, for one thing; and for another, they are often vapid in sentiment and artificial in effect. Now, his work for the *Museum* consisted largely in the adaptation of old rhymes and folk-songs to modern uses. Some he arranged, some he condensed, some he enlarged. some he reconstructed and rewrote. Stray snatches, phrases, lines, thin

echoes from a vanished past — nothing came amiss to him, nor was there anything he could not turn to good account. His appreciation was instant and inevitable, his touch unerring. Under his hand a patchwork of catch-words became a living song. He would take you two fragments of different epochs, select the best from each, and treat the matter of his choice in such a style that it is hard to know where its components end and begin : so that nothing is certain about his result except that here is a piece of art. Or he would capture a wandering old refrain, adjust it to his own conditions, and so renew its lyrical interest and significance that it seems to live its true life for the first time on his lips. Here, in fact, is his chief claim to perennial acceptance. He passed the folk-song of his nation through the mint of his mind, and he reproduced it stamped with his image and lettered with his superscription : so that for the world at large it exists, and will go on existing, not as he found but as he left it. Burns's knowledge of the older minstrelsy was unique ; he was saturate with its tradition, as he was absolute master of its emotions and effects ; no such artist in folk-song as he (so in other words Sir Walter said) has ever worked in literature. But a hundred forgotten singers went to the making of his achievement and himself. He did not wholly originate those master-qualities — of fresh and taking simplicity, of vigour and directness and happy and humorous ease, which have come to be regarded as distinctive of his verse ; for all these things, together with much of the thought, the romance, and the sentiment for which we read and love him, were included in the estate which he inherited from his nameless forebears : and he so assimilated them that what is actually those forebears' legacy to him has come to be regarded as his gift to them. Those forebears aiding, he stands forth as the sole great poet of the old Scots world ; and he thus is national as no poet has ever been, and as no poet ever will or ever can be again. Thus, too, it is that, being the " satirist and singer of a parish " — a fact which only the Common Burnsite could be crazy enough, or pigheaded enough, to deny — he is at the same time the least parochial — the most broadly and genuinely human — among the lyrists of his race.

[Many of the songs contributed to Johnson were afterward sent to Thomson, but in the collection which follows, Johnson's *Museum* is practically the authority for all up to *Wandering Willie*. That and the rest are from Thomson's *Scottish Airs*.]

YOUNG PEGGY

Margaret, daughter of Robert Kennedy, of Daljarroch, Ayrshire, and niece of Mr. Gavin Hamilton, was born 3d November, 1766; fell in love with (and finally succumbed to) Captain, afterwards Colonel, Andrew M'Doual ("Sculdudd'ry M'Doual" of the second *Heron Ballad*: see *ante*, p. 163) in 1784; bore him a daughter in January, 1794; raised an action for (1) declarator of marriage, or (2) damages for seduction; and died in February, 1795, before the case was decided. Meanwhile, M'Doual, who denied paternity as well as marriage, had wedded another lady; but in 1798 the Consistorial Court declared against him on both issues; and the Court of Session, having set aside its judgment as regards the marriage, ordered him to provide for his child in the sum of £3000.

Burns often met Miss Kennedy at Gavin Hamilton's. His song was enclosed to her in an undated letter: "I have in these verses attempted some faint sketches of your portrait in the unembellished simple manner of descriptive truth." This, and not *The Banks o' Doon*, (*post*, p. 243), which it is usual, but erroneous, to suppose was suggested by the lady's amour, must have been the song "on Miss Peggy Kennedy," which, with *The Lass o' Ballochmyle*, the "jury of literati" in Edinburgh "found defamatory libels against the fastidious powers of Poesy and Taste." Forbidden to print it (no doubt for the same reason as he was forbidden to print *The Lass o' Ballochmyle*, and not because it is not better than nine tenths of the Ramsay songs, of which it is an imitation) in the Edinburgh Edition, the writer sent it to Johnson, where it appears as alternative words to the tune, *Loch Errochside*.

I

YOUNG Peggy blooms our boniest lass:
　Her blush is like the morning,
The rosy dawn the springing grass
　With early gems adorning;
Her eyes outshine the radiant beams
　That gild the passing shower,
And glitter o'er the crystal streams,
　And cheer each fresh'ning flower.

II

Her lips, more than the cherries bright —
　A richer dye has graced them —
They charm the admiring gazer's sight,
　And sweetly tempt to taste them.
Her smile is as the evening mild,

When feather'd pairs are courting,
And little lambkins wanton wild,
　In playful bands disporting.

III

Were Fortune lovely Peggy's foe,
　Such sweetness would relent her:
As blooming Spring unbends the brow
　Of surly, savage Winter.
Detraction's eye no aim can gain
　Her winning powers to lessen,
And fretful Envy grins in vain
　The poison'd tooth to fasten.

IV

Ye Pow'rs of Honour, Love, and Truth,
　From ev'ry ill defend her !
Inspire the highly-favour'd youth
　The destinies intend her !
Still fan the sweet connubial flame
　Responsive in each bosom,
And bless the dear paternal name
　With many a filial blossom !

BONIE DUNDEE

A fragment of folk-ballad, with modifications and additions. Cromek states that Burns sent the draft of his version to Cleghorn with the following note : "DEAR CLEGHORN, — You will see by the above that I have added a stanza to *Bonny Dundee*. If you think it will do you may set it agoing upon a ten-stringed instrument and on the psaltery. — R. B."

I

"O, WHAR gat ye that hauver-meal bannock ?"
"O silly blind body, O, dinna ye see ?
I gat it frae a young, brisk sodger laddie
　Between Saint Johnston and bonie Dundee.
O, gin I saw the laddie that gae me 't !
　Aft has he doudl'd me up on his knee:
May Heaven protect my bonie Scots laddie,
　And send him hame to his babie and me !

II

"My blessin's upon thy sweet, wee lippie !
　My blessin's upon thy bonie e'e brie !
Thy smiles are sae like my blythe sodger laddie,
　Thou's ay the dearer and dearer to me !

But I 'll big a bow'r on yon bonie banks,
   Whare Tay rins wimplin by sae clear;
And I 'll cleed thee in the tartan sae fine,
   And mak thee a man like thy daddie
      dear."

TO THE WEAVER'S GIN YE GO

" The chorus of this song is old, the rest is
mine. Here once for all let me apologise for
many silly compositions of mine in this work.
Many beautiful airs wanted words, and in the
hurry of other avocations, if I could string a
parcel of rhymes together, anything nearly
tolerable, I was fain to let them pass. He
must be an excellent poet indeed whose every
performance is excellent."   (R. B.)

CHORUS

To the weaver's gin ye go, fair maids,
   To the weaver's gin ye go,
I rede you right, gang ne'er at night,
   To the weaver's gin ye go.

I

My heart was ance as blythe and free
   As simmer days were lang;
But a bonie, westlin weaver lad
   Has gart me change my sang.

II

My mither sent me to the town,
   To warp a plaiden wab;
But the weary, weary warpin o't
   Has gart me sigh and sab.

III

A bonie, westlin weaver lad
   Sat working at his loom;
He took my heart, as wi' a net,
   In every knot and thrum.

IV

I sat beside my warpin-wheel,
   And ay I ca'd it roun';
And every shot and every knock,
   My heart it gae a stoun.

V

The moon was sinking in the west
   Wi' visage pale and wan,
As my bonie, westlin weaver lad
   Convoy'd me thro' the glen.

VI

But what was said, or what was done
   Shame fa' me gin I tell;
But O ! I fear the kintra soon
   Will ken as weel 's mysel !

CHORUS

To the weaver's gin ye go, fair maids,
   To the weaver's gin ye go,
I rede you right, gang ne'er at night,
   To the weaver's gin ye go.

O, WHISTLE AN' I 'LL COME TO YE, MY LAD

The song has hitherto [1] been held pure Burns.
But he found his chorus in the Herd MS. : —

" Whistle and I 'll cum to ye, my lad !
   Whistle and I 'll cum to ye, my lad !
Gin father and mither and a' should gae mad,
   Whistle and I 'll cum to ye, my lad ! ' "

CHORUS

O, whistle an' I 'll come to ye, my lad !
O, whistle an' I 'll come to ye, my lad !
Tho' father an' mother an' a' should gae
      mad,
O, whistle an' I 'll come to ye, my lad !

I

But warily tent when ye come to court me,
And come nae unless the back-yett be a-jee;
Syne up the back-style, and let naebody see,
And come as ye were na comin to me,
And come as ye were na comin to me !

II

At kirk, or at market, whene'er ye meet me,
Gang by me as tho' that ye car'd na a flie;
But steal me a blink o' your bonie black e'e,
Yet look as ye were na lookin to me,
Yet look as ye were na lookin to me !

III

Ay vow and protest that ye care na for me,
And whyles ye may lightly my beauty a wee;
But court na anither tho' jokin ye be,
For fear that she wyle your fancy frae me,
For fear that she wyle your fancy frae me !

CHORUS

O, whistle an' I 'll come to ye, my lad !
O, whistle an' I 'll come to ye, my lad !

[1] That is, by previous editors.

Tho' father an' mother an' a' should gae
  mad,
O, whistle an' I 'll come to ye, my lad !

I'M O'ER YOUNG TO MARRY YET

"The chorus of this song is old ; the rest of it, such as it is, is mine." (R. B.)

CHORUS

I 'm o'er young, I 'm o'er young,
  I 'm o'er young to marry yet !
I 'm o'er young, 't wad be a sin
  To tak me frae my mammie yet.

I

I AM my mammie's ae bairn,
  Wi' unco folk I weary, Sir,
And lying in a man's bed,
  I 'm fley'd it make me eerie, Sir.

II

Hallowmass is come and gane,
  The nights are lang in winter, Sir,
And you an' I in ae bed —
  In trowth, I dare na venture, Sir !

III

Fu' loud and shrill the frosty wind
  Blaws thro' the leafless timmer, Sir,
But if ye come this gate again,
  I 'll aulder be gin simmer, Sir.

CHORUS

I 'm o'er young, I 'm o'er young,
  I 'm o'er young to marry yet !
I 'm o'er young, 't wad be a sin
  To tak me frae my mammie yet.

THE BIRKS OF ABERFELDIE

"I composed these stanzas standing under the Falls of Moness at or near Aberfeldy." (R. B.)

CHORUS

Bonie lassie, will ye go,
Will ye go, will ye go ?
Bonie lassie, will ye go
  To the birks of Aberfeldie ?

I

Now simmer blinks on flow'ry braes,
And o'er the crystal streamlets plays,
Come, let us spend the lightsome days
  In the birks of Aberfeldie !

II

The little birdies blythely sing,
While o'er their heads the hazels hing,
Or lightly flit on wanton wing
  In the birks of Aberfeldie.

III

The braes ascend like lofty wa's,
The foaming stream, deep-roaring, fa's
O'er hung with fragrant-spreading shaws,
  The birks of Aberfeldie.

IV

The hoary cliffs are crown'd wi' flowers,
White o'er the linns the burnie pours,
And, rising, weets wi' misty showers
  The birks of Aberfeldie.

V

Let Fortune's gifts at random flee,
They ne'er shall draw a wish frae me,
Supremely blest wi' love and thee
  In the birks of Aberfeldie.

CHORUS

Bonie lassie, will ye go,
Will ye go, will ye go ?
Bonie lassie, will ye go
  To the birks of Aberfeldie ?

M'PHERSON'S FAREWELL

"M'Pherson, a daring robber in the beginning of this century, was condemned to be hanged at the assizes of Inverness. He is said, when under sentence of death, to have composed this tune, which he calls his own Lament or Farewell." (R. B.)

The reputed son of a gipsy, James M'Pherson, a cateran of notable strength and prowess, was apprehended for robbery by the Laird of Braco, at Keith Market ; and, being haled before the Sheriff of Banff on 1st November, 1700, was hanged at the Cross of Banff on the 10th. The tradition that he played the *Lament* on his violin on the way to the tree, or at the foot of it, is absurd. It has, further, been pointed out that his legend may derive from an Irish story: of a tune called *M'Pherson*, with which its composer is said to have played himself to the gallows on the pipes.

There is a set in Herd (1769), but it is plainly a corruption of the old broadside — *The Last Words of James Mackpherson, Murderer* — (which seems in part an imitation of *Captain Johnston's Farewell*: he was hanged at Tyburn in 1690: in the Pepys Collection, v. 523), and opens thus: —

> "I spent my time in rioting,
>   Debauched my health and strength;
> I pillaged, plundered, murdered,
>   But now, alas! at length
> I'm brought to punishment condign;
>   Pale death draws near to me:
> The end I ever did project,
>   To hang upon a tree."

The most notable lines, however, are the four last: —

> "Then wantonly and rantingly
>   I am resolved to die;
> And with undaunted courage I
>   Shall mount this fatal tree:" —

which are the germ of Burns's refrain. But Burns, while preserving throughout the spirit of his original has expressed it in the noblest terms.

CHORUS

Sae rantingly, sae wantonly,
    Sae dauntingly gaed he,
He play'd a spring, and danc'd it round
    Below the gallows-tree.

I

FAREWELL, ye dungeons dark and strong,
    The wretch's destinie!
M'Pherson's time will not be long
    On yonder gallows-tree.

II

O, what is death but parting breath?
    On many a bloody plain
I've dar'd his face, and in this place
    I scorn him yet again!

III

Untie these bands from off my hands,
    And bring to me my sword,
And there's no a man in all Scotland
    But I'll brave him at a word.

IV

I've liv'd a life of sturt and strife;
    I die by treacherie:

It burns my heart I must depart,
    And not avengèd be.

V

Now farewell light, thou sunshine bright,
    And all beneath the sky!
May coward shame distain his name,
    The wretch that dare not die!

CHORUS

Sae rantingly, sae wantonly,
    Sae dauntingly gaed he,
He play'd a spring, and danc'd it round
    Below the gallows-tree.

MY HIGHLAND LASSIE, O

"This was a composition of mine in very early life, before I was known at all in the world. My 'Highland Lassie' was a warmhearted, charming young creature as ever blessed a man with generous love. After a pretty long tract of the most ardent reciprocal attachment we met by appointment on the second Sunday of May, in a sequestered spot by the Banks of Ayr, where we spent the day in taking farewell, before she should embark for the West Highlands to arrange matters for our projected change of life. At the close of the Autumn following she crossed the sea to meet me at Greenock, where she had scarce landed when she was seized with a malignant fever, which hurried my dear girl to the grave in a few days, before I could even hear of her illness." (R. B.)

The "Highland Lassie" was Mary Campbell, daughter of one Archibald Campbell, a Clyde sailor. The year of her birth is uncertain; its place is not beyond dispute; the date of her death is matter of debate; its exact circumstances are not authenticated; there is room for conjecture as to the place of her burial; little or no independent testimony exists as to her person and character — unless she be identified with a certain Mary Campbell of indifferent repute; there is scarce material for the barest outlines of her biography.

A part of *My Highland Lassie, O* is reminiscent of the chorus of Ramsay's *My Nannie O*, which traces back to a blackletter in the Pepys Collection [with the following chorus]: —

> "For Katy, Katy, Katy O,
>   The love I bear to Katy O:
> All the world shall never know
>   The love I bear to Katy O."

Another ballad, *The Scotch Wooing of Willy and Nanie,* has the same chorus, with "Nanie" for "Katy," and with this one Burns was probably as well acquainted as Ramsay himself. The old song, *Highland Lassie,* suggested to Burns scarce more than his title ; but it faintly resembles *The Highland Queen.*

CHORUS

Within the glen sae bushy, O,
Aboon the plain sae rashy, O,
I set me down wi' right guid will
To sing my Highland lassie, O !

I

NAE gentle dames, tho' ne'er sae fair,
Shall ever be my Muse's care:
Their titles a' are empty show —
Gie me my Highland lassie, O !

II

O, were yon hills and vallies mine,
Yon palace and yon gardens fine,
The world then the love should know
I bear my Highland lassie, O !

III

But fickle Fortune frowns on me,
And I maun cross the raging sea ;
But while my crimson currents flow
I 'll love my Highland lassie, O.

IV

Altho' thro' foreign climes I range,
I know her heart will never change ;
For her bosom burns with honour's glow,
My faithful Highland lassie, O.

V

For her I 'll dare the billows' roar,
For her I 'll trace a distant shore,
That Indian wealth may lustre throw
Around my Highland lassie, O.

VI

She has my heart, she has my hand,
My secret troth and honour's band !
Till the mortal stroke shall lay me low,
I 'm thine, my Highland lassie, O !

CHORUS

Farewell the glen sae bushy, O !
Farewell the plain sae rashy, O !
To other lands I now must go
To sing my Highland lassie, O.

THO' CRUEL FATE

THO' cruel fate should bid us part
Far as the pole and line,
Her dear idea round my heart
Should tenderly entwine.
Tho' mountains rise, and deserts howl,
And oceans roar between,
Yet dearer than my deathless soul
I still would love my Jean.

STAY, MY CHARMER

I

STAY, my charmer, can you leave me ?
Cruel, cruel to deceive me !
Well you know how much you grieve me:
Cruel charmer, can you go ?
Cruel charmer, can you go ?

II

By my love so ill-requited,
By the faith you fondly plighted,
By the pangs of lovers slighted,
Do not, do not leave me so !
Do not, do not leave me so !

STRATHALLAN'S LAMENT

" This air is the composition of the worthiest and best-hearted man living, Allan Masterton, schoolmaster in Edinburgh. As he and I were both sprouts of Jacobitism we agreed to dedicate our words and air to the cause. But to tell the matter of fact ; except when my passions were heated by some accidental cause, my Jacobitism was merely by way of ' *vive la bagatelle.*' " (R. B).

The Strathallan of the *Lament* was James Drummond, — eldest son of William, 4th Viscount Strathallan, killed at Culloden, 14th April, 1746, — who was included in the Act of Attainder, 4th June ; and, after staying for some time in hiding, escaped to France, where he died, 27th June, 1765, at Sens in Champagne. The titles were restored in 1824.

I

THICKEST night, surround my dwelling !
Howling tempests, o'er me rave !
Turbid torrents wintry-swelling,
Roaring by my lonely cave !

Crystal streamlets gently flowing,
　Busy haunts of base mankind,
Western breezes softly blowing,
　Suit not my distracted mind.

II

In the cause of Right engagèd,
　Wrongs injurious to redress,
Honour's war we strongly wagèd,
　But the heavens deny'd success.
Ruin's wheel has driven o'er us:
　Not a hope that dare attend,
The wide world is all before us,
　But a world without a friend.

MY HOGGIE

"Dr. Walker, who was minister in Moffat in 1772, and is now (1791) Professor of Natural History in the University of Edinburgh, told the following anecdote concerning this air. He said that some gentlemen riding a few years ago through Liddesdale, stopped at a hamlet consisting of a few houses, called Mosspaul (in Ewesdale); when they were struck with this tune, which an old woman, spinning on a rock at her door, was singing. All she could tell concerning it was, that she was taught it when a child, and it was called 'What will I do gin my Hoggie die?'" No person, except a few females at Mosspaul, knew this fine old tune, which in all probability would have been lost had not one of the gentlemen who happened to have a flute with him taken it down." (R. B.)

I

WHAT will I do gin my hoggie die?
　My joy, my pride, my hoggie!
My only beast, I had nae mae,
　And vow but I was vogie!
The lee-lang night we watched the fauld,
　Me and my faithfu' doggie;
We heard nocht but the roaring linn
　Amang the braes sae scroggie.

II

But the houlet cry'd frae the castle wa',
　The blitter frae the boggie,
The tod reply'd upon the hill:
　I trembled for my hoggie.
When day did daw, and cocks did craw,
　The morning it was foggie,
An unco tyke lap o'er the dyke,
　And maist has kill'd my hoggie!

JUMPIN JOHN

CHORUS

The lang lad they ca' Jumpin John
　Beguil'd the bonie lassie!
The lang lad they ca' Jumpin John
　Beguil'd the bonie lassie!

I

HER daddie forbad, her minnie forbad;
　Forbidden she wadna be:
She wadna trow't, the browst she brew'd
　Wad taste sae bitterlie!

II

A cow and a cauf, a yowe and a hauf,
　And thretty guid shillins and three:
A vera guid tocher! a cotter-man's dochter,
　The lass with the bonie black e'e!

CHORUS

The lang lad they ca' Jumpin John
　Beguil'd the bonnie lassie!
The lang lad they ca' Jumpin John
　Beguil'd the bonie lassie!

UP IN THE MORNING EARLY

"The chorus of this song is old; the two stanzas are mine." (R. B.)

CHORUS

Up in the morning's no for me,
　Up in the morning early!
When a' the hills are covered wi' snaw,
　I'm sure it's winter fairly!

I

CAULD blaws the wind frae east to west,
　The drift is driving sairly,
Sae loud and shrill's I hear the blast —
　I'm sure it's winter fairly!

II

The birds sit chittering in the thorn,
　A' day they fare but sparely;
And lang's the night frae e'en to morn —
　I'm sure it's winter fairly.

CHORUS

Up in the morning's no for me,
　Up in the morning early!

When a' the hills are cover'd wi' snaw,
  I 'm sure it 's winter fairly !

THE YOUNG HIGHLAND ROVER

Intended to commemorate his visit to Castle
Gordon in 1787, and made, seemingly, after
the discovery that *Castle Gordon* (*ante*, p. 121)
did not fit the tune *Morag*. To the same tune
he also wrote, *O, Wat ye wha that Lo'es Me*
(*post*, p. 284). The "rover" was probably the
Young Chevalier.

I

LOUD blaw the frosty breezes,
  The snaws the mountains cover.
Like winter on me seizes,
  Since my young Highland rover
Far wanders nations over.
Where'er he go, where'er he stray,
  May Heaven be his warden !
Return him safe to fair Strathspey
  And bonie Castle Gordon !

II

The trees, now naked groaning,
  Shall soon wi' leaves be hinging,
The birdies, dowie moaning,
  Shall a' be blythely singing,
And every flower be springing:
Sae I 'll rejoice the lee-lang day,
  When (by his mighty Warden)
My youth 's return'd to fair Strathspey
  And bonie Castle Gordon.

THE DUSTY MILLER

Stenhouse says vaguely that the verses "are
a fragment of the old ballad with a few verbal
alterations by Burns;" and Sharpe gives a
version of the "original" without saying where
he got it. It differs comparatively little from
the fragment (Herd MS.) upon which Burns
based his song : —

> "O, the Dusty Miller, O, the Dusty Miller!
> Dusty was his coat, Dusty was his cullour,
> Dusty was the kiss I got frae the Miller!
> O, the Dusty Miller with the dusty coat,
> He will spend a shilling ere he win a groat.
> O, the Dusty Miller."

I

HEY the dusty miller
  And his dusty coat !

He will spend a shilling
  Or he win a groat.
Dusty was the coat,
  Dusty was the colour,
Dusty was the kiss
  That I gat frae the miller !

II

Hey the dusty miller
  And his dusty sack !
Leeze me on the calling
  Fills the dusty peck !
Fills the dusty peck,
  Brings the dusty siller !
I wad gie my coatie
  For the dusty miller !

I DREAM'D I LAY

"These two stanzas I composed when I was
seventeen; they are among the oldest of my
printed pieces." (R. B.)

I

I DREAM'D I lay where flowers were spring-
    ing
  Gaily in the sunny beam,
List'ning to the wild birds singing,
  By a falling crystal stream;
Straight the sky grew black and daring,
  Thro' the woods the whirlwinds rave,
Trees with aged arms were warring
  O'er the swelling, drumlie wave.

II

Such was my life's deceitful morning,
  Such the pleasures I enjoy'd !
But lang or noon loud tempests, storming,
  A' my flowery bliss destroy'd.
Tho' fickle Fortune has deceiv'd me
  (She promis'd fair, and perform'd but
    ill),
Of monie a joy and hope bereav'd me,
  I bear a heart shall support me still.

DUNCAN DAVISON

Stenhouse affirms that this song is by Burns,
although he did not choose to avow it; also
that he (Stenhouse) had "recovered his
(Burns's) original manuscript, which is the

same as that inserted in the *Museum*." No doubt Stenhouse is right; but Burns did but act according to his wont in signing "Z," for not only was his *Duncan Davison* suggested by a song with the same title and something of the same motive preserved in *The Merry Muses* — from which his first, second, and fourth lines are lifted bodily — but it is, as regards his last stanza at least, a thing of shreds and patches; while the last half of this said stanza, containing a very irrelevant moral, is merely "conveyed" from a fragment, here first printed, in the Herd MS. : —

> " I can drink and no be drunk,
>   I can fight and no be slain;
>   I can kiss a bonie lass
>   And ay be welcome back again."

I

THERE was a lass, they ca'd her Meg,
  And she held o'er the moors to spin;
There was a lad that follow'd her,
  They ca'd him Duncan Davison.
The moor was dreigh, and Meg was skeigh,
  Her favour Duncan could na win;
For wi' the rock she wad him knock,
  And ay she shook the temper-pin.

II

As o'er the moor they lightly foor,
  A burn was clear, a glen was green;
Upon the banks they eas'd their shanks,
  And ay she set the wheel between:
But Duncan swoor a haly aith,
  That Meg should be a bride the morn;
Then Meg took up her spinnin-graith,
  And flang them a' out o'er the burn.

III

We will big a wee, wee house,
  And we will live like king and queen,
Sae blythe and merry's we will be,
  When ye set by the wheel at e'en !
A man may drink, and no be drunk;
A man may fight, and no be slain;
A man may kiss a bonie lass,
  And ay be welcome back again !

THENIEL MENZIES' BONIE MARY

CHORUS

Theniel Menzies' bonie Mary,
Theniel Menzies' bonie Mary,

Charlie Grigor tint his plaidie,
Kissin Theniel's bonie Mary !

I

IN comin by the brig o' Dye,
  At Darlet we a blink did tarry;
As day was dawin in the sky,
  We drank a health to bonie Mary.

II

Her een sae bright, her brow sae white,
  Her haffet locks as brown 's a berry,
And ay they dimpl't wi' a smile,
  The rosy cheeks o' bonie Mary.

III

We lap an' danc'd the lee-lang day,
  Till piper-lads were wae and weary;
But Charlie gat the spring to pay,
  For kissin Theniel's bonie Mary.

CHORUS

Theniel Menzies' bonie Mary,
Theniel Menzies' bonie Mary,
Charlie Grigor tint his plaidie,
Kissin Theniel's bonie Mary !

LADY ONLIE, HONEST LUCKY

CHORUS

Lady Onlie, honest lucky,
  Brews guid ale at shore o' Bucky:
I wish her sale for her guid ale,
  The best on a' the shore o' Bucky !

I

A' THE lads o' Thorniebank,
  When they gae to the shore o' Bucky,
They 'll step in an' tak a pint
  Wi' Lady Onlie, honest lucky.

II

Her house sae bien, her curch sae clean —
  I wat she is a dainty chuckie
And cheery blinks the ingle-gleede
  O' Ladie Onlie, honest lucky !

CHORUS

Lady Onlie, honest lucky,
  Brews guid ale at shore o' Bucky:
I wish her sale for her guid ale,
  The best on a' the shore o' Bucky !

THE BANKS OF THE DEVON

"These verses were composed on a charming girl, a Miss Charlotte Hamilton, who is now married to James M'Kittrick Adair, Esqr., physician. She is sister to my worthy friend Gavin Hamilton of Mauchline, and was born on the banks of Ayr, but was, at the time I wrote these lines, residing at Harvieston in Clackmannanshire, on the romantic banks of the little river Devon. I first heard the air from a lady in Inverness, and got the notes taken down for the work." (R. B.)

Burns visited Gavin Hamilton's mother and her family at Harvieston on Monday, 27th August, 1787, and wrote to Hamilton on the 28th: "Of Charlotte I cannot speak in common terms of admiration; she is not only beautiful but lovely. Her form is elegant; her features not regular, but they have the smile of sweetness and the settled complacency of good-nature in the highest degree; and her complexion, now that she has happily recovered her wonted health, is equal to Miss Burnet's." In the October following Burns stopped at Harvieston again, and introduced that Dr. Adair whom Miss Hamilton married, 16th November, 1789. She died a widow in 1806. On 2d September, 1787, Burns sent the first draft of his song to her friend, Miss Chalmers: "I am determined to pay Charlotte a poetic compliment in the second part of the *Museum*, if I could hit on some glorious Scotch air. You will see a small attempt on a shred of paper enclosed."

The "small attempt" is a poor enough performance, when all is said — not much above the stall level: but it appears to be pure Burns. [The tune was a Highland air, entitled *Phannerach dhon na chri*, or *The Pretty Milkmaid*.

Charlotte Hamilton may also have been the heroine of the song *Fairest Maid on Devon Banks*. (See *post*, p. 288). For Gavin Hamilton see *ante*, p. 41, Prefatory Note to *A Dedication*.]

I

How pleasant the banks of the clear winding Devon,
　With green spreading bushes and flow'rs blooming fair !
But the boniest flow'r on the banks of the Devon
　Was once a sweet bud on the braes of the Ayr.
Mild be the sun on this sweet blushing flower,
　In the gay rosy morn, as it bathes in the dew !

And gentle the fall of the soft vernal shower,
　That steals on the evening each leaf to renew !

II

O, spare the dear blossom, ye orient breezes,
　With chill, hoary wing as ye usher the dawn !
And far be thou distant, thou reptile that seizes
　The verdure and pride of the garden or lawn !
Let Bourbon exult in his gay gilded lilies,
　And England triumphant display her proud rose !
A fairer than either adorns the green vallies,
　Where Devon, sweet Devon, meandering flows.

DUNCAN GRAY

I

Weary fa' you, Duncan Gray !
　(Ha, ha, the girdin o't !)
Wae gae by you, Duncan Gray !
　(Ha, ha, the girdin o't !)
When a' the lave gae to their play,
Then I maun sit the lee-lang day,
And jeeg the cradle wi' my tae,
　And a' for the girdin o't !

II

Bonie was the Lammas moon
　(Ha, ha, the girdin o't !)
Glowrin a' the hills aboon
　(Ha, ha, the girdin o't !)
The girdin brak, the beast cam down,
I tint my curch and baith my shoon,
And, Duncan, ye 're an unco loun —
　Wae on the bad girdin o't !

III

But Duncan, gin ye 'll keep your aith
　(Ha, ha, the girdin o't !),
I 'se bless you wi' my hindmost breath
　(Ha, ha, the girdin o't !).
Duncan, gin ye 'll keep your aith,
The beast again can bear us baith,
And auld Mess John will mend the skaith
　And clout the bad girdin o't.

THE PLOUGHMAN

CHORUS

Then up wi't a', my ploughman lad,
  And hey, my merry ploughman !
Of a' the trades that I do ken,
  Commend me to the ploughman !

I

THE ploughman, he 's a bonie lad,
  His mind is ever true, jo !
His garters knit below his knee,
  His bonnet it is blue, jo.

II

I hae been east, I hae been west,
  I hae been at St. Johnston ;
The boniest sight that e'er I saw
  Was the ploughman laddie dancin.

III

Snaw-white stockings on his legs
  And siller buckles glancin,
A guid blue bonnet on his head,
  And O, but he was handsome !

IV

Commend me to the barn-yard
  And the corn mou, man !
I never got my coggie fou
  Till I met wi' the ploughman.

CHORUS

Then up wi't a', my ploughman lad,
  And hey, my merry ploughman !
Of a' the trades that I do ken,
  Commend me to the ploughman !

LANDLADY, COUNT THE LAWIN

Set to the tune, *Hey Tutti Taiti*. " I have
met the tradition universally over Scotland,
and particularly in the neighbourhood of the
scene, that this air was Robert Bruce's march
to Bannockburn." (R. B.) He afterwards
wrote *Scots Wha Hae* (*post*, p. 285) to it.

The present song is not an original, but a
patchwork of assorted scraps, with some few
verbal changes.

CHORUS

Hey tutti, taiti,
How tutti, taiti,

Hey tutti, taiti,
Wha 's fou now ?

I

LANDLADY, count the lawin,
The day is near the dawin;
Ye 're a' blind drunk, boys,
And I 'm but jolly fou.

II

Cog, an ye were ay fou,
Cog, an ye were ay fou,
I wad sit and sing to you,
If ye were ay fou !

III

Weel may ye a' be !
Ill may ye never see !
God bless the king
And the companie !

CHORUS

Hey tutti, taiti,
How tutti, taiti,
Hey tutti, taiti,
Wha 's fou now ?

RAVING WINDS AROUND HER BLOWING

" I composed these verses on Miss Isabella
Macleod of Rasa, alluding to her feelings on
the death of her sister, and the still more
melancholy death of her sister's husband, the
late Earl of Loudoun, who shot himself out
of sheer heart-break at some mortifications he
suffered owing to the deranged state of his
finances." (R. B.)

For Miss Isabella M'Leod see Prefatory
Note to *On the Death of John M'Leod, Esq.*,
(*ante*, p. 96), and *To Miss Isabella M'Leod*,
(*ante*, p. 137).

I

RAVING winds around her blowing,
Yellow leaves the woodlands strowing,
By a river hoarsely roaring,
Isabella stray'd deploring : —
" Farewell hours that late did measure
Sunshine days of joy and pleasure !
Hail, thou gloomy night of sorrow —
Cheerless night that knows no mor-
    row !

II

"O'er the Past too fondly wandering,
On the hopeless Future pondering,
Chilly Grief my life-blood freezes,
Fell Despair my fancy seizes.
Life, thou soul of every blessing,
Load to Misery most distressing,
Gladly how would I resign thee,
And to dark Oblivion join thee!"

HOW LANG AND DREARY IS THE NIGHT

"I met with some such words in a collection of songs somewhere, which I altered and enlarged; and to please you, and to suit your favourite air of *Cauld Kail*, I have taken a stride or two across my room, and have arranged it anew, as you will find on the other page." (R. B.)

CHORUS

For O, her lanely nights are lang,
And O, her dreams are eerie,
And O, her widow'd heart is sair,
That's absent frae her dearie!

I

How lang and dreary is the night,
When I am frae my dearie!
I restless lie frae e'en to morn,
Tho' I were ne'er sae weary.

II

When I think on the lightsome days
I spent wi' thee, my dearie,
And now what seas between us roar,
How can I be but eerie?

III

How slow ye move, ye heavy hours!
The joyless day how dreary!
It was na sae ye glinted by,
When I was wi' my dearie!

CHORUS

For O, her lanely nights are lang,
And O, her dreams are eerie,
And O, her widow'd heart is sair,
That's absent frae her dearie!

MUSING ON THE ROARING OCEAN

"I composed these verses out of compliment to a Mrs. M'Lachlan, whose husband is an officer in the East Indies." (R. B.)
They are reminiscent of divers Jacobitisms.

I

MUSING on the roaring ocean,
Which divides my love and me,
Wearying heav'n in warm devotion
For his weal where'er he be:

II

Hope and Fear's alternate billow
Yielding late to Nature's law,
Whispering spirits round my pillow,
Talk of him that's far awa.

III

Ye whom sorrow never wounded,
Ye who never shed a tear,
Care-untroubled, joy-surrounded,
Gaudy day to you is dear!

IV

Gentle night, do thou befriend me!
Downy sleep, the curtain draw!
Spirits kind, again attend me,
Talk of him that's far awa!

BLYTHE WAS SHE

"I composed these verses while I stayed at Ochtertyre with Sir William Murray. The lady, who was also at Ochtertyre at the same time, was a well-known toast, Miss Euphemia Murray of Lintrose, who was called, and very justly, 'the flower of Strathmore.'" (R. B.)
She married Mr. Smythe of Methven, who became one of the judges of the Court of Session.

CHORUS

Blythe, blythe and merry was she,
Blythe was she butt and ben,
Blythe by the banks of Earn,
And blythe in Glenturit glen!

I

By Oughtertyre grows the aik,
On Yarrow banks the birken shaw;
But Phemie was a bonier lass
Than braes o' Yarrow ever saw.

II

Her looks were like a flow'r in May,
  Her smile was like a simmer morn.
She trippèd by the banks o' Earn
  As light's a bird upon a thorn.

III

Her bonie face it was as meek
  As onie lamb upon a lea.
The evening sun was ne'er sae sweet
  As was the blink o' Phemie's e'e.

IV

The Highland hills I 've wander'd wide,
  As o'er the Lawlands I hae been,
But Phemie was the blythest lass
  That ever trod the dewy green.

CHORUS

Blythe, blythe and merry was she,
  Blythe was she butt and ben,
Blythe by the banks of Earn,
  And blythe in Glenturit Glen !

TO DAUNTON ME

CHORUS

To daunton me, to daunton me,
An auld man shall never daunton me !

I

THE blude-red rose at Yule may blaw,
The simmer lilies bloom in snaw,
The frost may freeze the deepest sea,
But an auld man shall never daunton me.

II

To daunton me, and me sae young,
Wi' his fause heart and flatt'ring tongue:
That is the thing you ne'er shall see,
For an auld man shall never daunton me.

III

For a' his meal and a' his maut,
For a' his fresh beef and his saut,
For a' his gold and white monfe,
An auld man shall never daunton me.

IV

His gear may buy him kye and yowes;
His gear may buy him glens and knowes;

But me he shall not buy nor fee,
For an auld man shall never daunton me.

V

He hirples twa-fauld as he dow,
Wi' his teethless gab and his auld beld
    pow,
And the rain rains down frae his red
    blear'd e'e —
That auld man shall never daunton me !

CHORUS

To daunton me, to daunton me,
An auld man shall never daunton me !

O'ER THE WATER TO CHARLIE

The " verses," Stenhouse says, were " re-
vised and improved by Burns ; " and, he adds,
" a more complete version of this song may be
seen in Hogg's *Jacobite Reliques* " (sic). " Many
versions of this song " — thus Buchan in a note
in Hogg and Motherwell, Part V. (1834) —
" have appeared in print. There is one in
Hogg's *Jacobite Relics*, and one in the *Ancient
Ballads and Songs of the North of Scotland*,
from which latter copy I infer that the original
had been written anterior to the days of Prince
Charles, commonly called the Pretender, and
the time of Charles the Second's restoration."
But Hogg's set is merely Ayrshire Bard *plus*
Ettrick Shepherd, and it were hard to say how
much Peter Buchan's, " taken down from re-
citation," is indebted to Peter Buchan — espe-
cially as internal evidence shows that, as he
gives it, it did not all exist before his own
days. No printed copy of any such ballad an-
terior to the Burns is quoted by Buchan. Nor
do we know more than three.

CHORUS

We 'll o'er the water, we 'll o'er the sea,
  We 'll o'er the water to Charlie !
Come weal, come woe, we 'll gather and go,
  And live and die wi' Charlie !

I

COME boat me o'er, come row me o'er,
  Come boat me o'er to Charlie !
I 'll gie John Ross another bawbee
  To boat me o'er to Charlie.

II

I lo'e weel my Charlie's name,
  Tho' some there be abhor him;

But O, to see Auld Nick gaun hame,
     And Charlie's faes before him !

III

I swear and vow by moon and stars
     And sun that shines so early,
If I had twenty thousand lives,
     I 'd die as aft for Charlie !

CHORUS

We 'll o'er the water, we 'll o'er the sea,
     We 'll o'er the water to Charlie !
Come weal, come woe, we 'll gather and
          go,
     And live and die wi' Charlie !

A ROSE–BUD, BY MY EARLY WALK

"This song I composed on Miss Jenny
Cruickshank, only child to my worthy friend
Mr. Wm. Cruickshank, of the High School,
Edinburgh. The air is by David Sillar, *quondam* merchant, and now schoolmaster in Irvine.
He is the 'Davie' to whom I address· my
printed poetical epistle in the measure of *The
Cherry and the Slae*." (R. B.)
     See Prefatory Note to *To Miss Cruickshank*
(*ante, p.* 95.)

I

A ROSE-BUD, by my early walk
Adown a corn-inclosèd bawk,
Sae gently bent its thorny stalk,
     All on a dewy morning.
Ere twice the shades o' dawn are fled,
In a' its crimson glory spread
And drooping rich the dewy head,
     It scents the early morning.

II

Within the bush her covert nest
A little linnet fondly prest,
The dew sat chilly on her breast,
     Sae early in the morning.
She soon shall see her tender brood,
The pride, the pleasure o' the wood,
Amang the fresh green leaves bedew'd,
     Awake the early morning.

III

So thou, dear bird, young Jeany fair,
On trembling string or vocal air
Shall sweetly pay the tender care

That tents thy early morning !
So thou, sweet rose-bud, young and gay,
Shalt beauteous blaze upon the day,
And bless the parent's evening ray
     That watch'd thy early morning !

AND I 'LL KISS THEE YET

CHORUS

And I 'll kiss thee yet, yet,
     And I 'll kiss thee o'er again,
And I 'll kiss thee yet, yet,
     My bonie Peggy Alison.

I

WHEN in my arms, wi' a' thy charms,
     I clasp my countless treasure, O,
I seek nae mair o' Heav'n to share
     Than sic a moment's pleasure, O !

II

And by thy een sae bonie blue
     I swear I 'm thine for ever, O !
And on thy lips I seal my vow,
     And break it shall I never, O !

CHORUS

And I 'll kiss thee yet, yet,·
     And I 'll kiss thee o'er again,
And I 'll kiss thee yet, yet,
     My bonie Peggy Alison.

RATTLIN, ROARIN WILLIE

" The last stanza of this song is mine ; it
was composed out of compliment to one of the
worthiest fellows in the world, William Dunbar, Esq., Writer to the Signet, Edinburgh, and
Colonel of the Crochallan Corps, a club of wits
who took that title at the time of raising the
fencible regiments." (R. B.)
     Dunbar, who became Inspector-General of
Stamp Duties in Scotland, died 18th February,
1807. He presented Burns in 1787 with a copy
of Spenser, and is often alluded to or addressed
in terms of warm regard.

I

O, RATTLIN, roarin Willie,
     O, he held to the fair,
An' for to sell his fiddle
     And buy some other ware;

But parting wi' his fiddle,
  The saut tear blin't his e'e —
And, rattlin, roarin Willie,
  Ye 're welcome hame to me !

II

"O Willie, come sell your fiddle,
  O, sell your fiddle sae fine !
O Willie, come sell your fiddle
  And buy a pint o' wine !"
"If I should sell my fiddle,
  The warld would think I was mad;
For monie a rantin day
  My fiddle and I hae had."

III

As I cam by Crochallan,
  I cannily keekit ben,
Rattlin, roarin Willie
  Was sitting at yon boord-en':
Sitting at yon boord-en',
  And amang guid companie !
Rattlin, roarin Willie,
  Ye 're welcome hame to me.

WHERE, BRAVING ANGRY WINTER'S STORMS

The heroine was Margaret, daughter of John
Chalmers of Fingland, and a cousin of Char-
lotte Hamilton, her particular friend. Burns
met her in Edinburgh during his first visit, and
also in October, 1787, at Harvieston. She mar-
ried in 1788 Mr. Lewis Hay, of Forbes and
Co.'s Bank ; and died in 1843. Thomas Camp-
bell affirmed that, according to Mrs. Hay,
Burns had asked her in marriage ; but this
scarce accords with the tone of his letters to
her. Still, he had a particular regard for the
lady, and she always called out the best in
him. His compliments in verse — or rather
his proposal to publish them — somewhat
alarmed her : her main objection being, pre-
sumably, not to the song in the text, but to
My Peggy's Face, My Peggy's Form (*post*, p.
263). "They are neither of them," he wrote
to her, 6th November, 1787, "so particular as
to point you out to the world at large ; and
the circle of your acquaintance will allow all I
have said."

I

WHERE, braving angry winter's storms,
  The lofty Ochils rise,
Far in their shade my Peggy's charms
  First blest my wondering eyes:

As one who by some savage stream
  A lonely gem surveys,
Astonish'd doubly, marks it beam
  With art's most polish'd blaze.

II

Blest be the wild, sequester'd glade,
  And blest the day and hour,
Where Peggy's charms I first survey'd,
  When first I felt their pow'r !
The tyrant Death with grim control
  May seize my fleeting breath,
But tearing Peggy from my soul
  Must be a stronger death.

O TIBBIE, I HAE SEEN THE DAY

"This song I composed about the age of
seventeen." (R. B.)
Mrs. Begg states that the heroine was one
Isabella Steenson, or Stevenson, the farmer's
daughter of Little Hill, which marched with
Lochlie. The song itself bears no small resem-
blance to a song (probably older) called *The
Saucy Lass with the Beard*.

CHORUS

O Tibbie, I hae seen the day,
  Ye wadna been sae shy !
For laik o' gear ye lightly me,
  But, trowth, I care na by.

I

YESTREEN I met you on the moor,
Ye spak na, but gaed by like stoure !
Ye geck at me because I 'm poor —
  But fient a hair care I !

II

When comin hame on Sunday last,
Upon the road as I cam past,
Ye snufft an' gae your head a cast —
  But, trowth, I care't na by !

III

I doubt na, lass, but ye may think,
Because ye hae the name o' clink,
That ye can please me at a wink,
  Whene'er ye like to try.

IV

But sorrow tak him that 's sae mean,
Altho' his pouch o' coin were clean,
Wha follows onie saucy quean,
  That looks sae proud and high !

V

Altho' a lad were e'er sae smart,
If that he want the yellow dirt,
Ye 'll cast your head anither airt,
  And answer him fu' dry.

VI

But if he hae the name o' gear,
Ye 'll fasten to him like a brier,
Tho' hardly he for sense or lear
  Be better than the kye.

VII

But, Tibbie, lass, tak my advice:
Your daddie's gear maks you sae nice,
The Deil a ane wad spier your price,
  Were ye as poor as I.

VIII

There lives a lass beside yon park,
I 'd rather hae her in her sark
Than you wi' a' your thousand mark,
  That gars you look sae high.

CHORUS

O Tibbie, I hae seen the day,
Ye wadna been sae shy !
For laik o' gear ye lightly me,
But, trowth, I care na by.

CLARINDA, MISTRESS OF MY SOUL

This song was written when Burns was about to leave Edinburgh. "I am sick of writing where my bosom is not strongly interested. Tell me what you think of the following. There the bosom was perhaps a little interested." (R. B. to Mrs. Dunlop.)

I

CLARINDA, mistress of my soul,
  The measur'd time is run !
The wretch beneath the dreary pole
  So marks his latest sun.

II

To what dark cave of frozen night
  Shall poor Sylvander hie,
Depriv'd of thee, his life and light,
  The sun of all his joy ?

III

We part — but, by these precious drops
  That fill thy lovely eyes,
No other light shall guide my steps
  Till thy bright beams arise !

IV

She, the fair sun of all her sex,
  Has blest my glorious day;
And shall a glimmering planet fix
  My worship to its ray ?

THE WINTER IT IS PAST

This song is largely and generously adapted from a song called *The Curragh of Kildare*. Only stanza ii. is wholly his own.

I

THE winter it is past, and the simmer comes at last,
  And the small birds sing on ev'ry tree:
The hearts of these are glad, but mine is very sad,
  For my love is parted from me.

II

The rose upon the brier by the waters running clear
  May have charms for the linnet or the bee:
Their little loves are blest, and their little hearts at rest,
  But my lover is parted from me.

III

My love is like the sun in the firmament does run —
  Forever is constant and true;
But his is like the moon, that wanders up and down,
  And every month it is new.

IV

All you that are in love, and cannot it remove,
  I pity the pains you endure,
For experience makes me know that your hearts are full of woe,
  A woe that no mortal can cure.

I LOVE MY LOVE IN SECRET

Stenhouse affirms that the old song was "slightly altered by Burns, because it was rather inadmissible in its original state;" but apparently he spoke by guesswork. There is no doubt that Burns got his original — here[1] printed for the first time — in the Herd MS.: —

> " My Sandy O, my Sandy O,
> My bonie, bonie Sandy O !
> Tho' the love that I owe,
> To thee I dare nae show,
> Yet I love my love in secret,
> My Sandie O.
>
> " My Sandy gied to me a ring
> Was a' beset wi' diamonds fine ;
> But I gied to him a far better thing :
> I gied to him my heart to keep
> In pledge of his ring."

It will be seen that all he did was to add a stanza to the original set, or what was left of it.

CHORUS

My Sandy O, my Sandy O,
My bonie, bonie Sandy O !
Tho' the love that I owe
To thee I dare na show,
Yet I love my love in secret,
My Sandy O !

I

My Sandy gied to me a ring
Was a' beset wi' diamonds fine;
But I gied him a far better thing,
I gied my heart in pledge o' his ring.

II

My Sandy brak a piece o' gowd,
While down his cheeks the saut tears row'd;
He took a hauf, and gied it to me,
And I 'll keep it till the hour I die.

CHORUS

My Sandy O, my Sandy O,
My bonie, bonie Sandy O !
Tho' the love that I owe
To thee I dare na show,
Yet I love my love in secret,
My Sandy O !

[1] That is, in the Centenary Edition.

SWEET TIBBIE DUNBAR

O, WILT thou go wi' me, sweet Tibbie Dunbar ?
O, wilt thou go wi' me, sweet Tibbie Dunbar ?
Wilt thou ride on a horse, or be drawn in a car,
Or walk by my side, O sweet Tibbie Dunbar ?

II

I care na thy daddie, his lands and his money;
I care na thy kin, sae high and sae lordly;
But say that thou 'lt hae me for better or waur,
And come in thy coatie, sweet Tibbie Dunbar.

HIGHLAND HARRY

" The chorus I picked up from an old woman in Dunblane. The rest of the song is mine." (R. B.)

CHORUS

O, for him back again !
O, for him back again !
I wad gie a' Knockhaspie's land
For Highland Harry back again.

I

My Harry was a gallant gay,
Fu' stately strade he on the plain,
But now he 's banish'd far away:
I 'll never see him back again.

II

When a' the lave gae to their bed,
I wander dowie up the glen,
I set me down, and greet my fill,
And ay I wish him back again.

III

O, were some villains hangit high,
And ilka body had their ain,
Then I might see the joyfu' sight,
My Highland Harry back again !

CHORUS

O, for him back again !
O, for him back again !

I wad gie a' Knockhaspie's land,
For Highland Harry back again.

THE TAILOR FELL THRO' THE BED

" This air is the march of the Corporation of Tailors. The second and fourth stanzas are mine. (R. B.)

I

THE tailor fell thro' the bed, thimble an' a',
The tailor fell thro' the bed, thimble an' a';
The blankets were thin, and the sheets they
      were sma' —
The tailor fell thro' the bed, thimble an' a' !

II

The sleepy bit lassie, she dreaded nae ill,
The sleepy bit lassie, she dreaded nae ill;
The weather was cauld, and the lassie lay
      still:
She thought that a tailor could do her nae
      ill !

III

Gie me the groat again, cannie young man !
Gie me the groat again, cannie young man !
The day it is short, and the night it is
      lang —
The dearest siller that ever I wan !

IV

There 's somebody weary wi' lying her
      lane,
There 's somebody weary wi' lying her
      lane !
There 's some that are dowie, I trow wad
      be fain
To see the bit tailor come skippin again.

AY WAUKIN, O

CHORUS

Ay waukin, O,
      Waukin still and weary:
Sleep I can get nane
      For thinking on my dearie.

I

SIMMER 's a pleasant time:
      Flowers of every colour,

The water rins owre the heugh,
      And I long for my true lover.

II

When I sleep I dream,
      When I wauk I 'm eerie,
Sleep I can get nane
      For thinkin on my dearie.

III

Lanely night comes on,
      A' the lave are sleepin,
I think on my bonie lad,
      And I bleer my een wi' greetin.

CHORUS

Ay waukin, O,
      Waukin still and weary:
Sleep I can get nane
      For thinking on my dearie

BEWARE O' BONIE ANN

" I composed this song out of compliment to Miss Ann Masterton, the daughter of my friend, Allan Masterton, the author of the air *Strathallan's Lament;* and two or three others in this work." (R. B.)
      The lady married Dr. Derbyshire, physician, of Bath and London, and died in August, 1834.

I

YE gallants bright, I rede you right,
      Beware o' bonie Ann !
Her comely face sae fu' o' grace,
      Your heart she will trepan.

II

Her een sae bright like stars by night,
      Her skin is like the swan.
Sae jimply lac'd her genty waist
      That sweetly ye might span.

III

Youth, Grace, and Love attendant move,
      And Pleasure leads the van :
In a' their charms, and conquering arms,
      They wait on bonie Ann.

IV

The captive bands may chain the hands,
      But Love enslaves the man :
Ye gallants braw, I rede you a',
      Beware o' bonie Ann !

LADDIE, LIE NEAR ME

CHORUS

Near me, near me,
Laddie, lie near me !
Lang hae I lain my lane —
Laddie, lie near me !

I

LANG hae we parted been,
Laddie, my dearie;
Now we are met again —
Laddie, lie near me !

II

A' that I hae endur'd,
Laddie, my dearie,
Here in thy arms is cur'd —
Laddie, lie near me !

CHORUS

Near me, near me,
Laddie, lie near me !
Lang hae I lain my lane —
Laddie, lie near me!

THE GARD'NER WI' HIS PAIDLE

"The title of the song only is old ; the rest is mine." (R. B.)

I

WHEN rosy May comes in wi' flowers
To deck her gay, green-spreading bowers,
Then busy, busy are his hours,
        The gard'ner wi' his paidle.

II

The crystal waters gently fa',
The merry birds are lovers a',
The scented breezes round him blaw —
        The gard'ner wi' his paidle.

III

When purple morning starts the hare
To steal upon her early fare,
Then thro' the dew he maun repair —
        The gard'ner wi' his paidle.

IV

When Day, expiring in the west,
The curtain draws o' Nature's rest,

He flies to her arms he lo'es best,
        The gard'ner wi' his paidle.

ON A BANK OF FLOWERS

The original was written by Theobald, set by Galliard, and sung by Mr. Park in *The Lady's Triumph :* —

> " On a Bank of Flowers
> In a summer's day,
> Inviting and undrest,
> In her bloom of youth bright Celia lay
> With love and sleep opprest,
> When a youthful swain with adoring eyes
> Wish'd he dared the fair maid surprise,
>   With a fa la la,
> But fear'd approaching spies."

Burns rather bungles his inspiration, and certainly diverts his motive to a more liberal conclusion. Both original and derivative belong to a type of pastoral in high favour after the Restoration, good examples being Dryden's *Chloe found Amyntas Lying* and *Beneath a Myrtle Shade.* Older and less farded, less artificial and immodest, are *As at Noon Dulcina Rested* (long attributed to Raleigh) and that charming ditty, *The Matchless Maid*, in the Second *Westminster Drollery* (1672).

I

ON a bank of flowers in a summer day,
For summer lightly drest,
The youthful, blooming Nelly lay
With love and sleep opprest;
When Willie, wand'ring thro' the wood,
Who for her favour oft had sued —
    He gaz'd, he wish'd,
    He fear'd, he blush'd,
And trembled where he stood.

II

Her closèd eyes, like weapons sheath'd,
Were seal'd in soft repose;
Her lips, still as she fragrant breath'd,
It richer dyed the rose:
The springing lilies, sweetly prest,
Wild-wanton kiss'd her rival breast:
    He gaz'd, he wish'd,
    He fear'd, he blush'd,
His bosom ill at rest.

III

Her robes, light-waving in the breeze,
Her tender limbs embrace;
Her lovely form, her native ease,
All harmony and grace.

Tumultuous tides his pulses roll,
A faltering, ardent kiss he stole:
    He gaz'd, he wish'd,
    He fear'd, he blush'd,
And sigh'd his very soul.

IV

As flies the partridge from the brake
    On fear-inspirèd wings,
So Nelly, starting, half-awake,
    Away affrighted springs.
But Willie follow'd — as he should:
He overtook her in the wood;
    He vow'd, he pray'd,
    He found the maid
Forgiving all, and good.

THE DAY RETURNS

TUNE: *Seventh of November*

" I composed this song out of compliment to one of the happiest and worthiest couples in the world: Robert Riddell, Esq. of Glenriddell, and his lady. At their fireside I have enjoyed more pleasant evenings than at all the houses of fashionable people in this country put together; and to their kindness and hospitality I am indebted for many of the happiest hours of my life." (R. B.)

For Captain Riddell, see *ante*, p. 142, Prefatory Note to *Impromptu to Captain Riddell*. The song was sent to him in a letter (unpublished) dated Tuesday evening (*i. e.* 9th September, 1788): "As I was busy behind my harvest folks this forenoon, and musing on a proper theme for your *Seventh of November*, some of the conversation before me accidentally suggested a suspicion that this said Seventh of November is a matrimonial anniversary with a certain very worthy neighbour of mine. I have seen very few who owe so much to a wedding-day as Mrs. Riddell and you; and my imagination took the hint accordingly, as you will see on the next page."

I

THE day returns, my bosom burns,
    The blissful day we twa did meet !
Tho' winter wild in tempest toil'd,
    Ne'er summer sun was half sae sweet.
Than a' the pride that loads the tide,
    And crosses o'er the sultry line,
Than kingly robes, than crowns and globes,
    Heav'n gave me more — it made thee
      mine !

II

While day and night can bring delight,
    Or Nature aught of pleasure give,
While joys above my mind can move,
    For thee, and thee alone, I live !
When that grim foe of Life below
    Comes in between to make us part,
The iron hand that breaks our band,
    It breaks my bliss, it breaks my heart !

MY LOVE, SHE'S BUT A LASSIE YET

CHORUS

My love, she's but a lassie yet,
My love, she's but a lassie yet !
We'll let her stand a year or twa,
She'll no be half sae saucy yet !

I

I RUE the day I sought her, O !
I rue the day I sought her, O !
Wha gets her need na say he's woo'd,
But he may say he has bought her, O.

II

Come draw a drap o' the best o't yet,
Come draw a drap o' the best o't yet !
Gae seek for pleasure whare ye will,
But here I never missed it yet.

III

We're a' dry wi' drinkin o't,
We're a' dry wi' drinkin o't !
The minister kiss't the fiddler's wife —
He could na preach for thinkin o't !

CHORUS

My love, she's but a lassie yet,
My love, she's but a lassie yet !
We'll let her stand a year or twa,
She'll no be half sae saucy yet !

JAMIE, COME TRY ME

CHORUS

Jamie, come try me,
Jamie, come try me !
If thou would win my love,
Jamie, come try me !

I

If thou should ask my love,
  Could I deny thee ?
If thou would win my love,
  Jamie, come try me !

II

If thou should kiss me, love,
  Wha could espy thee ?
If thou wad be my love,
  Jamie, come try me !

CHORUS

Jamie, come try me,
  Jamie, come try me !
If thou would win my love,
  Jamie, come try me !

THE SILVER TASSIE

"This air is Oswald's; the first half stanza : —

> " 'Go fetch to me a pint o' wine,
>   And fill it in a silver tassie,
>   That I may drink before I go
>   A service to my bonie lassie : ' " —

is old; the rest is mine." (R. B.) Nevertheless, on 17th December, 1788, he wrote to Mrs. Dunlop thus : " Now I am on my hobby horse, I cannot help inserting two other old stanzas which please me mightily."

I

Go, fetch to me a pint o' wine,
  And fill it in a silver tassie,
That I may drink before I go
  A service to my bonie lassie !
The boat rocks at the pier o' Leith,
  Fu' loud the wind blaws frae the Ferry,
The ship rides by the Berwick-Law,
  And I maun leave my bonie Mary.

II

The trumpets sound, the banners fly,
  The glittering spears are rankèd ready,
The shouts o' war are heard afar,
  The battle closes deep and bloody.
It 's not the roar o' sea or shore
  Wad mak me langer wish to tarry,
Nor shouts o' war that 's heard afar :
  It 's leaving thee, my bonie Mary !

THE LAZY MIST

I

The lazy mist hangs from the brow of the
  hill,
Concealing the course of the dark winding
  rill.
How languid the scenes, late so sprightly,
  appear,
As Autumn to Winter resigns the pale
  year !

II

The forests are leafless, the meadows are
  brown,
And all the gay foppery of summer is
  flown.
Apart let me wander, apart let me muse,
How quick Time is flying, how keen Fate
  pursues !

III

How long I have liv'd, but how much liv'd
  in vain !
How little of life's scanty span may re-
  main !
What aspects old Time in his progress has
  worn !
What ties cruel Fate in my bosom has
  torn !

IV

How foolish, or worse, till our summit is
  gain'd !
And downward, how weaken'd, how dark-
  en'd, how pain'd !
Life is not worth having with all it can
  give :
For something beyond it poor man, sure,
  must live.

THE CAPTAIN'S LADY

CHORUS

O, mount and go,
  Mount and make you ready !
O, mount and go,
  And be the Captain's Lady !

I

When the drums do beat,
  And the cannons rattle,

Thou shalt sit in state,
  And see thy love in battle:

II

When the vanquish'd foe
  Sues for peace and quiet,
To the shades we 'll go,
  And in love enjoy it.

CHORUS

O, mount and go,
  Mount and make you ready !
O, mount and go,
  And be the Captain's Lady !

OF A' THE AIRTS

"The air is by Marshall; the song I composed out of compliment to Mrs. Burns. *N. B.* It was during the honeymoon." (R. B.) The song was no doubt written shortly after his arrival in Ellisland, while his wife was yet in Ayrshire.

I

Of a' the airts the wind can blaw
  I dearly like the west,
For there the bonie lassie lives,
  The lassie I lo'e best.
There wild woods grow, and rivers row,
  And monie a hill between,
But day and night my fancy's flight
  Is ever wi' my Jean.

II

I see her in the dewy flowers —
  I see her sweet and fair.
I hear her in the tunefu' birds —
  I hear her charm the air.
There 's not a bonie flower that springs
  By fountain, shaw, or green,
There 's not a bonie bird that sings,
  But minds me o' my Jean.

CARL, AN THE KING COME

CHORUS

Carl, an the King come,
Carl, an the King come,

Thou shalt dance, and I will sing,
  Carl, an the King come !

I

An somebodie were come again,
Then somebodie maun cross the main,
And every man shall hae his ain,
  Carl, an the King come !

II

I trow we swappèd for the worse:
We gae the boot and better horse,
And that we 'll tell them at the Cross,
  Carl, an the King come !

III

Coggie, an the King come,
Coggie, an the King come,
I 'll be fou, and thou 'se be toom,
  Coggie, an the King come !

CHORUS

Carl, an the King come,
Carl, an the King come,
Thou shalt dance, and I will sing,
  Carl, an the King come !

WHISTLE O'ER THE LAVE O'T

The repeat is borrowed from the old song, *Whistle O'er the Lave O't.* [The fiddler of *The Jolly Beggars* models his solo upon the same ditty (see *ante*, p. 105).]

I

First when Maggie was my care,
Heav'n, I thought, was in her air;
Now we 're married, spier nae mair,
  But — whistle o'er the lave o't !
Meg was meek, and Meg was mild,
Sweet and harmless as a child:
Wiser men than me 's beguiled —
  Whistle o'er the lave o't !

II

How we live, my Meg and me,
How we love, and how we gree,
I care na by how few may see —
  Whistle o'er the lave o't !
Wha I wish were maggots' meat,
Dish'd up in her winding-sheet,
I could write (but Meg wad see 't) —
  Whistle o'er the lave o't !

O, WERE I ON PARNASSUS HILL

I

O, WERE I on Parnassus hill,
Or had o' Helicon my fill,
That I might catch poetic skill
    To sing how dear I love thee !
But Nith maun be my Muses' well,
My Muse maun be thy bonie sel',
On Corsincon I 'll glowr and spell,
    And write how dear I love thee.

II

Then come, sweet Muse, inspire my lay !
For a' the lee-lang simmer's day
I couldna sing, I couldna say
    How much, how dear I love thee.
I see thee dancing o'er the green,
Thy waist sae jimp, thy limbs sae clean,
Thy tempting lips, thy roguish een —
    By Heaven and Earth I love thee !

III

By night, by day, a-field, at hame,
The thoughts o' thee my breast inflame,
And ay I muse and sing thy name —
    I only live to love thee.
Tho' I were doom'd to wander on,
Beyond the sea, beyond the sun,
Till my last weary sand was run,
    Till then — and then — I 'd love thee !

THE CAPTIVE RIBBAND

I

MYRA, the captive ribband 's mine !
'T was all my faithful love could gain,
And would you ask me to resign
    The sole reward that crowns my pain ?

II

Go, bid the hero, who has run
    Thro' fields of death to gather fame —
Go, bid him lay his laurels down,
    And all his well-earn'd praise disclaim !

III

The ribband shall its freedom lose —
    Lose all the bliss it had with you ! —
And share the fate I would impose
    On thee, wert thou my captive too.

IV

It shall upon my bosom live,
    Or clasp me in a close embrace;
And at its fortune if you grieve,
    Retrieve its doom, and take its place.

THERE 'S A YOUTH IN THIS CITY

" The air is claimed by Neil Gow, who calls
it his Lament for his brother. The first half
stanza of the song is old; the rest is mine."
(R. B.)

Burns was never above vamping from him-
self; and the present piece is strongly reminis-
cent of *The Belles of Mauchline* (*ante*, p. 171).

I

THERE 'S a youth in this city, it were a
    great pity
    That he from our lasses should wander
    awa';
For he 's bonie and braw, weel-favor'd
    witha',
    An' his hair has a natural buckle an' a'.

II

His coat is the hue o' his bonnet sae blue,
    His fecket is white as the new-driven
    snaw,
His hose they are blae, and his shoon like
    the slae,
    And his clear siller buckles, they dazzle
    us a'.

III

For beauty and fortune the laddie 's been
    courtin:
    Weel - featur'd, weel - tocher'd, weel-
    mounted, an' braw,
But chiefly the siller that gars him gang
    till her —
    The penny 's the jewel that beautifies a' !

IV

There 's Meg wi' the mailen, that fain wad
    a haen him,
    And Susie, wha's daddie was laird of
    the Ha',
There 's lang-tocher'd Nancy maist fetters
    his fancy;
    But the laddie's dear sel he loes dearest
    of a'.

MY HEART'S IN THE HIGHLANDS

"The first half stanza of this song is old; the rest is mine." (R. B.)

Burns apparently refers to the first half stanza of the chorus. Sharpe quotes "from a stall copy" *The Strong Walls of Derry*, one stanza in which is almost identical with the Burns chorus.

CHORUS

My heart's in the Highlands, my heart
   is not here,
My heart's in the Highlands a-chasing
   the deer,
A-chasing the wild deer and following
   the roe —
My heart's in the Highlands, wherever
   I go !

I

FAREWELL to the Highlands, farewell to
   the North,
The birthplace of valour, the country of
   worth !
Wherever I wander, wherever I rove,
The hills of the Highlands for ever I love.

II

Farewell to the mountains high cover'd
   with snow,
Farewell to the straths and green valleys
   below,
Farewell to the forests and wild-hanging
   woods,
Farewell to the torrents and loud-pouring
   floods !

CHORUS

My heart's in the Highlands, my heart
   is not here,
My heart's in the Highlands a-chasing
   the deer,
A-chasing the wild deer and following
   the roe —
My heart's in the Highlands, wherever
   I go !

JOHN ANDERSON MY JO

I

JOHN Anderson my jo, John,
   When we were first acquent,

Your locks were like the raven,
   Your bonie brow was brent;
But now your brow is beld, John,
   Your locks are like the snaw,
But blessings on your frosty pow,
   John Anderson my jo !

II

John Anderson my jo, John,
   We clamb the hill thegither,
And monie a cantie day, John,
   We've had wi' ane anither;
Now we maun totter down, John,
   And hand in hand we'll go,
And sleep thegither at the foot,
   John Anderson my jo !

AWA', WHIGS, AWA'

CHORUS

Awa', Whigs, awa' !
   Awa', Whigs, awa' !
Ye're but a pack o' traitor louns,
   Ye'll do nae guid at a'.

I

OUR thrissles flourish'd fresh and fair,
   And bonie bloom'd our roses;
But Whigs cam like a frost in June,
   An' wither'd a' our posies.

II

Our ancient crown's fa'n in the dust —
   Deil blin' them wi' the stoure o't,
An' write their names in his black beuk,
   Wha gae the Whigs the power o't !

III

Our sad decay in church and state
   Surpasses my descriving.
The Whigs cam o'er us for a curse,
   And we hae done wi' thriving.

IV

Grim Vengeance lang has taen a nap,
   But we may see him waukin —
Gude help the day when Royal heads
   Are hunted like a maukin !

CHORUS

Awa', Whigs, awa' !
   Awa', Whigs, awa' !
Ye're but a pack o' traitor louns,
   Ye'll do nae guid at a'.

CA' THE YOWES TO THE KNOWES

"This beautiful song is in the true old Scotch taste, yet I do not know that either the air or words were in print before." (R. B.)

In sending a new version (*post*, p. 292) to Thomson in September, 1794, he wrote : " I am flattered at your adopting *Ca' the Yowes to the Knowes*, as it was owing to me that ever it saw the light. About seven years ago, I was well acquainted with a worthy little fellow, a Mr. Clunie [Rev. John Clunie, minister of Ewes, Dumfriesshire, author of *I Loe Na a Laddie but Ane*], who sang it charmingly ; and, at my request, Mr. Clarke took it down from his singing. When I gave it to Johnson I added some stanzas to the song and mended others ; but still it will not do for *you*." Stenhouse gives the old words, presumably those taken down from Clunie's singing. It can scarce be affirmed that Burns has improved them. The two last stanzas are his ; his two first are expanded from Clunie's first ; while his two middles, where they differ from Clunie, differ for the worse.

CHORUS

Ca' the yowes to the knowes,
Ca' them where the heather grows,
Ca' them where the burnie rowes,
    My bonie dearie !

I

As I gaed down the water-side,
There I met my shepherd lad:
He row'd me sweetly in his plaid,
    And he ca'd me his dearie.

II

" Will ye gang down the water-side,
And see the waves sae sweetly glide
Beneath the hazels spreading wide ?
    The moon it shines fu' clearly."

III

" I was bred up in nae sic school,
My shepherd lad, to play the fool,
An' a' the day to sit in dool,
    An' naebody to see me."

IV

" Ye sall get gowns and ribbons meet,
Cauf-leather shoon upon your feet,
And in my arms thou 'lt lie and sleep,
    An' ye sall be my dearie."

V

" If ye 'll but stand to what ye 've said,
I 'se gang wi' you, my shepherd lad,
And ye may row me in your plaid,
    And I sall be your dearie."

VI

" While waters wimple to the sea,
While day blinks in the lift sae hie,
Till clay-cauld death sall blin' my e'e,
    Ye sall be my dearie."

CHORUS

Ca' the yowes to the knowes,
Ca' them where the heather grows,
Ca' them where the burnie rowes,
    My bonie dearie !

O, MERRY HAE I BEEN

" Ramsay, as usual, has modernized this song. The original, which I learned on the spot, from the old hostess in the principal Inn there, is : —

' "Lassie, lend me your braw hemp-heckle,
    And I 'll lend you my thripplin kame."
" My heckle is broken, it canna be gotten,
    And we 'll gae dance the Bob o' Dumblane."
Twa gaed to the wood, to the wood, to the wood,
    Twa gaed to the wood — three came hame;
An it be na weel bobbit, weel bobbit, weel bobbit,
    And it be na weel bobbit we 'll bob it again.'

I insert this song to introduce the following anecdote, which I have heard well authenticated. In the evening of the day of the battle of Dunblane (Sheriffmuir) when the action was over, a Scots officer in Argyle's army observed to his Grace that he was afraid the rebels would give out to the world that they had gotten the victory. 'Weel, weel,' answered his Grace, alluding to the foregoing ballad, ' if they think it nae weel bobbit, we 'll bob it again.' " (R. B.)

I

O, MERRY hae I been teethin a heckle,
    An' merry hae I been shapin a spoon !
O, merry hae I been cloutin a kettle,
    An' kissin my Katie when a' was done !
O, a' the lang day I ca' at my hammer,
    An' a' the lang day I whistle an' sing !
O, a' the lang night I cuddle my kimmer,
    An' a' the lang night as happy 's a king !

II

Bitter in dool, I lickit my winnins
  O' marrying Bess, to gie her a slave.
Blest be the hour she cool'd in her linens,
  And blythe be the bird that sings on her
    grave !
Come to my arms, my Katie, my Katie,
  An' come to my arms, and kiss me
    again !
Drucken or sober, here 's to thee, Katie,
  And blest be the day I did it again !

A MOTHER'S LAMENT

"The words were composed to commemorate
the much lamented and premature death of
James Ferguson, Esq., Junior, of Craigdar-
roch." (R. B.)
In a letter to Mrs. Dunlop (27th September,
1788) Burns states that he made them on a
twenty-six mile ride from Nithsdale to Mauch-
line. The copy sent her is entitled *Mrs. Fer-
gusson of Craigdarroch's Lamentation for the
Death of her Son.* Young Fergusson died 5th
November, 1787, just after completing his
university course. The only son of Mrs. Stew-
art of Afton died 5th December, 1787, and
Burns inscribed the song in the *Afton Lodge
Book,* which he presented to the bereaved
mother, his title this time being *A Mother's
Lament for the Loss of Her Only Son.*

I

FATE gave the word — the arrow sped,
  And pierc'd my darling's heart,
And with him all the joys are fled
  Life can to me impart.
By cruel hands the sapling drops,
  In dust dishonor'd laid:
So fell the pride of all my hopes,
  My age's future shade.

II

The mother linnet in the brake
  Bewails her ravish'd young:
So I for my lost darling's sake
  Lament the live-day long.
Death, oft I 've fear'd thy fatal blow !
  Now fond I bare my breast !
O, do thou kindly lay me low,
  With him I love at rest !

THE WHITE COCKADE

CHORUS

O, he 's a ranting, roving lad !
He is a brisk an' a bonie lad !
Betide what may, I will be wed,
And follow the boy wi' the White Cock-
  ade !

I

MY love was born in Aberdeen,
The boniest lad that e'er was seen;
But now he makes our hearts fu' sad —
He takes the field wi' his White Cockade.

II

I 'll sell my rock, my reel, my tow,
My guid gray mare and hawkit cow,
To buy mysel a tartan plaid,
To follow the boy wi' the White Cockade.

CHORUS

O, he 's a ranting, roving lad !
He is a brisk an' a bonie lad !
Betide what may, I will be wed,
And follow the boy wi' the White Cock-
  ade !

THE BRAES O' BALLOCHMYLE

"I composed the verses on the amiable and
excellent family of Whitefoord's leaving Bal-
lochmyle, when Sir John's misfortunes had
obliged him to sell the estate." (R. B.) See
Prefatory Note to *Lines Sent to Sir John
Whitefoord, Bart. (ante,* p. 88).

I

THE Catrine woods were yellow seen,
  The flowers decay'd on Catrine lea;
Nae lav'rock sang on hillock green,
  But nature sicken'd on the e'e;
Thro' faded groves Maria sang,
  Hersel in beauty's bloom the while,
And aye the wild-wood echoes rang: —
  "Fareweel the braes o' Ballochmyle !

II

"Low in your wintry beds, ye flowers,
  Again ye 'll flourish fresh and fair;
Ye birdies, dumb in with'ring bowers,
  Again ye 'll charm the vocal air;

But here, alas ! for me nae mair
Shall birdie charm, or floweret smile:
Fareweel the bonie banks of Ayr !
Fareweel ! fareweel sweet Ballochmyle !"

THE RANTIN DOG, THE DADDIE O'T

"I composed this song pretty early in life, and sent it to a young girl, a very particular acquaintance of mine, who was at the time under a cloud." (R. B.)

The "young girl" may have been either Elizabeth Paton (see *A Poet's Welcome, ante*, p. 113) or Jean Armour. It matters not which.

I

O, WHA my babie-clouts will buy ?
O, wha will tent me when I cry ?
Wha will kiss me where I lie ? —
    The rantin dog, the daddie o't !

II

O, wha will own he did the faut ?
O, wha will buy the groanin maut ?
O, wha will tell me how to ca't ? —
    The rantin dog, the daddie o't !

III

When I mount the creepie-chair,
Wha will sit beside me there ?
Gie me Rob, I 'll seek nae mair —
    The rantin dog, the daddie o't !

IV

Wha will crack to me my lane ?
Wha will mak me fidgin fain ?
Wha will kiss me o'er again ? —
    The rantin dog, the daddie o't !

THOU LINGERING STAR

Enclosing this very famous lament — hypochondriacal and remorseful, yet riddled with adjectives, specifically amatorious, yet wofully lacking in genuine inspiration — in a letter to Mrs. Dunlop, 8th November, 1789, Burns described it as "made the other day." He also asked her opinion of it, as he was too much interested in the subject to be "a critic in the composition." For Mary Campbell see *ante*, p. 204, Prefatory Note to *My Highland Lassie, O*, and Notes, p. 343. To Mrs. Dunlop on 13th December, Burns, groaning "under the miseries of a diseased nervous system," refers with longing to a future life : "There should I, with speechless agony of rapture, again welcome my lost, my ever dear Mary, whose bosom was fraught with truth, honour, constancy, and love : —

" My Mary, dear departed shade," etc.

Currie states that a copy found among Burns's papers was headed *To Mary in Heaven;* but only seeing is believing.

I

THOU ling'ring star with less'ning ray,
    That lov'st to greet the early morn,
Again thou usher'st in the day
    My Mary from my soul was torn.
O Mary, dear departed shade !
    Where is thy place of blissful rest ?
See'st thou thy lover lowly laid ?
    Hear'st thou the groans that rend his breast ?

II

That sacred hour can I forget,
    Can I forget the hallow'd grove,
Where, by the winding Ayr, we met
    To live one day of parting love ?
Eternity cannot efface
    Those records dear of transports past,
Thy image at our last embrace —
    Ah ! little thought we 't was our last !

III

Ayr, gurgling, kiss'd his pebbled shore,
    O'erhung with wild woods thickening green;
The fragrant birch and hawthorn hoar
    'Twin'd amorous round the raptur'd scene;
The flowers sprang wanton to be prest,
    The birds sang love on every spray,
Till too, too soon, the glowing west
    Proclaim'd the speed of wingèd day.

IV

Still o'er these scenes my mem'ry wakes,
    And fondly broods with miser-care.
Time but th' impression stronger makes,
    As streams their channels deeper wear.
O Mary, dear departed shade !
    Where is thy place of blissful rest ?
See'st thou thy lover lowly laid ?
    Hear'st thou the groans that rend his breast ?

EPPIE ADAIR

CHORUS

An' O my Eppie,
My jewel, my Eppie !
Wha wadna be happy
Wi' Eppie Adair ?

I

By love and by beauty,
By law and by duty,
I swear to be true to
My Eppie Adair !

II

A' pleasure exile me,
Dishonour defile me,
If e'er I beguile thee,
My Eppie Adair !

CHORUS

An' O my Eppie,
My jewel, my Eppie !
Wha wadna be happy
Wi' Eppie Adair ?

THE BATTLE OF SHERRAMUIR

This song, in which the idiosyncrasies of the fight are summarised with excellent discrimination, is condensed from a ballad by the Rev. John Barclay (1734–1798), Berean minister at Edinburgh): "*The Dialogue Betwixt William Luckladle and Thomas Cleancogue*, Who were Feeding their Sheep upon the Ochil Hills, 13th November, 1715. Being the day the Battle of Sheriffmuir was Fought. To the tune of *The Cameron Men.*"

I

" O, cam ye here the fight to shun,
   Or herd the sheep wi' me, man ?
Or were ye at the Sherra-moor,
   Or did the battle see, man ? "
" I saw the battle, sair and teugh,
And reekin-red ran monie a sheugh;
My heart for fear gae sough for sough,
To hear the thuds, and see the cluds
O' clans frae woods in tartan duds,
   Wha glaum'd at kingdoms three, man.

II

" The red-coat lads wi' black cockauds
   To meet them were na slaw, man:

They rush'd and push'd and bluid out-
      gush'd,
   And monie a bouk did fa', man !
The great Argyle led on his files,
I wat they glanc'd for twenty miles;
They hough'd the clans like nine-pin kyles,
They hack'd and hash'd, while braid-swords
      clash'd,
And thro' they dash'd, and hew'd and
      smash'd,
   Till fey men died awa, man.

III

" But had ye seen the philibegs
   And skyrin tartan trews, man,
When in the teeth they daur'd our Whigs
   And Covenant trueblues, man !
In lines extended lang and large,
When baig'nets o'erpower'd the targe,
And thousands hasten'd to the charge,
Wi' Highland wrath they frae the sheath
Drew blades o' death, till out o' breath
   They fled like frighted dows, man ! "

IV

" O, how Deil ! Tam, can that be true ?
   The chase gaed frae the north, man !
I saw mysel, they did pursue
   The horseman back to Forth, man;
And at Dunblane, in my ain sight,
They took the brig wi' a' their might,
And straught to Stirling wing'd their flight;
But, cursed lot ! the gates were shut,
And monie a huntit poor red-coat,
   For fear amaist did swarf, man ! "

V

" My sister Kate cam up the gate
   Wi' crowdie unto me, man:
She swoor she saw some rebels run
   To Perth and to Dundee, man !
Their left-hand general had nae skill;
The Angus lads had nae good will
That day their neebors' bluid to spill;
For fear by foes that they should lose
Their cogs o' brose, they scar'd at blows,
   And hameward fast did flee, man.

VI

" They 've lost some gallant gentlemen,
   Amang the Highland clans, man !
I fear my Lord Panmure is slain,
   Or in his en'mies' hands, man.
Now wad ye sing this double flight,
Some fell for wrang, and some for right,

But monie bade the world guid-night:
Say, pell and mell, wi' muskets' knell
How Tories fell, and Whigs to Hell
    Flew off in frighted bands, man ! "

YOUNG JOCKIE WAS THE BLYTHEST LAD

I

YOUNG Jockie was the blythest lad,
    In a' our town or here awa:
Fu' blythe he whistled at the gaud,
    Fu' lightly danc'd he in the ha'.

II

He roos'd my een sae bonie blue,
    He roos'd my waist sae genty sma';
An' ay my heart cam to my mou',
    When ne'er a body heard or saw.

III

My Jockie toils upon the plain
    Thro' wind and weet, thro' frost and
        snaw;
And o'er the lea I leuk fu' fain,
    When Jockie's owsen hameward ca'.

IV

An' ay the night comes round again,
    When in his arms he taks me a',
An' ay he vows he 'll be my ain
    As lang 's he has a breath to draw.

A WAUKRIFE MINNIE

"I picked up the old song and tune from a country girl in Nithsdale. I never met with it elsewhere in Scotland." (R. B.)

The vamp — if vamp it be, and we have no-where found an original — is in Burns's happiest and most "folkish" vein.

I

"WHARE are you gaun, my bonie lass ?
    Whare are you gaun, my hinnie ? "
She answer'd me right saucilie: —
    "An errand for my minnie ! "

II

"O, whare live ye, my bonie lass ?
    O, whare live ye, my hinnie ? "

"By yon burnside, gin ye maun ken,
    In a wee house wi' my minnie ! "

III

But I foor up the glen at e'en
    To see my bonie lassie,
And lang before the grey morn cam
    She was na hauf sae saucy.

IV

O, weary fa' the waukrife cock,
    And the foumart lay his crawin !
He wauken'd the auld wife frae her sleep
    A wee blink or the dawin.

V

An angry wife I wat she raise,
    And o'er the bed she brought her,
And wi' a meikle hazel-rung
    She made her a weel-pay'd dochter.

VI

"O, fare-thee-weel, my bonie lass !
    O, fare-thee-weel, my hinnie !
Thou art a gay and a bonie lass,
    But thou has a waukrife minnie ! "

THO' WOMEN'S MINDS

"The song is mine, all except the chorus." (R. B.)

A new set of the Bard's song in *The Jolly Beggars* (*ante*, p. 106). [The verses were clearly suggested by an old Scots song beginning,

    "Put butter in my Donald's brose,"

and having a similar refrain. See also the song *Is There for Honest Poverty, post*, p. 294.]

CHORUS

For a' that, an' a' that,
    And twice as meikle 's a' that,
The bonie lass that I loe best,
    She 'll be my ain for a' that !

I

THO' women's minds like winter winds
    May shift, and turn, an' a' that,
The noblest breast adores them maist —
    A consequence, I draw that.

II

Great love I bear to a' the fair,
    Their humble slave, an' a' that;

But lordly will, I hold it still
  A mortal sin to thraw that.

III

In rapture sweet this hour we meet,
  Wi' mutual love an' a' that,
But for how lang the flie may stang,
  Let inclination law that !

IV

Their tricks an' craft hae put me daft,
  They 've taen me in an' a' that,
But clear your decks, and here 's: — "The
  Sex ! "
I like the jads for a' that !

CHORUS

For a' that, an' a' that,
  And twice as meikle 's a' that,
The bonie lass that I loe best,
  She 'll be my ain for a' that !

WILLIE BREW'D A PECK O' MAUT

"The air is Masterton's; the song mine.
The occasion of it was this: Mr. Wm. Nicol,
of the High School, Edinburgh, during the
autumn vacation being at Moffat, honest Allan
(who was at that time on a visit to Dalswinton)
and I went to pay Nicol a visit. We had such
a joyous meeting that Mr. Masterton and I
agreed, each in our own way, that we should
celebrate the business." (R. B.)

The meeting took place in the autumn of
1789. The song — a little masterpiece of
drunken fancy — is included in Thomson.
For William Nicol see *ante*, p. 195, Prefatory
Note to Epitaph *For William Nicol.* Allan
Masterton was appointed writing-master to
Edinburgh High School 10th October, 1789.
He died in 1799.

CHORUS

We are na fou, we 're nae that fou,
  But just a drappie in our e'e !
The cock may craw, the day may daw,
  And ay we 'll taste the barley-bree !

I

O, WILLIE brew'd a peck o' maut,
  And Rob and Allan cam to see.
Three blyther hearts that lee-lang night
  Ye wad na found in Christendie.

II

Here are we met three merry boys,
  Three merry boys I trow are we;
And monie a night we 've merry been,
  And monie mae we hope to be !

III

It is the moon, I ken her horn,
  That 's blinkin in the lift sae hie:
She shines sae bright to wyle us hame,
  But, by my sooth, she 'll wait a wee !

IV

Wha first shall rise to gang awa,
  A cuckold, coward loun is he !
Wha first beside his chair shall fa',
  He is the King amang us three !

CHORUS

We are na fou, we 're nae that fou,
  But just a drappie in our e'e !
The cock may craw, the day may daw,
  And ay we 'll taste the barley-bree !

KILLIECRANKIE

"The battle of Killiecrankie was the last
stand made by the clans for James after his
abdication. Here the gallant Lord Dundee
fell in the moment of victory, and with him
fell the hopes of the party. General M'Kay,
when he found the Highlanders did not pursue
his flying army, said : 'Dundee must be killed,
or he never would have overlooked this advan-
tage.' A great stone marks the place where
Dundee fell." (R. B.) But the fact is that
Dundee got his hurt further up the hill than
the "great stone." The battle was fought on
17th July, 1689.

CHORUS

An ye had been whare I hae been,
  Ye wad na been sae cantie, O !
An ye had seen what I hae seen
  On the braes o' Killiecrankie, O !

I

"WHARE hae ye been sae braw, lad ?
  Whare hae ye been sae brankie, O ?
Whare hae ye been sae braw, lad ?
  Cam ye by Killiecrankie, O ? "

II

"I faught at land, I faught at sea,
  At hame I faught my auntie, O;
But I met the Devil and Dundee
  On the braes o' Killiecrankie, O!

III

"The bauld Pitcur fell in a furr,
  An' Clavers gat a clankie, O,
Or I had fed an Athole gled
  On the braes o' Killiecrankie, O!"

CHORUS

An ye had been whare I hae been,
  Ye wad na been sae cantie, O!
An ye had seen what I hae seen
  On the braes o' Killiecrankie, O!

THE BLUE-EYED LASSIE

Enclosed in a letter to Mrs. Dunlop, 2d October, 1788: "How do you like the following song, designed for and composed by a friend of mine, and which he has christened *The Blue-Eyed Lassie*." The friend was Captain Robert Riddell.

The "blue-eyed lassie" was Jean, daughter of the Rev. Andrew Jeffrey, of Lochmaben. She married a Mr. Renwick, of New York, and died in October, 1850.

I

I GAED a waefu' gate yestreen,
  A gate I fear I'll dearly rue:
I gat my death frae twa sweet een,
  Twa lovely een o' bonie blue!
'T was not her golden ringlets bright,
  Her lips like roses wat wi' dew,
Her heaving bosom lily-white:
  It was her een sae bonie blue.

II

She talk'd, she smil'd, my heart she wyl'd,
  She charm'd my soul I wist na how;
And ay the stound, the deadly wound,
  Cam frae her een sae bonie blue.
But "spare to speak, and spare to speed"—
  She'll aiblins listen to my vow:
Should she refuse, I'll lay my dead
  To her twa een sae bonie blue.

THE BANKS OF NITH

I

THE Thames flows proudly to the sea,
  Where royal cities stately stand;
But sweeter flows the Nith to me,
  Where Cummins ance had high command.
When shall I see that honor'd land,
That winding stream I love so dear?
  Must wayward Fortune's adverse hand
For ever — ever keep me here?

II

How lovely, Nith, thy fruitful vales,
  Where bounding hawthorns gaily bloom,
And sweetly spread thy sloping dales,
  Where lambkins wanton thro' the broom!
Tho' wandring now must be my doom
Far from thy bonie banks and braes,
  May there my latest hours consume
Amang my friends of early days!

TAM GLEN

I

MY heart is a-breaking, dear tittie,
  Some counsel unto me come len'.
To anger them a' is a pity,
  But what will I do wi' Tam Glen?

II

I'm thinking, wi' sic a braw fellow
  In poortith I might mak a fen'.
What care I in riches to wallow,
  If I mauna marry Tam Glen?

III

There's Lowrie the laird o' Dumeller:
  "Guid day to you," brute! he comes ben.
He brags and he blaws o' his siller,
  But when will he dance like Tam Glen?

IV

My minnie does constantly deave me,
  And bids me beware o' young men.
They flatter, she says, to deceive me —
  But wha can think sae o' Tam Glen?

V

My daddie says, gin I'll forsake him,
  He'd gie me guid hunder marks ten.

But if it's ordain'd I maun take him,
  O, wha will I get but Tam Glen?

VI

Yestreen at the valentines' dealing,
  My heart to my mou gied a sten,
For thrice I drew ane without failing,
  And thrice it was written "Tam Glen!"

VII

The last Halloween I was waukin
  My droukit sark-sleeve, as ye ken —
His likeness came up the house staukin,
  And the very grey breeks o' Tam Glen!

VIII

Come, counsel, dear tittie, don't tarry!
  I'll gie ye my bonie black hen,
Gif ye will advise me to marry
  The lad I lo'e dearly, Tam Glen.

CRAIGIEBURN WOOD

"It is remarkable of this air, that it is the confine of that country where the greatest part of our lowland music (so far as from the title, words, etc., we can localize it) has been composed. From Craigieburn, near Moffat, until one reaches the West Highlands, we have scarcely one slow air of antiquity. The song was composed on a passion which a Mr. Gillespie, a particular friend of mine, had for a Miss Lorimer, afterwards a Mrs. Whepdale. The young lady was born in Craigieburn Wood. The chorus is part of an old foolish ballad." (R. B.)   For Jean Lorimer see *post*, p. 289.

CHORUS

Beyond thee, dearie, beyond thee, dearie,
  And O, to be lying beyond thee!
O, sweetly, soundly, weel may he sleep
  That's laid in the bed beyond thee!

I

SWEET closes the ev'ning on Craigieburn
    Wood
  And blythely awaukens the morrow;
But the pride o' the spring on the Craigie-
    burn Wood
  Can yield me naught but sorrow.

II

I see the spreading leaves and flowers,
  I hear the wild birds singing;

But pleasure they hae nane for me,
  While care my heart is wringing.

III

I can na tell, I maun na tell,
  I daur na for your anger;
But secret love will break my heart,
  If I conceal it langer.

IV

I see thee gracefu', straight, and tall,
  I see thee sweet and bonie;
But O, what will my torment be,
  If thou refuse thy Johnie!

V

To see thee in another's arms
  In love to lie and languish,
'T wad be my dead, that will be seen —
  My heart wad burst wi' anguish!

VI

But, Jeanie, say thou wilt be mine,
  Say thou lo'es nane before me,
And a' my days o' life to come
  I'll gratefully adore thee.

CHORUS

Beyond thee, dearie, beyond thee, dearie,
  And O, to be lying beyond thee!
O, sweetly, soundly, weel may he sleep
  That's laid in the bed beyond thee!

FRAE THE FRIENDS AND LAND I LOVE

"I added the four last lines by way of giving a turn to the theme of the poem, such as it is." (R. B.)

I

FRAE the friends and land I love
  Driv'n by Fortune's felly spite,
Frae my best belov'd I rove,
  Never mair to taste delight!
Never mair maun hope to find
  Ease frae toil, relief frae care.
When remembrance wracks the mind,
  Pleasures but unveil despair.

II

Brightest climes shall mirk appear,
  Desert ilka blooming shore,

Till the Fates, nae mair severe,
  Friendship, love, and peace restore:
Till Revenge wi' laurell'd head
  Bring our banish'd hame again,
And ilk loyal, bonie lad
  Cross the seas, and win his ain!

O JOHN, COME KISS ME NOW

Altered and expanded from a fragment in
Herd (1769):—

> "John, come kiss me now, now, now!
>   O John, come kiss me now!
> John, come kiss me by and by,
>   And make nae mair ado!

> "Some will court and compliment
>   And make a great ado,
> Some will make of their guidman,
>   And sae will I of you."

CHORUS

O John, come kiss me now, now, now!
  O John, my love, come kiss me now!
O John, come kiss me by and by,
  For weel ye ken the way to woo!

I

O, SOME will court and compliment,
  And ither some will kiss and daut;
But I will mak o' my guidman,
  My ain guidman—it is nae faut!

II

O, some will court and compliment,
  And ither some will prie their mou',
And some will hause in ither's arms,
  And that's the way I like to do!

CHORUS

O John, come kiss me now, now, now!
  O John, my love, come kiss me now!
O John, come kiss me by and by,
  For weel ye ken the way to woo!

COCK UP YOUR BEAVER

I

WHEN first my brave Johnie lad came to
  this town,
He had a blue bonnet that wanted the
  crown,

But now he has gotten a hat and a fea-
  ther—
Hey, brave Johnie lad, cock up your bea-
  ver!

II

Cock up your beaver, and cock it fu'
  sprush!
We'll over the border and gie them a
  brush:
There's somebody there we'll teach better
  haviour—
Hey, brave Johnie lad, cock up your bea-
  ver!

MY TOCHER'S THE JEWEL

I

O, MEIKLE thinks my luve o' my beauty,
  And meikle thinks my luve o' my kin;
But little thinks my luve I ken brawlie
  My tocher's the jewel has charms for
    him.
It's a' for the apple he'll nourish the tree,
It's a' for the hiney he'll cherish the bee!
  My laddie's sae meikle in luve wi' the
    siller,
He canna hae luve to spare for me!

II

Your proffer o' luve's an airle-penny,
  My tocher's the bargain ye wad buy;
But an ye be crafty, I am cunnin,
  Sae ye with anither your fortune may
    try.
Ye're like to the timmer o' yon rotten
  wood,
Ye're like to the bark o' yon rotten tree:
Ye'll slip frae me like a knotless thread,
  An' ye'll crack ye're credit wi' mair nor
    me!

GUIDWIFE, COUNT THE LAWIN

"The chorus of this is part of an old song,
one stanza of which I recollect:—

> 'Every day my wife tells me
>   That ale and brandy will ruin me;
> But if gude liquor be my dead,
>   This shall be written on my head—
>   Landlady, count the lawin,'" etc.

(R. B.)

CHORUS

Then, guidwife, count the lawin,
The lawin, the lawin !
Then, guidwife, count the lawin,
And bring a coggie mair !

I

GANE is the day, and mirk 's the night,
But we 'll ne'er stray for faut o' light,
For ale and brandy 's stars and moon,
And blude-red wine 's the risin sun.

II

There 's wealth and ease for gentlemen,
And semple folk maun fecht and fen';
But here we 're a' in ae accord,
For ilka man that 's drunk 's a lord.

III

My coggie is a haly pool,
That heals the wounds o' care and dool,
And Pleasure is a wanton trout:
An ye drink it a', ye 'll find him out !

CHORUS

Then, guidwife, count the lawin,
The lawin, the lawin !
Then, guidwife, count the lawin,
And bring a coggie mair !

THERE 'LL NEVER BE PEACE
TILL JAMIE COMES HAME

Burns enclosed a copy (" a song of my late composition ") to Alexander Cunningham, 11th March, 1791: " You must know a beautiful Jacobite air — *There 'll Never be Peace till Jamie Comes Hame.* When political combustion ceases to be the object of Princes and Patriots it then, you know, becomes the lawful prey of Historians and Poets." No doubt there was an old Jacobite song with this title; but the air and the title were all that Burns knew, and no authentic copy of the thing itself is known to survive.

I

BY yon castle wa' at the close of the day,
I heard a man sing, tho' his head it was grey,
And as he was singing, the tears doon came: —
" There 'll never be peace till Jamie comes hame !

II

" The Church is in ruins, the State is in jars,
Delusions, oppressions, and murderous wars,
We dare na weel say 't, but we ken wha 's to blame —
There 'll never be peace till Jamie comes hame !

III

" My seven braw sons for Jamie drew sword,
But now I greet round their green beds in the yerd;
It brak the sweet heart o' my faithfu' auld dame —
There 'll never be peace till Jamie comes hame !

IV

" Now life is a burden that bows me down,
Sin I tint my bairns, and he tint his crown;
But till my last moments my words are the same —
There 'll never be peace till Jamie comes hame ! "

WHAT CAN A YOUNG LASSIE

I

WHAT can a young lassie,
What shall a young lassie,
What can a young lassie
Do wi' an auld man ?
Bad luck on the penny
That tempted my minnie
To sell her puir Jenny
For siller an' lan' !

II

He 's always compleenin
Frae mornin to eenin;
He hoasts and he hirples
The weary day lang;
He 's doylt and he 's dozin;
His blude it is frozen —
O, dreary 's the night
Wi' a crazy auld man !

III

He hums and he hankers,
He frets and he cankers,

I never can please him
    Do a' that I can.
He's peevish an' jealous
    Of a' the young fellows —
O, dool on the day
    I met wi' an auld man!

IV

My auld auntie Katie
Upon me taks pity,
I'll do my endeavour
    To follow her plan:
I'll cross him an' wrack him
Until I heartbreak him,
And then his auld brass
    Will buy me a new pan.

THE BONIE LAD THAT'S FAR AWA

It is supposed to refer to old Armour's extrusion of his daughter in the winter of 1788.

I

O, HOW can I be blythe and glad,
    Or how can I gang brisk and braw,
When the bonie lad that I lo'e best
    Is o'er the hills and far awa?

II

It's no the frosty winter wind,
    It's no the driving drift and snaw;
But ay the tear comes in my e'e
    To think on him that's far awa.

III

My father pat me frae his door,
    My friends they hae disown'd me a';
But I hae ane will tak my part —
    The bonie lad that's far awa.

IV

A pair o' glooves he bought to me,
    And silken snoods he gae me twa,
And I will wear them for his sake,
    The bonie lad that's far awa.

V

O, weary Winter soon will pass,
    And Spring will cleed the birken shaw,
And my sweet babie will be born,
    And he'll be hame that's far awa!

I DO CONFESS THOU ART SAE FAIR

"This song is altered from a poem by Sir Robert Ayton, private secretary to Mary and Anne, Queens of Scotland. The poem is to be found in *Watson's Collection of Scots Poems*, the earliest collection published in Scotland. I think that I have improved the simplicity of the sentiments by giving them a Scots dress." (R. B.)

I

I DO confess thou art sae fair,
    I wad been o'er the lugs in luve,
Had I na found the slightest prayer
    That lips could speak thy heart could muve.
I do confess thee sweet, but find
    Thou art so thriftless o' thy sweets,
Thy favours are the silly wind
    That kisses ilka thing it meets.

II

See yonder rosebud rich in dew,
    Amang its native briers sae coy,
How sune it tines its scent and hue,
    When pu'd and worn a common toy!
Sic fate ere lang shall thee betide,
    Tho' thou may gaily bloom awhile,
And sune thou shalt be thrown aside,
    Like onie common weed, an' vile.

SENSIBILITY HOW CHARMING

I

.SENSIBILITY how charming,
    Thou, my friend, can'st truly tell!
But Distress with horrors arming
    Thou alas! hast known too well!

II

Fairest flower, behold the lily
    Blooming in the sunny ray:
Let the blast sweep o'er the valley,
    See it prostrate in the clay.

III

Hear the woodlark charm the forest,
    Telling o'er his little joys;
But alas! a prey the surest
    To each pirate of the skies!

IV

Dearly bought the hidden treasure
   Finer feelings can bestow:
Chords that vibrate sweetest pleasure
   Thrill the deepest notes of woe.

YON WILD MOSSY MOUNTAINS

"The song alludes to a part of my private
history which is of no consequence to the
world to know." (R. B.)
   In July, 1793, he recommended it to Thom-
son as suitable to the air of *There'll Never be
Peace till Jamie Comes Hame*, if he objected
to the Jacobite sentiments of that song. It is
held by some to refer to Mary Campbell; but
Burns occasionally visited a peasant-girl near
Covington, Lanarkshire.

I

Yon wild mossy mountains sae lofty and
   wide,
That nurse in their bosom the youth o' the
   Clyde,
Where the grouse lead their coveys thro'
   the heather to feed,
And the shepherd tents his flock as he
   pipes on his reed.

II

Not Gowrie's rich valley nor Forth's sunny
   shores
To me hae the charms o' yon wild, mossy
   moors;
For there, by a lanely, sequesterèd stream,
Resides a sweet lassie, my thought and my
   dream.

III

Amang thae wild mountains shall still be
   my path,
Ilk stream foaming down its ain green,
   narrow strath;
For there wi' my lassie the lang day I rove,
While o'er us unheeded flie the swift hours
   o' love.

IV

She is not the fairest, altho' she is fair;
O' nice education but sma' is her share;
Her parentage humble as humble can be;
But I lo'e the dear lassie because she lo'es
   me.

V

To Beauty what man but maun yield him
   a prize,
In her armour of glances, and blushes, and
   sighs?
And when Wit and Refinement hae polish'd
   her darts,
They dazzle our een, as they flie to our
   hearts.

VI

But kindness, sweet kindness, in the fond-
   sparkling e'e
Has lustre outshining the diamond to me,
And the heart beating love as I'm clasp'd
   in her arms,
O, these are my lassie's all-conquering
   charms!

I HAE BEEN AT CROOKIEDEN

I

I hae been at Crookieden—
   My bonie laddie, Highland laddie!
Viewing Willie and his men—
   My bonie laddie, Highland laddie!
There our foes that burnt and slew—
   My bonie laddie, Highland laddie!
There at last they gat their due—
   My bonie laddie, Highland laddie!

II

Satan sits in his black neuk—
   My bonie laddie, Highland laddie!
Breaking sticks to roast the Duke—
   My bonie laddie, Highland laddie!
The bloody monster gae a yell—
   My bonie laddie, Highland laddie!
And loud the laugh gaed round a' Hell—
   My bonie laddie, Highland laddie!

IT IS NA, JEAN, THY BONIE FACE

I

It is na, Jean, thy bonie face
   Nor shape that I admire,
Altho' thy beauty and thy grace
   Might weel awauk desire.

Something in ilka part o' thee
To praise, to love, I find;
But, dear as is thy form to me,
Still dearer is thy mind.

II

Nae mair ungen'rous wish I hae,
Nor stronger in my breast,
Than, if I canna mak thee sae,
At least to see thee blest:
Content am I, if Heaven shall give
But happiness to thee,
And, as wi' thee I wish to live,
For thee I 'd bear to dee.

MY EPPIE MACNAB

I

O, saw ye my dearie, my Eppie Macnab?
O, saw ye my dearie, my Eppie Macnab?
"She 's down in the yard, she 's kissin
the laird,
She winna come hame to her ain Jock
Rab !"

II

O, come thy ways to me, my Eppie Mac-
nab !
O, come thy ways to me, my Eppie Mac-
nab !
Whate'er thou has done, be it late, be it
soon,
Thou 's welcome again to thy ain Jock Rab.

III

What says she, my dearie, my Eppie Mac-
nab ?
What says she, my dearie, my Eppie Mac-
nab ?
"She lets thee to wit that she has thee
forgot,
And for ever disowns thee, her ain Jock
Rab."

IV

O, had I ne'er seen thee, my Eppie Mac-
nab !
O, had I ne'er seen thee, my Eppie Mac-
nab !
As light as the air and as fause as thou 's
fair,
Thou 's broken the heart o' thy ain Jock
Rab !

WHA IS THAT AT MY BOWER DOOR

Without any manner of doubt, Burns's ori-
ginal was *Who But I, quoth Finlay,* "a new
song, much in request, sung with its own proper
tune."

I

"WHA is that at my bower door?"
"O, wha is it but Findlay !"
"Then gae your gate, ye 'se nae be here."
"Indeed maun I !" quo' Findlay.
"What mak ye, sae like a thief?"
"O, come and see !" quo' Findlay.
"Before the morn ye 'll work mischief?"
"Indeed will I !" quo' Findlay.

II

"Gif I rise and let you in" —
"Let me in !" quo' Findlay —
"Ye 'll keep me wauken wi' your din?"
"Indeed will I !" quo' Findlay.
"In my bower if ye should stay" —
"Let me stay !" quo' Findlay —
"I fear ye 'll bide till break o' day?"
"Indeed will I !" quo' Findlay.

III

"Here this night if ye remain" —
"I 'll remain !" quo' Findlay —
"I dread ye 'll learn the gate again?"
"Indeed will I !" quo' Findlay.
"What may pass within this bower"
("Let it pass !" quo' Findlay !)
"Ye maun conceal till your last hour" —
"Indeed will I !" quo' Findlay.

BONIE WEE THING

"Composed on my little idol — 'the charm-
ing lovely Davies.'" (R. B.)
Miss Debora Davies, daughter of Dr. Davies
of Tenby, Pembrokeshire, and a relative of
Captain Riddell, was jilted by one Captain
Delany, and died of a decline. See further,
ante, p. 187, Epigram *On Miss Davies,* and the
song *Lovely Davies, post,* p. 237.

CHORUS

Bonie wee thing, cannie wee thing,
Lovely wee thing, wert thou mine,
I wad wear thee in my bosom
Lest my jewel it should tine.

I

WISHFULLY I look and languish
  In that bonie face o' thine,
And my heart it stounds wi' anguish,
  Lest my wee thing be na mine.

II

Wit and Grace and Love and Beauty
  In ae constellation shine!
To adore thee is my duty,
  Goddess o' this soul o' mine!

CHORUS

Bonie wee thing, cannie wee thing,
  Lovely wee thing, wert thou mine,
I wad wear thee in my bosom
  Lest my jewel it should tine.

THE TITHER MORN

I

THE tither morn, when I forlorn
  Aneath an aik sat moaning,
I did na trow I'd see my jo
  Beside me gin the gloaming.
But he sae trig lap o'er the rig,
  And dawtingly did cheer me,
When I, what reck, did least expeck
  To see my lad sae near me!

II

His bonnet he a thought ajee
  Cock'd sprush when first he clasp'd
    me;
And I, I wat, wi' fainness grat,
  While in his grips he press'd me.
"Deil tak the war!" I late and air
  Hae wish'd since Jock departed;
But now as glad I'm wi' my lad
  As short syne broken-hearted.

III

Fu' aft at e'en, wi' dancing keen,
  When a' were blythe and merry,
I car'd na by, sae sad was I
  In absence o' my deary.
But praise be blest! my mind's at rest,
  I'm happy wi' my Johnie!
At kirk and fair. I'se ay be there,
  And be as canty's onie.

AE FOND KISS

The germ of *Ae Fond Kiss* is found in *The
Parting Kiss*, by Robert Dodsley (1703-1764),
which was set by Oswald: —

> " One fond kiss before we part,
>   Drop a Tear and bid adieu;
> Tho' we sever, my fond Heart
>   Till we meet shall pant for you," etc.

It finishes with a repeat of the two first lines.

I

AE fond kiss, and then we sever!
Ae farewell, and then forever!
Deep in heart-wrung tears I'll pledge thee,
Warring sighs and groans I'll wage thee.
Who shall say that Fortune grieves him,
While the star of hope she leaves him?
Me, nae cheerfu' twinkle lights me,
Dark despair around benights me.

II

I'll ne'er blame my partial fancy:
Naething could resist my Nancy!
But to see her was to love her,
Love but her, and love for ever.
Had we never lov'd sae kindly,
Had we never lov'd sae blindly,
Never met — or never parted —
We had ne'er been broken-hearted.

III

Fare-the-weel, thou first and fairest!
Fare-the-weel, thou best and dearest!
Thine be ilka joy and treasure,
Peace, Enjoyment, Love and Pleasure!
Ae fond kiss, and then we sever!
Ae farewell, alas, for ever!
Deep in heart-wrung tears I'll pledge thee,
Warring sighs and groans I'll wage thee.

LOVELY DAVIES

For Miss Davies, see *ante*, p. 236, Prefatory
Note to *Bonie Wee Thing*.

I

O, HOW shall I, unskilfu', try
  The Poet's occupation?
The tunefu' Powers, in happy hours
  That whisper inspiration,

Even they maun dare an effort mair
　Than aught they ever gave us,
Ere they rehearse in equal verse
　The charms o' lovely Davies.

II

Each eye, it cheers, when she appears,
　Like Phœbus in the morning,
When past the shower, and every flower
　The garden is adorning !
As the wretch looks o'er Siberia's shore,
　When winter-bound the wave is,
Sae droops our heart, when we maun
　　part
Frae charming, lovely Davies.

III

Her smile 's a gift frae 'boon the lift
　That maks us mair than princes.
A sceptred hand, a king's command,
　Is in her darting glances.
The man in arms 'gainst female charms,
　Even he her willing slave is:
He hugs his chain, and owns the reign
　Of conquering lovely Davies.

IV

My Muse to dream of such a theme
　Her feeble powers surrenders;
The eagle's gaze alone surveys
　The sun's meridian splendours.
I wad in vain essay the strain —
　The deed too daring brave is !
I 'll drap the lyre, and, mute, admire
　The charms o' lovely Davies.

THE WEARY PUND O' TOW

CHORUS

The weary pund, the weary pund,
　The weary pund o' tow !
I think my wife will end her life
　Before she spin her tow.

I

I BOUGHT my wife a stane o' lint
　As guid as e'er did grow,
And a' that she has made o' that
　Is ae puir pund o' tow.

II

There sat a bottle in a bole
　Beyont the ingle low;
And ay she took the tither souk
　To drouk the stourie tow.

III

Quoth I : — " For shame, ye dirty dame,
　Gae spin your tap o' tow ! "
She took the rock, and wi' a knock
　She brake it o'er my pow.

IV

At last her feet — I sang to see 't ! —
　Gaed foremost o'er the knowe,
And or I wad anither jad,
　I 'll wallop in a tow.

CHORUS

The weary pund, the weary pund,
　The weary pund o' tow !
I think my wife will end her life
　Before she spin her tow.

I HAE A WIFE O' MY AIN

Made a few days after his marriage.

I

I HAE a wife o' my ain,
　I 'll partake wi' naebody:
I 'll take cuckold frae nane,
　I 'll gie cuckold to naebody.

II

I hae a penny to spend,
　There — thanks to naebody !
I hae naething to lend,
　I 'll borrow frae naebody.

III

I am naebody's lord,
　I 'll be slave to naebody.
I hae a guid braid sword,
　I 'll tak dunts frae naebody.

IV

I 'll be merry and free,
　I 'll be sad for naebody.
Naebody cares for me,
　I care for naebody.

WHEN SHE CAM BEN, SHE BOBBED

I

O, WHEN she cam ben, she bobbèd fu'
 law!
O, when she cam ben, she bobbèd fu'
 law!
And when she cam' ben, she kiss'd Cock-
 pen,
 And syne she deny'd she did it at a'!

II

And was na Cockpen right saucy witha'?
And was na Cockpen right saucy witha',
In leaving the dochter o' a lord,
 And kissin a collier lassie an' a'?

III

O, never look down, my lassie, at a'!
O, never look down, my lassie, at a'!
Thy lips are as sweet, and thy figure com-
 plete,
 As the finest dame in castle or ha'.

IV

" Tho' thou hast nae silk, and holland sae
 sma',
Tho' thou hast nae silk, and holland sae
 sma',
Thy coat and thy sark are thy ain handy-
 wark,
 And Lady Jean was never sae braw."

O, FOR ANE-AND-TWENTY, TAM

CHORUS

An' O, for ane-and-twenty, Tam !
 And hey, sweet ane-and-twenty, Tam !
I 'll learn my kin a rattlin sang
 An I saw ane-and-twenty, Tam.

I

THEY snool me sair, and haud me down,
 And gar me look like bluntie, Tam;
But three short years will soon wheel
 roun' —
 And then comes ane-and-twenty, Tam !

II

A gleib o' lan', a claut o' gear
 Was left me by my auntie, Tam.

At kith or kin I needna spier,
 An I saw ane-and-twenty, Tam.

III

They 'll hae me wed a wealthy coof,
 Tho' I mysel hae plenty, Tam;
But hear'st thou, laddie — there 's my loof:
 I 'm thine at ane-and-twenty, Tam !

CHORUS

An' O, for ane-and-twenty, Tam !
 And hey, sweet ane-and-twenty, Tam !
I 'll learn my kin a rattlin sang
 An I saw ane-and-twenty, Tam.

O, KENMURE 'S ON AND AWA, WILLIE

William Gordon, sixth Viscount Kenmure,
took up the Jacobite cause in 1715, — mainly
through the persuasion of his wife, Mary,
daughter of Robert Dalyell, sixth Earl of Carn-
wath, — and got Mar's commission to command
the forces in the south. After divers ineffec-
tive moves he passed into England, and, being
taken prisoner at Preston on 14th November,
was beheaded on Towerhill on 24th February,
1716.

I

O, KENMURE 's on and awa, Willie,
 O, Kenmure 's on and awa !
An' Kenmure 's lord 's the bravest lord
 That ever Galloway saw !

II

Success to Kenmure's band, Willie,
 Success to Kenmure's band !
There 's no a heart that fears a Whig
 That rides by Kenmure's hand.

III

Here 's Kenmure's health in wine, Willie,
 Here 's Kenmure's health in wine !
There ne'er was a coward o' Kenmure's
 blude,
 Nor yet o' Gordon's line.

IV

O, Kenmure's lads are men, Willie,
 O, Kenmure's lads are men !
Their hearts and swords are metal true,
 And that their faes shall ken.

V

They 'll live or die wi' fame, Willie,
    They 'll live or die wi' fame !
But soon wi' sounding victorie
    May Kenmure's lord come hame !

VI

Here 's him that 's far awa, Willie,
    Here 's him that 's far awa !
And here 's the flower that I lo'e best —
    The rose that 's like the snaw !

O, LEEZE ME ON MY SPINNIN-
WHEEL

One of the best and the most Burnsian of
Burns's vamps, this charming song was no
doubt suggested by *The Loving Lass and Spin-
ning-wheel* in Ramsay's *Tea-Table Miscellany*,
which Ramsay must have imitated from an old
blackletter broadside (Pepys Collection), "*The
Bonny Scott and the Yielding Lass*, to an excel-
lent new Tune : " —

> " As I sate at my spinning-wheel
>   A bonny lad there passèd by,
> I keen'd him round, and I lik'd him weel,
>   Geud faith he had a bony eye :
>   My heart new panting 'gan to feel,
>   But still I turned my spinning-wheel," etc.

I

O, LEEZE me on my spinnin-wheel !
And leeze me on my rock and reel,
Frae tap to tae that cleeds me bien,
And haps me fiel and warm at e'en !
I 'll set me down, and sing and spin,
While laigh descends the summer sun,
Blest wi' content, and milk and meal —
O, leeze me on my spinnin-wheel !

II

On ilka hand the burnies trot,
And meet below my theekit cot.
The scented birk and hawthorn white
Across the pool their arms unite,
Alike to screen the birdie's nest
And little fishes' caller rest.
The sun blinks kindly in the biel,
Where blythe I turn my spinnin-wheel.

III

On lofty aiks the cushats wail,
And Echo cons the doolfu' tale.

The lintwhites in the hazel braes,
Delighted, rival ither's lays.
The craik amang the claver hay,
The paitrick whirrin o'er the ley,
The swallow jinkin round my shiel,
Amuse me at my spinnin-wheel.

IV

Wi' sma to sell and less to buy,
Aboon distress, below envý,
O, wha wad leave this humble state
For a' the pride of a' the great ?
Amid their flaring, idle toys,
Amid their cumbrous, dinsome joys,
Can they the peace and pleasure feel
Of Bessy at her spinnin-wheel ?

MY COLLIER LADDIE

"I do not know a blyther old song than
this."   (R. B.)

I

" O, WHARE live ye, my bonie lass,
    And tell me how they ca' ye ? "
" My name," she says, " is Mistress Jean,
    And I follow the collier laddie."

II

" O, see you not yon hills and dales
    The sun shines on sae brawlie ?
They a' are mine, and they shall be thine,
    Gin ye 'll leave your collier laddie !

III

" An' ye shall gang in gay attire,
    Weel buskit up sae gaudy,
And ane to wait on every hand,
    Gin ye 'll leave your collier laddie ! "

IV

" Tho' ye had a' the sun shines on,
    And the earth conceals sae lowly,
I wad turn my back on you and it a',
    And embrace my collier laddie.

V

" I can win my five pennies in a day,
    An' spend it at night fu' brawlie,
And make my bed in the collier's neuk
    And lie down wi' my collier laddie.

VI

" Loove for loove is the bargain for me,
　Tho' the wee cot-house should haud me,
And the warld before me to win my
　　　bread —
　And fair fa' my collier laddie ! "

NITHSDALE'S WELCOME HAME

Lady Winifred Maxwell Constable (1735–
1801) was sole surviving child of William Lord
Maxwell, son of William, fifth Earl of Niths-
dale, who was sentenced to decapitation on
Towerhill, 24th February, 1716, for his share in
the Fifteen, but escaped the night before the
execution.　She married William Haggerston
Constable of Everinghame, and began rebuild-
ing the old family mansion, Terreagles, or
Terregles, Kirkcudbrightshire, in 1789.　Burns
has stated, for the sake of " *vive la bagatelle*,"
that his Jacobitism was mostly matter of sport.
But, in a letter of the 16th December, 1789,
he, as Sir Walter put it, plays " high Jacobite
to that singular old curmudgeon Lady Wini-
fred Constable : " roundly asserting that they
were " common sufferers in a cause where even
to be unfortunate is glorious, the cause of
heroic loyalty ; " and that his forefathers, like
her own, had shaken " hands with ruin for
what they esteemed the cause of their King
and country."

I

The noble Maxwells and their powers
　Are coming o'er the border;
And they 'll gae big Terreagles' towers,
　And set them a' in order;
And they declare Terreagles fair,
　For their abode they choose it:
There 's no a heart in a' the land
　But 's lighter at the news o't !

II

Tho' stars in skies may disappear,
　And angry tempests gather,
The happy hour may soon be near
　That brings us pleasant weather;
·The weary night o' care and grief
　May hae a joyfu' morrow;
So dawning day has brought relief —
　Fareweel our night o' sorrow !

IN SIMMER, WHEN THE HAY
WAS MAWN

I

In simmer, when the hay was mawn
　And corn wav'd green in ilka field,
While claver blooms white o'er the ley,
　And roses blaw in ilka field,
Blythe Bessie in the milking shiel
Says: — " I 'll be wed, come o't what will ! "
　Out spake a dame in wrinkled eild: —
" O' guid advisement comes nae ill.

II

" It 's ye hae wooers monie ane,
　And lassie, ye 're but young, ye ken !
Then wait a wee, and cannie wale
　A routhie butt, a routhie ben.
There Johnie o' the Buskie-Glen,
　Fu' is his barn, fu' is his byre.
Tak this frae me, my bonie hen:
It 's plenty beets the luver's fire ! "

III

" For Johnie o' the Buskie-Glen
　I dinna care a single flie:
He lo'es sae weel his craps and kye,
　He has nae love to spare for me.
But blythe 's the blink o' Robie's e'e,
　And weel I wat he lo'es me dear:
Ae blink o' him I wad na gie
For Buskie-Glen and a' his gear."

IV

" O thoughtless lassie, life 's a faught !
　The canniest gate, the strife is sair.
But ay fu'-han't is fechtin best:
　A hungry care 's an unco care.
But some will spend, and some will spare,
　An' wilfu' folk maun hae their will.
Syne as ye brew, my maiden fair,
Keep mind that ye maun drink the yill ! "

V

" O, gear will buy me rigs o' land,
　And gear will buy me sheep and kye !
Rut the tender heart o' leesome loove
　The gowd and siller canna buy !
We may be poor, Robie and I;
　Light is the burden luve lays on;
Content and loove brings peace and joy:
What mair hae Queens upon a throne ? "

FAIR ELIZA

Two copies in Burns's hand are in the Hastie Collection. In the earlier the lady's name is Robina. According to Stenhouse, she was "a young lady to whom Mr. Hunter, a friend of Mr. Burns, was much attached." Hunter died shortly after going to Jamaica. The verses appear, however, to have been written on some lady suggested by Johnson: "So much for your Robina — how do you like the verses? I assure you I have tasked my muse to the top of her performing. However, the song will not sing to your tune in Macdonald's Collection of Highland Airs, which is much admired in this country; I intended the verses to be sung to that air. It is in page 17th and No. 112. There is another air in the same collection, an Argyleshire Air, which, with a trifling alteration, will do charmingly." (R. B. to Johnson.)
Johnson set the words to both these tunes.

I

Turn again, thou fair Eliza !
 Ae kind blink before we part !
Rew on thy despairing lover —
 Canst thou break his faithfu' heart ?
Turn again, thou fair Eliza !
 If to love thy heart denies,
For pity hide the cruel sentence
 Under friendship's kind disguise !

II

Thee, dear maid, hae I offended ?
 The offence is loving thee.
Canst thou wreck his peace for ever,
 Wha for thine wad gladly die ?
While the life beats in my bosom,
 Thou shalt mix in ilka throe.
Turn again, thou lovely maiden,
 Ae sweet smile on me bestow !

III

Not the bee upon the blossom
 In the pride o' sinny noon,
Not the little sporting fairy
 All beneath the simmer moon,
Not the Poet in the moment
 Fancy lightens in his e'e,
Kens the pleasure, feels the rapture,
 That thy presence gies to me.

YE JACOBITES BY NAME

I

Ye Jacobites by name,
 Give an ear, give an ear !
Ye Jacobites by name,
 Give an ear !
Ye Jacobites by name,
Your fautes I will proclaim,
Your doctrines I maun blame —
 You shall hear !

II

What is Right, and what is Wrang,
 By the law, by the law ?
What is Right, and what is Wrang,
 By the law ?
What is Right, and what is Wrang ?
A short sword and a lang,
A weak arm and a strang
 For to draw !

III

What makes heroic strife
 Famed afar, famed afar ?
What makes heroic strife
 Famed afar ?
What makes heroic strife ?
To whet th' assassin's knife,
Or hunt a Parent's life
 Wi' bluidy war !

IV

Then let your schemes alone,
 In the State, in the State !
Then let your schemes alone,
 In the State !
Then let your schemes alone,
Adore the rising sun,
And leave a man undone
 To his fate !

THE POSIE

" *The Posie* in the *Museum* is my composition : the air was taken down from Mrs. Burns's voice. It is well known in the west country ; but the old words are trash." (Burns to Thomson, 19th October, 1794.) " It appears evident to me that Oswald composed his *Roslin Castle* on the modulation of this air. . . . The old verses to which it was sung, when I took down the notes from a country girl's voice, had no great merit. The following is a specimen : —

> " ' There was a pretty May, and a milkin she went,
> Wi' her red rosy cheeks, and her coal-black hair;
> And she had met a young man comin o'er the bent,
> With a double and adieu to the fair May,' etc.

and so on for four other stanzas." (R. B.)

I

O, LUVE will venture in where it daur na
    weel be seen !
O, luve will venture in, where wisdom
    ance hath been !
But I will doun yon river rove amang the
    wood sae green,
    And a' to pu' a posie to my ain dear
      May !

II

The primrose I will pu', the firstling o'
    the year,
And I will pu' the pink, the emblem o' my
    dear,
For she 's the pink o' womankind, and
    blooms without a peer —
    And a' to be a posie to my ain dear
      May !

III

I 'll pu' the budding rose when Phœbus
    peeps in view,
For it 's like a baumy kiss o' her sweet,
    bonie mou.
The hayacinth 's for constancy wi' its un-
    changing blue —
    And a' to be a posie to my ain dear
      May !

IV

The lily it is pure, and the lily it is fair,
And in her lovely bosom I 'll place the lily
    there.
The daisy 's for simplicity and unaffected
    air —
    And a' to be a posie to my ain dear
      May !

V

The hawthorn I will pu', wi' its locks o'
    siller gray,
Where, like an agèd man, it stands at
    break o' day;
But the songster's nest within the bush I
    winna tak away —
    And a' to be a posie to my ain dear
      May !

VI

The woodbine I will pu' when the e'ening
    star is near,
And the diamond draps o' dew shall be
    her een sae clear !
The violet 's for modesty, which weel she
    fa's to wear —
    And a' to be a posie to my ain dear
      May !

VII

I 'll tie the posie round wi' the silken band
    o' luve,
And I 'll place it in her breast, and I 'll
    swear by a' above,
That to my latest draught o' life the band
    shall ne'er remove,
    And this will be a posie to my ain
      dear May !

THE BANKS O' DOON

"An Ayrshire legend," according to Allan Cunningham, "says the heroine of this affecting song was Pegg Kennedy of Daljarroch;" and Chambers also supposed the ballad to be an allegory of the same "unhappy love-tale." See *ante*, p. 201, Prefatory Note to *Young Peggy*, but even if the "love-tale" were then known, it was not then "unhappy."

For other sets, *Sweet are the Banks* and *Ye Flowery Banks*, see *post*, pp. 309, 310.

I

YE banks and braes o' bonie Doon,
    How can ye bloom sae fresh and fair ?
How can ye chant, ye little birds,
    And I sae weary fu' o' care !
Thou 'll break my heart, thou warbling bird,
    That wantons thro' the flowering thorn !
Thou minds me o' departed joys,
    Departed never to return.

II

Aft hae I rov'd by bonie Doon
    To see the rose and woodbine twine,
And ilka bird sang o' its luve,
    And fondly sae did I o' mine.
Wi' lightsome heart I pu'd a rose,
    Fu' sweet upon its thorny tree !
And my fause luver staw my rose —
    But ah ! he left the thorn wi' me.

WILLIE WASTLE

The heroine is said to have been the wife of a farmer who lived near Ellisland. A cottage in Peeblesshire, which stood where a muirland burn, the Logan Water, joins the Tweed, was known by the name of Linkumdoddie, but probably it was so named after Burns wrote his song. The earliest authenticated appearance of Willie Wastle in rhyme is in Cockburn's (Governor of Dunse Castle) reply to Colonel Fenwick: —

> "I, Willie Wastle,
>   Am in my castle ;
>   All the dogges in the towne
>   Shall not dinge me downe."

This same rhyme was, and is, used in the mimic warfare of Scottish children; but whether they were the inspirers of Cockburn, or he of them, it is impossible to affirm.

I

WILLIE WASTLE dwalt on Tweed,
  The spot they ca'd it Linkumdoddie.
Willie was a wabster guid
  Could stown a clue wi' onie bodie.
He had a wife was dour and din,
  O, Tinkler Maidgie was her mither !
Sic a wife as Willie had,
  I wad na gie a button for her.

II

She has an e'e (she has but ane),
  The cat has twa the very colour,
Five rusty teeth, forbye a stump,
  A clapper-tongue wad deave a miller ;
A whiskin beard about her mou,
  Her nose and chin they threaten ither:
Sic a wife as Willie had,
  I wad na gie a button for her.

III

She 's bow-hough'd, she 's hem-shin'd,
  Ae limpin leg a hand-breed shorter;
She 's twisted right, she 's twisted left,
  To balance fair in ilka quarter;
She has a hump upon her breast,
  The twin o' that upon her shouther:
Sic a wife as Willie had,
  I wad na gie a button for her.

IV

Auld baudrans by the ingle sits,
  An' wi' her loof her face a-washin;
But Willie's wife is nae sae trig,
  She dights her grunzie wi' a hushion;
Her walie nieves like midden-creels,
  Her face wad fyle the Logan Water:
Sic a wife as Willie had,
  I wad na gie a button for her.

LADY MARY ANN

Burns got the germ of his song from a fragment in the Herd MS. "Lady Mary Ann" and "Young Charlie Cochrane" are his own, as are the last three stanzas of the ballad.

I

O, LADY Mary Ann looks o'er the Castle
  wa',
She saw three bonie boys playing at the ba',
The youngest he was the flower amang
  them a' —
  My bonie laddie 's young, but he 's
  growin yet !

II

"O father, O father, an ye think it fit,
We 'll send him a year to the college yet;
We 'll sew a green ribbon round about his
  hat,
  And that will let them ken he 's to
  marry yet ! "

III

Lady Mary Ann was a flower in the dew,
Sweet was its smell and bonie was its hue,
And the longer it blossom'd the sweeter it
  grew,
  For the lily in the bud will be bonier yet.

IV

Young Charlie Cochran was the sprout of
  an aik;
Bonie and bloomin and straucht was its
  make;
The sun took delight to shine for its sake,
  And it will be the brag o' the forest yet.

V

The simmer is gane when the leaves they
  were green,
And the days are awa that we hae seen;
But far better days I trust will come again,
  For my bonie laddie 's young, but he 's
  growin yet.

SUCH A PARCEL OF ROGUES IN A NATION

I

FAREWEEL to a' our Scottish fame,
    Fareweel our ancient glory !
Fareweel ev'n to the Scottish name
    Sae famed in martial story !
Now Sark rins over Solway sands,
    An' Tweed rins to the ocean,
To mark where England's province stands —
    Such a parcel of rogues in a nation !

II

What force or guile could not subdue
    Thro' many warlike ages
Is wrought now by a coward few
    For hireling traitor's wages.
The English steel we could disdain,
    Secure in valour's station;
But English gold has been our bane —
    Such a parcel of rogues in a nation !

III

O, would, or I had seen the day
    That Treason thus could sell us,
My auld grey head had lien in clay
    Wi' Bruce and loyal Wallace !
But pith and power, till my last hour
    I 'll mak this declaration: —
" We 're bought and sold for English gold " —
    Such a parcel of rogues in a nation !

KELLYBURN BRAES

The Kelly burn (*i. e.* brook) forms the northern boundary of Ayrshire, and the ballad has no connexion with Nithsdale or Galloway.

I

THERE lived a carl in Kellyburn Braes
    (Hey and the rue grows bonie wi' thyme !),
And he had a wife was the plague o' his days
    (And the thyme it is wither'd, and rue is in prime !).

II

Ae day as the carl gaed up the lang glen
    (Hey and the rue grows bonie wi' thyme !),
He met wi' the Devil, says: — " How do you fen ?"
    (And the thyme it is wither'd, and rue is in prime !).

III

" I 've got a bad wife, sir, that 's a' my complaint
    (Hey and the rue grows bonie wi' thyme !),
For, saving your presence, to her ye 're a saint."
    (And the thyme it is wither'd, and rue is in prime !).

IV

" It's neither your stot nor your staig I shall crave
    (Hey and the rue grows bonnie wi' thyme !),
But gie me your wife, man, for her I must have "
    (And the thyme it is wither'd, and rue is in prime !).

V

" O welcome most kindly ! " the blythe carl said
    (Hey and the rue grows bonie wi' thyme !),
" But if ye can match her ye 're waur than ye 're ca'd "
    (And the thyme it is wither'd, and rue is in prime !).

VI

The Devil has got the auld wife on his back
    (Hey and the rue grows bonie wi' thyme !),
And like a poor pedlar he 's carried his pack
    (And the thyme it is wither'd, and rue is in prime !).

VII

He 's carried her hame to his ain hallan-door
    (Hey and the rue grows bonie wi' thyme !),

Syne bade her gae in for a bitch and a
  whore
  (And the thyme it is wither'd, and rue is
  in prime !).

VIII

Then straight he makes fifty, the pick o'
  his band
  (Hey and the rue grows bonie wi'
  thyme !),
Turn out on her guard, in the clap o' a
  hand
  (And the thyme it is wither'd, and rue is
  in prime !).

IX

The carlin gaed thro' them like onie wud
  bear
  (Hey and the rue grows bonie wi'
  thyme !):
Whae'er she gat hands on cam near her
  nae mair
  (And the thyme it is wither'd, and rue is
  in prime !).

X

A reekit wee deevil looks over the wa
  (Hey and the rue grows bonie wi'
  thyme !): —
" O help, maister, help, or she 'll ruin us
  a' ! "
  (And the thyme it is wither'd, and rue
  is in prime !).

XI

The Devil he swore by the edge o' his
  knife
  (Hey and the rue grows bonie wi'
  thyme !),
He pitied the man that was tied to a wife
  (And the thyme it is wither'd, and rue is
  in prime !).

XII

The Devil he swore by the kirk and the bell
  (Hey and the rue grows bonie wi'
  thyme !),
He was not in wedlock, thank Heav'n, but
  in Hell
  (And the thyme it is wither'd, and rue is
  in prime !).

XIII

Then Satan has travell'd again wi' his pack
  (Hey and the rue grows bonie wi'
  thyme !),

And to her auld husband he 's carried her
  back
  (And the thyme it is wither'd, and rue is
  in prime !).

XIV

" I hae been a Devil the feck o' my life
  (Hey and the rue grows bonie wi'
  thyme !),
But ne'er was in Hell till I met wi' a
  wife "
  (And the thyme it is wither'd, and rue is
  in prime !).

THE SLAVE'S LAMENT

I

IT was in sweet Senegal
That my foes did me enthral
  For the lands of Virginia, -ginia, O !
Torn from that lovely shore,
And must never see it more,
  And alas ! I am weary, weary, O !

II

All on that charming coast
Is no bitter snow and frost,
  Like the lands of Virginia, -ginia, O !
There streams for ever flow,
And the flowers for ever blow,
  And alas ! I am weary, weary, O !

III

The burden I must bear,
While the cruel scourge I fear,
  In the lands of Virginia, -ginia, O !
And I think on friends most dear
With the bitter, bitter tear,
  And alas ! I am weary, weary, O !

THE SONG OF DEATH

I

FAREWELL, thou fair day, thou green earth,
  and ye skies,
  Now gay with the broad setting sun !
Farewell, loves and friendships, ye dear
  tender ties —
  Our race of existence is run !

Thou grim King of Terrors ! thou Life's
gloomy foe,
Go, frighten the coward and slave !
Go, teach them to tremble, fell tyrant, but
know,
No terrors hast thou to the brave !

II

Thou strik'st the dull peasant — he sinks
in the dark,
Nor saves e'en the wreck of a name !
Thou strik'st the young hero — a glorious
mark,
He falls in the blaze of his fame !
In the field of proud honour, our swords in
our hands,
Our king and our country to save,
While victory shines on Life's last ebbing
sands,
O, who would not die with the brave ?

SWEET AFTON

Flow Gently, Sweet Afton was sent to Mrs.
Dunlop, 5th February, 1789, and in the enclos-
ing letter Burns explicitly declares that it was
written for Johnson's *Musical Museum*, as a
" compliment " to the " small river Afton that
flows into Nith, near New Cumnock, which
has some charming wild romantic scenery on
its banks," etc. It seems certain, therefore,
that the name Mary was introduced *euphoniæ
gratiâ*, or at least that the heroine — if heroine
there were — was another than Mary Camp-
bell. Also, the song was clearly suggested by
one of David Garrick's, to the Avon, which
Burns saw in *A Select Collection of English
Songs* (London, 1763).

I

FLOW gently, sweet Afton, among thy
green braes !
Flow gently, I 'll sing thee a song in thy
praise !
My Mary 's asleep by thy murmuring
stream —
Flow gently, sweet Afton, disturb not her
dream !

II

Thou stock dove whose echo resounds thro'
the glen,
Ye wild whistling blackbirds in yon thorny
den,

Thou green-crested lapwing, thy screaming
forbear —
I charge you, disturb not my slumbering
fair !

III

How lofty, sweet Afton, thy neighbouring
hills,
Far mark'd with the courses of clear, wind-
ing rills !
There daily I wander, as noon rises high,
My flocks and my Mary's sweet cot in my
eye.

IV

How pleasant thy banks and green vallies
below,
Where wild in the woodlands the primroses
blow
There oft, as mild Ev'ning weeps over the
lea,
The sweet-scented birk shades my Mary
and me.

V

Thy crystal stream, Afton, how lovely it
glides,
And winds by the cot where my Mary
resides !
How wanton thy waters her snowy feet
lave,
As, gathering sweet flowerets, she stems thy
clear wave !

VI

Flow gently, sweet Afton, among thy green
braes !
Flow gently, sweet river, the theme of my
lays !
My Mary 's asleep by thy murmuring
stream —
Flow gently, sweet Afton, disturb not her
dream !

BONIE BELL

I

THE smiling Spring comes in rejoicing,
And surly Winter grimly flies.
Now crystal clear are the falling waters,
And bonie blue are the sunny skies.

Fresh o'er the mountains breaks forth the
    morning,
The ev'ning gilds the ocean's swell:
All creatures joy in the sun's returning,
    And I rejoice in my bonie Bell.

II

The flowery Spring leads sunny summer,
    The yellow Autumn presses near;
Then in his turn comes gloomy Winter,
    Till smiling Spring again appear.
Thus seasons dancing, life advancing,
    Old Time and Nature their changes tell;
But never ranging, still unchanging,
    I adore my bonie Bell.

THE GALLANT WEAVER

Supposed by some to refer to Armour's visit
to Paisley in the spring of 1786, [after the
quarrel, and to an unauthenticated story of a
flirtation with a weaver named Wilson. The
song *To the Weaver's Gin Ye Go* (ante, p. 202)
is also referred to the same episode, but with
little ground.] The Cart flows past Paisley.
A song, *The Lass of Cartside*, which we have
found in an old Dumfries chap, may or may
not have suggested this one to Burns : —

    " Where Cart gently glides thro' the vale,
      And nature, in beauty arrayed,
    Perfumes the sweet whispering gale,
      That wantons in every green shade," etc.

[As published in Thomson (vol. i.), the song
is of a gallant *sailor*.]

I

WHERE Cart rins rowin to the sea
By monie a flower and spreading tree,
There lives a lad, the lad for me —
    He is a gallant weaver!
O, I had wooers aught or nine,
They gied me rings and ribbons fine,
And I was fear'd my heart wad tine,
    And I gied it to the weaver.

II

My daddie sign'd my tocher-band
To gie the lad that has the land;
But to my heart I'll add my hand,
    And give it to the weaver.
While birds rejoice in leafy bowers,
While bees delight in opening flowers,
While corn grows green in summer showers,
    I love my gallant weaver.

HEY, CA' THRO'

CHORUS

Hey, ca' thro', ca' thro',
    For we hae mickle ado !
Hey, ca' thro', ca' thro',
    For we hae mickle ado !

I

UP wi' the carls of Dysart
    And the lads o' Buckhaven,
And the kimmers o' Largo
    And the lasses o' Leven !

II

We hae tales to tell,
    And we hae sangs to sing;
We hae pennies to spend,
    And we hae pints to bring.

III

We'll live a' our days,
    And them that comes behin',
Let them do the like,
    And spend the gear they win !

CHORUS

Hey, ca' thro', ca' thro',
    For we hae mickle ado !
Hey, ca' thro', ca' thro',
    For we hae mickle ado !

O, CAN YE LABOUR LEA

The first stanza and the chorus are well-nigh
word for word from the *Merry Muses* set,
which, however, may have been retouched by
Burns. The rest appears to be his own ; though
in one of his letters he describes his stanza iii.
as a favourite song "o' his mither's."

CHORUS

O, can ye labour lea, young man,
    O, can ye labour lea ?
Gae back the gate ye came again —
    Ye 'se never scorn me !

I

I FEE'D a man at Martinmas
    Wi' airle-pennies three;
But a' the faut I had to him
    He cauldna labour lea.

II

O, clappin 's guid in Febarwar,
  An' kissin 's sweet in May;
But what signifies a young man's love,
  An't dinna last for ay ?

III

O, kissin is the key o' love
  An' clappin is the lock;
An' makin of 's the best thing
  That e'er a young thing got !

CHORUS

O, can ye labour lea, young man,
  O, can ye labour lea ?
Gae back the gate ye came again —
  Ye 'se never scorn me !

THE DEUK 'S DANG O'ER MY DADDIE

I

THE bairns gat out wi' an unco shout: —
  "The deuk 's dang o'er my daddie, O !"
"The fien-ma-care," quo' the feirrie auld wife,
  "He was but a paidlin body, O !
He paidles out, and he paidles in,
  An' he paidles late and early, O !
This seven lang years I hae lien by his side,
  An' he is but a fusionless carlie, O !"

II

"O, haud your tongue, my feirrie auld wife,
  O, haud your tongue, now Nansie, O !
I 've seen the day, and sae hae ye,
  Ye wad na been sae donsie, O.
I 've seen the day ye butter'd my brose,
  And cuddl'd me late and early, O;
But downa-do 's come o'er me now,
  And och, I find it sairly, O !"

SHE 'S FAIR AND FAUSE

The general allusion is to the girl who jilted Alexander Cunningham (see *ante*, p. 95, Prefatory Note to *Song : Anna, Thy Charms;* and p. 140, Prefatory Note to *To Alexander Cunningham*).

I

SHE 's fair and fause that causes my smart;
  I lo'ed her meikle and lang;
She 's broken her vow, she 's broken my heart;
  And I may e'en gae hang.
A coof cam in wi' routh o' gear,
  And I hae tint my dearest dear;
But Woman is but warld's gear,
  Sae let the bonie lass gang !

II

Whae'er ye be that Woman love,
  To this be never blind:
Nae ferlie 't is, tho' fickle she prove,
  A woman has 't by kind.
O Woman lovely, Woman fair,
An angel form 's faun to thy share,
'T wad been o'er meikle to gien thee mair ! . . .
  I mean an angel mind.

THE DEIL'S AWA WI' TH' EXCISEMAN

CHORUS

The Deil 's awa, the Deil 's awa,
  The Deil 's awa wi' th' Exciseman !
He 's danc'd awa, he 's danc'd awa,
  He 's danc'd awa wi' th' Exciseman !

I

THE Deil cam fiddlin thro' the town,
  And danc'd awa wi' th' Exciseman,
And ilka wife cries: — "Auld Mahoun,
  I wish you luck o' the prize, man !

II

"We 'll mak our maut, and we 'll brew our drink,
  We 'll laugh, sing, and rejoice, man,
And monie braw thanks to the meikle black Deil,
  That danc'd awa wi' th' Exciseman."

III

There 's threesome reels, there 's foursome reels,
  There 's hornpipes and strathspeys, man,
But the ae best dance e'er cam to the land
  Was *The Deil 's Awa wi' th' Exciseman.*

CHORUS

The Deil's awa, the Deil's awa,
  The Deil's awa wi' th' Exciseman !
He's danc'd awa, he's danc'd awa,
  He's danc'd awa wi' th' Exciseman !

THE LOVELY LASS OF INVER-
NESS

I

THE lovely lass of Inverness,
  Nae joy nor pleasure can she see;
For e'en to morn she cries "Alas !"
  And ay the saut tear blin's her e'e: —

II

"Drumossie moor, Drumossie day —
  A waefu' day it was to me !
For there I lost my father dear,
  My father dear and brethren three.

III

"Their winding-sheet the bluidy clay,
  Their graves are growin green to see,
And by them lies the dearest lad
  That ever blest a woman's e'e.

IV

"Now wae to thee, thou cruel lord,
  A bluidy man I trow thou be,
For monie a heart thou hast made sair
  That ne'er did wrang to thine or thee !"

A RED, RED ROSE

I

O, MY luve is like a red, red rose,
  That's newly sprung in June.
O, my luve is like the melodie,
  That's sweetly play'd in tune.

II

As fair art thou, my bonie lass,
  So deep in luve am I,
And I will luve thee still, my dear,
  Till a' the seas gang dry.

III

Till a' the seas gang dry, my dear,
  And the rocks melt wi' the sun !

And I will luve thee still, my dear,
  While the sands o' life shall run.

IV

And fare thee weel, my only luve,
  And fare thee weel a while !
And I will come again, my luve,
  Tho' it were ten thousand mile !

AS I STOOD BY YON ROOFLESS
TOWER

The "roofless tower" was part of the ruins
of Lincluden Abbey, situate at the junction of
the Cluden with the Nith. See *ante*. p. 198, Pre-
fatory Note to Epitaph *On Grizzel Grimme*.

CHORUS

A lassie all alone was making her moan,
  Lamenting our lads beyond the sea: —
"In the bluidy wars they fa', and our
    honor's gane an' a',
  And broken-hearted we maun die."

I

As I stood by yon roofless tower,
  Where the wa'flow'r scents the dewy
    air,
Where the houlet mourns in her ivy bower,
  And tells the midnight moon her care:

II

The winds were laid, the air was still,
  The stars they shot along the sky,
The tod was howling on the hill,
  And the distant-echoing glens reply.

III

The burn, adown its hazelly path,
  Was rushing by the ruin'd wa',
Hasting to join the sweeping Nith,
  Whase roarings seem'd to rise and fa'.

IV

The cauld blae North was streaming forth
  Her lights, wi' hissing, eerie din :
Athort the lift they start and shift,
  Like Fortune's favours, tint as win.

V

Now, looking over firth and fauld,
  Her horn the pale-faced Cynthia rear'd,

When lo! in form of minstrel auld
A stern and stalwart ghaist appear'd.

VI

And frae his harp sic strains did flow,
  Might rous'd the slumbering Dead to
    hear,
But O, it was a tale of woe
  As ever met a Briton's ear!

VII

He sang wi' joy his former day,
  He, weeping, wail'd his latter times:
But what he said — it was nae play! —
  I winna ventur't in my rhymes.

CHORUS

A lassie all alone was making her moan
  Lamenting our lads beyond the sea: —
"In the bluidy wars they fa', and our
    honor's gane an' a',
  And broken-hearted we maun die."

O, AN YE WERE DEAD, GUID-MAN

CHORUS

Sing, round about the fire wi' a rung she
    ran,
An' round about the fire wi' a rung she
    ran: —
"Your horns shall tie you to the staw,
  An' I shall bang your hide, guidman!"

I

O, AN ye were dead, guidman,
A green turf on your head, guidman!
I wad bestow my widowhood
Upon a rantin Highlandman!

II

There's sax eggs in the pan, guidman,
There's sax eggs in the pan, guidman.
There's ane to you, and twa to me,
And three to our John Highlandman!

III

A sheep-head's in the pot, guidman,
A sheep-head's in the pot, guidman!
The flesh to him, the broo to me,
An' the horns become your brow, guidman!

CHORUS

Sing, round about the fire wi' a rung she
    ran,
An' round about the fire wi' a rung she
    ran: —
"Your horns shall tie you to the staw,
  An' I shall bang your hide, guidman!"

AULD LANG SYNE

Sent to Mrs. Dunlop, 17th December, 1788:
"*Apropos*, is not the Scotch phrase *Auld Lang-syne* exceedingly expressive? There is an old song and tune which has often thrilled through my soul," etc. To Thomson he wrote: "One song more and I have done — 'Auld Lang Syne.' The air is but mediocre; but the following song — the old song of the olden times, and which has never been in print, nor even in manuscript, until I took it down from an old man's singing, is enough to recommend any air." Thomson in *Scottish Airs* expressed the opinion that Burns thus wrote "merely in a playful humour." It may also be that the story was a device to make sure that he (Thomson) would accept a piece which the writer was far too modest to describe as his own improvement on the earlier sets, the one published in Watson (1711), the other credited to Allan Ramsay. But, after all, it is by no means impossible that he really got the germ of his set as he says he did.

CHORUS

For auld lang syne, my dear,
  For auld lang syne,
We'll tak a cup o' kindness yet
  For auld lang syne!

I

SHOULD auld acquaintance be forgot,
  And never brought to mind?
Should auld acquaintance be forgot,
  And auld lang syne!

II

And surely ye'll be your pint-stowp,
  And surely I'll be mine,
And we'll tak a cup o' kindness yet
  For auld lang syne!

III

We twa hae run about the braes,
  And pou'd the gowans fine,

But we 've wander'd monie a weary fit
  Sin' auld lang syne.

IV

We twa hae paidl'd in the burn
  Frae morning sun till dine,
But seas between us braid hae roar'd
  Sin' auld lang syne.

V

And there 's a hand, my trusty fiere,
  And gie 's a hand o' thine,
And we 'll tak a right guid-willie waught
  For auld lang syne !

CHORUS

For auld lang syne, my dear,
  For auld lang syne,
We 'll tak a cup o' kindness yet
  For auld lang syne !

LOUIS, WHAT RECK I BY THEE

Probably made soon after his marriage, and
certainly before the Revolution of 1795.

I

Louis, what reck I by thee,
  Or Geordie on his ocean ?
Dyvor beggar louns to me !
  I reign in Jeanie's bosom.

II

Let her crown my love her law,
  And in her breast enthrone me,
Kings and nations — swith awa !
  Reif randies, I disown ye.

HAD I THE WYTE?

I

Had I the wyte? had I the wyte?
  Had I the wyte? she bade me !
She watch'd me by the hie-gate side,
  And up the loan she shaw'd me;
And when I wadna venture in,
  A coward loon she ca'd me !
Had Kirk and State been in the gate,
  I 'd lighted when she bade me.

II

Sae craftilie she took me ben
  And bade me mak nae clatter: —
" For our ramgunshoch, glum guidman
  Is o'er ayont the water."
Whae'er shall say I wanted grace
  When I did kiss and dawte her,
Let him be planted in my place,
  Syne say I was the fautor !

III

Could I for shame, could I for shame,
  Could I for shame refus'd her ?
And wadna manhood been to blame
  Had I unkindly used her ?
He claw'd her wi' the ripplin-kame,
  And blae and bluidy bruis'd her —
When sic a husband was frae hame,
  What wife but wad excus'd her !

IV

I dighted ay her een sae blue,
  An' bann'd the cruel randy,
And, weel I wat, her willin mou'
  Was sweet as sugarcandie.
At gloamin-shot, it was, I wot,
  I lighted — on the Monday,
But I cam thro' the Tyseday's dew
  To wanton Willie's brandy.

COMIN THRO' THE RYE

CHORUS

O, Jenny 's a' weet, poor body,
  Jenny 's seldom dry:
She draigl't a' her petticoatie,
  Comin thro' the rye !

I

Comin thro' the rye, poor body,
  Comin thro' the rye,
She draigl't a' her petticoatie,
  Comin thro' the rye !

II

Gin a body meet a body
  Comin thro' the rye,
Gin a body kiss a body,
  Need a body cry ?

CHARLIE HE 'S MY DARLING

III

Gin a body meet a body
Comin thro' the glen,
Gin a body kiss a body,
Need the warld ken ?

CHORUS

O, Jenny 's a' weet, poor body,
Jenny 's seldom dry:
She draigl't a' her petticoatie,
Comin thro' the rye !

YOUNG JAMIE

I

YOUNG Jamie, pride of a' the plain,
Sae gallant and sae gay a swain,
Thro' a' our lasses he did rove,
And reign'd resistless King of Love.

II

But now, wi' sighs and starting tears,
He strays amang the woods and breers;
Or in the glens and rocky caves
His sad complaining dowie raves: —

III

" I, wha sae late did range and rove,
And chang'd with every moon my love —
I little thought the time was near,
Repentance I should buy sae dear.

IV

" The slighted maids my torments see,
And laugh at a' the pangs I dree;
While she, my cruel, scornful Fair,
Forbids me e'er to see her mair."

OUT OVER THE FORTH

I

OUT over the Forth, I look to the north —
But what is the north, and its Highlands
to me ?
The south nor the east gie ease to my breast,
The far foreign land or the wide rolling
sea !

II

But I look to the west, when I gae to rest,
That happy my dreams and my slumbers
may be;
For far in the west lives he I loe best,
The man that is dear to my babie and me.

WANTONNESS FOR EVERMAIR

WANTONNESS for evermair,
Wantonness has been my ruin.
Yet for a' my dool and care
It 's wantonness for evermair.
I hae lo'ed the Black, the Brown;
I hae lo'ed the Fair, the Gowden!
A' the colours in the town —
I hae won their wanton favour.

CHARLIE HE 'S MY DARLING

CHORUS

An' Charlie he 's my darling,
My darling, my darling,
Charlie he 's my darling —
The Young Chevalier !

I

'T WAS on a Monday morning
Right early in the year,
That Charlie came to our town —
The Young Chevalier !

II

As he was walking up the street
The city for to view,
O, there he spied a bonie lass
The window looking thro' !

III

Sae light 's he jimpèd up the stair,
And tirl'd at the pin;
And wha sae ready as hersel'
To let the laddie in !

IV

He set his Jenny on his knee,
All in his Highland dress;
For brawlie weel he kend the way
To please a bonie lass.

V

It's up yon heathery mountain
And down yon scroggy glen,
We daurna gang a-milking
For Charlie and his men !

CHORUS

An' Charlie he's my darling,
My darling, my darling,
Charlie he's my darling —
The Young Chevalier !

THE LASS O' ECCLEFECHAN

Burns, in the course of his " duty as super-
visor," was accustomed to " visit this unfortu-
nate wicked little village," and slept in it on
7th February, 1795 (R. B. to Thomson), about
two months after the birth of Thomas Carlyle.
It was long a favourite resort of such vaga-
bonds as are pictured in *The Jolly Beggars :*
which may — or may not — account in some
measure for Carlyle's affection for that admir-
able piece. Thus, in *The Trogger*, a ballad in
The Merry Muses, which may very well be from
Burns, the hero and heroine, their business
done, proceed to

"Tak the gate,
An' in by Ecclefechan,
Where the brandy stoup we gart it clink,
An' the strong beer ream the quaich in."

I

"GAT ye me, O, gat ye me,
Gat ye me wi' naething ?
Rock an' reel, an' spinning wheel,
A mickle quarter basin:
Bye attour, my gutcher has
A heich house and a laich ane,
A' forbye my bonie sel,
The toss o' Ecclefechan ! "

II

" O, haud your tongue now, Lucky Lang,
O, haud your tongue and jauner !
I held the gate till you I met,
Syne I began to wander:
I tint my whistle and my sang,
I tint my peace and pleasure;
But your green graff, now Lucky Lang,
Wad airt me to my treasure."

THE COOPER O' CUDDY

CHORUS

We 'll hide the cooper behint the door,
Behint the door, behint the door,
We 'll hide the cooper behint the door,
And cover him under a mawn, O.

I

THE Cooper o' Cuddy came here awa,
He ca'd the girrs out o'er us a',
An' our guidwife has gotten a ca',
That's anger'd the silly guidman, O.

II

He sought them out, he sought them in,
Wi' " Deil hae her ! " an' " Deil hae him ! "
But the body he was sae doited and blin',
He wist na where he was gaun, O.

III

They cooper'd at e'en, they cooper'd at
morn,
Till our guidman has gotten the scorn:
On ilka brow she's planted a horn,
And swears that there they sall stan', O !

CHORUS

We 'll hide the cooper behint the door,
Behint the door, behint the door,
We 'll hide the cooper behint the door,
And cover him under a mawn, O.

FOR THE SAKE O' SOMEBODY

I

My heart is sair — I dare na tell —
My heart is sair for Somebody:
I could wake a winter night
For the sake o' Somebody.
O-hon ! for Somebody !
O-hey ! for Somebody !
I could range the world around
For the sake o' Somebody.

II

Ye Powers that smile on virtuous love,
O, sweetly smile on Somebody !
Frae ilka danger keep him free,
And send me safe my Somebody !

O-hon ! for Somebody !
O-hey ! for Somebody !
I wad do — what wad I not ? —
For the sake o' Somebody !

THE CARDIN O'T

Suggested, perhaps, by Alexander Ross's : —

" There was a wifie had a wee pickle tow,
And she wad gae try the spinning o't."

CHORUS

The cardin o't, the spinnin o't,
The warpin o't, the winnin o't !
When ilka ell cost me a groat,
The tailor staw the lynin o't.

I

I COFT a stane o' haslock woo,
To mak a wab to Johnie o't,
For Johnie is my only jo —
I lo'e him best of onie yet !

II

For tho' his locks be lyart gray,
And tho' his brow be beld aboon,
Yet I hae seen him on a day
The pride of a' the parishen.

CHORUS

The cardin o't, the spinnin o't,
The warpin o't, the winnin o't !
When ilka ell cost me a groat,
The tailor staw the lynin o't.

THERE'S THREE TRUE GUID FELLOWS

I

THERE 's three true guid fellows,
There 's three true guid fellows,
There 's three true guid fellows,
Down ayont yon glen !

II

It 's now the day is dawin,
But or night do fa' in,
Whase cock 's best at crawin,
Willie, thou sall ken !

SAE FLAXEN WERE HER RING-
LETS

" Do you know, my dear sir, a blackguard
Irish song called *Oonagh's Waterfall ?* . . .
The air is charming, and I have often regretted
the want of decent verses to it. It is too much,
at least for *my* humble, rustic muse, to expect
that every effort of hers must have merit; still
I think that it is better to have *mediocre* verses
to a favourite air, than none at all. On this
principle I have all along proceeded in the
Scots Musical Museum; and, as that publica-
tion is at its last volume, I intend the follow-
ing song, to the air above-mentioned, for that
work." (R. B. to Thomson, September, 1794.)
For Chloris, see *post*, p. 289.

I

SAE flaxen were her ringlets,
Her eyebrows of a darker hue,
Bewitchingly o'er-arching
Twa laughing een o' bonie blue.
Her smiling, sae wyling,
Wad make a wretch forget his woe ,
What pleasure, what treasure,
Unto those rosy lips to grow !
Such was my Chloris' bonie face,
When first that bonie face I saw,
And ay my Chloris' dearest charm —
She says she lo'es me best of a' !

II

Like harmony her motion,
Her pretty ankle is a spy
Betraying fair proportion
Wad make a saint forget the sky !
Sae warming, sae charming,
Her faultless form and gracefu' air,
Ilk feature — auld Nature
Declar'd that she could dae nae mair !
Hers are the willing chains o' love
By conquering beauty's sovereign law,
And ay my Chloris' dearest charm —
She says she lo'es me best of a'.

III

Let others love the city,
And gaudy show at sunny noon !
Gie me the lonely valley,
The dewy eve, and rising moon,
Fair beaming, and streaming
Her silver light the boughs amang,
While falling, recalling,
The amorous thrush concludes his sang !

There, dearest Chloris, wilt thou rove
  By wimpling burn and leafy shaw,
And hear my vows o' truth and love,
  And say thou lo'es me best of a' ?

THE LASS THAT MADE THE BED

" *The Bonie Lass made the Bed to Me* was composed on an amour of Charles II. when skulking in the North about Aberdeen, in the time of the Usurpation. He formed *une petite affaire* with a daughter of the House of Port Letham, who was the lass that made the bed to him."

I

WHEN Januar' wind was blawin cauld,
  As to the North I took my way,
The mirksome night did me enfauld,
  I knew na where to lodge till day.
By my guid luck a maid I met
  Just in the middle o' my care,
And kindly she did me invite
  To walk into a chamber fair.

II

I bow'd fu' low unto this maid,
  And thank'd her for her courtesie;
I bow'd fu' low unto this maid,
  An' bade her mak a bed to me.
She made the bed baith large and wide,
  Wi' twa white hands she spread it down,
She put the cup to her rosy lips,
  And drank: — "Young man, now sleep
    ye soun'."

III

She snatch'd the candle in her hand,
  And frae my chamber went wi' speed,
But I call'd her quickly back again
  To lay some mair below my head:
A cod she laid below my head,
  And servèd me with due respeck,
And, to salute her wi' a kiss,
  I put my arms about her neck.

IV

" Haud aff your hands, young man," she
    said,
  " And dinna sae uncivil be;
Gif ye hae onie luve for me,
  O, wrang na my virginitie ! "

Her hair was like the links o' gowd,
  Her teeth were like the ivorie,
Her cheeks like lilies dipt in wine,
  The lass that made the bed to me !

V

Her bosom was the driven snaw,
  Twa drifted heaps sae fair to see;
Her limbs the polish'd marble stane,
  The lass that made the bed to me !
I kiss'd her o'er and o'er again,
  And ay she wist na what to say.
I laid her 'tween me an' the wa' —
  The lassie thocht na lang till day.

VI

Upon the morrow, when we raise,
  I thank'd her for her courtesie,
But ay she blush'd, and ay she sigh'd,
  And said: — " Alas, ye 've ruin'd me ! "
I clasp'd her waist, and kiss'd her syne,
  While the tear stood twinklin in her e'e.
I said: — " My lassie, dinna cry,
  For ye ay shall mak the bed to me."

VII

She took her mither's holland sheets,
  An' made them a' in sarks to me.
Blythe and merry may she be,
  The lass that made the bed to me !
The bonie lass made the bed to me,
  The braw lass made the bed to me !
I 'll ne'er forget till the day I die,
  The lass that made the bed to me.

SAE FAR AWA

I

O, SAD and heavy should I part
  But for her sake sae far awa,
Unknowing what my way may thwart —
  My native land sae far awa.

II

Thou that of a' things Maker art,
  That formed this Fair sae far awa,
Gie body strength, then I 'll ne'er start
  At this my way sae far awa !

III

How true is love to pure desert !
  So mine in her sae far awa,

And nocht can heal my bosom's smart,
While, O, she is sae far awa!

IV

Nane other love, nane other dart
I feel, but hers sae far awa;
But fairer never touched a heart,
Than hers, the Fair sae far awa.

THE REEL O' STUMPIE

I

WAP and rowe, wap and rowe,
Wap and rowe the feetie o't;
I thought I was a maiden fair,
Till I heard the greetie o't!

II

My daddie was a fiddler fine,
My minnie she made mantie, O,
And I myself a thumpin quine,
And danc'd the Reel o' Stumpie, O.

I 'LL AY CA' IN BY YON TOWN

CHORUS

I 'll ay ca' in by yon town
And by yon garden green again!
I 'll ay ca' in by yon town
And see my bonie Jean again.

I

THERE 's nane shall ken, there 's nane can
guess
What brings me back the gate again,
But she, my fairest faithfu' lass,
And stow'nlins we sall meet again.

II

She 'll wander by the aiken tree,
When trystin time draws near again;
And when her lovely form I see,
O haith! she 's doubly dear again.

CHORUS

I 'll ay ca' in by yon town
And by yon garden green again!
I 'll ay ca' in by yon town
And see my bonie Jean again.

O, WAT YE WHA 'S IN YON TOWN

Begun at Ecclefechan, where Burns was
storm-stayed, 7th February, 1795. "Do you
know an air — I am sure you must know it —
We'll Gang Nae Mair to Yon Town. I think,
in slowish time, it would make an excellent
song. I am highly delighted with it; and if
you should think it worthy of your attention,
I have a fair dame in my eye to whom I would
consecrate it; try with this doggrel until I give
you a better."

In the set sent to Johnson, Jeanie — either
Jean Armour or Jean Lorimer — is the heroine.
In that sent to Thomson, the name is Lucy;
and Burns, enclosing a copy to Syme in an
undated letter, explains its history: "Do you
know that among much that I admire in the
characters and manners of those great folks
whom I have now the honour to call my ac-
quaintances — the Oswald family, for instance
— there is nothing charms me more than Mr.
Oswald's unconcealable attachment to that
incomparable woman." The "incomparable
woman" was Oswald's wife. He was Richard
Oswald of Auchencruive, nephew of the Mrs.
Oswald to whose memory Burns had devoted
a savage *Ode* (*ante*, p. 81). Lucy, daughter of
Wynne Johnston, Esq., of Hilton, according to
Sharpe, was at this time "well turned of
thirty, and ten years older than her husband;
but still a charming creature." She died at
Lisbon in January, 1798.

CHORUS

O, wat ye wha 's in yon town
Ye see the e'enin sun upon?
The dearest maid 's in yon town
That e'enin sun is shining on!

I

Now haply down yon gay green shaw
She wanders by yon spreading tree.
How blest ye flowers that round her blaw!
Ye catch the glances o' her e'e.

II

How blest ye birds that round her sing,
And welcome in the blooming year!
And doubly welcome be the Spring,
The season to my Jeanie dear!

III

The sun blinks blythe in yon town,
Among the broomy braes sae green;

But my delight in yon town,
   And dearest pleasure, is my Jean.

IV

Without my Love, not a' the charms
   O' Paradise could yield me joy;
But gie me Jeanie in my arms,
   And welcome Lapland's dreary sky!

V

My cave wad be a lover's bower,
   Tho' raging Winter rent the air,
And she a lovely little flower,
   That I wad tent and shelter there.

VI

O, sweet is she in yon town
   The sinkin sun's gane down upon!
A fairer than's in yon town
   His setting beam ne'er shone upon.

VII

If angry Fate be sworn my foe,
   And suff'ring I am doom'd to bear,
I'd careless quit aught else below,
   But spare, O, spare me Jeanie dear!

VIII

For, while life's dearest blood is warm,
   Ae thought frae her shall ne'er depart,
And she, as fairest is her form,
   She has the truest, kindest heart.

CHORUS

O, wat ye wha's in yon town
   Ye see the e'enin sun upon?
The dearest maid's in yon town
   That e'enin sun is shining on!

WHEREFORE SIGHING ART THOU, PHILLIS?

I

WHEREFORE sighing art thou, Phillis?
   Has thy prime unheeded past?
Hast thou found that beauty's lilies
   Were not made for ay to last?

II

Know, thy form was once a treasure —
   Then it was thy hour of scorn!
Since thou then denied the pleasure,
   Now 't is fit that thou should'st mourn.

O MAY, THY MORN

Supposed to commemorate the parting with
Clarinda, 6th December, 1791.

I

O MAY, thy morn was ne'er sae sweet
   As the mirk night o' December!
For sparkling was the rosy wine,
   And private was the chamber,
And dear was she I dare na name,
   But I will ay remember.

II

And here's to them that, like oursel,
   Can push about the jorum!
And here's to them that wish us weel —
   May a' that's guid watch o'er 'em!
And here's to them we dare na tell,
   The dearest o' the quorum!

AS I CAME O'ER THE CAIRNEY MOUNT

CHORUS

O, my bonie Highland lad!
   My winsome, weel-faur'd Highland
   laddie!
Wha wad mind the wind and rain
   Sae weel row'd in his tartan plaidie!

I

As I came o'er the Cairney mount
   And down among the blooming heather,
Kindly stood the milking-shiel
   To shelter frae the stormy weather.

II

Now Phœbus blinkit on the bent,
   And o'er the knowes the lambs were
   bleating;
But he wan my heart's consent
   To be his ain at the neist meeting.

CHORUS

O, my bonie Highland lad!
   My winsome, weel-faur'd Highland
   laddie!
Wha wad mind the wind and rain
   Sae weel row'd in his tartan plaidie!

HIGHLAND LADDIE

This is chiefly an abridgment of the Jacobite ditty, *The Highland Lad and the Highland Lass*, published in *A Collection of Loyal Songs* (1750) and *The True Loyalist* (1779). The refrain is old; stanza i. is Burns; stanza ii. is substantially stanza i. of the older set; while stanza iii. is composed of the first halves of the older stanzas viii. and ix.

I

THE boniest lad that e'er I saw —
  Bonie laddie, Highland laddie !
Wore a plaid and was fu' braw —
  Bonie Highland laddie !
On his head a bonnet blue —
  Bonie laddie, Highland laddie !
His royal heart was firm and true —
  Bonie Highland laddie !

II

" Trumpets sound and cannons roar,
  Bonie lassie, Lawland lassie ! —
And a' the hills wi' echoes roar,
  Bonie Lawland lassie !
Glory, Honour, now invite —
  Bonie lassie, Lawland lassie ! —
For freedom and my King to fight,
  Bonie Lawland lassie ! "

III

" The sun a backward course shall take,
  Bonie laddie, Highland laddie !
Ere aught thy manly courage shake,
  Bonie Highland laddie !
Go, for yoursel' procure renown,
  Bonie laddie, Highland laddie,
And for your lawful King his crown,
  Bonie Highland laddie ! "

WILT THOU BE MY DEARIE?

In a MS. sent to Maria Riddell, "Jeanie" is substituted for "lassie." In view of the fact that Burns sent the song to Captain Miller's journal, this change confirms the statement that *Wilt Thou be My Dearie* was made in honour of Miss Janet Miller of Dalswinton.

I

WILT thou be my dearie ?
When Sorrow wrings thy gentle heart,

O, wilt thou let me cheer thee ?
By the treasure of my soul —
  That 's the love I bear thee —
I swear and vow that only thou
  Shall ever be my dearie !
Only thou, I swear and vow,
  Shall ever be my dearie !

II

Lassie, say thou lo'es me,
Or, if thou wilt na be my ain,
  Say na thou 'lt refuse me !
If it winna, canna be,
  Thou for thine may choose me,
Let me, lassie, quickly die,
  Trusting that thou lo'es me !
Lassie, let me quickly die,
  Trusting that thou lo'es me !

LOVELY POLLY STEWART

Polly or Mary Stewart was daughter of William Stewart, factor at Closeburn, to whom Burns addressed *To William Stewart (ante,* p. 146), and also the lines, *You 're Welcome, Willie Stewart (post,* p. 311). She was married first to her cousin, Ishmael Stewart, and then to a farmer, George Welsh (grand-uncle of Jane Welsh Carlyle). Being separated from Welsh, she fell in love with a French prisoner of war, whom she accompanied to his native Switzerland. She died in Italy at the age of seventy-two. The present song, together with *You 're Welcome, Willie Stewart,* is modelled on a Jacobite number in *Collection of Loyal Songs* (1750).

CHORUS

O lovely Polly Stewart,
O charming Polly Stewart,
There 's ne'er a flower that blooms in
    May,
  That 's half so fair as thou art !

I

THE flower it blaws, it fades, it fa's,
  And art can ne'er renew it;
But Worth and Truth eternal youth
  Will gie to Polly Stewart !

II

May he whase arms shall fauld thy charms
  Possess a leal and true heart !

To him be given to ken the heaven
He grasps in Polly Stewart !

CHORUS

O lovely Polly Stewart,
O charming Polly Stewart,
There 's ne'er a flower that blooms in
    May,
That 's half so fair as thou art !

THE HIGHLAND BALOU

Stenhouse states that it is " a versification,
by Burns, of a Gaelic nursery song, the literal
import of which, as well as the air, were com-
municated to him by a Highland lady." But
there are humorous touches in it which the
original (if there was an original) could not
have shown.

I

HEE balou, my sweet wee Donald,
Picture o' the great Clanronald !
Brawlie kens our wanton Chief
Wha gat my young Highland thief.

II

Leeze me on thy bonie craigie !
An thou live, thou 'll steal a naigie,
Travel the country thro' and thro',
And bring hame a Carlisle cow !

III

Thro' the Lawlands, o'er the Border,
Weel, my babie, may thou furder,
Herry the louns o' the laigh Countrie,
Syne to the Highlands hame to me !

BANNOCKS O' BEAR MEAL

CHORUS

Bannocks o' bear meal,
    Bannocks o' barley,
Here 's to the Highlandman's
    Bannocks o' barley !

I

WHA in a brulyie
    Will first cry " a parley " ?
Never the lads
    Wi' the bannocks o' barley !

II

Wha, in his wae days,
    Were loyal to Charlie ?
Wha but the lads
    Wi' the bannocks o' barley !

CHORUS

Bannocks o' bear meal,
    Bannocks o' barley,
Here 's to the Highlandman's
    Bannocks o' barley !

WAE IS MY HEART

I

WAE is my heart, and the tear 's in my e'e;
Lang, lang joy 's been a stranger to me:
Forsaken and friendless my burden I bear,
And the sweet voice o' pity ne'er sounds in
    my ear.

II

Love, thou hast pleasures — and deep hae
    I lov'd !
Love, thou hast sorrows — and sair hae I
    prov'd !
But this bruisèd heart that now bleeds in
    my breast,
I can feel by its throbbings, will soon be at
    rest.

III

O, if I were where happy I hae been,
Down by yon stream and yon bonie castle
    green !
For there he is wand'ring and musing on
    me,
Wha wad soon dry the tear frae his Phillis'
    e'e !

HERE 'S HIS HEALTH IN WATER

I

ALTHO' my back be at the wa',
    And tho' he be the fautor,
Altho' my back be at the wa',
    Yet here 's his health in water !
O, wae gae by his wanton sides,
    Sae brawly 's he could flatter !

Till for his sake I'm slighted sair
And dree the kintra clatter!
But, tho' my back be at the wa',
Yet here's his health in water!

THE WINTER OF LIFE

Burns sent a copy to Thomson, under the title of *The Old Man*. The song is included in Thomson (Vol. iii.).

Doubtless suggested by a song with the same title which we have found in *The Goldfinch* (Edinburgh, 1777): —

"In Spring, my dear Shepherds, your gardens are gay,
  They breathe all their sweets in the sunshine of May:
Their Flowers will drop when December draws near —
  The winter of life is like that of the year," etc.

I

But lately seen in gladsome green,
  The woods rejoiced the day;
Thro' gentle showers the laughing flowers
  In double pride were gay;
But now our joys are fled
  On winter blasts awa,
Yet maiden May in rich array
  Again shall bring them a'.

II

But my white pow — nae kindly thowe
  Shall melt the snaws of Age!
My trunk of eild, but buss and bield,
  Sinks in Time's wintry rage.
O, Age has weary days
  And nights o' sleepless pain!
Thou golden time o' youthfu' prime,
  Why comes thou not again?

THE TAILOR

I

The tailor he cam here to sew,
And weel he kend the way to woo,
For ay he pree'd the lassie's mou',
  As he gaed but and ben, O.
    For weel he kend the way, O,
    The way, O, the way, O!
    For weel he kend the way, O,
    The lassie's heart to win, O!

II

The tailor rase and shook his duds,
The flaes they flew awa in cluds!
And them that stay'd gat fearfu' thuds
  The Tailor prov'd a man, O!
    For now it was the gloamin,
    The gloamin, the gloamin!
    For now it was the gloamin,
    When a' the rest are gaun, O!

THERE GROWS A BONIE BRIER-BUSH

I

There grows a bonie brier-bush in our
  kail-yard,
There grows a bonie brier-bush in our kail-
  yard;
And below the bonie brier-bush there's a
  lassie and a lad,
And they're busy, busy courting in our
  kail-yard.

II

We'll court nae mair below the buss in
  our kail-yard,
We'll court nae mair below the buss in
  our kail-yard:
We'll awa to Athole's green, and there
  we'll no be seen,
Where the trees and the branches will be
  our safeguard.

III

Will ye go to the dancin in Carlyle's ha'?
Will ye go to the dancin in Carlyle's ha',
Where Sandy and Nancy I'm sure will
  ding them a'?
I winna gang to the dance in Carlyle-ha'!

IV

What will I do for a lad when Sandie
  gangs awa!
What will I do for a lad when Sandie
  gangs awa!
I will awa to Edinburgh, and win a pennie
  fee,
And see an onie lad will fancy me.

V

He's comin frae the north that's to marry
  me,
He's comin frae the north that's to marry
  me,

A feather in his bonnet and a ribbon at his
    knee —
He's a bonie, bonie laddie, an yon be he !

HERE'S TO THY HEALTH

I

HERE's to thy health, my bonie lass !
    Guid night and joy be wi' thee !
I'll come nae mair to thy bower-door
    To tell thee that I lo'e thee.
O, dinna think, my pretty pink,
    But I can live without thee:
I vow and swear I dinna care
    How lang ye look about ye !

II

Thou 'rt ay sae free informing me
    Thou hast nae mind to marry,
I'll be as free informing thee
    Nae time hae I to tarry.
I ken thy freens try ilka means
    Frae wedlock to delay thee
(Depending on some higher chance),
    But fortune may betray thee.

III

I ken they scorn my low estate,
    But that does never grieve me,
For I 'm as free as any he —
    Sma' siller will relieve me !
I'll count my health my greatest wealth
    Sae lang as I 'll enjoy it.
I'll fear nae scant, I'll bode nae want
    As lang's I get employment.

IV

But far off fowls hae feathers fair,
    And, ay until ye try them,
Tho' they seem fair, still have a care —
    They may prove as bad as I am !
But at twel at night, when the moon shines
    bright,
    My dear, I 'll come and see thee,
For the man that loves his mistress weel,
    Nae travel makes him weary.

IT WAS A' FOR OUR RIGHTFU' KING

[Suggested by the chap-book ballad of
Mally Stewart, circa 1746, of which the first
and last stanzas are as follows]: —

" ' The cold Winter is past and gone, and now comes in
    the Spring,
And I am one of the King's Life-guards, and must go
    fight for my King,
            My dear,
      I must go fight for my King.'

The trooper turn'd himself about all on the Irish shore,
He has given the bridal-reins a shake, saying ' Adieu
    for evermore,
            My dear,
      Adieu for evermore.' "

Burns used the last as his own central, grouping
his others, which are largely suggested by it,
round about it. He was also greatly influenced
by the first, which undoubtedly helped him to
his own beginning. For the rest, he took the
situation and the characters, and touched his
borrowings to issues as fine, perhaps, as the
Romantic Lyric has to show.

I

IT was a' for our rightfu' king
    We left fair Scotland's strand;
It was a' for our rightfu' king,
    We e'er saw Irish land,
          My dear —
    We e'er saw Irish land.

II

Now a' is done that men can do,
    And a' is done in vain,
My Love and Native Land fareweel,
    For I maun cross the main,
          My dear —
    For I maun cross the main.

III

He turn'd him right and round about
    Upon the Irish shore,
And gae his bridle reins a shake,
    With adieu for evermore,
          My dear —
    And adieu for evermore !

IV

The soger frae the wars returns,
    The sailor frae the main,
But I hae parted frae my love
    Never to meet again,
          My dear —
    Never to meet again.

V

When day is gane, and night is come,
    And a' folk bound to sleep,
I think on him that 's far awa
    The lee-lang night, and weep,
          My dear —
    The lee-lang night and weep.

THE HIGHLAND WIDOW'S LAMENT

[A similar refrain occurs in an old song in Johnson (Vol. i.), said to have been a lament for Glencoe.]

I

O, I AM come to the low countrie —
Ochon, ochon, ochrie ! —
Without a penny in my purse
To buy a meal to me.

II

It was na sae in the Highland hills —
Ochon, ochon, ochrie ! —
Nae woman in the country wide
Sae happy was as me.

III

For then I had a score o' kye —
Ochon, ochon, ochrie ! —
Feeding on yon hill sae high
And giving milk to me.

IV

And there I had three score o' yowes —
Ochon, ochon, ochrie ! —
Skipping on yon bonie knowes
And casting woo' to me.

V

I was the happiest of a' the clan —
Sair, sair may I repine ! —
For Donald was the brawest man,
And Donald he was mine.

VI

Till Charlie Stewart cam at last
Sae far to set us free:
My Donald's arm was wanted then
For Scotland and for me.

VII

Their waefu' fate what need I tell ?
Right to the wrang did yield:
My Donald and his country fell
Upon Culloden field.

VIII

Ochon ! O Donald, O !
Ochon, ochon, ochrie !
Nae woman in the warld wide
Sae wretched now as me !

THOU GLOOMY DECEMBER

I

ANCE mair I hail thee, thou gloomy December !
Ance mair I hail thee wi' sorrow and care !
Sad was the parting thou makes me remember:
Parting wi' Nancy, O, ne'er to meet mair !

II

Fond lovers' parting is sweet, painful pleasure,
Hope beaming mild on the soft parting hour;
But the dire feeling, O farewell for ever !
Anguish unmingled and agony pure !

III

Wild as the winter now tearing the forest,
Till the last leaf o' the summer is flown —
Such is the tempest has shaken my bosom,
Till my last hope and last comfort is gone !

IV

Still as I hail thee, thou gloomy December,
Still shall I hail thee wi' sorrow and care;
For sad was the parting thou makes me remember:
Parting wi' Nancy, O, ne'er to meet mair !

MY PEGGY'S FACE, MY PEGGY'S FORM

Written in 1787, and sent to Johnson with the following letter : " Dear Mr. Publisher, — I hope, against my return, you will be able to tell me from Mr. Clarke if these words will suit the tune. If they don't suit, I must think on some other air, as I have a very strong private reason for wishing them in the *second* volume. Don't forget to transcribe me the list of the Antiquarian Music. Farewell. — R. BURNS." No reason was given by Johnson for the delay in publishing ; but it is probable that Miss Chalmers (see *ante*, p. 214, Prefatory Note to *Where, Braving Angry Winter's Storms*) objected.

I

My Peggy's face, my Peggy's form
The frost of hermit Age might warm.
My Peggy's worth, my Peggy's mind
Might charm the first of human kind.

II

I love my Peggy's angel air,
Her face so truly heavenly fair,
Her native grace so void of art;
But I adore my Peggy's heart.

III

The lily's hue, the rose's dye,
The kindling lustre of an eye —
Who but owns their magic sway ?
Who but knows they all decay ?

IV

The tender thrill, the pitying tear,
The generous purpose nobly dear,
The gentle look that rage disarms —
These are all immortal charms.

O, STEER HER UP, AN' HAUD HER GAUN

The first half stanza is Ramsay's, from a set founded on an old, improper ditty.

I

O, STEER her up, an' haud her gaun —
　Her mither 's at the mill, jo,
An' gin she winna tak a man,
　E'en let her tak her will, jo.
First shore her wi' a gentle kiss,
　And ca' anither gill, jo,
An' gin she tak the thing amiss,
　E'en let her flyte her fill, jo.

II

O, steer her up, an' be na blate,
　An' gin she tak it ill, jo,
Then leave the lassie till her fate,
　And time nae langer spill, jo !
Ne'er break your heart for ae rebute,
　But think upon it still, jo,
That gin the lassie winna do 't,
　Ye 'll fin' anither will, jo.

WEE WILLIE GRAY

A nursery ditty for the tune *Wee Totum Fogg.*

I

WEE Willie Gray an' his leather wallet,
Peel a willow-wand to be him boots and
　jacket !
The rose upon the brier will be him trouse
　and doublet —
The rose upon the brier will be him trouse
　and doublet !

II

Wee Willie Gray and his leather wallet,
Twice a lily-flower will be him sark and
　gravat !
Feathers of a flie wad feather up his bon-
　net —
Feathers of a flie wad feather up his bon-
　net !

WE'RE A' NODDIN

The present ditty is a medley of two old songs with variations and amendments, *John Anderson My Jo* [not Burns's, but the sprightly old song that served as his model] — which gives us stanzas iv. and v., the best things in the Burns set, *verbatim* — and an unpublished fragment in the Herd MS. : —

"Cats like milk, and Dogs like Broo,
Lads like lasses and lasses lads too ;
And they 're a' nodding, nidding, nidding, nodding,
　They 're a' nodding at our house at hame.

"Kate sits i' the neuk supping hen broo,
Deil take Kate if she does not know it too ;
And they 're a' nodding, nidding, nidding, nodding,
　They 're a' nodding at our house at hame."

CHORUS

We 're a' noddin,
Nid nid noddin,
We 're a' noddin
At our house at hame !

I

"GUID e'en to you, kimmer,
　And how do ye do ? "
"Hiccup ! " quo' kimmer,
　" The better that I 'm fou ! "

II

Kate sits i' the neuk,
  Suppin hen-broo.
Deil tak Kate
  An she be na noddin too !

III

"How 's a' wi' you, kimmer ?
  And how do you fare ? "
"A pint o' the best o't,
  And twa pints mair ! "

IV

"How 's a' wi' you, kimmer ?
  And how do ye thrive ?
How monie bairns hae ye ? "
  Quo' kimmer, " I hae five."

V

" Are they a' Johnie's ? "
  " Eh ! atweel na:
Twa o' them were gotten
  When Johnie was awa ! "

VI

Cats like milk,
  And dogs like broo;
Lads like lasses weel,
  And lasses lads too.

CHORUS

We 're a' noddin,
  Nid nid noddin,
We 're a' noddin,
  At our house at hame !

O, AY MY WIFE SHE DANG ME

[Set to the tune of *My Wife She Dang Me.*]

CHORUS

O, ay my wife she dang me,
An' aft my wife she bang'd me !
If ye gie a woman a' her will,
Guid faith ! she 'll soon o'ergang ye.

I

On peace an' rest my mind was bent,
  And, fool I was ! I married;
But never honest man's intent
  Sae cursedly miscarried.

II

Some sairie comfort at the last,
  When a' thir days are done, man:
My " pains o' hell " on earth is past,
  I 'm sure o' bliss aboon, man.

CHORUS

O, ay my wife she dang me,
An' aft my wife she bang'd me !
If ye gie a woman a' her will,
Guid faith ! she 'll soon o'ergang ye.

SCROGGAM

I

There was a wife wonn'd in Cockpen,
          Scroggam !
She brew'd guid ale for gentlemen:
Sing Auld Cowl, lay you down by me —
Scroggam, my dearie, ruffum !

II

The guidwife's dochter fell in a fever,
          Scroggam !
The priest o' the parish fell in anither:
Sing Auld Cowl, lay you down by me —
Scroggam, my dearie, ruffum !

III

They laid the twa i' the bed thegither,
          Scroggam !
That the heat o' the tane might cool the
      tither:
Sing Auld Cowl, lay you down by me —
Scroggam, my dearie, ruffum !

O, GUID ALE COMES

CHORUS

O, guid ale comes, and guid ale goes,
Guid ale gars me sell my hose,
Sell my hose, and pawn my shoon
Guid ale keeps my heart aboon !

I

I had sax owsen in a pleugh,
And they drew a' weel eneugh:
I sell'd them a' just ane by ane —
Guid ale keeps the heart aboon !

II

Guid ale hauds me bare and busy,
Gars me moop wi' the servant hizzie,
Stand i' the stool when I hae dune —
Guid ale keeps the heart aboon !

CHORUS

O, guid ale comes, and guid ale goes,
Guid ale gars me sell my hose,
Sell my hose, and pawn my shoon —
Guid ale keeps my heart aboon !

ROBIN SHURE IN HAIRST

"I am still catering for Johnson's publication, and among others, I have brushed up the following old favourite song a little, with a view to your worship. I have only altered a word here and there ; but if you like the humour of it, we shall think of a stanza or two to add to it." (R. B. to Robert Ainslie, January 6th, 1789.)

CHORUS

Robin shure in hairst,
I shure wi' him:
Fient a heuk had I,
Yet I stack by him.

I

I GAED up to Dunse
To warp a wab o' plaiden
At his daddie's yett
Wha met me but Robin !

II

Was na Robin bauld,
Tho' I was a cottar ?
Play'd me sic a trick,
An' me the Eller's dochter !

III

Robin promis'd me
A' my winter vittle:
Fient haet he had but three
Guse feathers and a whittle !

CHORUS

Robin shure in hairst,
I shure wi' him:
Fient a heuk had I,
Yet I stack by him.

DOES HAUGHTY GAUL INVASION THREAT?

I

DOES haughty Gaul invasion threat ?
Then let the loons beware, Sir !
There 's wooden walls upon our seas
And volunteers on shore, Sir !
The Nith shall run to Corsincon,
And Criffel sink in Solway,
Ere we permit a foreign foe
On British ground to rally !

II

O, let us not, like snarling tykes,
In wrangling be divided,
Till, slap ! come in an unco loun,
And wi' a rung decide it !
Be Britain still to Britain true,
Amang oursels united !
For never but by British hands
Maun British wrangs be righted !

III

The kettle o' the Kirk and State,
Perhaps a clout may fail in 't;
But Deil a foreign tinkler loon
Shall ever ca' a nail in 't !
Our fathers' blude the kettle bought,
And wha wad dare to spoil it,
By Heav'ns ! the sacrilegious dog
Shall fuel be to boil it !

IV

The wretch that would a tyrant own,
And the wretch, his true-sworn brother,
Who would set the mob above the throne,
May they be damn'd together !
Who will not sing God save the King
Shall hang as high 's the steeple;
But while we sing God save the King,
We 'll ne'er forget the People !

O, ONCE I LOV'D A BONIE LASS

"The following composition was the first of my performances, and done at an early period of life, when my heart glowed with honest warm simplicity; unacquainted, and uncorrupted with the ways of a wicked world. The performance is, indeed, very puerile and silly: but I am always pleased with it, as it recalls to my mind those happy days when my heart was yet honest and my tongue was sincere. The subject of it was a young girl who really deserved all the praises I have bestowed on her." (R. B.) In the *Autobiographical Letter to Dr. Moore*, he states that the young girl was his partner in "the labors of harvest." "Among her other love-inspiring qualifications," so he further relates, "she sung sweetly; and 't was her favourite reel to which I attempted giving an embodied vehicle in rhyme. I was not so presumptive as to imagine that I would make verses like printed ones, composed by men who had Greek and Latin; but my girl sung a song which was said to be composed by a small country laird's son, on one of his father's maids, with whom he was in love; and I saw no reason why I might not rhyme as well as he, for except shearing sheep and casting peats, his father living in the moors, he had no more scholarcraft than I had."

His criticism of the song (in the *First Common Place Book*) is interesting enough to reprint in full: "The first distich of the first stanza is quite too much in the flimsy strain of our ordinary street ballads; and on the other hand, the second distich is too much in the other extreme. The expression is a little awkward, and the sentiment too serious. Stanza the second I am well pleased with, and I think it conveys a fine idea of that amiable part of the Sex — the agreeables; or what in our Scotch dialect we call a sweet sonsy Lass. The third stanza has a little of the flimsy turn in it; and the third line has rather too serious a cast. The fourth stanza is a very indifferent one; the first line is, indeed, all in the strain of the second stanza, but the rest is mostly an expletive. The thoughts in the fifth stanza come finely up to my favourite idea, a sweet sonsy Lass; the last line, however, halts a little. The same sentiments are kept up with equal spirit and tenderness in the sixth stanza, but the second and fourth lines ending with short syllables hurts the whole. The seventh stanza has several minute faults; but I remember I composed it in a wild enthusiasm of passion, and to this hour I never recollect it, but my heart melts, and my blood sallies at the remembrance."

I

O, ONCE I lov'd a bonie lass,
  Ay, and I love her still!
And whilst that virtue warms my breast,
  I 'll love my handsome Nell.

II

As bonie lasses I hae seen,
  And monie full as braw,

But for a modest gracefu' mien
  The like I never saw.

III

A bonie lass, I will confess,
  Is pleasant to the e'e;
But without some better qualities
  She 's no a lass for me.

IV

But Nelly's looks are blythe and sweet,
  And, what is best of a',
Her reputation is complete
  And fair without a flaw.

V

She dresses ay sae clean and neat,
  Both decent and genteel;
And then there 's something in her gait
  Gars onie dress look weel.

VI

A gaudy dress and gentle air
  May slightly touch the heart;
But it 's innocence and modesty
  That polishes the dart.

VII

'T is this in Nelly pleases me,
  'T is this enchants my soul;
For absolutely in my breast
  She reigns without controul.

MY LORD A-HUNTING

CHORUS

My lady's gown, there 's gairs upon 't,
And gowden flowers sae rare upon 't;
But Jenny's jimps and jirkinet,
My lord thinks meikle mair upon 't!

I

MY lord a-hunting he is gane,
But hounds or hawks wi' him are nane;
By Colin's cottage lies his game,
If Colin's Jenny be at hame.

II

My lady 's white, my lady 's red,
And kith and kin o' Cassillis' blude;
But her ten-pund lands o' tocher guid
Were a' the charms his lordship lo'ed.

III

Out o'er yon muir, out o'er yon moss,
Whare gor-cocks thro' the heather pass,
There wons auld Colin's bonie lass,
A lily in a wilderness.

IV

Sae sweetly move her genty limbs,
Like music notes o' lovers' hymns !
The diamond-dew in her een sae blue,
Where laughing love sae wanton swims !

V

My lady 's dink, my lady 's drest,
The flower and fancy o' the west;
But the lassie that a man lo'es best,
O, that 's the lass to mak him blest !

CHORUS

My lady 's gown, there 's gairs upon 't,
And gowden flowers sae rare upon 't;
But Jenny's jimps and jirkinet,
My lord thinks meikle mair upon 't !

SWEETEST MAY

An imitation, open and unabashed, of Ramsay's *My Sweetest May, Let Love Incline Thee.*

I

SWEETEST May, let Love inspire thee !
Take a heart which he designs thee:
As thy constant slave regard it,
For its faith and truth reward it.

II

Proof o' shot to birth or money,
Not the wealthy but the bonie,
Not the high-born but noble-minded,
In love's silken band can bind it.

MEG O' THE MILL

I

O, KEN ye what Meg o' the Mill has gotten ?
An' ken ye what Meg o' the Mill has gotten ?

A braw new naig wi' the tail o' a rottan,
And that 's what Meg o' the Mill has gotten !

II

O, ken ye what Meg o' the Mill lo'es dearly ?
An' ken ye what Meg o' the Mill lo'es dearly ?
A dram o' guid strunt in a morning early,
And that 's what Meg o' the Mill lo'es dearly !

III

O, ken ye how Meg o' the Mill was married ?
An' ken ye how Meg o' the Mill was married ?
The priest he was oxter'd, the clark he was carried,
And that 's how Meg o' the Mill was married !

IV

O, ken ye how Meg o' the Mill was bedded ?
An' ken ye how Meg o' the Mill was bedded ?
The groom gat sae fu' he fell awald beside it,
And that 's how Meg o' the Mill was bedded !

JOCKIE 'S TA'EN THE PARTING KISS

I

JOCKIE 's ta'en the parting kiss,
O'er the mountains he is gane,
And with him is a' my bliss —
Nought but griefs with me remain.

II

Spare my luve, ye winds that blaw,
Plashy sleets and beating rain !
Spare my luve, thou feathery snaw,
Drifting o'er the frozen plain !

III

When the shades of evening creep
O'er the day's fair gladsome e'e,
Sound and safely may he sleep,
Sweetly blythe his waukening be !

IV

He will think on her he loves,
Fondly he 'll repeat her name;
For where'er he distant roves,
Jockie's heart is still at hame.

O, LAY THY LOOF IN MINE, LASS

CHORUS

O, lay thy loof in mine, lass,
In mine, lass, in mine, lass,
And swear on thy white hand, lass,
That thou wilt be my ain!

I

A SLAVE to Love's unbounded sway,
He aft has wrought me meikle wae;
But now he is my deadly fae,
Unless thou be my ain.

II

There 's monie a lass has broke my rest,
That for a blink I hae lo'ed best;
But thou art queen within my breast,
For ever to remain.

CHORUS

O, lay thy loof in mine, lass,
In mine, lass, in mine, lass,
And swear on thy white hand, lass,
That thou wilt be my ain!

CAULD IS THE E'ENIN BLAST

I

CAULD is the e'enin blast
O' Boreas o'er the pool
An' dawin, it is dreary,
When birks are bare at Yule.

II

O, cauld blaws the e'enin blast,
When bitter bites the frost,
And in the mirk and dreary drift
The hills and glens are lost!

III

Ne'er sae murky blew the night
That drifted o'er the hill,
But bonie Peg-a-Ramsay
Gat grist to her mill.

THERE WAS A BONIE LASS

A cento of old catch words.

I

THERE was a bonie lass, and a bonie, bonie lass,
And she loed her bonie laddie dear,
Till War's loud alarms tore her laddie frae her arms
Wi' monie a sigh and a tear.

II

Over sea, over shore, where the cannons loudly roar,
He still was a stranger to fear,
And nocht could him quail, or his bosom assail,
But the bonie lass he loed sae dear.

THERE 'S NEWS, LASSES, NEWS

CHORUS

The wean wants a cradle,
And the cradle wants a cod,
An' I 'll no gang to my bed
Until I get a nod.

I

THERE 's news, lasses, news,
Guid news I 've to tell!
There 's a boatfu' o' lads
Come to our town to sell!

II

"Father," quo' she, "Mither," quo' she,
"Do what you can:
I 'll no gang to my bed
Until I get a man!"

III

I hae as guid a craft rig
As made o' yird and stane;

And waly fa' the ley-crap
For I maun till'd again.

CHORUS

The wean wants a cradle,
  And the cradle wants a cod,
An' I 'll no gang to my bed
  Until I get a nod.

O, THAT I HAD NE'ER BEEN MARRIED

CHORUS

Ance crowdie, twice crowdie,
  Three times crowdie in a day !
Gin ye crowdie onie mair,
  Ye 'll crowdie a' my meal away.

I

O, THAT I had ne'er been married,
  I wad never had nae care !
Now I 've gotten wife an' bairns,
  An' they cry " Crowdie " evermair.

II

Waefu' Want and Hunger fley me,
  Glowrin by the hallan en';
Sair I fecht them at the door,
  But ay I 'm eerie they come ben.

CHORUS

Ance crowdie, twice crowdie,
  Three times crowdie in a day !
Gin ye crowdie onie mair,
  Ye 'll crowdie a' my meal away.

MALLY 'S MEEK, MALLY 'S SWEET

CHORUS

Mally 's meek, Mally 's sweet,
Mally 's modest and discreet,
Mally 's rare, Mally 's fair,
Mally 's ev'ry way complete.

I

As I was walking up the street,
  A barefit maid I chanc'd to meet;
But O, the road was very hard
  For that fair maiden's tender feet !

II

It were mair meet that those fine feet
  Were weel laced up in silken shoon !
An' 't were more fit that she should sit
  Within yon chariot gilt aboon !

III

Her yellow hair, beyond compare,
  Comes tumbling down her swan-white
    neck,
And her twa eyes, like stars in skies,
  Would keep a sinking ship frae wreck !

CHORUS

Mally 's meek, Mally 's sweet,
Mally 's modest and discreet,
Mally 's rare, Mally 's fair,
Mally 's ev'ry way complete.

WANDERING WILLIE

I

HERE awa, there awa, wandering Willie,
  Here awa, there awa, haud awa hame !
Come to my bosom, my ae only dearie,
  And tell me thou bring'st me my Willie
    the same.

II

Loud tho' the Winter blew cauld at our
    parting,
  'T was na the blast brought the tear in
    my e'e:
Welcome now Simmer, and welcome my
    Willie,
  The Simmer to Nature, my Willie to me !

III

Rest, ye wild storms in the cave o' your
    slumbers —
  How your wild howling a lover alarms !
Wauken, ye breezes, row gently, ye billows,
  And waft my dear laddie ance mair to
    my arms.

IV

But O, if he 's faithless, and minds na his
    Nannie,
  Flow still between us, thou wide-roaring
    main !
May I never see it, may I never trow it,
  But, dying, believe that my Willie 's my
    ain !

BRAW LADS O' GALLA WATER

I

Braw, braw lads on Yarrow braes,
  They rove amang the blooming heather;
But Yarrow braes nor Ettrick shaws
  Can match the lads o' Galla Water.

II

But there is ane, a secret ane,
  Aboon them a' I loe him better;
And I 'll be his, and he 'll be mine,
  The bonie lad o' Galla Water.

III

Altho' his daddie was nae laird,
  And tho' I hae nae meikle tocher,
Yet, rich in kindest, truest love,
  We 'll tent our flocks by Galla Water.

IV

It ne'er was wealth, it ne'er was wealth,
  That coft contentment, peace, and plea-
    sure:
The bands and bliss o' mutual love,
  O, that 's the chiefest warld's treasure !

AULD ROB MORRIS

I

There 's Auld Rob Morris that wons in
    yon glen,
He 's the king o' guid fellows and wale of
    auld men:
He has gowd in his coffers, he has owsen
    and kine,
And ae bonie lassie, his dautie and mine.

II

She 's fresh as the morning the fairest in
    May,
She 's sweet as the ev'ning amang the new
    hay,
As blythe and as artless as the lambs on
    the lea,
And dear to my heart as the light to my e'e.

III

But O, she 's an heiress, auld Robin 's a
    laird,
And my daddie has nocht but a cot-house
    and yard !

A wooer like me maunna hope to come
    speed:
The wounds I must hide that will soon be
    my dead.

IV

The day comes to me, but delight brings
    me nane;
The night comes to me, but my rest it is
    gane;
I wander my lane like a night-troubled
    ghaist,
And I sigh as my heart it wad burst in my
    breast.

V

O, had she but been of a lower degree,
  I then might hae hop'd she wad smil'd
    upon me !
O, how past descriving had then been my
    bliss,
As now my distraction no words can ex-
    press !

OPEN THE DOOR TO ME, O

I

O, open the door some pity to shew,
  If love it may na be, O !
Tho' thou hast been false, I 'll ever prove
    true —
O, open the door to me, O !

II

Cauld is the blast upon my pale cheek,
  But caulder thy love for me, O :
The frost, that freezes the life at my heart,
  Is nought to my pains frae thee, O !

III

The wan moon sets behind the white wave,
  And Time is setting with me, O :
False friends, false love, farewell ! for mair
  I 'll ne'er trouble them nor thee, O !

IV

She has open'd the door, she has open'd it
    wide,
  She sees the pale corse on the plain, O,
"My true love !" she cried, and sank down
    by his side —
  Never to rise again, O !

WHEN WILD WAR'S DEADLY BLAST

I

WHEN wild War's deadly blast was blawn,
  And gentle Peace returning,
Wi' monie a sweet babe fatherless
  And monie a widow mourning,
I left the lines and tented field,
  Where lang I'd been a lodger,
My humble knapsack a' my wealth,
  A poor and honest sodger.

II

A leal, light heart was in my breast,
  My hand unstain'd wi' plunder,
And for fair Scotia, hame again,
  I cheery on did wander:
I thought upon the banks o' Coil,
  I thought upon my Nancy,
And ay I mind't the witching smile
  That caught my youthful fancy.

III

At length I reach'd the bonie glen,
  Where early life I sported.
I pass'd the mill and trysting thorn,
  Where Nancy aft I courted.
Wha spied I but my ain dear maid,
  Down by her mother's dwelling,
And turn'd me round to hide the flood
  That in my een was swelling!

IV

Wi' alter'd voice, quoth I : — " Sweet lass,
  Sweet as yon hawthorn's blossom,
O, happy, happy may he be,
  That 's dearest to thy bosom !
My purse is light, I 've far to gang,
  And fain wad be thy lodger;
I 've serv'd my king and country lang —
  Take pity on a sodger."

V

Sae wistfully she gaz'd on me,
  And lovelier was than ever.
Quo' she: — " A sodger ance I lo'ed,
  Forget him shall I never.
Our humble cot, and hamely fare,
  Ye freely shall partake it;
That gallant badge — the dear cockade —
  Ye 're welcome for the sake o't ! "

VI

She gaz'd, she redden'd like a rose,
  Syne, pale like onie lily,
She sank within my arms, and cried: —
  " Art thou my ain dear Willie ?"
" By Him who made yon sun and sky,
  By whom true love 's regarded,
I am the man ! And thus may still
  True lovers be rewarded !

VII

" The wars are o'er and I 'm come hame,
  And find thee still true-hearted.
Tho' poor in gear, we 're rich in love,
  And mair, we 'se ne'er be parted."
Quo' she: " My grandsire left me gowd,
  A mailen plenish'd fairly !
And come, my faithfu' sodger lad,
  Thou 'rt welcome to it dearly ! "

VIII

For gold the merchant ploughs the main,
  The farmer ploughs the manor;
But glory is the sodger's prize,
  The sodger's wealth is honour !
The brave poor sodger ne'er despise,
  Nor count him as a stranger:
Remember he 's his country's stay
  In day and hour of danger.

DUNCAN GRAY

Enclosed, together with *Auld Rob Morris*, to Thomson 4th December, 1792: "The foregoing I submit, my dear Sir, to your better judgment; acquit them or condemn them as seemeth good in thy sight. *Duncan Gray* is that kind of lighthorse gallop of an air which precludes sentiment. The ludicrous is its ruling feature."

I

DUNCAN GRAY cam here to woo
  (Ha, ha, the wooing o't !)
On blythe Yule-Night when we were fou
  (Ha, ha, the wooing o't !).
Maggie coost her head fu' high,
Look'd asklent and unco skeigh,
Gart poor Duncan stand abeigh —
  Ha, ha, the wooing o't !

II

Duncan fleech'd, and Duncan pray'd
  (Ha, ha, the wooing o't !),

Meg was deaf as Ailsa craig
  (Ha, ha, the wooing o't !).
Duncan sigh'd baith out and in,
Grat his een baith bleer't an' blin',
Spak o' lowpin o'er a linn —
  Ha, ha, the wooing o't !

III

Time and Chance are but a tide
  (Ha, ha, the wooing o't !):
Slighted love is sair to bide
  (Ha, ha, the wooing o't !).
"Shall I like a fool," quoth he,
"For a haughty hizzie die ?
She may gae to — France for me !" —
  Ha, ha, the wooing o't !

IV

How it comes, let doctors tell
  (Ha, ha, the wooing o't !):
Meg grew sick, as he grew hale
  (Ha, ha, the wooing o't !).
Something in her bosom wrings,
For relief a sigh she brings,
And O ! her een they spak sic things ! —
  Ha, ha, the wooing o't !

V

Duncan was a lad o' grace
  (Ha, ha, the wooing o't !),
Maggie's was a piteous case
  (Ha, ha, the wooing o't !):
Duncan could na be her death,
Swelling pity smoor'd his wrath;
Now they 're crouse and canty baith —
  Ha, ha, the wooing o't !

DELUDED SWAIN, THE PLEA-SURE

I

DELUDED swain, the pleasure
  The fickle Fair can give thee
Is but a fairy treasure —
  Thy hopes will soon deceive thee:
The billows on the ocean,
  The breezes idly roaming,
The cloud's uncertain motion,
  They are but types of Woman !

II

O, art thou not ashamèd
  To doat upon a feature ?

If Man thou would'st be namèd,
  Despise the silly creature !
Go, find an honest fellow,
  Good claret set before thee,
Hold on till thou art mellow,
  And then to bed in glory !

HERE IS THE GLEN

"I know you value a composition because it is made by one of the great ones as little as I do. However, I got an air, pretty enough, composed by Lady Elizabeth Heron of Heron, which she calls *The Banks of Cree.* Cree is a beautiful romantic stream, and, as her ladyship is a particular friend of mine, I have written the following song to it." (R. B. to Thomson.)

The tune did not please Thomson, who set the verses to *The Flowers of Edinburgh.* That they made a love-song for Maria Riddell, as some hold, is scarce consistent with Burns's statement. Moreover, he must have intended that Lady Elizabeth Heron should see them.

I

HERE is the glen, and here the bower
  All underneath the birchen shade,
The village-bell has toll'd the hour —
  O, what can stay my lovely maid ?
'T is not Maria's whispering call —
  'T is but the balmy-breathing gale,
Mixed with some warbler's dying fall
  The dewy star of eve to hail !

II

It is Maria's voice I hear ! —
  So calls the woodlark in the grove
His little faithful mate to cheer:
  At once 't is music and 't is love !
And art thou come ？ And art thou true ?
  O, welcome, dear, to love and me,
And let us all our vows renew
  Along the flowery banks of Cree !

LET NOT WOMEN E'ER COM-PLAIN

Alternative English words to the tune *Duncan Gray:* "These English songs gravel me to death. I have not that command of the language that I have of my native tongue. In fact, I think my ideas are more barren in English than in Scottish. I have been at *Dun-*

can Gray to dress it in English, but all I can do is deplorably stupid." (R. B. to Thomson, 19th October, 1794.) There is nothing to add to this, except that the song exists (if that can be said to exist which is never sung, never quoted, and if ever read, immediately forgotten) as pure Burns.

I

LET not women e'er complain
  Of inconstancy in love !
Let not women e'er complain
  Fickle man is apt to rove !
Look abroad thro' Nature's range,
Nature's mighty law is change:
Ladies, would it not be strange
  Man should then a monster prove ?

II

Mark the winds, and mark the skies,
  Ocean's ebb and ocean's flow.
Sun and moon but set to rise.
  Round and round the seasons go.
Why then, ask of silly man
To oppose great Nature's plan ?
We 'll be constant, while we can —
  You can be no more, you know !

LORD GREGORY

Written, at Thomson's request, to the air of *The Lass of Lochryan.*
Peter Pindar (Dr. Wolcott) wrote English verses for Thomson on the same theme. They are frigid rubbish; but "the very name of Peter Pindar is an acquisition to your work. His *Gregory* is beautiful. I have tried to give you a set of stanzas in Scots on the same subject, which are at your service. Not that I intend to enter the lists with Peter — that would be presumption indeed! My song, though much inferior in poetic merit, has, I think, more of the ballad simplicity in it." (R. B. to Thomson, 26th January, 1793.)

I

O, MIRK, mirk is this midnight hour,
  And loud the tempest's roar !
A waefu' wanderer seeks thy tower —
  Lord Gregory, ope thy door.

II

An exile frae her father's ha',
  And a' for sake o' thee,

At least some pity on me shaw,
  If love it may na be.

III

Lord Gregory, mind'st thou not the grove
  By bonie Irwine side,
Where first I own'd that virgin love
  I lang, lang had denied ?

IV

How aften didst thou pledge and vow,
  Thou wad for ay be mine !
And my fond heart, itsel' sae true,
  It ne'er mistrusted thine.

V

Hard is thy heart, Lord Gregory,
  And flinty is thy breast:
Thou bolt of Heaven that flashest by,
  O, wilt thou bring me rest !

VI

Ye mustering thunders from above,
  Your willing victim see,
But spare and pardon my fause love
  His wrangs to Heaven and me !

O POORTITH CAULD

Gilbert Burns told Thomson that Burns's heroine was "a Miss Jane Blackstock, afterwards Mrs. Whittier of Liverpool." But it was probably Jean Lorimer (see *post,* p. 289, Prefatory Note to *Lassie wi' the Lint-white Locks*), who was then contemplating the marriage of which she instantly repented. *O Poortith Cauld* is held to refer to her rejecting a gauger for the man she married (see *ante,* p. 231, Prefatory Note to *Craigieburn Wood*). It was sent to Thomson in January, 1793, for the tune of *Cauld Kail in Aberdeen;* but Thomson thought the verses had "too much of uneasy, cold reflection for the air." To this Burns : "The objections are just, but I cannot make it better. The stuff won't bear mending; yet for private reasons, I should like to see it in print." With a new chorus and other amendments, it was set in the end to *I Had a Horse and I Had Nae Mair.*

CHORUS

O, why should Fate sic pleasure have,
  Life's dearest bands untwining ?
Or why sae sweet a flower as love
  Depend on Fortune's shining ?

I

O POORTITH cauld and restless Love,
 Ye wrack my peace between ye !
Yet poortith a' I could forgive,
 An 't were na for my Jeanie.

II

The warld's wealth when I think on,
 Its pride and a' the lave o't —
My curse on silly coward man,
 That he should be the slave o't !

III

Her een sae bonie blue betray
 How she repays my passion;
But prudence is her o'erword ay:
 She talks o' rank and fashion.

IV

O, wha can prudence think upon,
 And sic a lassie by him ?
O, wha can prudence think upon,
 And sae in love as I am ?

V

How blest the wild-wood Indian's fate !
 He woos his artless dearie —
The silly bogles, Wealth and State,
 Can never make him eerie.

CHORUS

O, why should Fate sic pleasure have,
 Life's dearest bands untwining ?
Or why sae sweet a flower as love
 Depend on Fortune's shining ?

O, STAY, SWEET WARBLING WOOD-LARK

I

O, STAY, sweet warbling wood-lark, stay,
Nor quit for me the trembling spray !
A hapless lover courts thy lay,
 Thy soothing, fond complaining.
Again, again that tender part,
That I may catch thy melting art !
For surely that wad touch her heart,
 Wha kills me wi' disdaining.

II

Say, was thy little mate unkind,
And heard thee as the careless wind ?
O, nocht but love and sorrow join'd
 Sic notes o' woe could wauken !
Thou tells o' never-ending care,
O' speechless grief and dark despair —
For pity's sake, sweet bird, nae mair,
 Or my poor heart is broken !

SAW YE BONIE LESLEY

"Bonie Lesley" was Miss Leslie Baillie, daughter of Mr. Baillie of Mayfield, Ayrshire. She married, in June, 1799, Mr. Robert Cumming of Logie, and died in July, 1843. "The heart-struck awe, the distant humble approach, the delight we should have in gazing upon and listening to a messenger of Heaven, appearing in all the unspotted purity of his celestial home, among the coarse, polluted, far inferior sons of men, to deliver to them tidings that make their hearts swim in joy, and their imaginations soar in transport — such, so delighting and so pure were the emotions of my soul on meeting the other day with Miss Lesley Baillie, your neighbour at Mayfield. Mr. B., with his two daughters, accompanied with Mr. H. of G., passing through Dumfries a few days ago on their way to England, did me the honour of calling on me; on which I took my horse — though God knows I could ill spare the time — and accompanied them fourteen or fifteen miles, and dined and spent the day with them. 'T was about nine, I think, that I left them, and riding home I composed the following ballad, of which you will probably think you have a dear bargain, as it will cost you another groat of postage. You must know that there is an old ballad beginning with : —

'My Bonie Lizzie Baillie, I 'll rowe thee in my plaiddie,'

so I parodied it as follows, which is literally the first copy 'unanointed, unannealed,' as Hamlet says." (R. B. to Mrs. Dunlop, 22d August, 1792.)

I

O, SAW ye bonie Lesley,
 As she gaed o'er the Border ?
She 's gane, like Alexander,
 To spread her conquests farther !

II

To see her is to love her,
 And love but her for ever;

For Nature made her what she is,
  And never made anither !

III

Thou art a queen, fair Lesley —
  Thy subjects, we before thee !
Thou art divine, fair Lesley —
  The hearts o' men adore thee.

IV

The Deil he could na skaith thee,
  Or aught that wad belang thee:
He 'd look into thy bonie face,
  And say: — "I canna wrang thee !"

V

The Powers aboon will tent thee,
  Misfortune sha'na steer thee:
Thou 'rt like themsel' sae lovely,
  That ill they 'll ne'er let near thee.

VI

Return again, fair Lesley,
  Return to Caledonie !
That we may brag we hae a lass
  There 's nane again sae bonie.

SWEET FA'S THE EVE

I

Sweet fa's the eve on Craigieburn,
  And blythe awakes the morrow,
But a' the pride o' Spring's return
  Can yield me nocht but sorrow.

II

I see the flowers and spreading trees,
  I hear the wild birds singing;
But what a weary wight can please,
  And Care his bosom is wringing?

III

Fain, fain would I my griefs impart,
  Yet dare na for your anger;
But secret love will break my heart,
  If I conceal it langer.

IV

If thou refuse to pity me,
  If thou shalt love another,
When yon green leaves fade frae the tree,
  Around my grave they 'll wither.

YOUNG JESSIE

"I send you a song on a celebrated fashionable toast in this country to suit *Bonie Dundee*." (R. B. to Thomson.)

The lady was Miss Jessie Staig (daughter of Provost Staig of Dumfries), on whose recovery from a dangerous illness Burns afterwards wrote the epigram *To Dr. Maxwell* (see *ante*, p. 190). She married Major William Miller, son of Mr. Miller of Dalswinton, and died at twenty-six in the March of 1801.

I

True hearted was he, the sad swain o' the Yarrow,
  And fair are the maids on the banks of the Ayr;
But by the sweet side o' the Nith's winding river
  Are lovers as faithful and maidens as fair:
To equal young Jessie seek Scotia all over —
  To equal young Jessie you seek it in vain !
Grace, beauty, and elegance fetter her lover,
  And maidenly modesty fixes the chain.

II

Fresh is the rose in the gay, dewy morning,
  And sweet is the lily at evening close;
But in the fair presence o' lovely young Jessie
  Unseen is the lily, unheeded the rose.
Love sits in her smile, a wizard ensnaring;
  Enthron'd in her een he delivers his law;
And still to her charms she alone is a stranger:
  Her modest demeanour 's the jewel of a'.

ADOWN WINDING NITH

"Another favourite air of mine is *The Muckin o' Geordie's Byre*. When sung slow, with expression, I have wished that it had better poetry : that I have endeavoured to supply as follows. . . . Mr. Clarke begs you to give Miss Phillis a corner in your Book, as she is a particular Flame of his. She is a Miss Phillis M'Murdo, sister to the 'Bonie Jean' which I sent you some time ago. They are both pupils of his." (R. B. to Thomson, August, 1793.)

Phillis M'Murdo married Norman Lockhart, afterwards third baronet of Carnwath. Before this, Burns had sent Thomson another song on the same lady, *Phillis the Fair*, with which he did not pretend to be satisfied, and which Thomson did not accept (see *post*, p. 313).

CHORUS

Awa wi' your belles and your beauties —
    They never wi' her can compare !
Whaever hae met wi' my Phillis
    Has met wi' the Queen o' the Fair !

I

ADOWN winding Nith I did wander
    To mark the sweet flowers as they spring.
Adown winding Nith I did wander
    Of Phillis to muse and to sing.

II

The Daisy amus'd my fond fancy,
    So artless, so simple, so wild:
" Thou emblem," said I, " o' my Phillis " —
    For she is Simplicity's child.

III

The rose-bud 's the blush o' my charmer,
    Her sweet balmy lip when 't is prest.
How fair and how pure is the lily !
    But fairer and purer her breast.

IV

Yon knot of gay flowers in the arbour,
    They ne'er wi' my Phillis can vie:
Her breath is the breath of the woodbine,
    Its dew-drop o' diamond her eye.

V

Her voice is the song o' the morning,
    That wakes thro' the green-spreading
        grove,
When Phebus peeps over the mountains
    On music, and pleasure, and love.

VI

But Beauty, how frail and how fleeting !
    The bloom of a fine summer's day !
While Worth in the mind o' my Phillis
    Will flourish without a decay.

CHORUS

Awa wi' your belles and your beauties —
    They never wi' her can compare !
Whaever hae met wi' my Phillis
    Has met wi' the Queen o' the Fair !

A LASS WI' A TOCHER

" The other day I strung up a kind of rhapsody to another Hibernian melody that I admire much." (R. B. to Thomson, February, 1797.) The " Hibernian melody " was *Balinamona Ora*.

CHORUS

Then hey for a lass wi' a tocher,
Then hey for a lass wi' a tocher,
Then hey for a lass wi' a tocher,
    The nice yellow guineas for me !

I

AWA wi' your witchcraft o' Beauty's
        alarms,
The slender bit beauty you grasp in your
        arms !
O, gie me the lass that has acres o' charms !
O, gie me the lass wi' the weel-stockit
        farms !

II

Your Beauty 's a flower in the morning
        that blows,
And withers the faster the faster it grows ;
But the rapturous charm o' the bonie green
        knowes,
Ilk spring they 're new deckit wi' bonie
        white yowes !

III

And e'en when this Beauty your bosom has
        blest,
The brightest o' Beauty may cloy when
        possess'd;
But the sweet, yellow darlings wi' Geordie
        impress'd,
The langer ye hae them, the mair they 're
        carest !

CHORUS

Then hey for a lass wi' a tocher,
Then hey for a lass wi' a tocher,
Then hey for a lass wi' a tocher,
    The nice yellow guineas for me !

BLYTHE HAE I BEEN ON YON HILL

Suggested by Fraser the oboist's interpretation of *The Quaker's Wife*: "Mr. Fraser plays it slow, and with an expression that quite charms me. I got such an enthusiast in it that I made a song for it, which I here subjoin, and enclose Fraser's set of the tune. If they hit your fancy they are at your service; if not, return me the tune, and I will put it in Johnson's *Museum*. I think the song is not in my worst manner." (R. B. to Thomson, June, 1793.)

Later, in his remarks on Thomson's *List*, he inserted *Blythe Hae I Been on Yon Hill*: "which," he wrote, " is one of the finest songs ever I made in my life; and is composed on a young lady, positively the most beautiful lovely woman in the world. As I purpose giving you the name and designation of all my heroines to appear in some future edition of your work, perhaps half a century hence, you must certainly include the boniest lass in the world in your collection." For the " boniest lass in the world," see *ante*, p. 275, Prefatory Note to *Saw Ye Bonie Lesley*.

I

BLYTHE hae I been on yon hill
　As the lambs before me,
Careless ilka thought, and free
　As the breeze flew o'er me.
Now nae langer sport and play,
　Mirth or sang can please me:
Lesley is sae fair and coy,
　Care and anguish seize me.

II

Heavy, heavy is the task,
　Hopeless love declaring!
Trembling, I dow nocht but glow'r,
　Sighing, dumb despairing!
If she winna ease the thraws
　In my bosom swelling,
Underneath the grass-green sod
　Soon maun be my dwelling.

BY ALLAN STREAM

"I walked out yesterday evening with a volume of the *Museum* in my hand, when, turning up *Allan Water* ('What number shall my Muse repeat,' etc.), it appeared to me rather unworthy of so fine an air; and recollecting it is on your list, I sat and raved under the shade of an old thorn, till I wrote one to suit the measure. I may be wrong, but I think it is not in my worst style." (R. B. to Thomson, August, 1793.)

I

By Allan stream I chanc'd to rove,
　While Phebus sank beyond Benledi;
The winds were whispering thro' the grove,
　The yellow corn was waving ready;
I listen'd to a lover's sang,
　An' thought on youthfu' pleasures monie,
And ay the wild-wood echoes rang:—
　" O, my love Annie's very bonie!

II

" O, happy be the woodbine bower,
　Nae nightly bogle make it eerie!
Nor ever sorrow stain the hour,
　The place and time I met my dearie!
Her head upon my throbbing breast,
　She, sinking, said:—'I'm thine for
　　ever!'
While monie a kiss the seal imprest—
　The sacred vow we ne'er should sever."

III

The haunt o' Spring's the primrose-brae.
　The Summer joys the flocks to follow.
How cheery thro' her short'ning day
　Is Autumn in her weeds o' yellow!
But can they melt the glowing heart,
　Or chain the soul in speechless pleasure,
Or thro' each nerve the rapture dart,
　Like meeting her, our bosom's treasure?

CANST THOU LEAVE ME

Sent to Thomson, 20th November, 1794. "Well, I think this, to be done in two or three turns across my room, and with two or three pinches of Irish blackguard, is not far amiss. You see I am determined to have my quantum of applause from somebody." (R. B.)

CHORUS

Canst thou leave me thus, my Katie!
　Canst thou leave me thus, my Katie!
Well thou know'st my aching heart,
　And canst thou leave me thus for pity?

I

Is this thy plighted, fond regard:
　Thus cruelly to part, my Katie?
Is this thy faithful swain's reward:
　An aching broken heart, my Katie?

II

Farewell! And ne'er such sorrows tear
That fickle heart of thine, my Katie!
Thou may'st find those will love thee dear,
But not a love like mine, my Katie.

CHORUS

Canst thou leave me thus, my Katie!
Canst thou leave me thus, my Katie,
Well thou know'st my aching heart,
And canst thou leave me thus for pity?

COME, LET ME TAKE THEE

"That tune, *Cauld Kail*, is such a favourite
of yours that I once roved out yester evening for
a gloamin shot at the Muses; when the Muse
that presides o'er the shores of Nith, or rather
my old inspiring dearest nymph, Coila, whis-
pered me the following. I have two reasons for
thinking that it was my early, sweet Inspirer
that was by my elbow, 'smooth-gliding without
step,' and pouring the song on my glowing
fancy. In the first place, since I left Coila's
native haunts, not a fragment of a Poet has
arisen to cheer her solitary musings by catch-
ing inspiration from her, so I more than sus-
pect she has followed me hither, or at least
made me an occasional visit; secondly, the
last stanza of this song I sent you is the very
words that Coila taught me many years ago,
and which I set to an old Scots reel, in John-
son's *Museum*." (R. B. to Thomson, August,
1793.) The song referred to is *And I'll Kiss
Thee Yet* (*ante*, p. 213).

I

Come, let me take thee to my breast,
And pledge we ne'er shall sunder,
And I shall spurn as vilest dust
The world's wealth and grandeur!
And do I hear my Jeanie own
That equal transports move her?
I ask for dearest life alone,
That I may live to love her.

II

Thus in my arms, wi' a' her charms,
I clasp my countless treasure,
I'll seek nae mair o' Heav'n to share
Than sic a moment's pleasure!

And by thy een sae bonie blue
I swear I'm thine for ever,
And on thy lips I seal my vow,
And break it shall I never!

CONTENTED WI' LITTLE

I

Contented wi' little and cantie wi' mair,
Whene'er I forgather wi' Sorrow and Care,
I gie them a skelp, as they're creepin alang,
Wi' a cog o' guid swats and an auld Scot-
tish sang.

II

I whyles claw the elbow o' troublesome
Thought;
But Man is a soger, and Life is a faught.
My mirth and guid humour are coin in my
pouch,
And my Freedom's my lairdship nae mon-
arch daur touch.

III

A towmond o' trouble, should that be my
fa',
A night o' guid fellowship sowthers it a':
When at the blythe end o' our journey at
last,
Wha the Deil ever thinks o' the road he
has past?

IV

Blind Chance, let her snapper and stoyte
on her way,
Be't to me, be't frae me, e'en let the jade
gae!
Come Ease or come Travail, come Pleasure
or Pain,
My warst word is: — "Welcome, and wel-
come again!"

FAREWELL, THOU STREAM

The second set of a song which originally
began: —
"The last time I came o'er the moor
And left Maria's dwelling."
The heroine was Maria Riddell, to whom
Burns sent a copy. To this he added this note
(unpublished [1]): "On reading over the song, I

[1] That is, before the Centenary Edition.

see it is but a cold, inanimate composition. It will be absolutely necessary for me to get in love, else I shall never be able to make a line worth reading on the subject." In January, 1794, occurred the estrangement from Mrs. Riddell (see *ante*, pp. 178, 179, Prefatory Note to *Impromptu on Mrs. Riddell's Birthday*); and in July, 1794, Burns informed Thomson that he meant to set the verses he had sent him for *The Last Time I Came O'er the Moor* to *Nancy's to the Greenwood Gane*, and that he had "made an alteration in the beginning."

I

FAREWELL, thou stream that winding flows
  Around Eliza's dwelling !
O Mem'ry, spare the cruel throes
  Within my bosom swelling:
Condemn'd to drag a hopeless chain
  And yet in secret languish,
To feel a fire in every vein
  Nor dare disclose my anguish !

II

Love's veriest wretch, unseen, unknown,
  I fain my griefs would cover:
The bursting sigh, th' unweeting groan
  Betray the hapless lover.
I know thou doom'st me to despair,
  Nor wilt, nor canst relieve me;
But, O Eliza, hear one prayer —
  For pity's sake forgive me !

III

The music of thy voice I heard,
  Nor wist while it enslav'd me !
I saw thine eyes, yet nothing fear'd,
  Till fears no more had sav'd me !
Th' unwary sailor thus, aghast
  The wheeling torrent viewing,
'Mid circling horrors sinks at last
  In overwhelming ruin.

HAD I A CAVE

"That crinkum-crankum tune, *Robin Adair*, has run so in my head, and I succeeded so ill in my last attempt [*Phillis the Fair*, see *post*, p. 313], that I ventured in my morning's walk one essay more. You, my dear Sir, will remember an unfortunate part of our worthy friend Cunningham's story, which happened about three years ago. That struck my fancy, and I endeavoured to do the idea poetic justice, as follows." (R. B. to Thomson, August, 1793.)

See further, Prefatory Notes to *Anna* (*ante*, p. 95); *To Alex. Cunningham* (*ante*, p. 140); and *She's Fair and Fause* (*ante*, p. 249).

I

HAD I a cave
  On some wild distant shore,
Where the winds howl
  To the wave's dashing roar,
    There would I weep my woes,
    There seek my lost repose,
    Till grief my eyes should close,
  Ne'er to wake more !

II

Falsest of womankind,
  Can'st thou declare
All thy fond, plighted vows
  Fleeting as air ?
    To thy new lover hie,
    Laugh o'er thy perjury,
    Then in thy bosom try
  What peace is there !

HERE'S A HEALTH

"I once mentioned to you an air which I have long admired, *Here's Health to Them That's Awa, Hinney*; but I forget if you took notice of it. I have just been trying to suit it with verses ; and I beg leave to recommend the air to your attention once more." (R. B. to Thomson, May, 1796.) About a fortnight before his death he sent a copy to Alexander Cunningham : "Did Thomson show you the following song, the last I made, or probably will make for some time ? "
The heroine, Jessie Lewars, sister of John Lewars, a fellow-exciseman, was of great service to the Burns household during the last illness. She is also commemorated in certain complimentary verses (*ante*, pp. 148, 192), and in that very beautiful song, *O, Wert Thou in the Cauld Blast* (*post*, p. 315). On 3d June, 1799, she married Mr. James Thomson, Writer in Dumfries, and she died 26th May, 1855.

CHORUS

Here's a health to ane I loe dear !
Here's a health to ane I loe dear !
Thou art sweet as the smile when fond lov-
    ers meet,
  And soft as their parting tear,
          Jessy —
  And soft as their parting tear !

I

ALTHO' thou maun never be mine,
   Altho' even hope is denied,
'T is sweeter for thee despairing
   Than ought in the world beside,
         Jessy —
   Than ought in the world beside !

II

I mourn thro' the gay, gaudy day,
   As hopeless I muse on thy charms;
But welcome the dream o' sweet slumber !
   For then I am lockt in thine arms,
         Jessy —
   For then I am lockt in thine arms !

CHORUS

Here 's a health to ane I loe dear !
Here 's a health to ane I loe dear !
Thou art sweet as the smile when fond
      lovers meet,
And soft as their parting tear,
      Jessy —
And soft as their parting tear !

HOW CRUEL ARE THE PARENTS

" A song altered from an old English one "
(R. B.), [which begins] :
      " How cruel is that parent's care,
         Who riches only prizes."

I

How cruel are the parents
   Who riches only prize,
And to the wealthy booby
   Poor Woman sacrifice !
Meanwhile the hapless daughter
   Has but a choice of strife:
To shun a tyrant father's hate
   Become a wretched wife !

II

The ravening hawk pursuing,
   The trembling dove thus flies:
To shun impending ruin
   Awhile her pinion tries,
Till, of escape despairing,
   No shelter or retreat,
She trusts the ruthless falconer,
   And drops beneath his feet.

HUSBAND, HUSBAND, CEASE
YOUR STRIFE

I

" HUSBAND, husband, cease your strife,
   Nor longer idly rave, sir !
Tho' I am your wedded wife,
   Yet I am not your slave, sir."
" One of two must still obey,
   Nancy, Nancy !
Is it Man or Woman, say,
   My spouse Nancy ? "

II

" If 't is still the lordly word,
   Service and obedience,
I 'll desert my sov'reign lord,
   And so goodbye, allegiance ! "
" Sad will I be so bereft,
   Nancy, Nancy !
Yet I 'll try to make a shift,
   My spouse Nancy ! "

III

" My poor heart, then break it must,
   My last hour I am near it:
When you lay me in the dust,
   Think, how will you bear it ? "
" I will hope and trust in Heaven,
   Nancy, Nancy !
Strength to bear it will be given,
   My spouse Nancy."

IV

" Well, sir, from the silent dead,
   Still I 'll try to daunt you:
Ever round your midnight bed
   Horrid sprites shall haunt you ! "
" I 'll wed another like my dear,
   Nancy, Nancy !
Then all Hell will fly for fear,
   My spouse Nancy ! "

IT WAS THE CHARMING MONTH

Meant as English words to *Dainty Davie*,
and abridged from a song in *The Tea-Table
Miscellany*. " You may think meanly of this,
but take a look at the bombast original and
you will be surprised that I have made so
much of it." (R. B. to Thomson, November,
1794.)

All the same, Burns rather selected from than renewed and re-inspired the "bombast original." Practically nothing is his but the repeats and the chorus; and even these have their germs in the *Miscellany*. The rest of his set is "lifted" almost word for word, and simply edited and rearranged.

CHORUS

Lovely was she by the dawn,
    Youthful Chloe, charming Chloe,
Tripping o'er the pearly lawn,
    The youthful, charming Chloe!

I

It was the charming month of May,
When all the flow'rs were fresh and gay,
One morning, by the break of day,
    The youthful, charming Chloe,
From peaceful slumber she arose,
Girt on her mantle and her hose,
And o'er the flow'ry mead she goes —
    The youthful, charming Chloe!

II

The feather'd people you might see
Perch'd all around on every tree!
With notes of sweetest melody
    They hail the charming Chloe,
Till, painting gay the eastern skies,
The glorious sun began to rise,
Outrival'd by the radiant eyes
    Of youthful, charming Chloe.

CHORUS

Lovely was she by the dawn,
    Youthful Chloe, charming Chloe,
Tripping o'er the pearly lawn,
    The youthful, charming Chloe!

LAST MAY A BRAW WOOER

I

Last May a braw wooer cam down the
        lang glen,
    And sair wi' his love he did deave me.
I said there was naething I hated like
        men:
    The deuce gae wi'm to believe me, be-
        lieve me —
    The deuce gae wi'm to believe me!

II

He spak o' the darts in my bonie black een,
    And vow'd for my love he was diein.
I said, he might die when he liket for Jean:
    The Lord forgie me for liein, for liein —
    The Lord forgie me for liein!

III

A weel-stocket mailen, himsel for the laird,
    And marriage aff-hand were his proffers:
I never loot on that I kenn'd it, or car'd,
    But thought I might hae waur offers,
        waur offers —
    But thought I might hae waur offers.

IV

But what wad ye think? In a fortnight
        or less
    (The Deil tak his taste to gae near her!)
He up the Gate-Slack to my black cousin,
        Bess!
    Guess ye how, the jad! I could bear her,
        could bear her —
    Guess ye how, the jad! I could bear her.

V

But a' the niest week, as I petted wi' care,
    I gaed to the tryste o' Dalgarnock,
And wha but my fine fickle lover was
        there?
    I glowr'd as I'd seen a warlock, a war-
        lock —
    I glowr'd as I'd seen a warlock.

VI

But owre my left shouther I gae him a
        blink,
    Lest neebours might say I was saucy.
My wooer he caper'd as he'd been in
        drink,
    And vow'd I was his dear lassie, dear
        lassie —
    And vow'd I was his dear lassie!

VII

I spier'd for my cousin fu' couthy and
        sweet:
    Gin she had recover'd her hearin?
And how her new shoon fit her auld,
        shachl'd feet?
    But heavens! how he fell a swearin, a
        swearin —
    But heavens! how he fell a swearin!

VIII

He beggèd for gude sake, I wad be his wife,
  Or else I wad kill him wi' sorrow;
So e'en to preserve the poor body in life,
  I think I maun wed him to-morrow, to-
     morrow —
  I think I maun wed him to-morrow !

MY NANIE 'S AWA

"There is one passage in your charming letter. Thomson nor Shenstone never exceeded it, nor often came up to it. I shall certainly steal it, and set it in some future poetic production and get immortal fame by it. 'T is where you bid the scenes of Nature remind me of Clarinda." (Sylvander to Clarinda [see Prefatory Note, *ante*, p. 138], 7th February, 1788.) It may be, as some suppose, that this smooth and pleasant ditty represents the theft.

I

Now in her green mantle blythe Nature
  arrays,
And listens the lambkins that bleat o'er the
  braes,
While birds warble welcomes in ilka green
  shaw,
But to me it 's delightless — my Nanie 's
  awa.

II

The snawdrap and primrose our woodlands
  adorn,
And violets bathe in the weet o' the morn.
They pain my sad bosom, sae sweetly they
  blaw:
They mind me o' Nanie — and Nanie 's
  awa !

III

Thou lav'rock, that springs frae the dews
  of the lawn
The shepherd to warn o' the grey-breaking
  dawn,
And thou mellow mavis, that hails the
  night-fa,
Give over for pity — my Nanie 's awa.

IV

Come Autumn, sae pensive in yellow and
  grey,
And soothe me wi' tidings o' Nature's de-
  cay !

The dark, dreary Winter and wild-driving
  snaw
Alane can delight me — now Nanie 's awa.

NOW ROSY MAY

A *rifaccimento* of *The Gard'ner wi' his Paidle* (*ante*, p. 218), adapted to the tune of *Dainty Davie*. The original *Dainty Davie*, on which the chorus is modelled, is preserved in the Herd MS. and *The Merry Muses*. See also, *post*, p. 335, Notes to *The Jolly Beggars*. "The words 'Dainty Davie' glide so sweetly in the air, that to a Scots ear, any song to it, without Davie being the hero, would have a lame effect." (R. B. to Thomson, August, 1793.)

CHORUS

Meet me on the Warlock Knowe,
  Dainty Davie, Dainty Davie !
There I 'll spend the day wi' you,
  My ain dear Dainty Davie.

I

Now rosy May comes in wi' flowers
To deck her gay, green-spreading bowers;
And now comes in the happy hours
  To wander wi' my Davie.

II

The crystal waters round us fa',
The merry birds are lovers a',
The scented breezes round us blaw,
  A wandering wi' my Davie.

III

When purple morning starts the hare
To steal upon her early fare,
Then thro' the dews I will repair
  To meet my faithfu' Davie.

IV

When day, expiring in the west,
The curtain draws o' Nature's rest,
I flee to his arms I loe the best:
  And that 's my ain dear Davie !

CHORUS

Meet me on the Warlock Knowe,
  Dainty Davie, Dainty Davie !
There I 'll spend the day wi' you,
  My ain dear Dainty Davie.

NOW SPRING HAS CLAD

I

Now spring has clad the grove in green,
  And strew'd the lea wi' flowers;
The furrow'd, waving corn is seen
  Rejoice in fostering showers;
While ilka thing in nature join
  Their sorrows to forego,
O, why thus all alone are mine
  The weary steps o' woe !

II

The trout within yon wimpling burn
  Glides swift, a silver dart,
And, safe beneath the shady thorn,
  Defies the angler's art:
My life was ance that careless stream,
  That wanton trout was I,
But Love wi' unrelenting beam
  Has scorch'd my fountains dry.

III

The little floweret's peaceful lot,
  In yonder cliff that grows,
Which, save the linnet's flight, I wot,
  Nae ruder visit knows,
Was mine, till Love has o'er me past,
  And blighted a' my bloom;
And now beneath the withering blast
  My youth and joy consume.

IV

The waken'd lav'rock warbling springs,
  And climbs the early sky,
Winnowing blythe his dewy wings
  In Morning's rosy eye:
As little reck't I Sorrow's power,
  Until the flowery snare
O' witching Love in luckless hour
  Made me the thrall o' care !

V

O, had my fate been Greenland snows
  Or Afric's burning zone,
Wi' man and Nature leagu'd my foes,
  So Peggy ne'er I 'd known !
The wretch, whose doom is " hope nae
      mair,"
  What tongue his woes can tell,
Within whose bosom, save Despair,
  Nae kinder spirits dwell !

O, THIS IS NO MY AIN LASSIE

"*This is No My Ain House* puzzles me a good deal; in fact, I think to change the old rhythm of the first, or chorus part of the tune, will have a good effect. I would have it something like the gallop of the following." (R. B to Thomson, June, 1795.) In the first draft of the Chorus he wrote " Body" for " Lassie ; " but in August he directed Thomson to substitute " Lassie."

CHORUS

O, this is no my ain lassie,
  Fair tho' the lassie be:
Weel ken I my ain lassie —
  Kind love is in her e'e.

I

I SEE a form, I see a face,
Ye weel may wi' the fairest place:
It wants to me the witching grace,
  The kind love that 's in her e'e.

II

She 's bonie, blooming, straight, and tall,
And lang has had my heart in thrall;
And ay it charms my very saul,
  The kind love that 's in the e'e.

III

A thief sae pawkie is my Jean,
To steal a blink by a' unseen !
But gleg as light are lover's een,
  When kind love is in the e'e.

IV

It may escape the courtly sparks,
It may escape the learned clerks;
But well the watching lover marks
  The kind love that 's in her e'e.

CHORUS

O, this is no my ain lassie,
  Fair tho' the lassie be:
Weel ken I my ain lassie —
  Kind love is in her e'e.

O, WAT YE WHA THAT LO'ES ME

CHORUS

O, that 's the lassie o' my heart,
  My lassie ever dearer !

O, that 's the queen o' womankind,
And ne'er a ane to peer her !

I

O, WAT ye wha that lo'es me,
And has my heart a keeping ?
O, sweet is she that lo'es me
As dews o' summer weeping,
In tears the rosebuds steeping !

II

If thou shalt meet a lassie
In grace and beauty charming,
That e'en thy chosen lassie,
Erewhile thy breast sae warming,
Had ne'er sic powers alarming: —

III

If thou hadst heard her talking
(And thy attention 's plighted),
That ilka body talking
But her by thee is slighted,
And thou art all-delighted: —

IV

If thou hast met this fair one,
When frae her thou hast parted,
If every other fair one
But her thou hast deserted,
And thou art broken-hearted: —

CHORUS

O, that 's the lassie o' my heart,
My lassie ever dearer !
O, that 's the queen o' womankind,
And ne'er a ane to peer her !

SCOTS, WHA HAE

First published in *The Morning Chronicle*, May, 1794. Replying to Perry's offer of an engagement on that print, Burns wrote : " In the meantime they are most welcome to my ode ; only let them insert it as a thing they have met with by accident and unknown to me." Accordingly, the ode was thus ingenuously prefaced : " If the following warm and animating ode was not written near the times to which it applies, it is one of the most faithful imitations of the simple and beautiful style of the Scottish bards we ever read, and we know but of one living Poet to whom to ascribe it: " a piece of criticism which, if you reflect that in grammar, style, cast, sentiment, diction, and turn of phrase, the ode, though here and there

its spelling deviates into Scots, is pure Eighteenth Century English, says little for the soundness of Perry's judgment, however it may approve the kindness of his heart.

Varying accounts are given of the time and circumstances of its origin. John Syme connects it with a tour with Burns in Galloway in July, 1793 : " I told you that in the midst of the storm on the wilds of Kenmure, Burns was rapt in meditation. What do you think he was about ? He was charging the English army along with Bruce at Bannockburn. He was engaged in the same manner on our ride from St. Mary's Isle, and I did not disturb him. Next day he produced me the following address of Bruce to his troops, and gave me a copy for Dalzell." Burns tells a different tale. After some remarks to Thomson (August or September, 1793), on the old air *Hey Tutti Taiti*, and on the tradition that " it was Robert Bruce's march at the battle of Bannockburn," he introduces *Scots Wha Hae :* " This thought, in my yesternight's evening walk, roused me to a pitch of enthusiasm on the theme of liberty and independence, which I threw into a kind of Scots ode, fitted to the air, that one might suppose to be the gallant royal Scot's address to his heroic followers on that eventful morning." The two statements are irreconcilable ; and we must conclude either that Syme misdated the tour, and that the " yesternight " of Burns was the night of his return to Dumfries, or that Burns did not give Syme a copy until some time after his return, and that, like some other circumstances he was pleased to father, his " yester-night's evening walk " need not be literally interpreted.

Thomson reprobated the " idea of giving it a tune so totally devoid of interest or grandeur " as *Hey Tuttie Taitie*, and suggested certain additions in the fourth line of each stanza to fit it to that of *Lewie Gordon*. To accept these expletives was to ruin the effect ; but as in the case of *Ye Flowery Banks o' Bonie Doon*, accepted they were. Some other suggestions Burns declined : " I have scrutinized it over and over ; and to the world, some way or other, it shall go as it is." At the same time, he seems to have been scarce reconciled to the change to *Lewie Gordon*, for says he : " It will not in the least hurt me, tho' you leave the song out altogether, and adhere to your first idea of adopting Logan's verses." But having agreed to it, he adopted the changes in all such copies as he sent out in MS. After the publication of the *Thomson Correspondence*, general opinion pronounced in favour of *Hey Tuttie Taitie ;* and Thomson published the ode as written, and set it to the air for which it was made, and to which (as sung by Braham and others) it owes no little of its fortune.

In sending a copy (now in Harvard University Library) to Lord Buchan, Burns was moved to descant on the battle itself : "Independently of my enthusiasm as a Scotsman, I have rarely met with anything in history which interests my feelings as a man equal with the story of Bannockburn. On the one hand a cruel, but able usurper, leading on the finest army in Europe, to extinguish the last spark of freedom among a greatly-daring and greatly-injured people ; on the other hand, the desperate relics of a gallant nation, devoting themselves to rescue their bleeding country or perish with her. Liberty ! thou art a prize truly and indeed invaluable, for never canst thou be too dearly bought." Some have concluded therefrom that the writer had mixed his usurpers, and thought that the Edward beaten at Bannockburn was the *Malleus Scotorum*, the victor of Falkirk and the hangman of Sir William Wallace. But if he did, he was afterwards better informed ; for to a copy (now in the Corporation Council Chamber, Edinburgh) presented to Dr. Hughes of Hereford (8th August, 1795) he appended the following note : "This battle was the decisive blow which first put Robert the First, commonly called Robert de Bruce, in quiet possession of the Scottish throne. It was fought against Edward the Second, son to that Edward who shed so much blood in Scotland in consequence of the dispute between Bruce and Baliol." It is also to the purpose to note that, on the poet's own showing (letter to Thomson), this very famous lyric was inspired, not only by the thought of Bannockburn, but also "by the glowing ideas of some other struggles of the same nature *not quite so ancient :*" that, in other words, it is partly an effect of the French Revolution.

The stanza, binding-rhyme and all, is that of *Helen of Kirkconnel*, a ballad which Burns thought "silly to contemptibility : —

> "I wish I were where Helen lies !
> Night and day on me she cries ;
> O, that I were where Helen lies
> On fair Kirkconnel Lea ! "

I

SCOTS, wha hae wi' Wallace bled,
Scots, wham Bruce has aften led,
Welcome to your gory bed
        Or to victorie !

II

Now 's the day, and now 's the hour:
See the front o' battle lour,
See approach proud Edward's power —
        Chains and slaverie !

III

Wha will be a traitor knave ?
Wha can fill a coward's grave ?
Wha sae base as be a slave ? —
        Let him turn, and flee !

IV

Wha for Scotland's King and Law
Freedom's sword will strongly draw,
Freeman stand or freeman fa',
        Let him follow me !

V

By Oppression's woes and pains,
By your sons in servile chains,
We will drain our dearest veins
        But they shall be free !

VI

Lay the proud usurpers low !
Tyrants fall in every foe !
Liberty 's in every blow !
        Let us do, or die !

THEIR GROVES O' SWEET MYRTLE

" The Irish air, *Humours of Glen*, is a great favourite of mine, and as, except the silly verses in *The Poor Soldier*, there are not any decent words for it, I have written for it as follows." (R. B. to Thomson, April, 1795.)

I

THEIR groves o' sweet myrtle let foreign lands reckon,
    Where bright-beaming summers exalt the perfume !
Far dearer to me yon lone glen o' green breckan,
    Wi' the burn stealing under the lang, yellow broom;
Far dearer to me are yon humble broom bowers,
    Where the blue-bell and gowan lurk lowly, unseen;
For there, lightly tripping among the wild flowers,
    A-list'ning the linnet, aft wanders my Jean.

II

Tho' rich is the breeze in their gay, sunny
    vallies,
And cauld Caledonia's blast on the wave,
Their sweet-scented woodlands that skirt
    the proud palace,
What are they? — The haunt of the
    tyrant and slave !
The slave's spicy forests and gold-bubbling
    fountains
The brave Caledonian views wi' disdain:
He wanders as free as the winds of his
    mountains,
Save Love's willing fetters — the chains
    o' his Jean.

THINE AM I

Intended as English words to *The Quaker's
Wife.* It is possible that the verses had done
duty with Clarinda: " I have altered the first
stanza, which I would have to stand thus :

> " ' Thine am I, my faithful Fair,
>   Well thou may'st discover !
> Every pulse along my veins
> Tells the ardent Lover.' "

(R. B. to Thomson, 19th October, 1794.) But
on 2d August, 1795, being long, long off with
Clarinda and very much on with Jean Lorimer,
he wants his first line changed to " Thine am
I, my Chloris fair : " " If you neglect the al-
teration, I call on all the Nine conjunctly and
severally to anathematise you." A parallel
case is that of Mr. Arthur Pendennis, thriftily
turning his Fotheringay rhymes to account
with Miss Amory.

I

Thine am I, my faithful Fair,
  Thine my lovely Nancy !
Ev'ry pulse along my veins,
  Ev'ry roving fancy !
To thy bosom lay my heart
  There to throb and languish.
Tho' despair had wrung its core,
  That would heal its anguish.

II

Take away those rosy lips
  Rich with balmy treasure !
Turn away thine eyes of love,
  Lest I die with pleasure !

What is life when wanting love ?
  Night without a morning !
Love the cloudless summer's sun,
  Nature gay adorning.

THOU HAST LEFT ME EVER, JAMIE

Suggested to Thomson (September, 1793) as
words for *Fee Him Father :* " I enclose you
Fraser's set of this tune when he plays it slow :
in fact, he makes it the language of despair !
I shall here give you two stanzas in that style,
merely to try if it will be any improvement.
Were it possible, in singing, to give it half the
pathos which Fraser gives it in playing, it
would make an admirably pathetic song. I
do not give these verses for any merit they
have. I composed them at the time in which
' Patie Allan's mither de'ed ' — that was ' about
the back o' midnight ' — and by the leeside of
a bowl of punch, which had overset every mor-
tal in company except the *Hautbois* and the
Muse."

I

Thou hast left me ever, Jamie,
  Thou hast left me ever !
Thou hast left me ever, Jamie,
  Thou hast left me ever !
Aften hast thou vow'd that Death
  Only should us sever;
Now thou'st left thy lass for ay —
  I maun see thee never, Jamie,
  I 'll see thee never !

II

Thou hast me forsaken, Jamie,
  Thou hast me forsaken !
Thou hast me forsaken, Jamie,
  Thou hast me forsaken !
Thou canst love another jo,
  While my heart is breaking —
Soon my weary een I 'll close,
  Never mair to waken, Jamie,
  Never mair to waken !

HIGHLAND MARY

Sent to Thomson, 14th November, 1792:
" The foregoing song pleases myself; I think
it is in my happiest manner; you will see at
first glance that it suits the air. The subject

of the song is one of the most interesting passages of my youthful days; and I own that I would be much flattered to see the verses set to an air which would ensure celebrity. Perhaps, after all, 't is the still glowing prejudice of my heart that throws a borrowed lustre over the merits of the composition." For Mary Campbell see *ante*, p. 204, Prefatory Note to *My Highland Lassie, O*, and *post*, p. 343, Notes to the same.

I

Ye banks and braes and streams around
    The castle o' Montgomery,
Green be your woods, and fair your flowers,
    Your waters never drumlie !
There Summer first unfald her robes,
    And there the langest tarry !
For there I took the last fareweel
    O' my sweet Highland Mary !

II

How sweetly bloom'd the gay, green birk,
    How rich the hawthorn's blossom,
As underneath their fragrant shade
    I clasp'd her to my bosom !
The golden hours on angel wings
    Flew o'er me and my dearie:
For dear to me as light and life
    Was my sweet Highland Mary.

III

Wi' monie a vow and lock'd embrace
    Our parting was fu' tender;
And, pledging aft to meet again,
    We tore oursels asunder.
But O, fell Death's untimely frost,
    That nipt my flower sae early !
Now green 's the sod, and cauld 's the clay,
    That wraps my Highland Mary !

IV

O, pale, pale now, those rosy lips
    I aft hae kiss'd sae fondly;
And clos'd for ay, the sparkling glance
    That dwalt on me sae kindly;
And mouldering now in silent dust
    That heart that lo'ed me dearly !
But still within my bosom's core
    Shall live my Highland Mary.

MY CHLORIS, MARK

"On my visit the other day to my fair Chloris (that is the poetic name of the lovely goddess of my inspiration) she suggested an idea which on my return from the visit I wrought into the following song." (R. B. to Thomson in November, 1794.) For Chloris see *post*, p. 289, Prefatory Note to *Lassie wi' the Lint-white Locks.*

I

My Chloris, mark how green the groves,
    The primrose banks how fair !
The balmy gales awake the flowers,
    And wave thy flaxen hair.

II

The lav'rock shuns the palace gay,
    And o'er the cottage sings:
For Nature smiles as sweet, I ween,
    To shepherds as to kings.

III

Let minstrels sweep the skilfu' string
    In lordly, lighted ha':
The shepherd stops his simple reed,
    Blythe in the birken shaw.

IV

The princely revel may survey
    Our rustic dance wi' scorn;
But are their hearts as light as ours
    Beneath the milk-white thorn ?

V

The shepherd in the flowery glen
    In shepherd's phrase will woo:
The courtier tells a finer tale —
    But is his heart as true ?

VI

Here wild-wood flowers I 've pu'd, to deck
    That spotless breast o' thine:
The courtier's gems may witness love —
    But 't is na love like mine !

FAIREST MAID ON DEVON BANKS

Burns's last song. "I tried my hand on *Rothiemurchie* this morning. The measure is so difficult that it is impossible to infuse much genius into the lines; they are on the other side." (R. B. to Thomson. 12th July, 1796.) As in 1787 he had complimented Charlotte Hamilton in *The Banks of the Devon*, it may be that she is the "fairest maid" of the present song, although some refer it to a break in his friendship with Peggy Chalmers, or to her refusal to marry him (see *ante*, p. 214, Prefatory Note to *Where, Braving Angry Winter's Storms*). But, although the Devon is real enough, the "maid" in this case may have been pure fiction.

CHORUS

Fairest maid on Devon banks,
  Crystal Devon, winding Devon,
Wilt thou lay that frown aside,
  And smile as thou wert wont to do?

I

FULL well thou know'st I love thee dear —
Couldst thou to malice lend an ear!
O, did not Love exclaim: — "Forbear,
  Nor use a faithful lover so!"

II

Then come, thou fairest of the fair,
Those wonted smiles, O, let me share,
And by thy beauteous self I swear
  No love but thine my heart shall know!

CHORUS

Fairest maid on Devon banks,
  Crystal Devon, winding Devon,
Wilt thou lay that frown aside,
  And smile as thou wert wont to do?

LASSIE WI' THE LINT-WHITE LOCKS

"I have finished my song to *Rothiemurchie's Rant*. . . . The piece has at least the merit of being a regular pastoral; the vernal morn, the summer noon, the autumnal evening, and the winter night, are regularly rounded." (R. B. to Thomson, November, 1794.)

The Chloris who did duty as Burns's Muse for some time after his break with Maria Riddell was the daughter of William Lorimer, farmer and publican, Kemmishall, near Dumfries. She was born in September, 1775, at Craigieburn Wood, which her poet has associated with a Mr. Gillespie, a brother gauger (see p. 231), and his passion for her — Gillespie's disappointment, when she eloped to Gretna Green with a prodigal young Englishman, one Whepdale, tenant of a farm near Moffat, being shadowed forth in *O Poortith Cauld* (p. 274). The lady was still a bride, when her husband fled his creditors across the border; and, her illusion being no more, she returned to her parents and resumed her maiden name. Her misfortunes so touched the Bard that he became exceedingly enamoured of her. He re-wrote *Whistle and I'll Come to You My Lad* in her honour; on her behalf appropriated part of an earlier song, *And I'll Kiss Thee Yet* (p. 213), to complete *Come, Let Me Take Thee* (p. 279); celebrated her illness in a new set of *Ay Waukin, O* (p. 290, *Long, Long the Night*); and exalted her in such "reveries of passion" as the present song, as *My Chloris Mark* (p. 288), as *Mark Yonder Pomp* (p. 294), as *Forlorn, My Love* (p. 292), and as *Yon Rosy Brier* (p. 291), to name but these. He thus described to Thomson her relation to his work: "The lady on whom it [*Craigieburn Wood*] was made is one of the finest women in Scotland; and, in fact (*entre nous*) is, in a manner to me, what Sterne's Eliza was to him — a Mistress, or Friend, or what you will, in the guileless simplicity of Platonic love. (Now don't put any of your squinting constructions on this, or have any clishmaclavers about it among our acquaintances.) I assure you that to my lovely Friend you are indebted for many of your best songs of mine. Do you think that the sober gin-horse routine of existence could inspire a man with life, and love, and joy — could fire him with enthusiasm or melt him with pathos equal to the genius of your Book? No, No! Whenever I want to be more than ordinary in song — to be in some degree equal to your diviner airs — do you imagine I fast and pray for the celestial emanation? *Tout au contraire!* I have a glorious recipe; the very one that for his own use was invented to the Divinity of Healing and Poesy, when erst he piped to the flocks of Admetus. I put myself in the regimen of admiring a fine woman; and in proportion to the adorability of her charms, in proportion you are delighted with my verses." Towards the close of 1795 he (for whatever reason) grew disenchanted with the "adorability" of this particular "fine woman," and would rather, as we have seen, that neither her name nor her "charms" were associated with his fame. The poor lady's later years were unfortunate. Her father lost his money, and, compelled to support herself, she went into service, dying as late as September, 1831.

CHORUS

Lassie wi' the lint-white locks,
  Bonie lassie, artless lassie,

Wilt thou wi' me tent the flocks —
Wilt thou be my dearie, O ?

I

Now Nature cleeds the flowery lea,
And a' is young and sweet like thee,
O wilt thou share its joys wi' me,
And say thou 'lt be my dearie, O ?

II

The primrose bank, the wimpling burn,
The cuckoo on the milk-white thorn,
The wanton lambs at early morn
Shall welcome thee, my dearie, O.

III

And when the welcome simmer shower
Has cheer'd ilk drooping little flower,
We 'll to the breathing woodbine-bower
At sultry noon, my dearie, O.

IV

When Cynthia lights wi' silver ray
The weary shearer's hameward way,
Thro' yellow waving fields we 'll stray,
And talk o' love, my dearie, O.

V

And when the howling wintry blast
Disturbs my lassie's midnight rest,
Enclaspèd to my faithfu' breast,
I 'll comfort thee, my dearie, O.

CHORUS

Lassie wi' the lint-white locks,
Bonie lassie, artless lassie,
Wilt thou wi' me tent the flocks —
Wilt thou be my dearie, O ?

LONG, LONG THE NIGHT

A rather tawdry set of *Ay Waukin, O* (*ante*,
p. 217). See *ante*, p. 289, Prefatory Note to
Lassie wi' the Lint-white Locks.

CHORUS

Long, long the night,
Heavy comes the morrow,
While my soul's delight
Is on her bed of sorrow.

I

CAN I cease to care,
Can I cease to languish,
While my darling fair
Is on the couch of anguish !

II

Ev'ry hope is fled
Ev'ry fear is terror:
Slumber ev'n I dread,
Ev'ry dream is horror.

III

Hear me, Powers Divine:
O, in pity, hear me !
Take aught else of mine,
But my Chloris spare me !

CHORUS

Long, long the night,
Heavy comes the morrow,
While my soul's delight
Is on her bed of sorrow.

LOGAN WATER

"Have you ever, my dear Sir, felt your
bosom ready to burst with indignation on
reading, or seeing how these mighty villains
who divide kingdom against kingdom desolate
provinces and lay Nations waste, out of the
wantonness of ambition, or often from still
more ignoble passions ? In a mood of this
kind to-day, I recollected the air of *Logan
Water*, and it occurred to me that its queru-
lous melody probably had its origin from the
plaintive indignation of some swelling, suffer-
ing heart, fired at the tyrannic strides of some
Public Destroyer, and overwhelmed with pri-
vate distress, the consequences of a country's
ruin. If I have done anything like justice to
my feelings, the following song, composed in
three-quarters of an hour's lucubrations in my
elbow-chair, ought to have some merit." (R. B.
to Thomson, 25th June, 1793.)

"I remember two ending lines of a verse in
some of the old songs of *Logan Water* (for
I know a good many different ones) which I
think pretty : —

" ' Now my dear lad maun face his faes
Far, far frae me and Logan Braes.' "

(R. B. to Thomson, 3d April, 1793.)

I

O LOGAN, sweetly didst thou glide
That day I was my Willie's bride,
And years sin syne hae o'er us run
Like Logan to the simmer sun.
But now thy flowery banks appear
Like drumlie winter, dark and drear,
While my dear lad maun face his faes
Far, far frae me and Logan braes.

II

Again the merry month of May
Has made our hills and vallies gay;
The birds rejoice in leafy bowers,
The bees hum round the breathing flowers;
Blythe Morning lifts his rosy eye,
And Evening's tears are tears o' joy:
My soul delightless a' surveys,
While Willie's far fra Logan braes.

III

Within yon milk-white hawthorn bush,
Amang her nestlings sits the thrush:
Her faithfu' mate will share her toil,
Or wi' his song her cares beguile.
But I wi' my sweet nurslings here,
Nae mate to help, nae mate to cheer,
Pass widow'd nights and joyless days,
While Willie's far frae Logan braes.

IV

O, wae upon you, Men o' State,
That brethren rouse in deadly hate!
As ye make monie a fond heart mourn,
Sae may it on your heads return!
Ye mindna 'mid your cruel joys
The widow's tears, the orphan's cries;
But soon may peace bring happy days,
And Willie hame to Logan braes!

YON ROSY BRIER

I

O, BONIE was yon rosy brier
  That blooms sae far frae haunt o' man,
And bonie she — and ah, how dear! —
  It shaded frae the e'enin sun!

II

Yon rosebuds in the morning dew,
  How pure among the leaves sae green!

But purer was the lover's vow
  They witnessed in their shade yestreen.

III

All in its rude and prickly bower,
  That crimson rose how sweet and fair!
But love is far a sweeter flower
  Amid life's thorny path o' care.

IV

The pathless wild and wimpling burn,
  Wi' Chloris in my arms, be mine,
And I the warld nor wish nor scorn —
  Its joys and griefs alike resign!

WHERE ARE THE JOYS

"*Saw Ye My Father?* is one of my greatest favourites. The evening before last I wandered out, and began a tender song in what I think is its native style. . . . My song is but just begun; and I should like, before I proceed, to know your opinion of it." (R. B. to Thomson, in his comments on the latter's list of an hundred songs, September, 1793.) The completed song he sent to Thomson shortly afterwards, with the advice to set the air to the old words, and let his "follow as English verses."

I

WHERE are the joys I hae met in the
    morning,
  That danc'd to the lark's early sang?
Where is the peace that awaited my wan-
    d'ring
  At e'ening the wild-woods amang?

II

Nae mair a-winding the course o' yon river
  And marking sweet flowerets sae fair,
Nae mair I trace the light footsteps o'
    Pleasure,
  But Sorrow and sad-sighing Care.

III

Is it that Summer's forsaken our vallies,
  And grim, surly Winter is near?
No, no, the bees humming round the gay
    roses
  Proclaim it the pride o' the year.

IV

Fain wad I hide what I fear to discover,
  Yet lang, lang, too well hae I known:

A' that has causèd the wreck in my bosom
Is Jenny, fair Jenny alone !

V

Time cannot aid me, my griefs are immor-
tal,
    Not Hope dare a comfort bestow.
Come then, enamor'd and fond of my an-
guish,
    Enjoyment I 'll seek in my woe !

BEHOLD THE HOUR

" The following song I have composed for
Oran Gaoil, the Highland air that you tell me
in your last you have resolved to give a place
in your book. I have this moment finished
the song, so you have it glowing from the mint.
If it suit you, well ! if not 't is also well ! "
(R. B. to Thomson, September, 1793.)
    It is from a song sent to Clarinda in 1791 ;
but this itself was little more than a transcript
of a certain *Farewell to Nice*, to be found in
The Charmer and other books (see *post*, p. 312).

I

BEHOLD the hour, the boat arrive !
    Thou goest, the darling of my heart !
Sever'd from thee, can I survive ?
    But Fate has will'd and we must part.
I 'll often greet the surging swell,
    Yon distant isle will often hail : —
" E'en here I took the last farewell ;
    There, latest mark'd her vanish'd sail."

II

Along the solitary shore,
    While flitting sea-fowl round me cry,
Across the rolling, dashing roar,
    I 'll westward turn my wistful eye : —
"Happy, thou Indian grove," I 'll say,
    "Where now my Nancy's path may be !
While thro' thy sweets she loves to stray,
    O, tell me, does she muse on me ? "

FORLORN, MY LOVE

" How do you like the foregoing ? I have
written it within this hour ; so much for the
speed of my Pegasus, but what say you to his
bottom ? "   (R. B. to Thomson, May, 1795.)

CHORUS

O, wert thou, love, but near me,
But near, near, near me,
How kindly thou would cheer me,
    And mingle sighs with mine, love !

I

FORLORN, my love, no comfort near,
Far, far from thee I wander here ;
Far, far from thee, the fate severe,
    At which I most repine, love.

II

Around me scowls a wintry sky,
Blasting each bud of hope and joy,
And shelter, shade, nor home have I
    Save in these arms of thine, love.

III

Cold, alter'd friendship's cruel part,
To poison Fortune's ruthless dart !
Let me not break thy faithful heart,
    And say that fate is mine, love !

IV

But, dreary tho' the moments fleet,
O, let me think we yet shall meet !
That only ray of solace sweet
    Can on thy Chloris shine, love !

CHORUS

O, wert thou, love, but near me,
But near, near, near me,
How kindly thou would cheer me,
    And mingle sighs with mine, love !

CA' THE YOWES TO THE KNOWES

SECOND SET

Sent to Thomson in September, 1794, [four
years after the appearance of the first set in
Johnson's *Musical Museum*]. See *ante*, p. 224,
Prefatory Note to *Ca' the Yowes to the Knowes*
(first set).

CHORUS

Ca' the yowes to the knowes,
Ca' them where the heather grows,
Ca' them where the burnie rowes,
    My bonie dearie.

I

HARK, the mavis' e'ening sang
Sounding Clouden's woods amang ;
Then a-faulding let us gang,
  My bonie dearie.

II

We 'll gae down by Clouden side,
Thro' the hazels, spreading wide
O'er the waves that sweetly glide
  To the moon sae clearly.

III

Yonder Clouden's silent towers
Where, at moonshine's midnight hours,
O'er the dewy bending flowers
  Fairies dance sae cheery.

IV

Ghaist nor bogle shalt thou fear —
Thou 'rt to Love and Heav'n sae dear
Nocht of ill may come thee near,
  My bonie dearie.

CHORUS

Ca' the yowes to the knowes,
Ca' them where the heather grows,
Ca' them where the burnie rowes,
  My bonie dearie.

HOW CAN MY POOR HEART

"The last evening as I was straying out,
and thinking of *O'er the Hills and Far Away,*
I spun the following stanzas for it; but
whether my spinning will deserve to be laid
up in store, like the precious thread of the
silkworm, or brushed to the devil, like the
vile manufacture of the spider, I leave, my
dear sir, to your usual candid criticism. I was
pleased with several lines in it at first, but I
own that it appears rather a flimsy business.
. . . I give you leave to abuse this song, but do
it in the spirit of Christian meekness." (R. B.
to Thomson, 30th August, 1794.) Thomson
took him at his word, whereupon he replied:
"I shall withdraw my *O'er the Seas and Far
Away* altogether ; it is unequal, and unworthy
of the work. Making a poem is like begetting
a son ; you cannot know whether you have a
wise man or a fool, until you produce him to
the world and try him."

I

How can my poor heart be glad
When absent from my sailor lad ?
How can I the thought forego —
He 's on the seas to meet the foe ?
Let me wander, let me rove,
Still my heart is with my love.
Nightly dreams and thoughts by day
Are with him that 's far away.
  On the seas and far away,
  On stormy seas and far away —
  Nightly dreams and thoughts by day,
  Are ay with him that 's far away.

II

When in summer noon I faint,
As weary flocks around me pant,
Haply in this scorching sun
My sailor 's thund'ring at his gun.
Bullets, spare my only joy !
Bullets, spare my darling boy !
Fate, do with me what you may,
Spare but him that 's far away !
  On the seas and far away,
  On stormy seas and far away —
  Fate, do with me what you may,
  Spare but him that 's far away !

III

At the starless, midnight hour
When Winter rules with boundless power,
As the storms the forests tear,
And thunders rend the howling air,
Listening to the doubling roar
Surging on the rocky shore,
All I can — I weep and pray
For his weal that 's far away.
  On the seas and far away,
  On stormy seas and far away,
  All I can — I weep and pray
  For his weal that 's far away.

IV

Peace, thy olive wand extend
And bid wild War his ravage end;
Man with brother man to meet,
And as brother kindly greet !
Then may Heaven with prosperous gales
Fill my sailor's welcome sails,
To my arms their charge convey,
My dear lad that 's far away !
  On the seas and far away,
  On stormy seas and far away,
  To my arms their charge convey,
  My dear lad that 's far away !

IS THERE FOR HONEST POVERTY

" A great critic (Aikin) on songs says that
Love and Wine are the exclusive themes for
song-writing. The following is on neither sub-
ject, and consequently is no song. . . . I do
not give you the foregoing song for your book,
but merely by way of *vive la bagatelle;* for the
piece is not really poetry." - (R. B. to Thomson,
January, 1795.)

In all likelihood the oldest set of *For a' That*
is one in *The Merry Muses.* Apparently sug-
gested by the Highlander's imperfect Scots
(the hero is specifically some bare-breeched
Donald), the phrase was found effective for a
certain class of ditty — the ditty which (as
Burns says of this one) " is not really poetry."
A Jacobite derivative, which he knew likewise,
is included in a *Collection of Loyal Songs*, 1750.
It begins thus :

> " Tho' ——— reigns in ——— stead
> I 'm grieved, yet scorn to shaw that :
> I 'll ne'er look down nor hang my head
> On rebel Whig for a' that : "

and has this chorus :

> " For a' that and a' that,
> And twice as muckle 's a' that,
> He 's far beyond the seas the night,
> Yet he 'll be here for a' that."

Like *Scots Wha Hae* — " the Scottish *Mar-
seillaise* " (whatever that may mean) — this
famous song — " the *Marseillaise* of hu-
manity " (whatever *that* may mean) — which,
according to Chambers, " may be said to
embody all the false philosophy of Burns's
time and of his own mind," is very plainly
an effect of the writer's sympathies with the
spirit and the fact of the French Revolu-
tion, and of that estrangement from wealthier
loyalist friends, with which his expression
of these sympathies and his friendship with
such " sons of sedition " as Maxwell (see
ante, p. 188, Prefatory Note to *Ye True
Loyal Natives*, and p. 190, Prefatory Note to
To Dr. Maxwell) had been visited.

I

Is there for honest poverty
    That hings his head, an' a' that ?
The coward slave, we pass him by —
    We dare be poor for a' that !
For a' that, an' a' that,
    Our toils obscure, an' a' that,
The rank is but the guinea's stamp,
    The man 's the gowd for a' that.

II

What though on hamely fare we dine,
    Wear hoddin grey, an' a' that ?
Gie fools their silks, and knaves their
    wine —
A man 's a man for a' that.
For a' that, an' a' that,
    Their tinsel show, an' a' that,
The honest man, tho' e'er sae poor,
    Is king o' men for a' that.

III

Ye see yon birkie ca'd " a lord,"
    Wha struts, an' stares, an' a' that ?
Tho' hundreds worship at his word,
    He 's but a cuif for a' that.
For a' that, an' a' that,
    His ribband, star, an' a' that,
The man o' independent mind,
    He looks an' laughs at a' that.

IV

A prince can mak a belted knight,
    A marquis, duke, an' a' that !
But an honest man 's aboon his might —
    Guid faith, he mauna fa' that !
For a' that, an' a' that,
    Their dignities, an' a' that,
The pith o' sense an' pride o' worth
    Are higher rank than a' that.

V

Then let us pray that come it may
    (As come it will for a' that)
That Sense and Worth o'er a' the earth
    Shall bear the gree an' a' that !
For a' that, an' a' that,
    It 's comin yet for a' that,
That man to man the world o'er
    Shall brithers be for a' that.

MARK YONDER POMP

I

MARK yonder pomp of costly fashion
    Round the wealthy, titled bride !
But, when compar'd with real passion,
    Poor is all that princely pride.

II

What are the showy treasures ?
What are the noisy pleasures ?

The gay, gaudy glare of vanity and art !
  The polish'd jewel's blaze
  May draw the wond'ring gaze,
  And courtly grandeur bright
  The fancy may delight,
But never, never can come near the heart !

III

But did you see my dearest Chloris
  In simplicity's array,
Lovely as yonder sweet opening flower is,
  Shrinking from the gaze of day ?

IV

O, then, the heart alarming
And all resistless charming,
In love's delightful fetters she chains the
    willing soul !
Ambition would disown
The world's imperial crown !
Ev'n Avarice would deny
His worshipp'd deity,
And feel thro' every vein love's raptures
    roll !

O, LET ME IN THIS AE NIGHT

CHORUS

  O, let me in this ae night,
  This ae, ae, ae night !
  O, let me in this ae night,
  And rise, and let me in !

I

O LASSIE, are ye sleepin yet,
Or are ye waukin, I wad wit ?
For Love has bound me hand an' fit,
  And I would fain be in, jo.

II

Thou hear'st the winter wind an' weet :
Nae star blinks thro' the driving sleet !
Tak pity on my weary feet,
  And shield me frae the rain, jo.

III

The bitter blast that round me blaws,
Unheeded howls, unheeded fa's :
The cauldness o' thy heart 's the cause
  Of a' my care and pine, jo.

CHORUS

  O, let me in this ae night,
  This ae, ae, ae night !
  O, let me in this ae night,
  And rise and let me in !

HER ANSWER

CHORUS

  I tell you now this ae night,
  This ae, ae, ae night,
  And ance for a' this ae night,
  I winna let ye in, jo.

I

O, TELL me na o' wind an' rain,
Upbraid na me wi' cauld disdain,
Gae back the gate ye cam again,
  I winna let ye in, jo !

II

The snellest blast at mirkest hours,
That round the pathless wand'rer pours
Is nocht to what poor she endures,
  That 's trusted faithless man, jo.

III

The sweetest flower that deck'd the mead,
Now trodden like the vilest weed —
Let simple maid the lesson read !
  The weird may be her ain, jo.

IV

The bird that charm'd his summer day,
And now the cruel fowler's prey,
Let that to witless woman say : —
  "The gratefu' heart of man," jo.

CHORUS

  I tell you now this ae night,
  This ae, ae, ae night,
  And ance for a' this ae night,
  I winna let ye in, jo.

O PHILLY, HAPPY BE THAT DAY

" Did you not once propose *The Sow's Tail
to Geordie* as an air for your work ? I am
quite delighted with it ; but I acknowledge
that is no mark of its real excellence. I once
set about verses for it, which I meant to be in

the alternate way of a lover and his mistress chanting together. . . . I have just written four stanzas at random, which I intended to have woven somewhere into, probably at the conclusion of, the song." (R. B. to Thomson, September, 1794.) He finished the duet one morning in November, "though a keen blowing frost," in his "walk before breakfast." The portion written in September consisted of stanzas iv. and v.

CHORUS

He and She. For a' the joys that gowd can
    gie,
    I dinna care a single flie !
      The ⎰ lad ⎱ I love 's the
         ⎱ lass ⎰
         ⎰ lad ⎱ for me,
         ⎱ lass ⎰
    And that 's my ain dear
       ⎰ Willy ⎱
       ⎱ Philly ⎰

I

He. O PHILLY, happy be that day
    When, roving thro' the gather'd hay,
    My youthfu' heart was stown away,
      And by thy charms, my Philly !
She. O Willy, ay I bless the grove
    Where first I own'd my maiden love,
    Whilst thou did pledge the Powers
      above
    To be my ain dear Willy.

II

He. As songsters of the early year
    Are ilka day mair sweet to hear,
    So ilka day to me mair dear
      And charming is my Philly.
She. As on the brier the budding rose
    Still richer breathes, and fairer blows,
    So in my tender bosom grows
      The love I bear my Willy.

III

He. The milder sun and bluer sky,
    That crown my harvest cares wi' joy,
    Were ne'er sae welcome to my eye
      As is a sight o' Philly.
She. The little swallow's wanton wing,
    Tho' wafting o'er the flowery spring,
    Did ne'er to me sic tidings bring
      As meeting o' my Willy.

IV

He. The bee, that thro' the sunny hour
    Sips nectar in the op'ning flower,

Compar'd wi' my delight is poor
    Upon the lips o' Philly.
She. The woodbine in the dewy weet,
    When ev'ning shades in silence meet,
    Is nocht sae fragrant or sae sweet
      As is a kiss o' Willy.

V

He. Let Fortune's wheel at random rin,
    And fools may tyne, and knaves may
      win !
    My thoughts are a' bound up on ane,
      And that 's my ain dear Philly.
She. What 's a' the joys that gowd can gie ?
    I dinna care a single flie !
    The lad I love 's the lad for me,
      And that 's my ain dear Willy.

CHORUS

He and She. For a' the joys that gowd can
    gie,
    I dinna care a single flie !
      The ⎰ lad ⎱ I love 's the
         ⎱ lass ⎰
         ⎰ lad ⎱ for me,
         ⎱ lass ⎰
    And that 's my ain dear
       ⎰ Willy ⎱
       ⎱ Philly ⎰

O, WERE MY LOVE

The second stanza is a fragment preserved in Herd's Collection: "This thought is inexpressibly beautiful, and, so far as I know, quite original. It is too short for a song, else I would forswear you altogether except you gave it a place. I have often tried to eke a stanza to it, but in vain. After balancing myself for a musing five minutes on the hind-legs of my elbow-chair, I produced the following [*Were My Love Yon Lilac Fair*, etc.]. The verses are far inferior to the foregoing, I frankly confess; but, if worthy of insertion at all, they might be first in place, as every Poet who knows anything of his trade will husband his best thoughts for a concluding stroke." (R. B. to Thomson, June, 1793.)

In the Herd MS. there is also a set three stanzas in length :

    " O, if my love was a pickle of wheat,
      And growing upon yon lilly white lea,
    And I myself a bonny sweet bird,
      Away with that pickle I would flie.

    " O, if my love was a bonny red rose," *etc.*

I

O, WERE my love yon lilac fair
  Wi' purple blossoms to the spring,
And I a bird to shelter there,
  When wearied on my little wing,
How I wad mourn when it was torn
  By Autumn wild and Winter rude !
But I wad sing on wanton wing,
  When youthfu' May its bloom renew'd.

II

O, gin my love were yon red rose,
  That grows upon the castle wa',
And I mysel a drap o' dew
  Into her bonie breast to fa',
O, there, beyond expression blest,
  I 'd feast on beauty a' the night,
Seal'd on her silk-saft faulds to rest,
  Till fley'd awa by Phœbus' light !

SLEEP'ST THOU

I

SLEEP'ST thou, or wauk'st thou, fairest
      creature ?
  Rosy Morn now lifts his eye,
Numbering ilka bud, which Nature
  Waters wi' the tears o' joy.
Now to the streaming fountain
  Or up the heathy mountain
The hart, hind, and roe, freely, wildly-
      wanton stray;
  In twining hazel bowers
  His lay the linnet pours;
  The laverock to the sky
  Ascends wi' sangs o' joy,
While the sun and thou arise to bless the
      day !

II

Phœbus, gilding the brow of morning,
  Banishes ilk darksome shade,
Nature gladdening and adorning:
  Such to me my lovely maid !
  When frae my Chloris parted,
  Sad, cheerless, broken-hearted,
The night's gloomy shades, cloudy, dark,
      o'ercast my sky;
  But when she charms my sight
  In pride of Beauty's light,
  When thro' my very heart
  Her beaming glories dart,
'T is then — 't is then I wake to life and joy !

THERE WAS A LASS

The heroine was Jean M'Murdo, daughter
of Burns's friend, John M'Murdo (see *ante*, p.
143, Prefatory Note to *To John M'Murdo*).
To her he sent a copy: " In the inclosed ballad
I have, I think, hit off a few outlines of your
portrait. The personal charms, the purity of
mind, the ingenuous *naïveté* of heart and man-
ners in my heroine are, I flatter myself, a
pretty just likeness of Miss M'Murdo in a cot-
tage."

I

THERE was a lass, and she was fair !
  At kirk and market to be seen
When a' our fairest maids were met,
  The fairest maid was bonie Jean.

II

And ay she wrought her country wark,
  And ay she sang sae merrilie:
The blythest bird upon the bush
  Had ne'er a lighter heart than she !

III

But hawks will rob the tender joys,
  That bless the little lintwhite's nest,
And frost will blight the fairest flowers,
  And love will break the soundest rest.

IV

Young Robie was the brawest lad,
  The flower and pride of a' the glen,
And he had owsen, sheep, and kye,
  And wanton naigies nine or ten.

V

He gaed wi' Jeanie to the tryste,
  He danc'd wi' Jeanie on the down,
And, lang ere witless Jeanie wist,
  Her heart was tint, her peace was stown !

VI

As in the bosom of the stream
  The moon-beam dwells at dewy e'en,
So, trembling pure, was tender love
  Within the breast of bonie Jean.

VII

And now she works her country's wark,
  And ay she sighs wi' care and pain,
Yet wist na what her ail might be,
  Or what wad make her weel again.

VIII

But did na Jeanie's heart loup light,
  And did na joy blink in her e'e,
As Robie tauld a tale o' love
  Ae e'enin on the lily lea?

IX

While monie a bird sang sweet o' love,
  And monie a flower blooms o'er the dale,
His cheek to hers he aft did lay,
  And whisper'd thus his tender tale: —

X

" O Jeanie fair, I lo'e thee dear.
  O, canst thou think to fancy me ?
Or wilt thou leave thy mammie's cot,
  And learn to tent the farms wi' me ?

XI

" At barn or byre thou shalt na drudge,
  Or naething else to trouble thee,
But stray amang the heather-bells,
  And tent the waving corn wi' me."

XII

Now what could artless Jeanie do ?
  She had nae will to say him na !
At length she blush'd a sweet consent,
  And love was ay between them twa.

THE LEA–RIG

" On reading over *The Lea-Rig*, I imme-
diately set about trying my hand on it, and
after all, I could make nothing more of it than
the following, which Heaven knows is poor
enough." (R. B. to Thomson.) Here he prob-
ably referred to *The Lea-Rig* in Johnson's
Museum. This is his note on it in the Inter-
leaved Copy: " The old words of this song are
omitted here, though much more beautiful
than those inserted, which were mostly com-
posed by poor Fergusson in one of his merry
humours. The old words began thus :

' I 'll rowe thee o'er the lea-rig,
  My ain kind deary, O,
I 'll rowe thee o'er the lea-rig,
  My ain kind deary, O.
Altho' the night were ne'er sae wat,
  And I were ne'er sae weary, O.
I 'll rowe thee o'er the lea-rig,
  My ain kind deary, O.' "

A fuller set of the *Museum* words is in the
Herd MS., [which] also contains a fragment,
which is, perhaps, the archetypal original.

I

WHEN o'er the hill the eastern star
  Tells bughtin time is near, my jo,
And owsen frae the furrow'd field
  Return sae dowf and weary, O,
Down by the burn, where scented birks
  Wi' dew are hangin clear, my jo,
I 'll meet thee on the lea-rig,
  My ain kind dearie, O.

II

At midnight hour in mirkest glen
  I 'd rove, and ne'er be eerie, O,
If thro' that glen I gaed to thee,
  My ain kind dearie, O !
Altho' the night were ne'er sae wild,
  And I were ne'er sae weary, O,
I 'll meet thee on the lea-rig,
  My ain kind dearie, O.

III

The hunter lo'es the morning sun
  To rouse the mountain deer, my jo;
At noon the fisher takes the glen
  Adown the burn to steer, my jo:
Gie me the hour o' gloamin grey —
  It maks my heart sae cheery, O,
To meet thee on the lea-rig,
  My ain kind dearie, O !

MY WIFE 'S A WINSOME WEE THING

" In the air — *My Wife's a Wanton Wee
Thing* — if a few lines smooth and pretty can
be adapted to it, it is all you can expect. The
following I made *extempore* to it; and though,
on further study, I might give you something
more profound, yet it might not suit the light-
horse gallop of the air, so well as this random
clink." (R. B. to Thomson, 8th November,
1792.)

CHORUS

She is a winsome wee thing,
  She is a handsome wee thing,
  She is a lo'esome wee thing,
    This sweet wee wife o' mine !

I

I NEVER saw a fairer,
I never lo'ed a dearer,
And neist my heart I 'll wear her,
  For fear my jewel tine.

II

The warld's wrack, we share o't;
The warstle and the care o't,
Wi' her I 'll blythely bear it,
And think my lot divine.

CHORUS

She is a winsome wee thing,
She is a handsome wee thing,
She is a lo'esome wee thing,
   This sweet wee wife o' mine.

MARY MORISON

This little masterpiece of feeling and expression was sent to Thomson, 20th March, 1793. " The song prefixed is one of my juvenile works. I leave it among your hands. I do not think it very remarkable either for its merits or demerits." (R. B. to Thomson.) And Thomson sat on it for upwards of twenty-five years. Gilbert Burns told him that Mary Morison was the heroine of some light verses beginning: *And I'll kiss thee yet, yet* (see *ante*, p. 213). She has therefore been identified with Elison Begbie. But a Mary Morison, the daughter of one Adjutant Morison, who lived at Mauchline from 1784, is said to have been as beautiful as amiable. She died of consumption, 29th August, 1791.

I

O MARY, at thy window be !
It is the wish'd, the trysted hour.
Those smiles and glances let me see,
   That make the miser's treasure poor.
   How blythely wad I bide the stoure,
A weary slave frae sun to sun,
   Could I the rich reward secure —
The lovely Mary Morison !

II

Yestreen, when to the trembling string
   The dance gaed thro' the lighted ha',
To thee my fancy took its wing,
   I sat, but neither heard or saw:
   Tho' this was fair, and that was braw,
And you the toast of a' the town,
   I sigh'd and said amang them a': —
"Ye are na Mary Morison ! "

III

O Mary, canst thou wreck his peace
   Wha for thy sake wad gladly die ?
Or canst thou break that heart of his
   Whase only faut is loving thee ?
   If love for love thou wilt na gie,
At least be pity to me shown:
   A thought ungentle canna be
The thought o' Mary Morison.

MISCELLANEOUS SONGS

MORE than half the verse of Burns was published posthumously ; more than a third of it without his sanction. He was especially " unthrifty of his sweets ; " bestowing them on all and sundry, as if he had been denied the privilege of publication in any other form. Much of his work was in the strictest sense occasional ; written " by way of *vive la bagatelle* " on window-panes, in albums, in volumes, in letters to friends. He never dreamed, or not until the very last, that the world would cherish any curiosity about these fugitives ; and death came to him ere the chance of sifting gold from dross in a final Edition. Thus, his unrealised estate (so to speak) was not only of peculiar bulk : it was also of many qualities, and it was variously dispersed among a crowd of owners ; so that he provided the gull with

no defence against the gull-catcher, — he left the credulous wholly unarmed and unprepared against the contrivances of them that would deceive. Again, he was accustomed to jot down from recitation, or to copy from letters, or from odd volumes, such lines, such stanzas, or such whole pieces as took his fancy ; and more often than not he left his sources undenoted. Withal, he would dispatch songs got in this way — with or without retouches — for publication, especially in Johnson's *Museum ;* and, inasmuch as he signed not all those envoys which were his own, the task of separating false from true is one of very considerable difficulty. Often the probabilities are our only guides ; and in these cases we have summarised the evidence, and taken that direction in which the balance seemed to incline.

In others, any sort of evidence is of the scantest; and what there is has been made scanter still by the carelessness — or the romantic humour, to call it by no worse a name — of such Editors as Allan Cunningham, Hogg and Motherwell, and Robert Chambers. The chief exemplar in the other sense is certainly Scott Douglas, who, though he seems to have prepared himself for the work of editing Burns by resolutely declining to read any one else, was zealous in his quèst of MS. authorities, and, had he known something of literature, and been less given to putting on what Mr. Swin-

burne calls "a foolish face of praise" over any and every thing his author wrote, might have gone far to establish a sound tradition in the matter of text. But such a tradition was scarce indicated ere it succumbed to sentimentalism and pretence; the old, hap-hazard, irresponsible convention still holds its own; and editions professing to give the "complete text," the "true text," the "best text," and the like, continue to be issued, which set forth an abundance of proof that they are based — some wholly, all mainly — on the battered jog-trot hack-authorities of the prime.

A RUINED FARMER

Probably written during the crisis of William Burness's difficulties at Mount Oliphant: "The farm proved a ruinous bargain; and, to clench the curse, we fell into the hands of a factor, who sat for the picture I have drawn of one in my tale of *Twa Dogs*." (R. B. in Autobiographical Letter.) [See *ante*, p. xix, and footnote.]

I

THE sun he is sunk in the west,
All creatures retirèd to rest,
While here I sit, all sore beset
    With sorrow, grief, and woe:
And it 's O fickle Fortune, O !

II

The prosperous man is asleep,
Nor hears how the whirlwinds sweep;
But Misery and I must watch
    The surly tempests blow:
And it 's O fickle Fortune, O !

III

There lies the dear Partner of my breast,
Her cares for a moment at rest !
Must I see thee, my youthful pride,
    Thus brought so very low ? —
And it 's O fickle Fortune, O !

IV

There lie my sweet babies in her arms;
No anxious fear their little hearts alarms;
But for their sake my heart does ache,
    With many a bitter throe:
And it 's O fickle Fortune, O !

V

I once was by Fortune carest,
I once could relieve the distrest;
Now life's poor support, hardly earn'd,
    My fate will scarce bestow:
And it 's O fickle Fortune, O !

VI

No comfort, no comfort I have !
How welcome to me were the grave !
But then my wife and children dear —
    O, whither would they go !
And it 's O fickle Fortune, O !

VII

O, whither, O, whither shall I turn,
All friendless, forsaken, forlorn ?
For in this world Rest or Peace
    I never more shall know:
And it 's O fickle Fortune, O !

MONTGOMERIE'S PEGGY

"My Montgomerie's Peggy was my deity for six or eight months. She had been bred, tho', as the world says, without any just pretence for it, in a style of life rather elegant. But, as Vanburgh says in one of his comedies, 'my damn'd Star found me out' there too, for though I began the affair, merely in a *gaité de cœur*, or, to tell the truth, what would scarcely be believed, a vanity of showing my parts in courtship, particularly my abilities at a *billet doux*, which I always piqu'd myself upon, made me lay siege to her; and when, as I always do in my foolish gallantries, I had battered myself into a very warm affection for her, she told me one day, in a flag of truce, that her fortress had been for some time before the rightful property of another; but with the greatest friendship and politeness, she offered me every alliance, except actual possession." (R. B.) Mrs. Begg stated that the girl was housekeeper at Coilfield House.

I

ALTHO' my bed were in yon muir,
  Amang the heather, in my plaidie,
Yet happy, happy would I be,
  Had I my dear Montgomerie's Peggy.

II

When o'er the hill beat surly storms,
  And winter nights were dark and rainy,
I 'd seek some dell, and in my arms
  I 'd shelter dear Montgomerie's Peggy.

III

Were I a Baron proud and high,
  And horse and servants waiting ready,
Then a' 't wad gie o' joy to me —
  The sharin 't with Montgomerie's Peggy.

THE LASS OF CESSNOCK BANKS

The heroine is supposed to have been the Elison Begbie — daughter of a farmer in the parish of Galston — to whom Burns made what was probably his first offer of marriage, in letters (1780–81), included in his published *Correspondence*. By some she is also supposed to have been the heroine of *And I 'll Kiss Thee Yet* (*ante*, p. 213).

I

ON Cessnock banks a lassie dwells,
  Could I describe her shape and mien !
Our lasses a' she far excels —
  An' she has twa sparkling, rogueish een !

II

She 's sweeter than the morning dawn,
  When rising Phœbus first is seen,
And dew-drops twinkle o'er the lawn —
  An' she has twa sparkling, rogueish een!

III

She 's stately like yon youthful ash,
  That grows the cowslip braes between,
And drinks the stream with vigour fresh —
  An' she has twa sparkling, rogueish een!

IV

She 's spotless like the flow'ring thorn
  With flow'rs so white and leaves so
    green,
When purest in the dewy morn —
  An' she has twa sparkling, rogueish een !

V

Her looks are like the vernal May,
  When ev'ning Phœbus shines serene,
While birds rejoice on every spray —
  An' she has twa sparkling, rogueish een !

VI

Her hair is like the curling mist,
  That climbs the mountain-sides at e'en,
When flow'r-reviving rains are past —
  An' she has twa sparkling, rogueish een !

VII

Her forehead 's like the show'ry bow,
  When gleaming sunbeams intervene,
And gild the distant mountain's brow —
  An' she has twa sparkling, rogueish een !

VIII

Her cheeks are like yon crimson gem,
  The pride of all the flowery scene,
Just opening on its thorny stem —
  An' she has twa sparkling, rogueish een !

IX

Her teeth are like the nightly snow,
  When pale the morning rises keen,
While hid the murm'ring streamlets flow —
  An' she has twa sparkling, rogueish een !

X

Her lips are like yon cherries ripe,
  That sunny walls from Boreas screen:
They tempt the taste and charm the sight —
  An' she has twa sparkling, rogueish een !

XI

Her teeth are like a flock of sheep
  With fleeces newly washen clean,
That slowly mount the rising steep —
  An' she has twa sparkling, rogueish een !

XII

Her breath is like the fragrant breeze,
  That gently stirs the blossom'd bean,
When Phœbus sinks behind the seas —
  An' she has twa sparkling, rogueish een !

XIII

Her voice is like the ev'ning thrush,
  That sings on Cessnock banks unseen,
While his mate sits nestling in the bush —
  An' she has twa sparkling, rogueish een !

XIV

But it 's not her air, her form, her face,
Tho' matching Beauty's fabled Queen:
'T is the mind that shines in ev'ry grace —
An' chiefly in her rogueish een !

THO' FICKLE FORTUNE

"An extempore under the pressure of a
heavy train of misfortunes, which, indeed,
threatened to undo me altogether. It was just
at the close of that dreadful period mentioned
on page 8th [see *ante*, p. 37, Prefatory Note to
A Prayer in the Prospect of Death], and, though
the weather has brightened up a little with
me, yet there has always been, since, a ' tem-
pest brewing round me in the grim sky ' of
futurity, which I pretty plainly see will, some
time or other, perhaps ere long, overwhelm
me, and drive me into some doleful dell to pine
in solitary, squalid wretchedness." (R. B.)
He also states it to have been written "in
imitation of an old Scotch song well known
among the country ingle sides," and he sets
down one stanza thereof to mark the " debt I
owe to the author, as the repeating of that
verse has lighted up my flame a thousand
times : "

" When clouds in skies do come together
  To hide the brightness of the sun,
There will surely be some pleasant weather
When a' the storms are past and gone."

I

Tho' fickle Fortune has deceived me
  (She promis'd fair, and perform'd but ill),
Of mistress, friends, and wealth bereaved
  me,
  Yet I bear a heart shall support me still.

II

I 'll act with prudence as far as I 'm able;
  But if success I must never find,
Then come, Misfortune, I bid thee wel-
  come —
  I 'll meet thee with an undaunted mind !

RAGING FORTUNE

Inscribed in the *First Common Place Book*,
September, 1785, next to *Tho' Fickle Fortune*.
" 'T was at the same time I set about com-
posing an air in the old Scotch style. I am
not musical scholar enough to prick down my
tune properly, so it can never see the light;
and perhaps 't is no great matter, but the fol-
lowing were the verses I composed to suit it.
. . . The tune consisted of three parts, so that
the above verses just went through the whole
Air." (R. B.)

I

O, RAGING Fortune's withering blast
  Has laid my leaf full low !
O, raging Fortune's withering blast
  Has laid my leaf full low !

II

My stem was fair, my bud was green,
  My blossom sweet did blow;
The dew fell fresh, the sun rose mild,
  And made my branches grow.

III

But luckless Fortune's northern storms
  Laid a' my blossoms low !
But luckless Fortune's northern storms
  Laid a' my blossoms low !

MY FATHER WAS A FARMER

"The following song is a wild rhapsody,
miserably deficient in versification; but as the
sentiments are the genuine feelings of my
heart, for that reason I have a particular plea-
sure in conning it over." (R. B.)   It faintly
resembles a song in an old chap at Abbots-
ford, *My Father was a Farmer, and a Farmer's
Son am I.*

I

My father was a farmer upon the Carrick
    border, O,
And carefully he bred me in decency and
    order, O.
He bade me act a manly part, though I
    had ne'er a farthing, O,
For without an honest, manly heart no
    man was worth regarding, O.

II

Then out into the world my course I did
    determine, O:
Tho' to be rich was not my wish, yet to be
    great was charming, O.

My talents they were not the worst, nor
    yet my education, O —
Resolv'd was I at least to try to mend my
    situation, O.

III

In many a way and vain essay I courted
    Fortune's favour, O:
Some cause unseen still stept between to
    frustrate each endeavour, O.
Sometimes by foes I was o'erpower'd,
    sometimes by friends forsaken, O,
And when my hope was at the top, I still
    was worst mistaken, O.

IV

Then sore harass'd, and tir'd at last with
    Fortune's vain delusion, O,
I dropt my schemes like idle dreams, and
    came to this conclusion, O: —
The past was bad, and the future hid; its
    good or ill untrièd, O,
But the present hour was in my pow'r, and
    so I would enjoy it, O.

V

No help, nor hope, nor view had I, nor
    person to befriend me, O;
So I must toil, and sweat, and broil, and
    labour to sustain me, O !
To plough and sow, to reap and mow, my
    father bred me early, O:
For one, he said, to labour bred was a
    match for Fortune fairly, O.

VI

Thus all obscure, unknown, and poor, thro'
    life I 'm doom'd to wander, O,
Till down my weary bones I lay in ever-
    lasting slumber, O.
No view nor care, but shun whate'er might
    breed me pain or sorrow, O,
I live to-day as well 's I may, regardless
    of to-morrow, O !

VII

But, cheerful still, I am as well as a mon-
    arch in a palace, O,
Tho' Fortune's frown still hunts me down,
    with all her wonted malice, O:
I make indeed my daily bread, but ne'er
    can make it farther, O,
But, as daily bread is all I need, I do not
    much regard her, O.

VIII

When sometimes by my labour I earn a
    little money, O,
Some unforeseen misfortune comes gen'-
    rally upon me, O:
Mischance, mistake, or by neglect, or my
    good-natur'd folly, O —
But, come what will, I 've sworn it still,
    I 'll ne'er be melancholy, O.

IX

All you who follow wealth and power with
    unremitting ardour, O,
The more in this you look for bliss, you
    leave your view the farther, O.
Had you the wealth Potosi boasts, or na-
    tions to adore you, O,
A cheerful, honest-hearted clown I will
    prefer before you, O !

O, LEAVE NOVÉLS

I

O, LEAVE novéls, ye Mauchline belles —
    Ye 're safer at your spinning-wheel !
Such witching books are baited hooks
    For rakish rooks like Rob Mossgiel.

II

Your fine *Tom Jones* and *Grandisons*
    They make your youthful fancies reel !
They heat your brains, and fire your veins,
    And then you 're prey for Rob Mossgiel.

III

Beware a tongue that 's smoothly hung,
    A heart that warmly seems to feel !
That feeling heart but acts a part, —
    'T is rakish art in Rob Mossgiel.

IV

The frank address, the soft caress
    Are worse than poisoned darts of steel:
The frank address and politesse
    Are all finesse in Rob Mossgiel.

THE MAUCHLINE LADY

The Mauchline lady was no doubt Jean
Armour.

I

WHEN first I came to Stewart Kyle,
  My mind it was na steady:
Where'er I gaed, where'er I rade,
  A mistress still I had ay.

II

But when I came roun' by Mauchline toun,
  Not dreadin anybody,
My heart was caught, before I thought,
  And by a Mauchline lady.

ONE NIGHT AS I DID WANDER

ONE night as I did wander,
  When corn begins to shoot,
I sat me down to ponder
  Upon an auld tree-root:
Auld Ayr ran by before me,
  —And bicker'd to the seas;
A cushat crooded o'er me,
  That echoed through the trees.

THERE WAS A LAD

CHORUS

Robin was a rovin boy,
  Rantin, rovin, rantin, rovin,
Robin was a rovin boy,
  Rantin, rovin Robin !

I

THERE was a lad was born in Kyle,
But whatna day o' whatna style,
I doubt it 's hardly worth the while
  To be sae nice wi' Robin.

II

Our monarch's hindmost year but ane
Was five and twenty days begun
'T was then a blast o' Janwar' win'
  Blew hansel in on Robin.

III

The gossip keekit in his loof,
Quo' scho : — "Wha lives will see the
    proof,
This waly boy will be nae coof :
  I think we 'll ca' him Robin.

IV

"He 'll hae misfortunes great an' sma',
But ay a heart aboon them a'.
He 'll be a credit till us a':
  We 'll a' be proud o' Robin !

V

"But sure as three times three mak nine,
I see by ilka score and line,
This chap will dearly like our kin',
  So leeze me on thee, Robin !

VI

"Guid faith," quo' scho, "I doubt you,
    stir,
Ye gar the lasses lie aspar;
But twenty fauts ye may hae waur —
  So blessins on thee, Robin ! "

CHORUS

Robin was a rovin boy,
  Rantin, rovin, rantin, rovin,
Robin was a rovin boy,
  Rantin, rovin Robin !

WILL YE GO TO THE INDIES, MY MARY

Sent to Thomson in October, 1792, as a sub-
stitute for *Will Ye Gang to the Ewe-bughts,
Marion*, which Thomson, like the pedant he
was, could not approve. "In my very early
years, when I was thinking of going to the
West Indies, I took the following farewell of a
dear girl. It is quite trifling, and has nothing
of the merits of *Ewe-bughts*, but it will fill
up this page." Thomson replied that he did
not mean to supplant *The Ewe-bughts*, and
that what he wanted Burns to do was to try
his "hand on some of the inferior stanzas."
Burns took not the hint; nor did Thomson
accept his song: "This is a very poor song,
which I do not mean to include in my Collec-
tion." For Mary Campbell, the supposed
heroine (though this is at least doubtful), see
ante, p. 204, Prefatory Note to *My Highland
Lassie, O* [and *post*, p. 343, notes to the same,
also the account in Mr. Henley's essay, *ante*,
pp. xxxviii–xlii].

I

WILL ye go to the Indies, my Mary,
  And leave auld Scotia's shore ?
Will ye go to the Indies, my Mary,
  Across th' Atlantic roar ?

II

O, sweet grows the lime and the orange,
  And the apple on the pine;
But a' the charms o' the Indies
  Can never equal thine.

III

I hae sworn by the Heavens to my Mary,
  I hae sworn by the Heavens to be true,
And sae may the Heavens forget me,
  When I forget my vow!

IV

O, plight me your faith, my Mary,
  And plight me your lily-white hand!
O, plight me your faith, my Mary,
  Before I leave Scotia's strand!

V

We hae plighted our troth, my Mary,
  In mutual affection to join;
And curst be the cause that shall part us!
  The hour and the moment o' time!

HER FLOWING LOCKS

I

Her flowing locks, the raven's wing,
Adown her neck and bosom hing.
How sweet unto that breast to cling,
  And round that neck entwine her!

II

Her lips are roses wat wi' dew —
O, what a feast, her bonie mou!
Her cheeks a mair celestial hue,
  A crimson still diviner!

THE LASS O' BALLOCHMYLE

Sent to Miss Wilhelminia Alexander in a letter of 18th November, 1786: "The enclosed song was the work of my return home, and perhaps but poorly answers what might have been expected from such a scene. I am going to print a second edition of my Poems, but cannot insert those verses without your permission." The lady took no notice of the request; but a MS. copy sets forth this note: "The above song cannot be published without the consent of the lady, which I have desired a common friend to ask." In all probability this was the copy submitted to the "jury of literati" in Edinburgh. It went unpublished — not because the writer could not get Miss Alexander's consent, but because it and a song on Miss Peggy Kennedy (*Young Peggy*, *ante*, p. 201) were "found defamatory libels against the fastidious powers of Poesy and Taste." In *Polyhymnia* it is stated to "have been composed by Robert Burns, from the emotions of gratitude and esteem which he felt for the worthy family, for the kindness and attention they had shewn him" — a rather too Platonic theory of its origin.

Miss Wilhelminia Alexander was the sister of Claud Alexander, who succeeded the Whitefoords in Ballochmyle. She is referred to in one of the suppressed stanzas of *The Vision*:

"While lovely Wilhelminia warms
  The coldest heart."

Later in life she set a higher price than erst upon the compliment designed in Burns's verses. She died unmarried, as late as 1843.

I

'T WAS even: the dewy fields were green,
  On every blade the pearls hang,
The zephyr wanton'd round the bean,
  And bore its fragrant sweets alang,
  In ev'ry glen the mavis sang,
All nature list'ning seem'd the while,
  Except where greenwood echoes rang
Amang the braes o' Ballochmyle.

II

With careless step I onward stray'd,
  My heart rejoic'd in Nature's joy,
When, musing in a lonely glade,
  A maiden fair I chanc'd to spy.
  Her look was like the Morning's eye,
Her air like Nature's vernal smile.
  Perfection whisper'd, passing by:—
"Behold the lass of Ballochmyle!"

III

Fair is the morn in flowery May,
  And sweet is night in autumn mild,
When roving thro' the garden gay,
  Or wand'ring in the lonely wild;
  But woman, Nature's darling child —
There all her charms she does compile!
  Even there her other works are foil'd
By the bonie lass o' Ballochmyle.

IV

O, had she been a country maid,
  And I the happy country swain,

Tho' shelter'd in the lowest shed
 That ever rose on Scotia's plain,
 Thro' weary winter's wind and rain
With joy, with rapture, I would toil,
 And nightly to my bosom strain
The bonie lass o' Ballochmyle !

V

Then Pride might climb the slipp'ry steep,
 Where fame and honours lofty shine,
And thirst of gold might tempt the deep,
 Or downward seek the Indian mine !
Give me the cot below the pine,
To tend the flocks or till the soil,
 And ev'ry day have joys divine
With the bonie lass o' Ballochmyle.

THE NIGHT WAS STILL

The MS. was given to one of the daughters of Dr. Lawrie of Newmilns, and commemorates a dance — when Burns for the first time heard the spinet — in the manse of Newmilns on the banks of Irvine. (See *ante*, p. 70, Prefatory Note to *Prayer: O Thou Dread Power.*)

I

THE night was still, and o'er the hill
 The moon shone on the castle wa',
The mavis sang, while dew-drops hang
 Around her on the castle wa':

II

Sae merrily they danc'd the ring
 Frae eenin' till the cock did craw,
And ay the o'erword o' the spring
 Was: — "Irvine's bairns are bonie a' ! "

MASONIC SONG

Said to have been recited by Burns at his admission as an honorary member of the Kilwinning St. John's Lodge, Kilmarnock, 26th October, 1786. "Willie" was Major William Parker, Grand Master. (See *ante*, p. 139, Prefatory Note to *To Hugh Parker.*)

I

YE sons of old Killie, assembled by Willie
 To follow the noble vocation,

Your thrifty old mother has scarce such
  another
 To sit in that honourèd station !
I've little to say, but only to pray
 (As praying's the *ton* of your fashion).
A prayer from the Muse you well may excuse
 ('T is seldom her favourite passion): —

II

"Ye Powers who preside o'er the wind and
  the tide,
 Who markèd each element's border,
Who formèd this frame with beneficent
  aim,
 Whose sovereign statute is order,
Within this dear mansion may wayward
  Contention
 Or witherèd Envy ne'er enter !
May Secrecy round be the mystical bound,
 And brotherly Love be the centre ! "

THE BONIE MOOR-HEN

CHORUS

I rede you, beware at the hunting, young
  men !
I rede you, beware at the hunting, young
  men !
Take some on the wing, and some as
  they spring,
 But cannily steal on a bonie moor-hen.

I

THE heather was blooming, the meadows
  were mawn,
Our lads gaed a-hunting ae day at the
  dawn,
O'er moors and o'er mosses and monie a
  glen:
At length they discovered a bonie moor-
  hen.

II

Sweet-brushing the dew from the brown
  heather bells,
Her colours betray'd her on yon mossy
  fells !
Her plumage outlustred the pride o' the
  spring,
And O, as she wanton'd sae gay on the
  wing,

III

Auld Phœbus himsel', as he peeped o'er
    the hill,
In spite at her plumage he tryèd his skill:
He level'd his rays where she bask'd on
    the brae —
His rays were outshone, and but mark'd
    where she lay !

IV

They hunted the valley, they hunted the
    hill,
The best of our lads wi' the best o' their
    skill;
But still as the fairest she sat in their sight,
Then, whirr ! she was over, a mile at a flight.

CHORUS

I rede you, beware at the hunting, young
    men !
I rede you, beware at the hunting, young
    men !
Take some on the wing, and some as
    they spring,
But cannily steal on a bonie moor-hen.

HERE'S A BOTTLE

There 's nane that 's blest of human kind
But the cheerful and the gay, man.

Gilbert Burns expressed to Cromek his
doubts of Robert's authorship; but he may
have been influenced by a desire to disassociate
his brother from the sentiment of the song.
In any case it was possibly suggested by *The
Bottle and Friend*, in the *Damon and Phillis
Garland*, included in the Bell Collection at
Abbotsford :

"Bright glory is a trifle and so is ambition,
I despise a false heart and a lofty condition,
For pride is a folly, for it I 'll not contend,
But I will enjoy my bottle and friend :
    In a little close room
      So neat and so trim,
    O there I will enjoy
      My bottle and friend," etc.

I

HERE 's a bottle and an honest man !
    What wad ye wish for mair, man ?
Wha kens, before his life may end,
    What his share may be o' care, man ?

II

Then catch the moments as they fly,
    And use them as ye ought, man !
Believe me, Happiness is shy,
    And comes not ay when sought, man !

THE BONIE LASS OF ALBANIE

Charlotte Stuart, daughter of Charles Ed-
ward, the "Young Pretender," by Clementina
Walkinshaw, was baptized 29th October, 1753
(*Mémoire* in the Ministère des Affaires Etran-
gères, for an extract from which we are indebted
to Mr. Andrew Lang). In the register of bap-
tisms at Liège, the child is entered as the
daughter of D. Johnson and the noble dame
Charlotte Pitt; and there is other clear evi-
dence that, though at this time Charles treated
Miss Walkinshaw as his wife, she neither was
married to him nor supposed herself to be his
wife. After Charles's separation from his
wife, the Countess of Albany, he sent for his
illegitimate daughter Charlotte, who abode
with him till his death, 30th January, 1788.
In 1784 he made out letters of legitimation,
and these were confirmed by the Parlement of
Paris, 6th December, 1787, when she took the
style of Duchess of Albany. But the legiti-
mation did not imply (as was supposed at the
time in England, and as, of course, was credited
by Burns) that Miss Walkinshaw had been
married to the Prince, but rather that Miss
Walkinshaw had not. She died soon after her
father.

I

My heart is wae, and unco wae,
    To think upon the raging sea,
That roars between her gardens green
    An' the bonie lass of Albanie.

II

This noble maid 's of royal blood,
    That rulèd Albion's kingdoms three;
But O, alas for her bonie face !
    They hae wranged the lass of Albanie.

III

In the rolling tide of spreading Clyde
    There sits an isle of high degree,
And a town of fame, whose princely name
    Should grace the lass of Albanie.

IV

But there is a youth, a witless youth,
  That fills the place where she should be:
We 'll send him o'er to his native shore,
  And bring our ain sweet Albanie !

V

Alas the day, and woe the day !
  A false usurper wan the gree,
Who now commands the towers and lands,
  The royal right of Albanie.

VI

We 'll daily pray, we 'll nightly pray,
  On bended knees most fervently,
That the time may come, with pipe and
    drum
  We 'll welcome hame fair Albanie.

AMANG THE TREES

Written in honour of Niel Gow (1727–1807),
the famous fiddler, whom Burns met during
his Northern tour in 1787.

I

AMANG the trees, where humming bees
  At buds and flowers were hinging, O,
Auld Caledon drew out her drone,
  And to her pipe was singing, O.
'T was Pibroch, Sang, Strathspeys and
    Reels —
  She dirl'd them aff fu' clearly, O,
When there cam' a yell o' foreign squeels,
  That dang her tapsalteerie, O !

II

Their capon craws an' queer " ha, ha's,"
  They made our lugs grow eerie, O.
The hungry bike did scrape and fyke,
  Till we were wae and weary, O.
But a royal ghaist, wha ance was cas'd
  A prisoner aughteen year awa,
He fir'd a Fiddler in the North,
  That dang them tapsalteerie, O !

THE CHEVALIER'S LAMENT

"Yesterday, my dear sir, as I was riding
thro' a track of melancholy, joyless muirs, be-
tween Galloway and Ayrshire, it being Sun-
day, I turned my thoughts to psalms and
hymns, and spiritual songs, and your favourite
air, *Capt. O'Kean*, coming at length in my
head, I tried these words to it. You will see
that the first part of the tune must be re-
peated." (Burns to Cleghorn, 31st March,
1788.) Only stanza i. was sent to Cleghorn at
that time. " If I could hit on another stanza
equal to *The Small Birds Rejoice*, I do myself
honestly avow that I think it a very superior
song." (R. B. to Thomson, 1st April, 1793.)
He sent no more to Thomson either.

I

THE small birds rejoice in the green leaves
    returning,
  The murmuring streamlet winds clear
    thro' the vale,
The primroses blow in the dews of the
    morning,
  And wild scatter'd cowslips bedeck the
    green dale:
    But what can give pleasure, or what
      can seem fair,
    When the lingering moments are
      number'd by care ?
      No flow'rs gaily springing,
      Nor birds sweetly singing,
    Can soothe the sad bosom of joyless
      despair !

II

The deed that I dar'd, could it merit their
    malice,
  A king and a father to place on his
    throne ?
His right are these hills, and his right are
    those valleys,
  Where the wild beasts find shelter, tho'
    I can find none !
    But 't is not my suff'rings thus
      wretched, forlorn —
    My brave gallant friends, 't is your
      ruin I mourn !
      Your faith prov'd so loyal
      In hot bloody trial,
    Alas ! can I make it no better return ?

YESTREEN I HAD A PINT O'
WINE

The Anna of the song was Anna Park, niece
of Mrs. Hyslop of the Globe Tavern, Dumfries.
She bore a daughter to Burns, 31st March,
1791, which was first sent to Mossgiel, and af-

terwards fostered by Mrs. Burns along with
her baby, William Nicol, born ten days after
it. According to Chambers it was Mrs. Burns's
plain duty so to do, inasmuch as if she had n't
gone to visit relatives in Ayrshire, and thus
provided her spouse with both an opportunity
and an excuse, the child would never have been
begotten. Be this as it may, nothing is known
of the mother's after-life. Indeed, she is said
by some to have died in childbed of this girl.

The song was sent to Thomson in April,
1793 : " *Shepherds, I Have Lost My Love* is to
me a heavenly air — what would you think of
a set of Scots verses to it ? I have made one, a
good while ago, which I think is the best love
song I ever composed in my life, but in its
original state is not quite a lady's song. I en-
close the original, which please present with
my best compliments to Mr. Erskine, and I
also enclose an *altered* not *amended* copy for
you, if you choose to set the tune to it, and let
the Irish verses follow." (R. B.)

I

YESTREEN I had a pint o' wine
  A place where body saw na;
Yestreen lay on this breast o' mine
  The gowden locks of Anna.

II

The hungry Jew in wilderness
  Rejoicing o'er his manna
Was naething to my hiney bliss
  Upon the lips of Anna !

III

Ye monarchs take the East and West
  Frae Indus to Savannah :
Gie me within my straining grasp
  The melting form of Anna !

IV

There I 'll despise Imperial charms,
  An Empress or Sultana,
While dying raptures in her arms
  I give and take wi' Anna !

V

Awa, thou flaunting God of Day !
  Awa, thou pale Diana !
Ilk Star, gae hide thy twinkling ray,
  When I 'm to meet my Anna !

VI

Come, in thy raven plumage, Night
  (Sun, Moon, and Stars, withdrawn a'),

And bring an Angel-pen to write
  My transports with my Anna !

POSTSCRIPT

I

The Kirk an' State may join, and tell
  To do sic things I maunna:
The Kirk an' State may gae to Hell,
  And I 'll gae to my Anna.

II

She is the sunshine o' my e'e,
  To live but her I canna:
Had I on earth but wishes three,
  The first should be my Anna.

SWEET ARE THE BANKS

The first set of a song — of which the sec-
ond is *Ye Flowery Banks* (immediately follow-
ing) while the third — which, being the worst,
is naturally the most popular — *The Banks o'
Doon*, was published in Johnson's *Museum* (see
ante, p. 243). It was sent in a letter to Alex-
ander Cunningham, 11th March, 1791 : " My
song is intended to sing to a Strathspey reel of
which I am very fond, called in Cumming's
collection of Strathspeys, *Ballendaloch's Reel ;*
and in other collections that I have met with
it is known by the name of *Camdelmore*. It
takes three stanzas of four lines each to go
through the whole tune." (R. B.)

I

SWEET are the banks, the banks o' Doon,
  The spreading flowers are fair,
And everything is blythe and glad,
  But I am fu' o' care.
Thou 'll break my heart, thou bonie bird,
  That sings upon the bough !
Thou minds me o' the happy days
  When my fause Luve was true.
Thou 'll break my heart, thou bonie bird,
  That sings beside thy mate,
For sae I sat, and sae I sang,
  And wist na o' my fate !

II

Aft hae I rov'd by bonie Doon,
  To see the woodbine twine,
And ilka bird sang o' its luve,
  And sae did I o' mine.

Wi' lightsome heart I pu'd a rose
  Upon its thorny tree,
But my fause lover staw my rose,
  And left the thorn wi' me.
Wi' lightsome heart I pu'd a rose
  Upon a morn in June,
And sae I flourish'd on the morn,
  And sae was pu'd or noon.

YE FLOWERY BANKS

The second set of *Sweet are the Banks.* Sent
in an undated letter — probably of March,
1791 — to John Ballantine of Ayr: "While
here I sit, sad and solitary, by the side of a
fire in a little country inn, and drying my wet
clothes, in pops a poor fellow of a sodger, and
tells me he is going to Ayr. By heavens! say
I to myself, with a tide of good spirits which
the magic of that sound 'Auld Toon of Ayr'
conjured up, I will send my last song to Mr.
Ballantine."   (R. B.)

I

YE flowery banks o' bonie Doon,
  How can ye blume sae fair?
How can ye chant, ye little birds,
  And I sae fu' o' care?

II

Thou 'll break my heart, thou bonie bird,
  That sings upon the bough:
Thou minds me o' the happy days
  When my fause Luve was true!

III

Thou 'll break my heart, thou bonie bird,
  That sings beside thy mate:
For sae I sat, and sae I sang,
  And wist na o' my fate!

IV

Aft hae I rov'd by bonie Doon
  To see the woodbine twine,
And ilka bird sang o' its luve,
  And sae did I o' mine.

V

Wi' lightsome heart I pu'd a rose
  Frae aff its thorny tree,
And my fause luver staw my rose,
  But left the thorn wi' me.

CALEDONIA

I

THERE was on a time, but old Time was
    then young,
  That brave Caledonia, the chief of her
    line,
From some of your northern deities sprung
  (Who knows not that brave Caledonia's
    divine?).
From Tweed to the Orcades was her do-
    main,
  To hunt, or to pasture, or do what she
    would.
Her heav'nly relations there fixèd her reign,
  And pledged her their godheads to war-
    rant it good.

II

A lambkin in peace but a lion in war,
  The pride of her kindred the heroine
    grew.
Her grandsire, old Odin, triumphantly
    swore: —
  "Whoe'er shall provoke thee, th' en-
    counter shall rue!"
With tillage or pasture at times she would
    sport,
  To feed her fair flocks by her green
    rustling corn;
But chiefly the woods were her fav'rite
    resort,
  Her darling amusement the hounds and
    the horn.

III

Long quiet she reign'd, till thitherward
    steers
  A flight of bold eagles from Adria's
    strand.
Repeated, successive, for many long years,
  They darken'd the air, and they plun-
    der'd the land.
Their pounces were murder, and horror
    their cry;
  They 'd conquer'd and ravag'd a world
    beside.
She took to her hills, and her arrows let fly —
  The daring invaders, they fled or they
    died!

IV

The Cameleon-Savage disturb'd her repose,
  With tumult, disquiet, rebellion, and
    strife.

Provok'd beyond bearing, at last she arose,
  And robbed him at once of his hopes and
    his life.
The Anglian Lion, the terror of France,
  Oft, prowling, ensanguin'd the Tweed's
    silver flood,
But, taught by the bright Caledonian lance,
  He learnèd to fear in his own native
    wood.

V

The fell Harpy-Raven took wing from the
    north,
  The scourge of the seas, and the dread
    of the shore;
The wild Scandinavian Boar issued forth
  To wanton in carnage and wallow in gore;
O'er countries and kingdoms their fury
    prevail'd,
  No arts could appease them, no arms
    could repel;
But brave Caledonia in vain they assail'd,
  As Largs well can witness, and Lon-
    cartie tell.

VI

Thus bold, independent, unconquer'd, and
    free,
  Her bright course of glory for ever shall
    run,
For brave Caledonia immortal must be,
  I 'll prove it from Euclid as clear as the
    sun: —
Rectangle-triangle, the figure we 'll chuse;
  The upright is Chance, and old Time is
    the base,
But brave Caledonia 's the hypothenuse;
  Then, *ergo,* she 'll match them, and match
    them always !

YOU 'RE WELCOME, WILLIE
STEWART

Originally inscribed on a crystal tumbler,
now at Abbotsford, the song is modelled on
the same Jacobitism as *Lovely Polly Stewart.*
(See *ante,* p. 259. See also *ante,* p. 146, *To
William Stewart.*) Stewart, who was factor at
Closeburn, died in 1812.

CHORUS

You 're welcome, Willie Stewart !
  You 're welcome, Willie Stewart !

There 's ne'er a flower that blooms in
    May,
  That 's half sae welcome 's thou art !

I

COME, bumpers high ! express your joy !
  The bowl we maun renew it —
The tappet hen, gae bring her ben,
  To welcome Willie Stewart !

II

May foes be strong, and friends be slack !
  Ilk action, may he rue it !
May woman on him turn her back,
  That wrangs thee, Willie Stewart !

CHORUS

You 're welcome, Willie Stewart !
  You 're welcome, Willie Stewart !
There 's ne'er a flower that blooms in
    May,
  That 's half sae welcome 's thou art !

WHEN FIRST I SAW

Chambers states that the heroine was Miss
Jean Jeffrey, whom Burns celebrated in *The
Blue-eyed Lassie* (see *ante,* p. 230, Prefatory
Note to *The Blue-eyed Lassie*). But the song
is so poor that, had not Alexander Smith (Edi-
tion 1868) collated the text " with a copy in
the poet's handwriting," we should have classed
it with the " Improbables."

CHORUS

She 's aye, aye sae blithe, sae gay,
  She 's aye sae blithe and cheerie,
She 's aye sae bonie, blithe and gay,
  O, gin I were her dearie !

I

WHEN first I saw fair Jeanie's face,
  I couldna tell what ail'd me:
My heart went fluttering pit-a-pat,
  My een they almost fail'd me.
She 's aye sae neat, sae trim, sae tight,
  All grace does round her hover !
Ae look depriv'd me o' my heart,
  And I became her lover.

II

Had I Dundas's whole estate,
  Or Hopetoun's wealth to shine in;

Did warlike laurels crown my brow,
  Or humbler bays entwining;
I 'd lay them a' at Jeanie's feet,
  Could I but hope to move her,
And, prouder than a belted knight,
  I 'd be my Jeanie's lover.

III

But sair I fear some happier swain
  Has gain'd my Jeanie's favour.
If so, may every bliss be hers,
  Though I maun never have her !
But gang she east, or gang she west,
  'T wixt Forth and Tweed all over,
While men have eyes, or ears, or taste,
  She 'll always find a lover.

CHORUS

She 's aye, aye sae blithe, sae gay,
  She 's aye sae blithe and cheerie,
She 's aye sae bonie, blithe and gay,
  O, gin I were her dearie !

BEHOLD THE HOUR

FIRST SET

I

BEHOLD the hour, the boat, arrive !
  My dearest Nancy, O, farewell !
Sever'd frae thee, can I survive,
  Frae thee whom I hae lov'd sae well ?

II

Endless and deep shall be my grief,
  Nae ray of comfort shall I see,
But this most precious, dear belief,
  That thou wilt still remember me.

III

Along the solitary shore,
  Where flitting sea-fowl round me cry,
Across the rolling, dashing roar,
  I 'll westward turn my wistful eye.

IV

" Happy thou Indian grove," I 'll say,
  " Where now my Nancy's path shall be !
While thro' your sweets she holds her way,
  O, tell me, does she muse on me ? "

HERE 'S A HEALTH TO THEM THAT 'S AWA

I

HERE 's a health to them that 's awa,
  Here 's a health to them that 's awa !
And wha winna wish guid luck to our cause,
  May never guid luck be their fa' !
It 's guid to be merry and wise,
  It 's guid to be honest and true,
It 's guid to support Caledonia's cause
  And bide by the buff and the blue.

II

Here 's a health to them that 's awa,
  Here 's a health to them that 's awa !
Here 's a health to Charlie, the chief o' the
    clan,
  Altho' that his band be sma' !
May Liberty meet wi' success,
  May prudence protect her frae evil !
May tyrants and Tyranny tine i' the mist
  And wander their way to the Devil !

III

Here 's a health to them that 's awa,
  Here 's a health to them that 's awa !
Here 's a health to Tammie, the Norlan'
    laddie,
  That lives at the lug o' the Law !
Here 's freedom to them that wad read,
  Here 's freedom to them that would
    write !
There 's nane ever fear'd that the truth
    should be heard,
  But they whom the truth would in-
    dite !

IV

Here 's a health to them that 's awa,
  An' here 's to them that 's awa !
Here 's to Maitland and Wycombe ! Let
    wha does na like 'em
  Be built in a hole in the wa' !
Here 's timmer that 's red at the heart,
  Here 's fruit that is sound at the core,
And may he that wad turn the buff and
    blue coat
  Be turn'd to the back o' the door !

V

Here 's a health to them that 's awa,
  Here 's a health to them that 's awa,

Here 's Chieftain M'Leod, a chieftain worth
    gowd,
Tho' bred amang mountains o' snaw !
Here 's friends on baith sides o' the Firth,
    And friends on baith sides o' the Tweed,
And wha wad betray old Albion's right,
    May they never eat of her bread !

AH, CHLORIS

I

Ah, Chloris, since it may not be
    That thou of love wilt hear,
If from the lover thou maun flee,
    Yet let the friend be dear !

II

Altho' I love my Chloris mair
    Than ever tongue could tell,
My passion I will ne'er declare —
    I 'll say, I wish thee well.

III

Tho' a' my daily care thou art,
    And a' my nightly dream,
I 'll hide the struggle in my heart,
    And say it is esteem.

PRETTY PEG

I

As I gaed up by yon gate-end,
    When day was waxin weary,
Wha did I meet come down the street
    But pretty Peg, my dearie ?

II

Her air so sweet, her shape complete,
    Wi' nae proportion wanting —
The Queen of Love could never move
    Wi' motion mair enchanting !

III

With linkèd hands we took the sands
    Down by yon winding river;
And O ! that hour, and shady bow'r,
    Can I forget it ?   Never !

MEG O' THE MILL

SECOND SET

Sent to Thomson, April, 1793, along with
There Was a Lass. "I know these songs are
not to have the luck to please you, else you
might be welcome to them." (R. B.) It was
written for *Jackie Hume's Lament.* Thomson
asked him to write another song to this air,
but he replied: "My song, *Ken Ye What
Meg o' the Mill Has Gotten,* pleases me so much
that I cannot try my hand at another song to
the same air ; so I shall not attempt it. I
know you will laugh at this ; but ilka man
wears his belt his ain gait." For the first set
see *ante,* p. 268.

I

O, ken ye what Meg o' the mill has gotten ?
An' ken ye what Meg o' the mill has gotten ?
She 's gotten a coof wi' a claute o' siller,
And broken the heart o' the barley miller !

II

The miller was strappin, the miller was
    ruddy,
A heart like a lord, and a hue like a lady.
The laird was a widdifu', bleerit knurl —
She 's left the guid fellow, and taen the
    churl !

III

The miller, he hecht her a heart leal and
    loving.
The laird did address her wi' matter more
    moving:
A fine pacing-horse wi' a clear, chainèd
    bridle,
A whip by her side, and a bonie side saddle !

IV

O, wae on the siller — it is sae prevailing !
And wae on the love that is fixed on a
    mailen !
A tocher's nae word in a true lover's parl,
But gie me my love and a fig for the warl !

PHILLIS THE FAIR

Sent to Thomson, August, 1793. "I like-
wise tried my hand on *Robin Adair,* and you
will probably think with little success ; but it

is such a damned, crampt, out-of-the-way mea-
sure, that I despair of doing anything better
to it. . . . So much for namby-pamby. I may,
after all, try my hand on it in Scots verse.
There I always find myself at home." Thom-
son replied that he would be glad to see Burns
"give *Robin Adair* a Scottish dress," but that
"Peter" was furnishing him with an English
suit.

I

WHILE larks with little wing
    Fann'd the pure air,
Viewing the breathing Spring,
    Forth I did fare.
Gay, the sun's golden eye
Peep'd o'er the mountains high;
"Such thy bloom," did I cry —
    "Phillis the fair!"

II

In each bird's careless song,
    Glad, I did share;
While yon wild flowers among,
    Chance led me there.
Sweet to the opening day,
Rosebuds bent the dewy spray;
"Such thy bloom," did I say —
    "Phillis the fair!"

III

Down in a shady walk
    Doves cooing were;
I mark'd the cruel hawk
    Caught in a snare.
So kind may Fortune be!
Such make his destiny,
He who would injure thee,
    Phillis the fair!

O, SAW YE MY DEAR, MY PHILLY

I

O, SAW ye my Dear, my Philly?
O, saw ye my Dear, my Philly?
She's down i' the grove, she's wi' a new
    love,
    She winna come hame to her Willy.

II

What says she my Dear, my Philly?
What says she my Dear, my Philly?
She lets thee to wit she has thee forgot,
    And for ever disowns thee, her Willy.

III

O, had I ne'er seen thee, my Philly!
O, had I ne'er seen thee, my Philly!
As light as the air, and fause as thou's fair,
    Thou's broken the heart o' thy Willy.

'T WAS NA HER BONIE BLUE E'E

I

'T WAS na her bonie blue e'e was my ruin:
Fair tho' she be, that was ne'er my undoin.
'T was the dear smile when naebody did
    mind us,
'T was the bewitching, sweet, stoun glance
    o' kindness!

II

Sair do I fear that to hope is denied me,
Sair do I fear that despair maun abide me;
But tho' fell Fortune should fate us to sever,
Queen shall she be in my bosom for ever.

III

Chloris, I'm thine wi' a passion sincerest,
And thou hast plighted me love o' the
    dearest,
And thou'rt the angel that never can
    alter —
Sooner the sun in his motion would falter!

WHY, WHY TELL THY LOVER

I

WHY, why tell thy lover
Bliss he never must enjoy?
Why, why undeceive him,
And give all his hopes the lie?

II

O, why, while Fancy, raptur'd, slumbers,
"Chloris, Chloris," all the theme,
Why, why wouldst thou, cruel,
Wake thy lover from his dream?

THE PRIMROSE

Sent to Thomson, 1793: "For *Todlin Hame*
take the following old English song, which I
dare say is but little known." (R. B.) "*N.B.*

I have altered it a little." (R. B.) [This " old English song " is Carew's or Herrick's *Ask me why I send you here*.]

I

DOST ask me why I send thee here
The firstling of the infant year :
This lovely native of the vale,
That hangs so pensive and so pale ?

II

Look on its·bending stalk, so weak,
That, each way yielding, doth not break,
And see how aptly it reveals
The doubts and fears a lover feels.

III

Look on its leaves of yellow hue
Bepearl'd thus with morning dew,
And these will whisper in thine ears: —
" The sweets of loves are wash'd with tears."

O, WERT THOU IN THE CAULD BLAST

Written during his last illness in honour of Jessie Lewars (see *ante*, p. 280, Prefatory Note to *Here's a Health*), after she had played *The Wren* to him on the piano.

I

O, WERT thou in the cauld blast
  On yonder lea, on yonder lea,
My plaidie to the angry airt,
  I 'd shelter thee, I 'd shelter thee.
Or did Misfortune's bitter storms
  Around thee blaw, around thee blaw,
Thy bield should be my bosom,
  To share it a', to share it a'.

II

Or were I in the wildest waste,
  Sae black and bare, sae black and bare,
The desert were a Paradise,
  If thou wert there, if thou wert there.
Or were I monarch of the globe,
  Wi' thee to reign, wi' thee to reign,
The brightest jewel in my crown
  Wad be my queen, wad be my queen.

INTERPOLATIONS

[This heading is given to a few verses inserted by Burns in poems written by his contemporaries.]

YOUR FRIENDSHIP

I

YOUR friendship much can make me blest —
  O, why that bliss destroy ?
Why urge the only, one request
  You know I will deny ?

II

Your thought, if Love must harbour there,
  Conceal it in that thought,
Nor cause me from my bosom tear
  The very friend I sought.

FOR THEE IS LAUGHING NATURE

FOR thee is laughing Nature gay,
For thee she pours the vernal day:
For me in vain is Nature drest,
While Joy 's a stranger to my breast.

NO COLD APPROACH

Inserted in the song, *The Tears I Shed*, by Miss Cranstoun, afterwards the second wife of Professor Dugald Stewart, to complete the last octave, and so fit it for the tune in Johnson's *Museum*. " This song of genius was composed by a Miss Cranstoun. It wanted four lines to make all the stanzas suit the music, which I added, and are the first four of the last stanza." (R. B.)

No cold approach, no alter'd mien,
  Just what would make suspicion start,
No pause the dire extremes between :
  He made me blest — and broke my heart.

ALTHO' HE HAS LEFT ME

ALTHO' he has left me for greed o' the siller,
  I dinna envy him the gains he can win:

I rather wad bear a' the lade o' my sor-
　　row
Than ever hae acted sae faithless to him.

LET LOOVE SPARKLE

LET loove sparkle in her e'e,
Let her lo'e nae man but me:
That 's the tocher guid I prize,
There the luver's treasure lies.

AS DOWN THE BURN

As down the burn they took their way,
　　And thro' the flowery dale,
His cheek to hers he aft did lay,
　　And love was ay the tale,
With: — "Mary, when shall we return,
　　Sic pleasure to renew?"
Quoth Mary: — "Love, I like the burn,
　　And ay shall follow you."

IMPROBABLES

In our judgment few of [the poems that
follow] can justly be credited to Burns; and to
consider the quality of nearly all is to perceive,
and very clearly, that, partial as his Editors
were to the use of such epithets as "God-
gifted" and "heaven-inspired" and the like,
there was no rubbish so poor but they found
it good enough to father on the god of their
idolatry.

ON ROUGH ROADS

According to Scott Douglas, "it is very
familiarly quoted in Ayrshire, as a stray im-
promptu of Burns's." But he says not from
whom he got it, and an impromptu which had
lived for ninety years without getting written
or printed — *ça donne furieusement à penser!*

I 'M now arriv'd — thanks to the Gods! —
　　Through pathways rough and muddy:
A certain sign that makin' roads
　　Is no this people's study.
Yet, though I 'm no wi' scripture cramm'd,
　　I 'm sure the Bible says
That heedless sinners shall be damn'd,
　　Unless they mend their ways.

ELEGY ON STELLA

Inscribed in the *Second Common Place
Book:* "This poem is the work of some hap-
less son of the Muses who deserved a better
fate. There is a great deal of 'the voice
of Cona' in his solitary, mournful notes;
and had the sentiments been clothed in Shen-
stone's language, they would have been no
discredit to that elegant poet." (R. B.) He
sent a copy to Mrs. Dunlop in a letter of 7th
July, 1789, in which he said that he had met
the *Elegy* in MS., and marked the passages
which struck him most. These are stanzas i.
iv. xiii. xiv. (last two lines) xvii. xviii. and
xix.; and it is worth noting that he does not
include with them stanza xv., stanza xvi., or
stanza xx.

The theory of Scott Douglas and others,
that the verses were suggested by a visit to the
West Highlands in June, 1787, when Burns
may have visited Mary Campbell's grave — at
Greenock, which, in defiance of geography, ap-
pears "at the last limits of our isle" — is
sheer sentiment. The truth is, there is no
earthly reason, except the existence of that
sentiment, for attributing the thing to Burns;
and, as it is utterly unlike his work — especially
his work in English, which is far less easy and
less fluent — as, too, he suggests that another
wrote it, we see not why it should ever have
been printed as his.

I

STRAIT is the spot, and green the sod,
　　From whence my sorrows flow;
And soundly sleeps the ever dear
　　Inhabitant below.

II

Pardon my transport, gentle shade,
　　While o'er the turf I bow!
Thy earthly house is circumscrib'd,
　　And solitary now!

III

Not one poor stone to tell thy name
　　Or make thy virtues known!
But what avails to thee — to me —
　　The sculpture of a stone?

IV

I 'll sit me down upon this turf,
　　And wipe away this tear.
The chill blast passes swiftly by,
　　And flits around thy bier.

V

Dark is the dwelling of the dead,
  And sad their house of rest:
Low lies the head by Death's cold arm
  In awful fold embraced.

VI

I saw the grim Avenger stand
  Incessant by thy side;
Unseen by thee, his deadly breath
  Thy lingering frame destroy'd.

VII

Pale grew the roses on thy cheek,
  And wither'd was thy bloom,
Till the slow poison brought thy youth
  Untimely to the tomb.

VIII

Thus wasted are the ranks of men —
  Youth, health, and beauty fall!
The ruthless ruin spreads around,
  And overwhelms us all.

IX

Behold where, round thy narrow house,
  The graves unnumber'd lie!
The multitude, that sleep below,
  Existed but to die.

X

Some with the tottering steps of Age
  Trod down the darksome way;
And some in Youth's lamented prime,
  Like thee, were torn away.

XI

Yet these, however hard their fate,
  Their native earth receives:
Amid their weeping friends they died,
  And fill their fathers' graves.

XII

From thy lov'd friends, when first thy
    heart
  Was taught by Heaven to glow,
Far, far remov'd, the ruthless stroke
  Surpris'd, and laid thee low.

XIII

At the last limits of our Isle,
  Wash'd by the western wave,
Touch'd by thy fate, a thoughtful Bard
  Sits lonely on thy grave!

XIV

Pensive he eyes, before him spread,
  The deep, outstretch'd and vast.
His mourning notes are borne away
  Along the rapid blast.

XV

And while, amid the silent dead,
  Thy hapless fate he mourns,
His own long sorrows freshly bleed,
  And all his grief returns.

XVI

Like thee, cut off in early youth
  And flower of beauty's pride,
His friend, his first and only joy,
  His much-lov'd Stella died.

XVII

Him, too, the stern impulse of Fate
  Resistless bears along,
And the same rapid tide shall whelm
  The Poet and the Song.

XVIII

The tear of pity, which he shed,
  He asks not to receive:
Let but his poor remains be laid
  Obscurely in the grave!

XIX

His grief-worn heart with truest joy
  Shall meet the welcome shock;
His airy harp shall lie unstrung
  And silent on the rock.

XX

O my dear maid, my Stella, when
  Shall this sick period close,
And lead the solitary Bard
  To his belov'd repose?

POEM ON PASTORAL POETRY

Currie, from a MS. in Burns's hand; but
Gilbert Burns strongly doubted its authenti-
city, and internal evidence shows that it may
have been written by some contemporary of
Allan Ramsay. Thus in stanza vi. that maker
is referred to as alive; while no mention is
made of either Hamilton of Gilbertfield or
Fergusson, one or other of whom may well
have been the author. Burns, again, knew

nothing of Theocritus and nothing of Maro;
and, had he written of pastoral verse, would
certainly have quoted, not Pope but his fa-
vourite Shenstone.

I

HAIL, Poesie! thou Nymph reserv'd !
In chase o' thee, what crowds hae swerv'd
Frae common sense, or sunk enerv'd
      'Mang heaps o' clavers !
And och! o'er aft thy joes hae starv'd
      'Mid a' thy favours !

II

Say, Lassie, why thy train amang,
While loud the trump's heroic clang,
And sock or buskin skelp alang
      To death or marriage,
Scarce ane has tried the shepherd-sang
      But wi' miscarriage ?

III

In Homer's craft Jock Milton thrives;
Eschylus' pen Will Shakespeare drives;
Wee Pope, the knurlin, till him rives
      Horatian fame;
In thy sweet sang, Barbauld, survives
      Even Sappho's flame !

IV

But thee, Theocritus, wha matches ?
They 're no herd's ballats, Maro's catches !
Squire Pope but busks his skinklin patches
      O' heathen tatters !
I pass by hunders, nameless wretches,
      That ape their betters.

V

In this braw age o' wit and lear,
Will nane the Shepherd's whistle mair
Blaw sweetly in its native air
      And rural grace,
And wi' the far-fam'd Grecian share
      A rival place ?

VI

Yes ! there is ane — a Scottish callan !
There 's ane !   Come forrit, honest Allan !
Thou need na jouk behint the hallan,
      A chiel sae clever !
The teeth o' Time may gnaw Tantallan,
      But thou 's for ever.

VII

Thou paints auld Nature to the nines
In thy sweet Caledonian lines !
Nae gowden stream thro' myrtles twines,
      Where Philomel,
While nightly breezes sweep the vines,
      Her griefs will tell:

VIII

In gowany glens thy burnie strays,
Where bonie lasses bleach their claes,
Or trots by hazelly shaws and braes
      Wi' hawthorns gray,
Where blackbirds join the shepherd's lays
      At close o' day.

IX

Thy rural loves are nature's sel':
Nae bombast spates o' nonsense swell,
Nae snap conceits, but that sweet spell
      O' witchin love,
That charm that can the strongest quell,
      The sternest move.

ON THE DESTRUCTION OF DRUMLANRIG WOODS

First published in *The Scots Magazine* for
July (1803), where it is stated that the verses
had been found "written on the window-shutter
of a small inn on the banks of the Nith," and
that they were "supposed to have been written
by Burns." This is a little vague. Cromek,
who did n't print the verses, told Creech that
they were written by Henry Mackenzie, but
there is nothing beyond this statement to con-
firm the ascription; though one could credit
Mackenzie with them far more easily than one
could credit Burns.

I

As on the banks of winding Nith
  Ae smiling simmer morn I stray'd,
And traced its bonie holms and haughs,
  Where linties sang, and lammies play'd,
I sat me down upon a craig,
  And drank my fill o' fancy's dream,
When from the eddying deep below
  Up rose the Genius of the Stream.

II

Dark like the frowning rock his brow,
  And troubled like his wintry wave,

And deep as sughs the boding wind
   Amang his caves the sigh he gave.
" And come ye here, my son," he cried,
   " To wander in my birken shade ?
To muse some favourite Scottish theme,
   Or sing some favourite Scottish maid ?

III

" There was a time, it 's nae lang syne,
   Ye might hae seen me in my pride,
When a' my banks sae bravely saw
   Their woody pictures in my tide;
When hanging beech and spreading elm
   Shaded my stream sae clear and cool;
And stately oaks their twisted arms
   Threw broad and dark across the pool;

IV

" When, glinting thro' the trees, appear'd
   The wee white cot aboon the mill,
And peaceful rose its ingle reek,
   That, slowly curling, clamb the hill.
But now the cot is bare and cauld,
   Its leafy bield for ever gane,
And scarce a stinted birk is left
   To shiver in the blast its lane."

V

" Alas ! " quoth I, " what ruefu' chance
   Has twin'd ye o' your stately trees ?
Has laid your rocky bosom bare ?
Has stripp'd the cleeding aff your braes ?
Was it the bitter eastern blast,
   That scatters blight in early spring ?
Or was 't the wil'fire scorch'd their boughs ?
   Or canker-worm wi' secret sting ? "

VI

" Nae eastlin blast," the Sprite replied —
   " It blaws na here sae fierce and fell,
And on my dry and halesome banks
   Nae canker-worms get leave to dwell:
Man ! cruel man ! " the Genius sigh'd,
   As through the cliffs he sank him down:
" The worm that gnaw'd my bonie trees,
   That reptile wears a Ducal crown."

THE JOYFUL WIDOWER

This very squalid performance is attributed
by Stenhouse to Burns ; but he never acknow-
ledged it.

I

I MARRIED with a scolding wife
   The fourteenth of November:
She made me weary of my life
   By one unruly member.
Long did I bear the heavy yoke,
   And many griefs attended,
But to my comfort be it spoke,
   Now, now her life is ended !

II

We liv'd full one-and-twenty years
   A man and wife together.
At length from me her course she steer'd
   And gone I know not whither.
Would I could guess, I do profess:
   I speak, and do not flatter,
Of all the women in the world,
   I never would come at her !

III

Her body is bestowèd well —
   A handsome grave does hide her.
But sure her soul is not in Hell —
   The Deil would ne'er abide her !
I rather think she is aloft
   And imitating thunder,
For why ? — Methinks I hear her voice
   Tearing the clouds asunder !

WHY SHOULD WE IDLY WASTE OUR PRIME

I

WHY should we idly waste our prime
   Repeating our oppressions ?
Come rouse to arms ! 'T is now the time
   To punish past transgressions.
'T is said that Kings can do no wrong —
   Their murderous deeds deny it,
And, since from us their power is sprung,
   We have a right to try it.
Now each true patriot's song shall be: —
   " Welcome Death or Libertie ! "

II

Proud Priests and Bishops we 'll translate
   And canonize as Martyrs;
The guillotine on Peers shall wait;
   And Knights shall hang in garters.
Those Despots long have trode us down,
   And Judges are their engines:

Such wretched minions of a Crown
  Demand the people's vengeance !
To-day 't is *theirs.* To-morrow we
Shall don the Cap of Libertie !

III

The Golden Age we 'll then revive:
  Each man will be a brother;
In harmony we all shall live,
  And share the earth together;
In Virtue train'd, enlighten'd Youth
  Will love each fellow-creature;
And future years shall prove the truth
  That Man is good by nature:
Then let us toast with three times three
The reign of Peace and Libertie !

THE TREE OF LIBERTY

Chambers gave as his authority a MS. then
in the possession of Mr. James Duncan, More-
field, Glasgow. *The Tree of Liberty* reads like
a bad blend of *Scots Wha Hae* and *Is There
For Honest Poverty;* and as the MS. has not
been heard of since 1838, we may charitably
conclude that Burns neither made the trash
nor copied it.

I

HEARD ye o' the Tree o' France,
  And wat ye what 's the name o't ?
Around it a' the patriots dance —
  Weel Europe kens the fame o't !
It stands where ance the Bastile stood —
  A prison built by kings, man,
When Superstition's hellish brood
  Kept France in leading-strings, man.

II

Upo' this tree there grows sic fruit,
  Its virtues a' can tell, man:
It raises man aboon the brute,
  It mak's him ken himsel', man !
Gif ance the peasant taste a bit,
  He 's greater than a lord, man,
And wi' the beggar shares a mite
  O' a' he can afford, man.

III

This fruit is worth a' Afric's wealth:
  To comfort us 't was sent, man,
To gie the sweetest blush o' health,
  And mak' us a' content, man !

It clears the een, it cheers the heart,
  Mak's high and low guid friends, man,
And he wha acts the traitor's part,
  It to perdition sends, man.

IV

My blessings ay attend the chiel,
  Wha pitied Gallia's slaves, man,
And staw a branch, spite o' the Deil,
  Frae 'yont the western waves, man !
Fair Virtue water'd it wi' care,
  And now she sees wi' pride, man,
How weel it buds and blossoms there,
  Its branches spreading wide, man.

V

But vicious folk ay hate to see
  The works o' Virtue thrive, man:
The courtly vermin 's bann'd the tree,
  And grat to see it thrive, man !
King Louis thought to cut it down,
  When it was unco sma', man;
For this the watchman crack'd his crown,
  Cut aff his head and a', man.

VI

A wicked crew syne, on a time,
  Did tak' a solemn aith, man,
It ne'er should flourish to its prime —
  I wat they pledg'd their faith, man !
Awa they gaed wi' mock parade,
  Like beagles hunting game, man,
But soon grew weary o' the trade,
  And wish'd they 'd been at hame, man.

VII

Fair Freedom, standing by the tree,
  Her sons did loudly ca', man.
She sang a sang o' Liberty,
  Which pleas'd them ane and a', man.
By her inspir'd, the new-born race
  Soon drew the avenging steel, man.
The hirelings ran — her foes gied chase,
  And bang'd the despot weel, man.

VIII

Let Britain boast her hardy oak,
  Her poplar, and her pine, man !
Auld Britain ance could crack her joke,
  And o'er her neighbours shine, man !
But seek the forest round and round,
  And soon 't it will be agreed, man,
That sic a tree can not be found
  'Twixt London and the Tweed, man.

IX

Without this tree alake this life
    Is but a vale o' woe, man,
A scene o' sorrow mix'd wi' strife,
    Nae real joys we know, man;
We labour soon, we labour late,
    To feed the titled knave, man,
And a' the comfort we 're to get,
    Is that ayont the grave, man.

X

Wi' plenty o' sic trees, I trow,
    The warld would live in peace, man.
The sword would help to mak' a plough,
    The din o' war wad cease, man.
Like brethren in a common cause,
    We 'd on each other smile, man;
And equal rights and equal laws
    Wad gladden every isle, man.

XI

Wae worth the loon wha wadna eat
    Sic halesome, dainty cheer, man !
I 'd gie the shoon frae aff my feet,
    To taste the fruit o't here, man !
Syne let us pray, Auld England may
    Sure plant this far-famed tree, man;
And blythe we 'll sing, and herald the day
    That gives us liberty, man.

TO A KISS

Published in a Liverpool paper called *The
Kaleidoscope*, and there attributed to Burns.
It, however, appeared originally (and anony-
mously) in *The Oracle*, January 29, 1796, long
the favoured organ of the wretched Della
Cruscan shoal ; and it has the right Anna
Matilda smack throughout. After all, too,
that a thing is bad enough to have been written
by Burns for Thomson is no proof that it is
Burns's work.

I

HUMID seal of soft affections,
    Tend'rest pledge of future bliss,
Dearest tie of young connections,
    Love's first snow-drop, virgin kiss !

II

Speaking silence, dumb confession,
    Passion's birth and infant's play,

Dove-like fondness, chaste confession,
    Glowing dawn of brighter day !

III

Sorrowing joy, adieu's last action,
    Ling'ring lips — no more must join !
Words can never speak affection,
    Thrilling and sincere as thine !

DELIA

AN ODE

I

FAIR the face of orient day,
    Fair the tints of op'ning rose:
But fairer still my Delia dawns,
    More lovely far her beauty blows.

II

Sweet the lark's wild-warbled lay,
    Sweet the tinkling rill to hear:
But, Delia, more delightful still
    Steal thine accents on mine ear.

III

The flower-enamoured busy bee
    The rosy banquet loves to sip;
Sweet the streamlet's limpid lapse
    To the sun-brown'd Arab's lip:

IV

But, Delia, on thy balmy lips
    Let me, no vagrant insect, rove !
O, let me steal one liquid kiss !
    For O ! my soul is parch'd with love !

TO THE OWL

" Found among the Poet's MSS. in his own
handwriting, with occasional interlineations
such as occur in all his primitive effusions ; "
but attributed by him to John M'Creddie, of
whom nothing is known. To our mind, those
who give the verses to Burns would give him
anything.

I

SAD bird of night, what sorrow calls thee
    forth,
    To vent thy plaints thus in the midnight
      hour ?

Is it some blast that gathers in the north,
  Threat'ning to nip the verdure of thy
    bow'r ?

II

Is it, sad owl, that Autumn strips the shade,
  And leaves thee here, unshelter'd and
    forlorn ?
Or fear that Winter will thy nest invade ?
  Or friendless Melancholy bids thee
    mourn ?

III

Shut out, lone bird, from all the feather'd
    train,
  To tell thy sorrows to th' unheeding
    gloom,
No friend to pity when thou dost complain,
  Grief all thy thought, and solitude thy
    home,

IV

Sing on, sad mourner ! I will bless thy
    strain,
  And pleas'd in sorrow listen to thy song.
Sing on, sad mourner ! To the night
    complain,
  While the lone echo wafts thy notes along.

V

Is Beauty less, when down the glowing
    cheek
  Sad, piteous tears in native sorrows fall ?
Less kind the heart when anguish bids it
    break ?
  Less happy he who lists to Pity's call ?

VI

Ah no, sad owl ! nor is thy voice less
    sweet,
  That Sadness tunes it, and that Grief is
    there ?
That Spring's gay notes, unskill'd, thou
    can't repeat,
  That Sorrow bids thee to the gloom re-
    pair !

VII

Nor that the treble songsters of the day,
  Are quite estranged, sad bird of night,
    from thee !
Nor that the thrush deserts the evening
    spray,
  When darkness calls thee from thy rev-
    erie !

VIII

From some old tower, thy melancholy
    dome,
  While the gray walls and desert soli-
    tudes
Return each note, responsive to the gloom
  Of ivied coverts and surrounding woods:

IX

There hooting, I will list more pleased to
    thee,
  Than ever lover to the nightingale,
Or drooping wretch, oppress'd with misery,
  Lending his ear to some condoling tale !

THE VOWELS

A TALE

Found among the Poet's papers.

'T WAS where the birch and sounding thong
    are ply'd,
The noisy domicile of pedant pride;
Where Ignorance her darkening vapour
    throws,
And Cruelty directs the thickening blows !
Upon a time, Sir A B C the great,
In all his pedagogic powers elate,
His awful chair of state resolves to mount,
And call the trembling Vowels to account.

First enter'd A, a grave, broad, solemn
    wight,
But, ah ! deform'd, dishonest to the sight !
His twisted head look'd backward on his
    way,
And flagrant from the scourge he grunted,
    ai !

Reluctant, E stalk'd in ; a piteous case,
The justling tears ran down his honest
    face !
That name, that well-worn name, and all
    his own,
Pale, he surrenders at the tyrant's throne !
The Pedant stifles keen the Roman sound
Not all his mongrel diphthongs can com-
    pound;
And next the title following close behind,
He to the nameless, ghastly wretch as-
    sign'd.

The cobwebb'd gothic dome resounded, Y !
In sullen vengeance, I disdain'd reply:
The Pedant swung his felon cudgel round,
And knock'd the groaning vowel to the
    ground !

In rueful apprehension enter'd O,
The wailing minstrel of despairing woe:
Th' Inquisitor of Spain the most expert
Might there have learnt new mysteries of
    his art.
So grim, deform'd, with horrors entering, U
His dearest friend and brother scarcely
    knew !

As trembling U stood staring all aghast,
The Pedant in his left hand clutch'd him
    fast,
In helpless infants' tears he dipp'd his
    right,
Baptiz'd him *eu*, and kick'd him from his
    sight.

ON THE ILLNESS OF A FAVOUR-
ITE CHILD

It is hard to believe that Burns, though his
taste in English was none of the finest, could
even transcribe such immitigable rubbish.

I

Now health forsakes that angel face,
    Nae mair my dearie smiles.
Pale sickness withers ilka grace,
    And a' my hopes beguiles.

II

The cruel Powers reject the prayer
    I hourly mak' for thee:
Ye Heavens ! how great is my despair !
    How can I see him die !

ON THE DEATH OF A FAVOUR-
ITE CHILD

Burns's daughter, Elizabeth Riddell, died in
the autumn of 1795. But this fact can scarce
be regarded as proof of the authenticity of
verses altogether in the manner of Mrs. He-
mans.

I

O, SWEET be thy sleep in the land of the
    grave,
    My dear little angel, for ever !
For ever ? — O no ! let not man be a
    slave,
    His hopes from existence to sever !

II

Though cold be the clay, where thou pil-
    low'st thy head
    In the dark, silent mansions of sorrow,
The spring shall return to thy low, narrow
    bed,
    Like the beam of the day-star to-mor-
    row.

III

The flower-stem shall bloom like thy sweet
    seraph form
    Ere the spoiler had nipt thee in blos-
    som,
When thou shrank frae the scowl of the
    loud winter storm,
    And nestled thee close to that bosom.

IV

O, still I behold thee, all lovely in death,
    Reclined on the lap of thy mother,
When the tear-trickle bright, when the
    short, stifled breath
    Told how dear ye were ay to each other.

V

My child, thou art gone to the home of thy
    rest,
    Where suffering no longer can harm
    thee:
Where the songs of the Good, where the
    hymns of the Blest
    Through an endless existence shall charm
    thee !

VI

While he, thy fond parent, must sighing
    sojourn
    Through the dire desert regions of sor-
    row,
O'er the hope and misfortune of being to
    mourn,
    And sigh for this life's latest morrow.

THE MERRY MUSES OF CALEDONIA

The poems included in this collection are those accepted by the editors of the two best editions of *The Merry Muses of Caledonia*, James Barke, Sydney Goodsir Smith, and J. DeLancey Ferguson (Edinburgh, 1959, and New York, 1965) and G. Legman (New Hyde Park, New York, 1965). The reader is referred to the Editor's Note for more details.

I'LL TELL YOU A TALE OF A WIFE

TUNE: *Auld Sir Symon*

I'll tell you a tale of a Wife,
  And she was a Whig and a Saunt;
She liv'd a most sanctify'd life,
  But whyles she was fash'd wi' her ——— .
———

    Fal lal &c.

II

Poor woman! she gaed to the Priest,
  And till him she made her complaint;
"There's naething that troubles my breast
  "Sae sair as the sins o' my ——— . —

III

"Sin that I was herdin at hame,
  "Till now I'm three score & ayont,
"I own it wi' sin & wi' shame
  "I've led a sad life wi' my ——— . — "

IV

He bade her to clear up her brow,
  And no be discourag'd upon 't;
For holy gude women enow
  Were mony times waur't wi' ther ——— .
———

V

It's naught but Beelzebub's art,
  But that's the mair sign of a saunt,
He kens that ye're pure at the heart,
  Sae levels his darts at your ——— . —

VI

What signifies Morals & Works,
  Our works are no wordy a runt!
It's Faith that is sound, orthodox
  That covers the fauts o' your ——— . —

VII

Were ye o' the Reprobate race
  Created to sin & be brunt,

O then it would alter the case
  If ye should gae wrang wi' your ——— . —

VIII

But you that is Called & Free
  Elekit & chosen a saunt,
Will't break the Eternal Decree
  Whatever ye do wi' your ——— ? —

IX

And now with a sanctify'd kiss
  Let's kneel & renew covenant:
It's this — and it's this — and it's this —
  That settles the pride o' your ——— . —

X

Devotion blew up to a flame;
  No words can do justice upon't;
The honest auld woman gaed hame
  Rejoicing and clawin her ——— . —

XI

Then high to her memory charge;
  And may he who takes it affront,
Still ride in Love's channel at large,
  And never make port in a ——— !!!

BONIE MARY

TUNE: *Minnie's ay glowering o'er me—*

CHORUS —

Come cowe me, minnie, come cowe me;
Come cowe me, minnie, come cowe me;
The hair o' my a— is grown into my c—t,
And they canna win too [*sic*], to m—we me.

I

When Mary cam over the Border,
When Mary cam over the Border;
As eith 'twas approachin the C—t of a hurchin,
Her a— was in sic a disorder. —

fash'd: troubled *gaed:* went *sae sair:* so sorely *sin that:* since *ayont:* beyond *waur't:* worried *kens:* knows *wordy:* worth *brunt:* burned

elekit: elected *gaed:* went *cowe:* crop *minnie:* mother *win too:* wind in *mowe:* fuck *eith:* easy *hurchin:* hedgehog

II

But wanton Wattie cam west on't,
But wanton Wattie cam west on't,
He did it sae tickle, he left nae as meikle
'S a spider wad bigget a nest on't. —

III

And was nae Wattie a Clinker,
He m—w'd frae the Queen to the tinkler
Then sat down, in grief, like the Macedon
    chief
For want o' mae warlds to conquer. —

IV

And O, what a jewel was Mary!
And O, what a jewel was Mary!
Her face it was fine, & her bosom divine,
And her c—nt it was theekit wi' glory. —

Come cowe &c.

ACT SEDERUNT
OF THE SESSION

TUNE: *O'er the muir among the heather*

A SCOTS BALLAD —

In Edinburgh town they've made a law,
    In Edinburgh at the Court o' Session,
That standing pr—cks are fauteors a',
    And guilty of a high transgression. —

CHORUS

Act Sederunt o' the Session,
Decreet o' the Court o' Session,
That standing pr—cks are fauteors a',
And guilty of a high transgression.

II

And they've provided dungeons deep.
Ilk lass has ane in her possession;
Untill the wretches wail and weep,
    They there shall lie for their transgres-
        sion. —

CHORUS

Act Sederunt o' the Session,
Decreet o' the Court o' Session,
The rogues in pouring tears shall weep,
By act Sederunt o' the Session. —

sae: so   *tickle:* pleasingly   *meikle:*
much   *bigget:* build   *clinker:* crafty
rogue   *mae:* more
fauteors: transgressors   *ilk:* each, every

WHEN PRINCES
AND PRELATES

TUNE: *The Campbells are Coming*

When princes & prelates & het-headed
    zealots
    All Europe hae set in a lowe,
The poor man lies down, nor envies a
    crown,
    And comforts himself with a mowe. —

CHORUS —

And why shouldna poor folk mowe,
    mowe, mowe,
    And why shouldna poor folk mowe:
The great folk hae siller, & houses & lands,
Poor bodies hae naething but mowe. —

II

When Br—nsw—ck's great Prince cam a
    cruising to Fr—nce,
    Republican billies to cowe,
Bauld Br—nsw—c's great Prince wad hae
    shawn better sense,
    At hame with his Princess to mowe. —

And why should na &c.

III

Out over the Rhine proud Pr—ss—a wad
    shine,
    To *spend* his best blood he did vow;
But Frederic had better ne'er forded the
    water,
    But spent as he docht in a mowe. —

And why &c.

IV

By sea & by shore! the Emp—r—r swore,
    In Paris he'd kick up a row;
But Paris sae ready just leugh at the laddie
    And bade him gae tak him a mowe. —

And why &c.

V

Auld Kate laid her claws on poor Stanis-
    laus,

lowe: blaze   *mowe:* fuck   *billies:* fel-
lows   cowe: frighten   *docht:* could
leugh: laughed

And Poland has bent like a bow:
May the deil in her a— ram a huge pr—ck
    o' brass!
And damn her in h—ll with a mowe!

And why &c.

VI

But truce with commotions & new-fangled
    notions,
A bumper I trust you'll allow:
Here's George our gude king & Charlotte
    his queen
And lang may they tak a gude mowe!

WHILE PROSE-WORK
AND RHYMES

TUNE: *The Campbells are Coming*

A BALLAD

While Prose-work & rhymes
    Are hunted for crimes,
And things are — the devil knows how;
    Aware o' my rhymes,
    In these kittle times,
The subject I chuse is a ——— .

Some cry, Constitution!
    Some cry, Revolution!
And Politics kick up a rowe;
    But Prince & Republic,
    Agree on the Subject,
No treason is in a good ——— .

Th' Episcopal lawn,
    And Presbyter band,
Hae lang been to ither a cowe;
    But still the proud Prelate,
    And Presbyter zealot
Agree in an orthodox ——— .

Poor Justice, 'tis hinted —
    Ill natur'dly squinted,
The Process — but mum — we'll allow —
    Poor Justice has ever
    For C—t had a favor,
While Justice could tak a gude ——— .

Now fill to the brim —
    To her, & to him,

kittle: tricky   *mowe:* fuck   *ither:* each
other   *cowe:* horror

Wha willingly do what they dow;
    And ne'er a poor wench
    Want a friend at a pinch,
Whase failing is only a ——— .

NINE INCH WILL PLEASE
A LADY

To its ain tune—

I

"Come rede me, dame, come tell me, dame,
    "My dame come tell me truly,
"What length o' graith, when weel ca'd
    hame,
    "Will sair a woman duly?"
The carlin clew her wanton tail,
    Her wanton tail sae ready —
I learn'd a sang in Annandale,
    Nine inch will please a lady. —

II

But for a koontrie c—nt like mine,
    In sooth, we're nae sae gentle;
We'll tak tway thumb-bread to the nine,
    And that's a sonsy p—ntle:
O Leeze me on my Charlie lad,
    I'll ne'er forget my Charlie!
Tway roarin handfu's and a daud,
    He nidge't it in fu' rarely. —

III

But weary fa' the laithron doup,
    And may it ne'er be thrivin!
It's no the length that maks me loup,
    But it's the double drivin. —
Come nidge me, Tam, come nudge me,
    Tam,
    Come nidge me o'er the nyvel!
Come lowse & lug your battering ram,
    And thrash him at my gyvel!

dow: can
rede: advise *graith:* gear *ca'd:*
driven *sair:* serve *carlin:* old woman
koontrie: country *bread:* breadth *sonsy:*
jolly *pintle:* prick *leeze me:* how I love
tway: two *daud:* hunk *nidge't:* thrust
weary fa': damn *laithron:* lazy *doup:*
ass *loup:* jump *lowse:* loosen *lug:*
pull *gyvel:* gable

ODE TO SPRING

TUNE: *The tither morn*

When maukin bucks, at early f——s,
  In dewy grass are seen, Sir;
And birds, on boughs, take off their
    m——s,
  Amang the leaves sae green, Sir;
Latona's son looks liquorish on
  Dame Nature's grand impètus,
Till his p—go rise, then westward flies
  To r—ger Madame Thetis.

Yon wandering rill that marks the hill,
  And glances o'er the brae, Sir,
Glides by a bower where many a flower
  Sheds fragrance on the day, Sir;
There Damon lay, with Sylvia gay,
  To love they thought no crime, Sir;
The wild-birds sang, the echoes rang,
  While Damon's a—se beat time, Sir. —

First, wi' the thrush, his thrust & push
  Had compass large & long, Sir;
The blackbird next, his tuneful text,
  Was bolder, clear & strong, Sir;
The linnet's lay came then in play,
  And the lark that soar'd aboon, Sir;
Till Damon, fierce, mistim'd his a——,
  And f——'d quite out of tune, Sir. —

O SAW YE MY MAGGIE?

TUNE: *O Saw ye na my Peggy?*

I

Saw ye my Maggie?
Saw ye my Maggie?
Saw ye my Maggie?
  Comin oer the lea?

II

What mark has your Maggie,
What mark has your Maggie,
What mark has your Maggie,
  That ane may ken her be?

[IIa]

[Wry-c—d is she,
  Wry-c—d is she,

Wry-c—d is she,
  And pishes gain' her thie.]

III

My Maggie has a mark,
Ye'll find it in the dark,
It's in below her sark,
  A little aboon her knee.

IV

What wealth has your Maggie,
What wealth has your Maggie,
What wealth has your Maggie,
  In tocher, gear, or fee?

V

My Maggie has a treasure,
A hidden mine o' pleasure,
I'll howk it at my leisure,
  It's alane for me.

VIII

How meet you your Maggie,
How meet you your Maggie,
How meet you your Maggie,
  When nane's to hear or see?

VII

Ein that tell our wishes,
Eager glowing kisses,
Then diviner blisses,
  In holy ecstacy! —

VI

How loe ye your Maggy,
How loe [ye] your Maggy,
How loe ye your Maggy,
  An loe nane but she?

IX

Heavenly joys before me,
Rapture trembling o'er me,
Maggie I adore thee,
  On my bended knee!!!

TO ALEXANDER FINDLATER

Ellisland Saturday morning.

Dear Sir,

            our Lucky humbly begs
Ye'll prie her caller, new-laid eggs:

maukin bucks: male hares   *take off their mowes:* finish fucking   *pego:* prick   *roger:* fuck   *brae:* bank   *ane:* one   *ken:* know

sark: undershirt   *tocher:* dowry   *howk:* dig up   *ein:* eyes   *prie:* try   *caller:* fresh

L—d grant the Cock may keep his legs,
      Aboon the Chuckies;
And wi' his kittle, forket clegs,
      Claw weel their dockies!

Had Fate that curst me in her ledger,
A Poet poor, & poorer Gager,
Created me that feather'd Sodger,
      A generous Cock,
How I wad craw & strut and r—ger
      My kecklin Flock!

Buskit wi' mony a bien, braw feather,
I wad defied the warst o' weather:
When corn or bear I could na gather
      To gie my burdies;
I'd treated them wi' caller heather,
      And weel-knooz'd hurdies.

Na cursed CLERICAL EXCISE
On honest Nature's laws & ties;
Free as the vernal breeze that flies
      At early day,
We'd tasted Nature's richest joys,
      But stint or stay. —

But as this subject's something kittle,
Our wisest way's to say but little;
And while my Muse is at her mettle,
      I am, most fervent,
Or may I die upon a whittle!
      Your Friend & Servant —

        ROBt BURNS

THE FORNICATOR

TUNE: *Clout the Cauldron*

A NEW SONG

Ye jovial boys who love the joys,
    The blissful joys of Lovers,
Yet dare avow, with dauntless brow,
    When the bony lass discovers,
I pray draw near, and lend an ear,
    And welcome in a Frater,
For I've lately been on quarantine,
    A proven Fornicator.

kittle: tricky   *clegs:* spurs   *gager:* tax collector   *roger:* fuck   *kecklin:* cackling   *buskit:* dressed up   *bien:* rich   *braw:* beautiful   *bear:* barley   *weel-knooz'd:* well-kneaded   *hurdies:* backside   *whittle:* knife

Before the Congregation wide,
    I passed the muster fairly,
My handsome Betsy by my side,
    We gat our ditty rarely;
But my downcast eye did chance to spy
    What made my lips to water,
Those limbs so clean where I between
    Commenc'd a Fornicator.

With rueful face and signs of grace
    I pay'd the buttock-hire,
But the night was dark and thro' the park
    I could not but convoy her;
A parting kiss, I could not less,
    My vows began to scatter,
My Betsy fell — lal de dal lal lal,
    I am a Fornicator.

But for her sake this vow I make,
    And solemnly I swear it,
That while I own a single crown
    She's welcome for to share it;
And my roguish boy his Mother's joy
    And the darling of his Pater,
For him I boast my pains and cost,
    Although a Fornicator.

Ye wenching blades whose hireling jades
    Have tipt you off blue-joram,
I tell you plain, I do disdain
    To rank you in the Quorum;
But a bony lass upon the grass
    To teach her esse Mater,
And no reward but fond regard,
    O that's a Fornicator.

Your warlike Kings and Heros bold,
    Great Captains and Commanders;
Your mighty Caesars fam'd of old,
    And conquering Alexanders;
In fields they fought and laurels bought,
    And bulwarks strong did batter,
But still they grac'd our noble list,
    And ranked Fornicator!!!

MY GIRL SHE'S AIRY

TUNE: *Black Joke*

My Girl she's airy, she's buxom and gay,
Her breath is as sweet as the blossoms in
    May;

ditty: indictment   *blue-joram:* (possibly) chancre

A touch of her lips it ravishes quite;
She's always good natur'd, good humor'd
and free;
She dances, she glances, she smiles with a
glee;
Her eyes are the lightenings of joy and
delight;
Her slender neck, her handsome waist
Her hair well buckl'd, her stays well lac'd,
Her taper white leg, with an et, and a, ⊖
For her a, b, e, d, and her c, u, n, t,
And Oh, for the joys of a long winter
night!!!

THERE WAS TWA WIVES

There was twa wives, and twa witty wives,
As e'er play'd houghmagandie,
And they coost out, upon a time,
Out o'er a drink o' brandy;
Up Maggy rose, and forth she goes,
And she leaves auld Mary flytin,
And she f—rted by the byre-en'
For she was gaun a sh—ten.

She f—rted by the byre-en'
She f—rted by the stable;
And thick and nimble were her steps
As fast as she was able:
Till at yon dyke-back the hurly brak,
But raxin for some dockins,
The beans and pease cam down her thighs,
And she cackit a' her stockins.

BROSE AN' BUTTER

Gie my Love brose, brose,
Gie my Love brose an' butter;
An' gie my Love brose, brose,
Yestreen he wanted his supper.

Jenny sits up i' the laft,
Jocky wad fain a been at her;
There cam a win' out o' the wast
Made a' the windows to clatter.

Gie my Love brose &c.

houghmagandie: fornication   *coost out:*
quarreled   *flytin:* scolding   *byre-en':*
cowshed end   *hurly:* onrush   *raxin:*
stretching   *dockins:* leaves
brose: porridge   *laft:* loft   *wast:* west

A dow's a dainty dish;
A goose is hollow within;
A sight wad mak you blush,
But a' the fun's to fin'.

Gie my &c.

My Dadie sent me to the hill,
To pow my minnie some heather;
An' drive it in your fill,
Ye're welcome to the leather.

Gie my &c.

A mouse is a merry wee beast;
A modewurck wants the een;
An' O for the touch o' the thing
I had i' my nieve yestreen.

Gie my Love &c.

The lark she loves the grass;
The hen she loves the stibble;
An' hey for the Gar'ner lad,
To gully awa wi' his dibble. —

THE PATRIARCH

TUNE (in MMC): *The Auld Cripples Dow*

As honest Jacob on a night,
Wi' his beloved beauty,
Was duly laid on wedlock's bed.
And noddin' at his duty.

Tal de dal &c.

"How lang, she says, ye fumblin' wretch,
"Will ye be f——g at it?
"My eldest wean might die of age,
"Before that ye could get it.

"Ye pegh and grane, and groazle there,
"And mak an unco splutter,
"And I maun ly and thole you here,
"And fient a hair the better."

Then he, in wrath, put up his graith,
"The deevil's in the hizzie!

dow: pigeon   *pow:* pull   *minnie:*
mother   *modewurck:* mole   *nieve:* fist
gully: dig   *dibble:* tool
pegh: puff   *grane:* groan   *groozle:*
grunt   *unco:* uncommon, great   *thole:*
endure   *fient a hair:* not a bit   *graith:*
gear

"I m—w you as I m—w the lave,
  "And night and day I'm bisy.

"I've bairn'd the servant gypsies baith,
  "Forbye your titty Leah;
"Ye barren jad, ye put me mad,
  "What mair can I do wi you.

"There's ne'er a m—w I've gi'en the lave,
  "But ye ha'e got a dizzen;
"And d—n'd a ane ye'se get again,
  "Although your c—t should gizzen."

Then Rachel calm, as only lamb,
  She claps him on the waulies;
Quo' she, "ne'er fash a woman's clash,
  "In trowth ye m—w me braulies.

"My dear 'tis true, for mony a m—w,
  "I'm your ungratefu' debtor,
"But ance again, I dinna ken,
  "We'll aiblens happen better."

Then honest man! wi' little wark,
  He soon forgat his ire;
The patriarch, he coost the sark,
  And up and till't like fire!

THE BONNIEST LASS

The bonniest lass that ye meet neist
  Gie her a kiss an' a' that,
In spite o' ilka parish priest,
  Repentin' stool, an' a' that.

For a' that an' a' that,
  Their mim-mou'd sangs an' a' that,
In time and place convenient,
  They'll do't themselves for a' that.

Your patriarchs in days o' yore,
  Had their handmaids an' a' that;
O' bastard gets, some had a score
  An' some had mair than a' that.

mowe: fuck   lave: rest   bairn'd:
made pregnant   forbye: besides   titty:
sister   gizzon: dry up   waulies: buttocks
fash: bother with   clash: talk   braulies:
beautifully   ken: know   aiblens: per-
haps   coost: took off   sark: underwear
neist: next   ilka: any, every   mim-
mou'd: mealy-mouthed

For a' that an' a' that,
  Your langsyne saunts, an' a' that,
Were fonder o' a bonie lass,
  Than you or I, for a' that.

King Davie, when he waxed auld,
  An's bluid ran thin, an' a' that,
An' fand his cods were growin' cauld,
  Could not refrain, for a' that.

For a' that an' a' that,
  To keep him warm an' a' that,
The daughters o' Jerusalem
  Were waled for him, an' a' that.

Wha wadna pity thae sweet dames
  He fumbled at, an' a' that,
An' raised their bluid up into flames
  He couldna drown, for a' that.

For a' that an' a' that,
  He wanted pith, an' a' that;
For, as to what we shall not name,
  What could he do but claw that.

King Solomon, prince o' divines,
  Wha proverbs made, an' a' that,
Baith mistresses an' concubines
  In hundreds had, for a' that.

For a' that an' a' that,
  Tho' a preacher wise an' a' that,
The smuttiest sang that e'er was sung
  His Sang o' Sangs is a' that.

Then still I swear, a clever chiel
  Should kiss a lass, an' a' that,
Tho' priests consign him to the deil,
  As reprobate, an' a' that.

For a' that an' a' that,
  Their canting stuff, an' a' that,
They ken nae mair wha's reprobate
  Than you or I, for a' that.

GODLY GIRZIE

TUNE: *Wat ye wha I met Yestreen*

The night it was a haly night,
  The day had been a haly day;

langsyne: ancient   saunts: saints   bluid:
blood   cods: genitals   waled: picked
chiel: lad   ken: know
haly: holy

Kilmarnock gleamed wi' candle light,
  As Girzie hameward took her way.
A man o' sin, ill may he thrive!
  And never haly-meeting see!
Wi' godly Girzie met belyve,
  Amang the Cragie hills sae hie.

The chiel' was wight, the chiel' was stark,
  He wad na wait to chap nor ca',
And she was faint wi haly wark,
  She had na pith to say him na.
But ay she glowr'd up to the moon,
  And ay she sigh'd most piouslie;
"I trust my heart's in heaven aboon,
  "Whare'er your sinfu' p——e be."

WHA'LL MOW ME NOW?

TUNE: *Comin' thro' the rye*

O, I hae tint my rosy cheek,
  Likewise my waste sae sma';
O wae gae by the sodger lown,
  The sodger did it a'.

  O wha'll m——w me now, my jo,
    An' wha'll m——w me now:
  A sodger wi' his bandileers
    Has bang'd my belly fu'.

Now I maun thole the scornfu' sneer
  O' mony a saucy quine;
When, curse upon her godly face!
  Her c——t's as merry's mine.

Our dame hauds up her wanton tail,
  As due as she gaes lie;
An' yet misca's [a] young thing,
  The trade if she but try.

Our dame can lae her ain gudeman,
  An' m——w for glutton greed;
An' yet misca' a poor thing,
  That's m——n' for its bread.

Alake! sae sweet a tree as love,
  Sic bitter fruit should bear!
Alake, that e'er a merry a——e,
  Should draw a sa'tty tear.

belyve: by and by   *chiel':* lad   *wight:*
manly   *stark:* strong   *chap:* argue   *ca':*
urge   *pintle:* prick
  tint: lost   *wae gae by:* damn   *lown:*
bastard   *mowe:* fuck   *bandileers:* ammu-
nition box   *maun:* must   *thole:* endure
quine: bitch   *due:* readily

But deevil damn the lousy loon,
  Denies the bairn he got!
Or lea's the merry a——e he lo'ed,
  To wear a ragged coat!

HAD I THE WYTE
SHE BADE ME

TUNE: *Highland Hills*

Had I the wyte, had I the wyte,
  Had I the wyte she bad me;
For she was steward in the house,
  And I was fit-man laddie;
And when I wadna do't again,
  A silly cow she ca'd me;
She straik't my head, and clapt my cheeks,
  And lous'd my breeks and bad me

Could I for shame, could I for shame,
  Could I for shame deny['d] her;
Or in the bed was I to blame.
  She bad me lye beside her;
I pat six inches in her wame,
  A quarter wadna fly'd her;
For ay the mair I ca'd it hame,
  Her ports they grew the wider

My tartan plaid, when it was dark,
  Could I refuse to share it;
She lifted up her holland-sark,
  And bad me fin' the gair o't:
Or how could I amang the garse,
  But gie her hilt and hair o't;
She clasped her houghs about my a——e,
  And ay she glowr'd for mair o't.

DAINTY DAVIE

Being pursu'd by the dragoons,
  Within my bed he was laid down
And weel I wat he was worth his room,
  My ain dear dainty Davie.

bairn: child
  had I the wyte: was I to blame   *fit-man:*
footman   *lous'd:* loosened   *breeks:* britches
wame: womb, belly   *fly'd:* frightened
ca'd: drove   *fin':* find   *gair:* crotch
garse: grass   *houghs:* thighs

O leeze me on his curly pow,
  Bonie Davie, dainty Davie;
Leeze me on his curly pow,
  He was my dainty Davie.

My minnie laid him at my back,
  I trow he lay na lang at that,
But turn'd, and in a verra crack
  Produc'd a dainty Davie.

Then in the field amang the pease,
  Behin' the house o' Cherrytrees,
Again he wan atweesh my thies,
  And, splash! gaed out his gravy.

But had I goud, or had I land,
  It should be a' at his command;
I'll ne'er forget what he pat i' my hand,
  It was a dainty Davie.

THE TROGGER

TUNE: *Gillicrankie*

As I cam down by Annan side,
  Intending for the border,
Amang the Scroggie banks and braes
Wha met I but a trogger.
He laid me down upon my back,
  I thought he was but jokin',
Till he was in me to the hilts,
  O the deevil tak sic troggin!

What could I say, what could I do,
  I bann'd and sair misca'd him,
But whiltie-whaltie gaed his a—e,
  The mair that I forbade him:
He stell'd his foot against a stane,
  And doubl'd ilka stroke in,
Till I gaed daft amang his hands,
  O the deevil tak sic troggin!

Then up we raise, and took the road,
  And in by Ecclefechan,
Where the brandy-stoup we gart it clink,
  And the strang-beer ream the quech in.
Bedown the bents o' Bonshaw braes,
  We took the partin' yokin';
But I've claw'd a sairy c—t sinsyne,
  O the deevil tak sic troggin!

PUT BUTTER IN
MY DONALD'S BROSE

Put butter in my Donald's brose,
  For weel does Donald fa' that;
I loe my Donald's tartans weel
  His naked a—e and a' that.

For a' that, and a' that,
  And twice as meikle's a' that,
The lassie gat a skelpit doup,
  But wan the day for a' that.

For Donald swore a solemn aith,
  By his first hairy gravat!
That he wad fight the battle there,
  And stick the lass, and a' that.

His hairy b——s, side and wide,
  Hang like a beggar's wallet;
A p——e like a roaring-pin,
  She nicher'd when she saw that!!!

Then she turn'd up her hairy c—t,
  And she bade Donald claw that;
The deevil's dizzen Donald drew,
  And Donald gied her a' that.

HERE'S HIS HEALTH
IN WATER

TUNE: *The job o' journey wark*

Altho' my back be at the wa,
  An' tho' he be the fau'tor;

---

wat: knew   *leeze me on:* how I love
pow: head   *minnie:* mother   *trow:* swear
wan: won   *atweesh:* between   *thies:*
thighs   *goud:* gold
  braes: river side   *trogger:* peddler
bann'd: cursed   *sair:* sorely   *misca'd·*
abused   *whiltie-whaltie:* probably a made-
up expression   *stell'd:* fixed   *ilka:* every
gaed: went

stoup: tankard   *gart:* made   *ream:* foam
quech: cup   *bents:* ridges   *sinsyne:*
since then
  brose: porridge   *fa':* enjoy   *meikle:*
much   *skelpit doup:* slapped rump   *wan:*
won   *gravat:* necktie, muffler   *ballocks:*
balls   *pintle:* prick   *nicher'd:* laughed
deevil's dizzen: thirteen
  fau'tor: wrong doer

Altho' my back be at the wa',
 I'll drink his health in water.
O wae gae by his wanton sides,
 Sae brawly's he cou'd flatter.
I for his sake am slighted sair,
 An' dree the kintra clatter;
But let them say whate'er they like,
 Yet, here's his health in water.

He follow'd me baith out an' in,
 Thro' a' the nooks a' Killie;
He follow'd me baith out an' in,
 Wi' a stiff stanin' p-llie.
But when he gat atween my legs,
 We made an unco splatter;
An' haith, I trow, I soupled it,
 Tho' bauldly he did blatter;
But now my back is at the wa',
 Yet here's his health in water.

THE JOLLY GAUGER

TUNE: *We'll gang rae nair a rovin'*

There was a jolly gauger, a gauging he did
 ride,
And he has met a beggar down by yon
 river side.

An weel gang nae mair a rovin' wi' ladies
 to the wine,
When a beggar wi' her meal-pocks can
 fidge her tail sae fine.

Amang the broom he laid her; amang the
 broom sae green,
And he's fa'n to the beggar, as she had
 been a queen.

And we'll gang &c.

My blessings on thee, laddie, thou's done
 my turn sae weel,
Wilt thou accept, dear laddie, my pock
 and pickle meal?

And weel, &c.

Sae blyth the beggar took the bent, like
 ony bird in spring,
Sae blyth the beggar took the bent, and
 merrily did sing.

And weel, &c.

My blessings on the gauger, o' gaugers he's
 the chief,
Sic kail ne'er crost my kettle, nor sic a
 joint o beef.

And weel, &c.

O GAT YE ME WI
NAETHING?

TUNE: *Jacky Latin*

Gat ye me, O gat ye me,
 An' gat ye me wi' naething?
A rock, a reel, a spinning wheel,
 A gude black c—t was ae thing.
A tocher fine, o'er muckle far,
 When sic a scullion gat it;
Indeed, o'er muckle far, gudewife,
 For that was ay the fau't o't.

But had your tongue now, Luckie Lang,
 O had your tongue and jander,
I held the gate till you I met,
 Syne I began to wander;
I tint my whistle an' my sang,
 I tint my peace an' pleasure,
But your green grave now, Luckie Lang,
 Wad airt me to my treasure.

GIE THE LASS HER FAIRIN'

TUNE: *Cauld kail in Aberdeen*

O gie the lass her fairin' lad,
 O gie the lass her fairin',
An' something else she'll gie to you,
 That's waly worth the wearin';
Syne coup her o'er amang the creels,
 When ye hae taen your brandy,

---

wae gae by: damn   brawly: beautifully
  sair: sore   dree: suffer   kintra: country
pillie: prick   atween: between   unco: great
haith: faith   trow: swear   soupled: softened
bauldly: boldly   blatter: attack
  gauger: tax collector   gang: go   pocks:
bags   fidge: wiggle

bent: road   sic: such   kail: broth
gat: get   tocher: dowry   muckle: much
sic: such   jander: chatter   held the gate:
kept my virginity   syne: then   tint: lost
airt: guide
  fairin': deserts   waly: well
syne: then   coup: lay   creels: baskets

The mair she bangs the less she squeels,
An' hey for houghmagandie.

Then gie the lass a fairin', lad,
O gie the lass her fairin',
And she'll gie you a hairy thing,
An' of it be na sparin';
But coup her o'er amang the creels,
An' bar the door wi' baith your heels,
The mair she bangs the less she squeels,
An' hey for houghmagandie.

GREEN GROW
THE RASHES

O wat ye ought o' fisher Meg,
And how she trow'd the webster, O,
She loot me see her carrot c—t,
And sell'd it for a labster, O.

Green grow the rashes, O,
Green grow the rashes, O,
The lassies they hae wimble-bores,
The widows they hae gashes, O.

Mistress Mary cow'd her thing,
Because she wad be gentle, O,
And span the fleece upon a rock,
To waft a Highland mantle, O.

An' heard ye o' the coat o' arms,
The Lyon brought our lady, O,
The crest was, couchant, sable c—t,
The motto — "ready, ready," O.

An' ken ye Leezie Lundie, O,
The godly Leezie Lundie, O,
She m—s like reek thro' a' the week,
But finger f—s on Sunday, O.

TAIL TODLE

TUNE: *Chevalier's Muster-Roll* (says SD)

Our gudewife held o'er to Fife,
For to buy a coal-riddle;

Lang or she came back again,
Tammie gart my tail todle.

Tail todle, tail todle;
Tammie gart my tail todle;
At my a—e wi' diddle doddle,
Tammie gart my tail todle.

When I'm dead I'm out o' date;
When I'm sick I'm fu' o' trouble;
When I'm weel I step about,
An' Tammie gars my tail todle.

Jenny Jack she gae a plack,
Helen Wallace gae a boddle,
Quo' the bride, it's o'er little
For to mend a broken doddle.

I REDE YOU BEWARE
O' THE RIPPLES

TUNE: *The Taylor's faun thro the bed*

I rede you beware o' the ripples, young
man,
I rede you beware o' the ripples, young
man;
Tho' the saddle be saft, ye needna ride aft,
For fear that the girdin' beguile ye, young
man.

I rede you beware o' the ripples, young
man,
I rede you beware o' the ripples, young
man;
Tho' music be pleasure, tak' music in
measure,
Or ye may want win' i' your whistle, young
man.

I rede you beware o' the ripples, young
man,
I rede you beware o' the ripples, young
man;
Whate'er ye bestow, do less than ye dow,
The mair will be thought o' your kindness,
young man.

---

houghmagandie: fornication
wat: know   trow'd: trusted   wimble-
bores: small holes   cow'd: cropped   waft:
weave   ken: know   mowes: fucks   reek:
smoke, fire

lang or: before long   gart: made   gae:
gave   plack: coin   boddle: small coin
doddle: maidenhead
rede: warn   ripples: backache   girdin':
riding   dow: can

I rede you beware o' the ripples, young
    man,
I rede you beware o' the ripples, young
    man;
Gif you wad be strang, and wish to live
    lang,
Dance less wi' your a—e to the kipples,
    young man.

OUR JOHN'S BRAK
YESTREEN

Tune: *Gramachree*

Twa neebor wives sat i' the sun,
    A twynin' at their rocks,
An' they an argument began,
    An' a' the plea was c—ks.

'Twas whether they were sinnens strang,
    Or whether they were bane?
An' how they row'd about your thumb,
    An how they stan't themlane?

First, Raichie gae her rock a rug,
    An' syne she claw'd her tail;
"When our Tam draws on his breeks,
    "It waigles like a flail."

Says Bess, "they're bane I will maintain,
    "And proof in han' I'll gie;
"For our John's it brak yestreen,
    "And the margh ran down my thie."

GRIZZEL GRIMME

Grim Grizzel was a mighty Dame
    Weel kend on Cluden-side:
Grim Grizzel was a mighty Dame
    O' meikle fame and pride.

When gentles met in gentle bowers
    And nobles in the ha',
Grim Grizzel was a mighty Dame,
    The loudest o' them a'.

Where lawless Riot rag'd the night
    And Beauty durst na gang,
Grim Grizzel was a mighty Dame
    Wham nae man e'er wad wrang.

gif: if   *kipples:* couples
rocks: distaffs   *sinnens:* sinews   *bane:*
bone   *row'd:* rolled   *rug:* tug   *waigles:*
wiggles   *margh:* marrow
kend: known   *meikle:* much   *durst:*
dared   *gang:* go   *wad:* would

Nor had Grim Grizzel skill alane
    What bower and ha' require;
But she had skill, and meikle skill,
    In barn and eke in byre.

Ae day Grim Grizzel walkèd forth,
    As she was wont to do,
Alang the banks o' Cluden fair,
    Her cattle for to view.

The cattle sh—— o'er hill and dale
    As cattle will incline,
And sair it grieved Grim Girzzel's heart
    Sae muckle muck tae tine.

And she has ca'd on John o' Clods,
    Of her herdsmén the chief,
And she has ca'd on John o' Clods.
    And tell'd him a' her grief: —

"Now wae betide thee, John o' Clods!
    I gie thee meal and fee,
And yet sae meickle muck ye tine
    Might a' be gear to me!

"Ye claut my byre, ye sweep my byre,
    The like was never seen;
The very chamber I lie in
    Was never half sae clean.

"Ye ca' my kye adown the loan
    And there they a' discharge:
My Tammie's hat, wig, head and a'
    Was never half sae large!

"But mind my words now, John o' Clods,
    And tent me what I say:
My kye shall sh—— ere they gae out,
    That shall they ilka day.

"And mind my words now, John o' Clods,
    And tent now wha ye serve;
Or back ye'se to the Colonel gang,
    Either to steal or starve."

Then John o' Clods he lookèd up
    And syne he lookèd down;
He lookèd east, he lookèd west,
    He lookèd roun' and roun'.

His bonnet and his rowantree club
    Frae either hand did fa';
Wi' lifted een and open mouth
    He naething said at a'.

eke: also   *byre:* cowshed   *sair:* sorely
tine: lose   *gear:* property   *claut:* clean
kye: cattle   *loan:* pasture   *tent:* pay
attention to   *gang:* go   *rowantree:* ash
tree   *frae:* from   *een:* eyes

At length he found his trembling tongue,
 Within his mouth was fauld: —
"Ae silly word frae me, madám,
 Gin I daur be sae bauld.

"Your kye will at nae bidding sh——,
 Let me do what I can;
Your kye will at nae bidding sh——
 Of onie earthly man.

"Tho' ye are great Lady Glaur-hole,
 For a' your power and art
Tho' ye are great Lady Glaur-hole,
 They winna let a fart."

"Now wae betide thee, John o' Clods!
 An ill death may ye die!
My kye shall at my bidding sh——,
 And that ye soon shall see."

Then she's ta'en Hawkie by the tail,
 And wrung wi' might and main,
Till Hawkie rowted through the woods
 Wi' agonising pain.

"Sh——, sh——, ye bitch," Grim Grizzel
 roar'd,
 Till hill and valley rang;
"And sh——, ye bitch," the echoes roar'd
 Lincluden wa's amang.

TWO EPITAPHS

JOHANNES FUSCUS [JOHN BROWN]
HIC JACET
QUONDAM HOROLOGIORUM FABER
IN M[AUCHLINE]

Lament him, M[auchline] husbands a',
 He aften did assist ye!
Tho ye had bidden years awa
 Your wives [wad] ne'er hae miss't ye.

Ye M[auchline] bairns, as bye ye pass
 To school in bands thegither,
O tread but lightly on the grass,
 Perhaps he was your father!

fauld: enclosed   *gin:* if   *daur:* dare
rowted: bellowed
 bairns: children

EPITAPH FOR
H[UGH] L[OGAN], ESQ., OF L[AIGHT]

Here lyes Squire Hugh — ye harlot crew,
 Come mak' your water on him,
I'm sure that he weel pleas'd would be
 To think ye pish'd upon him.

YE HAE LIEN WRANG, LASSIE

TUNE: *Up and waur them a', Willie*

Your rosy cheeks are turn'd saw wan,
 Ye're greener than the grass, lassie,
Your coatie's shorter by a span,
 Yet deil an inch the less, lassie.

Ye hae lien wrang, lassie,
 Ye've lien a' wrang,
Ye've lien in some unco bed,
 And wi' some unco man.

Ye've loot the pounie o'er the dyke,
 And he's been in the corn, lassie;
For ay the brose ye sup at e'en,
 Ye bock them or the morn, lassie.

Fu' lightly lap ye o'er the knowe,
 And thro' the wood ye sang, lassie;
But herryin' o' the foggie byke,
 I fear ye've got a stang, lassie.

COMIN' O'ER THE HILLS O' COUPAR

TUNE: *Ruffian's Rant*

Donald Brodie met a lass,
 Comin' o'er the hills o' Coupar,
Donald wi' his Highland hand
 Graipit a' the bits about her.

Comin' o'er the hills o' Coupar,
 Comin' o'er the hills o' Coupar,
Donald in a sudden wrath
 He ran his Highland durk into her.

deil an: not one   *unco:* strange   *loot:* let   *pounie:* pony   *brose:* porridge   *bock:* vomit   *or:* before   *lap:* leaped   *knowe:* knoll   *herryin':* plundering   *byke:* beehive
graipit: gripped   *durk:* dagger

Weel I wat she was a quine,
    Wad made a body's mouth to water;
Our Mess John, wi's auld grey pow,
    His haly lips wad licket at her.

Up she started in a fright,
    Thro' the braes what she could bicker:
Let her gang, quo' Donald, now,
    For in him's nerse my shot is sicker.

COMIN' THRO' THE RYE

O gin a body meet a body,
    Comin throu the rye;
Gin a body f—k a body,
    Need a body cry.

    Comin' thro' the rye, my jo,
        An' comin' thro' the rye;
    She fand a staun o' staunin' graith,
        Comin' thro' the rye.

Gin a body meet a body,
    Comin' thro' the glen;
Gin a body f—k a body,
    Need the warld ken.

Gin a body meet a body,
    Comin' thro' the grain;
Gin a body f—k a body,
    C—t's a body's ain.

Gin a body meet a body,
    By a body's sel,
What na body f—s a body,
    Wad a body tell.

Mony a body meets a body,
    They dare na weel avow;
Mony a body f—s a body,
    Ye wadna think it true.

WAD YE DO THAT?

TUNE: *John Anderson, my jo*

Gudewife, when your gudeman's frae hame,
    Might I but be sae bauld,
As come to your bed-chamber,
    When winter nights are cauld;

As come to your bed-chamber,
    When nights are cauld and wat,
And lie in your gudeman's stead,
    Wad ye do that?

Young man, an ye should be so kind,
    When our gudeman's frae hame,
As come to my bed-chamber,
    Where I am laid my lane;
And lie in our gudeman's stead,
    I will tell you what,
He f—s me five times ilka night,
    Wad ye do that?

THERE CAM A CADGER

TUNE: *Clout the Cauldron*

There cam a cadger out o' Fife,
    I wat na how they ca'd him;
He play'd a trick to our gudewife,
    When fient a body bad him.

Fal lal, &c.

He took a lang thing stout and strang,
    An' strack it in her gyvel;
An' ay she swore she fand the thing
    Gae borin' by her nyvel.

Fal lal, &c.

JENNY MACRAW

TUNE: *The bonny moor-here*

Jenny Macraw was a bird o' the game,
An' mony a shot had been lows'd at her
        wame;
Be't a lang bearing arrow, or the sharp-
        rattlin' hail,
Still, whirr! she flew off wi' the shot in her
        tail.

Jenny Macraw to the mountains she's
        gaen,
Their leagues and their covenants a' she
        has taen;

---

wat: knew   *quine:* girl   *pow:* head
braes: banks   *bicker:* scamper   *gang:* go
him's: her   (satirically ungrammatical)
sicker: sure
    gin: if   *staunin':* standing   *graith:*
tool   *ken:* know

my lane: alone
cadger: peddler   *wat:* know   *fient a*
body: no one   *strack:* struck   *gyvel:*
gable
    lows'd: loosened   *wame:* womb, belly
gaen: gone   *taen:* taken

My head now, and heart now, quo' she.
   are at rest,
An' for my poor c—t, let the deil do his
   best.

Jenny Macraw on a midsummer morn,

She cut off her c—t and she hang't on a
   thorn;
There she loot it hing for a year and a day,
But, oh! how look'd her a—e when her
   c—t was away.

loot: let

NOTES

Page 2. THE TWA DOGS.
That bears the name of auld King Coil.
The "auld King Coil," from whom Kyle, the middle district of Ayrshire, is supposed to derive its name, is pure myth, though the castle is of unknown antiquity. The district itself is divided by the river Ayr into King's Kyle and Stewart Kyle. See *post*, p. 328, Notes to *The Vision*.
Page 3. *How they maun thole the factor's snash*, etc.
"My father's generous master died; the farm proved a ruinous bargain; and, to clench the curse, we fell into the hands of a factor, who sat for the picture I have drawn of one in my *Tale of Two Dogs*." (R. B. in *Autobiographical Letter*.)
Page 5. SCOTCH DRINK.
St. IV. l. 2. *Souple scones.*
The "souple scones" were very thin, pliable cakes of barley meal, long a favourite bread of the Scottish peasantry.
St. IV. l. 4. *Kail.*
The colewort or "green kale" was the chief vegetable of old Scotland. Hence the "kale-yard" was the common name for the cotter's garden, and "kale" the synonym for Scotch broth, of which barley also was an important ingredient.
St. IX. l. 4. *Cog or bicker.*
Both wooden vessels. From the larger "cog," the ale would probably be poured into the smaller "bicker" for drinking. A cog is properly a large wooden vessel from which the Scottish peasants sup porridge, or kale, in common. In the case of porridge — which is made very thick — each spoons in his own pit till the dividing walls are broken down. A "coggie" (*i. e.* a little cog) is a wooden porringer for one.
Page 6. St. XIX. l. 1. *Thee, Ferintosh! O sadly lost!*
By an Act of the Scottish Parliament of 1690, Duncan Forbes of Culloden, in recognition of his services during Dundee's rebellion and in compensation for the damage done his lands by the rebels, obtained, on payment of a small sum in lieu of excise, a perpetual liberty to distil grain at his "ancient brewery of *aqua vitæ* of Ferintosh." The privilege was withdrawn in 1785, over £20,000 being paid in compensation, when, of course, the price of whisky went up.
Page 6. THE AUTHOR'S EARNEST CRY AND PRAYER.
In the 1787 Edition Burns added a footnote: — "This was wrote before the Act anent the

Scotch Distilleries, of session 1786; for which Scotland and the author return their most grateful thanks." The Act superseded the duties on spirits by an annual tax on stills according to their capacity.
The passage in Milton parodied in the motto is: —

> "O fairest of creation! last and best . . .
> How art thou lost" . . .
> —*Paradise Lost*, ix. 896, 900.

St. I. l. 1. *Ye Irish lords, ye knights an' squires.*
Certain Irish lords had Scottish seats in the House of Commons, while eldest sons of Scottish peers were ineligible.
St. II. l. 1. *Roupet.*
Said of a vocal state which suggests the utterance of a chicken with a co'd.
Page 7. St. X. l. 3. *But could I like Montgomeries fight.*
From the time of Sir John Montgomerie, ancestor of the Earls of Eglinton, — who in 1388 vanquished Hotspur at Otterburne and took him prisoner, — many of the main branch had won distinction in arms; and, when Burns wrote, their tradition was worthily maintained by Archibald, eleventh Earl of Eglinton, who held the rank of General in the army, and by his cousin, Colonel Montgomerie of Coilsfield, the "sodger Hugh" of a subsequent stanza.
St. X. l. 4. *Or gab like Boswell.*
James Boswell, biographer of Samuel Johnson, who, succeeding to the Auchinleck estate on the death of his father in 1782, for some time thereafter took an active part in politics at county meetings, and even aspired to represent Ayrshire in Parliament.
St. XIII. l. 1. *Dempster, a true blue Scot I'se warran.*
George Dempster of Dunnichen, born at Dundee in February, 1732; educated at St. Andrews and Edinburgh; called to the Scottish bar in 1755; a friend of Hume and other Scottish *literati*; sat as member for the Forfar and Fife Burghs from 1762 to 1790; devoted much attention to agriculture, concerning which he published several works; died 13th February, 1818.
St. XIII. l. 2. *Thee, aith-detesting, chaste Kilkerran.*
Sir Adam Fergusson, third baronet of Kilkerran; entered Parliament in 1774 as member for Ayrshire, but in 1780 was defeated by Colonel Hugh Montgomerie, and at this time represented Edinburgh; in 1796 laid claim to the

earldom of Glencairn, but failed to establish his right to it; died 23d September, 1813.

St. XIII. l. 4. *The Laird o' Graham.*

James Graham, then Marquis of Graham; born 8th September, 1755; elected M. P. for Richmond, Yorkshire, 11th September, 1780; member for Great Bedwin, Wilts, from 1784 until, on the death of his father in 1790, he became third Duke of Montrose; was at this time a Lord of the Treasury under Pitt; subsequently held various important Ministerial and other offices; obtained the repeal of the Act of 1747 prohibiting the Highland costume; is described in Wraxall's *Memoirs* as possessing " a ready elocution, sustained by all the confidence in himself necessary for addressing the House; " died 30th December, 1836.

St. XIII. l. 6. *Dundas his name.*

Henry Dundas, the most distinguished Scottish statesman of his time; fourth son of Robert Dundas of Arniston, Lord President of the Court of Session; born 28th April, 1742; at this time member for Midlothian, and Treasurer of the Navy under Pitt, one of whose best trusted colleagues he was; was created Viscount Melville 24th December, 1802; and died 28th May, 1811.

St. XIV. l. 1. *Erskine, a spunkie Norland billie.*

Either Thomas Erskine, afterwards Lord Erskine (who, however, was not then in Parliament), or his elder brother, Henry Erskine, for a short time Lord Advocate under the Coalition Ministry; the chief rival of Dundas at the Scottish bar, whom he superseded as Lord Advocate, notwithstanding Dundas's boast: " No one shall venture to take my place."

St. XIV. l. 2. *True Campbells, Frederick and Ilay.*

Lord Frederick Campbell, third son of John, fourth Duke of Argyll, was born in 1729; sat for the Glasgow Burghs from 1761 to 1780, and for Argyllshire from 1780 to 1799; appointed Lord Clerk Register for Scotland in 1768; died 8th August, 1816. Sir Islay Campbell of Succoth was born 23d August, 1734; succeeded Henry Erskine as Lord Advocate in 1784; represented the Glasgow District of Burghs from 1784 to 1789, when as Lord Succoth he was appointed Lord President of the Court of Session; author of several works on Scots Law; died 28th March, 1823.

St. XIV. l. 3. *An' Livistone, the bauld Sir Willie.*

Sir William Augustus Cunynghame, fourth Baronet, of Milncraig, Ayrshire, and Livingstone, Linlithgowshire, sat for Linlithgowshire; died 17th March, 1828.

St. XV. This stanza was omitted by Burns from his press copy, and in an earlier MS. is marked to be " expunged." The " sodger Hugh " to whom it refers was Hugh Montgomerie of Coilsfield, who had seen service in the American War, and in 1778 became major of the Argyll Fencibles, of which Lord Frederick Campbell was colonel. He represented Ayrshire from 1780 to 1789; in 1793 became Major

of the West Lowland Fencibles, and in 1795 Lieutenant-Governor of Edinburgh Castle; succeeded to the earldom of Eglinton on the death of his cousin Archibald, eleventh earl, in 1796; in 1806 was raised to the British Peerage as Baron of Ardrossan; rebuilt Eglinton Castle and displayed great energy in the improvement and development of his property; was an accomplished musician, and a composer of popular tunes, among them *Lady Montgomerie's Reel* and *Ayrshire Lasses;* died 15th December, 1819.

St. XVII. l. 2. *Her lost Militia.*

The Militia Bill for Scotland was lost in 1782 by reason of the attempted insertion of a clause obnoxious to the Scottish representatives.

Page 8. St. XXI. l. 1. *Yon guid bluid of auld Boconnock's.*

The Premier Pitt was the grandson of Mr. Robert Pitt of Boconnock, Cornwall.

St. XXI. l. 3. *Nanse Tinnock's.*

" A worthy old hostess of the Author's in Mauchline, where he sometimes studies politics over a glass of gude auld 'Scotch Drink.' " (R. B.)

Page 10. THE HOLY FAIR.

St. VIII. l. 3. *A greedy glowr black-bonnet throws.*

The elder who " officiated " at the collecting-plate, which stood at the entrance, was accustomed to wear a black bonnet.

St. IX. l. 3. *There Racer Jess, an' twa-three whores.*

" Racer Jess " was Janet Gibson, the half-witted daughter of Mrs. Gibson or " Poosie Nansie " (see *post*, p. 334, Notes to *The Jolly Beggars*); being fleet of foot, she often ran errands. She died in February, 1813.

St. XI. l. 1. *O happy is that man an' blest !*

Psalm cxlvi. Line 1 of Verse 2, Scottish Metrical Version. The verse was probably sung at the tent-preaching.

St. XII. l. 3. *For Moodie speels the holy door.*

Alexander Moodie, minister of Riccarton, was born in 1722; ordained at Culross 20th February, 1759; translated to Riccarton 30th December, 1761; died 15th February, 1799, and was succeeded as minister of the parish by his eldest son. He almost rivalled Russel of Kilmarnock in enforcing the " terrors of the law." But, notwithstanding affinities of doctrine and character, the headstrong violence of both divines involved them in that " bitter black outcast " which is celebrated in *The Twa Herds* (ante, p. 107). In *The Kirk's Alarm* (ante, p. 112), Moodie is addressed as " Singet Sawnie."

St. XIV. l. 5. *Smith opens out his cauld harangues.*

George Smith, minister of Galston, son of William Smith of Cranston; ordained at Galston, 3d February, 1778; D.D. (Glasgow), 1806; died 20th April, 1823. Although really " moderate " or " New Light," — and here referred to in terms meant to be wholly laudatory, — his theological attitude was rather variable. At an earlier period the orthodox or " Old Light " party was inclined to set a certain reliance on him; but in *The Twa Herds* it describes him as "but a grey nick quill." On the other hand, the " New Light " party found him equally untrustworthy when it came to the pinch ; and in the " Irvine side " stanza of *The Kirk's Alarm* Burns, while allowing him the " figure " of manhood, affirms that even his friends " dare na say " he has " mair."

St. xvi. l. 3. *Peebles.*

William Peebles, minister of Newton-on-Ayr ; son of a draper at Inchture, Perthshire ; born about 1752 ; schoolmaster at Inchture, and afterwards assistant minister at Dundonald ; ordained at Newton-on-Ayr 25th June, 1778 ; clerk of the Presbytery of Ayr, 1782 ; D. D. (American), 1795 ; died 11th October, 1826. Author of " *The Great Things Which the Lord hath done for this Nation,* in two Sermons, preached on 5th November, 1788 [the second containing a veiled but obvious allusion to the doctrines of Dr. Macgill as heinous in themselves and inconsistent with his subscription to the Standards : see *The Kirk's Alarm*], to which is subjoined *An Ode to Liberty,*" Kilmarnock : Printed by J. Wilson [Burns's printer], 1788 ; *Sermons, with Hymns,* Edinburgh, 1794 ; *The Universality of Pure Christian Worship : A Sermon,* Air, 1796 ; *The Crisis, or the Progress of Revolutionary Principles,* Edinburgh, 1803 and 1804 ; and *Odes and Elegies,* Glasgow, 1810. He also published (anonymously) " *Burnomania :* the Celebrity of Robert Burns considered in a Discourse addressed to all real Christians of every Denomination, to which are added Epistles in Verse respecting Peter Pindar, Burns, &c., 1811 : " it especially condemns *The Holy Fair* and *Tam o' Shanter.* Peebles was a leader of the orthodox party in the Presbytery. In doctrine and sentiment his sermons are studiously correct, as they are invariably pompous in style. Burns makes a withering allusion to his *Ode to Liberty* in the " Poet Willie " stanza of *The Kirk's Alarm ;* and in *The Twa Herds* he appears as " Peebles Shaul."

St. xvi. l. 7. *While Common-sense has taen the road.*

" Common-sense," while generally used for the " New Light " party, is here traditionally supposed to mean Burns's friend, Dr. Mackenzie.

St. xvi. l. 8. *The Cowgate.*

" A street so called which faces the tent in Mauchline." (R. B. in Edinburgh Editions.)

St. xvii. l. 1. *Wee Miller niest, the guard relieves.*

" ' Wee Miller,' the assistant minister at St. Michael's." (R. B. in a copy of the 1786 Edition in the British Museum.) Alexander Millar, who was short and exceeding stout, was presented to the parish of Kilmaurs, 9th April, 1787 ; but, probably on account in part of this unflattering allusion to him, his settlement was bitterly opposed by the parishioners, who denied him access to preach, and abstained without exception from attending service when the call was moderated. He nevertheless was ordained 8th May, 1788, and died 22d December, 1804.

Page 11. St. xviii. l. 1. *Butt and ben.*

The entrance to the Scottish cottage was at the kitchen end, and the visitor passed through the " butt " or outer apartment into the " ben " or inner one.

St. xxi. l. 4. *Black Russell.*

John Russel, then minister of the chapel-of-ease, Kilmarnock, a native of Moray, born about 1740 ; for some time parochial teacher at Cromarty ; ordained at Kilmarnock 30th March, 1774 ; translated to the second charge of Stirling 18th January, 1800 ; died at Stirling 23d February, 1817, in his seventy-seventh year. Author of preface to Fraser's *Sermons on Sacramental Occasions,* Kilmarnock, 1785 ; *The Nature of the Gospel delineated in a Sermon,* August, 1796 ; *The Reason of our Lord's Agony,* a sermon, Stirling, 1801 ; and four sermons published in a posthumous volume of sermons by his son, Rev. John Russel of Muthill, Glasgow, 1826. Russel was a Calvinist of the sternest type, with a visage dark and morose and a tremendous voice : both combining to heighten the effect of his messages of wrath. As a schoolmaster he earned an altogether unique repute for severity, and astounding illustrations of the mingled dread and hatred cherished towards him by his scholars in Cromarty are given by Hugh Miller in his *Scenes and Legends of the North of Scotland.* Others relate that, being off duty, he was not without a certain geniality, and even humour. Over his parishioners he exercised a discipline well-nigh as rigid as that which he had maintained in his school. Such was the awe inspired by his mere presence that when, on Sunday afternoons, armed with a formidable cudgel, he began his wonted rounds in pursuit of Sabbath-breaking strollers, his appearance in the street was the signal for an instant breaking-up and a disappearing within-doors of gossiping groups. Russel is one of Burns's *Twa Herds,* and there are uncomplimentary allusions to him in *The Ordination, The Kirk's Alarm,* and the *Epistle to John Goldie.*

St. xxi. l. 8. *Our verra " sauls does harrow."*

" Shakespeare's Hamlet." (R. B.)

Page 15. POOR MAILIE'S ELEGY.

St. viii. l. 2. *Your chanters tune.*

In Lowland Scotland the bagpipe was at one time as common as it is and was in the Highlands. Its disuse was due to the action of the Kirk authorities in connexion with dancing.

Page 17. EPISTLE TO JAMES SMITH.

St. xxiii. l. 1. *Dempster.*

George Dempster of Dunnichen, M. P. See *ante,* p. 325, Notes to *The Author's Earnest Cry and Prayer.*

Page 18. A DREAM.

St. iv. l. 9. *Than did ae day.*

Before the American Colonies were lost.

Page 19. St. vii. l. 8. *Abridge your bonie barges.*

In the spring of 1785 it had been proposed to reduce the Navy.

St. x. l. 1. *Young Potentate o' Wales.*

Afterwards George IV.

St. xi. l. 5. *Him at Agincourt wha shone.*

" King Henry V." (R. B.)

St. xi. l. 7. *Funny, queer Sir John.*
"Sir John Falstaff, *vide* Shakespeare." (R. B.)

St. xii. l. 1. *Right rev'rend Osnaburg.*
Frederick Augustus, Duke of York and Albany, second son of George III.; born 16th August, 1763; elected to the Bishopric of Osnaburg in infancy (1764); had abandoned the title in 1784, on being created Duke of York and Albany; was appointed Commander-in-Chief in 1798; but in 1809 was compelled by the Clarke Scandals to resign. He died 5th January, 1827.

St. xiii. l. 3. *A glorious galley, stem an' stern.*
"Alluding to the newspaper account of a certain Royal sailor's amour." (R. B.) The royal sailor was Prince William Henry, — appointed captain in the Navy 10th April, 1786, — afterwards Duke of Clarence, and finally King William IV. His connexion with Dorothy Jordan did not begin till 1790.

Page 21. THE VISION.
Duan I. St. xvii. l. 2. *A race heroic.*
"The Wallaces." (R. B.)

St. xviii. l. 1. *His Country's Saviour.*
"William Wallace." (R. B.)

St. xviii. l. 2. *Bold Richardton's heroic swell.*
Adam Wallace of Richardton, cousin to the immortal preserver of Scottish independence." (R. B.) Richardton is now known as Riccarton.

St. xviii. l. 3. *The chief, on Sark who glorious fell.*
"Wallace, laird of Craigie, who was second in command, under Douglas, Earl of Ormond, at the famous battle on the banks of Sark, fought *anno* 1458. That glorious victory was principally owing to the judicious conduct and intrepid valour of the gallant laird of Craigie, who died of his wounds after the action." (R. B.) The Wallaces of Craigie were descended from the Wallaces of Riccarton, John Wallace of Riccarton having married Margaret, daughter and heiress of Sir John Lindsay of Craigie. The heiress of Craigie in Burns's time was his friend Mrs. Dunlop, whose maiden name was Frances Anne Wallace.

St. xix. l. 1. *A sceptr'd Pictish shade.*
"Coilus, King of the Picts, from whom the district of Kyle is said to take its name, lies buried, as tradition says, near the family seat of the Montgomeries of Coilsfield, where his burial place is still shown." (R. B.) See *ante,* p. 325, Note to *The Twa Dogs.*

St. xx. l. 1. *Thro' many a wild romantic grove.*
"Barskimming, the seat of the Lord Justice-Clerk." (R. B.) It lies two miles southwest of Mauchline.

St. xx. l. 5. *An aged Judge.*
[The owner of Barskimming], Sir Thomas Miller, son of William Miller of Glenlee, Kirkcudbrightshire; born 3d November, 1717; called to the Scottish Bar 21st February, 1742; appointed Lord Justice-Clerk 14th June, 1766, with the title of Lord Barskimming, afterwards changed to that of Lord Glenlee; Lord-President of the Court of Session 15th January, 1788; created a baronet 3d March of the same year;

died 27th September, 1789. The estate is still in the possession of the family.

St. xxi. l. 2. *The learned Sire and Son I saw.*
"Catrine, the seat of the late Doctor and present Professor Stewart." (R. B.) It is situate about two miles southeast of Mauchline. The estate came into the possession of Dr. Matthew Stewart, — born 1717, died 23d January, 1785, — Professor of Mathematics in the University of Edinburgh, through his marriage with Margaret, daughter of Archibald Stewart, Writer to the Signet; and here he spent the last years of his life. The "son," Professor Dugald Stewart, — born 22d November, 1753, died 11th June, 1828, the well-known metaphysician, — usually spent a part of the summer at Catrine, and there Burns made his acquaintance.

St. xxii. l. 1. *Brydon's brave ward I well could spy.*
"Colonel Fullarton." (R. B.) Colonel William Fullarton was descended from an Ayrshire family, which for five centuries had possessed the barony of Fullarton, near Irvine; born 12th January, 1754; educated at Edinburgh University; spent some time in foreign travel under the care of Patrick Brydone, author of a *Tour in Sicily;* in 1780 proposed an expedition to Mexico against the Spaniards; raised for this purpose the 98th Regiment, of which he was appointed Lieutenant-Colonel; was sent to the Cape of Good Hope — on account of the outbreak of the Dutch war — and thence to India, where in 1783 he was appointed to the command of the Southern army; published in 1787 *A View of the English Interests in India,* and in 1793 an *Account of the Agriculture of the County of Ayr;* raised the 23d or Fullarton's Dragoons in 1794, and the 101st Regiment in 1802; appointed in April, 1803, First Commissioner of Trinidad; died 13th February, 1808. In 1791 Fullarton introduced himself to Burns, who afterwards corresponded with him, and sent him verses in MS. In his *Account of Agriculture* he notes that the method of dishorning cattle therein recommended was suggested "by Mr. Robert Burns, whose general talents are no less conspicuous than the poetic powers which have done so much honour to the country in which he was born."

Duan II. St. xii. l. 2. *And this district as mine I claim.*
The district of Kyle.

St. xii. l. 3. *The Campbells, chiefs of fame.*
The Campbells of Loudoun, descended originally from Sir Duncan Campbell, of the house of Lochow, who in the reign of Robert I. married Sussanah Crawford, heiress of Loudoun. In 1620 Sir James Campbell of Lawers married Margaret Campbell, Baroness of Loudoun, and on 12th May, 1633, he was created Earl of Loudoun and Baron of Tarrinzean and Mauchline.

Page 23. HALLOWEEN.
"Is thought to be a night when witches, devils, and other mischief-making beings are all abroad on their baneful midnight errands; particularly those aerial people, the fairies, are

said on that night to hold a grand anniversary." (R. B.)

St. I. l. 2. *Cassilis Downans.*

"Certain little, romantic, rocky, green hills, in the neighbourhood of the ancient seat of the Earls of Cassilis." (R. B.) Cassilis, now a seat of the Marquis of Ailsa, who is also Earl of Cassilis, is the scene of the ballad of *Johnnie Faa.*

St. I. l. 7. *The Cove.*

"A noted cavern near Colean House, called the Cove of Colean; which, as well as Cassilis Downans, is famed, in country story, for being a favourite haunt of Fairies." (R. B.) Colean House, now known as Colzean Castle, is the principal seat of the Marquis of Ailsa. Of the Coves, Sir William Brereton in his *Travels* relates that there was to be seen in them in 1634 "either a notable imposture, or most strange and much-to-be-admired footsteps and impressions" of "men, children, dogs, coneys, and divers other creatures," which were "here conceived to be spirits."

St. II. l. 3. *Where Bruce ance ruled the martial ranks.*

"The famous family of that name, the ancestors of Robert, the great deliverer of his country, were Earls of Carrick." (R. B.)

Page 24. St. IV. l. 2. *Their stocks maun a' be sought ance.*

"The first ceremony of Halloween is, pulling each a 'stock' or plant of kail. They must go out, hand in hand, with eyes shut, and pull the first they meet with; its being big or little, straight or crooked, is prophetic of the size and shape of the grand object of all their spells, — the husband or wife. If any "yird," or earth, stick to the root, that is "tocher," or fortune; and the taste of the "custoc," that is, the heart of the stem, is indicative of the natural temper and disposition. Lastly, the stems, or, to give them their ordinary appellation, the 'runts,' are placed somewhere above the head of the door; and the Christian names of people whom chance brings into the house are, according to the priority of placing the 'runts,' the names in question." (R. B.)

St. VI. l. 2. *To pou their stalks o' corn.*

"They go to the barnyard, and pull each, at three several times, a stalk of oats. If the third stalk wants the 'tap-pickle,' that is, the grain at the top of the stalk, the party in question will come to the marriage-bed anything but a maid." (R. B.)

St. VI. l. 8. *The fause-house.*

"When the corn is in a doubtful state, by being too green or wet, the stack-builder, by means of old timber, etc., makes a large apartment in his stack, with an opening in the side which is fairest exposed to the wind; this he calls a 'fause-house.'" (R. B.)

St. VII. l. 1. *The auld guid-wife's weel-hoordet nits.*

"Burning the nuts is a favourite charm. They name the lad and lass to each particular nut, as they lay them in the fire; and according as they burn quietly together, or start from

beside one another, the course and issue of the courtship will be." (R. B.)

St. XI. l. 8. *And in the blue-clue throws then.*

"Whoever would, with success, try this spell, must strictly observe these directions: Steal out, all alone, to the kiln, and, darkling, throw into the 'pot' a clue of blue yarn; wind it in a new clue off the old one; and, towards the latter end, something will hold the thread: demand, 'Wha hauds?' *i. e.* who holds? and answer will be returned from the kiln-pot, by naming the Christian and surname of your future spouse." (R. B.)

St. XIII. l. 3. *I'll eat the apple at the glass.*

"Take a candle and go alone to a looking-glass; eat an apple before it, and some traditions say you should comb your hair all the time; the face of your conjugal companion, *to be*, will be seen in the glass, as if peeping over your shoulder." (R. B.)

Page 25. St. XIV. l. 1. *Ye little skelpie-limmer's-face!*

"A technical term in female scolding." (R. B.)

St. XVI. l. 5. *He gat hemp-seed.*

"Steal out, unperceived, and sow a handful of hemp-seed, harrowing it with anything you can conveniently draw after you. Repeat, now and then, 'Hemp-seed I saw thee, hemp-seed I saw thee; and him (or her) that is to be my true love, come after me and pou thee.' Look over your left shoulder, and you will see the appearance of the person invoked, in the attitude of pulling hemp. Some traditions say, 'Come after me and shaw thee,' that is, show thyself; in which case, it simply appears. Others omit the harrowing, and say, 'Come after me and harrow thee.'" (R. B.)

St. XXI. l. 2. *To winn three wechts o' naething.*

"This charm must likewise be performed unperceived and alone. You go to the barn, and open both doors, taking them off the hinges, if possible; for there is danger that the being about to appear may shut the doors, and do you some mischief. Then take that instrument used in winnowing the corn, which in our country dialect we call a 'wecht,' and go through all the attitudes of letting down corn against the wind. Repeat it three times, and the third time, an apparition will pass through the barn, in at the windy door, and out at the other, having both the figure in question, and the appearance or retinue, marking the employment or station in life." (R. B.) A "wecht" was a close sieve; *i. e.* the bottom was covered with leather.

St. XXII. l. 7. *Midden-hole.*

"A gutter at the bottom of the dunghill." (R. B. in *Glossary.*)

St. XXIII. l. 3. *The stack he faddom't thrice.*

"Take an opportunity of going (unnoticed) to a 'bear-stack,' and fathom it three times round. The last fathom of the last time, you will catch in your arms the appearance of your future conjugal yoke-fellow." (R. B.)

Page 26. St. XXIV. l. 7. *Whare three lairds' lands met at a burn.*

" You go out, one or more (for this is a social spell), to a south-running spring, or rivulet, where ' three lairds' lands meet,' and dip your left shirt-sleeve. Go to bed in sight of a fire, and hang your wet sleeve before it to dry. Lie awake; and, some time near midnight, an apparition, having the exact figure of the grand object in question, will come and turn the sleeve, as if to dry the other side of it." (R. B.)

St. XXVII. l. 2. *The luggies three are ranged.*

"Take three dishes, put clean water in one, foul water in another, and leave the third empty; blindfold a person, and lead him to the hearth where the dishes are ranged; he (or she) dips the left hand : if by chance in the clean water, the future (husband or) wife will come to the bar of matrimony a maid : if in the foul, a widow; if in the empty dish, it foretells, with equal certainty, no marriage at all. It is repeated three times, and every time the arrangement of the dishes is altered." (R. B.)

St. XXVIII. l. 5. *Butter'd sow'ns.*

"Sowens, with butter instead of milk to them, is always the Halloween Supper." (R. B.) Sowens are made from the liquor got by steeping the seeds of oats in water. When it has soured, it is boiled to the thickness of porridge.

Page 27. THE AULD FARMER'S NEW-YEAR MORNING SALUTATION TO HIS AULD MARE, MAGGIE.

St. VI. l. 5. *Kyle-Stewart.*

The northern division of the Ayrshire district of Kyle.

St. VII. l. 1. *Tho' now ye dow but hoyte and hobble.*

Burns explains " hoyte " as " the motion between a trot and a gallop," the old mare's stiffened joints preventing her from doing either properly.

St. XI. l. 1. *Thou was a noble fittie-lan'.*

" Fittie-Lan " was the near horse of the hindmost pair in the plough, which was then drawn by four horses. (See *post*, p. 338, Notes to *The Inventory*.)

St. XI. l. 2. *As e'er in tug or tow was drawn.*

" Tug, raw hides, of which in old times plough-traces were frequently made." (R. B. in *Glossary*.) They were also made of " tow " or rope.

Page 28. THE COTTER'S SATURDAY NIGHT.

St. I. l. 1. *My lov'd, my honor'd, much respected friend !*

Robert Aiken, eldest son of John Aiken, shipbuilder, Ayr, by Sarah Dalrymple, second daughter of James Dalrymple, sheriff-clerk of Ayrshire ; born 23d August, 1739; became solicitor and Surveyor of Taxes in Ayr ; was probably acquainted with the Burns household in the early years of Robert's life ; introduced him to Gavin Hamilton with a view to his taking Mossgiel ; displayed great skill and eloquence in his successful defence of Gavin Hamilton before the Presbytery of Ayr against the Kirk-Session of Mauchline ; especially excelled as an elocutionist, — so much so that Burns said that

he " read " him " into fame ; " and is mentioned by Burns in his letter to Richmond, 17th February, 1786, as " my chief patron," who " is pleased to express great approbation of my works." He is said by Burns in a supposed letter to John Ballantine, printed by Cunningham, but without date, to have been art and part in the destruction of his declaration of his marriage to Jean Armour; but Miss Grace Aiken, who had access to letters of Burns to her father, now lost, testifies that there " never was any interruption in their friendship or correspondence." (P. F. Aiken, *Memorials of Burns*, p. 102.) He subscribed for 105 copies of the Kilmarnock Edition ; and died at Ayr, 24th March, 1807. He is the " glib-tongued Aiken " of *Holy Willie's Prayer ;* the " Orator Bob " of *The Kirk's Alarm ;* and the " Aiken dear " of *The Farewell.*

Page 30. St. XII. l. 4. *The big ha' Bible.*

So called from its original use in the noble's hall, wherein the whole household assembled for religious services.

St. XVI. l. 3. *Hope " springs exulting on triumphant wing."*

" Pope's *Windsor Forest.*" (R. B.) The passage is : —

" See ! from the brake the whirring pheasant springs, And mounts exulting on triumphant wings."

Page 32. EPISTLE TO DAVIE.

St. I. l. 1. *While winds frae off Ben-Lomond blaw.*

Ben Lomond is visible in the distant northern horizon, from various points in Ayrshire.

St. II. l. 11. *" Mair spier na, nor fear na."*

" Ramsay." (R. B.) The line most nearly resembling this in Ramsay is " Nocht feirful, but cheirful," in *The Vision.* It closely resembles a line in *Ane Ballat of the Creation of the Warld :* " Nocht feiring, but speiring," and more faintly one in *The Cherry and the Slae :* " Then fear not, nor hear not," which also occurs in *The Banks of Helicon.*

Page 39. TO A MOUNTAIN DAISY.

St. IX. l. 3. *Stern Ruin's plough-share drives elate.*

Possibly, but not necessarily, a reminiscence of Young : —

" Stars rush, and final Ruin fiercely drives Her plough-share o'er creation."

Page 40. EPISTLE TO A YOUNG FRIEND.

St. VI. l. 3. *Th' illicit rove.*

The use of " rove " as a substantive is rare. Most likely Burns borrowed it from Young : " Thou nocturnal rove."

Page 41. ON A SCOTCH BARD.

St. V. l. 1. *Auld, cantie Kyle may weepers wear.*

Weepers are strips of muslin worn on the cuffs of mourners. Kyle is a district in Ayrshire ; not Kilmarnock, as stated by some editors.

Page 44. EPISTLE TO J. LAPRAIK.

St. II. l. 1. *Rockin.*

The term " rockin " is thus explained by Gilbert Burns : " Derived from those primitive times when the country-women employed their spare hours in spinning on the rock, or distaff. This simple implement is a very portable one, and well fitted on the social inclination of meeting in a neighbour's house; hence the phrase of *going a-rocking* or *with the rock*."

Page 47. SECOND EPISTLE TO J. LAPRAIK.

St. XII. l. 3. *Nae sheep-shank bane.*
That is, a personage of no small importance.

Page 47. TO WILLIAM SIMPSON OF OCHILTREE.

St. III. l. 1. *My senses wad be in a creel.*
A creel is an ozier basket. To be "in a creel" is to be perplexed, muddled, or fascinated: a sense probably derived from the old Scottish marriage custom of "creeling."

St. III. l. 3. *Wi' Allan, or wi' Gilbertfield.*
Allan Ramsay, of course, and his contemporary, Hamilton of Gilbertfield, whom, with Fergusson, Burns was accustomed to regard as his models; but, as he states in his Preface to the Kilmarnock Edition, "rather with a view to kindle at their flame, than for servile imitation."

Page 48. St. VI. l. 1. *Coila.*
The district of Kyle in Ayrshire.

Page 49. St. XIX. l. 4. *New-Light.*
In the Edinburgh Editions Burns refers to a note to *The Ordination:* "*New Light* is a cant phrase in the West of Scotland for those religious opinions which Dr. Taylor of Norwich has defended so strenuously." The names, "New Light" and "Old Light" were subsequently assumed by separate divisions of the Secession Church of Scotland, which became merged in the United Presbyterian Church.

Page 50. EPISTLE TO JOHN RANKINE.

St. I. l. 4. *Your dreams and tricks.*
"A certain humourous dream of his was then making a noise in the country-side." (R. B.)

St. IV. l. 2. *The Blue-gown badge an' claithing.*
This was the livery of a licensed order of beggars known as the King's bedesmen (no doubt in earlier years a religious fraternity, whose number coincided with that of the King's years. Every Maunday Thursday they received a new outfit, which included a blue gown and a pewter badge on which were inscribed the words: "Pass and Repass." Sir Walter immortalized the craft in the Edie Ochiltree of *The Antiquary.*

St. V. l. 5. *Yon sang ye'll sen't.*
"A song he had promised the author." (R. B.)

Page 51. St. XI. l. 4. *My gowd guinea.*
It was the custom of the Kirk-Session to require the person who had been disciplined for fornication to testify to the sincerity of his penance by contributing a guinea for the poor.

St. XI. l. 5. *Buckskin kye.*
"Buckskin" is slang for Virginian, and "kye" for negroes.

Page 53. THE FAREWELL.

St. IV. ll. 1, 2.
And you, farewell! whose merits claim
Justly that Highest Badge to wear.

The master of the Lodge at this date was Captain James Montgomerie, a younger brother of Colonel Hugh Montgomerie, afterwards Earl of Eglinton.

Page 54. FOR THE AUTHOR'S FATHER.
For "even his failings lean'd to virtue's side."
"Goldsmith." (R. B.)

Page 55. A BARD'S EPITAPH.

St. II. l. 3. *That weekly this aréa throng.*
Some editors substitute *arena* for *area;* but Burns did not regard the churchyard as an "arena" except on the occasion of a Holy Fair.

Page 57. DEATH AND DR. HORNBOOK.

St. V. l. 2. *Willie's mill.*
Tarbolton Mill, then occupied by William Muir, entitled by Burns in the heading to the *Epitaph* upon him (*ante*, p. 194) "My own friend and my father's friend."

St. VII. l. 6. *Cheeks o' branks.*
The wooden sides of an ox's bridle.

St. VIII. l. 2. *When ither folk are busy sawin'.*
"This rencontre happened in the seed-time, 1785." (R. B.)

St. X. ll. 3, 4.
But if I did, I wad be kittle
To be mislear'd.

This phrase has occasioned some discussion, Burns in his glossary explains "misleared" as "mischievous, unmannerly;" so that the most obvious interpretation is, "I would be quick to be mischievous." But "mislear'd" has a rather wider meaning, and would probably justify such a reading as "I would be hard to outwit." Either interpretation is to be preferred, in any case, before those attained by violent changes in punctuation, *e. g. :* —

"But if I did, I wad be kittle;
    To be mislear'd
I wad na mind it," etc. :

that is, "I would be dangerous; to be unmannerly, I would n't mind it," etc.

St. XI. l. 6. *At monie a house.*
"An epidemical fever was then raging in that country." (R. B.)

Page 58. St. XIV. l. 1. *Jock Hornbook.*
"This gentleman, Dr. Hornbook, is professionally a brother of the sovereign order of the ferula; but, by intuition and inspiration, is at once an apothecary, surgeon, and physician." (R. B.)

St. XIV. l. 2. *Deil mak his king's-hood in a spleuchan!*
The king's hood is the second stomach in a ruminant, but it is plain that here Burns uses the term in a very different sense. A spleuchan is a tobacco-pouch made of an animal's pelt.

St. XIV. l. 3. *Buchan.*
"Buchan's Domestic Medicine." (R. B.) This work by Dr. William Buchan (born 1729; died 1805) was first published in 1769, and continued to enjoy its popularity in country households long after the death of Burns.

St. XXIII. l. 1. *Johnie Ged's Hole.*
"The grave-digger." (R. B.) "Ged" is Scots for pike, whose greed is as the grave's.

Page 59. St. xxx. l. 6. *Fairin*.

Literally a present from a fair. It was long a custom of peasants returning from the fair to throw bags of confectionery to children. This was the children's "fairin." But the word came to be used, as here, sarcastically, to signify a beating. Cf. *Tam o' Shanter : —*

"Ah, Tam ! ah, Tam ! thou 'll get thy fairin !
    In hell they 'll roast thee like a herrin ! "

Page 60. THE BRIGS OF AYR.

And down by Simpson's wheel'd the left about.

"A noted tavern at the Auld Brig end." (R. B.)

The drowsy Dungeon - Clock had number'd two.

"Concerning the "clock" and the "Wallace Tower" of the next verse Burns notes: "The two steeples." The former stood 135 feet high, fronted the old jail near the new bridge, and was removed, together with the jail, in 1826; the latter — a small baronial structure in the High Street — was superseded in 1834 by a Gothic building 113 feet high, in which were placed the clock and bells of the old Dungeon Steeple.

Swift as the gos drives on the wheeling hare.

"The gos-hawk or falcon." (R. B.) [The goshawk is, however, distinct from the falcon both in ornithology and in falconry.]

Yet, teughly doure, he bade an unco bang.

"Bang " refers to the great number of years the bridge had stood. [See *Glossarial Index*.]

Page 61. *Nae sheep shank*.

See note to *Second Epistle to J. Lapraik*, *ante*, p. 331.

There 's men of taste would tak' the Ducat stream.

"A noted ford, just above the Auld Brig." (R. B.)

Or haunted Garpal draws his feeble source.

"The banks of Garpal water is one of the few places in the West of Scotland where those fancy-scaring beings, known by the name of Ghaists, still continue pertinaceously to inhabit." (R. B.)

And from Glenbuck down to the Ratton-Key.

R. B. explains that Glenbuck is " the source of the river Ayr," and that the Ratton-Key is " a small landing place above the large quay."

Fancies that our guid brugh denies protection.

Both Dr. M'Gill of Ayr and his colleague Mr. Dalrymple belonged to the New Light party in the Church, which party was consequently predominant in the burgh ; but this piece was written before the M'Gill prosecution. (See *ante*, p. 110, *The Kirk's Alarm*.)

Page 62. *O, had M'Lauchlan, thairm-inspiring sage.*

"A well-known performer of Scottish music on the violin." (R. B.) He was accustomed to give performances in the West of Scotland.

Page 63. *Next followed Courage.*

The reference is to the Montgomeries (see *ante*, p. 325, Notes to *The Author's Earnest Cry and Prayer*), through whose grounds the Teal flowed.

Benevolence, etc.

Mrs. Stewart of Stair.

Learning and Worth.

The reference is to Professor Dugald Stewart, who resided at Catrine House. (See *ante*, p. 328, Notes to *The Vision*.)

Page 63. THE ORDINATION.

St. I. l. 7. *Then aff to Begbie's in a raw.*

In 1786, apparently, Begbie succeeded Crookes [whose name appears in the line in a MS. form] in the inn — now the Angel Hotel — near the Laigh Kirk, with which it was connected by a close so narrow that worshippers had to traverse it in Indian file.

St. II. l. 1. *Curst Common-sense, that imp o' hell.*

"Common sense " was supposed to be a special attribute of the moderate clergy.

St. II. l. 2. *Cam in wi' Maggie Lauder.*

"Alluding to a scoffing ballad which was made on the admission of the late Reverend and worthy Mr. Lindsay to the Laigh Kirk." (R. B. in '87 and subsequent Editions.) — " I suppose the author here means Mrs. Lindsay, wife of the late Reverend and worthy Mr. Lindsay, as that was her maiden name, I am told. *N. B.* — He got the Laigh Kirk of Kilmarnock." (R. B. in MS.) The "scoffing ballad " is reprinted in M'Kay's *History of Kilmarnock*. According to current rumour, the Rev. William Lindsay, being minister at Cumbrae, was, through his wife's interest (she had been housekeeper, or governess, in the Glencairn family), presented to the Laigh Kirk, Kilmarnock, by the Earl of Glencairn, 30th November, 1762. But a Mr. Henderson, her descendant, maintains, in a series of letters to Robert Chambers (MS. correspondence in an interleaved copy of Chambers's *Burns*, 1851, vol. i., in the Kilmarnock Monument Museum), that she never was a member of the Glencairn household in any capacity ; and explains that Lindsay had been tutor to the Earl of Glencairn. The Presbytery refused to sustain the call, but it was finally sustained by the General Assembly, in the teeth of so determined an opposition that the ordination (12th July, 1764) took place in a public-house ; with the result that ten persons were tried before the criminal court at Ayr for riot and assault, of whom three were convicted and whipped through the town.

St. II. l. 3. *Oliphant.*

James Oliphant, born about 1734 ; Russell's predecessor in the chapel - of - ease or High Church, Kilmarnock, to which he was translated from Gorbals chapel-of-ease, Glasgow ; was ordained at Kilmarnock, 17th May, 1764 ; translated to Dumbarton, 23d December, 1772 ; died 10th April, 1818, in his eighty-fourth year. — Author of a *Mother's Catechism* (frequently reprinted), and a *Sacramental Catechism*.

St. II. l. 4. *Russell.*

See *ante*, p. 327, Notes to *The Holy Fair*.

St. II. l. 5. *Mackinlay.*

See Prefatory Note. [Also *post*, p. 333, Notes to *Tam Samson's Elegy*.]

St. III. l. 3. *Double verse.*

The Scottish *Metrical Psalms* are set forth in staves, each composed of a double quatrain.

St. III. l. 4. *Bangor.*

A favourite Scottish Psalm tune in the minor mode.

Page 64. St. IV. l. 3. *How graceless Ham leugh at his dad.*

"Genesis ix. 22." (R. B.)

St. IV. l. 7. *Zipporah, the scauldin jad.*

"Exodus iv. 25." (R. B.)

St. VIII. l. 3. *As lately Fenwick, sair forfairn.*

William Boyd, born 1747, was presented to the church of Fenwick by George, Earl of Glasgow, 20th September, 1780; but on account of the opposition of the parishioners (who barricaded the church) a settlement was not effected until 25th June, 1782, when by order of the Assembly the ordination took place at Irvine. Boyd afterward won the respect of his parishioners. He died 17th October, 1828.

St. IX. l. 1. *Robertson.*

John Robertson, ordained to the first charge, Kilmarnock, 25th April, 1765, died 5th June, 1799, in his sixty-seventh year. He belonged to the Common-sense party. See *ante*, p. 66, Prefatory Note to *Tam Samson's Elegy*, and *infra*, Notes to the same.

St. IX. l. 7. *The Netherton.*

A carpet-weaving district in Kilmarnock.

St. X. l. 1. *Mu'trie.*

John Multrie, Lindsay's successor, and predecessor of Mackinlay in the second charge of the Laigh Kirk, was ordained 8th March, 1775; he died 2d June, 1785, in his fortieth year.

St. XI. l. 8. *Jamie Beattie.*

Dr. James Beattie, author of *The Essay on Truth.*

Page 65. St. XIV. l. 3. *New Light.*

"'New Light' is a cant phrase in the West of Scotland for those religious opinions which Dr. Taylor of Norwich has so strenuously defended." (R. B.)

Page 66. ADDRESS TO THE UNCO GUID.

St. VII. l. 3. *A kennin wrang.*

"A kennin" means "a very little;" merely as much as can be perceived or known.

Page 66. TAM SAMSON'S ELEGY.

St. I. l. 2. *Mackinlay.*

"A certain preacher, a great favourite with the million. Vide *The Ordination*, St. II." (R. B.) [Also see *ante*, p. 63, Prefatory Note to *The Ordination*.]

St. I. l. 3. *Robertson.*

"Another preacher, an equal favourite with the *few*, who was at that time ailing. For him see also *The Ordination*. St. IX." (R. B.) [Also see *supra*, Notes to *The Ordination*.]

St. I. l. 4. *To preach an' read.*

The orthodox party strongly objected to a "read" sermon.

Page 67. St. V. l. 2. *To guard, or draw, or wick a bore.*

In curling, "to guard" is to defend a stone in a good position by placing another opposite it; "to draw" is to send it into a good position, by hitting it with just the right force; and "to

wick a bore" is to hit it obliquely and send it through an opening.

St. V. l. 5. *Death's hog-score.*

The hog-score is a line, which the curling stone must cross, or go out of play and be removed.

Page 68. St. XV. l. 4. *Yet what remead?*

Cf. *The Apocrypha*, Wisd. ii. 1: "In the death of a man there is no remedy;" and Sempill, *The Piper of Kilbarchan*, St. I. l. 4.

PER CONTRA, l. 2. *Killie.*

"Killie is a phrase the country folks sometimes use for the name of a certain town in the west." (R. B.)

Page 73. ADDRESS TO EDINBURGH.

St. IV. l. 5. *Fair Burnet.*

See *ante*, p. 176, *Elegy on the Late Miss Burnet of Monboddo.*

Page 79. NO CHURCHMAN AM I.

St. VI. l. 1. *Life's cares they are comforts.*

"Young's *Night Thoughts.*" (R. B.)

Page 85. TO ROBERT GRAHAM OF FINTRY, ESQ.

Late crippled of an arm and now a leg.

In a letter to Mrs. Dunlop (7th February, 1791, if the date be rightly given), Burns mentions that, his horse having fallen with him, for some time he had been unable to use his hand and arm in writing. If this accident happened before February, he had a similar mischance in the end of March, when, as he states in a letter to A. F. Tytler, his horse came down with him, and broke his right arm. The hurt to his leg is mentioned in a letter to Peter Hill, as well as in the letter to Graham of Fintry.

Page 90. TAM O' SHANTER.

Thou drank wi' Kirkton Jean till Monday.

The Jean referred to is supposed to have been Jean Kennedy of Kirkoswald, who with her sister kept a very respectable tavern, sometimes called the Ladies' House.

Page 91. *The landlord's laugh was ready chorus.*

On a MS. Robert Ainslie has noted that when Burns recited to him the poem at Ellisland he added these lines: —

"The crickets joined the chirping cry,
The kittlin chased her tail for joy."

Or like the snow falls in the river.

The relative "that" or "which" should be understood between "snow" and "fall." Chambers gave this preposterous attempt at amendment: "Or like the *snowfall* in the river;" and Scott Douglas took upon him to affirm that Burns would have preferred "snowflake" before "snowfall." Plainly Burns preferred the line as it is.

Page 116. *Nae cotillion, brent new frae France.*

Brent new [brand new] means quite new; new from the fire or forge. The term is no doubt agricultural.

Page 92. *Been snaw-white seventeen hunder linen.*

Woven in a reed of 1700 divisions.

Rigwoodie hags wad spean a foal.

The rigwoodie is the rope or chain that crosses

the saddle of a horse. Some editors translate the phrase as gallows-worthy. "Rig" is also a name for a strumpet, and the word read backwards might mean "gallows-strumpet." On the other hand, the simile refers to a mare, and it is probable that "rigwoodie" here means ancient or lean.

When plundering herds assail their byke.

Boy herds who were in the habit of plundering the hives of humble-bees.

Ah, Tam! ah, Tam! thou'll get thy fairin!

See *ante*, p. 332, Notes to *Death and Dr. Hornbook*.

And win the key-stane of the brig.

"It is a well known fact that witches, or any evil spirits, have no power to follow a poor wight any farther than the middle of the next running stream. It may be proper likewise to mention to the benighted traveller, that when he falls in with *bogles*, whatever danger may be in his going forward, there is much more hazard in turning back." (R. B. in Editions '93 and '94.)

Page 94. ON THE LATE CAPTAIN GROSE'S PEREGRINATIONS THRO' SCOTLAND.

St. III. l. 1. *By some auld, houlet-haunted biggin.*

"*Vide* his *Antiquities of Scotland*." (R. B.)

St. VI. l. 2. *Rusty airn caps and jinglin jackets.*

"*Vide* his treatise on ancient armour and weapons." (R. B.)

Page 95. St. VIII. l. 6. *Lang-kail gullie.*

A large knife used for cutting the stalks of the colewort.

Page 96. THE HUMBLE PETITION OF BRUAR WATER.

St. I. l. 8. *And drink my crystal tide.*

"Bruar falls are the finest in the country, but not a bush about them, which spoils much their beauty." (R. B. in MS.) "Bruar Falls in Atholl are exceedingly picturesque and beautiful; but their effect is much impaired by the want of trees and shrubs." (R. B. in Editions '93 and '94.)

Page 100. THE WHISTLE.

St. II. l. 1. *Old Loda, still rueing the arm of Fingal.*

"See Ossian's *Caric-thura*." (R. B.)

Page 101. St. VI. l. 3. *Trusty Glenriddel, so skilled in old coins.*

See *ante*, p. 142, Prefatory Note to *Impromptu to Captain Riddell*.

St. VIII. l. 3. *I'll conjure the ghost of the great Rorie More.*

"See Johnson's *Tour in the Hebrides*." (R. B.)

Page 102. THE JOLLY BEGGARS.

The personages of Burns's Cantata — ruffler and strolling mort, trull and tinker, balladsinger and bawdy-basket — are more or less the personages of the treatises and song-books. But they have been renewed by observation from the life, and they are made immortal by the fire of that inspiration through which they were passed. Burns, if we may believe his own words, could sympathise with such outcasts, and had at least a sentimental fancy for the life they led. . . .

As early as 1784 he is moved to confide to his *First Common Place Book* that he has "often observed, in the course of his experience of human life," — which already included Irvine and the Carrick smugglers, — "that every man, even the worst, has something good about him;" for which reason, "I have often courted the acquaintance of that part of mankind commonly known by the ordinary phrase of 'blackguards,' sometimes further than was consistent with the safety of my character." It is sheer impertinence to assume, with certain commentators, that he figured himself in the person of his own Ballad Singer. But it is undeniable that he set forth some of his own philosophy of life at that disreputable artist's lips; also with him it was ever "the heart ay's the part ay that makes us right or wrang;" and it is pretty safe to argue that his regard for the "fraternitie of vacabondes" was so far both temperamental and sincere. And this, in brief, is why Matthew Arnold prefers the Burns of *The Jolly Beggars* before the Goethe of the "Scene in Auerbach's Cellar." With a superb intelligence, the Scot creates his people from within; while the German's apprehension of his company is merely intellectual and pedantic.

Recitativo. St. I. l. 2. *The bauckie bird.*

"The old Scotch name for the bat." (R. B.) Perhaps because it hides in the roofs of houses near the "bauks" or crossbeams.

St. I. l. 9. *Poosie-Nansie.*

"The hostess of a noted caravanserai in Mauchline well known and much frequented by the lowest order of travellers and pilgrims." (R. B.) Also, "Luckie Nansie is Racer Jess's mother in my *Holy Fair*. Luckie kept a kind of caravansery for the lower order of wayfaring strangers and pilgrims." (R. B.) The epithet "Poosie" is of somewhat doubtful signification. A very similar word, "pousie," is a nickname for a cat; and in Scots and English slang a definite sense has attached to both these words ("cat" and "pousie") for over two centuries. "Pose" is also Scots for a purse, or a secret hoard of money. But most likely "Poosie" stands for pushing. Cf. *Reply to a Trimming Epistle*, p. 132, st. II. l. 2: in Eighteenth Century slang, "pushing-school" signifies brothel. The lady figures in the Kirk-Session Records for 1773, when she was handled for drunkenness as "Agnes Ronald, wife of George Gibson," with whom — and with her daughter — she appeared to answer a further charge of "fencing" stolen goods. As regards the earlier charge, she calmly but firmly "declared her resolution to continue in the sin of drunkenness," whereupon "the Session, considering the foresaid foolish resolution and expression," excluded her "from the privileges of the Church" until she should "profess her repentance." There is no evidence that she came to terms with the Session. She is clearly to be distinguished from Elizabeth Black, also the keeper of a "dosshouse," but in no way a connexion of George Gibson. See further *ante*, p. 115, Prefatory Note to *Adam Armour's Prayer.*

St. I. l. 14. *Girdle.*
The girdle is a round plate of metal used in Scotland from time immemorial in firing the oaten cake.

St. II. l. 2. *Mealy bags.*
The meal-bag was the beggar's main equipment, as oatmeal was the staple alms and might be taken as food or exchanged or sold. Cf. the ensuing song, "When the tother bag I sell," etc.

Song. St. II. l. 2. *The heights of Abram.*
Before Quebec, where Wolfe beat Montcalm on the 13th September, 1759.

Song. St. II. l. 4. *The Moro.*
El Moro, the castle defending the harbour of Santiago de Cuba, stormed by the British in August, 1762.

Page 103. First Song. St. III. l. 1. *Curtis.*
Sir Roger Curtis, Admiral, — born 1746, died 14th November, 1816, — who, being in command of the *Brilliant*, destroyed the French floating batteries before Gibraltar, 13th September, 1782.

St. III. l. 3. *Eliott.*
George Augustus Eliott, — born 25th December, 1717, died 6th July, 1790, — who, for his heroic defence of Gibraltar, was raised to the peerage as Lord Heathfield, Baron of Gibraltar, 14th June, 1787.

Second Song. St. IV. l. 3. *Spontoon.*
A weapon carried by soldier-officers instead of a half-pike.

St. V. l. 2. *Cunningham.*
The northern among the three ancient districts of Ayrshire. The Glencairns derive their family name from it.

Page 104. First Song. St. IV. l. 1. *Tyed up like a stirk.*
Punished with the "jougs," a sort of iron collar.

Second Recitativo. L. 3. *For monie a pursie she had hooked.*
"Hook" is old slang for (1) a finger, (2) a thief. Burns's heroine, who answers well enough to the "bawdy-basket" of the treatises, was, in fact, a pickpocket.

L. 8. *Braw.*
Here used in its original sense, and signifying gaily dressed, the reference being to the tawdry finery of the Highland vagabond. See st. II. of the succeeding song. For a curious instance of "braw" meaning good-looking as opposed to well-dressed, see *ante*, p. 23, *Halloween*, st. III. l. 2.

Page 105. First Recitativo. St. I. l. 2. *Trystes an' fairs.*
"Trystes" are cattle markets, and "fairs" are hiring fairs or "mops."

Page 106. First Song. St. II. l. 4. *Budget.*
A tinker's bag of tools. Cf. Shakespeare, *Winter's Tale*, Act IV. sc. 2, Autolycus' Song : —

> "If tinkers shall have leave to live
> And bear the sow-skin budget."

St. II. l. 6. *Kilbaigie.*
"A peculiar sort of whisky, a great favorite with Poosie Nansie's clubs." (R. B.) Kilbaigie Distillery was in Clackmannanshire, a little to the north of Kincardine-on-Forth.

First Recitativo. St. I. l. 8. *An' made the bottle clunk.*
"Clunk" (Fr. *faire glou-glou*) describes the sound of emptying a narrow-necked bottle, especially by application to the mouth.

St. II. l. 5. *A wight of Homer's craft.*
"Homer is allowed to be the oldest ballad singer on record." (R. B.)

St. II. ll. 8, 9.
> *An' shor'd them "Dainty Davie"*
> *O' boot that night.*

See the old song : —

> "Being pursued by the dragoons,
> Within my bed he laid him down,
> And weel I wat he was worth his room,
> For he was my Dainty Davie : " —

written to the praise of Mass David Williamson, and preserved in full in *The Merry Muses*, and in part by Herd (1769). It sets forth an adventure thus related by Captain Creichton in his *Memoirs*, as published by Swift (*Works*, ed. Scott, vol. xii. pp. 19, 20) : "I had been assured that Williamson did much frequent the house of my Lady Cherrytree, within ten miles of Edinburgh; but when I arrived with my party about the house, the lady, well knowing our errand, put Williamson to bed to her daughter, disguised in a woman's night-dress. When the troopers went to search in the young lady's room, her mother pretended that she was not well; and Williamson so managed the matter that, when the daughter raised herself a little in the bed to let the troopers see her, they did not discover him, and so went off disappointed. But the young lady proved with child, and Williamson, to take off the scandal, married her in some time after." Creichton is the sole authority for this *historiette*, which is placed in 1674, and whose hero died, at seventy-nine, in 1702. But it is certain that Miss Cherrytree became the third of his seven wives, although there is no record of her bearing him a child. Creichton's story was very generally believed. Williamson, whose exploit so nearly touched the heart of Charles II. that ('t is said) his attendance was commanded at Whitehall, did more, in fact, than endear himself both to writers of songs and to writers of such lampoons as *The Cardinal's Coach Couped* (1711 : in Burns's favourite stave) : —

> "You need not think I 'm speaking lies :
> Bear witness, House of Cherrytrees,
> Where Dainty Davie strove to please
> My lady's daughter
> And boldly crept . . .
> For fear of slaughter : " —

and the rather scandalous verses collected by Maidment in *A Handful of Pestilent Pasquils* (Privately Printed, no date). He added, in the "Dainty Davie" of the text, a synonym (susceptible, it seems, of more than one interpretation) to Scots venereal slang. What, in effect, is signified in Burns's lines is that there and then the Bard presented the Fiddler with that doxy from his train of three whom he had taken but now *in flagrante delicto;* and this is shown by the terms in which he presently (in the succeeding song) refers to the transaction: —

" I 've lost but ane, I 've twa behin',
I 've wife eneugh for a' that."

Second Song. St. II. l. 4. *Helicon.*

Burns's description may derive from Montgomerie's " fontaine Helicon " in *The Cherry and the Slae.* Again, it may be that, inasmuch as whisky was, and still is, named after the place of its production, and inasmuch as he regarded it as a source of inspiration, he simply meant his Bard to talk of " Helicon " as his Caird had spoken of " Kilbaigie." Cf. Byron, *English Bards* (1809) : " Fresh fish from Helicon ;" corrected (MS. 1816) to " Hippocrene."

Last chorus, l. 3. *My dearest bluid,* etc.

Cf. the sonnet attributed to Marlowe : —

" To do thee good,
I 'll freely spend my thrice-decocted blood."

Page 107. THE TWA HERDS.

" Herds " is old Scots for " shepherds."

Page 108. St. III. l. 1. *Moodie, man, an' wordy Russell.*

For notices of Moodie and Russell see *ante,* pp. 326, 327, Notes to *The Holy Fair.*

St. III. l. 3. *New-Light.*

See *ante,* p. 331, Notes to *Epistle to William Simpson of Ochiltree,* and the humorous dissertation in the *Epistle* itself (*ante,* p. 47).

St. IV. ll. 3-6. *Ye wha were no by lairds respeckit,* etc.

The construction is unusual, unless " respeckit " bears a somewhat strained meaning, and " respeckit to wear the plaid " signifies " esteemed fit to wear the plaid." If " respeckit " be used in its common sense, the lines may be read thus: " Ye who were elected to wear the plaid, not by respected lairds but by the brutes themselves to be their guide."

St. IV. l. 5. *By the brutes themselves eleckit.*
The reference is to popular election by the congregation.

St. x. l. 2. *Duncan deep, an' Peebles shaul.*
Robert Duncan, ordained minister at Dundonald 11th September, 1783 ; D. D., University of Glasgow, 1806 ; died 14th April, 1815 ; was deemed intellectual, and published *Infidelity the Growing Evil of the Times,* a sermon, Air, 1794. For Peebles, see *ante,* p. 327, Notes to *The Holy Fair.*

St. x. l. 3. *Apostle Auld.*
William Auld, minister of Mauchline, younger son of the laird of Ellanton, Ayrshire, was born in 1709 ; graduated M. A. at Edinburgh in 1733, and afterwards studied divinity at Glasgow and Leyden ; ordained minister of Mauchline in April, 1742 ; died 12th December, 1791, in his 83d year. He published *The Pastoral Duty Briefly Explained,* a sermon, Glasgow, 1763. Like his elder " Holy Willie," Auld was given to liquor, and, also like him, was a bitter Calvinist and a rigid disciplinarian. He is not alluded to in *The Holy Fair,* because as minister of the parish he had to preside at the services within the church. Auld's disciplinary dealings with Burns are referred to in the *Reply*

to a Trimming Epistle from a Tailor (see *ante,* p. 132). Several writers have credited him with a certain magnanimity with regard to his satirist. But Burns, though he certainly offended, did not attack him personally — except in the rather flattering allusion in the text — before he had left Ayrshire. He is not named in the earlier version of *Holy Willie's Prayer* except as " God's ain Priest ; " and as for magnanimity, there is no proof of any on his part. He rebuked Burns and Armour in 1786, together with other three, in terms applicable to all five. He could not with decency single Burns out for a special rebuke. On 5th August, 1788, Burns and Armour were rebuked for their irregular marriage, after which discipline they could not be rebuked for a second case of fornication. Auld was now an old man ; hence the epithet " Daddie " in a stanza of *The Kirk's Alarm,* with the line, " And gif ye canna bite, ye may bark."

St. XII. l. 1. *Dalrymple.*
William Dalrymple of Ayr, younger son of James Dalrymple, sheriff-clerk of Ayr ; born at Ayr, 29th August, 1723 ; ordained to the second charge of Ayr, December, 1746 ; translated to the first charge 13th May, 1756 ; D. D., St. Andrews, 1779 ; Moderator of the General Assembly of the Kirk of Scotland, 1781 ; died 20th January, 1814, in his 91st year. Author of *Sermons,* Glasgow, 1766 ; Edinburgh, 1782 ; *Family Worship Explained,* 1787 ; *History of Christ* (in which he referred with approval to his colleague M'Gill's *Practical Essay*), Edinburgh, 1787 ; *Faith in Jesus Christ,* Air, 1790, *etc.* Dalrymple was liked and respected even by his opponents. Burns, whom he baptized, devotes a stanza of admirable eulogy to him in *The Kirk's Alarm,* p. 111. He told Ramsay of Ochtertyre that his father was " so much pleased " with Dalrymple's strain of preaching and benevolent conduct that he embraced his religious opinions, " though he practically remained a Calvinist." (*Scotland and Scotsmen in the Eighteenth Century,* ii. 554.)

St. XII. l. 3. *M'Quhae.*
William M'Quhae, son of a magistrate of Wigton, was born 1st May, 1737 ; studied at Glasgow, where he was a favourite pupil of Adam Smith ; ordained at St. Quivox, 1st March, 1764 ; D. D., St. Andrews, 1794 ; died 1st March, 1823, in his 86th year. Author of *Difficulties which attend the Practice of Religion no just Argument against it,* a Sermon, Edinburgh, 1785.

St. XII. l. 4. *Baith the Shaws.*
Andrew Shaw, son of Andrew Shaw, Professor of Divinity at St. Andrews, was born in 1730 ; ordained at Craigie, 26th September, 1765 ; D. D., St. Andrews, 1795 ; died 14th September, 1805. He was scholarly, but somewhat diffident. David Shaw, no relation of Andrew, was son of Alexander Shaw, minister of Edenkillie ; ordained at Coylton, 29th June, 1749 ; D. D., St. Andrews, 1775 ; Moderator of the General Assembly, 1775 ; died 26th April, 1810, in his 92d year.

St. XIII. l. 1. *Auld Wodrow.*
Patrick Wodrow, Minister of Tarbolton, second son of John Wodrow, the ecclesiastical historian, born 1713; ordained at Tarbolton, 18th August, 1738; D. D., St. Andrews, 1784; died 17th April, 1793, in his 81st year. Author of a *Letter* (signed John Gillies) *addressed to the Elders of the Synod of Glasgow and Air with Observations Moral and Theological*, 1784.

St. XIII. l. 4. *Ane to succeed him.*
The assistant and successor was John M'Math — referred to by name in stanza xvii. — ordained 16th May, 1782; demitted his charge — on account of convivial habits — 21st December, 1791; retired to Mull, where he died 18th December, 1825. M'Math was an acquaintance of Burns, who at M'Math's request enclosed him a copy of *Holy Willie's Prayer*, adding the Rhymed Epistle (*ante*, p. 126), to himself.

St. XIV. l. 4. *Smith.*
Rév. George Smith of Galston. See *ante*, p. 326, Notes to *The Holy Fair*.

St. XIV. l. 5. *Greyneck.*
In English slang "gray" signifies a coin (for tossing) with two heads or two tails; while "gray-coat parson" signifies a lay-impropriator of tithes. A "greyneck," then, is a person of indeterminate principles, — one who is neither black nor white, but indifferent alike "to God and to His enemies."

Page 109. St. XVI. l. 3. *Common-sense.*
See *ante*, p. 332, Notes to *The Ordination*.

Page 110. HOLY WILLIE'S PRAYER.
St. XI. l. 5. *God's ain Priest.*
William Auld, minister of Mauchline. See *ante*, p. 336, Notes to *The Twa Herds*.

St. XII. l. 6. *Kail an' potatoes.*
One of the charges against Gavin Hamilton was that he sent his servants to dig potatoes on a Sunday.

St. XIII. l. 2. *Against that Presbyt'ry of Ayr.*
Because it vindicated Hamilton against the Mauchline Session.

St. XIV. l. 1. *That glib-tongu'd Aiken.*
Robert Aiken of Ayr, who successfully defended Hamilton. See *ante*, p. 330, Notes to *The Cotter's Saturday Night*.

Page 111. THE KIRK'S ALARM.
St. II. l. 1. *Dr. Mac.*
Dr. M'Gill, of course. See the Prefatory Note.

St. III. l. 3. *To meddle wi' mischief a-brewing.*
"See the advertisement." (R. B.) The magistrates of Ayr, when a complaint was laid before the Synod against Dr. M'Gill, inserted an advertisement in the newspapers, testifying to the respect of the community towards him.

St. III. l. 4. *Provost John.*
John Ballantine. Provost of Ayr, to whom Burns dedicated *The Brigs of Ayr* (*ante*, p. 59).

St. III. l. 6. *Orator Bob.*
Robert Aiken, Writer, who defended Dr. M'Gill as well as he had already defended Gavin Hamilton. See *ante*, p. 330, Notes to *The Cotter's Saturday Night*.

St. IV. l. 1. *D'rymple mild.*

William Dalrymple of Ayr. See *ante*, p. 336, Notes to *The Twa Herds*.

St. VI. l. 1. *Rumble John.*
John Russel of Kilmarnock. See *ante*, p. 327, Notes to *The Holy Fair*.

St. VII. l. 1. *Simper James.*
James M'Kinlay of Kilmarnock, whose settlement there is celebrated in *The Ordination* (see *ante*, p. 63).

Page 112. St. VIII. l. 1. *Singet Sawnie.*
Alexander Moodie of Riccarton. See *ante*, p. 326, Notes to *The Holy Fair*.

St. IX. l. 1. *Daddie Auld.*
William Auld of Mauchline. See *ante*, p. 336, Notes to *The Twa Herds*.

St. IX. l. 3. *A tod meikle waur than the clerk.*
Gavin Hamilton, whom Auld had previously prosecuted. See *ante*, p. 109, Prefatory Note to *Holy Willie's Prayer*, and *ante*, p. 41, Prefatory Note to *A Dedication*.

St. X. l. 1. *Davie Rant.*
David Grant of Ochiltree; born in Madderty, Aberdeenshire, in 1750; for some time teacher in George Watson's Hospital, Edinburgh; ordained Presbyterian minister at Newcastle-on-Tyne, 14th November, 1781; admitted to Etterick parish, 4th May, 1786; and translated to Ochiltree, 7th November of the same year; died 16th July, 1791. As convener of the Committee on M'Gill's publications, and one of the most persistent of his prosecutors, Grant made himself especially obnoxious to M'Gill's supporters; so much so, indeed, that his sudden death created the impression that it had been brought about by them. He was the author of two single sermons (Edinburgh, 1779 and 1782), and *Sermons Doctrinal and Practical*, 2 vols. (1785).

St. XI. l. 1. *Jamie Goose.*
"James Young of Cumnock, who had lately been foiled in an ecclesiastical prosecution against a Lieutenant Mitchell." (R. B.) He was ordained at New Cumnock, 3d May, 1758, and died 1st August, 1795, in his 85th year.

St. XII. l. 1. *Poet Willie.*
"William Peebles in Newton-upon-Ayr, a poetaster who, among other things, published an ode on the centenary of the Revolution, in which was the line: 'And bound in Liberty's endearing chain.'" (R. B.) For Peebles see also *ante*, p. 327, Notes to *The Holy Fair*.

St. XIII. l. 1. *Andro' Gowk.*
Andrew Mitchell of Monkton and Prestwick, son of Hugh Mitchell of Dalgain, his mother being one of the Campbells of Fairfield; ordained at Muirkirk, 11th July, 1751; translated to Monkton in November, 1774; died 11th October, 1811, in his 87th year. He possessed the estate of Avisyard, near Cumnock, and is said to have "kept a carriage." Being rich, he had a kind of influence among the Orthodox; but he was mentally the weakest of the brethren. He was author of *Causes of Opposition to the Gospel* (Edinburgh, 1764).

St. XIV. l. 1. *Barr Steenie.*
Stephen Young of Barr, who, after acting for some time as assistant at Ochiltree, was or-

dained at Barr, 8th March, 1780, and died 21st February, 1819, in his 75th year.

St. xv. l. 1. *Irvine-side.*
George Smith of Galston. (See *ante*, p. 326, Notes to *The Holy Fair.*) The town stands on the Irvine.

St. xvi. l. 1. *Muirland Jock.*
John Shepherd of Muirkirk, son of Rev. George Shepherd of Newbattle; ordained at Hemel-Hempstead, Herts, 30th October, 1772; translated to Muirkirk, 1st September, 1775; died 14th August, 1799, in his 59th year.

St. xvii. l. 1. *Holy Will.*
" *Vide* the 'Prayer' of this Saint." (R. B.) See *ante*, p. 109, Prefatory Note to *Holy Willie's Prayer.*

Page 113. Postscript 1, l. 1. *Afton's Laird.*
John Logan of Knockshinnoch and Afton.

Postscript 1, l. 6. *Clackleith.*
Mr. Johnson of Clackleith.

Postscript 2, l. 1. *Factor John.*
Either John Kennedy, factor to the Earl of Dumfries (see *ante*, p. 128, Prefatory Note to *To John Kennedy*), or John M'Murdo (see *ante*, Prefatory Note to *To John M'Murdo*, p. 143).

Page 114. THE INVENTORY.
My lan'-a-fore, etc.
The old wooden plough was drawn by four horses: two on the left hand, named respectively the "lan'-a-fore" (the foremost on the unploughed land side) and the "lan'-a-hind" (the hindmost on the unploughed land side); and two on the right hand, named respectively the "fur-a-fore" (the foremost in the furrow) and the "fur-a-hind" (the hindmost in the furrow).

As e'er in tug or tow was traced.
See *ante*, p. 330, Notes to *The Auld Farmer's Salutation.*

A gaudsman ane, a thrasher t' other.
The gaudsman was the driver of the plough-team. When it was drawn by oxen he used a gaud (= goad). Before cornmills were in use a "thrasher" had almost constant work with the flail.

Wee Davoc.
David Hutchieson, whose father, Robert, had been ploughman at Lochlie. The father died of fever, and Burns took care of the boy, to whom he also gave all the education he ever got.

I on the Questions *tairge them tightly.*
The *Shorter Catechism* of the Westminster Divines, on which the Kirk compelled housemasters to examine their servants and children every Sunday. To "tairge" = to "target," *i. e.* to pelt or riddle with importunities. Thus Callum Beg, intent on constraining Shamus an Snachad, "as he expressed himself 'targed him tightly' till the finishing of the job."

He'll screed you aff "*Effectual Calling.*"
The answer to the question, "What is Effectual Calling?" embodies the essence of Calvinism.

My sonsie, smirking, dear-bought Bess.
His daughter Elizabeth, by Elizabeth Paton. See *ante*, p. 113, Prefatory Note to *The Poet's Welcome.*

Page 115. A MAUCHLINE WEDDING.
St. ii. l. 1. *Blacksideen.*
"A hill." (R. B.)

St. ii. l. 3. *Nell and Bess.*
"Miller's two sisters." (R. B.) Nell was the eldest, — the Miss Miller of the *Belles of Mauchline* (see *post*, p. 171).

St. iv. ll. 1, 2.
*But now the gown wi' rustling sound
Its silken pomp displays.*
"The ladies' first silk gown, got for the occasion." (R. B.)

St. v. l. 1. *Sandy.*
"Driver of the Post-chaise." (R. B.)

St. v. l. 5. *Auld John Trot.*
"Miller's father." (R. B.)

Page 116. ADAM ARMOUR'S PRAYER.
St. v. l. 2. *Auld drucken Nanse.*
See *ante*, p. 334, Notes to *The Jolly Beggars.*

St. vi. l. 1. *Jock an' hav'rel Jean.*
They were the son and daughter. Jean or Jenny is the Racer Jess of *The Holy Fair.* See *ante*, p. 10, st. ix. l. 3, and Notes, p. 326.

Page 116. NATURE'S LAW.
St. iii. l. 3. *Coila's plains.*
Coila, identical with "Coil" in st. v., is poetic for Kyle, one of the districts of Ayrshire.

Page 117. LINES ON MEETING WITH LORD DAER.
St. ii. l. 5. *O' the Quorum.*
Certain Justices, without whom the Court could not sit.

St. iii. l. 4. *An' sic a Lord! — lang Scotch ell twa.*
A Scots ell is over a yard.

St. v. l. 2. *Or Scotia's sacred Demosthénes.*
This would seem to show that Dr. Hugh Blair was of the company.

Page 118. ADDRESS TO THE TOOTHACHE.
St. iv. l. 2. *Cutty-stools.*
Cutty = short or small. Some derive the use of the word in "cutty-stools" from "cutty" or "kitty," occasionally employed to signify a loose woman, as in the delightful ballad of *Robin Red-Breast* (Herd, 1769): —

"Then Robin turned him round about,
    E'en like a little king : —
'Go, pack ye out at my chamber door,
    Ye little cutty quean.'"

It is very commonly applied to a mischievous ungrown girl; it is also a nickname for a hare; it likewise signifies the three-legged milking-stool. The present reference is, of course, to the stool of repentance. This was conspicuously placed in front of the pulpit, and the penitent, the opening prayer being done, was conducted to it by the beadle; sat on it through the service, — in the olden time clothed in sackcloth (*Scotticé,* "a harn gown"); and at the close arose from it to receive the rebuke. There were two kinds of stools, a high and a low; the high being known as the "pillar."

Page 119. LAMENT FOR THE ABSENCE OF WILLIAM CREECH, PUBLISHER.
St. i. l. 1. *Auld chuckie Reekie.*
"Auld Reekie" = Edinburgh; not because

Edinburgh is abnormally smoky, but because her smoke is visible from many heights.

St. IV. l. 1. *Gawkies, tawpies, gowks, and fools.*

"Gawkies" and "tawpies" are here the diminutives or feminines of "gowks" and "fools." "Gawkie" (cf. the song *Bess the Gawkie*) is derived from "gowk" (the cuckoo, a giddy-pated bird), which is Scots, as "cuckoo" is Shakespearian English (cf. *First Henry IV.*, II. iv.: "O' horseback, ye cuckoo") for a daft or stupid person.

St. VII. l. 1. *Worthy Greg'ry's Latin face.*

James Gregory (*b.* 1753, *d.* 1821), the famous Professor of Medicine, was a great hand at Latin quotations, and is said by Cockburn to have had "a strikingly powerful countenance." For Gregory's stringent criticism of the *Wounded Hare*, see *ante*, p. 93, Prefatory Note to that poem.

St. VII. l. 2. *Tytler's and Greenfield's modest grace.*

Not William Tytler the historian, then an old man, but his son, A. F. Tytler (*b.* 1747, *d.* 1813), afterwards Lord Woodhouselee, at this time Professor of Civil History, who wrote a *Life of Lord Kames* (1807), an *Historical and Critical Essay on the Life of Petrarch* (1810), and a sensible essay on *The Genius and Writings of Allan Ramsay* (1800). He sat on that "jury of literati" to which Burns submitted the new material for the First Edinburgh, and assisted him in revising the proofs for a later edition. William Greenfield was minister of St. Andrew's parish and Professor of Rhetoric, but in 1798, being charged with a nameless offence, he demitted his offices and left Scotland. In his *Second Common Place Book* Burns extols "his good sense, his joyous hilarity, his sweetness of manners, and modesty."

St. VII. l. 3. *M'Kenzie, Stewart, such a brace.*

Henry M'Kenzie, author of *The Man of Feeling*, who had written an appreciation of Burns's *Poems* in *The Lounger* for December, 1786, and Dugald Stewart, described in the *Second Common Place Book* as "the most perfect character I ever saw."

Page 120. ELEGY ON THE DEPARTED YEAR, 1788.

An' cry till ye be haerse an' roupet.

For "roupet" see *ante*, p. 325, Notes to *The Author's Earnest Cry and Prayer.*

An' gied ye a' baith gear an' meal.

Even yet the clergymen of the Church of Scotland are paid in kind — their stipend being reckoned in chalders.

For Embro' wells are grutten dry!

During December, 1788, there was the coldest weather in Scotland, and the Edinburgh wells were all frozen.

Nae hand-cuff'd, mizzl'd, half-shackl'd Regent.

See *ante*, p. 154, Prefatory Note to *Ode to the Departed Regency Bill.*

Page 121. ON THE DUCHESS OF GORDON'S REEL DANCING.

St. I. l. 3. *Wallopèd.*

A motion, expressive at once of rapidity and a certain awkwardness: as (*e. g.*) of a fish out of water. It is used of galloping, as in David Lindsay, *Complaynt to the King*, line 179: "And wychtilie wallope ouer the sandis;" also, and very commonly, in a slightly sarcastic sense of dancing, as in the text and in the song of *Maggie Lauder*, sometimes attributed to Francis Sempill: —

"Meg up an' wallop'd ower the green,
For brawly she could frisk it."

St. II. l. 2. *The midden dub.*

Burns in his glossary defines the midden hole as "a gutter at the bottom of the dunghill."

Page 122. ON CAPTAIN GROSE.

St. v. l. 3. *As for the Deil, he daur na steer him.*

That is, attempt to carry him off, the reference being to Grose's exceeding corpulence. (See *ante*, p. 186, *Epigram on Captain Francis Grose.*)

Page 123. NEW YEAR'S DAY, 1791.

Coila's fair Rachel's care to-day.

"This young lady was drawing a picture of Coila from *The Vision*." (Note in Currie, 1800, probably supplied by Mrs. Dunlop.)

Page 124. FROM ESOPUS TO MARIA.

I see her face the first of Ireland's sons.

This Irishman is said to have been an officer named Gillespie.

The crafty Colonel.

Colonel M'Doual of Logan — "Sculdudd'ry" (*i. e.* Bawdy) M'Doual of the Second Heron Ballad (see *ante*, p. 166, St. x. l. 5, and Prefatory Note to *Young Peggie*, *ante*, p. 201).

The hopeful youth, in Scottish senate bred, Who owns a Bushby's heart without the head.

Mr. Maitland Bushby, advocate, the "Wigton's new sheriff" of the Second Heron Ballad (p. 165, St. III. l. 1), with "the heart" but not "the head" of his father, John Bushby, "honest man." (See *Epitaph on John Bushby*, *ante*, p. 198.)

Page 124. TO JOHN RANKINE.

St. II. l. 6. *A whaup 's i' the nest.*

This is a modification of the Scottish proverb: "There's a whaup in the rape" = "There is something wrong." In Ayrshire, "whaup" was also the name of a goblin supposed to haunt the eaves of houses. But in Burns's line "whaup" is probably curlew; and the meaning seems to be, "what is wrong will soon be known."

Page 125. TO JOHN GOLDIE.

St. II. l. 3. *Black Jock.*

Russell of Kilmarnock. See *ante*, p. 327, Notes to *The Holy Fair.*

St. IV. l. 5. *Haste, gie her name up in the chapel.*

Persons at the point of death are accustomed to request the prayers of the congregation.

Page 126. TO J. LAPRAIK. THIRD EPISTLE.

St. III. l. 5. *Whatt.*

From the Scots "white" or "wheat," meaning to cut with a knife, *i. e.* "whittle."

St. v. l. 5. *Browster wives.*

The old-world ale-wife always brewed the stuff she sold.

St. VII. l. 2. *Till kye be gaun without the herd.*

The grain being all harvested, the cattle could be allowed to crop at large. In olden times there were few or no fences on farms, and cattle were watched by a boy.

St. IX. l. 6. *Yours, Rab the Ranter.*

Cf. the old song *Maggie Lauder* : —

> " For I 'm a piper to my trade,
> My name is Rab the Ranter."

Page 126. TO THE REV. JOHN M'MATH.

St. II. l. 2. *Gown an' ban' an' douse black-bonnet.*

The clergyman, who on Sundays wears a gown and band ; and the elder, who in those days wore a black bonnet. Cf. *The Holy Fair, ante,* p. 10, St. VIII. l. 3.

Page 127. St. V. l. 1. *Gau'n.*

Gavin Hamilton. (See *ante,* p. 41, Prefatory Note to the *Dedication.*)

St. VI. l. 1.

> *The poor man's friend in need,*
> *The gentleman in word an' deed.*

Cf. *Dedication (ante,* p. 42).

Page 128. TO DAVIE. SECOND EPISTLE.

St. II. *Hale be your heart, etc.*

Cf. *Epistle to Major Logan,* St. III. (p. 133).

St. IV. [This stanza] describes the writer's mental condition and mode of life under Armour's repudiation.

St. IV. l. 1. *I'm on Parnassus' brink.*

That is, about to publish. Burns was preparing the Kilmarnock edition, and had sent a few numbers for Sillar's inspection.

St. VII. l. 5. *Rough an' raploch.*

Raploch = a coarse and undyed woollen.

Page 128. TO JOHN KENNEDY, DUMFRIES HOUSE.

St. II. l. 1. *Dow.*

[John Dow, or Dove — " dow " is Scots for " dove," — was] the landlord of the Whitefoord Arms, on whom Burns wrote one of his cleverest epitaphs. (See *ante,* p. 195.)

Page 129. TO GAVIN HAMILTON, ESQ., MAUCHLINE.

Like scrapin out auld Crummie's nicks.

The rings on a cow's horns tell her age.

Ay when ye gang yoursel.

Hamilton had been prosecuted for neglect of ordinances. Nor was he partial to the *Shorter Catechism.*

In Paisley John's.

John Dow's tavern. (See *supra.* Notes to *To John Kennedy.*)

I ken he weel a snick can draw.

" A snick can draw " = " can draw a latch."

The phrase is primarily applied to a stealthy entrance into another man's mind, so as to read his thoughts and take advantage of him.

Page 130. TO DR. MACKENZIE.

To get a blaud o' Johnie's morals.

The origin of morals was one of Mackenzie's favourite topics.

An' taste a swatch o' Manson's barrels.

Manson kept the tavern where the lodge met.

Page 132. REPLY TO A TRIMMING EPISTLE RECEIVED FROM A TAILOR.

St. I. l. 6. *Daddie Auld.*

The Rev. William Auld (see *ante,* p. 336, Notes to *The Twa Herds*), by whom Burns was rebuked before the congregation.

St. II. l. 2. *Pouse.*

See *ante,* p. 334, Notes to *The Jolly Beggars.*

Page 133. St. VII. l. 5. *Mess John.*

That is, " Mass John." Used in contempt. Dating from before the Reformation, the nick-name denotes, first, the small regard of the people for the old Catholic parish priest ; and secondly, that after the Reformation the majority held in extreme derision the authority which the minister essayed to wield — especially in respect of penal discipline. Writing in the opposite interest, Ramsay, in his *Address of Thanks From the Society of Rakes,* thus dramatises the latter sentiment : —

> " Down, down wi' the repenting-stools
> That gart the younkers look like fools
> Before the congregation ; "

and again in the same brisk copy of verses : —

> " For those wha Kirk affairs engross
> Their session books may burn all;
> Since fornication's pipe's put out
> What will they have to crack about
> Or jot into their journal ? "

See further, *ante,* p. 50, *Epistle to John Rankine.*

Page 133. TO MAJOR LOGAN.

St. III. *Hale be your heart, etc.*

Cf. St. II. of the *Second Epistle to Davie (ante,* p. 128).

Page 134. St. XI. l. 3. *A dear ane.*

The reference is to Jean Armour.

St. XIII. l. 2. *Sentimental sister Susie.*

See *To Miss Logan (ante,* p. 72).

St. XIII. l. 3. *Honest Lucky.*

The Major's mother. Though common Scots for " grandmother," " Lucky " has often an evil sense (as in the ill spring named by Willie Ste'enson in that story of his gudesire, which of itself would make *Redgauntlet* immortal, *Weel Hoddled, Luckie*). Derived from " luck," or " fortune," it was probably first used to designate a spae-wife (= a fortune-teller). Bawds and alewives were commonly called " Lucky," as in Ramsay's *Lucky Spence's Last Advice* and his *Elegy on Lucky Wood.*

Page 135. TO THE GUIDWIFE OF WAUCHOPE HOUSE.

St. V. l. 4. *The marl'd plaid.*

The " Guidwife " had offered to send Burns a party-coloured plaid.

Page 143. TO JAMES TENNANT OF GLEN-CONNER.

Perusing Bunyan, Brown, an' Boston.

[" Bunyan " needs no explanation. The other references are to] Brown's *Self-Interpreting Bible* and Boston's *Fourfold State,* long favourites with the pious Scottish peasant.

My heart-warm love to guid auld Glen.

The father, John Tennant, who was witness to the poet's baptism in 1759, and under whose advice he made an offer for Ellisland. The other references are to members or relations of the family.

Page 144. EPISTLE TO DR. BLACKLOCK.

St. II. l. 1. *The Heron.*

Robert Heron, son of a weaver; born at New Galloway, 6th November, 1764. When he visited Burns in 1789, he was a student of divinity. He was next assistant to Dr. Hugh Blair, but soon took to literary pursuits; got into debt, and while in Perth gaol began a *History of Scotland;* was liberated on engaging to' pay his creditors fifteen shillings in the pound from the proceeds thereof; was the author of many works, including a *Life of Burns,* 1797, by no means without merit; was in 1806 confined by his creditors in Newgate; took fever there; and died on his removal to St. Pancras Hospital, 13th April, 1807.

St. VI. l. 2. *Brose.*

Brose is properly meal and warm water, but the word is commonly used as a synonym for porridge.

Page 145. St. X. l. 2. *Honest Lucky.*

See *ante,* p. 340, Notes to *Epistle to Major Logan.*

Page 145. TO A GENTLEMAN WHO HAD SENT A NEWSPAPER.

That vile doup-skelper, Emperor Joseph.

A notorious whoremaster: died 20th February, 1790.

Or if the Swede, before he halt.

Gustavus III. of Sweden was then at war with Russia.

Page 146. TO WILLIAM STEWART.

In honest Bacon's ingle-neuk.

"Honest Bacon" (see *At Brownhill Inn, ante,* p. 187) was landlord of the inn at Brownhill, and a relative of Stewart, who was factor at Closeburn hard by (see *Lovely Polly Stewart, ante,* p. 259, and *You're Welcome, Willie Stewart, ante,* p. 311).

Page 148. TO COLONEL DE PEYSTER.

St. IV. l. 1. *Carmagnole.*

A violent Jacobin. Derived from the collarless jacket, not from the revolutionary song and dance.

Page 149. PROLOGUE SPOKEN BY MR. WOODS.

Philosophy.

The reference is to Dugald Stewart. See *ante,* p. 328, Notes to *The Vision.*

Here History.

Hume and Robertson.

Here Douglas *forms wild Shakespeare into plan.*

Home's *Douglas.* The ridiculous verse — one hopes the Bard knew better — reads like a variant on the Edinburgh pittite's "Whaur's your Wully Shakespeare noo?"

And Harley rouses all the God in man.

See Mackenzie's *Man of Feeling.*

Page 150. SCOTS PROLOGUE FOR MRS. SUTHERLAND.

Will bauldly try to gie us plays at hame.

Burns, at this time, had himself some thoughts of turning playwright. To Lady Elizabeth

Cunningham (probably) he wrote, 23d December, 1789, that for this purpose he had resolved to make himself "master of all the Dramatic Authors of any repute in both English and French;" and on 2d March, 1790, he ordered of Peter Hill copies of certain English playwrights, of Molière, and of "any other good French dramatic authors in their native language."

Page 151. *As able — and as cruel — as the Devil.*

Burns was a strong partisan of Mary Stuart, and a rabid anti-Elizabethan, as witnesses a passage (omitted, of course, by Currie) in a letter to Mrs. Dunlop, 20th February, 1791: "What a rocky-hearted, perfidious succubus was that Queen Elizabeth," etc.

Page 152. THE RIGHTS OF WOMAN.

Would swagger, swear, get drunk, kick up a riot.

According to Currie, the reference is to the Saturnalia of the Caledonian Hunt.

Page 156. A NEW PSALM FOR THE CHAPEL OF KILMARNOCK.

St. IV. l. 3. *That Young Man.*

William Pitt.

St. V. l. 3. *The Judge.*

Lord Thurlow. Cf. *Ode to the Departed Regency Bill, ante,* p. 155:

"By dread Thurlow's powers to awe —
Rhetoric, blasphemy, and law."

St. IX. l. 4. *That man M'Gill.*

Dr. M'Gill of Ayr. See *ante,* p. 110, Prefatory Note to *The Kirk's Alarm.*

Page 159. THE FÊTE CHAMPÊTRE.

St. I. l. 7. *Him wha led.*

James Boswell, the biographer of Samuel Johnson.

St. I. l. 8. *The meikle Ursa Major.*

Samuel Johnson.

St. II. l. 4. *Glencaird.*

Sir John Whitefoord of Cloncaird.

Page 160. St. VII. l. 2. *Ether-stane.*

Adder-stone. The adder-stone was used by the Druids as an amulet.

Page 160. THE FIVE CARLINS.

St. III. l. 1. *Maggie by the banks o' Nith.*

Dumfries.

St. III. l. 3. *And Marjorie o' the Monie Lochs.*

Lochmaben, situate in the midst of six small lochs.

St. IV. l. 1. *And Blinkin Bess of Annandale.*

Annan.

St. V. l. 1. *And Black Joan, frae Crichton Peel.*

"Sanquhar, near which is the old castle of the Crichtons." (R. B.)

Page 161. ELECTION BALLAD FOR WESTERHA'.

Cho. l. 1. *Up and waur them a'.*

In a note to *Up and Waur Them A', Willie* (interleaved copy of Johnson's *Museum*), Burns says: "The proper expression is 'Up and warn a', Willie,' alluding to the Crantara or warning of a Highland clan to arms. Notwithstanding this, the Lowlanders in the west and south say 'Up and *waur* them a', Willie.'" "Waur" is Scots for "worst."

Page 162. St. IV. l. 1. *Whistlebirk.*
Alexander Birtwhistle, Provost of Kirkcud-
bright.
Page 163. ELECTION BALLAD ADDRESSED
TO ROBERT GRAHAM OF FINTRY.
St. VI. l. 1. *Drumlanrig's haughty Grace.*
Drumlanrig was the residence of the Duke of
Queensberry. See *ante*, pp. 161 and 162, Prefa-
tory Notes to *Election Ballad for Westerha'*,
and *As I cam doon the Banks o' Nith.*
St. IX. l. 5. *Westerha' and Hopeton.*
Sir James Johnstone, the Tory candidate, and
the Earl of Hopetoun, his principal supporter.
St. XI. l. 1. *Mons-Meg.*
The old historic cannon which still stands on
the ramparts of Edinburgh Castle.
St. XII. l. 1. *M'Murdo and his lovely spouse.*
See *ante*, p. 143, Prefatory Note to *To John
M'Murdo.*
St. XIII. l. 1. *Craigdarroch.*
Fergusson of Craigdarroch, the hero of the
Whistle (see *ante*, p. 99).
St. XIII. l. 4. *Glenriddell.*
Captain Robert Riddell of Glenriddell (see
ante, p. 142, Prefatory Note to *Impromptu to
Captain Riddell*).
St. XIV. l. 2. *Redoubted Staig.*
Burns's friend, Provost Staig of Dumfries.
St. XIV. l. 4. *Welsh.*
Then Sheriff of the County.
St. XV. l. 1. *Miller.*
Patrick Miller of Dalswinton, Burns's land-
lord and the father of the Whig candidate,
Captain Miller.
St. XV. l. 4. *Maxwelton.*
Sir Robert Lawrie or Lowrie of Maxwelton,
of whom Craigdarroch won the whistle (see
ante, p. 100, Prefatory Note to *The Whistle*).
St. XV. l. 5. *Lawson.*
"The famous wine merchant." (R. B.)
Page 164. St. XIX. l. 6. *The Buchan Bullers.*
Caves on the Buchan littoral.
St. XX. l. 4. *The muffled murtherer of Charles.*
"Charles 1st was executed by a man in a
mask." (R. B.)
St. XXI. l. 2. *Bold Scrimgeour follows gallant
Graham.*
Burns gives "Dundee" for "Bold Scrim-
geour;" "Gallant Graham" he explains as
"Montrose." Apparently he supposed that
Claverhouse was a Scrimgeour.
St. XXIV. l. 6. *Stewart.*
"Stewart of Hillside." (R. B.)
Page 165. SECOND HERON ELECTION BAL-
LAD.
St. I. ll. 5, 6. *Murray commander, An' Gordon.*
Murray of Broughton was uncle of Gordon,
the Tory candidate. Murray had left his wife
and eloped with another lady (see *post*, p. 343,
Notes to *John Bushby's Lamentation*). There-
fore ll. 6–8 in one set run: —

"And Gordon *that keenly will start;
Why shameless her lane is the lassie?
E'en let her kind kin tak a part;*"

and for the same reason in l. 8 "kin" of the
text in another set reads "*sin.*"

St. II. l. 1. *And there'll be black-nebbit Johnie.*
John Bushby, see *ante*, p. 198, Prefatory Note
to *Epitaph on John Bushby.*
St. II. l. 5. *Kempleton's birkie.*
William Bushby, John's brother, who had
made a fortune in the East Indies.
St. III. l. 1. *An' there'll be Wigton's new
sheriff.*
Mr. Maitland Bushby, son of John Bushby.
See *ante*, p. 339, Notes to *From Esopus to Maria.*
St. III. l. 5. *Cardoness, Esquire.*
David Maxwell of Cardoness. See *ante*, p.
197, Prefatory Note to *Epitaph on a Galloway
Laird.*
St. IV. l. 1. *Douglasses doughty.*
Sir William and Mr. James Douglas. The
former got the name of Carlinwark changed to
Castle Douglas by royal warrant.
St. IV. l. 5. *Kenmure sae generous.*
John Gordon of Kenmure.
St. V. l. 1. *Redcastle.*
Walter Sloan Lawrie of Redcastle.
St. V. l. 5. *Our King's Lord Lieutenant.*
Lord Garlies, who was called to answer for
keeping the writ.
Page 166. St. VI. l. 2. *Muirhead.*
Minister of Urr, author of an epigram on
Burns, *To Vacerras.*
St. VI. l. 3. *Buittle's Apostle.*
Maxwell of Buittle.
St. VI. l. 5. *Folk frae St. Mary's.*
The Earl of Selkirk's family.
St. VII. l. 1. *Wealthy young Richard.*
Richard Oswald of Auchencruive, who inher-
ited Mrs. Oswald's fortune. See *ante*, p. 81,
Prefatory Note to *Ode, Sacred to the Memory of
Mrs. Oswald.*
St. VII. l. 5. *Rich brither nabobs.*
D. and J. Anderson of St. Germains.
St. VII. l. 7. *Collieston.*
Mr. Copeland of Collieston.
St. VII. l. 8. *Quinton.*
The son of Mr. M'Adam of Craigen-gillan.
See *ante*, p. 129, *To Mr. M'Adam of Craigen-
gillan.*
St. VIII. l. 1. *Stamp-Office Johnie.*
Mr. John Syme, Writer, Dumfries, an especial
friend of Burns. See *ante*, p. 191, Prefatory
Note to *To John Syme.*
St. VIII. l. 3. *Gay Cassencarry.*
Colonel M'Kenzie of Cassencarry.
St. VIII. l. 4. *Colonel Tam.*
In some sets "gleg" is inserted before "Colo-
nel Tam." He was Colonel Heron, according
to the Museum copy; but Colonel Goldie of
Goldielea is given elsewhere.
St. VIII. l. 5. *Trusty Kerroughtree.*
Mr. Heron of Kerroughtrie, the Whig candi-
date.
St. IX. l. 1. *The auld Major.*
He was brother of the Whig candidate.
St. IX. l. 5. *Maiden Kilkerran.*
Sir Adam Fergusson of Kilkerran. See *ante*,
p. 325, Notes to *The Author's Earnest Cry and
Prayer.*
St. IX. l. 6. *Barskimming's quid Knight.*
Sir William Miller of Barskimming, son of

Sir Thomas Miller, Lord Barskimming. See *ante*, p. 328, Notes to *The Vision*.

St. ix. l. 7. *Roaring Birtwhistle*.

Alexander Birtwhistle, Provost of Kircudbright.

St. x. l. 3. *Teuch Johnie*.

John Maxwell of Terraughtie. See *ante*, p. 146, Prefatory Note to *To John Maxwell, Esq.*

St. x. l. 5. *Logan's M'Doual*.

Colonel M'Doual of Logan. See *ante*, p. 201, Prefatory Note to *Young Peggy*.

St. x. l. 8. *Sogering, gunpowther Blair*.

Major Blair of Dunskey.

Page 166. JOHN BUSHBY'S LAMENTATION.

St. iii. l. 1. *Yerl Galloway*.

See *ante*, p. 189, Prefatory Note to *Epigrams against the Earl of Galloway*.

St. vii. l. 2. *Wi' wingèd spurs*.

The reference is to Murray's elopement, a winged spur being the crest of the house of Johnstone, to which the lady — " the auld grey yaud," as Burns genteelly describes her — belonged.

Page 170. THE RONALDS OF THE BENNALS.

St. xiii. l. 2. *Twal' hundred*.

Linen woven in a reed of twelve hundred divisions.

Page 172. THE FAREWELL.

St. i. l. 7. *My Bess*.

The poet's child by Elizabeth Paton, born in November, 1784. See *ante*, p. 113, Prefatory Note to *A Poet's Welcome*.

St. i. l. 12. *My Smith*.

See *ante*, p. 15, Prefatory Note to *Epistle to James Smith*.

St. ii. l. 7. *Thee, Hamilton, and Aiken dear*.

For Gavin Hamilton see *ante*, p. 41, Prefatory Note to *A Dedication;* for Aiken see *ante*, p. 330, Notes to *The Cotter's Saturday Night*.

Page 173. ELEGY ON THE DEATH OF SIR JAMES HUNTER BLAIR.

St. ii. l. 2. *Once the lov'd haunts of Scotia's royal train*.

" The King's Park, at Holyrood House." (R. B.)

St. iii. l. 3. *Where limpid streams, once hallow'd, well*.

" Saint Anthony's Well." (R. B.)

St. ii. l. 4. *Mould'ring ruins mark the sacred Fane*.

" St. Anthony's Chapel." (R. B.) The well and ruins are situated on the heights a little to the southeast of Holyrood House.

Page 182. SKETCH FOR AN ELEGY.

St. i. l. 1. *Craigdarroch*.

Alexander Fergusson of Craigdarroch, the hero of *The Whistle* (*ante*, p. 99).

St. ii. l. 1. *Black James*.

Possibly James Boswell.

St. iii. l. 1. *Philosophic Smellie*.

William Smellie. See *ante*, p. 181, Prefatory Note to *On William Smellie*.

Page 183. PASSION'S CRY.

"*I burn, I burn, as when thro' ripened corn By driving winds the crackling flames are borne*."

Quoted from Pope's *Sappho*.

Page 183. IN VAIN WOULD PRUDENCE.

"*Wrong'd, injur'd, shunn'd, unpitied, unredrest, The mock'd quotation of the scorner's jest*."

[These lines, slightly modified, appear in the preceding poem, *Passion's Cry* (*ante* p. 183).]

Page 193. ON MARRIAGE.

The best of things.

The nickname " the Best," or " the Best in Christendom," is classic slang. Cf. Dorset, Song, *Methinks the Poor Town:* " I know what I mean when I drink to the Best ; " and Rochester, *The Rehearsal* (*Works*, 1718, i. 131): " Mine Host drinks to the Best in Christendom, And decently my Lady quits the Room."

Page 194. ON JOHN RANKINE.

By Adamhill.

Rankine's farm. In Scotland it is still the custom among farmers to call each other by their territorial names.

Page 197. MONODY ON A LADY FAMED FOR HER CAPRICE.

St. v. l. 2. *Her idiot lyre*.

" The lady affects to be a poetess." (R. B.) He had carefully fostered the illusion.

Page 201. BONIE DUNDEE.

St. i. l. 1. *Hauver-meal bannock*.

A synonym (common in the North of England and some parts of Scotland) for the oaten cake, the staple bread of old Scotland.

Page 202. TO THE WEAVER'S GIN YE GO.

St. ii. l. 2. *To warp a plaiden wab*.

To form threads into a warp for a web of coarse woollen.

Page 203. I'M O'ER YOUNG TO MARRY YET.

St. i. l. 4. *Eerie*.

Apprehensive of ghosts, but the word is used here in a humorous sense. Perhaps the nearest English equivalent is " creepy."

Page 204. MY HIGHLAND LASSIE, O.

[It seemed inexpedient to lengthen the Prefatory note by a discussion of the relation held by Burns to Mary Campbell, but inasmuch as the subject is one much contested by commentators of Burns, the statement of the editors is reproduced here.] On the strength of sporadic allusions by Burns — meant, as it seems, to dissemble more than they reveal — and especially of certain ecstatic expressions in the song, *Thou Ling'ring Star* (*ante*, p. 226), and in a letter to Mrs. Dunlop — penned when the writer was " groaning under the miseries of a diseased nervous system " — Mary Campbell has come to be regarded less as an average Scots peasant, to whom a merry-begot was then, if not a necessary of life, at all events the commonest effect of luck, than as a sort of bare-legged Beatrice — a Spiritualised Ideal of Peasant Womanhood. Seriously examined, her cult — for cult it is — is found an absurdity ; but persons of repute have taken the craze, so that it is useful to remark that the Mary Campbell of tradition is a figment of the General Brain, for whose essential features not so much as the faintest outline is to be found in the confusion of amorous plaints and cries of repentance or remorse, which is all that we have to enlighten us from Burns. Further, it is forgotten that Mary Campbell's death revealed her to her Poet in a new and hallowed aspect. Whatever the date — whether 1786 or an earlier year: whether, that is to say, she preceded Armour in Burns's regard, or consoled him episodically after Armour's repudiation of him — assigned to the famous farewell on the banks of Ayr, the underhandedness of the engagement, with the extreme discretion of, not merely his references to it, but the references of his relatives and hers, leaves room for much conjecture. Here Burns, for once in his life, was reticent. Yet, what reason had he for reticence if, as is hotly contended by the more ardent among the Mariolaters, the affair belonged to 1784, or earlier? And why, in 1784, when he had no particular reputation, good or bad, should Mary's kinsfolk (or Mary herself) have conceived so arrant a grudge against him that it impelled them (or her) to obliterate the famous Inscription in his Bible, with its solemn scriptural oaths — which were unusual under the circumstances, and which, as being recorded for the girl's comfort, tend to show that those circumstances were peculiar — and to destroy his every scrap of writing to her? It were less difficult to explain the position if the amour belonged to 1786; for then the Armour business was notorious. But then, too, Burns's constancy in crying out for Jean must of necessity impeach the worth of his professions to Mary. In any case, it is a remarkable circumstance that the latter heroine left her situation with the vaguest possible outlook on marriage; for, though Burns does say that she went to make arrangements for their union, there is no scrap of proof that immediate espousals were designed. Indeed, no progress at all appears to have been made in such arrangements in all the five months preceding her death; and assuredly Burns did not intend to take her with him to Jamaica in 1786. Finally, there is the guarded, the official, statement of Currie that "the banks of Ayr formed the scene of youthful passions," the "history of which it would be *improper to reveal* were it even in one's power, and the traces of which will soon be discoverable only in those strains of nature and sensibility to which they gave birth." On the whole, it is a very pretty tangle; but the one thing in it worth acknowledgment and perfectly plain is that the Highland Mary of the Mariolater is but a "devout imagination."

Page 208. DUNCAN DAVISON.
St. I. l. 8. *Temper-pin.*
The pin which regulated the motion of the spinning-wheel. Cf. Allan Ramsay's vamp, *My Jo Janet:* —
"To keep the temper-pin in tiff
Employs right aft my hand, Sir."

Page 208. LADY ONLIE, HONEST LUCKY.
Cho. l. 1. *Honest Lucky.*
"Lucky" is a common designation for alewives. See further, *ante*, p. 340, Notes to *To Major Logan.*

Page 209. DUNCAN GRAY.
[For another set of *Duncan Gray* stanzas, see *ante*, p. 272. Both are] founded on a song preserved in the Herd MS.

Page 211. BLYTHE WAS SHE.
Cho. l. 2. *Butt and ben.*
See *ante*, p. 327, Notes to *The Holy Fair.*
Page 220. THE SILVER TASSIE.
St. I. l. 7. *The Berwick-Law.*
North Berwick Law, a conspicuous height in Haddingtonshire overlooking the Firth of Forth.
Page 222. O, WERE I ON PARNASSUS HILL.
St. I. l. 2. *Helicon.*
See *ante*, p. 336, Notes to *The Jolly Beggars.*
St. I. l. 7. *Cornsincon.*
Corsancone, a hill in New Cumnock parish, Ayrshire (visible from Ellisland), where the Bard (not quite correctly) placed the sources of the Nith.
Page 225. THE BRAES O' BALLOCHMYLE.
St. I. l. 1. *The Catrine woods.*
Catrine was the residence of Professor Dugald Stewart. (See *ante*, p. 328, Notes to *The Vision.*)
St. I. l. 5. *Maria.*
Mary Anne Whitefoord, the eldest daughter, who married Henry Kerr Cranstoun, grandson of William, fifth Lord Cranstoun.
Page 226. THE RANTIN DOG, THE DADDIE O' T.
St. II. l. 2. *The groanin maut.*
The ale for the midwife and her gossips. For the epithet, "groaning" is good English for a lying-in. Cf. *Hamlet*, iii. 2: "It would cost you a groaning to take my edge off."
St. III. l. 1. *The creepie-chair.*
The stool of repentance. See *ante*, p. 338, Notes to *Address to the Toothache.*
St. IV. l. 2. *Fidgin fain.*
Tingling with fondness. Cf. *Tam o' Shanter*, *ante*, p. 92:
"Even Satan glowr'd, and fidg'd fu' fain:" —
and the old song *Maggie Lauder:* —
"'Maggie,' quoth he, 'and by my bags
I'm fidgin fain to see thee.'"
Page 228. YOUNG JOCKIE WAS THE BLYTHEST LAD.
St. I. l. 3. *Gaud.*
The plough-oxen were driven with a goad.
Page 230. KILLIECRANKIE.
St. III. l. 1. *The bauld Pitcur.*
Haliburton of Pitcur, slain at Killiecrankie. A Jacobite song in the Pitcairn MS., entitled *Answer to Killiecrankie*, has this stanza: —
"My Lord Dundee the best o' ye
Into the fields did fa' then;
And great Pitcur fell in a furr
Wha could not win awa' then."
Page 230. THE BANKS OF NITH.
St. I. l. 4. *Where Cummins ance had high command.*
"My landlord Millar is building a house on the banks of the Nith, just on the ruins of the Comyn's Castle." (R. B.)
Page 231. TAM GLEN.
St. VII. *The last Halloween*, etc.
See *ante*, pp. 329, 330, Notes to *Halloween.*
Page 233. GUIDWIFE, COUNT THE LAWIN.
St. III. *My coggie is a haly pool*, etc.

[This stanza] was inscribed by Burns on a window-pane of the Globe Tavern, Dumfries (see *ante*, p. 188).

Page 238. I HAE A WIFE O' MY AIN.

St. IV. ll. 3, 4.

> *Naebody cares for me,*
> *I care for naebody.*

Cf. *The Jolly Miller*. He lived on the river Dee, and this was the burden of his song: —

> "I care for nobody, no, not I,
> And nobody cares for me."

Page 239. O, FOR ANE-AND-TWENTY, TAM.

St. II. l. 1. *A gleib o' lan'*.

The common meaning of gleib (*i. e.* glebe) in Scotland is church land — that is the land possessed by the parish minister. Here it probably means a portion of land about the average size of a kirk glebe — 30 acres or thereby.

Page 244. WILLIE WASTLE.

St. III. l. 1. *Hem-shin'd*.

Sometimes wrongly printed "Hen-shin'd," and more often "Hein-shin'd." The reference is to the "Haims" or "Hems" of a horse's collar, which bend outwards.

St. IV. l. 5. *Midden-creels*.

Manure-baskets slung across horses like panniers.

Page 248. HEY, CA' THRO'.

St. I. l. 1. *Upwi'*.

The phrase resembles the German *Hoch*.

Page 248. O, CAN YE LABOUR LEA.

Cho. l. 1. *O, can ye labour lea*.

"Labour lea" = plough pasture-land; but the phrase is used in an equivocal sense.

Page 249. St. III. l. 3. *Makin of*.

Probably not to be understood in the literal English sense, but as "fondling" or "petting."

Page 249. THE DEUK 'S DANG O'ER MY DADDIE.

St. II. l. 5. *Butter'd my brose*.

Cf. the song *For A' That* in *The Merry Muses*: "Put butter in my Donald's brose." Also, in the same collection the old song, *Brose and Butter*: —

> "O, gie my love brose, lasses,
> Gie my love brose and butter," *etc.*

St. II. l. 7. *But downa-do 's come o'er me now*.

This line is found in *She's Hoved Me Out of Lauderdale*, a song preserved in *The Merry Muses*.

Page 249. THE DEIL 'S AWA WI' TH' EXCISEMAN.

St. I. l. 3. *Mahoun*.

That is, Mahomet, an old name for the Devil. Cf. *Dunbar's Dance of the Seven Deadly Sins*:

> "Then cried Mahoun for a Hieland Padyane."

The scene of the song is a Highland village or clachan. Hence the reference to "hornpipes and strathspeys."

Page 251. AULD LANG SYNE.

Cho. l. 3. *A cup*.

Some sing "*kiss*" in place of "cup." (Note in Johnson, probably by R. B.)

Page 252. St. V. l. 3. *Guid-willie waught*.

There has been some unnecessary discussion as to the meaning of this phrase. It is of course analogous to that of "cup of kindness" in the Chorus.

Page 252. HAD I THE WYTE?

St. IV. l. 8. *Wanton Willie*.

Hamilton of Gilbertfield sometimes so signed himself; but there is a certain "Wanton Willie" referred to in the *Poems* of Alexander Tait (1790). As Tait made both Burns and Sillar subjects of his satire, it may be that Burns here refers to the same "Willie," whoever he may have been.

Page 253. CHARLIE HE 'S MY DARLING.

St. III. l. 2. *Tirl'd at the pin*.

Sounded the "rasping-pin," which was a notched rod of iron, with a ring attached.

Page 254. THE LASS O' ECCLEFECHAN.

St. I. l. 4. *Quarter basin*.

For holding meal. Cf. the song, *Woo'd and Married and A'*: "Ye 'll hae little to put in the bassie."

St. I. l. 6. *A heich house and a laich ane*.

A house with a porch, or it may be pantry, attached. Cf. the old song: —

> "He keepit ay a gude kale-yaird,
> A ha' house and a pantry."

St. II. l. 1. *Lucky*.

See *ante*, p. 340, Notes to *To Major Logan*.

Page 255. THE CARDIN O'T.

St. I. l. 1. *Haslock woo*.

Fine wool from the neck of the sheep.

St. II. l. 1. *Lyart gray*.

Here "hoary gray." Cf. Henryson's *Ressouning Betwen Age and Youth*, l. II, "Lyart lokkis hoir," and Sir Richard Maitland's *Folye of an Auld Man*, "Quhan that his hair is turnit lyart gray." "Lyart," though, like the Old English "lyard" (Latin *liardus*, Ital. *leardo*, Old Fr. *liart*), it originally was equivalent to "gray," and was also, like the English "lyard," used as a general nickname for a gray horse, gradually came, as in the preceding examples, to signify the peculiar discoloration caused by age and decay. Thus also in the ballad of *Jamie Telfer*: —

> "The Dinlay snaw was ne'er mair white
> Nor the lyart lockes of Harden's hair:"

and in Dunbar's *Petition*: "In lyart changed is his hue," the meaning really is that the "gray horse" (whose "mane is turned into quhyt") is no longer "gray." The most striking example of this use is probably that in the first line of *The Jolly Beggars* (*ante*, p. 102), "Lyart leaves," where "lyart" clearly means "old," "faded," or "withered." Cf. too, "Lyart Time," in Fergusson's *Ode to the Bee*.

Page 257. THE REEL O' STUMPIE.

St. II. l. 2. *Made mantie*.

"Manty" (from Fr. *manteau*) is Scots for a gown, and "Mantymaker" Scots for dressmaker. This seems to be the meaning here, unless the word be related to "mantic" (= prophetic), and the meaning be that she told fortunes.

Page 257. I'll ay ca' in by Yon Town.
"Town" in Scots is commonly applied to a set of farm-buildings.

Page 257. O, wat ye wha's in Yon Town.
See *supra*, Note to preceding song, *I'll ay ca' in by Yon Town*.

Page 263. Thou Gloomy December.
St. ii. l. 1. *Fond lovers' parting is sweet, painful pleasure.*
Cf. Shakespeare's *Romeo and Juliet*, Act ii. Scene 3: —
"Good night! Good night! parting is such sweet sorrow."

Page 266. Does Haughty Gaul Invasion Threat?
St. i. l. 5. *Corsincon.*
"A high hill at the source of the Nith." (R. B. in *Courant*, etc.) See *ante*, p. 344, Notes to *O, were I on Parnassus Hill.*
St. i. l. 6. *Criffel.*
"A mountain at the confluence of the Nith with the Solway Firth." (R. B. in *Courant*, etc.)

Page 268. Meg o' the Mill.
St. iv. l. 1. *O, ken ye how Meg o' the Mill was bedded?*
Among the Scots lower classes the newly married pair were bedded in presence of the company.

Page 272. When Wild War's Deadly Blast.
St. ii. l. 5. *Coil.*
A stream in the Kyle district of Ayrshire.

Page 272. Duncan Gray.
[For another set of *Duncan Gray* stanzas see *ante*, p. 209.] Both are founded on a song preserved in the Herd MS.

Page 273. St. ii. l. 3. *Ailsa craig.*
A rocky islet in the Firth of Clyde, opposite Ayr, much frequented by sea-fowl, whose screaming it has endured for ages without remonstrance.

Page 278. By Allan Stream.
St. i. l. 2. *Benledi.*
"A mountain to the north of Stirling." (R. B. in Lochryan MS.) "A mountain in Strathallan, 3009 feet." (R. B. in Thomson MS.) His geography is faulty; Strathallan is to the north of Stirling (the Allan flows by Dunblane and Bridge of Allan into the Forth) but Ben Ledi is about 20 miles west-north-west.

Page 279. Contented wi' Little.
St. i. l. 4. *Cog.*
See *ante*, p. 325, Notes to *Scotch Drink.*

Page 282. Last May a Braw Wooer.
St. iv. l. 3. *Gate-Slack.*
"'Gate-Slack,' the word you object to in my last ballad, is positively the name of a particular place, a kind of passage up among the Lowther hills, on the confines of this county [Dumfries]. . . . However, let the line run, 'He up the lang loan.'" (R. B. to Thomson.)
St. v. l. 2. *Dalgarnock.*
"Also the name of a romantic spot near the Nith, where are still a ruined church and a burial place." (R. B.)

Page 286. Scots wha hae.

St. vi.
"I have borrowed the last Stanza from the common stall edition of *Wallace:* —

'A false usurper sinks in every foe,
And liberty returns with every blow:'

a couplet worthy of Homer." (R. B. to Thomson.)

Page 291. Yon Rosy Brier.
St. iv. l. 2. *Chloris.*
See *ante*, p. 289, Prefatory Note to *Lassie wi' the Lint-white Locks.*

Page 292. Forlorn, my Love.
St. iv. l. 4. *Chloris.*
See *ante*, p. 289, Prefatory Note to *Lassie wi' the Lint-white Locks.*

Page 292. Ca' the Yowes to the Knowes.
St. i. l. 3. *A-faulding.*
To gather the sheep into the fold. Cf. the song, *My Peggy is a Young Thing*, in Ramsay's *Gentle Shepherd.*

Page 294. Is there for Honest Poverty.
St. iv. l. 4. *Fa' that.*
This phrase has puzzled the Editors. Here they usually translate it "attempt." But the common meaning is "have" (*i. e.* "possess"), or, better still, "claim," or "lay claim to," as in the following examples: "We Norlands mauna fa' To eat sae nice and gang sae braw" (Beattie); "The Whigs think a' that weal is won, But faith they mauna fa' that." (*Collection of Loyal Songs, ut sup.*) "He that some ells of this may fa'" (Fergusson); "Or wha in a' the country round, The best deserves to fa' that" (Burns). This, too, is the sense in the archetypal song: "Put butter in my Donald's brose, For weel does Donald fa' that:" as in the present derivative, where "Gude faith, he mauna fa' that" plainly means that the power of making an honest man, as a belted knight is made, is one no king can be allowed to claim.

Page 294. Mark Yonder Pomp.
St. iii. l. 1. *Chloris.*
See *ante*, p. 289, Prefatory Note to *Lassie wi' the Lint-white Locks.*

Page 297. There was a Lass.
St. v. l. 1. *Tryste.*
[The word] may here refer to the appointed meeting-place of lovers. (Cf. *Mary Morison*, st. i. l. 2. *ante*, p. 299, "the trysted hour.") It is also a common word for a cattle fair.

Page 302. The Lass of Cessnock Banks.
St. xiv.
See *ante*, p. 235, *It is na, Jean, thy Bonie Face.*

Page 304. The Mauchline Lady.
St. i. l. 1. *Stewart Kyle.*
The northern half of the Kyle district of Ayrshire. Burns removed from Mount Oliphant (in King's Kyle) to Lochlie (in Kyle Stewart) in 1777; and in March, 1784, he changed to Mossgiel (also in Kyle Stewart).

Page 304. There was a Lad.
St. i. l. 1. *Kyle.*
An ancient division of Ayrshire.
St. ii. l. 2. *Was five and twenty days begun.*
"Jan. 25th, 1759, the date of my Bardship's vital existence." (R. B.)

St. II. l. 4. *Hansel.*

The first gift. In Scotland, "Hansel Monday" is the first Monday of the New Year, when children are accustomed to go in bands to beg "hansel," which may be given either in bread or money.

Page 307. THE BONIE LASS OF ALBANIE.

St. III. l. 3. *A town of fame.*

Rothesay, in the Isle of Bute. The eldest sons of the Scottish Kings were Dukes of Rothesay.

Page 308. AMANG THE TREES.

St. I. l. 3. *Drone.*

The part of the bagpipe which produces the low bass note.

St. II. l. 1. *Capon craws.*

Castrate (*i. e.* squeaky) crowings.

St. II. l. 5. *A royal ghaist.*

James I. of Scotland, a great patron of musicians and artists.

Page 310. CALEDONIA.

St. IV. l. 1. *Cameleon-Savage.*

The Pict, who dyed and stained and variegated his person with woad.

Page 311. St. V. l. 8. *As Largs well can witness, and Loncartie tell.*

Haco the Norseman was defeated at Largs, according to the chroniclers, 2d October, 1263; and Kenneth III. of Scotland overthrew the Danes at Luncarty, Perthshire, in 970.

Page 311. YOU 'RE WELCOME, WILLIE STEWART.

St. I. l. 3. *The tappet hen.*

A bottle shaped like a hen, and holding three quarts of claret. Cf. Allan Ramsay's *An Ode to the Ph——* :—

> "That mutchkin stoup it hads but dribs,
> Then let 's get in the tappit hen : " —

and the old song, *Andrew Wi' His Cutty Gun:*

> "For weel she lo'ed a Hawick gill,
> And leugh to see a tappit hen."

Page 312. HERE 'S A HEALTH TO THEM THAT 'S AWA.

St. I. l. 5. *It 's guid to be merry and wise.*

Cf. the black-letter ballad (Roxburghe Collection), *The Good Fellow's Advice*, with the following refrain :—

> "Good fellows, great and small,
> Pray let me you advise
> To have a care withal :
> 'T is good to be merry and wise."

This counsel also forms the refrains of other black-letter ballads, as *The Father's Wholesome Admonition* (Crawford, Pepys, and Roxburghe Collections); and a late derivative, *Be Merry and Wise*, included in a chap, of which we have seen a copy with the date 1794 : —

> "To be merry and wise is a proverb of old,
> But a maxim so good can't too often be told.
> Then attend to my song, nor my maxims despise,
> For I mean to be merry, but merry and wise."

St. II. l. 3. *Charlie.*

Charles James Fox.

St. III. l. 3. *Tammie, the Norlan' laddie.*

The Hon. Thomas Erskine, afterwards Lord Erskine (1750–1823), who in 1792, being retained for Thomas Paine, resolved to obey the call to defend him, and was thereupon dismissed from his office as Attorney-General to the Prince of Wales.

St. IV. l. 3. *Maitland and Wycombe.*

"Maitland" was James, eighth Earl of Lauderdale (1759–1839), who in July, 1790, was elected a Scots representative peer, and during the debate in the House of Lords, 31st May, 1792, on the King's Proclamation "against seditious writings," had come forward "to vindicate himself, and those with whom he associated, from the gross calumnies levelled against them by the Proclamation," which he "stigmatised as a most malignant and impotent measure." In August following he left for France along with Dr. John Moore. He became a strong sympathiser with the French Revolution, protested against the war with France, and on one occasion appeared in the House of Lords "clothed in the rough garb of Jacobinism." "Wycombe" was John Henry Petty, second Marquis of Lansdowne (1765–1809), who, from 1784 until he succeeded his father in 1805, was styled Earl of Wycombe; at this time represented Chipping Wycombe; and in the House of Commons spoke against the Proclamation. His father, William Petty, first Marquis of Lansdowne (1739–1805), also in the House of Lords, supported Lauderdale.

Page 313. St. V. l. 3. *Chieftain M'Leod.*

Colonel Norman M'Leod of M'Leod (1754–1801), Member for Inverness.

Page 318. POEM ON PASTORAL POETRY.

St. VI. l. 5. *Tantallan.*

A famous historic stronghold on the east coast of Scotland, near North Berwick.

GLOSSARIAL INDEX

A', all.
A-back, (1) behind : "gaed a wee a-back," 9 ;
(2) away: "aback frae courts," 4.
Abeigh, abiegh, aloof, off : "stood abiegh," 27 ;
"stand abeigh," 272.
Ablins, v. *Aiblins*.
Aboon, (1) above (the usual sense) ; (2) up : "his
heart will never get aboon " = his heart will
never again rejoice, 15 ; "a lift aboon," 48 ;
"temper-pins aboon," 134 ; "heart aboon,"
265.
Abread, abroad : "beauties a' abread," 44.
Abreed, in breadth (R. B.) : "spread abreed thy
weel-fill'd brisket," 27.
Ado, to do : "mickle ado," 248.
Adle, cow-lant, putrid water : "deal brimstone
like adle," 111.
Ae, one.
Aff, off.
Aff-hand, at once : "a carpet weaver aff-hand,"
64 ; "marriage aff-hand," 282.
Aff-loof, off-hand, extempore : "just clean aff-
loof," 46.
A-fiel, afield.
Afore, before.
Aft, oft.
Aften, often.
Agley, askew : "gang aft agley," 32.
Ahin, behind.
Aiblins, ablins, may be, perhaps.
Aik, oak.
Aiken, oaken.
Ain, own.
Air, early.
Airle, arle, hansel, earnest money : "an airle-
penny," 232 ; "airle-pennies three," 248.
Airles, hansel : "the airles an' the fee," 129.
Airn, iron.
Airt, direction.
Airt, to direct : "airt me to my treasure," 254 ;
"airted till her a guid chiel," 143.
Aith, oath.
Aits, oats.
Aiver, an old horse (R. B.) : "a noble aiver," 19.
Aizle, a cinder : "an aizle brunt," 25.
A-jee, (1) ajar : "the back-yett be a-jee," 202 ;
(2) to one side ; "his bonnet he a thought
a-jee," 237.
Alake, alas.
Alane, alone.
Alang, along.
Amaist, almost.
Amang, among.
An, if.
An', and.
Ance, once.
Ane, one.
Aneath, beneath.

Anes, ones.
Anither, another.
Aqua-vitae, whisky.
Arle, v. *Airle*.
Ase, ashes.
Asklent, (1) askew, in an irregular manner :
"cam to the warl' asklent," 113 ; (2) askance :
"look'd asklent," 272.
Aspar, aspread : "the lasses lie aspar," 304.
Asteer, astir.
A'thegither, altogether.
Athort, athwart.
Atweel, in truth : "eh ! atweel na," 265.
Atween, between.
Aught, eight.
Aught, possession : "whase aught,"= who owns,
151.
Aughten, eighteen.
Aughtlins, at all, in any way : "aughtlins faw-
sont," 153. See also *Oughtlins*.
Auld, old.
Auldfarran, auldfarrant (old-favouring), seem-
ing to have the sagacity of age, sagacious,
shrewd : "a chap that 's damn'd auldfarran,"
7 ; "your auld-farrant frien'ly letter," 127.
Auld-Light. See Notes, p. 331.
Auld-warld, old-world.
Aumous, alms : "just like an aumous dish," 102.
Ava, at all, of all.
Awa, away. See *Here Awa*.
Awald, backways and bent together : "fell
awald beside it," 268.
Awauk, awake.
Awauken, awaken.
Awe, owe : "devil a shilling I awe, man," 170.
Awkart, awkward.
Awnie, bearded : "aits set up their awnie
horn," 5.
Ayont, beyond.

Ba', a ball.
Baby-clouts, babie-clouts, baby clothes ; "like
baby-clouts a-dryin," 64 ; "O, wha my babie-
clouts will buy," 226.
Backet, bucket or box : "auld saut-backets,"
94.
Backit, backed : "howe-backit now, an' knag-
gie," 26.
Backlins-comin, coming back, returning (R. B.),
49.
Back-yett, back gate : "the back-yett be a-jee,"
202.
Bade, asked : "and bade nae better," 144.
See also *Bid*.
Bade, endured : "bade an unco bang," 60. See
also *Bide*.
Baggie, the belly, the stomach : "a ripp to thy
auld baggie," 26.

Baig'nets, bayonets.
Bailie, baillie, magistrate of a Scots burgh.
Bainie, banie, bony, big-boned: the "brawnie, bainie, ploughman chiel," 5.
Bairn, child.
Bairntime, brood, issue: "thae bonie bairntime," 19; "my pleugh is now thy bairntime a'," 27.
Baith, both.
Bakes, biscuits: "bakes an' gills," 11.
Ballats, ballads.
Balou, lullaby: "The Highland Balou," 260.
Bamboozle, to trick by mystifying: "wicked men bamboozle him," 120.
Ban, swear (special Scottish meaning in addition to curse): "the devil-haet that I sud ban," 128.
Ban', band (*i. e.* of the Presbyterian clergyman): "gown an' ban'" = the clergyman, 126 (see also Notes, p. 340); "and band upon his breastie," 131.
Bane, bone.
Bang, an effort (R. B.), a blow, a large number: "he bade an unco bang," 60. See Notes, p. 332.
Bang, to thump: "bang your hide," 251 ; "she bang'd me," 265 ; "bang'd the despot," 320.
Banie, v. *Bainie*.
Bannet, bonnet.
Bannock, bonnock, a soft cake, generally of oat- and pease-meal, sometimes wholly of the latter: "twa mashlum bonnocks," 8; "saxpence, an' a bannock," 143 ; "hauvermeal bannock," 201 ; "bannocks o' bear meal, bannocks o' barley," 260. See also Notes, p. 343.
Bardie, dim. of *bard*.
Barefit, barefooted.
Barket, barked.
Barley-brie or *-bree*, barley-liquor = ale or whisky: "barley-brie cement the quarrel," 5; "taste the barley-bree," 229.
Barm, yeast: "that clarty barm should stain my laurels," 187.
Barmie, yeasty: "my barmie noddle," 16.
Barn-yard, stackyard, 210.
Bartie, the devil: "as fou as Bartie," 130.
Bashing, abashed: "bashing and dashing," 135.
Batch, a number, a company: "batch o' wabster lads," 10.
Batts, the botts (applied to horses), the colic: "a countra laird had taen the batts," 58.
Bauckie-bird, the bat: "wavering like the bauckie-bird," 102. See also Notes, p. 334.
Baudrons, baudrans, the cat: "a winkin baudrons," 64; "like baudrons by a ratton," 148; "auld baudrans by the ingle sits," 244.
Bauk, a cross-beam: "grapit for the bauks," 24.
Bauk, v. *Bawk*.
Bauk-en', a beam-end: "or whether 't was a bauk-en'," 24.
Bauld, bold.
Bauldest, boldest.
Bauldly, boldly.
Baumy, balmy.

Bawbee, a halfpenny (probably a "babie" penny).
Bawdrons, v. *Baudrons*.
Bawk, bauk, a field-path: "a corn-inclosèd bawk," 213.
Baws'nt, white-streaked: "sonsie, baws'nt face," 2.
Bawtie, pet name for a dog: "my auld teethless Bawtie," 120.
Bear, barley.
Beas', beasts, vermin (*i. e.* lice): "grey wi' beas'," 153.
Beastie, dim. of *beast*.
Beck, a curtsy: "she 'll gie ye a beck," 169.
Beet, to feed, kindle, fan, add fuel to: "or noble Elgin beets," 30; "it heats me, it beets me," 33; "beet his hymeneal flame," 43; "it 's plenty beets the luver's fire," 241. Cf. Chaucer, "Two fires on the autor [altar] gan she beete," *Knight's Tale, Canterbury Tales*, 2292.
Befa', befall.
Behin', behint, behind.
Beild, v. *Biel*.
Belang, belong.
Beld, bald.
Bellum, an assault: "brawlie ward their bellum," 119.
Bellys, bellows.
Belyve, by-and-by: "belyve the elder bairns," 28 ; "weel-swall'd kytes belyve are bent," 72.
Ben, a parlour. See Notes, p. 327.
Ben, into the spence or parlour (R. B.).
Benmost, inmost: "benmost bore," 103 ; "benmost neuk," 153.
Be-north, to the northward of.
Besom, a brush of twigs for sweeping.
Be-south, to the southward of.
Bethankit, the grace after meat (R. B.), 72.
Beuk, a book: "devil's pictur'd beuks" = playing-cards, 4.
Beyont, beyond.
Bicker, (1) a wooden cup: "in cog or bicker," 5 ; (2) a cupful, a glass: "a hearty bicker," 125. See also Notes, p. 325.
Bicker, a short run: "I took a bicker," 57.
Bicker, to flow swiftly and with a slight noise: "bickerin, dancin dazzle," 26 ; "bicker'd to the seas," 304. Cf. also "smoke and bickering flame," Milton's *Paradise Lost*, vi. 766.
Bickerin, noisy and keen contention: "there will be bickerin there," 165.
Bickering, hurrying: "bickering brattle," 31.
Bid, to ask, to wish, to offer: "bid nae better," 153 ; "ne'er bid better," 134. See also *Bade*.
Bide, abide. See also *Bade*.
Biel, bield, beild, a shelter, a sheltered spot: "the random bield o' clod or stane," 38 ; "hap him in a cozie biel," 41 ; "the sun blinks kindly in the biel," 240 ; "roses blaw in ilka bield," 241 ; "but buss and bield," 261 ; "thy bield should be my bosom," 315.
Bien, prosperous, comfortable: "bien an' snug," 32 ; "her house sae bien," 208.
Bien, bienly, comfortably: "bienly clad," 113 ; "that cleeds me bien," 240.

Big, to build.

Biggin, a structure, a dwelling : " the auld clay biggin," 20 ; " houlet-haunted biggin," 94.

Bike, v. *Byke*.

Bill, a bull : " as yell 's the bill," 13.

Billie, fellow, comrade, brother.

Bings, heaps : " potatoe-bings," 60.

Birdie, dim. of *bird*, also maiden : " bonie birdies," 115. See also *Burdie*.

Birk, the birch.

Birken, birchen.

Birkie, a fellow (usually implies conceit).

Birr, force, vigour : " wi' a' my birr," 162.

Birring, whirring : " birring paitricks," 67.

Birses, bristles: " tirl the hullions to the birses," 153.

Birth, berth : " a birth afore the mast," 41.

Bit, small.

Bit, nick of time : " just at the bit," 13.

Bitch-fou, completely drunk, 117.

Bizz, a flurry : " that day when in a bizz," 13.

Bizz, to buzz.

Bizzard, the buzzard.

Bizzie, busy.

Black-bonnet, the elder : " a greedy glowr blackbonnet throws," 10 ; " an' douse black-bonnet," 126. See also Notes, p. 340.

Black-nebbit, black - beaked : " black - nebbit Johnie," 165.

Blae, blue, livid.

Blastet, *blastit*, blasted (used in contempt and equivalent to *damn'd*) : " wee, blastit wonner," 2 ; " onie blastit, moorland toop," 15 ; " creepin, blastit wonner," 43.

Blastie, a blasted (*i. e.* damn'd) creature : " the blastie 's makin," 44 ; " red-wud Kilbirnie blastie," 114.

Blate, (1) modest : " owre blate to seek," 55 ; (2) bashful, shy : " nor blate nor scaur," 12 ; " some unco blate," 24 ; " but blate and laithfu'," 29 ; " young, and blate," 135 ; " steer her up, an' be na blate," 264.

Blather, *blether*, bladder.

Blaud, a large quantity, a screed : " a hearty blaud," 46 ; " a blaud o' Johnie's morals," 130.

Blaud, to slap : " he 's the boy will blaud her," 63.

Blaudin, driving, pelting : " the bitter, blaudin show'r," 126.

Blaw, (1) to blow ; (2) to brag, to boast : " blaw about mysel," 45 ; " he brags and he blaws o' his siller," 230.

Bleer, to blear.

Bleer't, bleared.

Bleeze, a blaze.

Bleeze, to blaze.

Blellum, (1) a babbler : " drunken blellum," 90 ; (2) a railer : " sour-mou'd, girnin blellum," 119 ; (3) a blusterer : " to cowe the blellums," 127.

Blether, *blethers*, nonsense. See also *Blather*.

Blether, to talk nonsense

Blin', blind.

Blin', to blind.

Blink, (1) a glance ; (2) a moment, a short period.

Blink, (1) to blink, to smirk, to leer : " are blinkin at the entry," 10 ; " Blinkin Bess of Annandale," 160 ; (2) to shine.

Blinkers, (1) spies : " seize the blinkers," 6 ; (2) oglers : " delicious blinkers," 134.

Blitter, the snipe : " blitter frae the boggie," 206.

Blue-gown, the livery of the licensed beggar : " the Blue-gown badge," 50. See also Notes, p. 331.

Bluid, blood.

Bluidy, bloody.

Blume, to bloom.

Bluntie, a stupid (*i.e.* one who is n't sharp) : " gar me look like bluntie," 239.

Blypes, shreds : " till skin in blypes cam haurlin," 26.

Bobbed, curtsied : " when she cam ben, she bobbèd," 239.

Bocked, vomited : " or thro' the mining outlet bocked," 68.

Boddle, a farthing (properly two pennies Scots, or one sixth of an English penny) : " he car'd na deils a boddle," 91 ; " I 'll wad a boddle," 61.

Bodkin, tailor's needle : " your bodkin 's bauld," 132.

Body, *bodie*, a person, a creature.

Boggie, dim. of *bog* : " the blitter frae the boggie," 206.

Bogle, a bogie, a hobgoblin : " lest bogles catch him unawares," 91 ; " the silly bogles, Wealth and State," 275 ; " nae nightly bogle make it eerie," 278 ; " ghaist nor bogle," 293.

Bole, a hole, or small recess in the wall : " there sat a bottle in a bole," 238.

Bonie, *bonnie*, pretty, beautiful.

Bonilie, prettily.

Bonnock, v. *Bannock*.

'Boon, above.

Boord, board, surface : " the jinglin icy boord," 13.

Boord-en', board-end: " sitting at yon boord-en'," 214.

Boortrees, " the shrub-elder, planted much of old in hedges of barnyards " (R. B.) : " thro' the boortrees comin," 13.

Boost, behove, must needs : " I shortly boost to pasture," 18 ; " like a blockhead, boost to ride," 114.

Boot, payment to the bargain : " the boot and better horse," 221. *O' boot* = to boot, gratis : " the saul o' boot," 54 ; " o' boot that night," 106.

Bore, a chink, a small hole, an opening : " to guard, or draw, or wick a bore," 67 (see Notes, p. 333) ; " thro' ilka bore the beams were glancing," 91 ; " the benmost bore," 103.

Botch, an angry tumour (R. B.) : " scabs and botches," 13.

Bouk, a human trunk (Eng. bulk : cf. " to shatter all his bulk," Shak. *Hamlet*, ii. 1.): " and monie a bouk did fa'," 227.

'Bout, about.

Bow-hough'd, bandy-thighed : " she 's bow hough'd, she 's hem-shin'd," 244.

Bow-kail, cabbage : "wandered thro' the bow-kail," 24 ; "his bow-kail runt," 24.

Bow't, bent : "like a sow-tail, sae bow't," 24.

Brachens, ferns : " amang the brachens," 26. See also *Breckan*.

Brae, a small hill, the slope of a hill.

Braid, broad.

Braid-claith, broad-cloth.

Braik, a harrow : "in pleugh or braik," 46.

Braing't, pulled rashly : " thou never braing't, an' fetch't, an' fliskit," 27.

Brak, brake, broke.

Brankie, spruce : " whare hae ye been sae bran-kie, O," 229.

Branks, a wooden curb, a bridle : " as cheeks o' branks," 57 ; "goavin 's he 'd been led wi' branks," 117 ; " if the beast and branks be spar'd," 126 ; " wi' braw new branks," 131.

Bran'y, brandy.

Brash, short illness : "monie a pain an' brash," 6.

Brats, small pieces, rags : "brats o' claes," 8 ; " brats o' duddies," 144.

Brats, small children : " our ragged brats and callets," 107 ; " wives an' dirty brats," 153.

Brattle, (1) a spurt, a scamper : "waur't thee for a brattle," 27 ; " wi' bickering brattle," 31 ; (2) noisy onset : " brattle o' winter war," 68.

Braw, gaily dressed, fine, handsome. See also Notes, p. 335.

Brawlie, finely, perfectly, heartily.

Braxies, sheep that have died of braxie (a disease) : "guid fat braxies," 49.

Breastie, dim. of *breast*.

Breastit, sprang forward : " thou never lap, an' sten't, an' breastit," 27.

Brechan, a horse collar : "a braw new brech-an," 131.

Breckan, ferns : " yon lone glen o' green breck-an," 286. See also *Brachens*.

Breedin, breeding, *i. e.* manners : "has nae sic breedin," 120.

Breeks, breeches.

Breer, briar.

Brent, brand : "brent new frae France," 91. See also Notes, p. 333.

Brent, straight, steep (*i.e.* not sloping from baldness) : "your bonie brow was brent," 223.

Brief, writ : " King David o' poetic brief," 133.

Brig, bridge.

Brisket, breast : "thy weel-fill'd brisket," 27.

Brither, brother.

Brock, a badger : "a stinking brock," 3 ; " wil-cat, brock, an' tod," 108.

Brogue, a trick : " an' play'd on man a cursed brogue," 13.

Broo, soup, broth, liquid, water : "the snaw-broo rowes," 61 ; "I 've borne aboon the broo," 62 ; "the flesh to him, the broo to me," 251 ; "suppin hen-broo," 265 ; "dogs like broo," 265.

Brooses, wedding races to the home of the bridegroom after the ceremony : "at brooses thou had ne'er a fellow," 27.

Brose, a thick mixture of meal and warm wa-ter, also a synonym for porridge : "they maun

hae brose," 144 ; "their cogs o' brose," 227 ; " ye butter'd my brose," 249. See Notes, p. 341.

Browst, malt liquor (and properly the whole liquor brewed at one time) : " the browst she brew'd," 206.

Browster wives, ale wives : "browster wives an' whisky-stills," 126. See also Notes, p. 339.

Brugh, a burgh, a borough.

Brulyie, brulzie, a brawl : "than mind sic brulzie," 50 ; "Hell mixed in the brulyie," 163 ; "wha in a brulyie," 260.

Brunstane, brimstone.

Brunt, burned.

Brust, burst.

Buckie, dim. of *buck*, a smart younker : "that daft buckie, Geordie Wales," 145 ; "envious buckies," 146.

Buckle, a curl : "his hair has a natural buckle," 222.

Buckskin, a Virginian : "the buckskins claw," 75.

Buckskin, Virginian : "the buckskin kye," 51. See also Notes, p. 331.

Budget, a tinker's bag of tools : "the budget and the apron," 106 ; "here 's to budgets," 107. See also Notes, p. 335.

Buff, to bang, to thump : "buff our beef," 108.

Bughtin, folding (*i. e.* gathering sheep into the fold) : "tells bughtin time is near, my jo," 298.

Buirdly, (1) stout, stalwart : "buirdly chiels," 3 ; (2) stately : "a filly buirdly," 26.

Bum, to hum : "yont the dyke she 's heard you bummin," 13 ; " bum owre their treasure," 48.

Bum-clock, a humming beetle : "the bum-clock humm'd wi' lazy drone," 4.

Bummle, a drone, a useless fellow : "some drowsy bummle," 41.

Bunker, a seat : "a winnock-bunker in the east," 91.

Bunters, harlots : "and kissing barefit bunt-ers," 163.

Burdie, dim. of *bird* or *burd* (a lady), a maiden : "ae blink o' the bonie burdies," 92. See also *Birdie*. Cf. *Burd Ellen*.

Bure, bore, did bear.

Burn, a rivulet.

Burnewin, the blacksmith (*i.e.* burn the wind) : "then Burnewin comes on like death," 5.

Burnie, dim. of *burn* (a rivulet).

Burr-thistle, spear-thistle : "the rough burr-thistle spreading wide," 135.

Busk, (1) to dress, to garb : "New Brig was buskit in a braw new coat," 60 ; "they 'll busk her like a fright," 119 ; " busking bowers," 159 ; (2) to dress up : "busks his skinklin patches," 318 ; (3) to trim, to adorn : "her bonie buskit nest," 119 ; " weel buskit up sae gaudy," 240.

Buss, a bush : "but buss and bield," 261. See *Rash-buss*.

Bussle, bustle.

But, without.

But, butt, in the kitchen (*i. e.* the outer apartment), "butt the house" = in the kitchen, 143. See also *Ben*.

By, past, aside.

By, beside.

By himsel, beside himself, off his wits : " monie a day was by himsel," 25.

Bye attour (*i. e.* "by and attour "), moreover : " bye attour my gutcher has," 254.

Byke, bike, (1) a bees' nest, a hive : " assail their byke," 92 ; (2) a swarm, a crowd : " the glow-rin byke," 106 ; " the hungry bike," 308.

Byre, a cowhouse.

Ca', a call, a knock.

Ca' (1) to call ; (2) to knock, to drive (*e. g.* a nail), to drive (*e. g.* cattle).

Cadger, a hawker : " a cadger pownie's death," 44 ; " like onie cadger's whup," 102.

Cadie, caddie, a varlet : " e'en cowe the cadie," 8 ; " Auld-Light caddies," 49.

Caff, chaff.

Caird, a tinker.

Calf-ward, a grazing plot for calves (*i. e.* a churchyard).

Callan, callant, a stripling.

Caller, cool, refreshing : " the caller air," 9 ; " little fishes' caller rest," 240.

Callet, a trull : " my bottle, and my callet," 103 ; " our ragged brats and callets," 107.

Cam, came.

Canie, cannie, (1) gentle, tractable : " tawie, quiet, an' cannie," 27 ; " cannie young man," 217 ; " bonie wee thing, cannie wee thing," 236 ; (2) quiet : " then cannie, in some cozie place," 17 ; " a cannie errand," 28 ; " a cannie hour at e'en," 77 ; " kind and cannie," 146 ; (3) prudent, careful : " wi' cannie care," 24, 50, 115, 139 ; " cannie for hoarding o' money," 170.

Cankrie, crabbed : " o' cankrie Care," 134.

Canna, cannot.

Cannie, v. *Canie*.

Cannie, (1) gently : " straik her cannie," 7 ; (2) quietly : " slade cannie to her bed," 58 ; (3) carefully, sensibly : " I maun guide it can-nie," 76 ; " and cannie wale," 241 ; (4) ex-pertly : " nickin down fu' cannie," 125.

Canniest, quietest : " the canniest gate, the strife is sair," 241.

Cannilie, cannily, quietly, prudently, cautious-ly : " cannilie he hums them," 11 ; " cannily keekit ben," 214 ; " cannily steal on a bonie moor-hen," 306.

Cantie, cheerful, lively, jolly, merry.

Cantraip, magic, witching : " by cantraip wit," 13 ; " cantraip sleight," 91 ; " some cantraip hour," 134.

Cants, (1) merry stories : " monie cracks and cants," 50 ; (2) sprees or merry doings : " a' my cants," 133.

Cape-stane, cope-stone.

Capon, castrate : " their capon craws," 308. See also Notes, p. 347.

Care na by, to care not, to care nothing, 76, 221, 214 ; " I car'd na by," 237.

Carl, carle (churl), a man, an old man.

Carl-hemp, male-hemp : " thou stalk o' carl-hemp," 145.

Carlie, a mannikin : " a fusionless carlie," 249.

Carlin, carline, a middle-aged, or old woman, a beldam, a witch.

Carmagnole, a violent Jacobin : " that curst carmagnole Auld Satan," 148. See also Notes, p. 341.

Cartes, playing cards.

Cartie, dim. of *cart :* " or hurl in a cartie," 130.

Catch-the-plack, the hunt for coin, 45.

Caudron, cauldron, a caldron : " fry them in his caudrons," 64 ; " clout the cauldron," 105.

Cauf, a calf.

Cauf-leather, calf-leather.

Cauk, chalk : " o' cauk and keel " = in chalk and ruddle, 94.

Cauld, cold.

Cauld, the cold.

Cauldness, coldness.

Cauldron, v. *Caudron*.

Caup, a wooden drinking-vessel (*i. e.* cup) : " th' lugget caup," 5 ; " yill-caup commentators," 11 ; " in cogs an' caups," 11 ; " that kiss'd his caup," 161.

Causey-cleaners, causeway-cleaners, street-cleaners.

Cavie, a hen-coop : " behint the chicken cavie," 106.

Chamer, chaumer, chamber.

Change-house, tavern.

Chanter, (1) bagpipes, the pipe of the bagpipes which produces the melody : " your chanters tune," 15 ; " chanters winna hain," 48 ; (2) syn. for *song :* " quat my chanter," 126, 143.

Chap, a fellow, a young fellow.

Chap, v. *Chaup*.

Chap, to strike : " ay chap the thicker," 125.

Chapman, a pedlar.

Chaumer, v. *Chamer*.

Chaup, chap, a stroke, a blow : " at ev'ry chaup," 5.

Chear, cheer.

Chear, to cheer.

Chearfu', cheerful.

Chearless, cheerless.

Cheary, cheery.

Cheek-for-chow, cheek-by-jowl (*i. e.* close beside, side by side) : " cheek-for-chow, a chuffie vintner," 7 ; " cheek-for-chow, shall jog thegither," 134.

Cheep, squeak, peep : " wi' tunefu' cheep," 64 ; " cheeps like some bewilder'd chicken," 119.

Chiel, chield (child) a fellow, a young fellow (indicates approval).

Chimla, chimney.

Chow, v. *Cheek-for-chow*.

Chows, chews.

Chuck, a hen, a dear : " the martial chuck," 103.

Chuckie, dim. of *chuck*, but usually signifies mother-hen, an old dear : " auld chuckie Reekie," 119 ; " a daintie chuckie," 145 ; " a dainty chuckie," 208.

Chuffie, fat-faced : " a chuffie vintner," 7.

Chuse, to choose.

Cit, the civet : " the cit and polecat stink," 85.

Cit, a citizen, a merchant.

Clachan, a small village about a church, a hamlet (R. B.) : " the clachan yill," 57 :

"Jock Hornbook i' the clachan," 58; "within the clachan," 115.

Claeding, claithing, clothing.

Claes, claise, clothes.

Claith, cloth.

Claithing, v. *Claeding.*

Claivers, v. *Clavers.*

Clankie, a severe knock: "Clavers gat a clankie, O," 230.

Clap, the clapper of a mill: "and still the clap plays clatter," 66.

Clark, a clerk: "like onie clark," 126.

Clark, clerkly, scholarly: "learned and clark," 173.

Clarkit, clerked, wrote: "in a bank and clarkit," 20.

Clarty, dirty: "clarty barm," 187.

Clash, an idle tale, the story of a day (R. B.): "the countra clash," 16.

Clash, to tattle: "e'en let them clash," 113.

Clatter, (1) noise: "the clap plays clatter," 66; "bade me mak nae clatter," 252; (2) tattle, gossip: "kintra clatter," 113, 261; (3) talk: "sangs and clatter," 91; "anither gies them clatter," 159; (4) disputation: "a' this clatter," 50; (5) babble: "rhymin clatter," 128.

Clatter, (1) to make a noise by striking: "the pint-stowp clatters," 11; "gar him clatter," 45; "clatter on my stumps," 103; (2) to babble, to prattle: "the gossips clatter bright," 5; "clatters, 'Tam Samson's dead,'" 67.

Claucht, claught, clutched, seized: "claught her by the rump," 92; "claucht th' unfading garland," 177. See also *Cleek.*

Claughtin, clutching, grasping: "claughtin 't together," 170.

Claut, (1) a clutch: "our sinfu' saul to get a claut on," 148; (2) a handful: "a claut o' gear," 239.

Claut, to scrape: "the laggen they hae clautet," 19.

Claver, clover.

Clavers, claivers, (1) gossip, nonsense: "clavers and havers," 135; "heaps o' clavers," 318.

Claw, a scratch, a blow.

Claw, to scratch, to strike.

Clay-cauld, clay-cold.

Claymore, a two-handed Highland sword: "an' guid claymore," 104; "wi' dirk, claymore," 153.

Cleckin, a brood: "its minnie and the cleckin," 119.

Cleed, to clothe.

Cleek, (1) to take hold: "they cross'd, they cleekit," 92; (2) to snatch: "cleek the sterlin," = pinch the ready, 104. See also *Claucht.*

Cleg, a gadfly: "the clegs o' feeling stang," 134.

Clink, (1) a sharp stroke: "her doup a clink," 116; (2) jingle: "o' rhymin clink," 128; (3) coin, money, wealth: "o' needfu' clink," 143; "the name o' clink," 214.

Clink, (1) to chink: "he'll clink in the hand," 169; (2) to jingle, to rhyme: "mak it clink," 46; "gar them clink," 128.

Clinkin, with a smart motion: "clinkin' down beside him," 10.

Clinkum, Clinkumbell, the beadle, the bellman: "auld Clinkum at the inner port," 133; "Clinkumbell, wi' rattlin tow," 11.

Clips, shears: "ne'er cross'd the clips," 15.

Clish-ma-claver, nonsense, idle talk, gossip, tale-telling: "for a' their clish-ma-claver," 19; "what farther clish-ma-claver might been said," 62.

Clockin-time, clucking- (= hatching-) time: "the clockin-time is by," 51.

Cloot, a cloven hoof, one of the divisions of a cloven hoof: "upon her cloot she coost a hitch," 14; "an' wear his cloots," 14.

Clootie, Cloots, Hoofie, Hoofs (a nickname of the devil): "Nick, or Clootie," 12; "Auld Cloots," 14; "auld Cloven-Clootie's haunts," 133.

Clour, a bump or swelling after a blow (R. B.): "clours an' nicks," 49.

Clout, (1) a cloth, a rag; (2) a patch: "perhaps a clout may fail in 't," 266. See also *Babie-clout.*

Clout, to patch: "reft and clouted," 18; "clout the cauldron," 105; "clout the bad girdin o't," 209; "cloutin a kettle," 224.

Clud, a cloud.

Clunk, to make a hollow sound: "made the bottle clunk," 106. See also Notes, p. 335.

Coatie, dim. of *coat.*

Coble, a broad and flat boat: "wintle like a saumont-coble," 27.

Cock, the mark (in curling): "station at the cock," 67.

Cockie, dim. of *cock* (applied to an old man): "my guid auld cockie," 145.

Cocks, fellows, good fellows: "my hearty cocks," 8; "the wale o' cocks," 50.

Cod, a pillow: "a cod she laid below my head," 256; "the cradle wants a cod," 269.

Coft, bought: "coft for her wee Nannie," 92; "I coft a stane o' haslock woo," 255; "that coft contentment," 271.

Cog, (1) a wooden drinking-vessel: "in cog or bicker," 5; "in cogs an' caups," 11; "cog, an ye were ay fou," 210; "a cog o' guid swats," 279; (2) a porridge-dish: "their cogs o' brose," 227; (3) a corn measure for horses: "thy cog a wee bit heap," 27. See also Notes, p. 325.

Coggie, dim. of *cog,* a little dish.

Coil, Coila, Kyle (one of the ancient districts of Ayrshire). See Notes, p. 325.

Collie, (1) a general, and sometimes a particular, name for country curs (R. B.); (2) a sheep-dog: "a ploughman's collie," 2.

Collieshangie, a squabble: "or how the collieshangie works," 145.

Cood, cud.

Coof, v. *cuif.*

Cookin, cooking.

Cookit, disappeared suddenly: "cookit underneath the braes," 26.

Coor, cover: "coor their fuds," 106.

Cooser, a stallion: "a perfect kintra cooser," 145.

Coost (cast), (1) looped : " coost a hitch," 14 ; (2) threw off : " coost their claise," 76 ; " coost her duddies," 92 ; (3) toss'd : " Maggie coost her head," 272 ; (4) chucked : " coost it in a corner," 191.

Cootie, a wooden dish : " the brunstane cootie," 12.

Cootie, leg-plumed : " cootie moorcocks," 67.

Corbies, ravens, crows : " corbies and clergy," 62.

Core, corps.

Corn mou, corn heap : " and the corn mou," 210.

Corn't, fed with corn (oats) : " thou was corn't," 27.

Corss, cross : " Mauchline Corss," 128.

Cou'dna, couldna, could n't.

Countra, country.

Coup, to capsize : " coup the cran" = upset the pot, 133.

Couthie, couthy, kind, loving, affable : " couthie Fortune," 146 ; " fu' couthy and sweet," 282.

Couthie, comfortably : " kindle couthie, side by side," 24.

Cowe, to cow, to scare, to daunt : " cowe the cadie," 8 ; " cowe the louns," 49 ; " cowe the lairds," 109 ; " cowe the blellums," 127 ; " cowe the rebel generation," 153.

Cowe, to crop : " cowe her measure shorter," 64.

Crack, (1) a tale : " tell your crack," 7 ; (2) a chat : " a hearty crack," 194 ; " ca' the crack," = have a chat, 44 ; (3) talk : " for crack that day," 11 ; " hear your crack," 45.

Crack, to converse, to chat, to talk : " crackin crouse," 3 ; " the father cracks of horses," 29 ; " wha will crack to me my lane," 226.

Cracks, (1) stories : " cracks and cants," 50 ; (2) conversation : " gashing at their cracks," 24 ; " an' friendly cracks," 26.

Craft, croft.

Craft-rig, croft-ridge.

Craig, the throat : " that nicket Abel's craig," 95.

Craig, a crag.

Craigie, dim. of *craig*, the throat : " weet my craigie," 106 ; " thy bonie craigie," 260.

Craigy, craggy.

Craik, the corn-crake, the land-rail : " mourn, clam'ring craiks, at close o' day," 83 ; " the craik amang the clover hay," 240.

Crambo-clink, crambo-jingle, rhyming : " live by crambo-clink," 40 ; " I to the crambo-jingle fell," 45.

Cran, the support for a pot or kettle : " coup the cran," 133.

Crankous, fretful : " in crankous mood," 7.

Cranks, creakings : " what tuneless cranks," 6.

Cranreuch, hoar - frost, rime : " cranreuch cauld," 32 ; " in hoary cranreuch drest," 102.

Crap, crop.

Crap, to crop : " that crap the heather bud," 82.

Craps, (1) tops : " craps o' heather " = heather-tops, 9 ; (2) crops : " his craps and kye," 241.

Craw, crow.

Creel, an osier basket : " my senses wad be in a

creel " = I should be perplexed, 47 (see also Notes, p. 331) ; " in Death's fish-creel," 67 ; " nieves, like midden-creels," 244 (see also Notes, p. 345).

Creepie-chair, stool of repentance : " mount the creepie-chair," 226. See also Notes, p. 338, (" Cutty-stools ").

Creeshie, greasy.

Crocks, old ewes : " tent the waifs an' crocks," 108.

Cronie, a crony.

Crood, to coo : " the cushat croods," 48 ; " a cushat crooded o'er me," 304.

Croon, (1) a moan : " wi' eldritch croon," 13 ; " the melancholious croon," 15 ; " gat up an' gae a croon," 26 ; " melancholious, sairie croon," 134.

Croon, (1) to boom : " jow an' croon," 11 ; (2) to hum : " crooning to a body's sel," 45 ; " crooning o'er some auld Scots sonnet," 91 ; " croon'd his gamut," 105.

Croose, crouse, (1) cocksure : " keen an' croose," 13 ; (2) lively, jolly : " when I grow crouse," 132 ; " crouse and canty," 273.

Crouchie, hunchbacked ; " crouchie Merran Humphie," 25.

Crouse, v. *Croose*.

Crouse, cheerfully : " crackin crouse," 3.

Crousely, confidently : " crousely craw," 67.

Crowdie, oatmeal and cold water, oatmeal and milk, porridge : " wi' crowdie unto me," 227 ; " ance crowdie, twice crowdie," etc., 270.

Crowdie-time, porridge-time (*i. e.* breakfast-time), 9.

Crowlin, crawling : " ye crowlin ferlie," 43.

Crummie, a horned cow : " auld Crummie's nicks," 129.

Crummock, cummock, a cudgel, a crooked staff (cf. the Gaelic or Welsh *cam* or *cum* = the crook of a stick, and *camon* = Irish hockey) : " louping and flinging on a crummock," 92 ; " on a cummock driddle," 134.

Crump, crisp : " farls . . . fu' crump," 10.

Crunt, a blow on the head with a cudgel : " wi' hearty crunt," 49.

Cuddle, to fondle : " bairns' bairns kindly cuddle," 128 ; " cuddle my kimmer," 224 ; " cuddl'd me late and early," 249.

Cuif, coof, a dull, spiritless fellow, a dolt, a ninny : " fumbling cuifs," 5 ; " blockhead ! coof ! " 20 ; " coofs on countless thousands rant," 32 ; " cuifs of later times," 61 ; " a cuif like him," 194 ; " a wealthy coof," 239 ; " a coof . . . wi' routh o' gear," 249 ; " he 's but a cuif," 294 ; " will be nae coof," 304.

Cummock, v. *Crummock*.

Curch, a kerchief for the head : " her curch sae clean," 208 ; " I tint my curch," 209.

Curchie, a curtsy : " wi' a curchie low did stoop," 9.

Curler, one who plays at curling (a game on the ice) : " the curlers quat their roaring play," 20 ; " to the loughs the curlers flock," 67.

Curmurring, rumbling : " curmurring in his guts," 58.

Curpin, the crupper of a horse : " haurls at his curpin," 25.

Curple, the crupper (*i. e.* buttocks): "hingin owre my curple," 135.

Cushat, the wood pigeon.

Custock, the stalk of the colewort: "gif the custock 's sweet or sour," 24.

Cutes, ankles: " her bonie cutes sae sma'," 121.

Cutty, short: "cutty sark," 92.

Cutty-stools, stools of repentance: " daft bargains, cutty-stools," 118. See also Notes, p. 338.

'D, it: " I maun till 'd again," 270.

Dad, *daddie*, father.

Daez't, dazed.

Daffin, larking, fun: " to spend an hour in daffin," 9; " fits o' daffin," 65; " towsing a lass i' my daffin," 104.

Daft, mad, foolish.

Dails, deals, planks: " some carryin dails," 10.

Daimen icker, an occasional ear of corn: " a daimen icker in a thrave," 31.

Dam, pent up water, urine: "ye tine your dam," 9.

Damie, dim. of *dame*.

Dang, *dung* (pret. of *ding*).

Danton, v. *Daunton*.

Darena, dare not.

Darg, *daurk*, labour, task, a day's labour: " nought but his han' darg," 3; " monie a sair darg," 27.

Darklins, in the dark : " an' darklins grapit for the bauks," 24.

Dashing, confounded, put to shame, abashed: " bashing and dashing, I fearèd ay to speak," 135. (This seems to be an intransitive and reflexive use of a word which is used not uncommonly in the sense of " to confound, to abash." " Bashing " is a similar case, but there is good authority for its use in this intransitive sense.)

Daud, to pelt: " set the bairns to daud her," 63; " the bitter, daudin showers," 126.

Daunton, *danton*, to daunt.

Daur, dare.

Daurk, v. *Darg*.

Daurna, dare not.

Daur't, dared.

Daut, *dawte*, to fondle, to pet: " dawtit, twalpint hawkie," 13; " unco muckle dautet," 19; " kiss and daut," 113, 232; " kiss and dawte," 252.

Daw, to dawn: " the day may daw," 229.

Dawds, lumps, large portions: " an' dawds that day," 11.

Dawtingly, pettingly, caressingly: " dawtingly did cheer me," 237.

Dead-sweer, extremely reluctant, 43.

Dearie, dim. of *dear*.

Dearthfu', high-priced.

Deave, to deafen.

Deevil, v. *Deil*.

Deil, *deevil*, devil.

Deil-haet, (1) nothing (the devil have it): " tho' deil-haet ails them," 4; (2) the devil have my soul; " the devil-haet that I sud ban," 128.

Deil-ma-care, no matter (the devil may care, but not I), 50, 58, 129.

Deleeret, delirious, mad : " an' liv'd an' died deleeret," 25.

Delvin, digging: "dubs of your ain delvin," 42.

Dern'd, hid (from the Old Eng. *dearn* or *dern*: " that dern time," Craig's Oxford Shak. *King Lear*, iii. 1. 62): " dern'd in dens and hollows," 116.

Descrive, to describe.

Deuk, a duck: "your deuks an' geese," 153; " the deuk 's dang o'er my daddie," 249.

Devel, a stunning blow : " an unco devel," 67.

Diddle, to move quickly (of fiddling) : "elbuck jink an' diddle," 128, 133.

Dight (1) to wipe ; (2) to winnow : "the cleanest corn that e'er was dight," 65.

Din, dun, muddy of complexion: " dour and din," 169, 244.

Ding, (1) to beat, to surpass ; (2) be beaten or upset : " facts are chiels that winna ding," 18.

Dink, trim : "my lady 's dink, my lady 's drest," 268.

Dinna, do not.

Dirl, a vibration ; " played dirl," 58.

Dirl, to vibrate, to ring : " roof and rafters a' did dirl," 91; " she dirl'd them aff fu' clearly," 308.

Diz'n, *dizzen*, dozen.

Dochter, daughter.

Doggie, dim. of *dog*.

Doited, muddled, stupid, bewildered: " doited Lear," 5; " a doited monkish race," 61; "doited stots," 121; " the doited beastie stammers," 131; "my very senses doited," 137; " sae doited and blin'," 254.

Donsie, (1) unlucky : " their donsie tricks," 66 ; (2) vicious, restive, testy: " ye ne'er was donsie," 27; " ye wad na been sae donsie, O," 249.

Dool, woe, sorrow: " sing dool " = lament, 55 ; " may dool and sorrow be his lot," 84 ; " dool to tell " = sad to tell, 108 ; " to sit in dool," 224; " bitter in dool," 225 ; " care and dool," 233 ; " O, dool on the day," 234 ; " dool and care," 253.

Doolfu', doleful, woful: " doolfu' clamour," 119; " the doolfu' tale," 240.

Dorty, pettish : " tho' a minister grow dorty," 8.

Douce, *douse*, sedate, sober, serious, prudent: " douce honest woman," 13; " O ye douce folk," 17 ; " douce or merry tale," 44 ; " douce conveeners," 62 ; " douce folk," 62 ; " thrifty citizens, an' douce," 62 ; " douce Wisdom's door," 66 ; " for you sae douce," 77 ; " sae cursèd douse," 143.

Douce, *doucely*, *dousely*, sedately, prudently : " douce hingin owre my curple," 135 ; " doucely manage our affairs," 6 ; " doucely fill a throne," 19.

Doudl'd, dandled : "doudl'd me up on his knee," 201.

Dought (pret. of *dow*), could : " as lang 's he dought," 75 ; " do what I dought," 137; " dought na bear us," 185.

Doukèd, ducked : " in monie a well been doukèd," 104.

Doup, the bottom, the buttocks.

Doup-skelper, bottom-spanker: "vile doup-skelper, Emperor Joseph," 145.

Dour, doure, (1) stubborn, obstinate: "teughly doure," 60; "and Sackville doure," 75; "the tither's dour," 120; "dour and din," 169, 244; (2) severe, stern: "fell and doure," 68.

Douse, v. *Douce*.

Douser, sedater: "oughtlins douser," 145.

Dow, dowe, am (is or are) able, can: "the best they dow," 11; "dow but hoyte and hobble," 27; "as lang's I dow," 46; "dow scarcely spread her wing," 50; "hirples twa-fauld as he dow," 212; "dow nocht but glow'r," 278. See also *Dought*.

Dow, a dove, a pigeon: "like frighted dows, man," 227.

Dowf, dowff, dull: "her dowff excuses," 46; "dowff an' dowilie," 120; "dowf and weary," 298.

Dowie, drooping, mournful: "our Bardie, dowie," 15; "dowie, stiff, and crazy," 26; "dowie she saunters," 139; "I wander dowie up the glen," 216; "some that are dowie," 217.

Dowie, mournfully: "his sad complaining dowie raves," 253.

Dowilie, drooping: "dowff an' dowilie they creep," 120.

Downa, cannot.

Downa-do, cannot-do, 249.

Doylt, stupid, stupefied: "doylt, drucken hash," 6; "he's doylt and he's dozin," 233.

Doytin, doddering: "cam doytin by," 14.

Dozen'd, torpid: "dearest member nearly dozen'd," 142.

Dozin, torpid: "he's doylt and he's dozin," 233.

Draigl't, draggled.

Drants, prosings: "to wait on their drants," 170.

Drap, drop.

Drappie, dim. of *drap*.

Draunting, tedious: "draunting drivel," 148.

Dree, to suffer, to endure: "the pangs I dree," 253; "dree the kintra clatter," 261.

Dreigh, v. *Driegh*.

Dribble, drizzle: "the winter's sleety dribble," 32.

Driddle, to toddle: "us'd to trystes an' fairs to driddle," 105; "on a cummock driddle," 134.

Driegh, dreigh, tedious, dull: "stable-meals . . . were driegh," 27; "the moor was dreigh," 208.

Droddum, the breech: "dress your droddum," 43.

Drone, part of the bagpipe. See Notes, p. 347.

Droop-rumpl't, short-rumped: "droop-rumpl't, hunter cattle," 27.

Drouk, to wet, to drench: "my droukit sark-sleeve," 231; "to drouk the stourie tow," 238.

Drouth, thirst: "Scotland's drouth," 6; "their hydra drouth," 117; "holy drouth," 168.

Drouthy, thirsty: "drouthy neebors," 90; "drouthy cronie," 91.

Druken, drucken, drunken.

Drumlie, (1) muddy, turbid: "drumlie German-water," 3; "the drumlie Dutch," 145; "drumlie wave," 207; "waters never drumlie," 288; (2) dull: "drumlie winter," 291.

Drummock, raw meal and cold water: "a belly-fu' o' drummock," 41.

Drunt, the huff: "took the drunt," 24.

Dub, a puddle: "gumlie dubs," 42; "thro' dub and mire," 45, 91; "the burning dub," 108; "thro' dirt and dub," 114. See *Midden dub*.

Duddie, ragged: "tho' e'er sae duddie," 2; "duddie weans," 3; "duddie boy," 44; "duddie, desperate beggar," 153.

Duddies, dim. of *duds*, rags: "coost her duddies," 92; "their orra duddies," 102; "brats o' duddies," 144.

Duds, rags, clothes: "wi' reekit duds," 13; "pawn'd their duds," 106; "flaffin wi' duds," 153; "tartan duds," 227; "shook his duds," 261.

Dung, v. *Dang*.

Dunted, throbbed: "wi' life-blood dunted," 147.

Dunts, blows, 238.

Durk, dirk.

Dusht, pushed: "eerie's I'd been dusht," 20.

Dwalling, dwelling.

Dwalt, dwelt.

Dyke, (1) a fence (of stone or turf), a wall: "a sheugh or dyke," 2; "biggin a dyke," 2; "yont the dyke," 13; "your lives a dyke," 17; "sun oursels about the dyke," 105; "about the dykes," 108; "owre a dyke," 121: "lap o'er the dyke," 206.

Dyke-back, the back of a fence, 44.

Dyke-side, the side of a fence: "a lee dyke-side," 129.

Dyvor, a bankrupt: "rot the dyvors," 153; "dyvor, beggar loons," 252.

Ear', early.

Eastlin, eastern.

E'e, eye.

E'ebrie, eyebrow.

Een, eyes.

E'en, even.

E'en, evening.

E'enin, evening.

Eerie, (1) apprehensive; (2) inspiring ghostly fear. See Notes, p. 343.

Eild, eld, age, old age.

Eke, also.

Elbuck, elbow.

Eldritch, (1) horrible, unearthly: "eldritch squeel," 10; "eldritch croon," 13; "an eldritch, stoor 'quaick, quaick,'" 13; "eldritch laugh," 58; "eldritch skriech," 92; (2) haunted, fearsome: "eldritch towen," 83; "eldritch part," 94.

Elekit, elected.

Ell (Scots), thirty-seven inches.

Eller, elder: "me the Eller's dochter," 266.

En', end.

Eneugh, enough.

Enfauld, infold.

Erse, Gaelic: "a Lallan tongue or Erse," 14.

Ether-stane, adder-stone : " and make his ether-stane," 160. See also Notes, p. 341.
Ettle, aim : " wi' furious ettle," 92.
Evermair, evermore.
Ev'n down, downright, positive : " ev'n down want o' wark," 4.
Expeckit, expected.
Eydent, diligent : " wi' an eydent hand," 29.

Fa', (1) a fall ; (2) a lot, a portion.
Fa', (1) to fall ; (2) to receive as one's portion : " best deserves to fa' that," 164 ; " weel does Selkirk fa' that," 165 ; (3) claim : " guid faith, he mauna fa' that," 294. See also Notes, p. 346 ; and, in addition, cf. Alexander Scott's *When His Wife Left Him* : " For fient a crumb of thee she fa's " [*i. e.* claims].
Faddom'd, fathomed.
Fae, foe.
Faem, foam.
Faiket, let off, excused : " sic han's as you sud ne'er be faiket," 128.
Fain, fond, glad. See *Fidgin-fain*.
Fainness, fondness, gladness : " wi' fainness grat," 237.
Fair fa', good befall : " fair fa' your honest sonsie face," 72 ; " fair fa' my collier laddie," 241. Cf. " fair fall the bones that took the pains for me," Shak., *King John*, Act i. sc. 1.
Fairin, a present from a fair : " he gets his fairin," 59 ; " thou 'll get thy fairin," 92. See Notes, p. 332.
Fallow, fellow.
Fand, found.
Far-aff, far-off.
Farls, small, thin oat-cakes : " farls, bak'd wi' butter," 10.
Fash, annoyance : " to gie ane fash," 113 ; " or fash o' fools," 118.
Fash, (1) to trouble, to bother, to worry : " they 're fash't eneugh," 2 ; " fash your thumb " = care a rap, 6 ; " I never fash " = I never trouble about, 16 ; " fash your head," 32 ; " fash me for 't," 50 ; " fash'd wi' fleshly lust," 110 ; " they seldom fash't him," 172 ; (2) to trouble one's self, to worry : " fash nae mair," 128.
Fashious, troublesome : " fin' them fashious," 143.
Fasten-e'en, Fasten's Even (the evening before Lent), 44.
Faught, a fight.
Fauld, the sheep-fold.
Faulding, folding, sheep-folding : " a-faulding let us gang," 293.
Faulding slap, fold gate : " steeks his faulding slap," 78.
Faun, fallen.
Fause, false.
Fause-house, hole in a cornstack : " kiutlin in the fause-house," 24 ; " the fause-house in her min'," 24. See also Notes, p. 329.
Faut, fault.
Fautor, transgressor : " syne, say I was a fautor," 252 ; " tho' he be the fautor," 260.
Fawsont, (1) seemly, decent : " honest, fawsont

folk," 3 ; (2) good-looking : " aughtlins faw-sont," 153.
Feat, spruce : " the lassies feat," 23.
Fecht, a fight.
Fecht, to fight.
Feck, (1) value, return : " for little feck," 120 ; (2) the bulk, the most part : " the feck of a' the Ten Comman's," 9 ; " the feck o' my life," 246.
Fecket, (1) sleeve-waistcoat (used by farm-servants as both vest and jacket) : " got me by the fecket," 147 ; (2) waistcoat (without sleeves) : " his fecket is white," 222.
Feckless, weak, pithless, feeble : " as feckless as a wither'd rash," 72 ; " an auld wife's tongue 's a feckless matter," 113.
Feckly, partly, or mostly : " carts . . . are feckly new," 114.
Feg, a fig.
Fegs, faith ! " but fegs ! the Session," 133.
Feide, feud : " wi' deadly feide," 67.
Feint, v. *Fient*.
Feirrie, lusty : " the feirrie auld wife," 249.
Fell, (1) keen, cruel, dreadful, deadly ; (2) pungent : " her weel-hain'd kebbuck fell," 30.
Fell, " the flesh immediately under the skin " (R. B.) : " the skin an' fell," 64. Cf. " flesh and fell," Shak. *King Lear*, v. 3.
Fell, to kill.
Felly, fell, relentless : " felly spite," 231.
Fen', a shift : " might mak a fen'," 230.
Fen', *fend*, (1) to look after, to care for : " fend themsel," 14 ; (2) keep off : " fend the show'rs," 10 ; (3) defend : " fecht and fen' " = shift for themselves, 233 ; (4) fare, prosper : " how do you fen' ? " 245.
Fenceless, defenceless.
Ferlie, *ferly*, (1) a wonder (used contemptuously) : " ye crowlin ferlie," 43 ; (2) " nae ferlie (y) " = no wonder, no marvel, 18, 249.
Ferlie, to marvel : " an' ferlie at the folk in Lon'on," 3.
Fetch, (1) to pull irregularly : " braing't, an' fetch't, an' fliskit," 27 ; (2) to catch : " fetch-es at the thrapple," 125.
Fey, doomed to death : " fey men died," 227.
Fidge, to fidget, to wriggle : " fidge your back," 7 ; " fidge fu' fain " = hug herself, 48 ; " fidge an' claw," 63 ; " fidg'd fu' fain " = fidgeted with eagerness, 92.
Fidgin-fain, tingling with pleasure, tingling with fondness, 226 ; " fidgin-fain to hear 't," 44. See Notes, p. 344.
Fiel, comfortable : " haps me fiel and warm," 240.
Fient, *feint*, fiend, a petty oath (R. B.).
Fient a, not a : " the fient a " = nothing of a.
Fient haet, nothing (fiend have it).
Fient haet o', not one of.
Fient-ma-care, the fiend may care (I don't !).
Fier, *fiere*, comrade : " my trusty fier," 144 ; " my trusty fiere," 252.
Fier, sound : " hale and fier," 32.
Fin', to find.
Fish-creel, v. *Creel*.
Fissle, tingle, fidget with delight (it is also used

of the agitation caused by frying) : " gar me fissle," 46.

Fit, foot.

Fittie-lan', the near horse of the hindmost pair in the plough : " a noble fittie-lan'," 27. See Notes, p. 330.

Flae, a flea.

Flaffin, flapping : " flaffin wi' duds," 153.

Flainin, flannen, flannel.

Flang, flung.

Flee, to fly.

Fleech, to wheedle : " a fleechin, fleth'rin Dedication," 42 ; " Duncan fleech'd, and Duncan pray'd," 272.

Fleesh, fleece : " a bonier fleesh ne'er cross'd the clips," 15.

Fleg, (1) either a scare (as the word is used by Ramsay), or a blow : " jirt an' fleg," 46 ; (2) kick : " uncouth kintra fleg," 162.

Fleth'rin, flattering : " fleth'rin Dedication," 42.

Flewit, a sharp lash : " a hearty flewit," 133.

Fley, to scare : " Want and Hunger fley me," 270 ; " fley'd awa," 297.

Fley'd, scared : " fley'd an' eerie," 25 ; " but be na fley'd," 57.

Flichterin', fluttering : as young nestlings when their dam approaches (R. B.) ; " flichterin' noise and glee," 28.

Flinders, shreds, broken pieces (R. B.) : " in flinders flee," 41.

Flinging, kicking out in dancing, capering : " louping and flinging on a crummock," 92.

Flingin-tree, a piece of timber hung by way of partition between two horses in a stable, a flail (R. B.) : " the thresher's weary flingin-tree," 20.

Fliskit, fretted, capered : " fetch't, an' fliskit," 27.

Flit, to shift.

Flittering, fluttering.

Flyte, scold : " e'en let her flyte her fill," 264.

Fock, focks, folk.

Fodgel, dumpy : " a fine, fat, fodgel wight," 94.

Foor, fared (*i. e.* went) : " o'er the moor they lightly foor," 208.

Foorsday, Thursday.

Forby, forbye, besides.

Forfairn, worn out, forlorn : " wi' crazy eild I 'm sair forfairn," 61 ; " Fenwick, sair forfairn," 64.

Forfoughten, exhausted (*i. e.* by labour or conflict) : " tho' forfoughten, sair eneugh," 135.

Forgather, to meet, to fall in (with).

Forgie, to forgive.

Forjesket, jaded with fatigue (R. B.) : " forjesket sair, with weary legs," 46.

Forrit, forward.

Fother, fodder.

Fou, fow, full (usually in the sense of drunk).

Foughten, troubled (*i. e.* by conflict with difficulties) : " sae foughten an' harass'd," 4. See *Forfoughten*.

Foursome, by fours : " foursome reels," 249.

Fouth, fulness, abundance : " fouth o' auld nicknackets," 94.

Fow, v. *Fou*.

Fow, a bushel.

Frae, from.

Freath, to froth.

Fremit, estranged : " is now a fremit wight," 161.

Fu', full. See also *Fou*.

Fu'-han't, full-handed (having abundance) : " ay fu'-han't is fechtin best," 241.

Fud, a short tail (of a rabbit or hare) : " cock your fud fu' braw," 67 ; " to coor their fuds," 106.

Fuff't, puffed : " she fuff't her pipe wi' sic a lunt," 25.

Fur, furr, a furrow.

Fur-ahin, the hindmost plough-horse in the furrow : " my fur-ahin 's a wordy beast," 114. See Notes, p. 338.

Furder, furtherance, success.

Furder, to succeed.

Furm, a wooden form.

Fusionless, pithless, sapless : " he is but a fusionless carlie," 249.

Fyke, fuss : " as bees bizz out wi' angry fyke," 92.

Fyke, to fuss, to fidget (*i. e.* from annoyance or pain) : " fyke an' fumble," 41 ; " until ye fyke," 128.

Fyle, to defile, to foul, to soil : " that fyl'd his shins," 10 ; " her face wad fyle the Logan Water," 244.

Gab, the mouth, the jaw : " set a' their gabs a-steerin," 26 ; " steek your gab for ever," 64 ; " his gab did gape," 92 ; " she held up her greedy gab," 102 ; " his teethless gab," 212.

Gab, to talk, to speak : " gab like Boswell," 7.

Gabs, talk : " some wi' gabs," 24.

Gae, gave.

Gae, to go.

Gaed, went.

Gaen, gane, gone.

Gaets, ways, manners : " learn the gaets," 14. See also *Gate*.

Gairs, gores, slashes : " my lady 's gown, there 's gairs upon 't," 267.

Gane, v. *Gaen*.

Gang, to go, to walk.

Gangrel, vagrant : " o' randie, gangrel bodies," 102.

Gar, to cause, to make, to compel.

Garten, garter.

Garten'd, gartered.

Gash, (1) wise, sagacious : " a gash an' faithfu' tyke," 2 ; (2) self-complacent (implying prudence and prosperity) : " here farmers gash," 9 ; (3) talkative and self-complacent : " a gawsie, gash guid-wife," 11.

Gashing, talking, gabbing : " gashing at their cracks," 24.

Gat, got.

Gate, way, road, manner. See also *Gaets*.

Gatty, gouty : " auld an' gatty," 126.

Gaucie, v. *Gawsie*.

Gaud, a goad, 228. See Notes, p. 344.

Gaudsman, goadsman, driver of the plough-team : " a gaudsman ane, a thrasher t' other," 114. See Notes, p. 344.

Gau'n, Gavin.

Gaun, going.

Gaunted, gaped, yawned: "I've grain'd and gaunted," 145.

Gawky, a foolish woman or lad (the feminine or diminutive of *gowk, q. v.*): "gawkies, tawpies, gowks, and fools," 119. See Notes, p. 339.

Gawky, cuckooing, foolish: "the senseless, gawky million," 129. Cf. *A Dream,* p. 18, St. II., ll. 3, 4.

> "*God save the King*'s a cuckoo sang
> That's unco easy said ay."

Gawsie, gaucie, (1) buxom: "her strappin limb an' gawsie middle," 105; (2) buxom and jolly: "a gawsie, gash guidwife," 11; (3) big and joyous: "his gawsie tail," 2.

Gaylies, gaily: "but they do gaylies," 153.

Gear, (1) money, wealth; (2) goods; (3) stuff: "taste sic gear as Johnie brews," 128.

Geck, (1) to sport: "may Freedom geck," 19; (2) to toss the head: "ye geck at me because I'm poor," 214.

Ged, a pike: "Johnie Ged's Hole" = the grave-digger (R. B.), 58, "and geds for greed," 67. See Notes, p. 331.

Gentles, gentry.

Genty, trim and elegant: "genty waist," 217; "her genty limbs," 268.

Genty, trimly: "sae genty sma'," 228.

Geordie, (1) dim. of *George;* hence (2) a guinea, bearing the image and superscription of King George.

Get, issue, offspring, breed: "nae get o' moorlan tips," 15; "a true, guid fallow's get," 19.

Ghaist, ghost.

Gie, to give.

Gied, gave.

Gien, given.

Gif, if.

Giftie, dim. of *gift.*

Giglets, giggling youngsters or maids: "the giglets keckle," 118. Cf. "a giglet wench" = a light woman, Shak. 1 *Henry VI.,* iv. 7.

Gillie, dim. of *gill* (glass of whisky).

Gilpey, young girl: "I was a gilpey then," 25.

Gimmer, a young ewe.

Gin, if, should, whether.

Gin, against, by: "their hearts o' stane, gin night, are gane," 11; "beside me gin the gloaming," 237.

Girdle, a plate of metal for firing cakes, bannocks, etc.; "the vera girdle rang," 102. See Notes, p. 335.

Girn, (1) to grin, to twist the face, (but from pain or rage, not joy); "it maks guid fellows girn an' gape," 15; "wi' girnin spite," 49, 134; "every sour-mou'd girnin blellum," 119; "thy girnin laugh," 148; (2) gapes: "that girns for the fishes and loaves," 166; (3) snarls: "girns and looks back," 125.

Gizz, wig: "an' reestit gizz," 13. See also *Jiz.*

Glaikit, foolish, thoughtless, giddy: "glaikit Folly's portals," 66; "I'm red ye're glaikit," 128; "ye glaikit, gleesome, dainty damies," 144; "glaikit Charlie," 145.

Glaizie, glossy, shiny: "sleek, an' glaizie," 26.

Glaum'd, grasped: "glaum'd at kingdoms three, man," 227.

Gled, a hawk, a kite (Anglo-Sax. "Gleida" = the glider): "a bizzard gled," 168; "or I had fed an Athole gled," 230.

Gleede, a glowing coal, a blaze (Anglo-Sax. "Glēd;" cf. "the cruel ire reed [red] as any gleede," Chaucer, *Knight's Tale, Canterbury Tales,* 1997): "cheery blinks the inglegleede," 208.

Gleg, sharp, quick, keen: "gleg as onie wumble," 41; "Death's gleg gullie," 68; "wee Davoc's grown sae gleg," 114; "as gleg's a whittle," 125; "he's gleg enough," 129; "gleg as light are lover's een," 284.

Gleg, smartly: "he'll shape you aff fu' gleg," 95.

Gleib, a glebe, a portion (of land): "a gleib o' lan," 239. See Notes, p. 345.

Glib-gabbet, smooth-tongued, 7.

Glint, (1) to shine, to gleam, to peep: "wi' glorious light was glintin," 9; "thou glinted forth," 38; (2) to flit: "glinted by," 211.

Gloamin, gloaming, twilight, dusk: "an' darker gloamin brought the night," 4; "when ance life's day draws near the gloamin," 17; "beside me gin the gloaming, 237; "now it was the gloamin," 261; "the hour o' gloamin grey," 298.

Gloamin-shot, sunset, 252.

Glow'r, a stare.

Glow'r, to stare.

Glowrin, staring.

Glunch, a frown, a sour look: "twists his gruntle wi' a glunch," 6.

Glunch, to frown, to look sour: "glunch an' gloom," 6.

Goavin, looking dazedly, mooning: "goavin's he'd been led wi' branks," 117; "idly goavin whyles we saunter," 133.

Gorcock, the moorcock: "the gorcock springs on whirring wings," 52; "whare gor-cocks thro' the heather pass," 268.

Gowan, the wild daisy.

Gowany, covered with wild daisies.

Gowd, gold.

Gowdie, the head: "heels o'er gowdie," 148.

Gowff'd, struck as in the game of golf: "gowff'd Willie like a ba', man," 76.

Gowk, (1) the cuckoo; (2) a dolt: "conceited gowk," 61; "Andro' Gowk," 112; "gowks and fools," 119. See Notes, p. 339.

Gowling, howling: "Misfortune's gowling bark," 43.

Graff, a grave, a tomb, a vault: "cauld in his graff," 54; "your marble graffs," 182; "your green graff," 254.

Grain'd, groaned.

Graip, a dung-fork.

Graith, (1) implements, tools, gear: "ploughmen gather wi' their graith," 5; "her spinnin-graith," 208; (2) furniture of all kinds: "a' my graith," 114; (3) attire, garb: "farmers gash in ridin graith," 9; "in shootin graith adorned," 67; "in heav'nly graith," 76.

(2) to peel: "till skin in blypes cam haurlin," 26; (3) to drag: "haurl thee hame to his black smiddie," 82.

Hause, to embrace, to cuddle: "hause in ither's arms," 232.

Haveril, hav'rel, one who talks nonsense, a half-witted person: "poor hav'rel Will," 24; "hav'rel Jean," 116.

Havers, haivers, nonsense.

Havins, good manners, good conduct: "pit some havins in his breast," 14; "havins, sense, an' grace," 45; "to havins and sense," 112.

Hawkie, a white-faced cow, a cow.

Heal, v. *Hale*.

Healsome, v. *Halesome*.

Hecht, (1) to promise: "they hecht him some fine braw ane," 25; "hecht them courtly gifts," 161; "hecht an honest heart," 161; (2) to menace: "some mortal heart is hecht-tin," 130.

Heckle, a flax-comb.

Heels-o'er-gowdie. See *Gowdie*.

Heeze, to hoist: "higher may they heeze ye," 19; "heeze thee up a constellation," 139.

Heich, heigh, high.

Hem-shin'd, crooked-shinned, 244. See Notes, p. 345.

Here awa, here about.

Herry, to harry, to plunder.

Herryment, spoliation: "the herryment and ruin of the country," 62.

Hersel, herself.

Het, hot.

Heugh, (1) a crag, a steep bank: "the water rins owre the heugh," 217; (2) a hollow or pit: "yon lowin heugh," 12.

Heuk, a hook, a reaping-hook.

Hilch, to hobble, to halt: "hilchin Jean M'Craw," 25; "hilch, an' stilt, an' jimp," 34.

Hiltie-skiltie, helter-skelter, 128.

Himsel, himself.

Hiney, hinny, honey.

Hing, to hang.

Hirple, to limp, to hobble: "the hares were hirplin down the furs," 9; "hirplin owre the field," 17; "November hirples o'er the lea," 99; "he hirpl'd up, an' lap like daft," 106; "he hirples twa-fauld as he dow," 212; "he hoasts and he hirples," 233.

Hissels, so many cattle as one person can attend (R. B.): "the herds an' hissels were alarm'd," 49.

Histie, bare: "histie stibblefield," 38.

Hizzie, a hussy, a wench, a young woman.

Hoast, a cough: "an' barkin hoast," 6; "hoast-provoking smeek," 20.

Hoast, host, to cough: "hoast up some pala-ver," 131; "he hoasts and he hirples," 233.

Hoddin, the motion of a sage countryman riding on a cart horse (R. B.): "gaed hoddin by their cotters," 9.

Hoddin-grey, coarse grey woollen (and retaining the natural colour of the wool): "wear hoddin grey, an' a' that," 294.

Hog, a young sheep.

Hoggie, dim. of *hog*: "my hoggie," 206.

Hog-score, a term in curling: "Death's hog-score," 67. See Notes, p. 333.

Hog-shouther, a kind of horse-play by justling with the shoulder, to justle (R. B.), 48.

Hoodie-craw, the hooded crow, 119.

Hoodock, grasping, miserly: "the harpy, hoo-dock, purse-proud race," 134.

Hooked, caught, stolen: "monie a pursie she had hookèd," 104. See Notes, p. 335.

Hool, a hull, a husk, an outer case: "poor Lee-zie's heart maist lap the hool," 26.

Hoolie, slowly: "something cries, 'Hoolie!'" 16.

Hoord, hoard.

Hoordet, hoarded.

Horn, a horn spoon: "horn for horn, they stretch an' strive," 72.

Hornie, the devil.

Host, v. *Hoast*.

Hotch'd, hitched, jerked (the action of a bag-piper's arm): "hotch'd and blew wi' might and main," 92.

Hough, to hamstring: "they hough'd the clans like nine-pin kyles," 227. (The word is not to be taken literally in this instance, of course, but rather as meaning "cut down.")

Houghmagandie, fornication (R. B.), 12.

Houlet, v. *Howlet*.

Houpe, hope.

Howdie, howdy, a midwife: "nae howdie gets a social night," 5; "afore the howdy," 133.

Howe, a hollow, a dell.

Howe, hollow.

Howk, (1) to dig out: "mice and moudieworts they howkit," 2; "howkit dead" = disin-terred dead, 13; (2) to dig: "howkin in a sheugh," 2.

Howlet, houlet, an owl.

Hoyse, a hoist: "they'll gie her on the rape a hoyse," 64.

Hoy't, urged (R. B.): "they hoy't out Will, wi' sair advice," 25.

Hoyte, to amble crazily (R. B.): "now ye dow but hoyte and hobble," 27. See also Notes, p. 330.

Hughoc, dim. of *Hugh*.

Hullions, slovens: "tirl the hullions to the birses," 153.

Hunder, a hundred.

Hunkers, hams: "upon his hunkers bended," 105.

Hurcheon, the hedgehog: "o'er hurcheon hides," 82.

Hurchin, urchin.

Hurdies, the loins, the crupper (R. B.) (*i. e.* the buttocks): "hung owre his hurdies wi' a swirl," 2; "row't his hurdies in a ham-mock," 41; "meekly gie your hurdies to the smiters," 62; "your hurdies like a distant hill," 72; "I wad hae gi'en them off my hurdies," 92; "their ample hurdies," 115.

Hurl, to be wheeled, to trundle: "or hurl in a cartie," 130.

Hushion, a footless stocking: "she dights her grunzie wi' a hushion," 244.

Hyte, furious: "hae put me hyte," 134.

I', in.

Icker, an ear of corn: "a daimen icker in a thrave," 31.

Ier-oe, a great-grandchild : "wee, curlie John's ier-oe," 43.

Ilk, ilka, each, every.

Ill o't, bad at it : "wretched ill o't," 43.

Ill-taen, ill-taken.

Ill-Thief, the devil: "the Ill-Thief blaw the Heron south," 144.

Ill-willie, ill-natured, malicious, niggardly (R. B.) : "your native soil was right ill-willie," 41.

Indentin, indenturing : "his saul indentin," 3.

Ingine, (1) genius, ingenuity (R. B.): "he had ingine," 44 ; (2) wit: "wi' right ingine," 128.

Ingle, the fire, the fireplace.

Ingle-cheek, fireside (properly the jamb of the fireplace) : "lanely by the ingle-cheek," 20.

Ingle-gleede, v. *Gleede*.

Ingle-lowe, ingle low, the flame or light of the fire : "by my ingle-lowe I saw," 20 ; "beyont the ingle low " = at the back of the fireplace, 238.

I'se, I shall, I will.

Ither, other, each other, one another.

Itsel', itself.

Jad, a jade.

Janwar, January.

Jauk, (1) to trifle, to dally : "she made nae jaukin," 24 ; "to jauk or play," 29.

Jauner, foolish talk : "haud your tongue and jauner," 254.

Jauntie, dim. of *jaunt:* "your wee bit jauntie," 144.

Jaup, to splash : "that jaups in luggies," 72.

Jaups, splashes: "dash the gumlie jaups up to the pouring skies," 61.

Jaw, talk, impudence : "deil-ma-care about their jaw," 129.

Jaw, to throw, to dash: "and in the sea did jaw, man," 75.

Jeeg, to jog: "and jeeg the cradle wi' my tae," 209.

Jeuk, v. *Jouk*.

Jillet, a jilt: "a jillet brak his heart at last," 41.

Jimp, small, slender: "thy waist sae jimp," 222.

Jimply, neatly : "sae jimply lac'd," 217.

Jimps, stays : "but Jenny's jimps," 267.

Jink, the slip: "our billie's gien us a' a jink," 40.

Jink, (1) to frisk, to sport, to move nimbly : "thro' wimplin worms thou jink," 5 ; "and jinkin hares, in amorous whids," 48 ; "jink an' diddle " = dance and shake, 128, 133 ; (2) to dodge, to dart about : "he 'll turn a corner jinkin," 14 ; "Rab slips out, an' jinks about," 24 ; "jink there or here," 115 ; "the swallow jinkin," 240; (3) move out and in: "and drawers jink," 115.

Jinker, (1) one who moves quickly: "a jinker noble," 27 ; (2) a gay, sprightly girl : "earth-ly jinkers," 134.

Jirkinet, bodice : "jimps and jirkinet," 267.

Jirt, a jerk : "monie a jirt an' fleg," 46.

Jiz, a wig, "his Sunday's jiz," 115. See also *Gizz*.

Jo, a sweetheart: "John Anderson my jo," 223.

Jocteleg, a jack-knife, 24, 95, 126.

Jouk, jeuk, to duck, to crouch : "jouk beneath Misfortune's blows," 17 ; "to Nobles jeuk," 165 ; "jouk behint the hallan," 318.

Jow, a verb which includes both the swinging motion and pealing sound of a large bell (R. B.) : "to jow an' croon," 11.

Jundie, to justle (R. B.), to jostle : "hog-shouther, jundie, stretch, an' strive," 48.

Jurr, a servant wench : "Geordie's jurr," 115.

Kae, a jackdaw : "thievish kaes," 8.

Kail, kale, (1) the colewort (also cabbage, but see *Bow-kail*) ; (2) Scots broth. See also *Lang-kail*.

Kail-blade, a leaf of the colewort, 58.

Kail-runt, the stem of the colewort, 58.

Kail-whittle, a cabbage knife, 115.

Kail-yard, a kitchen garden.

Kain, kane, rents in kind : "his kain, an' a' his stents," 2 ; "to Death she 's dearly pay'd the kain," 67.

Kale, v. *Kail*.

Kame, a comb : "claw'd her wi' the ripplin-kame," 252.

Kebars, rafters: "he ended ; and the kebars sheuk," 103.

Kebbuck, a cheese: "syne draws her kebbuck an' her knife," 11 ; "a kebbuck-heel," 11 ; "her weel-hain'd kebbuck, fell," 30.

Keckle, to cackle, to giggle loudly (as a girl): "the giglets keckle," 118.

Keek, a look, a glance, a peep, a stolen glance: "he by his shouther gae a keek," 25 ; "at ev'ry kindling keek," 135.

Keek, (1) to look, to peep, to glance : "now the sinn keeks in the wast," 126 ; "I cannily keekit ben," 214 ; "the gossip keekit in his loof," 304 ; (2) to look searchingly : "but keek thro' ev'ry other man," 40.

Keekin-glass, a looking-glass, 188.

Keel, v. *Cauk*.

Kelpies, river-demons (usually shaped as horses): "water-kelpies haunt the foord," 13 ; "fays, spunkies, kelpies," 60.

Ken, to know.

Kend, kent, known.

Kenna, know not.

Kennin, a very little (merely as much as can be perceived) : "a kennin wrang," 66.

Kent, v. *Kend*.

Kep, to catch (a thing thrown or falling): "shall kep a tear," 83.

Ket, the fleece on a sheep's body: "tawted ket, an' hairy hips," 15.

Key, quay.

Key-stane, key-stone.

Kiaugh, cark, anxiety : "his weary kiaugh and care beguile," 28.

Kilt, to tuck up: "her tartan petticoat, she 'll kilt," 7 ; "she kiltit up her kirtle weel," 121.

Kimmer, (1) a wench, a gossip : "despite the kit-tle kimmer " [Dame Fortune], 46 ; "loosome kimmers " = lovable girls, 130; "ye weel ken, kimmers a'," 161; "guid e'en to you, kimmer," 264; (2) a wife or bed-fellow: "I cuddle my kimmer," 224; "the kimmers o' Largo," 248.

Kin', kind.

King's-hood, the second stomach in a ruminant (equivocal for the scrotum): "Deil mak his king's-hood in a spleuchan," 58.

Kintra, country.

Kirk, church.

Kirn, a churn: "plunge an' plunge the kirn in vain," 13.

Kirn, harvest - home: "the jovial, ranting kirns," 3; "an' ay a rantin kirn we gat," 25; "at kirns an' weddins we'se be there," 105.

Kirsen, to christen: "and kirsen him wi' reekin water," 45.

Kist, (1) a chest; (2) a counter (humorous): "behint a kist to lie an' sklent," 47.

Kitchen, to relish (to add relish to): "thou kitchens fine," 5.

Kittle, difficult, ticklish, delicate, vexatious: "despite the kittle kimmer," 46; "kittle to be mislear'd," 57 (see Notes, p. 331); "are a shot right kittle," 62; "to paint an angel's kittle wark," 184.

Kittle, to tickle: " to kittle up our notion," 11; "kittle up your moorland harp," 46; "I kittle up my rustic reed," 48; "while I kittle hair on thairms," 105.

Kittlin, a kitten: "as cantie as a kittlin," 26.

Kiutlin, cuddling: "kiutlin in the fause-house," 24.

Knaggie, knobby: "tho' thou's howe-backit now, an' knaggie," 26.

Knappin - hammers, hammers for breaking stones (from *knap*, to crack, to break in pieces with blows), 45.

Knowe, a knoll, a hillock.

Knurlin, a dwarf.

Kye, kine, cows.

Kyles, skittles: "they hough'd the clans like nine-pin kyles," 227.

Kytes, bellies: "weel-swall'd kytes," 72.

Kythe, to show: "fu' sweetly kythe hearts leal," 23.

Labour, to plough.

Laddie, dim. of *lad*.

Lade, a load.

Lag, slow: "thou's neither lag nor lame," 12.

Laggen, the angle between the side and the bottom of a wooden dish: "the laggen they hae clautet," 19.

Laich, *laigh*, low.

Laik, lack.

Lair, lore, learning.

Laird, landowner (the lord of houses or lands).

Lairing, sticking or sinking when wading in snow, moss, or mud: "deep-lairing, sprattle," 68.

Laith, loath, loth.

Laithfu', (loathful) sheepish: "but blate and laithfu', scarce can weel behave," 29.

Lallan, *Lalland*, Lowland: "wad ding a Lallan tongue, or Erse," 14; "the Lalland laws he held in scorn," 104; "a Lalland face he feared none," 104.

Lallans, Scots Lowland vernacular: "in plain, braid Lallans," 49.

Lammie, dim. of *lamb*.

Lan', land.

Lan'-afore, the foremost horse on the unploughed land side, 114. See Notes, p. 338.

Lan'-ahin, the hindmost horse on the unploughed land side, 114. See Notes, p. 338.

Lane, lone. *My lane, thy lane*, etc. = alone.

Lang, long.

Lang-kail, coleworts not cut or chopped. See also *Kail*.

Lang syne, long since, long ago.

Lap, leapt.

Lassie, dim. of *lass*.

Lave, the rest, the remainder, the others.

Laverock, *lav'rock*, the lark.

Lawin, the reckoning, "landlady, count the lawin," 210; "guidwife, count the lawin," 232, 233.

Lawlands, the Lowlands.

Lea, grass land, untilled land, pasture land (also used in an equivocal sense).

Lear, lore, learning.

Leather, (1) leather; (2) leather breeches; (3) skin.

Leddy, lady.

Lee-lang, live-long.

Leesome, agreeable, pleasant: "the tender heart o' leesome loove," 241.

Leeze me on (from *leis me* = dear is to me), how well I love, blessings on, commend me to: "leeze me on thee, John Barleycorn," 5; "leeze me on drink," 11; "leeze me on rhyme," 128; "leeze me on the calling," 207; "O, leeze me on my spinnin-wheel," 240; "leeze me on thy bonie craigie," 260.

Leister, a fish-spear: "a three-tae'd leister on the ither," 57.

Len', to lend.

Leugh, laughed: "how graceless Ham leugh at his dad," 64.

Leuk, look.

Ley-crap, lea-crop (used equivocally): "waly fa' the ley-crap," 270.

Libbet, castrate: "how libbet Italy was singing," 145.

Licket, *lickit*, licked, beaten, whipt: "ye sud be lickit," 128; "how I've been licket," 147.

Licks, a beating, punishment: "monie a fallow gat his licks," 49.

Lien, lain.

Lieve, lief.

Lift, the sky.

Lift, as much as one may lift, a load: "gie me o' wit an' sense a lift," 47.

Lightly, (1) to disparage: "whyles ye may lightly my beauty a wee," 202; (2) to scorn: "for laik o' gear ye lightly me," 214.

Lilt, to sing: "lilt wi' holy clangor," 63.

Limmer, (1) a jade: "ye little skelpie-limmer's-face," 25 (see Notes, p. 329); "still persecuted by the limmer," 46; (2) a mistress: "or speakin lightly o' their limmer," 4.

Lin, v. *Linn*.
Link, (1) to trip or dance with activity: "and linket at it in her sark," 92; (2) to trip along: "will send him linkin," 14.
Linn, lin, a waterfall.
Lint, flax: "sin' lint was i' the bell," 30; "I bought my wife a stane o' lint," 238.
Lint-white, flax-coloured (a pale yellow), flaxen: "lassie wi' the lint-white locks," 289.
Lintwhite, the linnet: "the lintwhites chant amang the buds," 48; "the mavis and the lintwhite sing," 77; "the blackbird strong, the lintwhite clear," 97; "the lintwhites in the hazel braes," 240; the little lintwhite's nest," 297.
Lippen'd, trusted: "I lippen'd to the chiel," 144.
Lippie, dim. of *lip*.
Loan, a lane, a field-path, the private road to a farm or house: "the kye stood rowtin i' the loan," 4; "and up the loan she shaw'd me," 252.
Loanin, the open grassy place where the cows are milked: "wi' double plenty o'er the loanin," 147.
Lo'ed, loved.
Lon'on, London.
Loof, (pl. *looves*), the palm of the hand: "an's loof upon her bosom," 10; "an' heav'd on high my waukit loof," 20; "wi' weel-spread looves, an' lang, wry faces," 42; "hear'st thou, laddie — there's my loof," 239; "an wi' her loof her face a-washin," 244; "O, lay thy loof in mine, lass," 269; "the gossip keekit in his loof," 304.
Loon, loun, lown, a clown, a rascal.
Loosome, lovable: "loosome kimmers," 130.
Loot, let, uttered: "loot a winze," 26; "I never loot on that I kenn'd it," 282.
Loove, v. *Luve*.
Looves, v. *Loof*.
Losh, a minced oath (a mild form of "Lord"): "Losh, man, hae mercy wi' your natch," 132.
Lough, a loch, a lake: "ayont the lough," 13; "when to the loughs the curlers flock," 67.
Loun, v. *Loon*.
Loup, lowp, to leap.
Louse, v. *Lowse*.
Low, lowe, a flame: "the sacred lowe o' weel-plac'd love," 40. See also *Ingle-lowe*.
Lowin, lowing, (1) flaming: "lowin brunstane," 11; "tho' yon lowin heugh 's thy hame," 12; (2) burning: "to quench their lowin drouth," 106.
Lown, v. *Loon*.
Lowp, a leap.
Lowp, v. *Loup*.
Lowse, louse, (1) to loose, to untie: "lowse his pack," 106; (2) let loose: "lows'd his ill-tongu'd wicked scaul," 14; "lows'd his tink-ler jaw," 75; "louse Hell upon me," 126.
Lucky, (1) a grandmother, an old woman: "honest Lucky," 134, 145; (2) an ale-wife: "Lady Onlie, honest Lucky," 208. See Notes, p. 340.

Lug, the ear.
Lugget, having a handle: "lugget caup," 5.
Luggie, a small wooden dish with a handle: "the luggies three are ranged," 26; "that jaups in luggies," 72.
Lum, the chimney.
Lume, (1) a utensil: "wark-lume" = a tool, 13; (2) a loom.
Lunardi, a balloon-bonnet (named after Lunardi, a famous balloonist): "Miss's fine Lunardi,' 44.
Lunches, full portions: "dealt about in lunches," 11.
Lunt, a column of smoke or steam: "she fuff't her pipe wi' sic a lunt," 25; "butter'd sown's, wi' fragrant lunt," 26.
Luntin, smoking: "the luntin pipe," 3.
Luve, loove, love.
Lyart, (1) grey in general: "but ane wi' lyart lining," 9; (2) grey from decay or old age, faded: "lyart haffets wearing thin and bare," 30; "lyart pow," 46; "lyart leaves," 102; "lyart gray," 255. See Notes, p. 345.
Lynin, lining.

Mae, more.
Mailen, mailin, a farm: "than stocket mailins," 113; "there's Meg wi' the mailen," 222; "a mailen plenish'd fairly," 272; "a weel-stocket mailen," 282.
Mailie, Molly. See also *Mall*.
Mair, more.
Maist, most.
Maist, almost.
Mak, make.
Mak o', make o', to pet, to fondle: "I will mak o' my guidman," 232; "makin of 's the best thing," 249.
Mall, Mally, Moll, Molly, (nickname for Mary).
Mantie, a gown: "she made mantie," 257. See Notes, p. 345.
Manteele, a mantle, 9.
Mark, merk, an old Scots coin (13½d. sterling).
Mashlum, of mixed meal: "mashlum bonnocks," 8.
Maskin-pat, a teapot, 75.
Maukin, a hare: "hunger'd maukin taen her way," 20; "ye maukins, cock your fud fu' braw," 67; "ye maukins, whiddin through the glade," 82; "and coward maukin sleep secure," 97; "skip't like a maukin owre a dyke," 121; "are hunted like a maukin," 223.
Maun, must.
Mauna, maunna, must not.
Maut, malt.
Mavis, the thrush.
Maw, to mow.
Mawn, mown.
Mawn, a large basket: "and cover him under a mawn, O," 254. Cf. "A thousand favors from a maund she drew," Shakespeare, *Lover's Complaint*, l. 36.
Mear, a mare.
Meikle, mickle, muckle, (1) much, (2) great.
Melder, the quantity of corn sent to be ground: "ilka melder wi' the miller," 90.

Oughtlins, aughtlins, aught, in the least, at all : "oughtlins douser," 145 ; v. *Aughtlins.*
Ourie, shivering, drooping (R. B.) : "the ourie cattle," 68.
Oursel, oursels, ourselves.
Outler, unhoused, in the open fields: "an outler quey," 26.
Owre, over, too.
Owsen, oxen.
Oxter'd, held up under the arms : "the priest he was oxter'd," 268.

Pack an' thick, confidential : "unco pack an' thick thegither," 2.
Paidle, a spade.
Paidle, (1) to paddle, to wade : "thro' dirt and dub for life I'll paidle," 114 ; "we twa hae paidl'd in the burn," 252 ; (2) to walk with a weak action : "he was but a paidlin body, O," 249 ; "he paidles out, and he paidles in," 249.
Painch, the paunch.
Paitrick (1) a partridge ; (2) used equivocally, (the bird was once esteemed salacious) : "an' brought a paitrick to the grun'," 50.
Pang, to cram : "it pangs us fou o' knowledge," 11.
Parishen, the parish (*i. e.* the persons of the parish) : "the pride of a' the parishen," 255.
Parritch, porridge.
Parritch-pats, porridge-pots.
Pat, pot.
Pat, put.
Pattle, pettle, a plough-staff : "my new pleugh-pettle," 7 ; "wi' murdering pattle," 31 ; "as ever drew before a pattle," 114.
Paughty, haughty : "yon paughty dog," 19 ; "the paughty feudal thane," 47.
Paukie, pauky, pawkie, artful, sly : "the slee'st, pawkie thief," 16 ; "her pauky een," 135 ; "a thief sae pawkie is my Jean," 284.
Pechan, the stomach : "the ha' folk fill their pechan," 2.
Pechin, panting, blowing : "up Parnassus pechin," 131.
Penny wheep, small beer : "be 't whisky-gill or penny wheep," 11.
Pettle, v. *Pattle.*
Philibeg, the Highlander's kilt : "Adam's philibeg," 95 ; "with his philibeg an' tartan plaid," 104 ; "the philibegs and skyrin tartan trews," 227.
Phraise, phrase, to flatter, to wheedle : "phraisin terms," 47 ; "to phrase you an' praise you," 129.
Pickle, a few, a little : "a pickle nits," 25 ; "a pickle siller," 143.
Pint (Scots), two English quarts.
Pit, put.
Plack, four pennies Scots (but only the third of an English penny).
Plackless, penniless : "poor, plackless devils like mysel," 6.
Plaiden, coarse woolen cloth : "to warp a plaiden wab," 202 ; "a wab o' plaiden," 266. See Notes, p. 343.
Plaister, plaster.

Plenish'd, stocked : "a mailen plenish'd fairly," 272.
Pleugh-pettle, v. *Pattle.*
Pleugh, plew, a plough.
Pliskie, a trick : "play'd her that pliskie," 7.
Pliver, a plover.
Pock, a pouch, a small bag, a wallet : "the auld guidman raught down the pock," 25 ; "they toom'd their pocks," 106.
Poind, to seize, to distrain, to impound : "poind their gear," 3.
Poind, subjected to distraint : "poind and herriet," 153.
Poortith, poverty.
Pou, pu', to pull.
Pouch, a pocket.
Pouk, to poke : "and pouk my hips," 58.
Poupit, pulpit.
Pouse, a push : "a random pouse," 132. See Notes, p. 334.
Poussie, a hare (also a cat) : "poussie whiddin seen," 44. See also *Pussie.*
Pouther, powther, powder.
Pouts, chicks : "an' the wee pouts begun to cry," 51.
Pow, the poll, the head.
Pownie, a pony.
Pow't, pulled : "an' pow't, for want o' better shift," 24.
Pree'd, pried (proved), tasted : "Rob, stownlins, pried her bonie mou'," 24 ; "for ay he pree'd the lassie's mou'," 261.
Preen, a pin : "my memory 's no worth a preen," 49.
Prent, print.
Pried, v. *Pree'd.*
Prief, proof : "for ne'er a bosom yet was prief," 16 ; "stuff o' prief," 146.
Priggin, haggling : "priggin owre hops an' raisins," 62.
Primsie, dim. of *prim,* precise : "primsie Mallie," 24.
Proveses, provosts (chief magistrate of a Scots burgh) : "ye worthy proveses," 62.
Pu', v. *Pou.*
Puddock-stools, toad-stools, mushrooms : "like simmer puddock-stools," 119.
Puir, poor.
Pun', pund, pound.
Pursie, dim. of *purse.*
Pussie, a hare : "as open pussie's mortal foes," 92. See also *Poussie.*
Pyet, a magpie : "cast my een up like a pyet," 143.
Pyke, to pick : "sae merrily the banes we 'll pyke," 105.
Pyles, grains : "may hae some pyles o' caff in," 65.

Quat, quit, quitted.
Quean, a young woman, a lass : "now Tam, O Tam ! had thae been queans," 92 ; "the sonsie quean," 135 ; "wha follows onie saucie quean," 214.
Queir, quire, choir.
Quey, a young cow (that has not calved), a heifer.

Quo', *quod*, quoth.

Rab, Rob (nickname for *Robert*).
Rade, rode.
Raep, *rape*, a rope.
Ragweed, ragwort, benweed (*Senecio Jacobœa*, Linn.): " on ragweed nags," 13. See p. 89, Prefatory Note to *Tam o' Shanter*.
Raible, to gabble: " an' orthodoxy raibles," 10.
Rair, to roar.
Raise, *rase*, rose.
Raize, to excite: " that daur't to raize thee," 26.
Ramfeezl'd, exhausted: " the tapetless, ramfeezl'd hizzie," 46.
Ramgunshoch, rough: " our ramgunshoch, glum guidman," 252.
Ram-stam, thoughtless, rash, headstrong: " harum-scarum, ram-stam boys," 18.
Randie, lawless, obstreperous: " a merrie core o' randie, gangrel bodies," 102.
Randie, *randy*, a sturdy beggar, a ruffian: " reif randies, I disown ye," 252; " bann'd the cruel randy," 252.
Rant, to be jovial in a noisy way.
Rantin, *ranting*, rollicking, roistering.
Rantingly, with boisterous jollity.
Rants, (1) merry meetings, sprees: " our fairs and rants," 5; " drucken rants," 50, 133; (2) rows: " an' bloody rants," 133.
Rape, v. *Raep*.
Raploch, homespun: " tho' rough an' raploch be her measure," 128.
Rash, a rush: " as feckless as a wither'd rash," 72; " green grow the rashes," 76, 77.
Rash-buss, a clump of rushes: " ye, like a rash-buss, stood in sight," 13.
Rashy, rushy: " aboon the plain sae rashy, O," 205.
Rattan, *ratton*, a rat: " an' heard the restless rattons squeak," 20; " a ratton rattl'd up the wa'," 25 ; " while frighted rattons backward leuk," 103; " like baudrons by a ratton," 148; v. *Rottan*.
Ratton-Key, the Rat-Quay, 61. See Notes, p. 332.
Raucle, (1) rash, fearless: " a raucle tongue," 8; (2) sturdy: " a raucle carlin," 104.
Raught, reached: " the auld guidman raught down the pock," 25.
Raw, a row.
Rax, to stretch, to extend: " an' may ye rax Corruption's neck," 19 ; " rax your leather " = stretch your hide, fill your stomach, 27; " ye wha leather rax," 63; " raxin conscience " = elastic conscience, 126; " how cesses, stents, and fees were rax'd," 145.
Ream, foam: " the nappie reeks wi' mantling ream," 3.
Ream, to foam: " ream owre the brink," 5; " thou reams the horn in," 5; " wi' reaming swats, that drank divinely," 91; " the swats sae ream'd in Tammie's noddle," 91 ; " but there it streams, and richtly reams," 106.
Reave, to rob: " reave an' steal," 14.
Rebute, rebuff: " ne'er break your heart for ae rebute," 264.

Red, afraid: " I 'm red ye 're glaikit," 128.
Red, *rede*, to advise, to counsel.
Rede, counsel: " and may ye better reck the rede," 40. Cf. " Recks not his own rede," Shakespeare, *Hamlet*, i. 3.
Red-wat-shod, red-wet-shod, wading in blood: " still pressing onward, red-wat-shod," 48.
Red-wud, stark mad: " an' now she 's like to rin red-wud," 7.
Reek, smoke.
Reek, to smoke.
Reekie, *reeky*, smoky.
Reekit, smoked, smoky.
Reestit, singed: " wi' reekit duds an' reestit gizz," 13.
Reestit, refused to go, balked: " in cart or car thou never reestit," 27.
Reif, thieving: " reif randies," 252. See also *Rief*.
Remead, remedy.
Rickles, ricklets (small stacks of corn in the fields): " nor kick your rickles aff their legs," 126.
Rief, robbery: " that e'er attempted stealth or rief," 16. See also *Reif*.
Rig, a ridge (of land).
Riggin, a ridge (of a house), a roof: " rattons squeak about the riggin," 20 ; " or kirk deserted by its riggin," 94.
Rigwoodie, ancient, lean: " rigwoodie hags wad spean a foal," 92. See Notes, p. 333.
Rin, to run.
Ripp, a handful of corn from the sheaf: " teats o' hay an' ripps o' corn," 14 ; " there 's a ripp to thy auld baggie," 26.
Ripplin-kame, a flax-comb: " he claw'd her wi' the ripplin-kame," 252.
Riskit, made a cracking sound: " wad rair't an' riskit," 27.
Rive, (1) to split, to cleave, to rend, to tear: " are riven out baith root an' branch," 3; " he rives his father's auld entails," 3 ; " rives 't aff their back," 50 ; " they 'll rive it wi' the plew," 58 ; " rivin the words to gar them clink," 128 ; " till him rives Horatian fame," 318; (2) to be split, to split, to burst: " maist like to rive," 72.
Rock, a distaff.
Rockin, a social meeting, 44. See Notes, p. 330.
Roon, shred: " wore by degrees, till her last roon," 49.
Roose, to praise, to flatter.
Roose, reputation: " ye hae made but toom roose," 112.
Roosty, rusty.
Rottan, a rat: " the tail o' a rottan," 268. See also *Rattan*.
Roun', round.
Roupet, exhausted in voice: " my roupet Muse is haerse," 6; " till ye be haerse an' roupet," 120. See Notes, p. 325.
Routh, v. *Rowth*.
Routhie, well-stocked: " a routhie butt, a routhie ben," 241.
Row, *rowe*, (1) to roll: " if bowls row right," 151; (2) to roll or flow, as a river ; (3) to roll or wrap.

Rowte, to low, to bellow : "the kye stood row-tin," 4; "while new-ca'd kye rowte at the stake," 46; "rowte out-owre the dale," 64; "to hear you roar and rowte," 65.

Rowth, *routh*, plenty, a store: "rowth o' rhyme," 6; "rowth o' rhymes," 17; "ay a rowth," 148; "routh o' gear," 249.

Rozet, rosin: "mercurial rozet," 43.

Run-deils, downright devils, 4, 114.

Rung, a cudgel: "she 's just a devil wi' a rung," 8; "a meikle hazel-rung," 228; "round about the fire wi' a rung she ran," 251; "wi' a rung decide it," 266.

Runkl'd, wrinkled : "yon runkl'd pair," 9.

Runt, a cabbage- or colewort-stalk: "a runt, was like a sow-tail," 24; "his bow-kail runt," 24; "runts o' grace," 64.

Ryke, to reach: "let me ryke up," 105.

Sab, to sob.

Sae, so.

Saft, soft.

Sair, sore, hard, severe, strong.

Sair, to serve : "what sairs your grammers"= what avail your grammars, 45; "I 'd better gaen an' sair't the king," 50; "some less maun sair," 128; "your clerkship he should sair," 129; "he 'll sair them as he sair't his King," 162; "your billie Satan sair us," 185.

Sair, *sairly*, sorely, etc.

Sairie, (1) sorrowful : "the melancholious, sairie croon," 134; (2) sorry : "some sairie comfort at the last," 265.

Sall, shall.

Sandy, Sannock, Sawney, dim. of *Alexander*.

Sark, a shirt, a shift.

Saugh, a sallow, a willow : "o' saugh or hazle," 27; "saugh woodies" = willow withes, 145.

Saul, soul.

Saumont, sawmont, the salmon.

Saunt, saint.

Saut, salt.

Saut-backets, v. *Backets*.

Saw, to sow.

Sawney, v. *Sandy*.

Sax, six.

Scaith, v. *Skaith*.

Scar, to scare.

Scathe, v. *Skaith*.

Scaud, to scald.

Scaul, scold : "his ill-tongu'd wicked scaul," 14.

Scauld, to scold.

Scaur, scary, timid : "nor blate nor scaur," 12.

Scaur, a jutting cliff or bank of earth : "whyles round a rocky scaur it strays," 26; "beneath a scaur," 68.

Scho, she.

Scone, a soft cake: "souple scones," 5; "hale breeks, a scone, an' whisky gill," 6; "an' barley-scone shall cheer me," 129. See Notes, p. 325.

Sconner, loathing, 72.

Sconner, to sicken (with disgust) : "until they sconner," 17.

Scraichin, calling hoarsely : "and paitricks scraichin loud at e'en," 44.

Screed, a rip, a rent: "a screed some day," 9; "or lasses gie my heart a screed," 48.

Screed, to repeat rapidly, to rattle : "he 'll screed you aff ' Effectual Calling,' " 114.

Scriechin, screeching : "and scriechin out pro-saic verse," 6. See also *Skriech*.

Scriegh, v. *Skriegh*.

Scrievin, moving swiftly : "gae downhill, scrievin," 5; "owre the hill gaed scrievin," 26; "then hiltie-skeltie, we gae scrievin," 128.

Scroggie, scroggy, scrubby ; "amang the braes sae scroggie," 206; "down yon scroggy glen," 254.

Sculdudd'ry, bawdry : "sculdudd'ry an' he will be there," 166.

See'd, saw (pret. of *see*).

Seisins, freehold possessions : "in bonds and seisins," 62.

Sel, sel', sell, self.

Sell'd, sell't, sold.

Semple, simple : "semple folk " = humble folk, 233.

Sen', send.

Set, (1) to set off, to start : "while for the barn she sets," 25; "for Hornbook sets," 59; (2) to become, to suit : "it sets you ill," 6; "nane sets the lawn-sleeve sweeter," 19.

Set, sat.

Shachl'd, shapeless : "how her new shoon fit her auld, shachl'd feet," 282.

Shaird, a shred, a shard : "the hindmost shaird," 50.

Shangan, a cleft stick: "he 'll clap a shangan on her tail," 63.

Shanna, shall not.

Shaul, shallow : "an' Peebles shaul," 108.

Shaver, a funny fellow: "he was an unco shaver," 19.

Shaw, a wood.

Shaw, to show.

Shearer, a reaper.

Sheep-shank, "nae sheep-shank bane " = a person of no small importance, 47; "nae sheep-shank " = a person of no small import-ance, 61.

Sheerly, absolutely, wholly : "priests wyte them sheerly," 134.

Sheers, shears, scissors.

Sherra-moor, Sheriffmuir.

Sheugh, a ditch, a furrow: "as ever lap a sheugh or dyke," 2; "a cotter howkin in a sheugh," 2; "they 'll a' be trench'd wi' monie a sheugh," 58; "and reekin-red ran monie a sheugh," 227.

Sheuk, shook.

Shiel, a shed : "the swallow jinkin round my shiel," 240. See also *Milking-shiel*.

Shill, shrill.

Shog, a shake : "an' gied the infant warld a shog," 13. Cf. "His gang garis all your chalmeris schog," Dunbar, *On James Dog*.

Shool, a shovel.

Shoon, shoes.

Shore, (1) to offer : "even as I was, he shor'd me," 96; "an' shor'd them ' Dainty Davie,' " 106; "I doubt na Fortune may you shore,"

131; (2) to menace, to threaten: "had shor'd them with a glimmer of his lamp," 62; "has shor'd the Kirk's undoin," 64; "an' shore him weel wi' ' Hell,' " 129; "if e'er Detraction shore to smit you," 130; "like good mithers, shore before ye strike," 151; "first shore her wi' a gentle kiss," 264.

Short syne, a little while ago: "as short syne broken-hearted," 237.

Shouldna, should not.

Shouther, *showther*, shoulder.

Shure, sheared, reaped: "Robin **shure** in hairst," 266.

Sic, such.

Siccan, such, such like, such kind of.

Sicker, secure, firm, certain: "to keep me sicker," 57; "sicker score" = strict conditions, 113; "thy sicker treasure," 148.

Sidelins, sideways: "sidelins sklented," 47.

Siller, silver, money in general, wealth.

Simmer, summer.

Sin, a son: "his sin gat Eppie Sim wi' wean," 25.

Sin', since.

Sindry, sundry.

Singet, singed, "singet Sawnie," 112.

Sinn, the sun: "the sinn keeks," 126.

Sinny, sunny: "in the pride o' sinny noon," 242.

Skaith, scaith, scathe, damage.

Skaith, to harm, to injure: "think, wicked sinner, wha ye're skaithing," 50; "the Deil he couldna skaith thee," 276.

Skeigh, skiegh, skittish: "when thou an' I were young and skiegh," 27; "and Meg was skeigh," 208; "look'd asklent and unco skeigh," 272.

Skellum, a good-for-nothing: "thou was a skellum," 90; "ilk self-conceited critic-skellum," 119; "by worthless skellums," 127.

Skelp, a slap: "skelp — a shot" = crack — a shot, 8; "I gie them a skelp, as they're creepin alang," 279.

Skelp, (1) to spank, to slap, to strike: "to skelp and scaud poor dogs like me,' 12; "or else, I fear, some ill ane skelp him," 42; "wi' your priest-skelping turns," 112; (2) to hasten, to move quickly: "cam skelpin up the way," 9; "skelpin barefit," 10; "the words come skelpin rank an' file," 34; "Tam skelpit on thro' dub and mire," 91; "skelpin at it " = driving at it, 126; "and barefit skelp," 131; (3) "skelpin jig an' reel" = dancing jig and reel, 147; (4) "a skelpin kiss " = a sounding kiss, 102.

Skelpie-limmer's-face, a technical term in female scolding (R. B.): "ye little skelpie-limmer's-face," 25.

Skelvy, shelvy: "foaming down the skelvy rocks," 97.

Skiegh, v. *Skeigh*.

Skinking, watery: "nae skinking ware," 72.

Skinklin, small: "skinklin patches," 318.

Skirl, to cry or sound shrilly, to squeal, to squall: "skirlin weanies," 5; "loud skirl'd a' the lasses," 24; "an' skirl up the *Bangor*," 63; "he screw'd his pipes, and gart them **skirl**," 91; "he skirl'd out *Encore*," 103.

Sklent, a slant. a turn: "my notion 's taen **a** sklent," 16.

Sklent, (1) to slant, to squint: "wi' sklentin light," 13; "an' sklented on the man of Uzz," 13; (2) to cheat: "to lie an' sklent," 47; (3) to cast obliquely: "ironic satire, sidelins sklented," 47; "an' sklent on poverty their joke," 128.

Skouth, vent: "to gie their malice skouth," 127.

Skriech, a screech: "wi' monie an eldritch skriech and hollo," 92. See also *Scriechin*.

Skriegh, scriegh, to scream, to whinny: "prance an' snore an' skriegh," 27.

Skyrin, flaring: "skyrin tartan trews, man," 227.

Skyte, a dash, a sudden and violent shower (the primary meaning of *to skyte* is to eject forcibly = to stool): "when hailstanes drive wi' bitter skyte," 102.

Slade, slid.

Slae, the sloe.

Slap, (1) a breach in a fence, an opening: "at slaps the billies halt a blink," 11; "to slink thro' slaps," 14; "the mosses, waters, slaps, and styles," 90; (2) a gate: "the sheep-herd steeks his faulding slap," 78.

Slaw, slow.

Slee, sly, ingenious.

Sleekit, (1) sleek: "wee, sleekit, cow'rin, tim'rous beastie," 31; (2) crafty: "sleekit Chatham Will," 145.

Slidd'ry, slippery: "Fortune's slidd'ry ba'," 53.

Sloken, to slake: "their hydra drouth **did** sloken," 117.

Slypet, slipped: "an' slypet owre " = fallen smoothly over, 27.

Sma', small.

Smeddum, a powder: "or fell, red smeddum," 43.

Smeek, smoke.

Smiddy, smithy.

Smoor'd, smothered.

Smoutie, smutty.

Smytrie, a large collection of small individuals, a litter: "a smytrie o' wee duddie weans," 3.

Snakin, sneering: "wi' hingin lip an' snakin," 110.

Snapper, to stumble: "Blind Chance let her snapper and stoyte on her way," 279.

Snash, abuse: "how they maun thole a factor's snash," 3.

Snaw, snow.

Snaw-broo, snow-broth or melted snow: "the snaw-broo rowes," 61. Cf. "A man whose blood is very snow-broth," Shak., *Measure for Measure*, i. 4.

Sned, to lop, to cut: "an' legs, an' arms, an' heads will sned," 72; "I'll sned besoms," 145.

Sneeshin mill, a snuff-box: "the luntin pipe, the sneeshin mill," 3.

Snell, bitter, biting: "snell and keen," 31; "the snellest blast at mirkest hours," 295.

Snick, a latch: "when click! the string the snick did draw," 20; snick-drawing = scheming: "ye auld, snick-drawing dog," 13; "he weel a snick can draw '' = he is good at cheating, 129. See Notes, p. 340. Cf. Engl. *draw-latch*.

Snirtle, to snigger: "he feign'd to snirtle in his sleeve," 105.

Snood, a fillet worn by maidens: "and silken snoods he gae me twa," 234.

Snool, (1) to cringe, to crawl: "owre proud to snool," 55; (2) to snub: "they snool me sair," 239.

Snoove, to go smoothly and constantly: "thou snoov't awa'" = thou jogged along, 27; "snoov'd awa'" = toddled off, 133.

Snowkit, snuffed (expressive of the sound made by the dog's nose): "snuff'd and snowkit," 2.

Sodger, *soger*, a soldier.

Sonsie, *sonsy*, pleasant, good-natured, jolly: "his honest, sonsie, bawsn't face," 2; "an' unco sonsie," 27; "fair fa' your honest, sonsie face," 72; "sonsie, smirking, dear-bought Bess," 114; "women sonsie, saft, and sappy," 125; "the sonsie quean," 135; "sae sonsy and sweet," 170.

Soom, to swim.

Soor, sour.

Sough, v. *Sugh*.

Souk, suck: "and ay she took the tither souk," 238.

Soupe, v. *Sowp*.

Souple, supple, flexible: "souple scones," 5; "souple tail," 67; "souple jad," 92.

Souter, cobbler, a shoemaker: "Souter Hood," 54; "Souter Johnie," 91.

Sowp, *soupe*, a sup, a quantity of liquid: "wi' sowps o' kail," 8; "the soupe (= milk) their only hawkie does afford," 29; "sowps o' drink," 40.

Sowth, to hum or whistle in a low tone: "we'll sit an' sowth a tune," 33.

Sowther, to solder: "sowther a' in deep debauches," 4; "a night o' guid fellowship sowthers it a'," 279.

Spae, to foretell: "to spae your fortune," 25.

Spails, chips: "a' to spails," 153.

Spairge, (1) to splash: "spairges about the brunstane cootie," 12; (2) to spatter: "a name not envy spairges," 19.

Spak, spoke.

Spate, *speat*, a flood: "the roaring speat," 61; "bombast spates," 318.

Spavie, the spavin.

Spavit, spavined.

Spean, to wean: "wad spean a foal" (by disgust), 92.

Speat, v. *Spate*.

Speel, to climb: "Moodie speels the holy door," 10: "ance that five-an'-forty's speel'd," 16; "to speel . . . the braes o' fame," 47; "if on a beastie I can speel," 130; "now sma' heart hae I to speel the steep Parnassus," 147.

Speer, *spier*, to ask.

Speet, to spit: "to speet him like a pliver," 105.

Spence, the parlour: "keeps the spence," 15; "ben i' the spence," 20.

Spier, v. *Speer*.

Spleuchan, (1) tobacco-pouch made of some sort of peltry: "Deil mak his king's-hood in a spleuchan," 58; (2) (equivocally): "hurt her spleuchan," 115.

Splore, (1) a frolic, a carousal: "a random-splore," 41; "in Poosie-Nansie's held the splore," 102; (2) a row: "he bred sic a splore," 110.

Spontoon, a kind of halberd, 103. See Notes, p. 335.

Sprachl'd, clambered: "I sprachl'd up the brae," 117.

Sprattle, to scramble: "sprawl, and sprattle," 43; "deep-lairing, sprattle," 68.

Spreckled, speckled.

Spring, a lively tune, a dance: "I've play'd mysel a bonie spring," 50; "he play'd a spring, and danc'd it round," 204; "Charlie gat the spring to pay," 208; "the o'erword o' the spring," 306.

Sprittie, full of roots of sprits (a kind of rush): "sprittie knowes," 27.

Sprush, spruce.

Spunk, (1) a match: "we'll light a spunk," 65; (2) a spark: "a spunk o' Allan's glee," 45; (3) fire, spirit: "a man o' spunk," 106; "life and spunk," 139.

Spunkie, spirited: "a spunkie Norland billie," 7.

Spunkie, liquor, spirits: "and spunkie ance to mak us mellow," 128.

Spunkie, a will-o'-the-wisp, a jack-o'-lanthorn: "moss-traversing spunkies," 13; "fays, spunkies, kelpies," 60.

Spurtle, a stick used for stirring porridge, etc.: "spurtle-blade" (used humorously of a sword), 94.

Squattle, to squat, to settle: "in some beggar's hauffet squattle," 43.

Stacher, to stagger, to totter: "th' expectant wee-things, toddlin, stacher through," 28; "I stacher'd whyles," 57; "except when drunk he stacher't thro' it," 139.

Staggie, dim. of *staig* (a young horse).

Staig, a young horse.

Stan', stand.

Stane, stone.

Stang, sting.

Stank, a ditch, a pool: "out-ower a stank," 26; "the Muses' stank," 106; "soor Arminian stank," 108.

Stan't, stood.

Stap, to stop.

Stapple, a stopple: "for every hole to get a stapple," 125.

Stark, strong: "an' thou was stark," 26; "baith wight and stark," 172.

Starnie, dim. of *starn* or *star:* "ye twinkling starnies bright," 83.

Starns, stars: "ye hills, near neebors o' the starns," 82.

Startle, to course: "or down Italian vista startles," 3.

Staumrel, half-witted: "staumrel, corky-headed, graceless gentry," 62.

Staw, a stall: "your horns shall tie you to the staw," 251.

Staw, to surfeit, to disgust: "*olio* that wad staw a sow," 72.

Staw, stole: "auld hermit Ayr staw thro' his woods," 21; "the lasses staw frae 'mang them a'," 24; "staw my rose," 243, 310; "staw the linin o't," 255; "staw a branch," 320.

Stechin, cramming, stuffing: "the gentry first are stechin," 2.

Steek, a stitch: "thro' the steeks," 2; "ne'er a wrang steek in them a', man," 170.

Steek, to shut, to close: "their solemn een may steek," 8; "steek their een," 24; "steek your gab for ever," 64; "the sheep-herd steeks his faulding slap," 78; "and bonie bosoms steekit" (*i. e.* closed in), 115.

Steer, (1) to stir: "steer about the toddy," 11; (2) to rouse, to stir: "O, steer her up," 264; (3) to meddle with, to molest: "nae cauld nor hunger e'er can steer them," 4; "thy servant true wad never steer her," 110; "the Deil, he daurna steer," 122, 146; "misfortune sha'na steer thee," 276; (4) to move, to stir: "set a' their gabs a-steerin," 26.

Steeve, stiff, stanch, compact: "a filly, buirdly, steeve, an' swank," 26.

Stell, a still.

Sten, a leap: "foaming, strang, wi' hasty stens," 82; "my heart to my mou gied a sten," 231.

Sten't, sprang: "thou never lap an' sten't an' breastit," 27.

Stented, appointed: "my watchman stented," 7.

Stents, assessments, dues, taxes: "an' a' his stents,'" 2; "how cesses, stents, and fees were rax'd," 145.

Steyest, steepest: "the steyest brae thou wad hae fac't it," 27.

Stibble, stubble.

Stibble-rig, chief harvester (with the hook), 25.

Stick-an-stowe, completely: "ruin'd stick-an-stowe," 49.

Stilt, limp: "hilch, an' stilt, an' jump," 34.

Stimpart, "the eighth part of a Winchester bushel" (R. B.): "a heapet stimpart," 27.

Stirk, a young bullock or heifer (more than one year old).

Stock, a plant of cabbage or colewort.

Stoited, stumbled: "down George's Street I stoited," 137. See also *Stoyte*.

Stoiter, to stagger: "stoiter'd up" = struggled up, 104; "stoit'ring out thro' the midden dub," 121.

Stoor, (1) hoarse: "an eldritch, stoor 'quaick, quaick,'" 13; (2) stern: "a carlin stoor and grim," 161.

Stot, a steer.

Stoun, *stound*, a sudden sharp pain: "life's various stounds," 99; "my heart it gae a stoun," 202; "the stound, the deadly wound," 230.

Stound, to ache, to smart: "my heart it stounds wi' anguish," 237.

Stoure, dust.

Stoure, conflict, strife.

Stourie, dusty.

Stown, stolen.

Stownlins, by stealth: "Rob, stownlins, prie'd

her bonie mou," 24; "an' stow'nlins we sall meet again," 257.

Stoyte, to stagger: "let her snapper and stoyte on her way," 279. See also *Stoited*.

Strae death, death in bed (*i. e.* on straw), 58.

Straik, to stroke.

Strak, struck.

Strang, strong.

Straught, straight.

Straught, to stretch: "will straught on a board," 170.

Streekit, stretched: "ance ye were streekit owre frae bank to bank," 61; "streekit out to bleach," 120.

Striddle, to straddle, to stride: "striddle owre a rig," 46.

Stroan't, pissed, 2.

Strunt, liquor: "a social glass o' strunt," 26; "a dram o' guid strunt," 268.

Strunt, to strut: "ye strunt rarely," 43.

Studdie, an anvil: "till block an' studdie ring an' reel," 5; "come o'er his studdie," 82.

Stumpie, dim. of *stump* (applied playfully to a worn quill): "doun gaed stumpie in the ink," 46.

Sturt, worry, trouble: "sturt and strife," 184, 204.

Sturt, to trouble, to vex: "ay the less they hae to sturt them," 4.

Sturtin, frighted, staggered: "tho' he was something sturtin," 25.

Styme, the faintest outline: "or see a styme," 125.

Sucker, sugar: "gusty sucker," 5.

Sud, should.

Sugh, *sough*, a sough, a moan, a sound as of the wind, a sigh: "wi' waving sugh," 13; "wi' angry sugh," 28; "the clanging sugh of whistling wings," 60; "sough for sough," 227.

Sumph, a blockhead: "ye surly sumphs," 135.

Sune, soon.

Suthron, Southern (*i. e.* English).

Swaird, the sward.

Swall'd, swelled.

Swank, limber: "steeve, an' swank," 26.

Swankies, strapping fellows: "swankies young," 9.

Swarf, to swoon: "amaist did swarf, man," 227.

Swat, sweated.

Swatch, a sample: "a chosen swatch," 10; "a swatch o' Hornbook's way," 59; "a swatch o' Manson's barrels," 130.

Swats, new ale: "reaming swats, that drank divinely," 91; "the swats sae ream'd in Tammie's noddle," 91.

Sweer, v. *Dead-sweer*.

Swirl, a curl: "hung owre his hurdies wi' a swirl," 2.

Swirlie, twisted, knaggy: "a swirlie, auld moss-oak," 26.

Swith, (1) haste! off and away! "then swith! an' get a wife to hug," 19; "swith! in some beggar's hauffet squattle," 43; "swith! to the Laigh Kirk," 63; "swith awa," 252.

Swither, hesitation, doubt: "a hank'ring

swither," 8; "an eerie swither," 57; "I've little swither," 134.

Swoom, swim.

Swoor, swore.

Sybow, a young onion: "a sybow-tail," 129.

Syne, since, then, ago.

Tack, a lease, a holding: "stand as tightly by your tack," 7; "or Poland, wha had now the tack o't," 145; "a tack o' seven times seven," 146.

Tacket, a hob-nail: "wad haud the Lothians three in tackets," 94.

Tae, to.

Tae, toe.

Tae'd, toed: "a three-tae'd leister," 57.

Taed, toad; "sprawlin like a taed," 168.

Taen, taken.

Tairge, vex with questions, to catechise strictly: "I on the *Questions* tairge them tightly," 114. See Notes, p. 338.

Tak, to take.

Tald, told.

Tane, one (in contrast to other): "the tane is game," 120; "the heat o' the tane," 265.

Tangs, tongs.

Tap, top.

Tap o' tow, the quantity of flax that is put upon the distaff at one time: "spin your tap o' tow," 238.

Tapetless, heedless, foolish: "the tapetless, ramfeezl'd hizzie," 46.

Tapmost, topmost.

Tappet hen, (crested hen) a pot or bottle holding about three English quarts of claret or ale: "the tappet hen, gae bring her ben," 311. See Notes, p. 347.

Tap-pickle, the grain at the top of the stalk: "her tap-pickle maist was lost," 24. See Notes, p. 329.

Tapsalteerie, topsy-turvy: 77, 308.

Tarrow, (1) to tarry (the original sense in Henryson and the older writers, a secondary sense being to haggle), to hesitate: "if you on your station tarrow," 153; (2) to murmur: "that yet hae tarrow't at it," 19.

Tassie, a cup: "the silver tassie," 220.

Tauk, talk.

Tauld, told.

Tawie, tractable: "hamely, tawie, quiet, an' cannie," 27.

Tawpie, a foolish young woman: "gawkies, tawpies, gowks, and fools," 119. See Notes, p. 339.

Tawted, matted, with matted hair: "nae tawted tyke," 2; "wi' tawted ket," 15.

Teats, small quantities: "wi' teats o' hay," 14.

Teen, vexation: (common in Shakespeare, e. g. "of sorrow and of teen," *Love's Labour's Lost*, iv. 3); "spite and teen," 96.

Tell'd, told.

Temper-pin, (1) a fiddle-peg: "screw your temper-pins," 134; (2) the regulating pin of the spinning-wheel: "and ay she shook the temper-pin," 208.

Tent, heed: "tak [or took] tent" = take [or took] care, 16, 57, 166.

Tent, to tend, to heed, to observe.

Tentie, watchful, careful, heedful: "wi' tentie e'e," 24; 'wi' tentie care," 27; "some tentie rin," 28; "wi' joy the tentie seedsman stalks," 77.

Tentier, more watchful: "a tentier way," 147.

Tentless, careless, heedless: "tentless heed," 16, 51.

Tester (Old Fr. *Test*, a head), an old Scots silver coin about sixpence in value: "till she has scarce a tester," 18. Cf. "Hold, here's a tester for thee," Shak., 2 *Henry IV*., iii. 2.

Teugh, tough.

Teuk, took.

Thack, thatch: "thack and rape" = the covering of a house, and therefore used as a simile for home necessities, 3; "thack and rape" (of a corn-stack), 60.

Thae, those.

Thairm, (1) an intestine: "painch, tripe, or thairm," 72; (2) catgut (a fiddle-string): "thairm - inspiring," 62, 133; "o'er the thairms be tryin," 64; "kittle hair on thairms," 105.

Theckit, thatched: "an' theckit right," 126.

Thegither, together.

Themsel, *themsels*, themselves.

Thick, v. *Pack an' thick*.

Thieveless, forbidding: "thieveless sneer," 61.

Thiggin, begging: "come thiggin at your doors an' yetts," 153.

Thir, these.

Thirl'd, thrilled: "it thirl'd the heart-strings," 44.

Thole, to endure, to suffer: "thole a factor's snash," 3; "thole the winter's sleety dribble," 32; "thole their blethers," 51; "thole their mither's ban," 133; "the scathe and banter we're forced to thole," 133.

Thou'se, thou shalt, thou wilt.

Thowe, thaw.

Thowless, lazy: "'Conscience,' says I, 'ye thowless jad,'" 46.

Thrang, (1) crowded: "the lasses, skelpin barefit, thrang," 10; "thick an' thrang," 11; (2) busy: "that were na thrang at hame," 2; "aiblins thrang a parliamentin," 3; "thrang winkin on the lasses," 10.

Thrang, busily: "complimented thrang," 18; "are whistling thrang," 16.

Thrang, a throng: "aff the godly pour in thrangs," 10; "the jovial thrang," 106.

Thrapple, the windpipe: "but now she fetches at the thrapple," 125; "as Murther at his thrapple shor'd," 163.

Thrave, twenty-four sheaves of corn: "a daimen icker in a thrave," 31.

Thraw, a twist: "she turns the key wi' cannie thraw," 25.

Thraw, (1) to twist, to turn: "for thrawin" = against twisting or bending, 25; "great Mackinlay thrawn his heel," 66; "did our hellim thraw," 75; "thraw saugh woodies," 145; (2) to thwart: "the German chief to thraw, man," 75; "did his measures thraw," 75; "a mortal sin to thraw that," 106.

Thraws, throes: "ease the thraws," 278.

Threap, maintain (with asseverations): " wad threap auld folk the thing misteuk," 49.
Threesome, by threes: " there 's threesome reels," 249.
Thretteen, thirteen.
Thretty, thirty.
Thrissle, thistle.
Thristed, thirsted.
Through: " mak to through " = make good, 62.
Throu'ther, (through other) in confusion: " cry a' throu'ther," 24.
Thummart, polecat, 108.
Tight. girt, prepared: " he should been tight that daur't to raize thee," 26.
Till, to.
Till'd, till it, plough it: " I maun till'd again," 270.
Till't, to it.
Timmer, (1) timber; (2) material (as also timber in English), " the timmer is scant, when ye 're taen for a saunt " = the saintly material is scant when you are taken for one, 112. (Some wiseacres affirm the meaning to be *the wood* (for the gallows) *is scant :* but (1) if this were the meaning the article " the " would be superfluous; (2) it is absurd to suppose that there was then not wood enough to erect a gallows; (3) wood was less essential than a rope, and (4) " material " is quite a common meaning of " timmer.")
Tine, tyne, (1) to lose, (2) to be lost.
Tinkler, a tinker.
Tint, lost: " tint as win " = lost as soon as won, 250.
Tip, v. *Toop*.
Tippence, twopence.
Tippenny, two-penny ale: " wi' tippenny we fear nae evil," 91.
Tirl, (1) to strip, to uncover, to unroof: " tirlin the kirks," 12; " tirl the hullions to the birses," 153; (2) to rattle: " tirl'd at your door," 185; " tirl'd at the pin," 253. See Notes, p. 345.
Tither, the other.
Tittlin, whispering: " a raw o' tittlin jads," 10.
Tocher, dowry.
Tocher, to give a dowry.
Tod, the fox.
To-fa', the fall: " to-fa' o' the night," 166.
Toom, empty.
Toop, tip, a tup, a ram.
Toss, a toast: " the toss o' Ecclefechan," 254.
Tousie, shaggy: " his tousie back," 2; " a tousie tyke," 91.
Tow, (1) flax, (2) a rope.
Towmond, towmont, a twelve-month.
Towsing, tousling, rumpling (equivocal): " towsing a lass i' my daffin," 104. Cf. " Damn me if he sha't have the tousling of her," Fielding, *Tom Jones.*
Toyte, to totter: " toyte about wi' ane anither," 27.
Tozie, tipsy: " the tozie drab," 102.
Trams, shafts (of a barrow or cart) : " baith the trams are broken," 114.
Trashtrie, small trash: " sauce, ragouts, an' sic like trashtrie," 2.

Trews, trousers: " skyrin tartan trews," 227. See also *Trouse.*
Trig, neat, trim : " the lads sae trig," 24 ; " and trig an' braw," 119 ; " he sae trig lap o'er the rig," 237 ; " Willie's wife is nae sae trig," 244.
Trin'le, a wheel (especially of a wheel-barrow), 114.
Troggin, wares : " buy braw troggin," 167.
Troke, to barter, to exchange: " wi' you nae friendship I will troke," 128.
Trouse, trousers: " will be him trouse and doublet," 264. See also *Trews.*
Trowth, truth, In truth !
Tryste, a fair, a cattle-market : " to trystes an' fairs to driddle," 105 ; " the tryste o' Dalgarnock," 282 ; " he gaed wi' Jeanie to the tryste," 297. See Notes, p. 346.
Trysted, appointed, agreed upon : " the trysted hour," 299.
Trystin, trysting, meeting : " trystin time," 257 ; " trysting thorn," 272.
Tulyie, tulzie, a squabble, a broil: " in logic tulzie," 50 ; " The Holy Tulyie," 107 ; " the tulyie 's teugh 'tween Pitt and Fox," 120 ; " amid this mighty tulyie," 163.
Twa, two.
Twafauld, two-fold. double : " he hirples twafauld " = he hobbles bent double, 212.
Twal, twelve ; " the twal " = twelve at night, 59.
Twalpennie worth = a penny worth (sterling), 3.
Twang, a twinge, 118.
Twa-three, two or three.
Tway, two : " ne'er a ane but tway," 160.
Twin, twine, to deprive, to rob : " twins . . . o' half his days," 6 ; " may twin auld Scotland o' a life," 153 ; " has twin'd ye o' your stately trees," 319.
Twistle, a twist, a wrench: " the Lord's cause gat na sic a twistle," 108.
Tyke, a dog.
Tyne, v. *Tine.*
Tysday, Tyseday, **Tuesday.**

Ulzie, oil : " wi' powther and wi' ulzie," 115.
Unchancy, dangerous: " an' mair unchancy," 128. See also *Wanchancie.*
Unco, remarkably, uncommonly, very.
Unco, (1) strange : " unco folk," 203 ; (2) remarkable, uncommon.
Uncos, strange things, wonders, news: " each tells the uncos that he sees or hears," 29.
Unkend, unknown.
Unsicker, unsecure, uncertain : " feeble, and unsicker," 148.
Unskaithed, unscathed, unhurt.
Usquabae, usquebae, whisky.

Vauntie, vain, proud: " and she was vauntie," 92 ; " vauntie o' my hap," 135 ; " your letter made me vauntie," 144.
Vera, very.
Virls, ferrules, rings (such as those around the ends of canes, etc.): " virls and whirlygigums," 60.
Vittel, vittle, (victual) (1) provisions : " a' my

winter vittle," 266 ; (2) grain : " a' the vittel in the yard," 126.
Vogie, vain : " and vow but I was vogie," 206.

Wa', *waw*, a wall.
Wab, a web.
Wabster, a weaver.
Wad, to wager : " I 'll wad my new pleugh-pettle," 7 ; " I 'll wad a groat," 59 ; " wad a boddle," 61.
Wad, to wed : " and or I wad anither jad," 238.
Wad, would, would have.
Wad 'a, would have.
Wadna, would not, would not have.
Wadset, a mortgage : " here 's a little wadset," 168.
Wae, woful, sorrowful (also used sarcastically).
Wae, woe : " wae 's me " = woe is to me.
Waesucks, alas ! " waesucks ! for him that gets nae lass," 11.
Wae worth, woe befall.
Wair, v. *Ware*.
Wale, to choose.
Wale, choice.
Walie, *waly*, *wawlie*, ample, large, robust : " walie nieve," 72 ; " ae winsome wench ard wawlie," 92 ; " walie nieves," 244 ; " this waly boy," 304.
Wallop, to move quickly but clumsily : " may Envy wallop in a tether," 49 ; " walloped about the reel," 121 ; " wallop in a tow," 238 ; See Notes, p. 329.
Waly, good fortune, prosperity : " waly fa' " = may good fortune befall, 270.
Wame, the belly.
Wamefou, bellyful.
Wan, won.
Wanchancie, dangerous : " that vile, wanchancie thing — a rape," 15. See *Unchancy*.
Wanrestfu', restless : " wanrestfu' pets," 14.
Ware, *wair*, to spend, bestow : " and ken na how to ware 't," 32 ; " to ware his theologic care on," 144 ; " tho' wair'd on Willie Chalmers," 131.
Ware, worn : " gratefully be ware," 135.
Wark, work.
Wark-lume, v. *Lume*.
Warl', *warld*, world.
Warlock, a wizard.
Warl'y, *warldly*, worldly.
Warran, warrant.
Warse, worse.
Warsle, *warstle*, wrestle.
Wast, west.
Wastrie, waste : " downright wastrie," 2.
Wat, wet.
Wat, *wot*, know.
Water-fit, water-foot (the river's mouth), 10.
Water-kelpies, v. *Kelpies*.
Wauble, to wobble : " ran them till they a' did wauble," 27.
Waught, a deep draught : " a right guid-willie waught," 252.
Wauk, to awake, to watch.
Wauken, to waken.
Waukin, awake, watching.

Waukit, horny, (with toil) : " my waukit loof," 20.
Waukrife, wakeful : " till waukrife morn," 83 ; " waukrife winkers," 134 ; " a waukrife minnie," 228 ; " the waukrife cock," 228.
Waur, worse.
Waur, to worst, to beat : " might aiblins waur't thee for a brattle," 27 ; " and faith ! he 'll waur me," 57 ; " waur them a'," 161.
Wean, (wee one) a child.
Weanies, babies : " when skirlin weanies see the light," 5.
Weary fa', woe befall.
Weason, the weasand, the windpipe.
Wecht, a leather-covered hoop, resembling a sieve, but without holes, used for winnowing grain : " three wechts o' naething," 25. See Notes, p. 329.
Wee, little.
Wee, a little, a short space or time.
Wee-things, children, 24, 28.
Weel, well.
Weel-faured, well-favoured.
Weel-gaun, well-going.
Weel-hain'd, well-saved : " her weel-hain'd kebbuck," 30 ; " well-hain'd gear," 62.
Weepers, strips of cambric or muslin worn on the sleeves as a badge of mourning : " auld cantie Kyle may weepers wear," 41.
Weet, wet.
Weet, to wet.
Werena, were not.
We 'se, we shall, we will.
Westlin, western.
Wha, who.
Whaizle, wheeze : " an' gar't them whaizle," 27.
Whalpit, whelped.
Wham, whom.
Whan, when.
Whang, a large slice : " in monie a whang," 10.
Whang, flog : " and gloriously she 'll whang her," 63.
Whar, *whare*, *whaur*, where.
Wha 's, *whase*, whose.
What for, *whatfore*, wherefore, why : " what for no " = why not, 133.
Whatna, what, what kind of, (partly in contempt) : " whatna day o' whatna style," 304.
What reck, what matter, nevertheless : " but yet, what reck, he at Quebec," 75 ; " when I, what reck, did least expeck," 237.
Whatt, whittled, 126. See Notes, p. 339.
Whaup, the curlew, 124. See Notes, p. 339.
Whaur, where.
Wheep, v. *Penny-wheep*.
Wheep, to jerk : " to see our elbucks wheep," 64.
Whid, a fib : " a rousing whid at times to vend," 57.
Whiddin, scudding : " an' morning poussie whiddin seen," 44 ; " ye maukins whiddin through the glade," 82.
Whids, gambols : " jinkin hares, in amorous whids," 48.
Whigmeleeries, crotchets : " whigmeleeries in your noddle," 61.

Whingin, whining: "if onie whiggish, whingin sot," 84.

Whins, furze: "thro' the whins, an' [and] by the cairn," 26, 91.

Whirlygigums, flourishes, 60.

Whisht, silence: "held my whisht" = kept silence, 20.

Whissle, a whistle.

Whissle, to whistle.

Whitter, a hearty draught: "tak our whitter," 45.

Whittle, a knife.

Whyles, sometimes, now and then.

Wi', with.

Wick: "wick a bore," 67. See Notes, p. 333.

Wi's, with his.

Wi't, with it.

Widdifu', deserving the halter: "a widdifu', bleerit knurl," 313.

Widdle, a wriggle, a struggle: "the weary widdle," 128, 134.

Wiel, a whirlpool: "whyles in a wiel it dimpl't," 26.

Wight, strong, stout, valiant, active: "wight an' wilfu'," 114; "wight and stark," 172.

Wighter, comp. of *wight:* "five wighter carlins," 160.

Wilcat, a wildcat.

Willyart, bashful: "willyart glow'r," 117.

Wimple, to meander.

Win, won: "tint as win" = lost as soon as won, 250.

Winn, to winnow: "to winn three wechts o' naething." 25.

Winna, will not.

Winnin, winding: "the warpin o't, the winnin o't," 255.

Winnock, window.

Winnock-bunker, v. *Bunker*.

Win't, wound (did wind): "an' ay she win't," 24.

Wintle, a stagger, a reel, a roll: "tumbl'd wi' a wintle," 25.

Wintle, (1) to stagger: "wintle like a saumont-coble," 27; (2) to wriggle: "wintle in a woodie," 116; "that wintles in a halter," 194.

Winze, a curse: "loot a winze," 26.

Wiss, wish.

Won, to dwell: "there was a wife wonn'd in Cockpen," 265; "there wons auld Colin's bonie lass," 268; "Auld Rob Morris that wons in yon glen," 271. Cf. "The wild beast, where he wons," Milton, *Paradise Lost*, vii. 457.

Wonner, a wonder, a marvel, (sometimes used contemptuously), "blastit wonner," 2, 43.

Woo', wool.

Woodie, woody, a rope (originally of withes): (1) "the meikle Devil wi' a woodie," 82; (2) a gallows rope: "the waefu' woodie," 104; "Learning in a woody dance," 109; "wintle in a woodie," 116.

Woodies, twigs, withes: "saugh woodies," 145.

Wooer-babs: love-knots (tied in the garters), 24.

Wordy, worthy: "wordy of a grace," 72; "a wordy beast," 114.

Worset, worsted: "her braw, new, worset apron," 25.

Worth, v. *Wae worth*.

Wrack, wreck, destruction, ruin.

Wrang, wrong.

Wud, mad, angry, raging: "as wud as wud can be," 5; "like onie wud bear," 246. See also *Red-wud*.

Wumble, a wimble, a gimlet: "gleg as onie wumble," 41.

Wyliecoat, undervest, 44.

Wyte, blame: "Had I the wyte?" = Was I to blame? 252.

Wyte, to blame, to reproach, "to wyte her countrymen," 5; "priests wyte them sheerly," 134.

Yard, a garden, a stackyard.

Yaud, a jade, an old mare: "auld grey yaud," 166, 167.

Yealings, coevals: "my dear-remember'd, ancient yealings," 62.

Yearth, v. *Yerd*.

Yell, dry (milkless): "as yell's the bill," 13.

Yerd, yird, yearth, earth: "their green beds in the yerd," 233.

Yerkit, jerked: "yerkit up sublime," 16.

Yerl, Earl.

Ye'se, ye shall.

Yestreen, last night.

Yett, a gate.

Yeuk, to itch: "If Warren Hastings' neck was yeukin," 145; "yeuks wi' joy," 148.

Yill, ale.

Yill-caup, v. *Caup*.

Yird, v. *Yerd*.

Yokin, (yoking) as much work as is done by the draught animals at one time, a spell: "a yokin at the pleugh," 135; "a hearty yokin at sang about," 44.

'Yont, beyond.

Yowe, ewe.

Yowie, dim. of *ewe*.

Yule, Christmas.

INDEX OF PERSONS AND PLACES

INDEX OF FIRST LINES

[The first lines of Choruses to Songs are included in this Index]

INDEX OF TITLES